PSYCHOANALYSIS—A GENERAL PSYCHOLOGY

Essays in Honor of Heinz Hartmann

HEINZ HARTMANN

PSYCHOANALYSIS—
A GENERAL
PSYCHOLOGY

Essays in Honor of Heinz Hartmann

Edited by

RUDOLPH M. LOEWENSTEIN,
LOTTIE M. NEWMAN, MAX SCHUR, *and*
ALBERT J. SOLNIT

Editorial Board

K. R. Eissler, m.d.
Ruth S. Eissler, m.d.
Anna Freud, ll.d., sc.d.
Maxwell Gitelson, m.d.†
Phyllis Greenacre, m.d.

George S. Klein, ph.d.
Robert P. Knight, m.d.†
Marianne Kris, m.d.
Richard Newman, m.d.
Martin H. Stein, m.d.

INTERNATIONAL UNIVERSITIES PRESS, INC.

NEW YORK

Manufactured in the United States of America
by Hallmark Press, New York

Contents

Part IV
Contributions to Psychoanalytic Theory

Part V
Clinical Problems

Part VI
Correlations and Applications of Psychoanalysis

Preface

There have been many direct tributes to Heinz Hartmann, but perhaps the more important and lasting are the indirect ones, those psychoanalytic studies and publications which others have derived from his pioneering theoretical contributions. These scientific works are so numerous and represent so many aspects of psychoanalysis that it would require a large psychoanalytic index to indicate how comprehensive his influence has been.

Heinz Hartmann has set forth guidelines and posed fruitful questions for a generation of psychoanalytic research. This research, as it continues, will enable us to refine, systematize, and increase our present knowledge, thus advancing psychoanalysis as a general psychological theory of human development and behavior. One way of describing Hartmann's contributions is to state that he has always asked why and how adaptation succeeds and what interferes with and determines the deviations in human development. There is hardly a clinical problem or question about human behavior that is not clarified by Hartmann's perspectives and specific theoretical contributions. Because of the fructifying and clarifying functions of his theoretical work, the fact is often overlooked that Hartmann would not have succeeded in helping so many workers in all areas of psychoanalysis, and in particular those in child development, if he were not an inspiring teacher. His style of writing, especially the economy of his expression, may not suit everyone; yet the elegance of his thinking and his ability to transmit highly condensed but specific observational and theoretical data have resulted in productive learning by all who study his work.

In previously published tributes,[1] explicit efforts have been made to comment upon Hartmann the physician, the psychoanalyst, the scientist, the humanist, the philosopher, the classicist, the musicologist, the explorer. He is a man of many interests and talents, with a special intellectual vitality and grace that defy categorization.

"Heinz Hartmann, in addition to his talents, has in his development imposed on himself many duties and obligations which have formed his character; amongst these, objectivity may well rank first. Objectivity is one of the main pillars of his moral position. It is maintained by a constant vigilance against self deception, from whatever quarter it may threaten. This has required a renunciation of over-idealization and comfortable wishful thinking. This moral obligation requires severe self-discipline and brings in its train the requirement to think through all possible answers to any question. As a consequence, which we readily accept, his values are firmly held and are not quickly modified when differences of opinion arise. One is reminded of Freud, who said of himself in *The History of the Psychoanalytic Movement*, 'My confidence in my own judgment was by no means slight.' Because of his objectivity and clarity of thought, we are even tempted to let Heinz do our thinking; yet quite characteristically he seldom presents a 'prepared statement' in his discussions. Rather his comments are an uninterrupted flow of fresh responses reflecting his great pleasure in surprise. He welcomes any thought, new fact or unexpected turn of phrase. Then his eyes widen and his head is tilted back, perhaps to achieve a slightly greater distance, as he assesses the new information in terms of its specificity and the order of generalization. These are instantly mastered and responded to with epigrammatic briefness and precision. This readiness to receive fresh stimulation from all sources explains his generous sociability" (Bak, 1965).

The papers in this *Festschrift* speak for themselves but at the same time elaborate formulations or questions suggested by Hartmann's work. Their range demonstrates the richness of his ideas and the scope

[1] See R. C. Bak (*Bull. Phila. Assn. Psa.*, 15:1-3, 1965); R. S. & K. R. Eissler (*Bull. Menninger Clin.*, 28:289-301, 1964); A. Freud (*J. Am. Psa. Assn.*, 13:195-196, 1965); M. Gitelson (*Int. J. Psa.*, 46:2-4, 1965); N. H. Holland (*Bull. Phila. Assn. Psa.*, 15:4-9, 1965); G. S. Klein (*Contemp. Psychol.*, 10:358-360, 1965); J. Lampl-de Groot (*Psyche*, 18:321-329, 1964); R. M. Loewenstein (*Psychoanalytic Pioneers*. NY: Basic Books, 1966, 469-483); L. Rangell (*Int. J. Psa.*, 46:5-30, 1965); A. J. Solnit (*Psa. Q.*, 33:475-484, 1964).

of his inquiries. The Editors have grouped the papers under various headings which logically suggested themselves.

Part I, The Man and His Work, contains a biographical essay and papers evaluating Hartmann's work in 1939 and from 1939 to the present.

Part II, History of Psychoanalysis, is comprised of a paper illuminating the discovery period of analysis and a study tracing the precursors of Freud's death instinct concept.

The seven papers in Part III trace aspects of normal and pathological development from infancy through childhood and adulthood to old age.

Part IV contains contributions to psychoanalytic theory. Several papers deal with the concept superego; one introduces a new concept, reality constancy; others discuss problems of memory and repression, and methodology.

Part V, Clinical Problems, describes the adaptive function of amnesias, such syndromes as depersonalization and depression, and problems of differential diagnosis.

Part VI contains papers correlating psychoanalytic theory with physiological and ethological findings and studies applying analysis to other disciplines.

The Editors regret that many excellent papers submitted to them could not be included because of the space limitations imposed by the format of a single volume.

An arrangement such as this results of course in an oversimplification in terms of the individual essays. It is in the nature of analysis that clinical and developmental papers reflect and add to theory, and theoretical studies present clinical data and may also contribute to technique. The interdependence of clinical observations and theory building has always characterized Heinz Hartmann's work. In addition, he has always made an attempt to present his theoretical formulations in a way that facilitates interchange with other disciplines. This attempt is reflected in the range and sequence of the papers—and also justifies the title of this book.

To provide a balanced tribute to Heinz Hartmann's unique complexity, the Editors are delighted to present a poetic prologue to this scientific volume.

For the Seventieth Birthday of My Father: November 4, 1964

In six and thirty years, when you are old,
May you look back on some of this and smile!

When eagles ruled the sky, my father came.
Some say the sun stood still, while comets soared;
And Jupiter and Neptune, sages claim,
Combined with Mars and Saturn; lions roared;
Tornadoes leapt; and Etna spoke a name!
(Some others say it rained all day and, bored,
They strolled Grillparzerstrasse, took their tea,
Got splashed by someone's horse, and slept 'til three.)

The century was still six years unborn.
Victoria sat content (despite the lack
On sunsets in her realm). Franz Joseph, torn
Between two soft champagnes, just at the crack
Of dawn, drank both. Top hats and canes were worn
By gaslight. Brahms played on, while at his back
America's frontier had closed the hall.
Dear Father hadn't noticed this at all.

Presumably he yowled—now there's a thought!
Distinguished thinker, teacher, wisdom's tongue
Emerged and—well, one really hardly ought
To state that laurels sometimes grow on dung,
Or that great Phidias, young, may well have wrought
Bright Kewpie dolls—at any rate, the lung
Capacity of Father, new unwalled,
Responded to the world: my father bawled.

Irreverent! What nonsense! Cavalier!
Ah well, but you're still reading, and suspect
That further disrespect will come. Don't fear!
He passed through Childhood!! (Now it's said! I've wrecked
Th' immaculate adulthood concept here!)
He came, full-fledged in skill and intellect,
Like Pallas from Jove's brain! I've got more shocks:
He had blond hair, a sister, and a fox.

He grew and waxed, as some old book might say.
What added to the polish? Let's drop names:
Freud, Mozart, Goethe, Plato came to play
With Haydn, Nietzsche, Homer, Kant—whose fames
Met Shakespeare, Dante, Brahms and Bach's bouquet,
Joined Leonardo, Sophocles at games—
And Aristotle fired Father's soul.
His parents also may have played a role.

The analyst emerged; the smoker too.
They're both well known; we'll let them be.
He also was a noble father who
Could sail from Martha's Vineyard 'cross the sea
Like some firm whaling captain battling through
A storm—yet still find muffins there for me.
O may your sails and muffins ever soar!
Good Father: Happy Birthday! Many more!

Larry

I

The Man and His Work

Heinz Hartmann: A Biographical Sketch

RUTH S. EISSLER, M.D.
and K. R. EISSLER, M.D.

Heinz Hartmann is the scion of a family renowned for its scholarly and artistic achievements. On his father's side, the family tree goes back to Adolf Gans (1541-1613) who was an astronomer and historiographer, famous in his days and personally acquainted with Kepler and Tycho Brahe. His grandfather, Moritz Hartmann (1821-1872), was a leading politician, deputy in the first German Parliament of 1848, author, poet, satirist, reporter, librettist, and professor of German literature. The ten volumes of his collected works (Moritz Hartmann, 1873/74) contain only part of his literary output. Many publications have been written on his life and work.[1] His son, Ludo Moritz Hartmann (1856-1924), became a great historian; he continued Theodor Mommsen's work on the history of Rome, and was full professor of history at the University of Vienna. His work culminated in the editorship of a world history. He, too, was a leading politician and became the Austrian ambassador to Germany after the First World War. His memory is revered in Vienna, where he was the principal organizer of educational centers at university level for the laboring class (*Volkshochschulen*). His life and work were also extensively written about.[2]

On his mother's side, one encounters equally great personages. His grandfather was Rudolf Chrobak (1843-1910), a professor of

---

[1] See Neumann (1854), Bamberger (1872), Kürnberger (1872), Wittner (1906/07), anonymous (1910/11), Wittner (1911), D. B. (1921), Kisch (1921), Wolkan (1921), Steinberg (1953), Lass (1963).

[2] Stern (1910), anonymous (1924), Lampa (1924), Bauer (1926), Stowasser (1926), Koenig (1954), *Österreichisches Biographisches Lexikon 1815-1950* (1959). A complete bibliography of Ludo Hartmann's publications has not yet been produced. For a bibliography of his historical writings, see von Below et al. (1925).

gynecology and obstetrics at the University of Vienna, a man of such excellence that Freud (1914) could call him "the most eminent of all our Vienna physicians"—no minor praise for a contemporary of Billroth's, and at a time when the medical faculty was bristling with illustrious names.[3] His mother's uncle, Rudolf Eitelberger von Edelberg, was a prominent art historian. He was the founder and first director of two well-known Viennese institutions, the Museum of Art and Industry and the School of Applied Art (*Kunstgewerbeschule*). His collected papers (1879/84) cover 1,625 pages.

Heinz Hartmann was born November 4, 1894 in Vienna. As a growing child, he was surrounded by the best prototypes for identification that a talented youngster could wish for. The foremost influence, of course, was his father, but his grandfather Chrobak's influence ought not to be underestimated. The mere fact that Heinz Hartmann studied medicine and did not choose the humanities as his principal field of endeavor, although he was equally endowed for them, warrants the conclusion that the grandfather did not necessarily hold a second place in the formation of young Heinz's ego ideal.

Like his own father before him, Ludo Hartmann did not hold with the general custom of giving one's children a religious training. Since attendance at any school would have entailed this, Heinz and his sister, who was one and a half years older, were taught at home. This provided the benefit of individualized instruction, which Heinz enjoyed up to the age of 14; from that age on, he attended public schools, since religious instruction was compulsory only for the younger students.

His private tutoring was supervised by a man of no minor stature. This was Karl Seitz (1869-1950), who in later years became renowned as a beloved Mayor of Vienna and a great Social-Democratic leader.

The artistic element was strong in Heinz's upbringing. Music had been quite a tradition in the Chrobak household, at which Brahms had been a frequent visitor, and Heinz's mother continued it. Not only Austrian intellectuals met in Ludo Hartmann's home; the atmosphere there was an international one. Consequently, Heinz not only had the privilege of meeting many of the outstanding personalities of his time, he was also introduced to a great variety of problems and ideas, of ways of looking at the world, of possible solutions—and not

[3] For writings about Chrobak, consult Chrobak-Feier (1908), Bucura (1910), Peham (1910), Schönbauer (1957), Lesky (1965).

through book learning, but by the live disputes of unusually talented and original minds.

Under such extraordinary stimulation, a superabundance of talents took shape. Heinz played the violin and was a self-taught pianist; he wrote remarkable poetry and painted in watercolors.

Prior to graduating from medical school at the University of Vienna in 1920, he had to serve in the Army.

His study years were unusually productive. Heinz Hartmann had the incomparable advantage of being trained in a large variety of scientific pursuits. The study of medicine was organized at the University of Vienna in such a way that the student was not squeezed into the rigid armor of the usual medical training. Instead, anyone who was eager to enlarge his horizon could readily attend lectures of his choice. Thus Heinz Hartmann audited lectures on psychology and philosophy under Friedrich Jodl (1849-1914), Adolf Stöhr (1855-1921), Heinrich Gomperz (1873-1943), Hermann Swoboda (1873-1963). Later, when he spent time in Berlin, he came into contact with Kurt Lewin (1890-1947) and his work.

As a student, he worked under the renowned pharmacologist, Hans Horst Mayer (1853-1939). Two early papers on the metabolism of quinine, published before his graduation (1917, 1918), testify to his early expertise in the experimental method. A lasting effect was produced in him by the privilege he enjoyed of being permitted to attend a half-year seminar held in Vienna by the great sociologist, Max Weber (1864-1920).

Within this period, he also worked as secretary to his father, then Ambassador in Berlin. In this way, Heinz Hartmann was able to study history as a living process, meeting the foremost politicians of the new German Republic, such as Friedrich Ebert (1871-1925), the first president of the German Republic. It was an enriching experience to be able to feel the pulse of a historical center—particularly for a young man whose background must have created in him a disposition toward theory. Yet, despite the fascination created by this close observation of political events, the profession of politics was one of the few he never contemplated entering.

After graduation, Hartmann started his career at the Psychiatric and Neurological University Clinics in Vienna under Wagner-Jauregg (1857-1940). There he remained until 1934. The chief influence on him came from Paul Schilder (1866-1940), who had recently joined

Wagner-Jauregg's staff; four papers resulted from their collaboration.[4] Thus, he had the advantage of integrating psychiatry in its classical and most conservative, as well as in its most revolutionary and modern, forms. Later in Berlin, he had the opportunity of working for a time at the clinic of Bonhöffer (1868-1948).

Four years after graduation, he published, together with Betlheim, what must be considered a classic; it still remains the best paper in the field of experimental psychoanalysis: "On Parapraxes in the Korsakow Psychosis." In it, he proved by experiment that Freud's theory of symbols, which appeared to be the most "far-fetched" among his many theories, was in fact correct and could no longer be doubted. It was a stroke of genius on the part of the young scientist. Around this masterpiece are clustered Hartmann's important clinical papers, which so felicitously combine classical psychiatry with psychoanalytic insights.

In 1927, without any foreshadowings, in his previous publications, of this sort of effort, he published *Die Grundlagen der Psychoanalyse* (*The Fundamentals of Psychoanalysis*). It was written in Berlin, while he was undergoing his first training analysis with Sandor Rado. In this book, the position of psychoanalysis among the *Geistes- und Naturwissenschaften* is set forth, and the theory of psychoanalytic methodology explicated. Written at a time when psychoanalytic work was mainly clinically directed, and methodological questions were not fashionable among analysts, the book did not meet initially with the esteem that it deserved, although it has since also become a classic. In any case, with its publication, Hartmann's prestige as a psychoanalytic theoretician was established.

Upon his return to Vienna, and during the rest of his stay at the Psychiatric Clinics, Hartmann continued his research, which combined psychoanalysis with psychiatry. Now began his work on twins, which led to six publications in the field of the psychopathology of twins, for which he earned a unique position in the field. The fact that he was assigned to write thirteen articles in the *Handwörterbuch für medizinische Psychologie* demonstrates the eminence he had already acquired in mental science.

It may have been a stroke of luck for psychoanalysis that Heinz Hartmann's university career was cut short. Disagreements with the successor to Wagner-Jauregg made it advisable for him to leave the

[4] For a complete listing of Hartmann's writings see pp. 679-684.

University Clinics and to take up full-time private practice—which meant exclusive devotion to psychoanalysis. His farewell to the University Clinics may have been eased for him by his regrets that Paul Schilder had already departed for the United States six years earlier —an irreplaceable loss to the Viennese psychiatric school.

It is also noteworthy that Heinz Hartmann never officially became a Dozent, that highly prized appointment to membership of the medical faculty of the University of Vienna. After he submitted his qualifying thesis (one of his twin studies), the College of Professors recommended that he be appointed. But the government never confirmed his appointment, for Hartmann refused to declare membership in a religious group and instead stated that he was *"konfessionslos,"* an unpardonable defect in the eyes of a bigoted government.

In 1933 he became, in collaboration with Paul Federn and Sandor Rado (later with Edward Bibring), editor of the *Internationale Zeitschrift für Psychoanalyse;* during the same year, the editorship of *Imago* was reorganized and entrusted to Ernst Kris and Robert Waelder. The second generation of psychoanalysts thus moved in and began to take over what the first had so brilliantly built up under Freud's guidance. This also had the effect of bringing Heinz Hartmann into closer association with Ernst Kris, which led to their Dioscurian friendship of later years, and proved a great blessing for the growth of psychoanalysis in this country.

When Heinz Hartmann left the Clinics, he was invited by Freud to continue his training analysis with him, one of the two instances known of that sort, and the greatest honor that a psychoanalyst could be accorded in those days. There is still another sidelight to Hartmann's second training analysis (1934-1936). Josef Breuer, who had been the family physician to Moritz and Ludo Hartmann, also occasionally treated Heinz, of course—which probably makes him the only analyst who was treated by both Breuer and Freud.

There is a gap of four years (1935-1939) in Heinz Hartmann's bibliography. This was a quadrennium of productive silence. On November 17, 1937, Hartmann read to the Viennese Society a paper on ego psychology and the problem of adaptation, part of his later more extended publication of the same title (1939). The audience was stunned by his presentation. There were probably few who grasped instantly the far-reaching consequences of his presentation, which extended psychoanalysis into new areas, and opened up a host of new

problems that had laid dormant in Freud's theories, but were here for
the first time set forth explicitly within the framework of a general
theory of psychoanalysis.

In 1928 Heinz married the pediatrician Dora Karplus, who later
became an analyst. She is a member of a professionally outstanding
Viennese family, her maternal great-uncle being Josef Breuer, and her
paternal uncle the famous neurologist, Johann Paul Karplus (1866-
1933), who, with Alois Kreidl (1864-1928) wrote the classical treatise
on the physiology of the diencephalon. Two sons—Ernest and Law-
rence (who became a Rhodes scholar)—were born to them. The
invasion of Austria forced the Hartmanns into exile, and they had to
leave Vienna in the spring of 1938. However, Heinz Hartmann's roots
in the classical soil of Europe seem to have been particularly strong,
for only in 1941 did he and his family at last arrive in New York,
after some time spent in Paris, Geneva, and Lausanne.

It was on the new continent that Hartmann brought to full fruition
his unusual gifts and the vast knowledge and experience he had accumulated. Systematically, he went over the ground of all fields of psychoanalysis, setting forth the results that obtain, in the light of their
structural aspect. In carrying out this task, he had, of course, to
include all other aspects of theory. Thus one may call the aggregate
of Heinz Hartmann's papers since 1941 a *Gesamtdarstellung* of psychoanalysis. A psychoanalytic thrust into entirely new fields, such as
the theory of values, was one of the many side effects.

Heinz Hartmann is a great teacher, and has been a fertilizing
influence on the work of many analysts. The number of papers he has
stimulated or enriched by his criticism among friends and pupils we
shall probably never know, but it must reach into the hundreds. His
work has become an integral part of that stream of psychoanalysis that
continues Freud's tradition; it is characterized by an insistence upon
the primacy of the psychoanalytic situation as the source and center
of observation and research, without the neglect of data obtained by
other methods, and by a balance of views: biological and cultural;
dynamic, economic, topographic, structural, and adaptational—and,
always, genetic.

Heinz Hartmann is, intellectually speaking, an aristocrat; his is
an essentially unpolemical mind, although probably no other analyst
has ever been engaged in as many discussions as he has. He is unpolemical, not because he is eclectic—the aristocratic spirit and eclecticism

are altogether incompatible—but because, in the history of abstract ideas, there are debates and not polemics. He himself has made valid contributions to the great debates that have continued through the centuries, from ancient Greek philosophy down to our own times, and that will continue for many centuries to come, until man has arrived at certainty about those questions on which one is forced to take a stand, well knowing that no lasting answer may ever be found.

In the great scientific tradition of the 19th century, Heinz Hartmann's work stands firmly rooted in clinical observation—that is to say, in data that are empirically and scientifically ascertainable. Yet this empirical root of his work has not impeded his psychological understanding of the metaphysical tradition that is so significant in Western civilization. The tendency to extract from that tradition those thoughts that reflect reality, whether they concern man's psychic reality or his relationship to objective reality—this is implicit in his work. In consideration of the width and extent of the areas brought by Heinz Hartmann into the psychoanalytic orbit, one may say that, among all of Freud's disciples, he has probably demonstrated the greatest synthetic power.

Aside from the sort of objections that every mental product is likely to arouse in the intellectual community, the criticism has been made that since 1939 Heinz Hartmann's work has been mainly of an abstract character, tending to shy away from clinical exemplification. This is true and it is quite surprising for a scholar who, in a score of papers, has shown his own clinical mastery. But if the objection means that Hartmann's papers do not provide any clues to the verifiability of the theories set forth in them, then it is wrong. The astute reader knows where to look, in the empirical realm, in order to test the contents and the concatenation of the magnificent abstract edifice that Heinz Hartmann has built.

On the formal side, Heinz Hartmann's psychoanalytic work can be described as the architectonic frame within which psychoanalytic research will have to be carried on for many decades to come. It is precisely its abstract austerity that gives it its beauty and individuality, while its roots in empiricism are what give it its solidity and vitality. The synthesis of psychology, sociology, history, philosophy, biology, and medicine—that is to say, the synthesis of *Geisteswissenschaften* and the natural sciences into the framework of a psychoanalytic theory—is the result of Hartmann's universality.

Heinz Hartmann cannot be called a popular analyst, in the true sense of the word. There are others, among those who have come here from Europe, who have become far better known to the American public. His contribution is still known to a comparatively small group, and only the expert can measure his achievements. Yet there is no doubt that, if he had sought popularity, he would have succeeded in attaining it—although that might have proven incompatible with his membership in that aristocracy of mind to which the chosen few belong.

A word about Heinz Hartmann as the man who is loved and admired by both friend and opponent: the happy man who has no enemy, just as his father (of whom a political foe once said: "One wishes to shake hands with him before one attacks him") had none. In the midst of his activities as physician, teacher, scientist, and as editor and cofounder of *The Psychoanalytic Study of the Child*, he rarely spends a day without meeting at least one of the large number of his friends. He is devoted to music, which is a prime passion with him, and to the arts, and is equally at home in the ancient ruins of Sicily and the *chefs d'oeuvre* of the Louvre. Yet he could also write on the latest novels (English, German, or French), being *au courant* not only with modern science and its history, but with the totality of artistic creations reflecting the genius of the Western mind.

Nobility does not display its wealth unnecessarily. Thus Heinz Hartmann's true profundity of mind is not fully revealed but only adumbrated in his published works, which—following the trend of our times—are limited to those fields in which he is a professional expert. He is certainly not the sort of writer who pretends to say— and even sometimes does say—more than he is truly equipped to. Whoever would want to plumb Hartmann's true depth must have the opportunity for intimate conversation with him.

If his "Conversations" were collected and published, one would see at once that in him is exemplified the type of mind that now stands at the brink of passing out of existence (it has already become a rarity), the type of mind that can be traced back to the Renaissance, that glorious period whose end (in its most general terms) we may well be witnessing now.

The Renaissance tradition, which came into being with Petrarch, cannot, of course, be discussed at length here. For want of a better name, let us call it "liberal humanism." The liberal humanist is, to be sure, encyclopedic, but the wide range of facts that he has mastered is only, so to speak, "minimum requirement." It is his original, individual synthesis that makes the liberal humanist what he is. He integrates the cultural tradition, without being overwhelmed by it; he transforms it into his own domain. This becomes especially impressive when one listens to Hartmann quoting or citing. Others use what has already been said as a source of confirmation for what they are now saying. When Hartmann introduces a quotation into his conversation, the new context adds new meaning to the words of his predecessors. By his individual understanding of the tradition that he shares, the liberal humanist organically enhances its growth.

The mind of the liberal humanist is raised above provincial prejudices; it has freed itself of any conformism (in this case, it had probably never been its victim, for Hartmann had already been both brilliant and original during his prep school days, as his classmates can well remember). To every new piece of knowledge or shade of stimulus, such a mind reverberates with its own individual subtlety, sensitiveness, and originality. The liberal humanist, at his best, is therefore not a "mirror" of the cultural tradition: with each new turn that he gives it, its pieces fall into new and surprising patterns.

How liberal such humanism may be can perhaps be best exemplified by a remark that Hartmann made after a speaker had demonstrated the fallacy of the theories that a former colleague had produced, following his leaving psychoanalysis. Hartmann agreed with the speaker's critique. "But," he added, "we should be grateful that he [the former colleague] has taken the trouble of thinking through one aspect consistently to its end, and has thus demonstrated to us its limitations and its errors." This is true liberalism, for each step taken in the history of ideas is close to its heart and meaningful, in so far as it represents the particular, perhaps momentary—and yet perhaps ultimately necessary—form of a general pattern. Such liberalism has become vastly extended by Freud's new psychology, which owes so much to the fact that Hartmann made it the center of his professional career.

In our accepting an idea, it makes a big difference whether the acceptance is "a casual flirtation," as Freud so aptly said, or "a legal marriage with all its duties and difficulties." In view of the broad cultural stream in which Heinz Hartmann was brought up, and the constant temptation to espouse one or the other of the many systems that are far more attractive and far more aesthetic than the psycho-analytic system, we have indeed reason to be grateful that a "casual flirtation" with psychoanalysis did not suffice him (as it has so many!), but that he underwent a "legal marriage" with it, and bore all the consequent duties and difficulties.

If Hartmann had indeed limited his contact with psychoanalysis to a casual flirtation, there easily might have been a way open for him to a professorship in psychiatry at one of the highly prized German universities, which offered positions of high prestige. But such a flirtation would have added up to a betrayal of liberal human-ism, which—notwithstanding its aspirations to attaining adequate recognition of its excellence—gives first place to a self-imposed per-fection of self and personality. Thus, since this was by no means a marriage of convenience, it became a happy marriage, in which both parties have had reason to be rightly grateful for the fact that they met and concluded an alliance. Both have remained faithful, and each has brought much to the other. Hartmann and psychoanalysis have grown together; they are right to be proud of each other.

Although Hartmann is part of a tradition which has had to be no more than sketched here, there is one aspect of his personality that may be touched on, even though with a regrettable brevity. Many of his professional papers are outstanding for the almost classic auster-ity of their sharply hewn abstractness. With Nietzsche, one might say that they are "Apollonian" in style and outlook. Yet, when one listens to Hartmann talking about music, nature, art, beauty, one discovers in him that Dionysiac element that Nietzsche also delineated. That Hartmann has succeeded in synthesizing the Apollonian and the Dionysiac (despite the pressure of some very un-Dionysiac special-ization!) is his own personal merit; it adds a special beauty to the many others he possesses.

The psychoanalyst, of course, would like to know how so many praiseworthy qualities came to be united in one person.

Two factors are clear enough: the cultural one, in the form of the eminence of the subjects of early identification; and the biological one, in the form of intellectual endowment, which comprises not only the highest intelligence but also an enviable memory, unusual quickness to grasp essentials, and a rare facility of the organization of thought.

Yet what the analyst would like to know, beyond these obvious factors, is what have been "the intervening variables."

The outstanding characteristic of Heinz Hartmann is his creativity—by which more is meant here than the totality of printed output, but a fundamental attitude. When Robert Bak (1965) in his tribute emphasized Heinz Hartmann's objectivity, he hit the nail on the head; this is the creative objectivity of a mind to whom truth is never, as it is to so many, a threat. Objectivity in some specific area is not rarely found; it is general objectivity toward all sectors of reality that is rather rare. What it requires is that cheerful tranquillity that one feels so strongly when one shares Heinz Hartmann's presence. It is by no means accidental that Heinz Hartmann introduced the concept of the "conflict-free sphere" in human personality. The vast area in his own personality in which freedom from conflict reigns is the backbone of that serenity of his that makes for creative objectivity. It is also the backbone of the incredible generosity with which he distributes the treasures of his mind, without concern for questions of priority: truth to the serene, the conflict-free mind is a universal property; it should belong to everyone and, in so doing, give up any of its narcissistic contaminations. It was to this very innocence of Heinz Hartmann's mind that Anna Freud (1965) was probably referring in her Tribute when she wrote: "In spite of this precarious position at the top of a profession, Heinz Hartmann, in his teaching activities and publications, seems to have completely disregarded or even remained oblivious to the battle which was staged around him. In the place of polemics, criticism of fellow workers, or bids to win approval, there is only the author's deep immersion into the problems which engage his own interest and for which he tries to gain the students', the readers', or the audiences' attention."

Yet, is such serenity and innocence the end result of having resolved crises and conflicts in the past, or is Heinz Hartmann distinguished by the privilege of possessing an unusually large inborn conflict-free sphere?

The authors recall vividly when they had the privilege of meeting Heinz Hartmann for the first time, some three decades or more ago. Although he has grown in stature and eminence since then, the basic and essential image of serenity and freedom from conflict was already fully grown then, and it was as appealing as it is at present.

What actually occurs deep down, where freedom from conflict must stop, remains his secret, as befits the man who never burdens others with concerns and worries of his own.

Two traits that are rarely met with—one having to do with Hartmann, the public man, and one with the person himself—should be recorded here, for they are so very characteristic of him. The type of person who ardently seeks offices and, provided he desires them strenuously enough, does succeed in the fulfillment of his heart's desire, is too well known to need description here. Heinz Hartmann was elected to the highest offices in almost every group that he honored by his membership; had he accepted every offer that was made, he could have had even more of this type of distinction; yet no instance is known in which he aspired to office, not to speak of making a move toward it. Groups to which he belongs consider it to be a matter of course, without the need for deliberation or doubt, that he should fill the highest office available. This unique rise without effort, in his public career, reflects that lack of ambivalence that is significant of Heinz Hartmann. Ambition always contains a grain of ambivalence, and groups respond sensitively, although frequently unconsciously, to the degree of ambition in the office-seeker, who counteracts in turn by means of intrigue. The very effortlessness of Heinz Hartmann in his public career seems to be present also in his professional work. His publications—which could be, in number, many times what they are, if he were an ambitious writer—impress the reader as effortless effusions of what has come to his mind; in fact, they may appear as if their content were known by everyone, as if the publications were written only because it so happened that no one had done so before. Thus it happens that his ratiocination too reveals an absence of ambivalence.

The other trait we have referred to above is likewise rare. For the last two decades, disease and its consequent physical discomfort have played a not inconsiderable role in Heinz Hartmann's life. Many were the moments when his friends were alarmed and worried greatly for him; yet Heinz Hartmann bore his misfortune and discomfiture without evoking in his friends those feelings of guilt that, even though one knows them to be irrational, one cannot usually avoid when a beloved person is suffering and in danger. This rare ability to spare friends what might have been a feeling of guilt may be taken as an indirect proof, if such were necessary, of Heinz Hartmann's predominantly serene, positive, and loving attitude, so delightfully free of ambivalence toward the world.

BIBLIOGRAPHY

Anonymous (1910/11), Moritz Hartmann. *Encyclopaedia Britannica*, 11th ed., 13:36.
—— (1924), Ludo Hartmann. *Arbeiter-Zeitung*, Nov. 15.
Bak, R. C. (1965), Heinz Hartmann: A Tribute to the Person. *Bull. Phila. Assn. Psa.*, 15:1-3.
Bamberger, L. (1872), Moritz Hartmann. *Die Presse*, May 18.
Bauer, S. (1926), Ludo Moritz Hartmann. In *Neue Österreichische Biographie 1815-1918*. Erste Abteilung Biographien. III. Band. Wien: Amalthea Verlag, 1926.
Bucura, C. J. (1910), Rudolf Chrobak. *Dtsch. Med. Wschr.*, No. 46.
D. B. (1921), Moritz Hartmann. *Arbeiter-Zeitung*, Oct. 21.
Die Chrobak-Feier am 22. März 1908. *Wien. klin. Wschr.*, Vol. 21, No. 13.
Eitelberger von Edelberg, R. (1879/84), *Gesammelte kunsthistorische Schriften*, 4 Vols. Vienna: Braumüller.
Freud, A. (1965), Heinz Hartmann: A Tribute. *J. Am. Psa. Assn.*, 13:195-196.
Freud, S. (1914), The History of the Psycho-Analytic Movement. *S.E.*, 14:7-66.
Hartmann, M. (1873/74), *Gesammelte Werke*, 10 Vols. Stuttgart: Cotta.
Kisch, P. (1921), Der Dichter von "Kelch und Schwert." Zum hundertsten Geburtstage Moritz Hartmanns am 15. Oktober. *Neue Freie Presse*, Oct. 16.
Koenig, O. (1954), Ludo Hartmann zum Gedächtnis. *Arbeiter-Zeitung*, Nov. 14.
Kürnberger, F. (1872), Moritz Hartmann. In: *Literarische Herzenssachen, Reflexionen und Kritiken*. Wien: L. Rosner, 1877, 233-238.
Lampa, A. (1924), Ludo Hartmann zum Gedächtnis. *Volksbildung*, 5:235-241.
Lass, H. (1963), Moritz Hartmann: Entwicklungsstufen des Lebens und Gestaltwandel des Werkes. Unpublished dissertation, Hamburg University.
Lesky, E. (1965), *Die Wiener Medizinische Schule im 19. Jahrhundert*. Graz & Köln: Böhlau, 471-475.
Neumann, W. (1854), *Moritz Hartmann: Eine Biographie*. Cassel: Ernst Balde.
Österreichisches Biographisches Lexikon, 1815-1950 [publ. by Österreichische Akademie der Wissenschaften]. Graz & Köln: Böhlau, 1959, 2:195-196.
Peham, H. (1910), Rudolf Chrobak. *Wien. klin. Wschr.*, 23:1507-1510.
Schönbauer, L. (1944), *Das medizinische Wien*. Vienna: Urban & Schwarzenberg, 1947, 409-411.
—— (1957), Chrobak, Rudolf. In *Neue Deutsche Biographie* [publ. by Bayerische Akademie der Wissenschaften]. Berlin: Duncker & Humblot, 3:249-250.
Steinberg, S. H. (1953), Moritz Hartmann. In *Cassel's Encyclopedia of Literature*. London: Cassel, 1:999.
Stern, J. L. (1910), *Wiener Volksbildungswesen*. Jena: Eugen Diederichs.
Stowasser, O. H. (1926), Ludo Moritz Hartmann. *Mitteil. Österreich. Inst. Geschichte*, 41:380-384.
von Below, G., Stein, E., Ciccotti, E., Salvioli, G., & Bauer, S. (1925), Zur Erinnerung an L. M. Hartmann. *Vierteljahrschr. Sozial. & Wirtschaftgeschichte*, 18:312-339.
Wittner, O. (1906/07), *Moritz Hartmanns Leben und Werke*, 2 Vols. Prag: J. G. Calve.
—— (1911), ed., *Briefe aus dem Vormärz: Eine Sammlung aus dem Nachlass Moritz Hartmanns*. Prag: J. G. Calve.
Wolkan, R. (1921), Moritz Hartmann als Politiker. *Neue Freie Presse*, Nov. 8.

Links Between Hartmann's Ego Psychology and the Child Analyst's Thinking

ANNA FREUD, LL.D., D.Sc.

To speak to an audience in honor of Heinz Hartmann on the occasion of his 70th birthday is not an assignment to be taken lightly. With Hartmann himself present as a listener, obviously nothing will fulfill the purpose of a tribute except an address which approximates his own, exacting level of thinking. To the lecturer this presents the task of showing himself fully conversant with the body of theories which owe their origin to Hartmann, of proving her appreciation of them by measuring against them her own notions and opinions, for whatever these are worth, and of surveying beyond this the superior achievement of a brilliant mind trained to rigorous scientific effort.

Opposition and Acceptance

In their Preface to Hartmann's *Ego Psychology and Problem of Adaptation*, the editors speak of "the remarkable degree to which Hartmann's ideas have shaped, and become assimilated into current psychoanalytic thinking" (p. viii). If, thereby, they create a picture of an author's ideas being accepted easily and quickly, the impression is misleading. On the contrary: although this had no power to deter him, Hartmann's ego psychology met with an extraordinary amount of opposition in the analytic world. There were many analytic colleagues who took exception to the degree to which he turned his mind away from the problems of psychopathology to contemplate instead the possibility of securing for psychoanalysis the status of a

Lecture in honor of Heinz Hartmann's 70th birthday, New York Academy of Medicine, November 4, 1964.

16

general psychology. Others had misgivings on principle concerning the manner in which, in Hartmann's writings, theoretical thinking took precedence over the clinical concerns of the analyst in practice. But, above all, there were many who feared that the explicit introduction of an ego psychology into psychoanalysis endangered its position as a depth psychology, a discipline concerned exclusively with the activity of the instinctual drives and the functioning of the unconscious mind. Taking the stand that work on the ego was an unwarranted extension of analysis, they ignored the fact that, from its beginnings, psychoanalytic metapsychology was intended to embrace all the agencies within the mental apparatus, plus their interactions.

However this may be, it took years until by the mere weight of his published work, opposition was silenced sufficiently to allow one after the other of his notions to become accepted, to penetrate to the knowledge of the membership at large, and to infiltrate gradually into the teaching programs of many of the official training institutes. By now, concepts such as the conflict-free sphere of the ego; primary and secondary ego autonomy; intrasystemic conflicts within the ego; the notion of energy change in sublimation; interest in the undifferentiated id-ego sphere, etc., are familiar elements in the analytic theory.

Hartmann's Theories and Child Analysis

If "the assimilation of Hartmann's ideas into current analytic thinking" applies to the analytic world in general, it does so even more in the area of child analysis. The child analyst's thinking, governed as it is by the developmental aspects of the human personality, does not thrive on the basis of drive psychology alone, but needs to range freely in the whole theoretical field of psychoanalysis, according equal significance to id, ego, and superego, to depth and surface, as Hartmann does. This creates the specific links between his work and the child analyst's thinking, which is indicated in the title.

Some Interrelations Between Hartmann and Myself, Past and Present

Since I had myself in mind in this title, as the representative of at least one brand of child analysis, and since it is my own thinking which I propose to compare with Hartmann's, some personal remarks concerning our common past will be needed here.

Heinz Hartmann and I entered the Vienna Psychoanalytic Society almost simultaneously, some forty years ago, he being analytically my slightly elder brother, or half brother, since in some respect we even shared the same father. In the field of ego psychology, too, we appeared almost at the same time, in the 1930s. I came into it, more conventionally, from the side of the ego's defensive activity against the drives; Hartmann, in a more revolutionary manner, from the new angle of ego autonomy, which until then had lain outside analytic study. This revealed itself openly for the first time in the Vienna Society in the discussion following the presentation of my first two chapters of *The Ego and the Mechanisms of Defense* in 1936. Hartmann showed himself appreciative on the whole, but he emphasized the point that to show the ego at war with the id was not the whole story; that there were many additional problems of ego growth and ego functioning which needed consideration. My views were more restricted at the time, and this was news to me which I was not yet ready to assimilate.

From that point onward we went ahead, each of us very much immersed in our special field, respecting each other, quoting each other, but not in active interchange. In production and achievement, Hartmann always remained some way ahead, owing to his genuinely scientific mind and thorough scientific training, both of which I lacked and had to acquire slowly. It was not easy for me, or for anybody at the time, to catch up with the rapid development of his systematic thinking.

Our ideas met fully and squarely for the first time in the Symposium on "The Mutual Influences in the Development of Ego and Id," held at the Amsterdam Congress, 1951, and they remained firmly linked since then. In his and my contribution presented there already can be found the germs and nuclei of all the topical links on which I propose to enlarge in what follows.

Links Between Hartmann's and My (The Child Analyst's) Thinking

Although the connections may be infinitely more numerous when traced in detail, I single out for the present purpose seven of them which seem to me to represent basic concepts in Hartmann's scheme as well as cornerstones in my recent account of work in the Hampstead Child-Therapy Clinic (1965). This may be an unorthodox procedure of approaching another author's work, but one which will, I hope, serve the present purpose and in turn elicit some reactions from the other side.

THE CONFLICT-FREE SPHERE OF THE EGO

Following his discussion remarks in 1936, Hartmann presented his paper on *Ego Psychology and the Problem of Adaptation* in 1937. There we find for the first time the exhortation to analysts that "we must recognize that, though the ego grows on conflicts, these are not the only roots of ego development." Obvious though this point of view seemed to him, no one found it easy at the time to turn his interest away from the internal conflicts between ego and drive activity and the symptomatology resulting from them, and to become concerned with the purely maturational and developmental side of ego growth, that is, with events which proceed silently, without clamor, outside the realm of conflict. On the other hand, since these processes determine the shape of the very ego apparatus and ego functions which are later drawn into the orbit of conflict, and which serve as tools in the ego's struggle for mastery over the id, this—as Hartmann stressed—is no less decisive for the upkeep of normality or for psychopathology than all the other items of mental functioning which traditionally come under the analyst's scrutiny.

As indicated above, the correctness of this point has been accepted in the analytic world by now, although the analysts of adults often pay no more than lip service to it. Where child analysis is concerned, on the other hand, as in our Hampstead Clinic, it has been put into action very vigorously in the Diagnostic Profile, used for the assessment of a child's development in general or his psychopathology in particular. With the Profile scheme used as a guide, the diagnostician's attention is directed as decisively to "conflict-free," autonomous ego growth, and the irregularities and failures of building up ego apparatuses and functions, as it is directed to the ego's defense organization or the vicissitudes of drive development.[1] To my mind, these sections of the Profile carry out the suggestions introduced and up-

[1] See Profile, Section V, B, Ego and Superego Development, (a), (b), and (c) (A. Freud, 1965, p. 142).

held by Hartmann during the past thirty years. Whether this application to diagnosis is in fact far-reaching enough and meets his demands in full remains for him to confirm.

THE INTRASYSTEMIC APPROACH

Moving from the concept of a conflict-free area to that of conflict, Hartmann wishes analysts to pay attention also to those clashes which occur not between the mental agencies but within the particular systems. Intrasystemic conflicts had of course always been prominent in psychoanalytic theory. Within the id, they are known to be only potential ones, since drive opposites such as passive-active, feminine-masculine, love-hate, are contained without contradiction so long as they remain unconscious and turn into "conflict" only when they rise to the surface and approach the conscious ego. Within the super-ego, clashes have been shown to arise between conflicting identifications with and internalizations of external figures of authority, which genetically have served as its sources. But what Hartmann has in mind here are the ways in which, during its growth, the ego is torn within itself, the development of one side of it acting as an obstacle to the intactness of another side. In his "Technical Implications of Ego Psychology" (1951), for example, Hartmann emphasizes the necessity to examine "whether the autonomous ego functions are interfered with by the defensive functions."

This, to me, too, has seemed an important point for years. It is true that in clinical descriptions of analytic cases it has always been implied and that it has been alluded to under terms such as "the price paid by the ego for the upkeep of its defense organization"; the "harm done by pathology to normal functioning," as, for example, the damage done to normal motility by a hysterical paralysis, or the damage done to rational thinking by the obsessional devices. But what Hartmann and I have in mind goes beyond these facts encountered in pathology, to events which happen normally in every individual's development. As I have expressed it elsewhere (1965):

> As the ego of the child grows and improves its functioning, better *awareness* of the internal and external world brings it into contact with many unpleasurable and painful aspects; the increasing dominance of the *reality principle* curtails wishful thinking; the improvement of *memory* leads to retaining not only pleasurable but frightening and painful items; the *synthetic function* prepares the ground for conflict

between the inner agencies, etc. The resultant influx of unpleasure and anxiety is more than the human being can bear without relief; consequently it is warded off by the defense mechanisms which come into action to protect the ego.

Thus, *denial* interferes with accuracy in the perception of the outer world by excluding the unpleasurable. *Repression* does the same for the inner world by withdrawing conscious cathexis from unpleasurable items. *Reaction formations* replace the unpleasurable and unwelcome by the opposite. All three mechanisms interfere with memory, i.e., with its impartial functioning, regardless of pleasure and unpleasure. *Projection* runs counter to the synthetic function by eliminating anxiety-arousing elements from the image of the personality and attributing them to the object world.

In short, while the forces of maturation and adaptation strive toward the increasing, reality-governed efficiency in all ego functioning, the defense against unpleasure works in the opposite direction and, in its turn, invalidates the ego functions [p. 104f.].[2]

OTHER INTRASYSTEMIC ASPECTS

In the same paper, "Technical Implications of Ego Psychology," Hartmann speaks of "the relative preponderance of certain ego functions over others," and in his "Psychoanalysis and Developmental Psychology" (1950) he advocates that it should "be feasible and useful to replace the global . . . terms like 'precocious' or 'retarded' ego development by more detailed statements specifying what ego functions have actually undergone a precocious or retarded development in relation to the drives and in relation to one another" (p. 107).

In fact, for the accurate assessment of any child's developmental status, no point can be of greater assistance than this particular one which complements what has always happened in analytic diagnosis with regard to the sequence of libidinal, later also of aggressive, stages. So far as I am concerned, I have tried to take care of this by establishing the concept of *developmental lines*, contributed to both from the side of id and of ego development; these developmental lines lead from the child's state of immaturity to the gradual setting up of a mature personality and are, in fact, the result of interaction between maturation, adaptation and structuralization (1965, p. 62ff.). While what enters into this combination from the side of the drives is better

---

[2] See also A. Freud (1945). In the Profile this point of Hartmann's is taken care of in section B (d) (A. Freud, 1965, p. 143).

known to us at present, the obvious need to fill in the missing data on the side of the ego spurs us on to greater efforts in exploring those aspects of ego growth which Hartmann has in mind.

The disharmony and disequilibrium between the lines of development, in their turn, serve to highlight precocity or retardation of specific ego functions as well as "the relative preponderance of certain ego functions over others," in Hartmann's sense.

"THE SIGN AND SIGNAL FUNCTION OF BEHAVIOR"

With regard to the observation of behavior for the purpose of assessments of development, it gives me particular pleasure to find in Hartmann's attitude that of a fellow rebel. He writes in "Psychoanalysis and Developmental Psychology" (1950) as follows: "We come to the conclusion that psychoanalytic psychology is not limited to what can be gained through the use of the psychoanalytic method" (p. 103). And further: "Such [developmental] studies will of necessity lead to a growing awareness of the sign- or signal-function which behavior details may have for the observer, that is, to a better or more systematic understanding of how data of direct observation can be used as indicators of structurally central and partly unconscious developments—in a sense that by far transcends the possibilities of sign interpretation accessible to the various methods of testing" (p. 102).

The suggestion made here by Hartmann—that development, finished character structures, and even pathological formations can be assessed outside of the analytic session—runs of course counter to the beliefs of many analysts who wish to rely exclusively on the material produced by their patients via the analytic method. On the other hand, it is a point to which I subscribe fully (1965, Chapter 1). I have also tried to demonstrate in detail that in the historical development of psychoanalysis such complete restriction of observation to the privacy of the analytic setting is a fiction rather than reality; that derivatives of the unconscious, observed in normal people not under analysis, were considered a legitimate source of information at all times, viz., faulty and symptomatic actions, daydreams, children's dreams (see Freud, 1900, 1901); that, at a later date, the same became true of the revealing functions of certain characters.[3]

[3] As emphasized by S. Freud (1933), concerning the obsessional character, with the expectation ". . . that other character traits as well will turn out similarly to be precipitates or reaction-formations related to particular pregenital libidinal structures" (p. 102).

Personally, I can see no difficulty in extending this conviction of certain fixed relationships existing between surface appearance and id content from the mental phenomena named above to particular items of behavior, especially of children, as they can be observed in the areas of play; in hobbies; in the attitude to illness, food, clothing, etc. I believe, what deters the majority of analysts from accepting this suggestion is not so much a disbelief in the validity of this material, but a reminder of certain phases in the history of psychoanalysis when such items were used profusely and disadvantageously for the purpose of symbolic interpretation within analysis, which is a technical mistake, of course.

That the intellectual ego functions as such can be assessed in surface observation, i.e., testing, naturally needs no further proof.

PROBLEMS OF THE INFANTILE NEUROSIS

Nowhere, of course, does Hartmann come nearer to the concerns of the child analyst than in his paper on the "Problems of Infantile Neurosis" (1954).

He asserts that "at present we have more questions than answers" and that "what Freud said about infantile neurosis long ago remains true today. But it is also obvious that in the course of the development of analysis reformulations are inevitable"; that it is "actually not easy to say what we call an infantile neurosis." He speaks also of neurotic problems in children "limited to a single functional disturbance" and of the fact that "the way from conflict to symptom is often shorter than in adult neurosis" (p. 208f.).

The problems alluded to here by Hartmann are precisely those which engage our interest in the Hampstead Clinic and which have given rise to some of our publications.[4] We agree with Hartmann that the term "infantile neurosis" has been overused, and extended to cover a large variety of disturbances which do not come under the heading of neuroses since they are either not the result of conflict at all or, in any case, not of the type of internal conflict where danger comes to a head during the oedipus complex, regression takes place from there to earlier, prephallic fixation points, and a pathogenic conflict arises between these reawakened pregenital strivings and the ego—conflicts which are solved by compromise, i.e., by symptom formation. Far from corresponding to this classical definition of the infantile neurosis,

[4] See, for example, A. Freud (1965, Chapter 5) and Nagera (1966).

many of the childhood disturbances seen in the Clinic are (nonorganic) disturbances of vital body needs ("limited to one functional disturbance," in Hartmann's terms); or they represent excessive delays in acquiring vital ego functions; or primary disturbances of narcissism (Sandler, 1966) or of object relatedness; or lack of ego control or faulty superego development or both. We subscribe to the same view as Hartmann, that some of the quasi-pathological formulations "represent the best possible solution of a given infantile conflict," and we agree wholeheartedly with him that the whole subject of diagnostic categorization needs reformulation so far as childhood pathology is concerned.

One of our suggestions in this direction is to clear the field by establishing as a separate diagnostic category the so-called *developmental disturbances*, namely, disorders which arise owing to the particular external and internal strains and stresses, dangers and anxieties connected with particular developmental phases, and which are transitory in the sense that they fade away with the passing of the developmental level on which they have emerged. As shown by Nagera (1966), it is a long way from this type of childhood problem to the infantile neuroses proper, and the gap can be filled by a whole hierarchy of other forms of infantile pathology.

Hartmann shows himself concerned further with "the simple clinical question of what the actual correlations between childhood neurosis and form and intensity of adult neurosis are" (p. 209f.), and he quotes the Wolf Man case as one of the rare opportunities where such a correlation can be found in the literature. Simple as the question may be, the answer is not easy to give, and at present no more can be offered than a few tentative ideas. While we know for certain that every adult neurosis is based on an infantile one, it has been demonstrated by experience that this statement is not reversible: not every infantile neurosis is followed by an adult neurosis. Moreover, in childhood there are many more dissocial individuals, exhibitionists, fetishists, and transvestites than there are adult delinquents or perverts, notwithstanding the fact that adult delinquency, criminality, and perversion invariably begin in early life. Hartmann is right in asserting that "more systematic study" of these problems is needed before we can predict with any degree of certainty what will be the further fate of an infantile neurosis or any other childhood disorder: whether, as phase-determined, it will be "outgrown"; whether it will persist unaltered into adulthood, as some of the perversions do; or whether it will change form, as it happens from the dissocial to the compulsive, or the phobic-hysteric to the obsessional, or from the obsessional to the schizophrenic, etc.

THE PROBLEM OF MORALITY

As regards the problem of morality, my developmental study of the attainment of law abidingness in individual life does not in any way come up to Hartmann's closely argued, beautiful, objective essay on the whole relationship between psychoanalysis and moral values (1960). But, at least, as it seems to me, I have managed to fulfill Hartmann's demands in one particular respect, namely, to trace how, to use his terminology, "the various ego functions and acquisitions enter into the final result as independent variables." Like Hartmann, I have been impressed by the state of affairs which exists in this respect. Although, intrinsically, ego functions such as memory, secondary-process thinking, reality testing, integration, control of motility have neither a moral connotation nor the opposite, social behavior and law abidingness cannot come about without them, nor can they without ego mechanisms such as imitation, identification, introjection. It is a fascinating developmental study in itself to see each ego attribute, as it appears during the individual's growth, contribute to the unfolding of the socially adapted, moral personality. Memory is indispensable for the individual's acting on experience and foresight; reason and logic for understanding cause and effect in relation to behavior; ego control of motility for preventing action on impulse; identification and introjection for internalizing the external social norms, etc.

I am well aware that this does not cover the problem of morality, nor does it touch on the value issues, as they are raised by Hartmann. My exposition merely serves to demonstrate the double pull within the personality, the various ego characteristics helping the individual toward morality while the id strivings exert their urge in the opposite direction.

THE CONCEPT OF HEALTH

Finally, Hartmann and I come very close together in our approach to the concept of health, which, like the study of normality, is a neglected area in the analytic literature.

We agree with each other in *not* conceiving of psychic health in terms of the *opposite of neurosis,* since phenomena such as conflict, defense, compromise formations are necessary for both, and are merely quantitatively and not qualitatively different in the mentally ill and mentally healthy.

We also agree that mental health cannot be characterized by the absence of *suffering.* Hartmann (1939b) expresses this by writing "that a limited amount of suffering and illness forms an integral part of the scheme of health" (p. 7). For me it is an important point that, regarding children, the presence of suffering is no reliable indicator for the presence of pathology; that, on the contrary, mental distress has to be accepted as a normal by-product of the child's dependency, his exposure to frustrations, and the inevitable strains and stresses of development; more than this: that the absence of suffering in an individual child may be an ominous sign of ill-health, pointing to organic damage, mental backwardness, or extreme passivity.

So far as the *location and maintenance* of mental health are concerned, Hartmann points above all to the intactness of the synthetic and adaptive functions of the ego. I assess in a more global way the intactness of the whole trend of progressive id-ego development, asserting that children in whom these progressive tendencies outweigh the regressive ones are more safely anchored in health, and are helped to maintain health by the pleasure gains which they experience during maturation, development, and adaptation.

There is no doubt that we both regard personal characteristics such as frustration tolerance, anxiety tolerance, and a high potential for sublimation and neutralization of drives as substantial aids in maintaining the status of health.

Altogether, I cannot help feeling that it is in this particular area of the concept of mental health where the links between Hartmann's and my thinking become most obvious. While other psychoanalytic authors emphasize what ego and superego do to make us neurotic, Hartmann and I both have given added weight to that side of the analytic theory which convincingly shows the immense efforts made by the ego and superego to keep us healthy.

Conclusion

One concluding remark: there were occasions in the past when Hartmann used to refer to me as his "silent critic." Obviously, he misunderstood my attitude since, though I have have been silent, while waiting for increased understanding, I was never critical. I hope I have convinced him now, at this late date, that far from being a silent critic, I am an eloquent supporter of his work.

BIBLIOGRAPHY

Freud, A. (1936), *The Ego and the Mechanisms of Defense*. NY: IUP, 1946.
—— (1945), Indications for Child Analysis. *Psa. Study Ch.*, 1:127-149.
—— (1952), The Mutual Influences in the Development of Ego and Id: Introduction to the Discussion. *Psa. Study Ch.*, 7:42-50.
—— (1965), *Normality and Pathology in Childhood*. NY: IUP.
Freud, S. (1900), The Interpretation of Dreams. *S.E.*, 4 & 5.
—— (1901), The Psychopathology of Everyday Life. *S.E.*, 6.
—— (1933), New Introductory Lectures on Psycho-Analysis. *S.E.*, 22:3-182.
Hartmann, H. (1939a), *Ego Psychology and the Problem of Adaptation*. NY: IUP, 1958.
—— (1939b), Psychoanalysis and the Concept of Health. *Essays*, 1-18.
—— (1950), Psychoanalysis and Developmental Psychology. *Essays*, 99-112.
—— (1951), Technical Implications of Ego Psychology. *Essays*, 142-154.
—— (1952), The Mutual Influences in the Development of Ego and Id. *Essays*, 155-181.
—— (1954), Problems of Infantile Neurosis. *Essays*, 207-217.
—— (1960), *Psychoanalysis and Moral Values*. NY: IUP.
Nagera, H. (1966), *Early Childhood Disturbances, the Infantile Neurosis, and the Adulthood Disturbances*. NY: IUP.
Sandler, J. (1966), Disorders of Narcissism (in preparation).

Discussion of Hartmann's Ego Psychology and the Problem of Adaptation

JOHN D. BENJAMIN, M.D.

I am pleased to have the opportunity to discuss with you Hartmann's *Ego Psychology and the Problem of Adaptation,* a work which has had such a major impact on the development of psychoanalytic science and psychoanalytic thinking. In so doing, I shall of necessity be historical, in an informal and at times even personal way. I know that there are some who feel that the historical approach to psychoanalysis, as to science in general, is often overdone; and I, too, am of the opinion that sometimes psychoanalytic history tends to become a sort of psychoanalytic archeology, revealing more an antiquarian than a developmental point of view. Nonetheless, I am in full agreement with Hartmann when he states, in an introductory note explaining why he chose to leave the English translation of this work in 1958 essentially unchanged in content from the original 1939 German version, "I feel that a close study of historical developments in psychoanalysis is still one main prerequisite for its fuller understanding" (p. xi). To which I would add, as I have in the past (1959), that this fuller understanding is in turn a prerequisite for meaningful theory revision when that is indicated.

In emphasizing the great impact of this work, I should add that for a number of years it stood in remarkable contrast to the number of people who had actually read the paper. One might almost say, "Never had so much been read by so few!" I am referring not only

This paper was read at the Meeting of the Chicago Psychoanalytic Society, January 28, 1964. The editors do not know whether Dr. Benjamin would have published it in this form had he lived. They want to express appreciation to Mrs. Katherine Tennes and Dr. Herbert S. Gaskill for their work in preparing this for publication.

to the obvious fact that no English translation at all was available until 1951 and no complete one until 1958, and that this automatically excluded a large number of potential readers; but also to the less obvious finding that among many German-speaking and -reading colleagues the number of conversational references to this publication far exceeded the bits of evidence that it had been read carefully, or, in some instances, even read at all. Part of the explanation for this lies, no doubt, in the length of the article and the rather difficult style in which it was written; another part, in the frequent references to it in later works by Hartmann himself and by others, giving the reader the feeling that he knew the work well even though he had not read it. We are perhaps more accustomed to this phenomenon in the cases of literary than of scientific classics, but it unquestionably occurs frequently enough in the latter sphere as well.

At this point I find it appropriate to confess that my own first reading of this paper was also quite inadequate. I liked it in most respects, and quoted it as being in substantial agreement with some ideas of my own (1950). But it was not until I reread it much later that I read it carefully enough to understand more precisely just what were the areas of agreement and disagreement, and to recognize the full magnitude of Hartmann's achievement.

Today the situation is an entirely different one. An excellent translation by Rapaport is available, following an earlier partial but annotated version by the same author. Ego psychology is now taught more or less systematically in most Institutes, and this monograph as well as later works of Hartmann are assigned reading. Presumably, therefore, not only most analytic students and recent graduates, but most of their teachers as well, are thoroughly familiar with it. Under these circumstances, I would consider it superfluous, and a waste of your time and mine, for me to review the book with you in a systematic condensation. Later on, I shall summarize and discuss a few of its most salient points. Before that, however, I should like to give, not so much even a sketchy picture, as a reminder, of the status of psychoanalytic ego psychology at the time this publication appeared.

For the purpose of such a preliminary general orientation, I choose the year 1937, when Hartmann presented the chief substance of this paper to the Viennese Psychoanalytic Society. This was the same year that Freud published "Analysis Terminable and Interminable," which included his first major discussion of ego psychology since 1933, following his concentration on this topic in 1921, 1923, and 1926. A year earlier, Anna Freud's *The Ego and the Mechanisms of Defense* had been published. Waelder's "Principle of Multiple Functioning" had appeared in 1930, and his paper on reality testing in 1936. Nunberg, who in 1930 had published his paper on "The Synthetic Function of the Ego," had participated with Glover, Fenichel, and others in the 1936 "Symposium on the Theory of the Therapeutic Results of Psychoanalysis" (published in 1937), in which ego-psychological points of view were prominent. Fenichel's major paper on "Early Stages of Ego Development" also appeared in 1937, as did Balint's paper on "Early Developmental Stages of the Ego." In 1936 E. Bibring had considered some of the interrelationships of instinctual drive psychology and ego psychology as it then stood. A few years earlier, in 1934, Kris had already introduced the concept of regression in the service of the ego. In this country Hendrick published in 1936 on ego development in terms of character problems, and in 1937 French had considered the issue of adaptation to reality in terms of the repetition compulsion.

All the publications I have mentioned so far are actually touched on by Hartmann in the monograph and included in his bibliography; and some of them, particularly Anna Freud's book, are referred to frequently for purposes of supporting or clarifying some of his theses.

It is clear in retrospect that from the standpoint of the history of psychoanalysis the time was ripe in 1937 for major developments and shifts of emphasis, all of them involving some aspects of ego psychology. In particular there was an increasing readiness to pay more attention to external reality as a *source* of variability in ego development, on the one hand; and, on the other, to the ego itself, or many of its functions, as an instrument of adaptation *to* external reality in a broader sense than had hitherto been considered. Some of these attempts—namely, Hartmann's, Anna Freud's, and, in my opinion, though not everyone's, Erikson's—were able to expand the field of psychoanalysis importantly while remaining entirely within the main body of psychoanalytic thought and experience; others were destined to depart so far from this background as to lose meaningful contact with psychoanalysis proper, as most of us understand this term. For those of us who strongly believe, on what we think is good evidence, that the basic data and many of the concepts of psychoanalysis are and must remain a cornerstone of human individual and social psychology (despite the need for revision as well as elaboration of much of our theory [Benjamin, 1950, 1959, 1961a, 1965]), this departure constitutes a serious limitation of potential. Since we are not concerned here with surveying the present scene, however, I shall merely point out that the first publications in this direction of such diverse authors as Horney (1936), Kardiner (1939), and Sullivan (1938) also date from this period. Of more direct pertinence to psychoanalytic ego psychology is the fact that the first of Erikson's main series of investigations (1950, 1946/56) which, starting off in predominantly libido-theoretical terms, have significantly enriched our concepts of adaptation and of ego development, was published in 1937. In contrast to Hartmann, however, Erikson himself has never succeeded in delineating a coherent theoretical synthesis of his work with the rest of modern psychoanalytic ego psychology. Rapaport's (1958a, 1959) efforts to do this for him, while brilliant as well as enlightening, were not, in my opinion, entirely successful. I might add that Rapaport (1958a) shared this opinion.

One more topic should be mentioned at this point, with a brevity that is disproportionate to its importance, in itself and in creating that climate of interest in the ego that we are discussing. I refer to the whole series of clinical-therapeutic-theoretical developments in the '20s and '30s that can best be indicated in shorthand by such words as defense analysis, character resistances, character analysis, character neuroses, theory of technique, and theory of therapeutic results (e.g., Fenichel, 1935; Reich, 1933; Kaiser, 1934; Glover et al., 1937; and others). Again in my opinion, the best in psychoanalytic theory to date has usually been derived in major part from clinical experience. Despite opinions to the contrary, I believe this also holds true for many of Hartmann's best contributions.

In this connection it is scarcely necessary to correct any impression I may have given, from the works I chose to cite, that this period in psychoanalysis was in any way *dominated* by ego psychology as such. Mere mention of such significant publications as those of Lewin (1935, 1937) on claustrophobia and on hypomania, and of Fenichel (1936) on the equation girl=phallus and on the scoptophilic instinct, to which many more by other authors could be added, will suffice to dispel any such impression if it exists.

With this introduction, I shall now turn to Hartmann as of 1939, and with that to Freud also. For it is quite impossible, within any reasonable time limit for this presentation, to attempt even a greatly shortened version of the fascinating story of Freud's changing concepts of the nature, genesis, and functions of the ego and of the role of external reality, from the very earliest days of psychoanalysis on, during the fifty-two years from 1887 to 1939 (see Kris, 1951; Jones, 1957; Hartmann, 1956; Rapaport, 1958a, 1959; Gill, 1963; Benjamin, 1961a, 1965). I propose, therefore, to summarize at this point some of the major theses advanced in Hartmann's monograph, and refer to Freud's views while discussing Hartmann's.

Of the many concepts advanced in this rich and logically coherent work, I choose the following for brief consideration: (1) the activity of the ego; (2) ego constitution; (3) change of function; (4) primary and secondary autonomy; and (5) the conflict-free sphere.

Ego Activity and Ego Constitution

When Freud first formulated the tripartite structural theory as such in 1923, following the beginnings of this concept in 1921, he took many steps in the direction of his and others' later ego-psychological formulations; e.g., the ego's coherent organization, the role of identification in its formation, its relationship to perception, the unconscious nature of its resistances and defenses, and the sources of its energies. Yet with respect to both the relative *activity* of the ego and the question of *ego constitution*, our first two topics, Freud was explicitly negative in this work. As regards the former, he compared the ego to the rider who is obliged to guide the id horse where *it* wants to go (p. 25). It is "a poor creature owing service to three masters," menaced by dangers from the external world, the id, and the superego. "It is not only a helper to the id; it is also a submissive slave" (p. 56). As regards ego constitution, Freud stated flatly: "it is not possible to speak of direct inheritance in the ego" (p. 38).

A short three years later, in *Inhibition, Symptoms and Anxiety* (1926), a major shift had occurred with respect to the active position of the ego in dealing with external as well as internal reality. Though still limited largely to external and internal *dangers*, the role of the ego in anticipating these and taking appropriate action through signal anxiety is clearly a description of an active adaptive process. Freud spoke of the ego exercising its "power," and even explicitly asked the question how he could reconcile this emphasis on the "might of the ego" with the description of its powerless and apprehensive position that he had given in *The Ego and the Id* (p. 95). His answer (p. 97ff.), which need not concern us here, was in part a confusing one. But it is of some interest to note that it contained statements about the relationship of ego and id that are pertinent to some of the present-day concerns about structural theory in its classic form (see, for example, Hartmann, 1952; Benjamin, 1961a; Gill, 1963).

These concepts of Freud, repeated and expanded in 1933, even imply a relative secondary functional autonomy of the ego, although in no sense do they imply a *developmental* autonomy.

Hartmann, of course, went far beyond Freud, and beyond Nunberg (1930), Waelder (1930, 1936), and Anna Freud (1936), too, in advancing and generalizing the concept of a powerful ego serving the function of adaptation to reality. Nevertheless, in this respect he was in a direct line of continuity with the development of Freud's own views.

The same statement does not hold true, at least not in the same way, for the problem of *ego constitution*. As you will remember, toward the end of his monograph Hartmann addresses himself specifically to this question (pp. 101-107), with the comment that the components of ego constitution deserve our attention just as much as do the components of drive constitution. He cites evidence from twin studies in support of the thesis that not only ego apparatuses, but the ego itself as a regulative agency, have constitutional roots. He speaks of inherited ego *characteristics*, and then quotes the passage from "Analysis Terminable and Interminable": "nor does it imply any mystical overvaluation of heredity if we think it credible that, even before the ego has come into existence, the lines of development, trends and reactions . . . are already laid down for it" (1937, p. 240).

This passage from Freud is of interest in two different directions. In the one, it is consistent with a general tendency in Freud to look upon hereditary factors as *predetermining* rather than codetermining highly complex interactive functions. As one out of many examples, I quote from "The Dissolution of the Oedipus Complex" (1924, p. 174): "Although the majority of human beings go through the Oedipus complex as an individual experience, it is nevertheless a phenomenon which is determined and laid down by heredity and which is bound to pass away according to programme when the next pre-ordained phase of development sets in" (see also Freud, 1919, p. 188).

In its ego-psychological context, however, the passage *is* unique for Freud. Not only is it in apparent sharp contradiction to the passage from *The Ego and the Id* already cited ("It is not possible to speak of direct inheritance in the ego."), and to his references to heredity in 1926 and 1933, but it is equally contradictory to what he said subsequent to 1937 in *Moses and Monotheism* (1939) and in the *Outline* (1940), where he stated: "It [the id] contains everything that is inherited, that is present at birth, that is laid down in the constitution" (p. 145).

Two considerations make this contradiction less glaring than it seems at first sight. The quotation cited by Hartmann actually starts with the phrase *"But we shall not overlook the fact that id and ego are originally one;* nor does it imply any mystical overvaluation of heredity . . ."* (my italics). And the passage from *The Ego and the Id* is preceded by a discussion of the origins of the superego in the archaic experiences leading to totemism, as well as by the statement that "The question whether it was the ego or the id that experienced and acquired these things soon comes to nothing," since one must not "forget that the ego is a specially differentiated part of the id" (1923, p. 38). From the point of view of Freud's convictions about Lamarckian inheritance on the one hand (e.g., 1913, 1923, 1937, 1939, 1940), and the development of the ego out of the id, on the other, he was entirely right in his opinion that a distinction between ego and id inheritance was really not very important. Hartmann, on the contrary, offered the concept of independent ego roots and, although not yet under that name (Hartmann, Kris, Loewenstein, 1946), of the undifferentiated phase (1939, p. 102f.). Under these assumptions, new to the psychoanalytic literature at that time, the distinction assumes major importance conceptually and for empiric investigation.

Nevertheless, it remains true that in 1937 Freud spoke for the first and last time of "original, innate distinguishing characteristics of the ego" (p. 240). This fact calls for an explanation. I have only a speculative one to offer. Moreover, it is one that cannot be confirmed. I shall nonetheless advance it because of its pertinence to our general topic. I suggest that in this instance Freud may have been directly influenced by Hartmann, rather than the other way around. In support of this speculation we know that Freud had very great respect for Hartmann's abilities, that Hartmann was a "favorite pupil" of his (Jones, 1957, p. 24), and that they had frequent opportunities for

discussions in the years immediately preceding the writing and publication of "Analysis Terminable and Interminable." True or not, I
find the idea appealing. And it does not, to my mind, imply a mystical
overvaluation of Hartmann!

With respect to Freud's Lamarckian views on heredity, Hartmann
took no stand (p. 24). The topic is directly pertinent, however, to
differences between Freud and Hartmann with respect to the role
of external reality in both the genesis and functions of the ego. As
we have seen, external reality only slowly regained the place in
Freud's ego-psychological thinking that he gave to it originally; and
it never did approach Hartmann's, and Anna Freud's, in generality.
Why? I have considered this question in some detail in a previous
publication (1961a, p. 21ff.) and shall only summarize my thoughts
on the subject here. They concern Freud's famous discovery, about
which so much has been written (see my 1961a paper for references),
that the reports by his patients of sexual traumata were in large part
fantasies, i.e., psychic rather than external reality. Throughout his
life Freud repeatedly referred to this discovery as a turning point
in his thinking; and there can be no doubt of the validity of this statement, nor of the enormously positive impact it had, in conjunction
with his self analysis, in terms of his discovery of the oedipus complex,
of unconscious as well as conscious fantasies, and of the role of these
and the drives they represent in shaping and organizing reality experiences. But it had another effect, too. It led him for a long time
to an underestimation of the importance of reality experiences, and
to the opinion that "the factor of hereditary predisposition regains
a sphere of influence from which I had made it my business to oust
it" (Freud, 1950, p. 216). Since at the same time Freud remained
convinced of the enormous importance of experience, he was led
to displace a great part of it from the ontogenetic to the phylogenetic
sphere, and thus to the Lamarckism of *Totem and Taboo* (1913),
which we find essentially unaltered in *The Ego and the Id* (1923)
and in *Moses and Monotheism* (1939).

Change of Function

The idea of change of function is a fundamental one to some of
Hartmann's theses, leading directly to that of secondary autonomy,
with which we shall be dealing shortly. His discussions of this topic
are, in my opinion, among his best ego-psychological and develop-

mental contributions. The general description he gave was that "a behavior-form which originated in a certain realm of life may, in the course of development, appear in an entirely different realm and role" (p. 25f.). What was once a means may become a goal (p. 26). What once served a defensive function may become a relatively independent structure, and may in turn serve the function of synthesis or of adaptation (pp. 26, 51). The defensive intellectualization of adolescence, for example, may lead to the adaptive and productive use of intelligence (p. 13f.; see also A. Freud, 1936, p. 179). Regression, too, may serve adaptation in a change of function (p. 53), in Hartmann's elaboration of Kris's (1934) earliest statement on regression in the service of the ego. And also, though not in this monograph, what was once an instinctual gratification may become a defense, as, for example, introjection (Hartmann, 1950b, p. 82). (Cf. also A. Freud [1936, p. 192] and Gill [1963, p. 108f.].)

The concept is not purely a developmental one, since apparatuses or mechanisms can sometimes serve defense and adaptation simultaneously (p. 51); a point previously made by Anna Freud, as Hartmann pointed out. But it is *predominantly* conceptualized in developmental terms, as is apparent from the definition I have just quoted. This fact may account for its occasional confusion with another, related, but in a sense opposite mechanism, one that could analogously be termed "change of apparatus," or "change of means." Here the same *function*, for example, defense, may utilize different *means* or *mechanisms* at different stages of development, as contrasted to the previous examples in which the same "means" are used for different *functions* (cf. Benjamin, 1965). Hartmann discusses this phenomenon, too; in the monograph (p. 49f.), and at greater length in subsequent publications (e.g., 1950a, 1950b). Here the original conceptualization was Freud's, in "Instincts and Their Vicissitudes" (1915, p. 132), and particularly in *Inhibitions, Symptoms and Anxiety*, where he stated: "It may well be that before its sharp cleavage into an ego and an id, and before the formation of a super-ego, the mental apparatus makes use of different methods of defence from those which it employs after it has reached these stages of organization" (1926, p. 164).

Further discussion of this concept of "change of means" would take us too far afield from our topic, the 1939 monograph, since it would lead us directly into the complex and difficult, if alliterative, area of precursors, prototypes, and predispositions. (Cf. Hartmann

[1950a, 1950b], Spitz [1957, 1961], and Benjamin [1959, p. 47ff.; 1961b, pp. 654-658; and 1965; other references there].)

Primary and Secondary Autonomy and the Conflict-Free Sphere

With that, we come to our last topics: primary and secondary autonomy and the so-called conflict-free, or nonconflictual, sphere of ego development and ego functioning. There can be no question but that these constitute the essence, though far from the totality, of Hartmann's ego-psychological writings (as contrasted to his contributions to other aspects of theory). What we have covered so far in this monograph, as well as much of what we shall have to leave untouched, is intimately related to these basic and in part still controversial concepts.

Before discussing the concepts themselves, I should like to touch on one aspect of what I meant when I just said that they are in part still controversial. I refer to the feeling, not infrequently expressed in private or group discussions, though seldom in publications, that they are in some vague sense not really psychoanalytic or clinically significant, on the one hand; or, on the other, that they are a statement of the obvious, of something that has always been known and accepted. Both of these objections seem to me to be entirely wrong as well as essentially beside the point.

Probably the best known expression of the first point of view was Fenichel's comment in 1945 that "the term sphere without conflict seems misleading, as tending toward an undynamic point of view" (p. 52). I agree with Fenichel that the term can be misleading, in that it is easily misunderstood; and shall return to this point later. But I strongly disagree with the idea that there is anything undynamic or unclinical about this or any other of Hartmann's ego-psychological conceptualizations (Benjamin, 1950, p. 151). The term "undynamic" itself, although unquestionably in one sense of the word a highly dynamic one, is sufficiently global and undifferentiated to lend itself all too easily to epithetical rather than clarifying usage (Benjamin, 1952, p. 4), as, for example, when studies of hereditary and constitutional contributions to development are thought of as being in some way "opposed" to dynamic theories of learning and personality development (Benjamin, 1950, p. 150ff.; 1952, p. 7). The issue here, however, is not whether these particular conceptualizations of Hartmann are dynamic or not (which they assuredly are), but rather to what degree they are useful for explanation and prediction, as well as for the acquisition of new knowledge through investigation; and to what extent they are supported by such investigation.

What Fenichel and others may well have meant, and what is unquestionably true, is that much of modern ego psychology *can* be utilized, and sometimes is, in the service of resistances, to the detriment of integrated psychoanalytic practice, theory, and research. This is unfortunate, when it occurs, but has little to do with the validity, or lack of it, of Hartmann's or anyone else's ego-psychological formulations. I belabor this truly obvious point, not for the first time, only because I find opinions to the contrary to be still prevalent, if less widespread and much less vocal than in earlier times. In my opinion, they represent one form of what some time ago (1950, p. 140) I somewhat facetiously but essentially seriously called counterresistance, or *Gegenwiderstand;* a phenomenon that has interfered with communication between psychoanalysis and other sciences almost as much as has resistance itself.

The second and less frequently expressed objection—that there was little that was really new in these conceptualizations, that they are self-evident, so to speak, and have always been tacitly accepted —is an equally untenable one, in my view. Outside the field of psychoanalysis, to be sure, there have been many to whom the concept of autonomy from conflict and from drive determination would seem self-evident. But to speak of *relative* autonomy from the instinctual drives has no meaning unless at the same time one subscribes to the direct or indirect determination of much behavior *by* the instinctual drives.[1] Although K. Bühler, Woodworth, and others had previously offered somewhat related ideas, the only nonanalytic psychologist who delineated a concept truly comparable to Hartmann's secondary autonomy was Allport, whose concept of "functional autonomy" was advanced in the same year to which we have so often referred, 1937. Interestingly enough, Hartmann seems to underestimate the originality of his own contribution to psychoanalysis when he speaks of Allport as being closer to psychoanalytic thinking than he (Allport)

[1] More generally, to speak of relative autonomy from developmentally primary motivations would have no meaning for essentially *nonmotivational* psychological systems, such as that of Piaget, for example. But the findings and constructs of Piaget are nonetheless pertinent to the further development of psychoanalytic ego psychology.

seemed to assume (1951, p. 41). Allport was quite right in 1937 in considering his point of view different from that of psychoanalysis as it then existed; and the fact that in this one important respect psychoanalysis is now closer to Allport than it then was is due largely to the original and independent contributions of Hartmann and his collaborators, so many of which were either explicitly stated or clearly implied in the 1939 monograph we are discussing. The fact is that Hartmann's concepts of primary and secondary autonomy *were* essentially new to psychoanalysis. After they had been delineated, it was of course possible to see certain anticipations of them in Freud, Anna Freud, Waelder, and others. But even this exercise has the usual number of pitfalls associated with the *post facto* reading into Freud of what we are not really certain he meant. For example, if we turn for a moment to energy theory, which is hardly touched on in this monograph, but to which Hartmann and his collaborators devoted much subsequent consideration,[2] it seems entirely justified to say that the concept of "neutral" energy is closely related to primary, that of "neutralized" energy to secondary autonomy (Hartmann, 1955, pp. 25, 28). But when we read what Freud had to say on the subject of "neutral" (*indifferente*) energy, we find that he is in fact talking about "neutralized" (i.e., desexualized) libido (1923, p. 44f.). Nor can we assume with confidence that when Freud spoke in *The Interpretation of Dreams* of "the mobile cathectic energy" available to the system *Pcs.*, and related it to attention (1900, p. 615), he had in mind anything comparable to the neutral (noninstinctual) energy which, in terms of energy theory, is conceptually a necessary condition for primary autonomy, and which Hartmann in a later publication calls "primary ego energy" (1955, p. 28).[3]

Closing Comments

A natural extension of these remarks would be to discuss other related ideas advanced or implied by Hartmann in this monograph; to

[2] See, e.g., Hartmann (1948; 1950b, pp. 85-90; 1952, pp. 20-25; 1955); Hartmann, Kris, and Loewenstein (1949); Kris (1955).

[3] For a somewhat different reading of Freud, as well as for a statement, with which the writer is in full agreement, about the necessity for distinguishing more sharply between neutral and neutralized energy, see Gill (1963, p. 13). (Cf. also Holt [1962] and Rapaport [1959].) My comments above are phrased in terms of classical psychoanalytic energy theory despite some major reservations on my part about many aspects of it, since this does not seem an appropriate occasion for discussion of these issues.

follow their subsequent development by him (1947, 1958, 1959, 1964) and his collaborators (with Kris, 1945; with Kris and Loewenstein, 1946; Loewenstein, 1950); and to examine their impact on current theorizing by others (Erikson, 1950; 1946/56; Rapaport, 1951, 1958b, 1959; Spitz, 1957). This will not be possible on this occasion. Nevertheless, I would like to conclude with a more general statement of my views on the extent of Hartmann's contributions.

In other writings and particularly in discussions I have expressed a number of reservations about some of Hartmann's views. They have to do with such matters as his conceptualizations of biopsychological relationships (Benjamin, 1961a, 1965), his appraisal of the present state of psychoanalytic theory (Benjamin, 1950, 1959) and its relationship to primary data (1959), and, as a more specific example, even with such a highly popular and generally accepted concept as energy neutralization (cf. 1959, p. 31). Although I do not consider any of these reservations trivial, they do seem relatively unimportant to me when contrasted to what I perceive as the great positive impact that he has had on psychoanalytic and psychological science. He has functioned, and still does, not only as a clarifier of difficult issues, and as a corrector of one-sided theoretical points of view (1959, p. 7), but also in a genuinely original and creative fashion. Beyond his own major contributions, his direct and indirect influence on a new generation of clinical and experimental investigators will, I believe, continue to be as great and as beneficial as it has been in the recent past.

Finally, I would add a further historical note. The year 1964 is the 25th anniversary of the publication of *Ego Psychology and the Problem of Adaptation*. It is also the year in which Heinz Hartmann's 70th birthday will occur. Whatever other celebrations may take place, I like to look upon this evening's discussion, and my participation in it, as being in a spirit of appreciation of a first-rate man.

BIBLIOGRAPHY

Allport, G. W. (1937), *Personality*. NY: Holt.
Balint, M. (1937), Frühe Entwicklungsstadien des Ichs. Primäre Objectliebe. *Imago*, 23:270-288.
Benjamin, J. D. (1950), Methodological Considerations in the Validation and Elaboration of Psychoanalytical Personality Theory. *Am. J. Orthopsychiat.*, 20:139-156.
———— (1952), Directions and Problems in Psychiatric Research. *Psychosom. Med.*, 14:1-9.

—— (1959), Prediction and Psychopathological Theory. *Dynamic Psychopathology in Childhood*, ed. L. Jessner & E. Pavenstedt. NY: Grune & Stratton, 6-77.

—— (1961a), The Innate and the Experiential in Development. *Lectures in Experimental Psychiatry*, ed. H. W. Brosin. Pittsburgh: Univ. Pittsburgh Pr., 19-42.

—— (1961b), Some Developmental Observations Relating to the Theory of Anxiety. *J. Am. Psa. Assn.*, 9:652-668.

—— (1965), Developmental Biology and Psychoanalysis. *Psychoanalysis and Current Biological Thought*, ed. N. Greenfield & W. Lewis. Madison: Univ. Wisc. Pr., 57-80.

Bibring, E. (1936), The Development and Problems of the Instincts. *Int. J. Psa.*, 22:102-131, 1941.

Erikson, E. H. (1937), Configurations in Play. *Psa. Q.*, 6:139-214.

—— (1950), *Childhood and Society*. NY: Norton.

—— (1946/56), *Identity and the Life Cycle. Psychol. Issues*, 1.

Fenichel, O. (1935), Concerning the Theory of Psychoanalytic Technique. *C.P.*, 1:332-348. NY: Norton, 1953.

—— (1936), The Symbolic Equation: Girl=Phallus. *C.P.*, 2:3-18. NY: Norton, 1954.

—— (1937), Early Stages of Ego Development. *C.P.*, 2:25-48. NY: Norton, 1954.

—— (1945), *The Psychoanalytic Theory of Neurosis*. NY: Norton.

French, T. M. (1937), Reality and the Unconscious. *Psa. Q.*, 6:23-61.

Freud, A. (1936), *The Ego and the Mechanisms of Defense*. NY: IUP, 1946.

Freud, S. (1900), The Interpretation of Dreams. *S.E.*, 4 & 5.

—— (1913), Totem and Taboo. *S.E.*, 13:1-161.

—— (1915), Instincts and Their Vicissitudes. *S.E.*, 14:117-140.

—— (1919), 'A Child is Being Beaten.' *S.E.*, 17:179-204.

—— (1921), Group Psychology and the Analysis of the Ego. *S.E.*, 18:69-143.

—— (1923), The Ego and the Id. *S.E.*, 19:12-56.

—— (1924), The Dissolution of the Oedipus Complex. *S.E.*, 19:173-179.

—— (1926), Inhibitions, Symptoms and Anxiety. *S.E.*, 20:87-174.

—— (1933), New Introductory Lectures on Psycho-Analysis. *S.E.*, 22:5-182.

—— (1937), Analysis Terminable and Interminable. *S.E.*, 23:209-253.

—— (1939), Moses and Monotheism. *S.E.*, 23:3-137.

—— (1940), An Outline of Psychoanalysis. *S.E.*, 23:141-207.

—— (1950), Letter No. 69 [1897]. *The Origins of Psychoanalysis*. NY: Basic Books, 1954.

Gill, M. M. (1963), *Topography and Systems in Psychoanalytic Theory. Psychol. Issues*, 10.

Glover, E., Fenichel, O., Strachey, J., Bergler, E., Nunberg, H., & Bibring, E. (1937), Symposium on the Theory of the Therapeutic Results of Psychoanalysis. *Int. J. Psa.* 18:9-189.

Hartmann, H. (1939), *Ego Psychology and the Problem of Adaptation*. NY: IUP, 1958.

—— (1947), On Rational and Irrational Action. *Psa. & Soc. Sci.*, 1:359-392. NY: IUP.

—— (1948), Comments on the Psychoanalytic Theory of Instinctual Drives. *Psa. Q.*, 17:368-388.

—— (1950a), Psychoanalysis and Developmental Psychology. *Psa. Study Ch.*, 5:7-17.

—— (1950b), Comments on the Psychoanalytic Theory of the Ego. *Psa. Study Ch.*, 5:74-96.

—— (1951), Technical Implications of Ego Psychology. *Psa. Q.*, 20:31-43.

—— (1952), The Mutual Influences in the Development of Ego and Id. *Psa. Study Ch.*, 7:9-30.

—— (1955), Notes on the Theory of Sublimation. *Psa. Study Ch.*, 10:9-29.

—— (1956), The Development of the Ego Concept in Freud's Work. *Int. J. Psa.,* 37:425-438.

—— (1958), Comments on the Scientific Aspects of Psychoanalysis. *Psa. Study Ch.,* 13:127-146.

—— (1959), Psychoanalysis as a Scientific Theory. *Psychoanalysis, Scientific Method and Philosophy,* ed. S. Hook. NY: New York Univ. Pr., 3-37.

—— (1964), *Essays on Ego Psychology.* NY: IUP.

—— & Kris, E. (1945), The Genetic Approach in Psychoanalysis. *Psa. Study Ch.,* 1:11-30.

———— & Loewenstein, R. M. (1946), Comments on the Formation of Psychic Structure. *Psa. Study Ch.,* 2:11-38.

————— (1949), Notes on the Theory of Aggression. *Psa. Study Ch.,* 3/4:9-36.

Hendrick, I. (1936), Ego Development and Certain Character Problems. *Psa. Q.,* 5:320-346.

Holt, R. R. (1962), A Critical Examination of Freud's Concept of Bound vs. Free Cathexis. *J. Am. Psa. Assn.,* 10:475-525.

Horney, K. (1936), *The Neurotic Personality of Our Time.* NY: Norton.

—— (1939), *New Ways in Psychoanalysis.* NY: Norton.

Jones, E. (1957), *The Life and Work of Sigmund Freud,* 3. NY: Basic Books.

Kaiser, H. (1934), Probleme der Technik. *Int. Z. Psa.,* 20:490-522.

Kardiner, A. (1939), *The Individual and His Society.* NY: Columbia Univ. Pr.

Kris, E. (1934), The Psychology of Caricature. *Psychoanalytic Explorations in Art.* NY: IUP, 173-188.

—— (1951), The Development of Ego Psychology. *Samiksa,* 5:153-168.

—— (1955), Neutralization and Sublimation. *Psa. Study Ch.,* 10:30-46.

Lewin, B. D. (1935), Claustrophobia. *Psa. Q.,* 4:227-233.

—— (1937), A Type of Neurotic Hypomanic Reaction. *Arch. Neurol. Psychiat.,* 37:868-873.

Loewenstein, R. M. (1950), Conflict and Autonomous Ego Development during the Phallic Phase. *Psa. Study Ch.,* 5:47-52.

Nunberg, H. (1930), The Synthetic Function of the Ego. *Int. J. Psa.,* 12:123-140, 1931.

Rapaport, D. (1951), The Autonomy of the Ego. *Bull. Menninger Clin.,* 15:113-123.

—— (1958a), An Historical Survey of Psychoanalytic Ego Psychology. *Bull. Phila. Assn. Psa.,* 8:105-120.

—— (1958b), The Theory of Ego Autonomy. *Bull. Menninger Clin.,* 22:13-35.

—— (1959), *The Structure of Psychoanalytic Theory. Psychol. Issues,* 6.

Reich, W. (1933), *Character Analysis.* NY: Orgone Inst. Pr., 1949.

Spitz, R. A. (1957), *No and Yes.* NY: IUP.

—— (1961), Some Early Prototypes of Ego Defenses. *J. Am. Psa. Assn.,* 9:626-651.

Sullivan, H. S. (1938), Psychiatry: I. *Psychiatry,* 1:121-134.

Waelder, R. (1930), The Principle of Multiple Functioning. *Psa. Q.,* 5:45-62, 1936.

—— (1936), The Problem of Freedom in Psychoanalysis and the Problem of Reality-Testing. *Int. J. Psa.,* 17:89-108.

II
History of Psychoanalysis

Some Additional "Day Residues" of "The Specimen Dream of Psychoanalysis"

MAX SCHUR, M.D.

The centenary of Freud's birthday in 1956 provided a fitting occasion for both a review of the past and a look into the future of psychoanalysis, in the spirit of the genetic point of view, which, as applied in that science, establishes links between past, present, and future.

At the centennial celebration in London, Heinz Hartmann delivered the main scientific lecture, later published under the title "The Development of the Ego Concept in Freud's Work" (1956). In his paper Hartmann stated:

> None of Freud's own historical writings is aimed at a really comprehensive or detailed presentation of all the adventures of discovery and adventures of inventive thought that went into the making of psychoanalysis. . . . More recently, we have witnessed a renaissance of historical awareness in analysis. There is . . . Jones's imposing work (1953-57); . . . there is Kris's brilliant introduction to Freud's letters to Fliess (1950); there are the invaluable introductions and notes by Strachey in the *Standard Edition*, the detailed investigations of Bernfeld (1944-1953) and a few others [p. 269f.].

Hartmann's essay is an excellent example of the value of the genetic-developmental approach. But he has given us another example, too, of the creative value of such a genetic study in his "Com-

Clinical Professor of Psychiatry, State University of New York, Downstate Medical College, Brooklyn, New York.

This paper has been supported in part by a grant from the Foundation for Research in Psychoanalysis, Berkeley, California. I am also indebted to the Sigmund Freud Copyright, Ltd. for permission to use certain of the unpublished letters of Sigmund Freud to Wilhelm Fliess.

ments on the Psychoanalytic Theory of Instinctual Drives" (1948), where he says: "we may say that even at present an understanding of analysis is hardly possible without a detailed knowledge of its history" (p. 69).

It might therefore be appropriate to honor Heinz Hartmann on his 70th birthday by offering this historically oriented essay, which certainly illustrates "the adventures of discovery and adventures of inventive thought that went into the making of psychoanalysis," and which thus not only helps to illuminate the origins of our science but encourages us to look with confidence into its future.

I

On June 12, 1900, following the publication of *The Interpretation of Dreams*, Freud wrote to Fliess:

> Life at the Bellevue[1] is turning out very pleasantly for everyone. The evenings and mornings are enchanting; the scent of acacia and jasmine has succeeded that of lilac and laburnum, the wild roses are in bloom, and everything, as even I notice, seems suddenly to have burst out.[2]

Was it this expansive mood, a response to witnessing the miracle of spring, which made it possible for Freud to continue as follows:

> Do you actually suppose that some day this house will have a marble plaque with the inscription:
> "Here, on July 24, 1895, the mystery
> of dreams revealed itself to Dr. Sigm.
> Freud."

Or were there still other determinants?

This letter was written after Freud had overcome the letdown following the feverish effort of completing *The Interpretation of Dreams*. It had been the kind of letdown which frequently had certain characteristics of a depressive mood. He had by then also mastered his disappointment over the almost total neglect of the book by both the professional and the general public.[3] Once before, in a letter

---

[1] A house situated on a hill in one of the suburbs of Vienna, where Freud and his family were spending the summer, as they had also done the summer of 1895.

[2] The translations in this essay differ somewhat from the published versions. Unpublished letters will be given both in German and in my translation.

[3] According to J. Strachey's introduction to *The Interpretation of Dreams*, only 351 copies were sold in the first six years after this book's publication!

written on May 21, 1894, when his cardiac episode was at its height (see Schur, 1966), Freud had expressed a similarly exuberant evaluation of his work, saying: "I have the distinct feeling of having touched upon one of the great mysteries of nature."

On the one hand, the letter of June 12, 1900 clearly indicates that Freud was unshaken in the firm conviction, held throughout his life, that *The Interpretation of Dreams* represented his *magnum opus*. On the other hand, it points to the fact that his interpretation of the Irma dream ("of July 23rd-24th, 1895") represented an important milestone in the development of his work.

We can trace Freud's interest in dreams to his betrothal letters (Freud, 1960; Jones, Vol. I; Eissler, 1964). In a footnote to his first case history in the *Studies on Hysteria* (1895), Freud reports his attempts to understand some of his own dreams. This effort was necessitated in part by the more and more frequent reporting of dreams on the part of patients in the course of their associations. In a letter to Fliess of March 4, 1895, Freud not only reports to Fliess about the dream of Rudi Kaufmann,[4] indicating that he had already formulated the wish-fulfillment hypothesis of dreams (1900, p. 125; 1950, Letter 22), but also alludes to the "dream psychosis" of one of his patients, Emma, about whom we shall hear quite a lot further on in this paper. This passage in his letter indicates that Freud had already concluded that there were certain analogies between the dream and neurotic and psychotic symptom formation.

Freud indicates in a footnote to the preamble of the Irma dream that this was the first dream he had submitted to a "thorough interpretation." The letter quoted at the beginning of this paper also claims that the secret of the dream had been unveiled to Freud on the occasion of his analysis of the Irma dream.

This statement has been tacitly accepted in the psychoanalytic literature (see, for example, Erikson, 1954). We may assume, however, that this *systematic* dream interpretation was only the culmination of an ongoing process, which must have lasted for quite some time.

The previously quoted remarks from the Fliess correspondence indicate that by that time Freud took it for granted that dreams were meaningful and could be understood. He tried to understand the

---

[4] Rudolf Kaufmann, who later became one of Vienna's leading cardiologists.

dreams of his patients and to relate them to the latter's symptomatology. In 1914 he stated that *The Interpretation of Dreams* had to a great extent been finished by 1896. In the book itself (p. 104) he mentions that he has "analyzed over a thousand dreams" of his neurotic patients. The reference to the dreams of Rudi Kaufmann (a nephew of Breuer) indicates that Freud's friends and colleagues must have been aware of his interest in dreams and were "collecting" them for him. Even if Freud's recollection that *The Interpretation of Dreams* was practically finished in 1896 (with the exception of Chapters VI and VII) proved to be not entirely accurate, as shown by the Fliess correspondence, he must have partly analyzed an ample number of his own and his patients' dreams in those earlier years.

What Freud may have been attempting for the first time with the Irma dream was the systematic application of free association to every single element of the manifest dream, after which he connected these associations until a meaningful trend emerged. While the meaningfulness of dreams and their importance in our mental life were already familiar to Freud, this systematic analysis alone enabled him to discover the mechanism of the "dream work," which was of course the unveiling of a mystery, the stripping off of one of the "seven veils."

The Fliess correspondence points to an additional reason for Freud's interest in his own dreams. He reveals his increasing awareness that progress in understanding the intricacies of neurotic symptoms would have to be paralleled by an understanding of normal phenomena, all of which he could achieve in part by self analysis. The letters to Fliess indicate that Freud's systematic self analysis began some time in the spring of 1897, when the crucial importance of the first years of life had become apparent to him.

This *systematic* self analysis, however, was preceded by a prolonged introductory phase, during which Freud had to develop the tools necessary for this effort. This was analogous to the prolonged phase of dream interpretation which had preceded the *systematic* attempt to interpret the Irma dream. During this introductory phase of Freud's analysis, the interpretation of his own dreams probably played an important part, as it did to an even greater extent after he had "unraveled the mystery of the dream" by analyzing the Irma dream.

This introductory phase showed many of the aspects common to the unfolding of the analytic situation so familiar to us through the treatment of our patients and students and our own firsthand experience with analysis. The most important ingredient of this preliminary phase was what we would recognize in the light of present-day concepts as full-fledged transference phenomena, which in Freud's unique case manifested themselves to a large extent in his relationship to Fliess. Certain aspects of this transference situation were apparent during Freud's cardiac episode, the most severe symptoms of which preceded the Irma dream (for a detailed discussion, see Schur, 1966).

The material to be presented will make apparent the manner in which these transference phenomena manifested themselves in an episode preceding the Irma dream, influenced the content of that dream and Freud's associations to it, and probably also interfered to some extent with his interpretation.

Freud indicates in several passages of his interpretation of the Irma dream that he will not pursue a certain train of thought any further. In the last paragraph of the chapter dealing with the Irma dream, Freud says:

> I will not pretend that I have completely uncovered the meaning of this dream or that its interpretation is without a gap. I could spend much more time over it, derive further information from it and discuss fresh problems raised by it. I myself know the points from which further trains of thought could be followed. But considerations which arise in the case of every dream of my own restrain me from pursuing my interpretative work. If anyone should feel tempted to express a hasty condemnation of my reticence, I would advise him to make the experiment of being franker than I am [p. 120f.].

Many passages of the dream lend themselves to speculation about additional meanings. An ingenious "supplement" to Freud's interpretation of the Irma dream was attempted by Erikson (1954), who used this "dream specimen" to elaborate on some of his theoretical concepts. I shall refrain from speculation and limit myself to comparing and contrasting some additional day residues of the Irma dream with Freud's associations and the interpretations derived from them.

On the assumption that the Irma dream[5] is sufficiently familiar to the reader, I shall omit a verbatim quotation of the whole dream and Freud's associations (see 1900, pp. 106-121 and 292-295).

[5] This dream is frequently called the dream of Irma's injection, thus singling out one element to represent the whole.

Freud gives us the following background for this dream (the italicized portions pertain to the supplementary information supplied to the hitherto unpublished material).

Freud was spending the summer of 1895 at the Bellevue (see footnote 1), slowly recovering from a severe cardiac episode which had started in the fall of 1893 and had reached a critical phase in the spring of 1894. He had recently resumed smoking in defiance of Fliess's strict orders (see Freud, 1950, Letter 25 of June 12, 1895). His wife, who had arranged a party for her birthday on July 26, was in the fourth month of her sixth pregnancy.

Freud had broken off for the summer months the treatment of his patient Irma, who had shown partial improvement. *At that point the concepts of resistance and working through had not yet occurred to Freud*, so that he had been blaming Irma for not accepting his "solution" to her symptoms. He was aware (as opposed to Breuer) of the importance of a positive, sexualized transference in the treatment of hysterics, *but was not yet familiar with the intricacies of the transference neurosis* and the difficulties inherent in its dissolution, especially under the contaminated circumstances of a close social relationship.

Freud was faced with a special dilemma, which has haunted all succeeding generations of analysts. Irma was still suffering from certain (gastric) somatic symptoms; *were they due to an unresolved element of her neurosis or to an organic condition? Was he blaming her unjustly for not accepting his interpretations and thereby preventing her own full recovery, when in reality she was suffering from an organic illness?*[6] He had the impression of mild reproof from a remark made with reference to Irma by his friend "Otto,"[7] *and he had sat down that evening and written a long report to M.* (Breuer), who had obviously referred Irma to Freud for treatment, *"in order to justify himself."*

Freud's relationship to Breuer had been quite strained during the year 1894, but in a letter to Fliess of May 25, 1895, Freud emphasized that Breuer had changed his attitude completely and had fully accepted Freud's theory of sexuality.

I quote below first the pertinent facts from the Irma dream, and

[6] Freud added a footnote in 1909 stating that Irma's "unresolved" gastric pains were forerunners of gallstones, thus indicating his ongoing concern about this matter.

[7] Dr. Oskar Rie, one of Freud's oldest and most devoted friends, the pediatrician of Freud's children, and the future brother-in-law of Fliess.

later Freud's associations. I shall italicize what seem to me the salient features.[8]

> A large hall—numerous guests, whom we were receiving.—Among them was Irma. I at once took her on one side, as though to answer her letter and to *reproach her for not having accepted my* 'solution' yet. I said to her: '*If you still get pains, it's really only your fault.*' She replied: 'If you only knew what pains I've got now *in my throat* and stomach and abdomen—it's choking me'—I was alarmed and looked at her. She looked pale and puffy. I thought to myself that after all I must be missing some organic trouble. I took her to the window and looked down her throat, and she showed signs of recalcitrance. . . . *She then opened her mouth properly* and on the right I found a big white patch; at another place I *saw extensive whitish grey scabs* upon some remarkable curly structures which were *evidently modelled on the turbinal bones of the nose.—I at once called in Dr. M., and he repeated the examination and confirmed it.* . . . *My friend Otto was now standing beside her as well*, and my friend Leopold was percussing her through her bodice and saying: 'She has a dull area low down on the left.' . . . M. said: 'There's no doubt it's an infection, but no matter; dysentery will supervene and the toxin will be eliminated.' . . . *We were directly aware, too, of the origin of the infection.* Not long before, when she was feeling unwell, *my friend Otto had given her an injection* of a preparation of propyl, propyls . . . propionic acid . . . trimethylamin (and I saw before me the formula for this printed in heavy type). . . . *Injections of that sort ought not to be made so thoughtlessly. . . And probably the syringe had not been clean* [p. 107].

The chain of Freud's associations to the individual elements of the dream led him far afield. They brought back painful memories of situations in which he could not have failed to feel self-reproach. This applied, above all, to the episode involving Fleischl, Freud's admired friend and brilliant senior colleague, a man of high social standing and wealth, endowed with unusual physical and intellectual qualities. Fleischl had been a victim of his profession and succumbed to the consequences of what had first been a morphine addiction and then, as

---

[8] Throughout this essay *all* italics in quotations are mine. To distinguish them from Freud's italics in the original, the latter will be designated by asterisks. In the original German letters reproduced below, Freud's spelling and abbreviations have been retained.

Freud had tried to cure him by cocaine, a cocaine addiction even more tragic than the original (see Jones, I, pp. 78-97).

Freud was also reminded of the patient who had actually died of *toxicity* from the sulphonal he had prescribed for her.

However, all of his associations led Freud to the interpretation that he had succeeded in displacing all blame to others—his friend Otto (Rie), Dr. M. (Breuer), Irma, who would not accept his solutions, other female patients, even his pregnant wife. The hostile associations were directed mainly against Otto, who had given Irma the injection with a dirty syringe, and Dr. M., who as a consultant had to some extent made a fool of himself by confusing dysentery and diphtheria. They were also directed against Irma and most of the other females he associated with her.

Freud summarizes the wish fulfillment of the Irma dream as follows:

> The conclusion of the dream . . . was *that I was not responsible for the persistence of Irma's pains, but that Otto was.* Otto had in fact annoyed me by his remarks about Irma's incomplete cure, and the dream gave me my revenge by throwing the reproach back on to him. The dream acquitted me of the responsibility for Irma's condition by showing that it was due to other factors—it produced a whole series of reasons. The dream represented a particular state of affairs as I should have wished it to be. *Thus its content was the fulfilment of a wish and its motive was a wish.**
>
> Thus much leapt to the eyes. But many of the details of the dream also became intelligible to me from the point of view of wish-fulfilment. Not only did I revenge myself on Otto for being too hasty in taking sides against me by representing him as being too hasty in his medical treatment (in giving the injection); but I also revenged myself on him for giving me the bad liqueur which had an aroma of fusel oil. . . . This did not satisfy me and I pursued my revenge further by contrasting him with his more trustworthy competitor. I seemed to be saying: 'I like *him** better than *you.'** But Otto was not the only person to suffer from the vials of my wrath. I took revenge as well on my disobedient patient by exchanging her for one who was wiser and less recalcitrant. Nor did I allow Dr. M. to escape the consequences of his contradiction but showed him by means of a clear allusion that he was an ignoramus on the subject. (*'Dysentery will supervene,** etc.') Indeed I seemed to be appealing from him to someone else with greater knowledge (to my friend who had told me of trimethylamin) just as

I had turned from Irma to her friend and from Otto to Leopold. . . .
The groundlessness of the reproaches was proved for me in the dream
in the most elaborate fashion. *I** was not to blame for Irma's pains,
since she herself was to blame for them by refusing to accept my solution. *I** was not concerned with Irma's pains, *since they were of an
organic nature and quite incurable by psychological treatment.* . . .
Irma's pains had been caused by Otto giving her an incautious injection
of an unsuitable drug—a thing *I** should never have done. Irma's pains
were the results of an injection with a dirty needle . . . [p. 118f.].

This friend "with greater knowledge" was, of course, Fliess, who
entered the chain of Freud's associations to the dream in connection
with the word "trimethylamin" and also with the association of
"pyemia":

> What was it, then, to which my attention was to be directed in this
> way by trimethylamin? It was to a conversation with another friend
> who had for many years been familiar with all my writings during the
> period of their gestation, just as I had been with his. He had at that
> time confided some ideas to me on the subject of the chemistry of the
> sexual processes, and had mentioned among other things that he be-
> lieved that one of the products of sexual metabolism was trimethylamin
> [p. 116].
>
> I began to guess why the formula for trimethylamin had been so
> prominent in the dream. So many important subjects converged upon
> that one word. Trimethylamin was an allusion not only to the im-
> mensely powerful factor of sexuality, *but also to a person whose agree-
> ment I recalled with satisfaction whenever I felt isolated in my opinions.
> Surely this friend who played so large a part in my life must appear again
> elsewhere in these trains of thought. Yes. For he had a special knowl-
> edge of the consequences of affections of the nose and its accessory
> cavities;* and he had drawn scientific attention to some very remarkable
> connections between the *turbinal bones* and the female organs of sex.
> (Cf. the three curly structures in Irma's throat.) *I had had Irma exam-
> ined by him to see whether her gastric pains might be of nasal origin.*
> But *he suffered himself from suppurative rhinitis, which caused me
> anxiety;* and no doubt there was an allusion to this in the *pyaemia*
> which vaguely came into my mind in connection with the metastases
> in the dream [p. 117].

Freud returns to this part of his associations in his discussion of
the process of condensation in dreams:

On the one hand we see the group of ideas attached to my friend Otto, who did not understand me, who sided against me, and who made me a present of liqueur with an aroma of amyl. On the other hand we see—linked to the former group by its very contrast—the group of ideas attached to my friend in Berlin [Wilhelm Fliess], who *did** understand me, who would take my side, and to whom I owed so much valuable information, dealing, amongst other things, with the chemistry of the sexual process.

The recent exciting causes—the actual instigators of the dream—determined what was to attract my attention in the 'Otto' group; the amyl was among these selected elements, which were predestined to form part of the dream-content. The copious 'Wilhelm' group was stirred up precisely through being in contrast to 'Otto', and those elements in it were emphasized which echoed those which were already stirred up in 'Otto'. All through the dream, indeed, I kept on turning from someone who annoyed me to someone else who could be agreeably contrasted with him; point by point, I called up a friend against an opponent [p. 294f.].

We may therefore add to Freud's summation that his associations and interpretations reaffirm the exalted position of his friend Wilhelm Fliess, who *knows better* than Otto or M. and *understands Freud fully*.

After this lengthy introduction, I come now to the supplementary background material for the Irma dream which will constitute, so to speak, a preamble to Freud's preamble.

We are accustomed to applying the term "day residues" to material originating during the few days preceding a dream. We know, however, that preconscious material resulting from events of previous weeks can actually influence both the manifest and the latent contents of a dream if, on the one hand, more recent events provide the means for representing such preconscious material, and, on the other hand, this preconscious material contains id derivatives of sufficient intensity to press for discharge through representation in the dream (see also Fisher, 1954).

In the course of preparing another publication (Schur, 1966), I studied the unpublished letters of Freud to Fliess. From a series of these letters the following facts emerged: Freud had treated a female patient, Emma, for hysteria. In the correspondence, this patient is first mentioned in the previously quoted letter of March 4, 1895. Like

Irma, Emma had been examined by Fliess, at Freud's request, to determine if there was a partly "nasal origin" of her somatic symptoms.[9] Fliess had come to Vienna, recommended surgery (apparently of the turbinate bone and one of the sinuses—compare the Irma dream), and had operated on her there, returning to Berlin a few days later.

The letter of March 4, 1895 begins with the following passages:

Vienna, March 4, 1895

Dearest Wilhelm,

We really can't be satisfied with Emma's condition; persistent swelling, going up and down "like an avalanche," pain to the point where morphine is indispensable, poor nights. The purulent secretion has somewhat decreased since yesterday. The day before yesterday (Saturday) she had a massive hemorrhage, probably because a bone chip the size of a penny had come loose; there were about two bowlfuls. Today we encountered some resistance on irrigation, and because the pain and edema had increased, I let myself be persuaded to call in G. [Gersuny, a prominent Viennese surgeon]. (By the way, he greatly admired an etching of "The Isle of the Dead" [by Böcklin].) He stated that the access [to the cavity] had considerably contracted and was insufficient for drainage. He inserted a rubber tube and threatened to break it [the bone] open if this didn't stay in. To judge by the smell,[10] all this is probably right. Please send me your authoritative advice. I don't look forward to new surgery on this girl. . . .

Wien 4.3.95

Liebster Wilhelm

Mit der Emma kann man nicht zufrieden sein. Anhaltend noch Schwellung auf und ab, "wie eine Lawine", Schmerzen, so dass das Morphin nicht zu entbehren ist, schlechte Nächte. Die Eiterung hat

[9] Fliess, who had started his medical career as a nose and throat specialist, claimed on the grounds of his clinical observations that the application of cocaine to nasal mucous membranes and the performing of certain surgical procedures on the turbinate bone and the nasal sinuses could favorably influence a wide variety of symptoms such as migraine, Ménière's syndrome, neuralgias not restricted to the head, gastrointestinal disorders, and, above all, disturbances of various sexual functions. He coined the term nasal-reflex neurosis, and on Freud's suggestion published in 1897 a monograph entitled *Die Beziehungen zwischen Nase und weiblichen Geschlechtsorganen in ihren biologischen Bedeutungen dargestellt*. For further details and bibliography, see Freud (1950).

[10] See next letter.

sich seit gestern ermässigt. Vorgestern (Samstag) gab es eine massen-
hafte Blutung wahrscheinlich in Folge der Abstossung eines Heller-
grossen Knochenplättchens, es waren 2 Eiterschalen voll. Heute stiessen
wir auf Widerstand beim Ausspülen u da Schmerzen u sichtbares
Oedem sich gesteigert hatten, liess ich mich bewegen G. zu holen
(Nebenbei, er hat einen Stich von der "Todteninsel" sehr bewundert).
Er erklärte den Zugang für sehr verengt u ungenügend zur Drainirg,
legte ein Drainrohr ein u drohte mit Aufbrechen, wenn es nicht hielte.
Nach dem Geruch ist das wol richtig. Ich bitte um Deinen massge-
benden Rath. Auf neue Operationen mit dem Mädel freue ich mich
nicht. . . .

On March 8, 1895, Freud wrote to Fliess:

March 8, 1895

Dearest Wilhelm,

Just received your letter and am able to answer it immediately. Fortunately I am finally seeing my way clear and feel reassured about Miss
Emma, about whom I can give you a report which will probably upset
you as much as me; but I hope you will also get over it as fast I have.

I wrote you that the swelling and bleeding wouldn't let up, and
that suddenly a foetid odor set in along with an obstacle to irrigation
(or was the latter new?). I arranged for Gersuny to be called in, and
he inserted a drain, hoping that things would work out if discharge
were re-established. Otherwise he behaved in a rather rejecting way.
Two days later I was awakened early in the morning—quite profuse
bleeding had started again, with pain, etc. I got a telephone message
from G[ersuny] that he could come only in the evening, so I asked
R.[11] to meet me [at Miss Emma's apartment]. This we did at noon.
There was moderate bleeding from the nose and mouth; the foetid
odor was very bad. R. cleaned the area surrounding the opening, removed some blood clots which were sticking to the surface, and suddenly pulled at something like a thread. He kept right on pulling, and
before either of us had time to think, at least half a meter of gauze had
been removed from the cavity. The next moment came a flood of
blood. The patient turned white, her eyes bulged, and her pulse was
no longer palpable. However, immediately after this he packed the
cavity with fresh iodoform gauze, and the hemorrhage stopped. It had

---

[11] An E.N.T. specialist. Cf. the Irma dream: "I at once called in Dr. M."

lasted about half a minute, but this was enough to make the poor creature, who by then we had lying quite flat, unrecognizable. In the
meantime, or actually afterwards, something else happened. At the
moment the foreign body came out, and everything had become obvious to me, immediately after which I was confronted with the sight
of the patient, I felt sick. After she had been packed I fled to the next
room, drank a bottle of water, and felt rather miserable. The brave
Frau Doktor then brought me a small glass of cognac [cf. the liqueur
of the Irma dream], and I felt like myself again.

R. remained with the patient until I arranged to have both of them
taken to the Loew Sanatorium [a private hospital] by S. Nothing
more happened that evening. The following day, i.e., yesterday,
Thursday, the operation was repeated with the assistance of G. The
bone was broken wide open, the packing removed, and the wound
curetted. There was hardly any further bleeding. She had not lost
consciousness during the severe hemorrhage scene,[12] and when I returned to the room somewhat shaky, she greeted me with the con-
descending remark: "This is the strong sex."

I don't think I had been overwhelmed by the blood; affects were
welling up in me at that moment. *So we had done her an injustice.
She had not been abnormal at all, but a piece of iodoform gauze had
gotten torn off when you removed the rest, and stayed in for fourteen
days,*[13] interfering with the healing process, after which it had torn
away and provoked the bleeding.[14] The fact that this mishap should
have happened to *you*, how you would react to it when you learned
about it, what others would make of it, how wrong I had been to
press you to operate in a foreign city where you couldn't handle the
aftercare, how my intention of getting[15] the best for the poor girl was
insidiously thwarted, with the resultant danger to her life—all this
came over me simultaneously. I have worked it off[16] by now. *I was*

---

[12] The literal translation of "*Verblutungsszene*" would be "the scene of bleeding
to death."

[13] There is hardly a more sickeningly foetid odor than that of iodoform gauze
left in a wound for fourteen days. There is also an absorption of iodoform with
toxic effects (cf. associations to the Irma dream: sulphonal, cocaine toxicity; the
poisonous, smelly fusel oil).

[14] There is a subtle slip in the wording of this sentence; Freud does not say: "sie
wurde losgerissen, was die Blutung provociert hat"—"it [the gauze] was torn away,
which provoked the bleeding." In Freud's wording, the gauze tore away, thus becoming the sole culprit! Here begins the displacement operative in the Irma dream, of
which we shall see further evidence.

[15] Freud's use of the word "*anzuthun*" from "*anthun*" is quite ambiguous. The
correct translation is "inflict"—used prevalently in the sense of inflicting violence,
pain, etc.

[16] See footnote 19.

not sufficiently clear-headed to think of reproaching R. at that moment.[17] That occurred to me only ten minutes later; he should have thought immediately: "There is something there; don't pull it out or you'll start a hemorrhage; stick some more in, take her to Loew and do the cleaning and widening [of the opening to the cavity—obviously the sinus] at the same time.[18] But he was just as surprised as I was.

Now that I have assimilated[19] all this, nothing remains but sincere compassion for my "child of sorrow" [*Schmerzenskind*]. Indeed, I shouldn't have tortured you, but I had every reason to entrust you with such a matter and with even more than this. You handled it as well as possible. The tearing off of the iodoform gauze was one of those accidents[20] that happen to the most fortunate and cautious of surgeons. . . . G[ersuny] mentioned that he had had a similar experience, and that he therefore used iodoform wicks instead of gauze (you must remember this from your own case).[21] Of course no one blames you in any way, nor do I know why they should.[22] And I only hope that you will come as quickly as I did to feel only pity.[23] Rest assured that I felt no need to restore my trust in you. I only want to add that I hesitated for a day to tell you all about it, and that then I began to be ashamed, and here is the letter.

In view of all this, any other news has obviously faded into the background. As far as my condition is concerned, you are certainly right. In some peculiar way I'm never more productive than when I have mild symptoms like these. So I've been writing page after page of "The Therapy of Hysterias."

[17] Now R. has become the culprit. The displacement operative in the Irma dream is continuing full force.

[18] Freud's medical reasoning is also highly subjective at this point. The need for displacement still holds sway. The removal of the old iodoform gauze would inevitably have been followed by a hemorrhage, even if done in the hospital, and R. must have had things quite well under control if the hemorrhage lasted only half a minute and he had another packing ready. However, at the end of the paragraph, Freud is somewhat more charitable with poor R.

[19] Freud's use of the word "*verarbeiten*" (assimilate) here, and of the word "*aufarbeiten*" (work off) in the paragraph above, indicates that he was going through progressive phases of a process to which he later assigned the term "*durcharbeiten*" (working through), an important technical concept of psychoanalysis.

[20] Freud had not yet written *The Psychopathology of Everyday Life!*

[21] Apparently Fliess had been operated on by Gersuny. This is about as far as Freud goes in expressing a veiled reproach: "Why didn't *you* use wicks on Emma instead of gauze, as G. did with you?"

[22] Freud did not yet know that such protestations and negations stood for their opposite!

[23] Freud's use of the word "*Bedauern*" is also ambiguous. While it can be used in the sense of pity, commiseration, the common meaning is that of regret.

There is a peculiar idea of a different kind that I'll confess to you only after we have Emma off our minds.

With cordial greetings,

Your

Sigm.

8.3.95

Liebster Wilhelm

Eben Deinen Brief erhalten u in der Lage ihn gleich zu beantworten. Ich bin zum Glück endlich klar und beruhigt über Frl. Emma u kann Dir den Bericht geben über den Du Dich wol ebenso kränken wirst wie ich, aber es hoffentlich ebenso rasch überwinden.

Ich schrieb Dir dass Schwellg u Blutg kein Ende nehmen wollten, dass dann plötzlich Foetos und Hinderniss beim Ausspülen auftrat. (Oder letzteres neu?) Ich liess Gersuny bitten, der ein Drainrohr einsetzte, hoffte, es werde bei hergestelltem Abfluss wieder gehen, sonst aber eigentlich sich ablehnend verhielt. Zwei Tage später weckte man mich des morgens, es blute wieder so stark Schmerzen u dgl. Ich erhielt von G. die telephonische Antwort, er könne erst abends, bat also R. mit mir zusammenzutreffen. Das war Mittags. Es blutete mässig fort aus Nase u Mund, der Foetos war sehr arg. R. reinigte sich die Umgebg der Öffnung, zog Blutgeriensel heraus, die anhafteten u plötzlich zog er an etwas wie einem Faden, zog weiter an; ehe einer von uns Zeit zum Überlegen gehabt hatte, war ein gut ½ Meter langes Stück Gaze aus der Höhle herausbefördert. Im nächsten Moment folgte ein Blutstrom, die Kranke wurde weiss, mit hervorquellenden Augen u pulslos. Allerdings im nächsten wieder hatte er frische Jodoformgaze hineingestopft u die Blutung stand, sie hatte ½ Minute etwa gedauert, aber ausgereicht um das Geschöpf, das wir dann flach niederlegten, unkenntlich zu machen. Dazwischen dh darnach eigentlich geschah noch etwas. In dem Moment, da der Fremdkörper herauskam u mir alles klar wurde u ich gleich darnach den Anblick der Kranken hatte, wurde mir übel; nachdem sie ausgestopft war, flüchtete ich ins Nebenzimmer, trank eine Flasche Wasser aus u kam mir kläglich vor. Die tapfere Doktorin brachte mir dann ein Gläschen Cognac u ich wurde wieder ich.

R. blieb bei der Kranken bis ich ihn u sie durch S. ins Sanatorium Loew holen liess. An dem Abend geschah nichts mehr. Tags darauf d.i. gestern Donnerstag wurde unter Assistenz von G. die Operation wiederholt, weit aufgebrochen der Tampon herausgezogen u ausgekratzt. Es blutete kaum. Sie ist seither ausser Gefahr natürlich sehr bleich u elend mit frischen Schmerzen u Schwellg. Sie hatte während der Verblutgsscene ihre Besinng nicht verloren, als ich etwas wankend ins Zimmer kam, empfing sie mich mit der überlegenden Bemerkung: Das ist das starke Geschlecht.

Ich glaube nicht, dass mich das Blut überwältigt hat,—es drängten sich damals bei mir die Affekte. Wir hatten ihr also unrecht getan, sie war gar nicht abnorm gewesen sondern ein Stück Jodoformgaze war Dir beim Herausziehen abgerissen, 14 Tage lang liegen geblieben u hatte die Heilung verhindert, zum Schluss losgerissen die Blutung provocirt. Dass dieses Malheur Dir geschehen konnte, wie Du darauf reagiren wirst es zu hören, was die Anderen daraus machen können, wie unrecht ich gehabt, Dich zu einer Operation in der Fremde zu drängen, wo Du nicht nachbehandeln kannst, wie meine Absicht dem armen Mädel das Beste anzuthun, tückisch vereitelt worden u sich Lebensgefahr für sie daran geknüpft, diess alles kam zusammen über mich. Ich habe es jetzt aufgearbeitet. Ich war nicht klar genug, mir auch gleich damals einen Vorwurf für R. zu concipieren. Das fiel mir erst 10 M. später ein, dass er sofort hätte denken sollen: Da ist etwas darin, ich zieh es nicht heraus, sonst kommt eine Blutung sondern stopf' noch was herein, fahr mit ihr zu Loew u mache dort Säuberg u Erweiterg in Einem. Aber er war ebenso überrascht wie ich.

Jetzt nachdem ich es verarbeitet, bleibt davon nichts übrig als herzliches Mitleid mit meinem Schmerzenskind. Ich hätte Dich freilich hier nicht quälen sollen, allein ich durfte Dir dergl u mehr zutrauen. Du hast es so gut gemacht, als man kann. Das Abreissen der Jodoformgaze bleibt unter den Zufällen, die dem glücklichsten u umsichtigsten Chirurgen passieren. . . . G. sagte, er hätte schon so eine Erfahrung u darum nehme er Jodoformdochte anstatt Gaze (Du erinnerst Dich, bei Dir.) Es macht Dir natürlich niemand einen Vorwurf, ich wüsste, auch nicht, woher. Und ich möchte nur, dass Du ebenso schnell wie ich beim Bedauern anlangst u versichert bleibst, dass ich nicht nothwendig hatte, mein Vertrauen in Dich erst wieder herzustellen. Ich will nur noch hinzufügen, dass ich einen Tag lang gescheut habe, es Dir mitzutheilen, dann habe ich begonnen mich zu schämen u hier ist der Brief.

Daneben verschwinden wol andere Neuigkeiten. Mit meinem Zustand hast Du gewiss ganz Recht, merkwürdiger Weise produzire ich nie leichter als unter solchen leichten Beschwerden. Ich schreibe also jetzt Therapie der Hysterie Bogenweise.

Eine komische Idee anderer Art vertraue ich Dir erst an, wenn wir die Emma wieder aus dem Kopf haben. . . .

Mit herzlichst Gruss

Dein

Sigm.

However, this was not the end of the Emma affair. Nearly three weeks later, Freud writes:

Vienna, March 28, 1895

Dearest Wilhelm,

I know what you want to hear first: *she* is doing tolerably well, completely calmed down, no fever, no hemorrhage. The packing which was inserted six days ago is still in, and we hope to be safe from new surprises. Of course, she is starting to develop new hysterias from this past period, which then are being dissolved by me.

I must take it in my stride that you are not quite so well either. I hope this won't be for long. I suppose you will work your way out of it pretty soon. . . .

My own condition is not especially bad, but keeps me out of sorts. A pulse as irregular as that seems after all to preclude well-being. The motoric insufficiency was intolerable for several days.[24] I would like to accept your proposition, but the present time is obviously not propitious. Besides this, my practice is particularly poor at the moment, and as far as my mood is concerned, I'm mostly quite useless.

April 2.[25] These past days I have really felt abjectly unconcerned. Writing has been difficult; at such times I am unbearable; the slightest indications of fluctuating changes of mood. Now I'm of a piece again, and also "strong of heart," but wildly thirsty to enjoy some of the spring. Perhaps it is not so important how I felt or feel. But I have little that is important to report. . . .

In general I miss you badly. Am I really the same person who was overflowing with ideas and projects as long as you were within reach? When I sit down at my desk in the evening, I often don't know *what**
I should work on.[26]

[24] For a discussion of Freud's cardiac symptoms, see Schur (1966). As far as the Irma dream is concerned, I shall mention only that Freud himself was uncertain whether he was suffering from an organic heart condition or nicotine toxicity.

[25] Freud only rarely allowed a letter to remain unposted for several days.

[26] This is the kind of mood which Freud frequently described in 1897, during the time of his *systematic* self analysis, indicating clearly that he had already been "in analysis" well before that year.

She, Miss Emma, is doing well; she is a nice, decent girl who does not blame either of us in this affair, and who speaks of you with high esteem.

Keep quite well; give me detailed reports about yourself and don't take me to task this time. Another time I'll swamp you with letters and enclosures. *You are steady; I am not.*

Cordially your

Sigm.

Wien 28. 3. 95.

Liebster Wilhelm

Ich weiss was Du zuerst erfahren willst. Es geht *ihr* also erträglich, volle Beruhigg kein Fieber, keine Blutg, der vor 6 Tagen angelegte Tampon liegt noch, wir hoffen vor neuen Ueberraschungen sicher to sein. Natürlich beginnt sie mit der Neubildg von Hysterien aus diesen Zeiten, die dann von mir zersetzt werden.

Dass es Dir noch nicht recht ordentlich geht, muss ich auch so hinnehmen, hoffentlich nicht für lange. Ich meine Du wirst Dich bald herausgearbeitet haben. . . .

Mein eigenes Befinden ist nicht besonders schlecht aber fortgesetzt verstimmend. Ein so unregelmässiger Puls scheint doch Wolbehagen auszuschliessen, die motorische Insufficienz war wieder Tage lang unerträglich. Ich möchte gerne Deinen Vorschlag annehmen, die Zeit ist offenbar jetzt nicht günstig dazu. Es ist übrigens auch bes. schlechte Praxis u dann bin ich meist in der Stimmung ganz unbrauchbar.

2.4. Ich bin wirklich niederträchtig unbekümmert diese Tage gewesen. Das Schreiben war mir schwer, Zeiten in denen ich nicht geniessbar bin, leichteste Andeutg eines wellenförmigen Stimmgs-wechsels. Jetzt bin ich wieder beisammen auch herzkräftig, nur wild u durstig etwas vom Frühling zu geniessen.—Es ist vielleicht gar nicht so wichtig, wie ich war u bin. Ich habe Dir aber sonst wenig Ernstes zu berichten. . . .

Im Allgemeinen fehlst Du mir sehr. Bin ich wirklich derselbe, der von Einfällen u Entwürfen überströmte, solange Du erreichbar warst? Wenn ich mich abends an den Schreibtisch setze, weiss ich oft nicht, *worüber* arbeiten

Ihr, der Emma geht es gut, es ist ein sehr liebes anständiges Mädel das keinem von uns Beiden die Affäre übel nimmt u Dich mit grosser Achtung nennt.

Leb mir recht wol, gib ausführliche Nachricht von Dir u rechte nicht mit mir für diesmal. Ein andermal überhäufe ich Dich ja wieder mit Briefen u Sendungen. Du bist, ich bin nicht gleichmässig.

Herzlich Dein

Sigm.

The calm did not last long. After two weeks Freud reports again:

Vienna, April 11, 1895

Dearest Wilhelm,

Gloomy times, unbelievably gloomy. Mainly this business with Emma which is rapidly deteriorating. I reported to you last time that G. had inspected the cavity under general anesthesia, palpated it, and declared it satisfactory. We indulged our hopes and the patient was gradually recovering. However, eight days ago she began to bleed with the packing in place, something which had not happened before. She was packed again. The bleeding was minimal. Two days ago a new hemorrhage, again with the packing in place, and by now more than ample. New packing, renewed helplessness. Yesterday, R. wanted to re-examine the cavity. A new hypothesis about the source of the hemorrhage after the first operation (the one performed by you) had by chance been suggested by Weil.[27] As soon as the packing was partly out, there was a new, highly dangerous hemorrhage, which I witnessed. It didn't spurt,[28] but it surged, something like a [fluid] level rising exceedingly fast and then overflowing everything. It must have been a large vessel; but which one, and where? We of course couldn't see anything, and were glad that the packing was inside again. Add to this the pain, the morphine, the demoralization resulting from the obvious medical helplessness, and the whole air of danger, and you can picture the state the poor girl is in. We don't know what can be done. R. has been resisting the suggestion that he perform a ligation of the carotid artery. The danger that she will start to run a fever is also not far off.[29] I'm really quite shaken that such a misfortune

[27] Another E.N.T. specialist. While Freud was protesting adamantly that no one could possibly accuse Fliess of any negligence, his hint about Weil's remark had far-reaching repercussions (see below).

[28] Cf. Irma's injection: "Es spritzte nicht."

[29] Cf. the Irma dream: "there is no doubt it is an infection"; the association: pyemia might set in; the allusion to Fliess's suppurative rhinitis.

can have arisen from this operation, which was depicted as harmless.[30]

I am not sure that I should attribute exclusively to this depressing business the fact that my cardiac condition is so much below par for this year of my illness.[31] After an interruption of several months I have started to take strophantus[32] again so as to have a less miserable pulse, but I have not yet succeeded. Mood and strength are very low. I shall spend Easter with Rie ["Otto"] on the Semmering, and perhaps pull myself together there. . . .

With cordial regards to you and your dear wife,

Your

Sigm.

Wien 11. 4. 95

Liebster Wilhelm

Trübe Zeiten, unglaublich trübe. Vor Allem diese Geschichte mit der Emma, die zu keinem guten Ende hineilt. Ich habe Dir zuletzt berichtet, dass G. Die Höhle in der Narkose beaugenscheint, ausgetastet u für ordentlich erklärt hat. Wir gaben uns guten Hoffnungen hin u die Kranke erholte sich allmälich. 8 Tage begann sie bei liegendem Tampon zu bluten, was bislang nicht der Fall gewesen war. Sie wurde sofort neu tamponiert, die Blutg war geringfügig. Zwei Tage neue Blutg wiederum bei liegendem Tampon u bereits überreichlich. Neue Tamponade, neuerliche Rathlosigkeit. Gestern wollte R. die Höhle wieder untersuchen, es war durch Zufall eine Version von Weil über die Entstehg der Blutg bei der ersten Operation (Deiner) aufgetaucht. Sowie der Tampn halb heraus war, kam eine neue, lebensgefährliche Blutung, die ich mit ansah. Es spritzte nicht, aber es wogte. Etwas wie ein Niveau hob sich ausserordentlich rasch u überströmte dann alles. Es muss ein grosses Gefäss gewesen sein; aber welches u woher? Man sah natürlich nichts, war froh, dass man wieder einen Tampon drin hatte. Nimm dazu die Schmerzen, das Morphin, die Demoralisation durch die offenkundige ärztliche Rathlosigkeit u den Anstrich von Gefahr u Du wirst Dir den Zustand der Armen vorstellen können. Man weiss sich nicht zu helfen. R. sträubt sich gegen die vorge-

---

[30] This is a less disguised but still not conscious accusation of Fliess.

[31] Freud's worst attack of anginal pain with paroxysmal tachycardia had occurred just one year before this letter was written (Schur, 1966).

[32] A digitalislike drug.

schlagene Carotisunterbindung. Die Gefahr, dass sie zu fiebern beginnen wird, ist auch nicht mehr weit. Ich bin doch sehr erschüttert, wenn dergl. Malheur aus der für harmlos ausgegeben Operation entstehen kann.

Ich weiss nicht, ob ich es ausschliesslich dieser deprimirenden Angelegenheit zuschreiben soll, dass mein Herzbefinden so sehr unter dem Mittel dieses Krankheitsjahres verweilt. Ich habe nach viel monatlicher Unterbrechg wieder strophantus vorgenommen um einen minder schmählichen Puls zu haben, was noch nicht recht gelungen ist. Stimmg u Kräfte sind sehr a bas. Ich werde über Ostern mit Rie auf den Semmering gehen, vielleicht klaub' ich mich dort zusammen. . . .

Mit herzlichst Grüssen für Dich u Deine liebe Frau

Dein

Sigm.

Fliess must have been quite offended by Weil's remark as reported to him by Freud (see letter of April 11, 1895). The immediate consequence was that Fliess probably demanded some kind of "testimonial" from Gersuny (who was the more renowned surgeon) that the latter did not share Weil's belief in the connection between Emma's continuing hemorrhage and the operation performed on her by Fliess. To this demand Freud replied with the following letter:

Vienna, April 20, 1895

Dearest Wilhelm,

The Easter trip and one day in Abbazia have delayed my answer to your letter. I shall mail to you today the proofs of the second part of our book;[33] do not be bothered by the misprints. I am delighted that for once I can write about something [other][34] than the two tedious states of health. Your health is fortunately no longer on the agenda. We are so ungrateful; how hesitant we were about surgery and all the dangers it entailed.[35] Now we hardly say a word about it having been successful and your being able to work again. I want to rejoice out loud, and I now wait to hear about your scientific discoveries.

Of course I immediately informed R. of your suggestions con-

---

[33] Breuer and Freud: *Studies on Hysteria* (1893/95).
[34] See footnote 36.
[35] Fliess had had to undergo some surgery.

cerning Emma. Naturally things look different from close up, for
example, the hemorrhage. I can assure you that for the surgeons, to
sit around and wait would have been out of the question. It was
bleeding as though from the carotid artery. Within half a minute she
would have bled to death. However, she is doing better now. The
packing was carefully and gradually removed. There was no mishap,
and she is now in the clear.

The writer of this is still very miserable, but is also quite offended
that you should deem it necessary to have a testimonial from G. for
your rehabilitation. Even if G. should have the same opinion of your
skill as Weil, for me you remain the healer, the prototype of the man
into whose hands one confidently entrusts one's life and that of one's
family. I wanted to tell you of my misery, perhaps ask you for some
advice about Emma, but not reproach you for anything. *This would
have been stupid, unjustified, in clear contradiction to my feelings. . . .*

Wien, 20.4.95

Liebster Wilhelm,

Der Osterausflug u. ein Tag in Abbazia haben die Beantwortung
Deines Schreibens verzögert. Ich schicke Dir heute die Korrektur-
bögen von der zweiten Hälfte unseres Buches, lass Dich durch die
Druckfehler nicht stören. Es ist mir lieb, wenn ich so einmal von
etwas[36] als von den zwei langweiligen Gesundheiten schreiben kann.
Deine Gesundheit setzt sich ja zum Glück von der Tagesordnung ab.
Wir sind so undankbar; was haben wir gezagt mit Operation u. allen
daran haftenden Gefahren? Jetzt fällt kaum ein Wort darüber, dass
es gelungen u. Du wieder arbeitsfähig bist. Ich will mich laut darüber
freuen u. jetzt auf die Mitteilung Deiner wissenschaftlichen Funde
warten.

Deine Vorschläge in Betreff der Emma habe ich R. natürlich gleich
mitgeteilt. Es sieht sich aus der Nähe natürlich anders an, so die
Blutungen; ich kann bestätigen dass bei ihnen von Zuwarten nicht die
Rede sein kann. Es blutet wie aus der Carotis, in einer halben Minute
wäre sie wieder exsanguis [exsanguiniert]. Es geht ihr jetzt übrigens
besser. Der Tampon ist sachte u. allmählich entfernt worden, es hat
kein Malheur gegeben, sie ist jetzt frei.

Schreiber dieses ist noch sehr miserabel, ist aber auch beleidigt, dass
Du ein Zeugniss von G. für notwendig zur Rehabilitierung erachtest.

---

[36] The word *"anderem,"* which obviously belongs in here, was omitted, raising a
doubt about what Freud really wanted to say.

Für mich bleibst Du der Arzt, der Typus des Mannes dem man vertrauensvoll sein Leben u. das der Seinigen in die Hände legt auch wenn G. von Deiner Kunst dasselbe meinen würde wie Weil. Ich hab Dir was vorjammern u. vielleicht Rath für die Emma von Dir haben wollen, nicht Dir etwas vorwerfen. Es wäre dumm, unberechtigt u. in hellem Wiederspruch mit all meinem Gefühl. . . .

With this letter Freud probably reached the high watermark of his transference relationship to Fliess. It also tells us why his positive feelings were so strong. In this letter Freud is addressing not only Fliess the "mentor,"[37] the substitute analyst, but the healer who is also his physician. The last sentence of this letter clearly illustrates the "transference" situation. Freud stresses that any doubt about Fliess's skill would be in clear contradiction to his *feelings*. "Transference" is mainly an expression of "feelings" and not of logical thinking.

The last letter referring to the Emma episode prior to the Irma dream was written on May 25, 1895. Emma's condition was finally stabilized and the bleeding had stopped. She was convalescing and continuing with her treatment. An epilogue with a "happy ending" followed about a year later and will be quoted further on.

II

The link between the Emma episode and the Irma dream is self-evident, and I shall single out only a few links to the manifest dream content and to Freud's associations, as reported by him.

Here was a patient being treated by Freud for hysteria who *did* have an organic, largely "iatrogenic" illness; who had narrowly escaped death because a physician really had committed an error; whose pathology was located in the nasal cavity; whose case had confronted Freud with a number of emergencies requiring him urgently to call in several consultants, all of whom had been helpless and confused; Emma's lesion had a foetid odor (propylamyl); Freud had had to look repeatedly into her nose and mouth.

The most pertinent link is to be found in Freud's attitude toward Fliess, reflected in his letters about the Emma affair, his associations about Fliess in connection with the manifest dream content, and his final interpretation of the dream.

[37] In another (unpublished) letter, Freud even begins with the salutation "*Lieber Zauberer*" ("Dear Magician").

The second letter of March 8th already contains the whole conflict: Freud was shocked by the outcome of Emma's symptoms, the
severe hemorrhage, and the "slip" of Fliess. In his letter Freud attributes his spell of faintness not to the impact of Emma's hemorrhage
but to the affects which were welling up in him at that moment. "So
we had done her an *injustice.*" Hence, the first, overwhelming affect
was guilt, because "we"—Freud and Fliess—shared in the responsibility. To accuse both himself *and* Fliess was apparently intolerable;
hence his spell of weakness,[38] after which the process of displacement
began. Freud had hesitated for an entire day about telling Fliess of
the complication. However, within a matter of ten minutes he had
already, at least tentatively, displaced all his reproaches first to the
gauze and then to R. Compare this with the Irma dream, in which
his dear friend Otto became the culprit. At that time Freud did not
yet know that negations of reproaches, solemn protestations of trust
can only mean a defense against their opposite. When Freud confesses his shame about hesitating to write the letter to Fliess, he is
confessing his guilt for actually having blamed Fliess.

This letter, which expresses such painful emotions, is full of contradictions arising from largely unconscious conflicts between positive
and highly critical—hence hostile—feelings. Showing clearly the very
mechanisms that Freud was soon to detect as the elements of the
dream work (e.g., displacement, condensation, etc.), it reads like a
record of an analytic session.[39] The explanation is obvious. Freud was
by that time already "in analysis," at a stage where the "material" was
pouring out in free associations. While Freud was in the main his own
analyst, he was manifesting at this stage in his relationship with Fliess
what we would now call transference phenomena, and he could not
yet afford to abandon his positive "transference" to Fliess.

Only after the death of his father in 1896, which occurred at a
time when he had already been engaged for a year and a half in
systematically analyzing his own dreams and those of his patients, and
when the crucial importance of early childhood events had begun to

---

[38] In later years, Freud had two fainting spells in the presence of Fliess and two
in the presence of Jung (see Jones, I, p. 317; II, pp. 55, 146). Freud himself linked
the last of these fainting spells (in 1912) to Fliess and to the death of his younger
brother when Freud was about two years old. This brother had died in 1858—the
year Fliess was born (Schur, 1966).

[39] The Fliess correspondence, especially some of the unpublished letters, contains
many similar examples.

dawn on him, could he also begin what was to be his most heroic feat —his *systematic* self analysis. This led to the reconstruction of early infantile material; the discovery of the oedipus complex, anality, and other aspects of early infantile fantasies; and eventually to the dissolution of this "transference" relationship to Fliess.

And this brings us back to the beginning of this paper, and Freud's challenging, proud letter about the Irma dream. That letter was written on June 12, 1900.

A study of the Fliess correspondence (including the unpublished letters) indicates clearly that while the actual final break in the relationship between Freud and Fliess did not occur until their last meeting, during the summer of 1900, the change in Freud's attitude was a gradual one, with many ups and downs (Schur, 1966). Freud's letter of March 23, 1900 (1950, Letter 131) represents one of the final turning points in his inner relationship to Fliess.[40]

Could the triumphant letter referring to the Irma dream have been an (unconscious) challenge to Fliess, telling him, in essence: "One part of me thinks in terms of *ere perennius*—lasting fame—and that part of me already knew at the time of the Irma dream who had committed an error and whom I really had to protect because the other part of me was not yet as strong, sure, and *steady* [see letter of March 28, 1895] as it is now"? Could this episode have been the first step, therefore, in the direction of loosening the "transference"?

The two letters that followed, especially the second, indicate some of Freud's doubts: was the hemorrhage connected with something which had happened during the first operation, apart from the "lost" gauze packing? Are operations of this kind really necessary, especially if they are not all that harmless? We may also speculate that another doubt arose at this point: is the theory of the nasal origin of abdominal, and more especially, genital symptoms really cogent? Should I really have all my patients examined by Fliess? Should I constantly treat my own nose with cocaine?

And what of Fliess's symptoms? Why does he have such persistent headaches and nasal suppurations?

Is the defiance of Fliess (the resumption of smoking [see Freud, 1950, Letter 25 of June 12, 1895]) another indication of the growing

[40] See Kris's introduction to Freud (1950), and his footnote to Letter 138 of July 7, 1900.

conflict? And the praise of Breuer in the preceding letter of May 25, 1895 (No. 24)?

However, none of this could have reached consciousness in 1895. In the Irma dream Fliess had again to be put in the exalted role of the knowing, understanding, superior friend. The blame had to be displaced to Rie (Otto), while M. (Breuer) had to be ridiculed.

Does this addition detract from the historical importance of the Irma dream? In no way. In the interpretation of the Irma dream Freud first used the systematic analysis of each individual element of the dream. He discovered such mechanisms of the dream work as condensation, displacement, overdetermination, multiple representation, the wish-fulfillment function of dreams, etc. He had thus unveiled most, but not all, of the mysteries of the dream. He was, for example, not yet aware of the transference implication of dreams. Freud was right in claiming that the wish fulfillment of the Irma dream was a displacement of his responsibility for any failure with his patients, and a disclaimer that he had not been conscientious. Moreover, the complex process of displacement, which had started during the traumatic scene of Emma's hemorrhage, had freed Freud at least temporarily from guilt, thereby facilitating a similar displacement in the Irma dream.

But it was not only his own exculpation that he achieved; it was the need to exculpate Fliess from responsibility for Emma's nearly fatal complications that was probably the strongest (immediate) motive for the constellation of his dream. Why was this so?

Fliess was not only Freud's admired friend, his sounding board and therefore a substitute analyst; he was also the only one who not only believed in Freud's theories but also took the repeated changes of Freud's tentative formulations for granted, encouraged any new discovery, however revolutionary, and provided Freud's only "audience," his only protection from complete isolation.

Fliess was even more than this. Freud was just emerging from a severe cardiac episode which had started in the fall of 1893 and reached its culmination in April, 1894. During this period one of Fliess's roles was that of trusted physician, the source of constant support. Nothing describes this role better than a passage of what was in a sense Freud's (unpublished) farewell letter to Fliess, written on June 9, 1901, at a time when the break between them had in essence already taken place.

You have reminded me of that beautiful and difficult time when I was forced to believe that I was very close to the end of my life, and when it was your confidence that kept me going. I certainly did not behave either very bravely or very wisely then. I was too young, my instincts still too hungry, my curiosity still too great to be able to remain indifferent. However, I have always lacked your optimism. It is certainly foolish to want to banish suffering and dying from the earth, as we do in our New Year's wishes, and it was not for this that we did away with our dear Lord God, only to shift both of these things from ourselves and our dear ones to strangers.

I am thus more humble now, and more ready to bear whatever may come. There is no doubt that not all wishes can be fulfilled. Many a thing for which I have striven ardently is today no longer possible; why shouldn't I be obliged to bury some new hope each year? If you don't agree, this may be an attempt to soothe me, or it may be an appraisal led astray by friendship.

It is true that it is hard to tolerate complainers. This, too, I have learned to understand. I have been quite pleased with my mood for many weeks now.

I hope to have good news about you and yours soon and greet you cordially.

Your,

Sigm.

Du hast mich an die schöne u schwere Zeit erinnert, da ich mich dem Ende des Lebens sehr nahe glauben musste u Deine Zuversicht mich gehalten hat. Ich habe mich dabei gewiss nicht sehr mutig u nicht sehr weise benommen. Ich war zu jung, die Instinkte noch alle zu hungrig, die Neugierde noch zu gross, als dass ich hätte gleichgültig bleiben können. Dein Optimismus aber hat mir immer gefehlt. Es ist gewiss thöricht, Leiden u Sterben aus der Welt weisen zu wollen, wie wir's in unseren Neujahrsgratulationen thun, u nicht dazu haben wir uns den lieben Herrgott abgeschafft, u Beides von uns u den unserigen auf die Fremden zu wälzen.

Heute bin ich also ergebener u bereiter zu ertragen, was kommen wird. Es ist kein Zweifel, dass nicht alle Wünsche in Erfüllung gehen. Einiges, wonach ich heiss gestrebt, ist schon heute ausser Möglichkeit gekommen; warum soll ich nicht jedes Jahr eine neue Hoffnung begraben müssen? Stimmst Du nicht bei, so kann es ein Versuch der Beschwichtigg, es kann auch durch Freundschaft abgelenktes Urtheil sein.

Richtig ist, dass man die Klagenden schwer verträgt. Auch das habe ich einsehen gelernt. Ich bin jetzt mit meiner Stimmung seit vielen Wochen sehr zufrieden.

Ich hoffe bald von Dir u den Deinigen Gutes zu hören u grüsse Dich herzlich

Dein

Sigm.

This letter is made even more meaningful by the fact that it, too, opens with the theme of an injection.

Vienna, June 9, 1901

Dear Wilhelm,

I am taking advantage of this strange Sunday to write to you once again. It is the first Sunday I have been completely free, with nothing to remind me that at other times I am a physician. My aged lady, whom I have been visiting twice a day at fixed hours, was taken to the country yesterday, and I have been looking at my watch every fifteen minutes to see whether I am not keeping her waiting too long for her injection. *Thus we still feel the shackles even after they are removed, and do not really know how to enjoy our freedom.*

Wien, 9. 6. 1901

Theurer Wilhelm

Ich benütze diesen sonderbaren Sonntag, um Dir wieder einmal zu schreiben. Es ist der erste, an dem ich ganz frei bin, durch nichts erinnert werde, dass ich sonst Arzt bin. Meine uralte Dame, die ich täglich zweimal zu bestimmten Zeiten besuche, ist gestern auf's Land gebracht worden u ich schaue alle Viertelstuden auf die Uhr, ob ich sie nicht schon zu lange auf die Injektion warten lasse. So verspürt man noch die abgenommene Fessel u weiss sich seiner Freiheit nicht zu freuen.

How clearly the last sentence of this paragraph expresses the pain of being "free!" Gratitude for what Fliess had done for him persisted long after the dissolution of the transference and left Freud with an unresolved feeling of guilt (Schur, 1966).

For all these reasons Freud was still obliged in 1895 to exculpate

Fliess, because only by keeping Fliess strong and "steady" could he preserve both his ego ideal and his own security.

However, we find at one point in Freud's associations a highly aggressive wish against Fliess, *disguised as concern:* the association that Fliess "suffered himself from suppurative rhinitis, which caused me anxiety; and no doubt there was an allusion to this in the pyaemia which vaguely came into my mind in connection with the metastases in the dream." Here Fliess *is* being punished for Emma's fate!

For all these reasons, both the Emma episode and the Irma dream were important milestones. With the discovery of the necessary tools and the concepts for dream interpretation, Freud took another important step not only toward the understanding of psychic phenomena, but toward his own liberation—ultimately inescapable—from the necessity for his "transference" relationship to Fliess.

The following question might be raised: is it possible that Freud was aware of this meaning of the Irma dream which I have just discussed, specifically when he referred to certain omissions of material because of the limits to be placed on divulging associations pertaining to his innermost secrets?

Freud certainly was aware of *omissions* in his discussions of the Irma dream (see, for example, 1900, p. 113; p. 105, n. 2; p. 118, n. 2, added in 1909). However, the highly complimentary associations and interpretations pertaining to Fliess in the Irma dream were not *omissions* but *positive* conclusions involving one of the main elements of the dream. Knowing as we do that Freud wrote the final version of *The Interpretation of Dreams* in 1899, and knowing his superb honesty, we must assume that by that time any connection between the Irma dream and the Emma episode had been even more thoroughly repressed than before. Moreover, Freud did not change any of these passages after his break wtih Fliess, in any of his many revisions of *The Interpretation of Dreams.*

One further question might be raised in connection with the history of the Irma dream. Careful readers of the Fliess correspondence and of J. Strachey's introduction to *The Interpretation of Dreams* are aware of the fact that Fliess closely scrutinized and even "censored" the manuscript and proofs of *The Interpretation of Dreams.* There is a somewhat cryptic passage in Freud's letter to Fliess of October 23, 1898 (Letter 99), which Strachey quotes (p. xix): "Freud writes that the book 'remains stationary, unchanged; I have no motive for preparing it for publication, and the gap in the psychology [i.e., Chapter VII] as well as the gap left by removing the completely analysed sample dream [Chapter II] are obstacles to my finishing it which I have not yet overcome.' "

Strachey's translation "sample" dream for the German *"Beispiel,"* rather than the more correct "example," and his insertion of the reference to Chapter II (which contains the Irma dream), added to his remark (p. xx) that Fliess seems "to have been responsible for the omission (evidently on grounds of discretion) of an analysis of one important dream of Freud's own" would seem to indicate that Strachey believes the dream omitted on Fliess's recommendation to have been the Irma dream. (See Strachey's translation of the heading of Chapter II as "specimen" dream (*Traummuster*), a term much closer to "sample" than to "example.") This opinion is shared by a number of others.

However, there are various indications that the Irma dream was not the one "censored" by Fliess and wtihdrawn by Freud.

First, of course, is the fact that the Irma dream *does* appear in *The Interpretation of Dreams*. If it had been withdrawn on Fliess's objections and subsequently restored before publication, it is likely that some indication of this change of decision on Freud's part would have appeared in his correspondence with Fliess, but in fact none does.

Secondly, Freud never referred to the Irma dream as a *completely* (*"zu Grunde"*) analyzed dream. Instead, he spoke of it as the first dream subjected to a "thorough" (*"eingehend"*) analysis.

Most important is the evidence found in a number of letters to Fliess, pointing to an entirely different dream which in fact *was* (regretfully) removed by Freud and replaced by several others.

On June 9, 1898 Freud writes (in an unpublished portion of Letter 90):

> I also thank you cordially for your criticism. I am aware of the fact that you have undertaken a very thankless task. I am reasonable enough to recognize that I need your critical help, because in this instance I myself have lost the feeling of shame required of an author. So this dream is condemned. However, now that the sentence has been passed, I would like to shed a tear for it and confess that I regret it and that I cannot hope to find a better one as a substitute. You must know that a beautiful dream and no indiscretion d not go together. At least write me to which topic you took exception, and where you

feared an attack by a malicious critic. Was it my anxiety, or Martha, or the *Dalles*,[41] or my being without a fatherland? [Please let me know] so I can omit the topic you designate in a substitute dream, because I can have dreams like that to order. . . .

Herzlichen Dank ferner für Deine Kritik. Ich weiss, Du hast da ein undankbares Geschäft auf Dich genommen. Ich bin verständig zu erkennen, dass ich Deine kritische Mithilfe brauche, weil ich selbst in diesem Falle das dem Autor nöthige Schamgefühl verloren habe. Der Traum ist also verdammt. Aber nachdem das Urtheil gefällt ist, will ich ihm eine Thräne nachweinen u gestehen, dass er mir leid thut, u dass ich keinen besseren als Ersatz zu finden hoffe. Du weisst ja, ein schöner Traum u keine Indiscretion—das trifft nicht zusammen. Schreib mir wenigstens, an welchem Thema Du den Anstoss genommen hast, u wo Du den Angriff von dem boshaften Kritiker fürchtest. Ob es meine Angst, oder Martha oder der Dalles oder die Vaterlandslosigkeit ist? Damit ich das von Dir bezeichnete im Ersatztraum auslassen kann, denn ich kann mir solche Träume bei mir bestellen. . . .

This is the first mention of the rejected dream which I found in the Fliess correspondence.

Of the topics mentioned by Freud as possibly objectionable in Fliess's opinion, only the reference to his wife applies also to the Irma dream. No special anxiety and no allusion to Freud's poverty or his lack of a fatherland can be found in the Irma dream. Nor is there any reference to Fliess which might be offensive to the latter.

In an unpublished paragraph of his letter of June 20, 1898 (Letter 91), Freud writes:

My mourning for the lost dream is not yet over. As if in spite I recently had a substitute dream in which a house constructed of building blocks collapsed (we had built a *staatliches*[42] house); this dream, therefore, because of that reference, cannot be used either.

Die Trauer um den verlorenen Traum ist noch nicht zu Ende. Wie zum Trotz war unlängst ein Ersatztraum, in dem ein aus Bausteinen erbautes Haus zusammenstürtzte ("Wir hatten gebauet ein staatliches Haus"), der also wegen dieser Beziehg nicht zu brauchen war.

[41] A Jewish word for poverty, frequently used colloquially by Viennese Jews.

[42] The words in parentheses represent one of Freud's associations. The word "*staatliches*" is a pun combining the two words: "*stattlich*"—stately, imposing, grand; and "*staatlich*"—pertaining to the state, to public affairs, to politics.

This letter and dream on the one hand express Freud's resentment and regrets in a characteristically witty way. On the other hand—and this is of course much more important to my topic—the pun indicates that the main bone of contention in the rejected dream must have been something "political," probably connected with Freud's allusion in the previous letter to "being without a fatherland."[43]

The next reference to the rejected dream is the passage in the letter of October 23, 1898 (Letter 99) where Freud for the first time speaks of the *completely analyzed* example. At that time Freud had already "discovered" the oedipus complex and other aspects of infantile sexuality. It is therefore most unlikely that he would still consider the Irma dream to be a *completely* analyzed dream. For this reason Freud himself later referred to the Irma dream as the first one subjected to a "thorough" analysis.[44]

The dream book was put aside until Freud caught up with his self analysis and his new understanding of the material of his patients. In May, 1899 began one of his periods of feverish activity, and after only two months he was able to announce to Fliess that the first chapter had gone to the printer. Fliess was now regularly receiving the manuscripts and first galleys of each chapter.

In a letter of August 1, 1899 (Letter 113), Freud again mentions the omitted dream:

> The gap made by the big dream which you took out is to be filled by a small collection of dreams (innocent and absurd dreams, calculations and speeches in dreams, affects in dreams). Real revision will only be required for the last, psychological chapter [VII]. . . .

This letter clearly indicates that "the" dream actually was left out, and was replaced by others. Early in October, 1899 *The Interpretation of Dreams* was published with the Irma dream included. We may therefore safely claim that the omitted dream was not the Irma dream.

Among the many other possible links between the Emma episode and the Irma dream I shall mention only two.

Freud's need to exculpate Fliess and also, indirectly, himself resulted in a displacement of hostile accusations to the person of his

---

[43] The collapsed house could, of course, pertain to Freud's relationship with Fliess as well as to the collapse or threatened collapse of other hopes and expectations.

[44] Freud's letters written between January 3 and March 3, 1899 (1950, letters 101-107) explain the actual reasons for the long interruption in the progress of *The Interpretation of Dreams*.

innocent friend "Otto." But there were also hostile associations directed against Irma and other female figures. If the reproaches against "Otto" were meant as a displacement from Fliess (hence belonging to the category of what Freud later described as "hypocritical" dreams), could the hostility expressed against Irma also have been a displacement from Emma?

Emma had certainly caused Freud a great deal of trouble and concern. She had shaken Freud's trust in Fliess—even though he had denied this at the time—and this trust was absolutely essential for Freud's equilibrium. But she had done even more. She had seen Freud at a weak moment and mocked him with her remark: "This is the strong sex." Is it possible that Freud, who at the time of the Irma dream was recovering from his cardiac episode and was enjoying his stay at the beautiful villa (which he described so vividly in his letter of June 12, 1900) as a sign of beginning prosperity, who had resumed smoking in defiance of Fliess, who had realized that he was on the threshold of "touch[ing] upon one of the great mysteries of nature" (Letter 18, May 21, 1894), and, last but not least, whose wife was pregnant with her sixth child, was "getting even" with the "weak woman" who dared to doubt his interpretations and even to mock him? Was he "getting even," too, with the "recalcitrant" girl friend of Irma's who had "shown herself strong enough to master her condition without outside help" (1900, p. 110)? Was he in fact retaliating against "brave women"—the "brave Frau Doktor" of the Emma episode and the "Frau Professor," his courageous wife, against whom he directed his somewhat deprecatory associations to the Irma dream?

Finally, in the preamble to the Irma dream (p. 106), Freud indicated his annoyance over a passing remark of his friend O. (Dr. Oskar Rie) in which he "fancied" he detected skeptical reproof about his therapeutic results in the Irma case. Freud thought that M. (Breuer), "at that time the leading figure in our circle," might share this skepticism, and that same evening he wrote out Irma's case history with the idea of giving it to Breuer in order to justify himself. In his letter of April 11, 1895 Freud had *told* Fliess about a similarly critical remark of Weil's, to which Fliess had taken strong exception, necessitating in turn a rather humble apology from Freud. I have already mentioned the far-reaching repercussions which Freud's "*telling*" had for him. This theme of "telling" on or about someone was one of the main motives of another of Freud's most revealing dreams, which he re-

ported in *The Interpretation of Dreams*—the *"non vixit"* dream. It
played a decisive role in the final break between Freud and Fliess,
especially in the latter's accusation against Freud in connection with
Otto Weininger's publication (see Freud, 1950, p. 41).

That the Irma dream—like any other—was overdetermined, that
its latent content comprised genetic material from Freud's childhood,
that it had sexual connotations is self-evident. Erikson, for example,
in his 1954 study, tried to reanalyze this "specimen dream of psychoanalysis" by using biographical data on Freud's early childhood
obtained from various sources.

I have deliberately refrained from attempting any such reinterpre-
tation of the "deeper" sources of the dream, and restricted myself to
the use of material presented in Freud's own words, which quite obviously represented the background residuum both for the manifest
dream and for the most important associations and interpretations
given by Freud. I have also refrained from tracing *all* the links between the Emma material and each single element of the Irma dream
—something that can easily be done but seems superfluous for the
purposes of this paper.

The background material and the use made of it by Freud throw
important light on the earlier stages of Freud's self analysis and on the
role which his "transference" phenomena, reflected in his relationship
to Fliess, played in the "specimen dream," as well as in his progressive
unveiling of the secrets of the mind. The whole Emma episode also
throws an important and more intimate light on the period of trial
and error through which Freud's therapeutic technique had to pass.
It explains why Freud eventually had to stress the role of abstinence
in the transference situation. But all this was contingent upon Freud's
progress in his self analysis and the concomitant dissolution of his
transference relationship.

In his introduction to the Irma dream, Freud quotes the French
psychologist Delboeuf: "Every psychologist is under an obligation to
confess even his own weaknesses, if he thinks that it may throw light
upon some obscure problem" (p. 105).

Freud certainly followed this exhortation, and did not hesitate to
divulge in *The Interpretation of Dreams* a number of intimate details
about his own life and the life of those around him. To do this in the
service of science was not "weakness" but courage and strength. We
are all inclined to look upon Freud as the incarnation of strength,

wisdom, and courage. But Freud could not have been Freud without being intensely human, and this condition included deep suffering.

Nothing shows this quality better than his lettters. K. R. Eissler (1964) could therefore have chosen no better title for his review of Freud's collection of letters than "Mankind at Its Best."

In my discussion of a small segment of Freud's development, I have chosen to speak of his "transference phenomena." In so doing I wished to demonstrate, on the one hand, how intensely human Freud showed himself to be even in this phase which included severe physical illness, and how, on the other hand, Freud was able to emerge from this period of conflict and suffering having accomplished one of his greatest feats—the discovery of the secret of the dream.

Epilogue

And now we come to the denouement and epilogue of the drama, which illustrate Freud's ability even at that early stage to achieve therapeutic results and arrive at new insights in a case which confronted him with many seemingly insurmountable obstacles.

On April 16, 1896, approximately one year after the last-quoted letter about Miss Emma, Freud wrote to Fliess upon his return from one of their periodic meetings:

Vienna, April 16, 1896

Dearest Wilhelm,

I felt the same way. With my head full of periods and hunches about summations,[45] proud of having achieved some recognition, and with a bold feeling of *independence*,[46] I came back with a real sense of well-being, and have been quite lazy ever since, because that state of semi-misery[47] which is essential for intensive work won't re-establish itself. I have only some sparse hunches to set down about the "in-

[45] This word probably pertains both to Fliess's theories on periodicity, to which Freud was thus paying somewhat tongue-in-cheek lip service, and to his own feeling that his ideas and concepts were starting to fall into place.

[46] Does the use of this term in the context of his expansive mood herald Freud's gradual shift from a "transference" relationship to a more independent one?

[47] Freud had remarked repeatedly in his correspondence that he was most creative during periods of mild physical distress (Schur, 1966). This mood was also characteristic of periods in which new material was coming up in his self analysis and in the treatment of his patients.

between realm"[48] which have come out of my daily work, plus a
general reinforcement of the impression that *everything** is the way
I have surmised it to be and that everything will thus become clear.
Among all these things is a quite surprising explanation of Emma's
hemorrhages, which will give you great satisfaction. I have already
guessed what the story is, but I shall wait to communicate it until
the patient herself has caught up with it. . . .

Wien, 16. 4. 96

Liebster Wilhelm

Es gieng mir ebenso; den Kopf voll von Terminen u Summations-
ahnungen, stolz auf manche Anerkennung und mit einem frechen
Gefühl von Selbstständigkeit bin ich zu gutem Wolbefinden zurück-
gekehrt u bin seither sehr faul gewesen, weil sich das zur intensiven
Arbeit nöthige Mittelelend nicht einstellen will. Nur einige wenige
aus der täglichen Arbeit aufsteigende Ahnungen über das Zwischenreich habe ich zu verzeichnen wie im Allgemeinen die Verstärkg des
Eindrucks, dass *alles* so ist, wie ich es vermuthe u dass sich also alles
klären wird. Darunter eine ganz überraschende Aufklärung über die
Blutungen bei der Emma, mit denen Du Deine Freude haben wirst.
Ich habe die Geschichte schon errathen, warte aber mit der Mittheilg
bis die Pat. selbst nachgekommen ist. . . .

In a letter of April 26, 1896, Freud provides more specific information:

. . . with regard to Emma, I shall be able to prove to you that you
were right; her hemorrhages were hysterical, brought on by *longing,**
probably at the "sexual period"[49] (out of sheer resistance that
Frauenzimmer[50] has not yet given me the dates). . . .

. . . mit der Emma: Ich werde Dir nachweisen können, dass Du Recht
hast, dass ihre Blutungen hysterische waren, aus *Sehnsucht* erfolgt

---

[48] Freud coined the term "*Zwischenreich*," combining "*zwischen*" (between, in-
between) and "*Reich*" (realm, state, empire). This probably refers to the "Unconscious," and also to his self analysis.

[49] Freud is apparently using the awkward word "*Sexualtermine*" instead of *Menstruation*, in accordance with Fliess's theory about the link between periodicity and
menstruation.

[50] "Literally, 'woman's apartment'. The word is very often used in German as a
slightly derogatory synonym for 'woman'." See Strachey's note in *S.E.*, 15:162.

sind u wahrscheinlich zu Sexualterminen (das Frauenzimmer hat nur aus Widerstand die Daten noch nicht besorgt). . . .

This letter is full of hidden ambiguities obviously related to Freud's increasing ambivalence toward Fliess, which also expresses itself in doubts about Fliess's theory of periodicity. On the one hand, he is giving Fliess credit by agreeing that Emma's hemorrhages were hysterical, thus exculpating Fliess even more than heretofore. He also refers to Fliess's theory of periodicity. On the other hand, he asserts that Emma's hysterical hemorrhages were based on an unconscious (sexual) wish, and therefore on an emotional conflict. What Fliess expected was an unconditional acceptance of his theory that periodicity was the main cause of pathology. (See Kris's footnote to Freud's Letter 43 and Chapter IV of the introduction to this book [1950].)

In a letter of May 4, 1896, Freud finally divulges the analytic material underlying his assumption that the hemorrhages were hysterical in origin:

Vienna, May 4, 1896

. . . Concerning Emma, about whose history I am making notes to send you, I know so far that she was bleeding out of *longing*.* She had been a bleeder all along, whenever she cut herself, etc. As a child she suffered from severe nosebleeds. During her prepuberty years [she] started to have headaches, which were interpreted to her as malingering, which in fact had been due to [auto]suggestion, so that she greeted her intense menstrual bleeding with pleasure, as a proof of the genuineness of her illness, a proof which was even accepted as valid. She has [the image of] a *scene* from her fifteenth year, where she suddenly starts to bleed from the nose, with the wish to be treated by a particular young physician who was present at the time (and also appears in the dream). When she became aware of my deep emotion during her first hemorrhage while in the hands of R., she experienced the realization of an old wish to be loved in her sickness, and during the next few hours, despite her danger, felt happy as never before. Then in the sanatorium, during the night, she began to feel restless out of unconscious longing and the intention of drawing me to her side. And since I did not come during the night, she renewed the hemorrhage as an unfailing means of reawakening my affection. She bled spontaneously three times, and each hemorrhage lasted approximately four days, which must be significant. She still owes me details and specific dates.

My heartfelt greetings to you and do not forget to write as often as your head permits.[51]

Yours,

Sigm.

. . . Von der Emma, deren Geschichte ich notiere so dass ich sie Dir schicken kann, weiss ich bis jetzt, dass sie aus *Sehnsucht* geblutet hat. Sie war von jeher eine Bluterin, wenn sie sich schnitt udgl, litt als Kind an heftigen Nasenbluten, bekam in den Jahren vor der Periode Kopfschmerzen, die ihr als Simulation ausgelegt wurden, die in Wahrheit durch Suggestion entstanden waren u begrüsste darum die heftigen Periodenblutgen mit Freude als Beweis für die Echtheit ihres Krankseins der ihr auch gelten gelassen wurde. Sie hat eine Scene aus ihrem 15. Jahr, in der sie plötzl Nasenbluten bekommt mit dem Wunsch, von einem bestimmten dabei anwesenden jungen Arzt (der auch im Traum vorkommt) behandelt zu werden. Als sie meine Ergriffenheit bei der ersten Blutg unter R.'s Händen sah, fand sie einen alten Wunsch nach Liebe im Kranksein verwirklicht, fühlte sich die nächsten Stunden trotz ihrer Gefahr so glücklich wie nie, bekam dann im Sanat. nächtl. Unruhe aus der unbew. Sehnsuchtsabsicht, mich hinzulocken, u da ich nachts nicht kam, erneuerte sie die Blutg, als unfehlbares Mittel meine Zärtlichkeit wieder zu wecken. Sie hat 3 mal spontan geblutet und jede Blutg hielt über 4 Tage an, was eine Bedeutg haben muss. Details u Termine ist sie mir noch schuldig.

Sei mir herzliche gegrüsst u vergiss nicht, mir zu schreiben so oft Dein Kopf es erlaubt.

Dein

Sigm.

Nowadays we would of course expect a careful hematological work-up to establish what kind of "bleeder" Emma was. But in this letter Freud was—without mentioning it—continuing with the exculpation of Fliess! The iodoform gauze was buried and forgotten! However, Freud had obviously also conceived of the possibility of "hysterical" nose-bleeding and probably of vicarious menstrual nasal bleeding as well, a step from the concept of conversion to that of "resomatization" (Schur, 1955).

---

[51] Fliess was suffering from persistent headaches which he attributed to his nose, for which he had undergone repeated surgery.

On January 17, 1897, Freud wrote Fliess a letter, most of which was published in *The Origins of Psychoanalysis* (Letter 56). This letter is remarkable for many reasons. It introduces, among other points, the link between the symptomatology of hysterics and the accusations of possession by the devil made by the Inquisition. (See Kris's footnote to this letter.)

In the unpublished portion of the letter Freud writes:

> Emma has a scene [in mind] where the *Diabolus* sticks pins into her finger and puts a piece of candy on each drop of blood. As far as the blood is concerned,[52] you are altogether innocent! As a counterpart to this: the fear of needles and pointed objects from the second psychic period.[53] As for cruelty in general: the fear of hurting someone with a knife or in some other way.[54]

> Die Emma hat eine Scene, wo ihr der Diabolus Nadeln in die Finger sticht u auf jeden Blutstropfen ein Zuckerl legt. An dem Blut' bist Du überhaupt unschuldig! Gegenstück dazu: Die Angst vor Nadeln u spitzen Gegenständen aus der zweiten psych. Periode. Zur Grausamkeit überhpt: Angst jemanden mit Messer oder sonst zu verletzen.

The allusions to Emma continue, this time with a reminder of Fliess's surgery!

In an unpublished part of Letter 57, written on January 24, 1897, Freud writes:

> ... Think of it; I have been given a scene[55] about the circumcision of a girl, involving the cutting off of a piece of one of the labia minora (which is shorter even now) and the sucking off of the blood, after which the child got to eat a piece of the skin. This child at the age of

---

[52] Meaning the hemorrhage. Now Fliess has been completely vindicated, even of having left the iodoform strip in the wound!

[53] At that time Freud already distinguished several periods of mental development.

[54] An allusion to what Freud later described as the sadistic component of phallic strivings.

[55] The use of the word "scene" here and in the two previous letters is very significant. We know from Freud's correspondence with Fliess that he still believed in the "seduction etiology" of hysteria. However, in the published portion of this letter and the preceding one he clearly describes what he later called fantasies. This holds true for Emma's "scenes." It would therefore seem that Emma was one of the first patients who offered Freud a clue to the crucial realization that what his patients had described to him as actual seduction episodes were fantasies. As we know, this realization opened the way to the discovery of early infantile sexuality and its manifestations in infancy.

thirteen once claimed that she could swallow a piece of an earthworm, which she actually did. And an operation once performed by you had to come to grief from a hemophilia based on all this. . . .

. . . Denke Dir, dass ich eine Scene von Mädchenbeschneidg bekommen habe. Abschneiden eines Stückes von einem kleinen Labium (das heute noch kürzer ist), Aufsaugen des Blutes, wonach das Kind das Stückchen Haut zu essen bekommt. Dieses Kind behauptete einmal mit 13 J, dass es ein Stück von einem Regenwurm schlukken könne u führte es auch aus. Unter der so begründeten Haemophilie hat einmal eine Operation von Dir gelitten. . . .

This is the last reference to the case of Emma I was able to find in Freud's correspondence with Fliess.[56] One more attempt has been made here to exculpate Fliess. The further—post-Irma-dream—additions pertaining to the case of Emma confirm my elaboration of the interpretations of that dream. Moreover, the little snatches of material, when put together, give us a fascinating clinical vignette of those early cases of hysteria treated by Freud. On the one hand, these sparse portions of a case history add to our satisfaction that the correspondence between Freud and Fliess has been preserved (see Kris's Introduction to Freud [1950]; Schur [1965]). On the other hand, they add to our feeling of loss that so many of Freud's early case histories—for example, that of Emma, about whom Freud was obviously writing to Fliess—have remained unknown to us.

Summary

The material of this essay gives us a fascinating glimpse into the "workshop" of a genius during a heroic and dramatic phase of his struggle to unveil the mysteries of the mind.

Giving us an insight into the early phases of Freud's unique analytic situation, this material provides an unusually vivid example of how a transference relationship can almost simultaneously reach its climax and show the signs of its incipient dissolution. The material provides highly illuminating examples of displacement *in statu nascendi;* these found their way into a dream which took place more than three months later. We find a confirmation of the hypothesis that the "day residue" includes elements originating much earlier than

---

[56] I plan at a later date to study once again the originals of this correspondence, because some of the letters still have to be transcribed.

the day immediately preceding the dream. Finally, it provides a brilliant example of the transition from fantasy to conversion and resomatization through the interplay of psychopathology, "somatic compliance," and traumatization.

BIBLIOGRAPHY

Breuer, J. & Freud, S. (1893/95), Studies on Hysteria. *S.E.*, 2.

Eissler, K. R. (1964), Mankind at Its Best. *J. Am. Psa. Assn.*, 12:187-222.

Erikson, E. H. (1954), The Dream Specimen of Psychoanalysis. *J. Am. Psa. Assn.*, 2:5-56.

Fisher, C. (1954), Dreams and Perception. *J. Am. Psa. Assn.*, 2:389-445.

Freud, S. (1900), The Interpretation of Dreams. *S.E.*, 4 & 5.

—— (1950), *The Origins of Psychoanalysis*. NY: Basic Books, 1954.

—— (1960), *Briefe 1873-1939*. Frankfurt: Fischer.

Hartmann, H. (1948), Comments on the Psychoanalytic Theory of Instinctual Drives. *Essays*, 69-89.

—— (1956), The Development of the Ego Concept in Freud's Work. *Essays*, 268-296.

Jones, E. (1953/57), *The Life and Work of Sigmund Freud*, 3 Vols. NY: Basic Books.

Schur, M. (1955), Comments on the Metapsychology of Somatization. *Psa. Study Ch.*, 10:119-164.

—— (1965), Editor's Introduction. *Drives, Affects, Behavior*. NY: IUP, 2:9-20.

—— (1966), *The Problem of Death in Freud's Writings and Life*. NY: IUP (in preparation).

Precursors of the Concept of the Death Instinct

MAURITS KATAN, M.D.

In *Civilization and Its Discontents* Freud (1930) writes: "I remember my own defensive attitude when the idea of an instinct of destruction first emerged in psycho-analytic literature, and how long it took before I became receptive to it" (p. 120). This remark clearly refers to two publications—one by Sabina Spielrein (1912), the other a Dutch translation by Stärcke (1914) of Freud's paper "Civilized Sexual Morality"—in which the authors expressed speculative ideas about the destructive character of the sexual instinct.[1] Thus, according to his own admission, Freud could have started to formulate his new ideas about the death instinct only some years after 1914. This conclusion, however, seems to be challenged by the following considerations.

It was approximately twenty years ago that my attention was drawn to the strong similarity between a passage in Freud's article on Schreber (1911) and one in *The Ego and the Id* (1923). In the former Freud developed the theory that delusional formation is an attempt at recovery. Relationships to objects that were relinquished are restored in a delusional form, although relationships that originally were affectionate have now become hostile. "We may say, then, that the process of repression proper consists in a detachment of the libido from people—and things—that were previously loved. It happens silently; we receive no intelligence of it, but can only infer it from subsequent events. What forces itself so noisily upon our attention is the process of recovery, which undoes the work of repression and brings back the libido again on to the people it had abandoned" (1911, p. 71).

[1] Freud points this out in a footnote in *Beyond the Pleasure Principle* (1920, p. 55).

And here is the similar passage from *The Ego and the Id:* "Over and over again we find, when we are able to trace instinctual impulses back, that they reveal themselves as derivatives of Eros. If it were not for the considerations put forward in *Beyond the Pleasure Principle*, and ultimately for the sadistic constituents which have attached themselves to Eros, we should have difficulty in holding to our fundamental dualistic point of view. But since we cannot escape that view, we are driven to conclude that the death instincts are by their nature mute and that the clamour of life proceeds for the most part from Eros" (1923, p. 46).

It is a pity that the translators, owing to the chronological gap of twelve years between the two passages, were unaware of their conspicuous similarity and so unwittingly obscured the meaningful relation existing between them in the original German text. I shall try to restore the similarity by showing that in both passages Freud used exactly the same words in comparable key positions.

1911: "It proceeds *mutely;* we receive no message of it, *we feel necessitated to conclude* it from the processes that follow. What forces itself so *noisily* upon our attention is the process of recovery, which undoes the work of repression and brings back the libido again on to the people it had abandoned."

1923: "*But since we feel necessitated to it* [namely, to hold to our fundamental dualistic point of view], we gain the impression that the death instincts are by their nature *mute* and that the *noise* of life proceeds for the most part from Eros."[2]

The similarity between the two passages is striking. The *noise* of the libidinal attempt at recovery is comparable to the *noise* of the life instinct. *We feel compelled to conclude* that there is a process of withdrawal, just as *we feel compelled to conclude* that there are two basic instincts, namely, that in addition to a life instinct, a death instinct also exists. The process of withdrawal occurs *mutely*, just as the death instinct is *mute*.

Notwithstanding a gap of twelve years, Freud used exactly the same words in comparable key positions, although he certainly had many synonyms at his disposal from which to choose. This fact points to the question whether during the writing of the Schreber article ideas were already begging for expression, ideas which at that time

[2] I have translated "*sind genötigt*," "*Lärm*" ("*lärmend*"), and "*stumm*" as "feel necessitated," "noise" ("noisy"), and "mute."

Freud could not sufficiently conceptualize and which as a result were forgotten. Under completely different circumstances the same basic ideas again begged for admittance, and Freud formulated them anew, as if they had never knocked on the door twelve years before.

Briefly, the problem is this: can Freud's formulation of the psychotic process be viewed as a precursor of his ideas of life and death instincts which were developed a decade later? In an attempt to arrive at an answer, let us study Freud's early formulation in the article on Schreber.

We should keep well in mind what Freud's main viewpoints were when he began this work. The years following the publication of *The Interpretation of Dreams* (1900) had been used principally for the exploration of the unconscious. As far as instincts were concerned, he considered one group, the ego instincts, as working for self preservation; the other group, the libidinal instincts, had the task of preserving the species.

In the very beginning of his article on Schreber, Freud reveals his *plan de campagne*. The study of psychotics would be totally impossible if they did not betray, although in a distorted form, what all the other neurotics keep hidden as a secret. It does not require much deliberation to see expressed here the idea that the return of the repressed makes possible the study of the psychoses. First, we have to ask what returns from the repressed. The answer sounded at first unbelievable to Freud, but the other analysts, Ferenczi and Jung, reached the same conclusion. The homosexual attachment to the father, which attachment Freud then formulated in the sentence, "I love him," influences the content of the psychotic symptoms.

Next, we have to turn to that part of Freud's basic approach where he states that the secret which no longer remains hidden is not revealed by the psychotic in its original form but is now distorted. Thus, when the repressed returns, it occurs in a distorted form. The influence of the ego comes to the fore by causing the distortion. The stage is set for the entry of a scientific ego psychology.

Freud approaches the problem of psychotic phenomena in two different ways. In the one, he considers symptom formation; in the other, the mechanism of repression. In the first method he follows the course of the homosexual urge as a return of the repressed, i.e., on its way up to consciousness, from the depths up to the surface. In the second method he looks more at the ego side of the problem.

Let us begin with the homosexual urge itself. In the article on Leonardo da Vinci (1910), which preceded the Schreber paper, Freud had already revealed a clear insight into the final stages of the development of the homosexual perversion, emphasizing the role of the positive oedipus complex. He described how the boy, in his strong attachment to the mother, cannot shift his libidinal strivings over to a girl of his own age but instead identifies with his mother and then loves other boys who possess the features he himself has. He forms a narcissistic object choice, as Freud later called it. Simultaneously Freud showed that in this homosexual attachment regressive elements are also incorporated, namely, repetitions of the early relationship between mother and child.

In the Schreber study, Freud developed a completely different picture of the homosexual urge, which is so predominant in the psychoses. The boy, in his narcissism, attaches great value to his penis; next, in his object choice, he turns to the man, who possesses the same organ. Thus Freud introduces a very early form of homosexuality which occurs before the boy loves his mother. The homosexual libido is not changed into a heterosexual type but is sublimated, and its desexualized energy lends great support to the ego in the form of love for mankind, *esprit de corps,* etc. When ego regression takes place and, as a result, the sublimation is undone, the homosexual urge consequently becomes increasingly strong and finally acquires an overwhelming character.

I have intentionally stressed the different viewpoints on homosexuality which Freud developed in describing the homosexual perversion versus the homosexual urge in the psychosis. In the latter the mother figure does not play a role at all. We may say that homosexuality, as it is painted in the Schreber study, has a prephallic early narcissistic nature. Freud, in his later work, never applied the same reasoning. Nevertheless, one may ask whether there is not a prephallic early stirring of this turning by the boy to his father, which stirring under very special circumstances can acquire a pernicious influence.

Let us see what becomes of this homosexual urge on its way up to consciousness. The ego does not admit homosexuality in its original form. The result is either a delusion of persecution, or of jealousy, or of erotomania, depending upon whether the verb or the subject or the object of the basic "I love him" is contradicted. In these three forms of delusion, projection is the primary means of defense. There is still a fourth form of delusion to be considered, namely, megalomania. Here the basic sentence as a whole is contradicted: "I don't love anybody, I love only myself." The delusion of grandeur is then a return to the infantile ego state of megalomania. Thus, in megalomania, projection does not occur. Here the defense is an ego regression, whereas in the other three delusional forms the defense is based on projection.

By conceiving of the psychotic symptoms as the result of the warding off of "I love him," we see that Freud tried to give an explanation of the content of the delusions.

Next, Freud turned from symptom formation to the mechanism of repression. At that time Freud still thought that any neurotic or psychotic defensive process took place within the framework of repression. He concluded that the psychotic process consisted of two phases. The first phase was the mute withdrawal of the libido from the object. This first phase was then followed by the noisy process of restitution, through which the destroyed relationships were repaired.

Before embarking upon a critical discussion, I want to stress the great advantage of Freud's stimulating idea that a delusion is the result of an attempt at restitution. The first phase consists of the withdrawal of the libidinal relationships. Thus a break with reality has developed. This hypothesis offers an opportunity to define the difference between neurosis and psychosis. In the neurosis no such rift occurs in the relationships. Between normal and neurotic processes, all possible gradations exist. This rift enables us to explain why the thinking of a psychotic cannot be corrected by our arguments. The patient has become impervious to these arguments, for he has broken down the bridge at exactly that place where we want to reach him. As Freud later formulated it (1924c), the delusion is the sewed-up patch which repairs the rent in the relationship with the outside world.

Our conclusion greatly enhances the value of Freud's revolutionary idea. Accordingly, it becomes very important to know why Freud abandoned this attractive theory in his later work.

The delusion is the result of an attempt at restitution. Freud drew this conclusion from his observation that Schreber had formed the idea that the world in which he used to live no longer existed. In my opinion, the idea of the world coming to an end is a delusional conviction with which the patient approaches his environment. We must then conclude that the theory of the attempt at restitution is based upon the fact that one delusion of a certain type, namely, "the end of the world," is followed by a number of other delusions. Accordingly, we are forced to distinguish between a primary delusion and secondary delusions. The conclusion that the delusion is the result of an attempt at restitution would be valid only for secondary delusions. The primary delusion must be explained in a different way. Freud thought that the idea of the end of the world was expressive of the fact that the patient had withdrawn the libidinal cathexis from the object representation.[3]

I do not believe that the idea of a world catastrophe has anything to do with a withdrawal of libido from object representations. We know that the newborn baby does not yet have a cathexis of such representations. A decathexis of object representations would mean a regression to the state of mind of a newborn baby. In this case it is clear that Schreber would never be able to observe that everyone else in the world was dead. This delusional idea shows only that his concept of the persons around him has changed radically. But such a process is, of course, not synonymous with the process of decathexis.

In addition to my theoretical objections, I want to mention a clinical one. The idea of the end of the world is not an isolated symptom but is a part of a complicated delusion of persecution. Because Flechsig had interfered in the relationship that Schreber maintained with God, a conflict arose which resulted in the destruction of the world. Thus it is difficult to see how the delusion of the end of the world could be a primary delusion.

This negative result should not prevent us from continuing our study. Let me bring a final objection. As mentioned above, Freud approached the problem of the delusion by two different avenues: symptom formation and repression. These two avenues of approach should lead to insights which supplement each other, or at least these insights should not contradict each other. In the first avenue of approach, the basic "I love him" is warded off, and, depending upon what part of the basic sentence the defense concentrates upon, the

[3] Of course, in addition to the psychotic part of the personality, there are other parts that are still in contact with reality. However, we do not have to consider these more realistic parts because they do not lead to delusion formation.

content of the various delusions can be explained. The second avenue of approach reveals that the libidinal energy is withdrawn from the object representation.

Let us put these two results together. The "I love him" is affected by this withdrawal. The "him" stands for an object and therefore loses its cathexis. Thus the whole striving represented by "I love him" has lost its meaning. A defense against this abandoned homosexual striving has no longer any *raison d'être;* for lack of an opponent, the defense at this point also has to be abandoned. The delusion formation is then nipped in the bud before it can lead to any delusional production. Thus the theoretical elaborations about symptom formation are irreconcilable with elaborations about the attempt at restitution.

Notwithstanding our negative results, many new vistas are opened up by Freud in his Schreber study. Especially important is the subject of projection, of which Freud gives two different descriptions. First he describes this process: an inner perception is suppressed, whereupon its content, after undergoing a certain distortion, becomes conscious as an outer perception. We may conceive of this form of projection as constituting an ego defense. For instance, by accusing somebody else of homosexuality, the ego may ward off the same striving in itself. This form of projection has nothing to do, of course, with a psychotic mechanism.

Next, Freud gives another description of projection, a description which is valid for the psychotic process. According to him, it is not correct to say that the inwardly suppressed sensation is projected to the outside. Rather we discover that what is inwardly abolished returns from the outside (p. 71). In my opinion, Freud is stressing here that the psychotic form of projection differs from the neurotic one. The warded-off is abolished; or, let us say, the loss of its cathexis causes it to disappear. When, next, the abolished part returns from the outside, we may conclude that the attempt at restitution erects something in the outside world after it has lost its cathexis in the inner world. In comparing these two forms of projection with each other, we must emphasize that in neurotic projection the unconscious representations, etc., maintain their cathexis, in contrast to the psychotic form of projection through which the unconscious ideas lose their energetic charge. We are justified in distinguishing a primary form of projection from a secondary form. Primary projection is used in psychoses, whereas the secondary form is mainly a neurotic defense.

We observe the similarity between this psychotic form of projection and projection in very early child development. The child, ruled by the pleasure-pain principle, differentiates between pleasurable and painful events. Pleasurable events are considered to have their origin within the self; the disagreeable ones are ascribed to the outside world.

In the application of projection, therefore, the psychotic may make use of the earliest mechanisms of development. However, the mechanism of psychotic projection should not be confused with the mechanism of these early reactions. The latter accomplish the first, although still faulty, differentiation between the self and the object world. In the course of normal development, these first reactions are exchanged for more appropriate ones, and an intricate set of relations is formed between ego and objects.

In the psychoses, the ego uses these early reactions for the purpose of staying away from objective reality. Thus the psychotic ego applies these mechanisms for completely different reasons than for the reasons existing in the beginning of life.

Actually, Freud made only one further elaboration of the theory of the attempt at restitution. He applied the theory to those symptoms in which the psychotic process has also affected the language (1915b). In making a distinction between word and thing representations (1891), he thought that the thing representation did not play a role in the schizophrenic language. Whereas the word representation occurs in the preconscious, the thing would be represented primarily in the unconscious. In the schizophrenically affected language, the primary process would take over and henceforward the words would be manipulated as if they were things. Therefore Freud thought that the attempt at restitution had withdrawn the energy from the unconscious representation of the thing and then used this energy to charge the preconscious representation of the word. Through this hypercathexis, the word representation became conscious. This explanation of the language changes in schizophrenia makes it clear that this symptom is delusional in itself. The explanation considers only an economic aspect; it does not offer any psychological understanding (Katan, 1939).

Prior to the publication of "A Metapsychological Supplement to the Theory of Dreams" (1917), Freud defined narcissism as a libidinal cathexis of the ego. At that time he regarded the instincts as being divided into ego instincts and libidinal ones. However, it was possible to make this distinction between the two instincts (ego and libidinal) only after a clear differentiation had been made between ego and object, i.e., after object cathexis had been developed.

The relation between autoerotism and narcissism was still obscure, and Freud (1914) thought that a new psychic act was necessary to bind the various autoerotisms together into narcissism.

In "A Metapsychological Supplement to the Theory of Dreams" Freud took a decisive step in concluding that at birth the mind is already in a state of primary narcissism. Thus the assumption had been dropped that an ego had to be present before narcissism could enter into the picture. It was no longer essential for any development to take place in order for narcissism to exist. We see that the state of primary narcissism coincides with the undifferentiated state, as Hartmann (1950) has called it. We must keep in mind that the undifferentiated state is more than a state of primary narcissism, for it contains not only libido but the other basic instinctual drive as well.

In sleep, man returns to this original state of primary narcissism. Accordingly, one may say that a regression of the entire personality takes place toward the beginning of mental development.

This article shows clearly that Freud is at the point of changing his thoughts about psychosis. His new insight into dream formation seemed to offer him a better opportunity to explain psychotic phenomena than had been afforded by the theory of the attempt at restitution.

During sleep, an unconscious wish may resist this general regression, and as a result the ego has to erect a defense. Now a dream may follow. This viewpoint led Freud to reconsider his concept of the psychosis. "A restrictive modification of this kind [a warded-off wish resisting the process of regression] is, as we shall discover later, necessary in the theory of dementia praecox as well" (1917, p. 225).

It is conspicuous, at least as far as my knowledge extends, that this sentence has failed to arouse any comments. The translator has even appended to this sentence a footnote: "It is not clear what this refers to."

Actually, Freud's remark is not obscure at all. I have drawn attention to his descriptions of what I call the primary form of projec tion and also the schizophrenic language. The representations of the objects and of the unconscious drives, etc., were affected by the psychotic process of withdrawal and thus had lost their cathexis. These conclusions, however, are diametrically opposed to his newest insight. His reasoning that unconscious wishes, etc., in the dream resist the regressive movement and keep (or regain) their cathexis, convinced him that the same had to be true for the psychotic process. "As we shall discover later" is evidence that Freud postponed the elaboration of this new opinion to a future date. Indeed, "Neurosis and Psychosis" (1924b) and "The Loss of Reality in Neurosis and Psychosis" (1924c) fulfilled this promise.

The theory of the attempt at restitution had run its course, and Freud no longer applied it, at least not in its original form.

In "Neurosis and Psychosis" Freud defended the viewpoint that the id demands force the ego to relinquish its ties with reality, whereupon psychotic symptom formation occurs under the dominance of the id. Thus Freud's new concept of the psychosis was exactly the opposite of his original formulation.

Let us return to our starting point. We wanted to find out more about the possibility of a precursor in Freud's thoughts regarding the concept of the death instinct. This precursor was interwoven with the new theoretical assumption of the two-phase attempt at restitution. We followed this theoretical assumption through its short-lived existence. It did not lead to a successful ending; the theory did not seem able to account for the very intricate processes.

Meanwhile we are better prepared to find an answer to a question that has lingered with us from the very beginning. What motivated Freud to write these remarkable few sentences which, in form as well as in content, are so similar to comparable sentences in *The Ego and the Id*?

In order to arrive at a solution, we have to know first from which observations Freud started, and what theoretical conclusions he drew from these central observations. It must have struck him that the schizophrenic patient lives in a world of his own and that the patient's thinking follows rules far removed from those valid for normality. Thus the patient must have relinquished the normal set of rules and exchanged these rules for new ones of his own making. In his new world he has abandoned the objects to which he was previously attached.

Next, the patient either remains in a withdrawn position or pro-
claims a new and frequently bizarre relationship to other people.
Accordingly, Freud divided the psychotic process into two phases:
the first, one of withdrawal; the second, one of filling the void left
by the withdrawal.

The withdrawal cannot be observed. There are no signs of a
strong tide running in an inward direction. One can make the observation only after the withdrawal has taken place. Originally I thought
that Freud was wrong in assuming that the process of withdrawal
occurred *mutely*. For instance, Schreber devoted the fourth chapter
of the account of his illness to a description of his prepsychotic phase,
when he was changing his attitude toward the world without yet
breaking his ties with reality. Finally I saw that the symptoms which
Schreber showed during that period were the result of the ego's
desperate struggle not to abandon contact with reality. These symptoms hid the tendency to withdraw. The second phase portrays the
development of the psychosis proper. The resulting psychotic symptoms command all the attention. Thus the first phase is replete with
symptoms, bearing witness to attempts to hold on to reality; in the
second phase, bearing witness to attempts to return to reality. This
new reality, however, is of the patient's own fabrication. Thus it
makes excellent sense that Freud felt forced by necessity to conclude
that a process of withdrawal had occurred of which one received no
direct indication. Having accepted the proposition of two successive
processes of withdrawal and repair, one cannot fail to consider next
where the turning point lies, namely, where withdrawal stops and
the rebuilding begins.

Still another question now becomes unavoidable. Does this process
of withdrawal take place on a horizontal level, so to say, or does it
move more or less vertically? If the latter, the turning point would
have to be found on a regressed level.

Having gone this far with my "reconstruction" of Freud's
thoughts, my next step is to conclude that Freud, at that moment,
would have looked for a clinical symptom indicative of this turning
point! It does not take much deliberation to see that, according to
Freud's thinking, the idea of the end of the world expressed just such
an indication. From the content of this delusion, Freud deduced that
the representations of the objects had lost their energetic charge. He
must have concluded that this loss of charge was an indication that

the turning point had been reached. However, in our theoretical digressions we reached the conclusion that a clinical symptom will never be able to express this loss of cathexis. The patient cannot have any awareness of thoughts that are not cathected.

We may ask why Freud at that time did not make this deduction himself. The bone of contention is to be found in the instinctual theory. The division into ego and libidinal instincts formed an obstacle to better understanding. In order for the two instincts to function, ego as well as object cathexes had to be present. The libido could travel only from ego to object representations; or, in the case of withdrawal, from object to ego. According to this theory, all that happened was that the object representation lost its charge to the ego. However, it was impossible for the cathexis to be withdrawn from both ego and object at the same time. Thus the old instinctual theory excluded a consideration that a regression might take place to the undifferentiated state.

Apparently missing from my thoughts is the possibility that the entire amount of libidinal energy would have been transferred from the ego to the object representations. Freud's idea was that this might happen in a state of love. However, as I see it, object cathexis without ego cathexis is unthinkable; for instance, in love, the ego function of loving must be strongly cathected.

The weakness of the instinctual theory led Freud to conceive erroneously of the idea of the end of the world as indicating a decathexis of the object world. This theory created a distinct disadvantage: for years to come, it blocked the insight that if the object world loses its cathexis, the ego has to share the same fate! Thus it happened that from the beginning there was no uniform explanation of delusion formation. Megalomania, i.e., the group of delusions concerned with the ego, was thought to be caused by a regressive withdrawal of the libido; the other group, in which projection played a role, was thought to be caused by the attempt at restitution.

In the Schreber study Freud was already well aware of the shortcomings of the instinctual theory. He considered the possibility that the withdrawal of libido alone could not cause the idea of the end of the world, but that a disturbance in the cathexis of the ego might also play a role in it. "But these are problems which we are still quite helpless and incompetent to solve. *It would be otherwise if we could start out from some well-grounded theory of instincts;* but in fact we have nothing of the kind at our disposal" (p. 74; my italics).

Freud even hoped that the study of the psychoses would enable him to form "some conclusions on questions connected with the theory of instincts."

We may assume it was this hope that inspired Freud to write the remarkable passage which has so much in common with his later formulations about life and death instincts. Therefore I believe that he was already hinting at a new division of instincts!

In addition, notwithstanding his theoretical objections, Freud started at least to consider that loss of cathexis of the object representations, as well as of the ego itself, might be responsible for the idea of the end of the world. The fact that Freud considered this possibility is very valuable to us. It contains the ingredients of the formulation that a regression might occur to the phase in which no mental systems are cathected. In this formulation I see a corroboration of my construction that Freud was looking for a clinical symptom indicative of what I have called the turning point. For Freud, the idea of the end of the world fulfilled this requirement. To him, this idea contained evidence of a state of no cathexis. He was still too much involved in the assumption of an ego instinct and therefore he had to exempt the ego from inclusion in this state of *no cathexis;* the latter referred only to the object representations.[4]

This conclusion enables us to expand the comparison between the two passages. The noisy attempt at restitution is carried out by the libido and is comparable to the life instinct, whose performance, through its noise, attracts attention. We encounter greater difficulties when we try to compare the mute withdrawal of the libido in schizophrenia with the muteness of the death instinct. A process of

---

[4] The discovery that the ego was narcissistically cathected posed great difficulties for Freud. In order to save the instinctual theory, he had to form a helping hypothesis. The ego performed its functions with two different types of energy. The ego had at its disposal the ego energy proper and, in addition, the sublimated homosexual libido. This sublimated energy, in the form of "leaning-upon instincts," supported the normal task of the ego. (These instincts were pictured by Freud as if they were leaning upon the already existing ego.)

Therefore, when Freud spoke of a regression of the ego to its narcissistic state, he referred only to this libidinal aspect of the ego. The ego instinct itself was not involved. The first signs of a change of opinion in this respect occurred when he remarked that, at that moment, the theory was still too much in its beginning stages to consider the possibility that not only the withdrawal of libido, but also the loss of energetic charges of the ego, might be responsible for "the end of the world."

libidinal withdrawal as such is a description of a regressive movement of libidinal energy, but it does not contain any evidence that death is its goal. This is really an unexpected difficulty, which threatens to destroy our idea that the frequently cited passage in the article on Schreber was a precursor of Freud's concept of life and death instincts.

A brief historical review is needed to clarify this point. In his early work on hysteria, written in collaboration with Breuer (1893/ 95),[5] Freud was very much influenced by Fechner's concept of the stability principle. The mental apparatus possessed the function of keeping the amount of excitation at a constant level. In the "Project" Freud stated that pleasure led to a discharge of tension (1950, p. 373). It is clear that Freud's thoughts about the functioning of the pleasure principle fitted within the frame of the stability principle.

In "Instincts and Their Vicissitudes" (1915a) Freud returned to these earlier ideas. According to this article, the function of the mental apparatus is to keep the excitation at as low a level as possible; if possible, to keep the mind in a state of no excitation at all. These ideas formed the basis for Freud's further explorations in *Beyond the Pleasure Principle*. He wrote a review, showing how the stability principle was deduced from the same facts which had led him to assume the existence of the pleasure principle. The latter was subordinated, as a special case, to Fechner's stability principle (1920, p. 9). One of the new additions was the concept of the Nirvana principle. This principle, which was far more original than the pleasure principle, was also marked by the tendency to dissolve all excitation. Both principles had the same goal, but the methods of achieving this goal were completely different.

In "The Economic Problem of Masochism" (1924a) Freud no longer maintained that the pleasure principle and the Nirvana principle had a common denominator. He now ascribed different goals to these two principles. The pleasure principle did not strive for a release of tension, inasmuch as situations existed of a pleasurable increase of excitation, and also of an unpleasurable decrease. From then on, the basic tendency of striving to keep the mental apparatus without any stimulation was valid only for the Nirvana principle.

In "A Metapsychological Supplement to the Theory of Dreams"

---

[5] See Freud's letter to Fliess (June 28, 1892) and his study on the hysterical attack (November, 1892) (Freud, 1950).

(1917) Freud concluded that in sleep the mind returns to the level before any mental development exists. We may conceive of this process as one of total regression. Every faculty of the personality loses its cathexis. There is no indication that when Freud came to this conclusion he thought of this regressive process as being different from the pleasure principle. After all, one may reason, this regression was in harmony with the wish to sleep. Accordingly, there was no need to separate this regressive process from the functioning of the pleasure principle, which, as Freud still thought at that time, also had a state of no excitation as its goal.

Are we compelled to draw the same conclusion from the by now very well-known passage in the article on Schreber? Freud distinguished in the psychosis two different movements, each of them antagonistic to the other. The first movement is one of withdrawal of libidinal energy. As we have discovered, Freud had in mind that this withdrawal led to a state of no cathexis, but at that time the acceptance of an ego instinct made it impossible for him to define his idea clearly. The second movement contains the attempt at restitution, which is a libidinal process and therefore falls within the frame of the pleasure principle. In my opinion, the passage expresses the following thought:

Freud pictures a conflict between the Nirvana principle and the pleasure principle. During the first phase of the psychosis (the pre-psychotic phase) the Nirvana principle is dominant. During the second phase (the psychosis proper) the pleasure principle returns to the foreground.

This conclusion contains the key to the solution of the question whether this concept (1911) can be considered a precursor of the concept of the death instinct. The answer has to be in the negative, for we do not find any evidence (except in the wording) which comes close to that concept. Nevertheless, a precursor is present: the concept of the Nirvana principle is clearly detectable. Thus we observe that the birth of the concept of this principle precedes the birth of the concept of the death instinct by many years. This sequence is, of course, exactly the reverse of the sequence as presented by Freud.

Our deduction of the chronological sequence encourages us to make a further distinction between the two concepts. The Nirvana principle represents the regressive tendency to return to the state existing at the beginning of life, whereas the death instinct has a completely different goal, namely, to undo the source of life.

Hartmann's opinion regarding the concepts of life and death instincts is exceedingly important in considering the subject under discussion. "These concepts are of a different order, as Freud clearly realized, and the corresponding hypotheses have to be proved or disproved biologically; . . . and so far have not added much to our understanding of the specific functions of drives (in the psychological sense) in contradistinction to other psychic functions" (1948, p. 72).

We may make use of Hartmann's opinion. Whereas the death instinct is a biological concept, the Nirvana principle is a concept which can be applied to a number of clinical phenomena, such as sleep and psychotic development.

In normal life the reality principle, the pleasure principle, and the Nirvana principle cooperate together and achieve a state of balance. Under abnormal conditions the balance is disturbed and a state of imbalance results. Freud's concepts of fusion and defusion may be applied to the states of balance and imbalance. In normal life fusion of the three principles occurs. In the state of dreamless sleep there also is a cooperation among the three principles: the reality principle and the pleasure principle do not resist being taken over by the Nirvana principle. If a wish disturbs the peace of sleep, the reality principle is forced to react and creates the dream in an effort to quiet down the pleasure principle. In so doing, the reality principle is still on the side of the Nirvana principle in order to keep the level of stimulation at as low a level as possible under the existing circumstances.

The state of imbalance in prepsychotic development is most interesting. During this development the Nirvana principle, not in sleep, but in waking life, threatens to take over. In contradistinction to the dream, it is now the reality principle which resists the Nirvana principle and clings to reality testing.

We have to emphasize that the ego relations with reality are not confined solely to the ego. The greater the threat that the ego will have to relinquish these relations, the more the ego has to rely upon *warded-off* id strivings, which are also directed toward reality. The ego is now in a precarious position. On the one hand, it needs the id strivings; on the other, these strivings constitute a danger. Thus the ego, by maintaining its existence, causes the id to be maintained as well. We may express this as follows: the reality principle, as a result of resisting the Nirvana principle, has a conflict with the pleasure principle on its hands.

Almost always the reality principle is unsuccessful in clinging to reality. This means that the Nirvana principle has then reached its goal of a total regression of that part of the personality which is involved. Now the psychosis proper starts and the attempt at restitution sets in, using the energy which has become available through the total regression. The Nirvana principle now works again in harmony with the pleasure principle, allowing the latter a limited field of action, namely, a field which no longer has any ties with reality. The reality principle also joins in the plot. This principle has suffered most of all, for it is permitted to establish only a pseudo (namely, psychotic) reality.

We may observe that our description of the prepsychotic phase comes close to Freud's concept that in the psychosis the id drives the ego away from reality. Thus Freud's last formulation is, in my opinion, valid only for the prepsychotic phase. His first theory, namely, that of the attempt at restitution, is still valid for the psychosis proper.

The prepsychotic phase seems to bear a certain similarity to the dream. According to our understanding, the difference is this: in the dream, the Nirvana principle and the reality principle are united against the pleasure principle. In the prepsychosis, however, the Nirvana principle and the pleasure principle join forces against the reality principle. The prepsychotic phase is a clear example of a state of imbalance. There is a strong defusion of all three principles. In the psychosis a new balance is found, but this new balance has very little similarity with the balance of the normal personality.

BIBLIOGRAPHY

Breuer, J. & Freud, S. (1893/95), Studies on Hysteria. S.E., 2.
Freud, S. (1891), On Aphasia, NY: IUP, 1953.
—— (1900), The Interpretation of Dreams. S.E., 4 & 5.
—— (1910), Leonardo da Vinci and a Memory of His Childhood. S.E., 11:63-137.
—— (1911), Psycho-Analytical Notes on an Autobiographical Account of a Case of Paranoia (Dementia Paranoides). S.E., 12:3-82.
—— (1914), On Narcissism. S.E., 14:67-102.
—— (1915a), Instincts and Their Vicissitudes. S.E., 14:111-140.
—— (1915b), The Unconscious. S.E., 14:159-215.
—— (1917 [1915]), A Metapsychological Supplement to the Theory of Dreams. S.E., 14:217-235.
—— (1920), Beyond the Pleasure Principle. S.E., 18:7-64.
—— (1923), The Ego and the Id. S.E., 19:3-66.

—— (1924a), The Economic Problem of Masochism. *S.E.*, 19:159-170.

—— (1924b), Neurosis and Psychosis. *S.E.*, 19:149-153.

—— (1924c), The Loss of Reality in Neurosis and Psychosis. *S.E.*, 19:183-187.

—— (1930), Civilization and Its Discontents. *S.E.*, 21:59-145.

—— (1950), *The Origins of Psychoanalysis*. NY: Basic Books, 1954.

Hartmann, H. (1948), Comments on the Psychoanalytic Theory of Instinctual Drives. *Essays*, 69-89.

—— (1950), Comments on the Psychoanalytic Theory of the Ego. *Essays*, 113-141.

Katan, M. (1939), A Contribution to the Understanding of Schizophrenic Speech. *Int. J. Psa.*, 20:353-362.

Spielrein, S. (1912), Die Destruktion als Ursache des Werdens. *Jb. Psa.*, 4:465-503.

Stärcke, A. (1914), tr. & intro. of S. Freud (1908): 'Civilized' Sexual Morality and Modern Nervous Illness. Baarn: Hollandia Drukkerij.

III

Aspects of Normal and Pathological Development

Some Aspects of Early Ego Development

Data From a Longitudinal Study

SALLY PROVENCE, M.D.

Two of Hartmann's essays on ego psychology provided the stimulation for the focus of this paper written in his honor. In "Psychoanalysis and Developmental Psychology" (1950a) he wrote:

> Among the functions of the ego most systematically studied in relation to the drives and to reality are no doubt the mechanisms of defense (Anna Freud, 1936). Still, certain aspects of their psychology confront us with unsolved problems. A chronology of defense mechanisms has been attempted, but so far only its bare outlines are visible; and we know little about the factors which determine the individual choice of defense methods. Here I only want to point to the possibility of approaching these problems by observing in children such primitive functions of the autonomous ego which we may consider the first developmental elements of what later will be used in the process of defense. . . . There may well be a correlation between observable individual differences in such primary factors and later defense mechanisms, and this is why I mention this point here. It is likely that the methods by which infants deal with stimuli are later used by the ego in an active way, and especially for defense. This may add to our understanding of the choice of defense mechanisms, and maybe also to their chronology. But such autonomous factors are relevant not only for the understanding of the "negative" aspects of defense. Factors in the conflict-free sphere also codetermine other aspects of the methods by which instinctual stimuli are dealt with—their neutralization, their utilization for a variety of ego functions, and so forth—and thus influence in many ways individual modes of solving conflicts. . . . These are some

From the Child Study Center and the Department of Pediatrics, Yale University School of Medicine.

essential points in which the direct observation of early autonomous ego development can be expected to prove helpful for the understanding of those later situations of conflict we meet in our clinical work [p. 106f.].

And again in "Comments on the Psychoanalytic Theory of the Ego" (1950b) Hartmann says:

It might well be that the ways in which infants deal with stimuli—also those functions of delaying, of postponing discharge . . . —are later used by the ego in an active way. . . . This hypothesis of a genetic correlation between individual differences in primary factors of this kind and the later defense mechanisms . . . is intended as an appeal to those analysts who have the opportunities for conducting longitudinal developmental studies on children. I think that this hypothesis will prove to be accessible to direct verification or refutation [p. 125f.].

This paper follows Hartmann's thought by presenting material from the first 13 months in the life of one child and comparing it with material from her analysis. The infancy data were obtained from developmental tests, observations of infant behavior and mother-infant interaction, physical examinations, and from interviews with the parents, primarily the mother. The child, Margaret, was in analysis with Dr. A. J. Solnit from age 3½ years to age 7 years and has been seen in several follow-up visits since that time, most recently a few months ago at age 14 years. Margaret and her family were participants in a longitudinal study of personality development at the Yale Child Study Center organized by Ernst Kris and Milton Senn.[1] It utilized a multidiscipline team of psychoanalytically trained or oriented observers in a service-centered investigation. I was the pediatrician for the child and also administered the developmental tests. The data to be presented support Hartmann's hypothesis of a genetic correlation between the infant's way of dealing with stimuli and later defense mechanisms. Some of the data also support Hartmann's view (quoted above) that infantile antecedents of ego functions in the conflict-free sphere can be observed which "codetermine other aspects of the methods by which instinctual stimuli are dealt with . . . and thus influence in many ways the individual modes of solving conflicts."

[1] The research project was supported by a grant from the Commonwealth Fund, New York.

Margaret has been the subject of a number of other papers from various members of the longitudinal study staff (Coleman, E. Kris, and Provence, 1953; M. Kris, 1957; Ritvo and Solnit, 1958, 1960). It is a reflection of the psychoanalytic view of the complexity of human development that observational data used in one paper to emphasize a particular formulation or sequence can be used in another context to illustrate another aspect of psychoanalytic developmental psychology. Thus parts of the following description of Margaret as an infant will seem familiar to those who have read other reports from this longitudinal study. Some events of her first year and some characteristics of the maternal care will be described before the developmental data are presented.

Background

Margaret was delivered at term after a prolonged labor necessitating spinal anesthesia and low forceps delivery. She was a well-formed, vigorous little girl who was in good condition at birth and weighed 7 lbs. Twelve hours later there was cause for some concern: she had a high-pitched cry of poor quality, reacted sluggishly to stimulation, had poor sucking and rooting responses, and appeared excessively somnolent. There was a mild, unilateral facial weakness. However, over the period of the next 3 days she became more wakeful and alert, the facial paresis disappeared, and the sucking and rooting responses became active and normal. By the time she was 6 days of age she was described as an attractive, well-formed, vigorous infant who was active, sensitive to external stimuli (touch, position change, temperature change, etc.), and startled easily. She cried loudly for feedings, could not be easily quieted at such times for the few minutes needed to prepare the breast or bottle, and was characterized by the nurse in the newborn nursery as a "screamer." It was not easy for the experienced nurse to comfort her and almost impossible for the inexperienced mother.

We expected that Margaret would be a difficult baby to live with because of her physiological make-up, and it seemed unfortunate that this infant whose needs seemed to overwhelm her was to be cared for by such an anxious and inept mother. In this prediction we were eminently correct. Mrs. C. described this period as the worst 3 months of her life, a period in which she lost all confidence in herself, was not able to make decisions, did not feel successful in what she did for the baby, and was repeatedly confused by suggestions from neighbors and relatives. She was encouraged to call the pediatrician whenever she needed to and frequently did so. It was discovered quite early in the contact (by the time Margaret was 2 weeks of age) that it was almost impossible for Mrs. C. to choose between two acceptable methods of child care. She had to be given very specific instructions with the advice that there was more than one way to do things, and if the suggested one did not work with Margaret she should call the doctor. This seemed to be the only way in which she could be helped during those first three months, and for many months thereafter she could not carry over the reasoning behind one child-care situation to another. She had to ask separately about hun-dreds of small—but to her vital—points.

The baby grew and developed well, but she was physiologically unstable and difficult to satisfy. She was partially breast-fed for 6 weeks, but the mother finally gave this up in anger and discourage-ment because although "the books say breast feeding is best for babies," Margaret spit up her mother's breast milk more frequently than she did the bottle feeding. On the occasion of Margaret's first visit to the clinic at the age of 6 weeks, I characterized her as being very sensitive to loud or sudden sounds or sudden changes in move-ment, a very easy startler, and difficult to comfort when crying. Muscle tone was heightened though not abnormal. While the findings were not considered pathological, it was not possible at this time categorically to exclude a mild insult to the central nervous system in view of the reactions during the first two days of life described above. This possibility was not mentioned to the parents.

At the 3-month visit Margaret looked good, had grown well, and was performing at or above her chronological age on all items of the developmental tests. We were no longer concerned about her central nervous system. Particular efforts were made to explain to Mrs. C. how well the child was doing. During the 4th and 5th months Mrs. C. continued to need much support and reassurance. By this time Margaret had very beautiful fair skin and rosy cheeks, and it was quite easy and natural to comment on her attractiveness. Socially she became increasingly responsive, and it was hoped that her smiling, laughing, and reaching out toward her mother could be recognized by Mrs. C. as signs of favorable development. This was a period when

Mrs. C. accepted momentarily the evidences of Margaret's attractiveness and good health and then reminisced about how terrible the first 3 months had been and how inadequate she had felt as a mother.

At the 5-month visit it became apparent that Mrs. C., evidently in an effort to reduce the necessity to make decisions, had become extremely rigid about feeding and failed to notice or disregarded the clues the baby gave her. For example, it was revealed that she always waited until the baby became loud and insistent in her crying for food before she fed her (and by this time the infant was expressing her needs by slight crying, followed only later by vigorous crying); she was stopping the feeding exactly after each 2 oz. to wait for an exact number of bubbles regardless of the baby's state of hunger or satiation.

I felt that mother and child were caught in a situation difficult for both, and that the mother was relying upon compulsive devices to insure that she could function as a mother. I therefore decided to interrupt the mother's self-imposed rigid regime and for another period to give the mother advice that would avoid the anxiety associated with making decisions regarding the baby's care. After a few weeks of this kind of support Mrs. C. became somewhat more relaxed in her care of the child.

The examination of the baby at that visit (age 5 months) revealed excellent development. She was able to roll from supine to prone, would support a large fraction of her weight when placed in standing position, and was (as expected at this age) more involved and active in sitting and in moving about. She gave her usual good performance with the test materials, exploiting them with interest and vigor. The most striking change to the staff at that visit was her anxiety reaction to strangers and her marked preference for her mother. She was sufficiently apprehensive of me and the room, that it was necessary for the first time to permit her to sit on her mother's lap for the developmental and physical examinations. Mrs. C. confirmed that this had been present also in other situations for about two weeks.

A few weeks later, Mrs. C., apparently taking encouragement from Margaret's increased motor ability (creeping) and her obvious preference for her mother, began to feel much better about the child. This was the beginning of a period of much improved, though less than ideal, relationship between them in which Mrs. C. could enjoy Margaret and could communicate increasingly with her, and the pleasure and comfort in the child's experiences with her mother and with her environment were increased.

I now turn to some of the data from the developmental examination and other observations made during the clinic sessions which form the basis for the discussion of my topic.

Observations and Test Data

At 3 months of age Margaret was described as a well-nourished, somewhat tense and sensitive infant, whose development was excellent as measured by the infant tests. For example, those items designated as Perception on the tests were advanced for her age: she focused visually both on toys and on people when near to her and across the room; she looked around observing her environment when carried from place to place; she "searched" with her eyes the contours and surfaces of the toys. There was no doubt about the activity of her perception. She also was advanced in the social sphere and in her interest in and manipulation of the toys. In addition to social stimulation, she initiated a social interchange by smiling spontaneously at the adult. She was able to grasp a toy held near her hand and to hold it actively (not reflexly) while she looked at it. She "recognized" her bottle and anticipated the feeding when she observed its preparation. Gross motor development was age adequate, but not spectacular; fine motor development (mainly at this age the maturation and use of prehension) was advanced. It was interesting that in respect to gross motor behavior, she tended to be still and passive when lying in supine and to become more active and to demonstrate more body skills when placed in prone.

Margaret was also tested at age 22 weeks (0;5+4), 30 weeks (0;6+29), 41 weeks (0;9+16), and 46 weeks (0;10+20) during the first year. Of these tests only the data obtained at 9½ months will be given in some detail. However, as background to this a few relevant observations from the period of 3 to 9½ months are included.

We know that Margaret discriminated between her mother and other adults by the age of 4½ months and was apprehensive at the sight of the pediatrician when she came to the clinic at age 5 months. She could, however, be made comfortable when approached slowly or by being close to her mother. Her interest both in toys and in people was high. Her approaches to toys were more active and more immediate than to people, and it was already apparent that (at least in the test situation) she needed a period of visual examination and "warming up" before she approached either new people or toys. At the 30-week test (0;6+29) she was characterized as a "scrutinizing observer of her environment."[2] Her anxiety reaction to me, and according to reports to unfamiliar people, was intense. I noted that the calming effect of the toys was greater than that of people, i.e., she was using the relationship to the person much less directly as a protection than one would expect at this age. Her mother, for example, could comfort her more effectively if she moved close to her and gave her a toy, than if she tried to comfort her by holding, speaking, patting, etc.

During the period beginning at 5 months Margaret became a serious-looking infant whose smiles were rare and tentative. People were interesting and acceptable if they did not come close too quickly. At the 8-month physical examination she objected strenuously to being touched by me, apparently remembering previous examinations (with injections) and fearful of an assault. Her mother said Margaret "likes to do the touching but doesn't want to be touched." She was creeping skillfully, sleeping well, and was beginning to be active about finger feeding herself. The relationship between infant and mother continued to improve, and Mrs. C. expressed much more satisfaction and pride in Margaret than before.

Several observations made at the clinic at the 41-week (0;9+16) visit are of special relevance to my subject. Margaret performed at a superior level on the developmental tests. A quotation from the record of that day will convey the impressions she made: "Margaret continues to surprise us by performing at a very high level with the test materials. I am not sure why this always comes as something of a surprise. Perhaps it is because she at times looks so tentative in her approaches and is less robust and noisy in her play than most babies of her age. Her pleasure is never exuberantly expressed. When given the toys and left in peace she performs extremely well with them and displays considerable interest and drive." She was very advanced in those test items that assess memory for the hidden toy and those that reflect a discriminatory and investigative interest in her environment. She was also impressively competent in her ability to handle two toys simultaneously and to combine them in various ways. Items of imita-

[2] By Katherine M. Wolf, who participated in the longitudinal study for the first three years.

tion of the adult were also high, both imitation of action (gestures, games, etc.) and imitation of words. She was socially responsive when comfortable with people; but when in a situation of "danger" (from people) her gross motor activity lessened markedly, she looked extremely serious and sometimes cried, and *could be comforted or put at ease most effectively by being given something to play with.* Visual contact with the mother, physical nearness, or being talked to by the mother were reassuring to her, but very much more so if a toy was included. Being held by the mother was rarely as comforting as with most infants.

The above data from Margaret's first year are of course selective, but they do designate predominant characteristics at the indicated ages. Descriptions have been pared considerably, so that the behaviors that indicate antecedents of the autonomous ego functions and the infant's methods of coping with stress can be made more easily visible.

I shall now examine the connections between these observations and later characteristics of the child's ego functioning.

Discussion

ANTECENDENTS OF INTELLECTUALIZATION AS DEFENSE

Margaret's turning to toys, the energy and interest she directed toward them, and her progressively more capable exploitation of them from the point of view of "knowing them" (their qualities and uses) were early forms of one aspect of what is later designated as intelligence. In her first year, this behavior was facilitated and heightened by (1) her interest in toys which was derived in part from the mother's sponsorship of play with toys (libidinal cathexis);[3] (2) her advanced ability to *perceive, discriminate,* and to *act* in regard to toys, an ability which reflects characteristics of the ego constitution; (3) the alleviation of anxiety by playing with toys when she was in a strange place or when a strange person came too close to her, that is, when there was a danger situation. In the clinic setting, one was always

[3] Mrs. C. far more than most mothers characteristically utilized an intermediate object (toy, bottle, diaper) in her contacts with the child. It was part of her style of mothering, and was prominent not only when she was trying to comfort the child but also when she played with Margaret. This probably served as a strong reinforcer to the child's interest in toys. While I cannot deal with it in detail here, the mother's use of the intermediate object seemed partly to have a defensive function in her, and the child's defensive use of toys via identification may also have played a role, especially later.

impressed with her use of toys to relieve anxiety and with the probability that this also stimulated intellectual development. This method of coping with danger in the first year—a part of the ego's primary autonomy—was followed later by a heavy reliance upon intellectualization as a mechanism of defense which was prominent in her analysis. Her later intellectual development, of course, partly functioned autonomously, and this, too, influenced her development in many ways. The point I wish to make, however, is that a line can be drawn from this child's mode of handling anxiety in infancy by the inspection, examination, and manipulation of toys to the use of intellectualization as defense, as revealed in her analysis from age 3½. To illustrate this point I shall present some descriptive material, beginning with my characterization of Margaret at the age of 9 months.

When I entered the waiting room Margaret was seated in the large rocking chair chewing on a piece of Zwieback. She looked up at me very soberly and penetratingly and continued to watch me as I talked with her mother. Her general appearance remains very much as before. She has scanty blond hair, big blue eyes and finely chiseled facial features. Her face is serious much of the time, especially in the presence of strangers, but it is not immobile. She frowns fairly often, wrinkling her forehead with vertical furrows between her eyebrows, and her smiles at me are tentative and small. . . . She looks out at the world through her large blue eyes often with a quizzical and investigating expression. Today she had to be tested while sitting on her mother's lap because she was apprehensive about the crib and would not permit me to pick her up for more than a very brief moment. She would not accept any toys directly from me, but when I placed them on the table and left them, *she began to play and her discomfort diminished appreciably*. Her way of approaching toys is already highly individual. First there is a period of visual examination. She then picks up the toy, turning it over, inspecting it from all angles apparently examining its possibilities and characteristics. While doing so she keeps me in her peripheral field of vision but looks as if she is pretending not to notice me and gets quite involved with the toys. As long as I do nothing suddenly or unexpectedly she continues to work and begins to look relaxed and the pleasure in the toys becomes visible. When I wish to introduce another toy and remove the old one, I must do it unhurriedly and respectfully—otherwise her activity ceases and she looks anxious. There is no doubt in my mind that she continues to explore all the possibilities of the toys repeatedly in order to avoid contact with me. There is another interesting and probably relevant observation: it takes several minutes before one sees her maximal performance with the materials; for example, with the one-inch cubes, after several minutes of looking, manipulating, mouthing, and putting cubes into the cup, she eventually builds a tower. It is as though she continues to work and think until she discovers all of the possibilities. According to her mother's report, Margaret currently is absorbed with one kind of toy or one activity here in the clinic longer and more completely than she is when she is in the safety of her home. She seems to enjoy toys she has not seen before fully as much as the old ones as long as she is given time to deal with them in her own way.

To the above description of the first year I add, as a link to material from the analysis, some data from a research staff meeting when Margaret was 15 months of age. These indicate some of our formulations and predictions at that time.

Margaret has learned to lower the level of apprehension brought on by strong stimuli (or danger situations). She has developed a technique of exploration and observation, of becoming familiar with things. She substitutes an intellectual operation for an immediate (action) response to stimulation. Her resultant achievements in problem solving are sometimes astonishing. Her avoidance of pressure is also manifest at times in her *deliberate* ignoring of mother's prompting. . . . Her anxiety about the stranger (in the first year) has spread to a general apprehension in regard to human beings (including to some extent the mother). . . . Her intellectualization extends to high performance in other areas on the symbolic level. She has developed language very early and has names for many objects. In addition, physical contact with the mother is reduced (i.e., much less than it was a few months ago) in the test situation. It is as though she "recharges" herself symbolically from a supplementary source of power to help solve a problem. . . . The lack of joy or ebullience is not explained by this tendency to intellectualization. It might be considered her most pathognomic sign.

At this time Ernst Kris, who earlier had suggested that she might become a passionate intellectual because of her apparent investment in the *process* of ideation, stated that this might not be true. It seemed to him more likely that intellectualization would be prominently used as defense.

In the analytic treatment Margaret, age 5 years 3 months, was reviewing her curiosity and anxiety about the differences between boys and girls. This concern was associated with her own separation anxiety in relation to starting kindergarten as well as reflecting the separation anxiety her younger sister was experiencing in nursery school. Margaret's envy of the boy she had seen with her analyst two days earlier was also incorporated in these reactions. Adding to this overdetermined review was Margaret's tender ankle resulting from a misstep a few days earlier while looking for her mother, who had momentarily disappeared from sight, at a department store where they had been shopping. Characteristically Margaret set out to depict and understand the differences between boys and girls, acting bossy and grown-up, as she warded off her anxiety through drawing a boy and discussing in quite an intellectual way the attributes of the draw-ing. Later in that session, under the influence of an interpretation about her wish for and fear of knowing, Margaret conveyed her anxiety about how girls are constituted and wondered apprehensively if one could always be certain who was a boy and who was a girl.

At the age of 14½ years, about half-way through a follow-up visit, Margaret said to the analyst that he had asked her and talked to her about the things she expected he would discuss. She laughed and said she always prepares herself in that way—by trying to anticipate what will take place at the beginning of a situation she is afraid will surprise her. She said that she is getting pretty good at predicting such things. This was all said in a friendly, relaxed, and pleased manner.[4]

It has remained characteristic of Margaret that she continues to use intellectualization for defensive as well as adaptive purposes. A statement by Hartmann (1951) is especially apt here: "we can as-sume that many defense mechanisms are traceable to primitive de-fensive actions against the outside world, which in part probably belong to the ego's primary autonomy, and that only later, in situa-tions of psychic conflicts, do they develop into what we specifically call mechanisms of defense. Also, we can say of many of them that after having been established as such, they become in a secondary way invested with other functions (intellectualization for example)" (p. 151f.). The degree of which Margaret's intellectual activity has been put into defensive action has varied over the years. However,

---

[4] I wish to thank Dr. A. J. Solnit for this material from the analysis.

there has always also been evidence of pleasure—sometimes more, sometimes less—in intellectual activity.

ANTECEDENTS OF THE ORGANIZING FUNCTION OF THE EGO

From early infancy Margaret showed a capacity to discriminate and adapt differentially to stimuli; moreover, in spite of her sensitivity, she remained well organized under the impact of multiple stimuli as long as they were not intense. From around 6 months on, one aspect of the capacity to deal with multiple stimuli and to coordinate them can be discerned (in the test situation) in the ability to manipulate simultaneously and to combine two or more toys in a definite relationship to each other. This adaptive ability probably reflects the biological organization that is the somatic prerequisite for the development of the synthetic function of the ego. This speculation is supported by our clinical experience with infants and young children in whom difficulties with these tasks in infancy have later been followed by disturbances in integrative capacities of the ego. In Margaret, this adaptive integrating ability developed at an advanced rate and probably was an important factor in her good general development in spite of some areas of hypersensitivity and some problems in the maternal care. This quality can be considered a particular area of strength in the developing ego. Among other benefits, it probably enabled her to resist the potentially impeding effects of the perceptual sensitivity and predisposition to anxiety (Greenacre, 1941). In this very important respect she differed from the infants with unusual sensitivities described by Bergman and Escalona (1949) who were characterized by precocious ego development in some areas and whose organization then broke down under stress.[5] In Margaret, this capacity for integration later became a prominent and continuing characteristic of her ego functioning. Some of its aspects were revealed in her excellent intellectual performance and probably in her ability to adjust to school and to life with her family and peers with reason-

[5] In Margaret's early infancy I had a number of discussions about Margaret with Ernst Kris in which I maintained, somewhat stubbornly, that Margaret was not a potentially psychotic infant in spite of her impressive sensitivity. What I was not able to formulate at that time was the meaning of the test and observational data in terms of the excellent development of many early ego functions and especially the synthetic function. Twelve years later some answers to Kris's stimulating questions are proposed. A clinical judgment formulated earlier as "but she does well in too many ways to be considered potentially psychotic" can now be conceptualized more explicitly.

ably good harmony and no severe distress. Without discounting the influence of the analytic treatment upon the neurotic difficulties she developed, one might speculate that the autonomous capacity for synthesis contributed an important dimension to the situation that resulted in relatively healthy development rather than a serious impairment involving an ego defect.

RELATIONSHIPS BETWEEN OTHER EARLY AND LATER
MODES OF FUNCTIONING

Another set of reactions characteristic of Margaret in infancy is relevant to my thesis. From 4 to 5 months on, it was clear that she was psychologically uneasy in any situation that was not familiar or predictable. Repetition of an experience or a familiar sequence was reassuring to her, except of course when it signaled a danger such as the physical examination by the pediatrician. Her pleasure in controlling the toys was evident by 8 to 9 months in the variety of ways in which she examined and manipulated them. These characteristics, while present in all normal infants to some degree, were especially prominent in Margaret. At this time and far into the future she strongly preferred play materials that were structured and predictable. Early in the second year her precision in lining up the blocks and other toys in a very orderly, systematic way was unusual. By one year she was able to recognize the cues that signaled that my direct contact with her on a given day was about to end; she anticipated the end of her "ordeal" and relaxed visibly. At any change of clinic routine she appeared apprehensive, for example, if the testing session was omitted and a free play situation with the pediatrician was arranged. Thus by the beginning of the second year, Margaret exhibited behavior in which the need for and pleasure in control, orderliness, and sameness of experience were noteworthy.

An interpretation of the possible meaning of some of this behavior was suggested in the following statement from the record of a research staff meeting in which Margaret was discussed early in her second year. "It is possible that this child may be constitutionally so formed that it has been necessary for her to evolve a systematization of the stimuli of the external world in order to cope with them. Certain thresholds must not be trespassed. . . . Categorization (ordering) of the world enables her to find attitudes to it more easily and establish cues to find out whether a stimulating object be friend or enemy. It reduces the problem to a symbolic and less dangerous level." This is seen as an example of the situation in which behavior usually associated with the anal phase appeared prior to the expected time. Later, with the onset of the anal phase in Margaret, the control system was heightened and reinforced. The neatness and orderliness took on added and more complex meanings.[6]

Other infantile reactions of special prominence in Margaret have to do with the postponement of discharge. Her behavior from 4 to 5 months on was characterized by a conspicuous inhibition in respect to motor activity. The relationship between inhibition of motor impulse and the functioning of inhibition as defense as well as the autonomous capacities for delay of discharge in the psychic sphere should not be glibly assumed. However, there is a congruence of observations which may have relevance: (1) Margaret's capacity for smooth modulation and control of motor impulse was reflected early and continuously in an exquisite precision of fine motor skills (i.e., hand and finger skills). I am inclined to speculate that such control is one reflection of the capacity for delay of discharge considered a part of the ego's primary autonomy. It may be that this is similar to the relationship between the adaptive combining activities and the synthetic function of the ego suggested earlier, i.e., that the control of motor impulse reflects the biological organization of the somatic prerequisites for delay of psychic energy discharge. The excellent autonomous capacities for postponement and delay must have strongly influenced Margaret's personality organization and intellectual functioning. (2) "Freezing" (massive inhibition) of large muscle activity in danger situations characterized Margaret from the moment we could recognize she was experiencing psychic discomfort, and some remnants of this motor inhibition are still visible. The possible explanation and the vicissitudes of this motility trait are beyond the scope of this paper. I wish only to make the point that a plausible connection—not simply a parallel—is suggested between the motoric inhibition, which must have had psychic accompaniments, and Margaret's later problems of inhibition of certain ego functions and of some aspects of her object relations as well as the use of inhibition as a defense.[7]

[6] M. Kris (1957) has also dealt with some aspects of this behavior in Margaret.
[7] Another thought along this line which is to be explored in Margaret's biography concerns the availability and use of these inhibitory mechanisms—both autonomous

The several thoughts presented in this section might be drawn together as follows: in the advanced perception discrimination, anticipation, and memory, which influenced and reflected the early ideation; in her attempts to organize and control the external environment; and in her motoric inhibition—in these characteristics the psychic defenses of intellectualization, reaction formation, isolation, and inhibition are impressively foreshadowed.

Thus, again, in the first year one could observe characteristic modes of dealing with stress (danger) which formed the model for and probably partially determined the choice of defense. Over and beyond that, the functions of memory, anticipation, acuteness of perception, capacity for delay of discharge, and the good over-all intellectual growth strongly influenced her approaches to situations of all kinds, including those involving the solving of problems. She became more a "thinker" than a "doer," if one can oversimplify for purposes of communicating her style of functioning. While I am intrigued with the plausibility of these connections, such claims must be made cautiously and with respect for the complexity of development. This is, of course, one of the hallmarks of Heinz Hartmann's scientific approach. To cite only one simple example, the effect of the child's identification with the compulsiveness of her mother as another determinant of some of the previously described behavior must also be considered.

There are other comparable avenues that might be explored as connections between the infancy data and Margaret's later characteristics. One could attempt a comprehensive inventory of antecedents and earliest manifestation of the autonomous ego functions and try to compare them, relating the comparison to later development. We know, for example, that visual perception was acute and she was active in its use; memory also developed early as did intentionality (Hartmann's term), which was first discernible in her visual activity. The acute visual perception played a role in the early discrimination of the familiar vs. unfamiliar, the safe vs. the dangerous, and hence participated both in the predisposition to anxiety and the development of defensive actions to cope with it. Undoubtedly it

---

and defensive—as they influenced her emotional expressiveness as well as her ideation. Some of the data suggest that Margaret's inhibitory capacities may have allowed more energies to be used in mental activity while impeding the expression and perhaps also recognition of her own feelings.

also was one of the determinants of her good intellectual development. She was delayed in large muscle activity compared to the rest
of her development though never below the norms for her age, and
one might speculate about the relationships between this relative delay
as a characteristic of the ego and the previously described fact that
Margaret's psychic discomfort in infancy (and far beyond) was
accompanied by an inhibition of large muscle activity. Further, one
might examine the possibility that the child's early and persistently
impressive mental activity as compared with motor action was reinforced by this tendency to massive motoric inhibition in danger situations. The interrelationship between these various antecedents of the
autonomous functions and, for example, the cognitive aspects of her
object relations is another one of the possibilities that suggest themselves.

   In short, numerous reactions to the infancy data along the lines
Hartmann suggests are possible, but the examples given seem sufficient
to illustrate—and I believe to confirm in this one child—the hypothesis with which this paper began. Hartmann's thinking and scientific
approach provide the analyst who ventures into the preverbal period
of life a frame of reference that enables him to focus upon observations pertinent to psychoanalytic developmental psychology, the caution against unjustified and adultomorphic interpretation of infancy
data, and the encouragement to persist in the study of early phases.

BIBLIOGRAPHY

Bergman, P. & Escalona, S. K. (1949), Unusual Sensitivities in Very Young Children.
      Psa. Study Ch., 3/4:333-352.
Coleman, R. W., Kris, E., & Provence, S. (1953), The Study of Variations of Early
      Parental Attitudes. *Psa. Study Ch.*, 8:20-47.
Greenacre, P. (1941), The Predisposition to Anxiety. *Psa. Q.*, 10:66-95; 610-638.
Hartmann, H. (1950a), Psychoanalysis and Developmental Psychology. *Essays*, 99-112.
────── (1950b), Comments on the Psychoanalytic Theory of the Ego. *Essays*, 113-141.
────── (1951), Technical Implications of Ego Psychology. *Essays*, 142-154.
Kris, M. (1957), The Use of Prediction in a Longitudinal Study. *Psa. Study Ch.*,
      12:175-189.
Ritvo, S. & Solnit, A. J. (1958), Influences of Early Mother-Child Interaction on
      Identification Processes. *Psa. Study Ch.*, 13:64-85.
────── ────── (1960), The Relationships of Ego Identifications to Superego Forma-
      tion. *Int. J. Psa.*, 41:295-300.
Solnit, A. J. & Kris, M. (1966), Trauma and Infantile Experiences (in press).

Metapsychology and Direct Infant Observation

RENÉ A. SPITZ, M.D.

Since its definite formulation by Freud in 1915, metapsychology has occupied a central position in the thinking of theoreticians in psychoanalysis. At times exciting new ideas of Freud such as the introduction of ego psychology took the limelight away from his interest in the earlier model of metapsychology, though it never ceased to govern analytic thinking.

Freud's first model, consisting of the topographic, dynamic, and economic viewpoints, was elaborated over a number of years. In 1921 he introduced the structural viewpoint, adding thereby a fourth item to the three already existing aspects of metapsychology. In the following years, ego psychology assumed a leading role in psychoanalytic theory and practice, so that the structural viewpoint overshadowed temporarily the topographic approach, though it never displaced it in Freud's thinking.[1]

While psychoanalysis has always been genetically oriented (Freud, 1905), Hartmann and Kris (1945) emphasized the genetic approach, based on Hartmann's studies (1929) of genetic principles in psychological development. The genetic approach became a logical necessity when adaptation was recognized as one of the decisive factors in producing and shaping psychological phenomena and structure.

Actually, it is only due to Hartmann's personal modesty that the adaptational and the genetic viewpoints were made basic elements of

Adapted, enlarged, and reformulated from a paper presented at the 26th Congrès des Psychanalystes de Langues Romanes in Paris, October 29, 1965.

I am indebted to W. Godfrey Cobliner, Ph.D. for his critical comments as well as for his stylistic suggestions.

[1] See his use of this viewpoint as late as 1937, and Kurt Eissler's discussion of the preconscious (1962).

metapsychology only by Rapaport and Gill (1959). The genetic viewpoint pertains to the laws of nature, applies to all living matter (and in a certain sense also to inanimate matter), and therefore cannot be ignored in psychology and *a fortiori* in psychoanalysis. The fact that some psychologies—and I mention only Gestalt psychology —dispense with it and thus come to be ahistoric represents an impoverishment of these schools.

The genetic procedure is one of the pivotal aspects of psychoanalysis, and is part and parcel of the concept of psychic determinism. Freud formulated this concept in 1901, and from then on stressed it again and again throughout his work. I feel justified in using it to point up the difference between the psychoanalytic approach and the principles invoked by other psychologies.

In addition to the genetic approach, I shall also deal in detail with the topographic viewpoint. Its application fell somewhat into disfavor when the ego and the ego defenses moved into the center of psychoanalytic thinking and therapy. That is understandable, for the topographic viewpoint refers to a relatively static and descriptive approach to psychological phenomena, while the structural viewpoint stresses function in the first place and therefore lends itself better to dynamic explanations.

In the case of my own research, however, the structural viewpoint can be applied only to a very limited extent. During the first part of infancy, the ego is either still nonexistent or in the act of becoming. At the same time, with the absence of speech one cannot make use of the classical tool of psychoanalysis, i.e., free association. Thus one is forced to resort to a descriptive method and has to follow the emergence of consciousness from the topographic viewpoint. We therefore observe the operations taking place within the psyche, or rather their derivatives, from the economic and dynamic viewpoints as well as from the topographic viewpoint up to that moment when definite signs of an emerging ego appear, however rudimentary it may be. From then on the topographic approach is complemented by the structural one, and our attention will shift to the functioning of the ego.

My first basic finding, derived from these observations (later supported by many other researchers), confirms Freud's proposition on the question of the early existence of the ego, to which he refers in many of his writings; e.g., in 1914, he said: "we are bound to suppose that a unit comparable to the ego cannot exist in the individual from the start; the ego has to be developed" (p. 76f.). This statement was elaborated by Tausk (1919), who maintained that during the neonatal period, no "object" of the external world exists for the newborn and therefore no external world as such; nor is the newborn conscious of himself. Tausk adds that ideation also is absent in the entity which we call the ego, before intellect, before the psyche has arrived at the stage of mnemonic representation.

Direct observation and experiments made on newborns inform us that during the first days after birth one cannot demonstrate either memory in the usual sense of the term or directed activity. There is one exception to the latter: the reflex behavior connected with what is commonly called "sucking reflex" shows an observable directed behavioral sequence. This comprises, among others, the orientation reflex, commonly called rooting; oral prehension, swallowing; and all that follows. This action sequence is coherent, coordinated, and directed toward a goal; it is demonstrable, however, not only *after* birth, but long *before*, in the fetus. As I have explained elsewhere (1957), it is an innate behavior, phylogenetically developed and transmitted through heredity, and can be found either in the same or in a modified form in the so-called altricial mammals and birds.

The fact that this behavior, which is at the origin of our concept of the oral phase, has its antecedents in a behavior that has evolved in the course of phylogenesis raises the following points:

1. Like Hartmann and Kris (1945) I distinguish between *maturation* and *development*. By maturation I mean the unfolding of phylogenetically evolved and therefore inborn functions of the species, which emerge in the course of embryonic development or are carried forward after birth as Anlage and become manifest at later stages in life. Conversely, by development I mean the emergence of forms, functions, and behavior which are the outcome of exchanges between the organism on the one hand, the environment (comprising both inner and outer environment) on the other. It is a purely semantic question whether we want to include in the concept of development those modifications which intrapsychic processes impose on the organism and which are secondary consequences of the exchanges taking place between the subject and the surround.

2. We must continue to search for phylogenetic prototypes of behaviors, structures, functions, which we observe in grownup and child.

3. The natural history of the development of the human psyche still remains to be written.

To carry out these assignments the analysts of the future will have recourse in the first place to those insights which we have gained with the help of psychoanalysis. Then they will have the obligation to take cognizance of the existence of manifest connections between phenomena observed by us and those discovered by disciplines conterminous with our own, such as phylogenesis, embryology, ethology, etc. Thus we shall become able to discern the innate from the experiential (Benjamin, 1961); that is, we shall be able to separate what we have inherited from that which results from interaction with the surround.

The very first thing which one learns from direct observation of the newborn is the universality of the evolutionary process. The more I observed newborns, the more I realized that in them both soma and psyche are in a process of rapid development. Both start as entities with imperceptible differentiation, from which they progress to an increasing differentiation and an ever greater complexity. This applies to their physical person no less than to their psychic development. The latter can be observed clearly in those sections of the psyche which we have subsumed in constructs to facilitate our orientation and comprehension. I am referring of course to the psychic apparatus, its various structures, and the details and aspects of these systems.

Freud advanced the notion that the ego has to be developed. Hartmann (1950), following his reasoning, called the phase before this development has taken place "the undifferentiated phase." I prefer to speak of the "stage of nondifferentiation." Hartmann's formulation implies that at the stage of which he is speaking, namely, the first 3 months of life, there is no differentiation between conscious and unconscious, or between the structural elements of the personality, in short, between intrapsychic elements. In my concept nondifferentiation applies to the organization of the psyche as well as to its functioning, or, as one would say in the vernacular, to the newborn's "manner of being." Thus nondifferentiation refers to the fact that the newborn is incapable of distinguishing between outside and inside, of differentiating the objects or modalities of perception, and so on. It includes the elements impinging from the surround.

Actually, the state of nondifferentiation encompasses even more. In my opinion, at birth the drives too are not yet differentiated from each other. This differentiation will come about only as a result of development in the following months. With this proposition we have entered the domain of metapsychology: for it is evident that if at birth the drives are not differentiated from each other, then we cannot apply the dynamic or economic viewpoints.

We might illustrate these propositions by citing experiments made on newborns during the first weeks of life by Watson and other members of his school of behaviorism. Their experiments were always conclusive in the case of the "approach" response—that is, love. This is not surprising because these experiments were performed in the sector of survival, i.e., in that of nursing at the breast.

Obviously, the newborn need not be able to discern diacritically what the stimulus he received represents in order to be able to recognize that what he needs is food. To respond positively in this sector the newborn has available a series of phylogenetically preformed behavior patterns. In animals these responses belong to the all-or-none category. This statement is strikingly illustrated by some experiments performed by one of our colleagues, Bertram Lewin.[2] He demonstrated on the opossum (*Didelphis virginiana*) that the newborn opossum finds his way to the marsupial pouch and the nipple by successively sucking from hair to hair until he reaches the nipple itself. If on his way he misses a hair he will perish inevitably, because he will no longer be able to find his way to the nipple.

In man, evolution has provided in the person of the mother an insurance against the inexorable functioning of the all-or-none law; in the help, care, and love which she lavishes on her newborn. Nevertheless, in man too, the newborn and even the infant have retained certain behaviors preformed by phylogenesis. Such are the orientation reflex, commonly called rooting; the snapping at the nipple.

Yet, at birth, in his subjection to the all-or-none law of survival, the Nirvana principle, the human newborn is basically not different from the opossum. The human newborn opens his mouth wide, when hungry, and screams. When the nipple is put inside his mouth, the

[2] In collaboration with Carl G. Hartmann.

food is actually already inside him, yet he continues screaming without snapping at the nipple and sucking. The behavior is the same as that of the opossum which, on losing a hair on its way to the nipple, is unable to snap at the next one and perishes.

The human baby survives, however, thanks to his mother. This difference between the opossum and the human baby has its origin in phylogenesis: the altricial[3] mother sweeps the young toward herself with her paws if they do not find the nipple on their own with the help of their scanning movements. Maternal behavior of this kind is evident in cat and dog, and is more pronounced in monkeys where the baby *may* cling to the maternal fur, but certainly is *clutched* to the breast by the maternal animal.

In *man* a decisive step is added to maternal behavior: the nipple is *placed* in the baby's mouth by the mother again and again, and the mouth titillated until the infant grasps the nipple firmly. Accordingly, the orientation of the newborn toward the nipple is complemented in the course of evolution by the orientation of the maternal animal toward the offspring, culminating in what I called elsewhere (1956) the mother's *diatrophic* attitude.

Without this complementation the situation of the baby losing the nipple and screaming without making an effort to achieve it again is identical with that of the opossum which loses its way to the pouch. *Both will die* without outside intervention. This outside intervention, which has approach characteristics of a libidinal nature, is different in kind from the defense of the young, manifest both in altricial and precocial maternal animals. Here it is the *aggressive* drive which is placed in the service of survival.

As already pointed out, Watson and his school had no difficulty in demonstrating the existence of the first in their series of affects recognizable at birth, namely, "approach"; for it corresponds to the unrolling of a phylogenetically evolved sequence of inborn responses.

By contrast, the experiments carried out by the Watsonians to demonstrate the existence of hostility and flight (or rather "approach with the intention of removal" and "withdrawal") remained inconclusive. In the first place, the newborn is unable to localize in space a stimulus which causes him unpleasure, so that naturally he cannot avoid it. Nor can he perform a directed action; he can only squirm,

---

[3] *Altricial:* animals that depend on maternal care after birth in contrast to *precocials* which do not.

kick, wriggle, writhe randomly. If, as a result of these random activities, he succeeds in avoiding the unpleasure stimulus, the noxious agent, that also will be accidental and random. This has led to severe burns being inflicted on newborns by the careless use of an electric heating pad.

To produce "rage" Watson suggested immobilizing the newborn. He alleged that in this case the baby became angry. I repeated this experiment on a long series of newborns—I have even filmed it—and never succeeded in enraging a single one of them. By and large, if I held the fidgeting newborn immobilized for a sufficient length of time, he quieted down; and in a not inconsiderable percentage of the cases he fell asleep.

This, incidentally, is common knowledge among good nurses; when during the first weeks of life a child gets restless and cries, the nurse usually wraps him up tightly in his blanket; thereupon the child mostly becomes quiet and goes to sleep. Small wonder! After all, we are dealing with a being who a few hours or days earlier was firmly supported and comfortably protected.

Another suggestive aspect of this picture is offered by the familiar maternal behavior of mammals who lick their newborn for prolonged periods. Ashley Montagu (1953) stresses the importance of this maternal stimulation which in our culture we replace—quite improperly, I believe—by a bath and soaping down administered immediately after delivery. I believe that this is a residue, which we are pleased to call "hygienic," of the prejudice that everything which comes out of the genitals is dirty. Nowadays, in certain delivery clinics with which I am familiar, the newborn is not deprived of the protective layer which covers his skin, of the vernix caseosa, he is not given a bath, and, as far as I know, he fares all the better.

It may be useful in this context to call attention to what was observed in certain mammals, among them rodents: namely, that they perish unless they are licked after birth by the mother animal. Rats, raised in a bacteria-free environment so that they could serve as sterile experimental subjects, regularly died; the newborn could not start urinating unless the mother animal licked their genitals.

To a certain extent, soaping the newborn human baby in a bath may have served a similar function. But we know far too little about the human newborn to be able to determine what is really useful and what is not, what should be provided and what should be avoided, in a word, to make any definitive statements about this subject. I mentioned before that in the uterus, the fetus is securely pillowed and protected in every direction by the amniotic fluid; actually, during delivery it is under considerable pressure. From this situation of being supported in this firm manner on every part of his body, on every square inch of his skin, he is shifted to complete supportlessness in the outside world. This cannot fail to have a far-reaching impact on the coenesthetic system of the newborn.

What I am advancing is a speculation, for to my knowledge experiments in this direction have never been made. But I do believe that to leave the newborn during the first days of his life knocking around in his crib without any support can hardly be the best way to handle him. The crib is small only in our adult eyes. In proportion to the newborn it is a vast expanse, and when we allege that this permits him to use his body and his extremities freely, it is my belief that this is an adultomorphic rationalization and that the transition from the security of the uterus to the insecurity of the crib is too brutal.

It may be assumed that this measure results in an acceleration of bodily development and a premature development of the infantile body ego. This is a parallel, as it were, to Greenacre's (1945) proposition of birth stimulation resulting in a rudimentary erotization of different body parts and early development of anxiety. I believe that during the first weeks of life the method of our forebears, which consisted in swaddling the newborn firmly, has much to commend it; but that will have to be proved experimentally. I believe that the indication to stop the swaddling will be given when on relieving the newborn from his confining wrappings, one sees him stretching himself and showing pleasure or something like appreciation of being liberated from restraint. (See, however, the recent work of Lipton, et al., 1965.)

Coming back to Watson, I believe that at birth it is difficult, if not impossible, to distinguish by his simple methods the manifestations of the aggressive drive from those of the libidinal drive. As far as one is able to classify the various pathognomonic expressions observable in the newborn, these occur mostly in the wake of an unpleasure stimulus. This is why our grandmothers used to say that when the newborn smiles, he has a bellyache.

What can we say now of the newborn from the metapsychological viewpoint beyond stating that he is at the stage of nondifferentiation? From the viewpoint of libido theory we can say that he is in the primary narcissistic stage and that drives will have to be separated from each other, beginning with their inchoate existence in the great reservoir of narcissistic energy. Here I find myself in good agreement with the opinions expressed by Jacobson (1964).

This is not the place to describe in detail the development of the newborn, of his psyche, of his object relations, and the implications for metapsychology of these extraordinary metamorphoses (Spitz, 1965a); but let me outline them briefly.

As one would expect, correspondence is close between these sectors of development and the different aspects of the metapsychological viewpoint. Obviously, the very establishment of the topographic viewpoint, the separation of conscious and unconscious, is predicated on development. Vice versa, however, the existence of a topographic separation into unconscious and conscious, the proportions of the two to each other, the sectors of development which become conscious and those which remain unconscious, will in their turn have vitally important consequences for the subject's subsequent development. The interaction of the inborn with the experiential, on the one hand, and the topographic stratification, on the other, are surely dissimilar and incommensurable. Yet the fact that one or the other sector of development remains located in the unconscious or becomes located in the conscious will change its mode of function radically. Furthermore, interacting and circular reverberating processes of change will take place between these heterogeneous factors, often leading to what Maruyama (1963) dscribed as "The Second Cybernetics." Comparable considerations apply to the dynamic viewpoint (from which we consider the distribution of energies) or to the economic viewpoint (from which we consider shifts in quantities within the psychic apparatus). It is apparent that many factors are interrelated and interacting in the course of this evolution. Even a sketchy description of these processes would immeasurably complicate our present task.

I shall therefore limit my presentation to certain cardinal points at the successive stages of the first year of life. The first of these stages is marked by the newborn's ability to distinguish inside from outside. This is demonstrated when he turns intentionally and in a directed manner *toward* an external stimulus or *away* from it. Anna Freud called this the stage of *need fulfillment*. At this stage (approximately the first 3 months) the newborn's predominant need relates to feeding, which corresponds to his being in the oral phase. The first signs that the newborn becomes conscious of what is outside can also be observed in the feeding situation; to be more exact, in his behavior in respect to the circumstances connected with the intake of food.

These signs still form part of a behavior which is in the nature of the conditioned reflex. I have postulated that the conditioned reflex represents the transition from the somatic neurological reflex, the stimulus-reflex arc, toward the psychological process. On the one hand, the conditioned reflex is solidly rooted in phylogenesis and neurology; on the other, it is the first manifestation of anticipation, of prolepsis, which is purely psychological. This function and its manifestations were investigated first by Volkelt (1929), and later in detail by Rubinow and Frankl (1934).

I have repeated these experiments; based on my own observations of babies in the first 8 to 12 weeks of life, I arrived at the following conclusions:

1. The stage of nondifferentiation continues during this period for both the libidinal and the aggressive drives. Any differentiation which takes place between the two is still vague; one can observe only certain preliminary signs of such differentiation, the most important of which is the reciprocal social smiling response. So much for the dynamic viewpoint.

2. The same obtains for the economic and topographic viewpoints, though the visible signs of their functioning are still more difficult to demonstrate.

3. Regarding the structural viewpoint the situation is different. My observations confirm Glover's (1930, 1932) proposition, according to which discreet nuclei of what later is to become the ego show an organizing tendency from the beginning. These are nuclei which originate in phylogenetically preformed functions, somatically established and probably innate.

One can, for example, observe a progressive organization and synchronization of certain volitional functions into larger behavioral entities which then operate on a higher level of efficiency and flexibility. In conceptual terms, we refer to this newly organized coherent system as an ego nucleus.

The process is well demonstrated in the behavior sequences centering around the sucking response. Initially the response serves the ingestion of food, but soon a link to visual perception becomes established; for during the whole period of the nursing act the newborn fixes his eyes on his mother's face. As a result, need fulfillment during nursing and the visual perception of the face will be inevitably linked. Furthermore, the laying down of the memory traces of this experience will be reinforced by its repetitiveness and through the relief of tension associated with it.

In the course of this process meaningful perception and recognition are established in this particular sector. The three functions (the laying down of memory traces, recognition, and meaningful perception) will in due time become an ego apparatus. In the same archaic system a further link to a phylogenetically transmitted behavior, the so-called "pressor" movements (Spitz, 1957), will be established simultaneously. These are movements of the hands and feet; they represent the beginning of both the tactile perceptive functions and the function of prehension.

A further elaboration of this example would lead beyond the scope of this paper. I trust, though, that my remarks have clearly indicated how these nuclei of behavior are transformed into psychological functions, the prototypes and precursors of which are located within the emerging ego around the activities of the oral zone and its nascent representation.

In the terms of Erikson (1950) this is a modal zone. The mode of the oral zone is incorporation. This is a mode which characterizes the intake of food with its metabolic assimilation, its perception, and a taking in in the form of mnemonic traces; furthermore, prehension, with the assimilation of mnemonic motoric traces of taking, of manipulating; it also includes the beginning of the volitional apparatus, that is, conation; and many more, which would lead us too far.

Therefore, it is my opinion that the observations made in this first trimester of life serve to elucidate the most obscure elements in the origins of the ego in its structural sense. Here is situated a first rudiment of the ego as an entity. This is a nuclear *structure*. It crystallizes because in the organism a synthetic tendency is at work, a tendency which assembles, arranges, and links phylogenetically preformed nuclei, so that they gradually form a coherent entity. However, this structure is not yet an ego—not even a body ego as envisaged by Freud. We are still fully in the soma, in physiology.

In my opinion, this synthetic tendency which has linked the

nuclei with one another is an attribute of all living organisms. It is equally present in psychic unfolding as in the course of somatic embryonic development before the existence of the psyche. In the psychic domain the tendency constitutes the precursor of the synthetic function of the ego, first formulated by Nunberg (1930) and elaborated by Waelder (1930). Synthesis is one of the most important functions of the ego and its importance in psychic life cannot be overrated.

In regard to the dynamic viewpoint, I have stated earlier that the development of the two drives parallels that of the ego. At birth it is impossible to distinguish the libidinal from the aggressive drive, but in the two months following birth the derivatives of these two drives gradually become discernible; one should add: "more or less." They still cannot be distinguished from each other in their aims, sources, or implications. As long as perception and memory are not developed in a more stable manner, the manifestations of the two drive derivatives in identical circumstances will remain interchangeable. In her recent book, Edith Jacobson (1964) raised a point which I find as correct as it is interesting. She notes that during the phase of primary narcissism or—to avoid a terminology which may lend itself to argument— in what I call the phase of nondifferentiation, it is true that we deal with discharge processes, but she underscores that this discharge can occur toward the outside as well as toward the inside and that these two processes must be kept clearly apart.

I am in complete agreement with her, and I am grateful to her, as I feel many others will be, for having introduced this notion, which permits us to account for the nature of phenomena and functions which derive from the two directions of discharge, so different from each other. Perhaps it should be added that in the beginning the nondifferentiation shows itself in the fact that the direction of the discharge probably occurs randomly and is not predictable. However, the results differ from each other, and this very difference will determine, in a circular process (involving perhaps positive entropy as mentioned before), further and divergent development.

It seems indeed likely that the crude unmodulated discharge toward the outside, for instance, will usher in the function of communication. Freud remarked on this as early as 1895. We may add to this the mimetic function and aggression. In my use of the term the latter

involves action and aggressivity, which in turn involves hostility—
in one word, all the elements of alloplastic adaptation.

Conversely, it is to be expected that discharge toward the inside
will lead to autoplastic development. Here, however, conditions are
more complicated: unmodified raw energy, discharged outward, is
channeled into motor activities and actions. When the discharge is
directed inward, this may, for instance, in the physical sector, lead to
somatization. On the other hand, in the sphere of psychology, which
for man is of decisive importance, we shall find the development of
thought processes—that is, trial actions with the help of displacement
of minimal quanta of energy (Freud, 1911). Leibniz called it "apperception."

We may assume that such a discharge to the inside, be it somatization
or ideational, can represent only a detour function, which ultimately
will find its way to the outside. In the course of the detour, however,
raw energy undergoes a transformation; in this way a better adaptation to environmental reality is achieved than would be through direct
motor discharge to the outside (Hartmann, 1939). Here then would
be the point at which the reality principle has its origin.

It seems to me that any distinction between discharge processes is
futile as long as the Nirvana principle rules unchecked, as long as the
newborn is compelled to discharge his drives without delay. Rudiments of the pleasure principle must be present; it is necessary that
gratification be actively sought and unpleasure be actively avoided if
such distinctions are to be meaningful.

This occurs indeed in the 3rd month of life: the infant smiles on
beholding the human face; and at 4 months he cries when the adult
with whom he was playing leaves him. Before he can achieve these
feats, before he has acquired this ability, several steps, different from
each other but similar in their metapsychological significance, must be
achieved:

A forerunner of the reality principle must emerge. The reality
principle refers to the introduction of a detour function, that is, to
man's capacity to delay the immediate gratification of a desire for the
purpose of achieving its more effective gratification.

If one places the nipple (food) into the open mouth of a 4-week-
old infant screaming with hunger, he is unaware that the food *is*
already in his mouth and continues screaming. As long as he is unable
to delay the gratification of his drive for the moment needed to per-

ceive this food in his mouth, he is under the sway of the Nirvana principle. He perceives only his own sensations, and not outside reality. He is unable to use apperceptive mnemonic procedures which are needed to recognize food as such. As Freud (1925) stated, cognition is recognition. There is no direct, immediate psychological cognition.

A fortiori the infant can react with a smile to the human face only after he has assimilated the rudiments of the reality principle, as it were. The human face then becomes the signal of the approaching gratification (to the exclusion of all other percepts).

When the infant indicates by his smile that he "recognizes" the human face, we may conclude:

a. He *recognized* a signal, the signal of nursing, of pleasure. If we wish to be rigorous, we should say that it is the signal indicating that the unpleasure he is experiencing will be removed. The "will be" in the preceding statement indicates that he is performing a psychological act, that of *anticipation.*

b. He is past the stage of exclusive contact perception and has progressed toward distance perception.

c. He can distinguish between sensations coming from inside and percepts coming from outside; in other terms, he has acquired the capacity to distinguish the "I" from what I have called the "non-I." In one word, the first nucleus of the ego is manifested by the inception of the reality principle and by the capacity to distinguish the "I" from the "non-I." The 6 months which follow this first 3-month period are characterized by the progressive development and constitution of the ego proper.

It is hardly necessary to stress the role of the mother in this process. In the past twelve years I have written on little else (1963, 1964, 1965a, 1965b). Viewed from the angle of metapsychology, the infant's efforts, strivings, experiments represent attempts to use his instinctual drives, which have now become progressively separated and organized into two different "units." These experiments go on endlessly, repetitively, iteratively. They are applied to every situation, to every object, to every person encountered by the infant.

These recurring experiences cannot fail to leave corresponding mnemonic traces; this is all the more true since most of these experiences do not lead to immediate discharge or even to an adequate discharge of drive energy. Because of this circumstance the infant (or theoretically speaking, his ego) is spurred to ever-renewed efforts of synthesis. Concurrently the baby will progressively modify his experiments according to the mode of trial-and-error learning.

So much for the immediate factors achieved by the baby through experience. At the same time intrapsychic energies are released by these selfsame events. It follows that in addition to the physical and observable conditions and consequences of each experience, a further element needs consideration: the intrapsychic factors engaged in the given experience, namely, the dynamic and economic distribution of the aggressive and libidinal drive. A law of learning, derived from careful experiments—Thorndike's law of effect (1913)—governs the baby's acquisition of experiential knowledge throughout the first year of life. When the baby's experiment leads to satisfaction, he tends to remember it; what is more, he will repeat it. Conversely, when the experiment leads to disappointment, repetition will become progressively infrequent.

These developments combine with the growing memory, while apperception of mnemonic traces becomes more and more efficient. Both are instrumental in helping the baby to achieve a stable, consistent memory image of his mother. Hartmann (1952) refers to this as the establishment of object constancy.

Up to this point, one and the same person, the mother, was alternatively a good or a bad object. She became a bad object when she refused to gratify the desire of the baby, for this refusal triggered his aggressive drive; when shortly thereafter she gratified his wish, or rather his need, she became the good mother, toward whom libidinal drives were directed.

In the second half of the first year, the infant pursues a constant, persistent, and tenacious experimentation, which is greatly aided by his progressively more efficient mnemonic apparatus. This experimentation brings him to a landmark in his perceptual sphere, an extraordinary achievement in recognition and insight: he comes to realize that the "good" and the "bad" mother are one and the same person. The baby can now direct both his libidinal and his aggressive drive on the person of the mother and in so doing achieves their fusion for the first time.

In this description I have deliberately viewed events exclusively from the vantage point of development, while keeping the role of maturation in the background.

It is the apperceptive processes going on in the course of the baby's experimentation which form the basis of his capacity to merge and fuse memory traces cathected with aggressive and libidinal drive. To make these memory traces available to the infantile psyche, maturation has to take place in the central nervous system, specifically myelinization of nervous tracts, activation of internuncial fibers, leading to organized intercommunication.

De Ajuriaguerra (1965) recently coined the epigram *"L'homme se fait en faisant"* ("Man is made by doing"). Maturation is certainly the basis of development; but without the exercise of function and the activation of behavior patterns (e.g., von Senden's report [1932] on operated blind-born individuals) maturation will be arrested. I described this phenomenon in children deprived of affective supplies (Spitz, 1945, 1946); Harlow's (1958, 1959) experiments on primates have recently furnished strong support for this assumption.

Once the stage of object constancy is acquired, a new dimension will be added to the relations of the baby with his mother. In the first half year of life, the preverbal dialogue between infant and mother takes place as a function of the child's needs, as expressed by Anna Freud's term of "need fulfillment." Once the memory image of the mother is established as a distinct integrated individual, of whom one can be certain, as an individual who provides the gratification of the libidinal drive at the same time as that of the aggressive drives, the mother-child dialogue acquires a wealth of novel possibilities. The baby will experiment with the consequences of alternately satisfying one or the other of his drives, and vary the proportions from experiment to experiment. His behavior can now be understood from the economic viewpoint.

Let us return to the developmental level before the fusion of the aggressive and libidinal drive has taken place and the significance of this archaic condition for developments in the perceptual area.

We have the good fortune to possess certain data gathered by von Senden (1932) on 66 subjects born with infantile cataracts who were operated upon when they were adolescents or adults. Von Senden's data suggest that at birth differentiation does not exist in the perceptual sphere, just as we have postulated the absence of differentiation in all other sectors of the personality. Von Senden's observations were recently duplicated on primates by Riesen (1965). Not only are visual stimuli not distinguished from each other, but they are not even distinguished from stimuli originating in other perceptual modalities. Perhaps the most striking example in von Senden's book is an adult operated for infantile cataract who compared his first perception of color to the smell of varnish.

From this inchoate beginning visual and other percepts will have to develop as a function of the relations of the newborn with the outside world. I tried to show, and my findings were confirmed by the experiments of Harlow and others on primates, that the givens necessary for this development are mediated to the baby by the libidinal object. After birth, a relatively long period will elapse before the newborn becomes capable of recognizing a signal outside of himself, namely, the Gestalt signal inherent in the human face.

I have advanced the hypothesis that in the breast-fed infant (other rules prevail for bottle-fed infants), this signal owes the privilege of being the first one to be perceived to circumstances which correspond exactly to the postulate of Freud (1925): "A precondition for the setting up of reality-testing is that objects shall have been lost which once brought real satisfaction" (p. 238). In the case of the first consistently established signal, the process is as follows: the nursing infant, as soon as he arrives at the stage where he keeps his eyes open during feeding, stares at the mother's face from the beginning to the end of his meal. Thus there are two percepts which become operative during nursing: one, the tactile perception of the food, of the nipple in the infant's mouth; and second, the visual percept of the mother's face. Of the two only the visual percept remains invariable.

In contrast, the perception of the nipple is discontinuous. It is absent before the beginning of nursing and after its end. And when during nursing the nipple is removed from the mouth of the baby— a procedure which takes place frequently during every nursing— the percept of the mother's face remains unchanged. In other terms, the face of the mother is the stable element in an experience of need fulfillment interrupted by gaps of frustration, the loss of the part object, the nipple, which had responded to the need of the child.

The gratification of the libidinal drive during nursing insures the increasingly conscious perception of the Gestalt characteristics of the human face. Less obviously but no less powerfully, this conscious perception is enforced by the aggressive drive evoked through the loss of the nipple in the course of nursing. This is probably the first occasion in life when the two drives, only recently emerged from the stage of undifferentiation, will alternate in quick succession in a situation in which a large portion of the perceptual field (mainly the visual one) remains unchanged.

From this point onward the interaction of maturation and development brings about, by the second half of the first year, an extraordinary advance in the psychic apparatus, of which I have chosen to present the perceptual manifestations only.

In the perceptual field, between the 3rd and the 6th months of life, the infant is exposed, again and again, to opposite emotions while contemplating his mother's face, which of course remains identical. In my opinion, this identity of the visual percept permits the infant to combine the "giving" mother's *face* with the "frustrating" mother's *face* into the unified percept of the mother's *person*. This development is a progressive one, and results from the maturation of the child's central nervous system and the unfolding of his psychic capacity.

This then is the road which the infant's development has to follow to arrive at the percept of the mother's *person* independent of the situation in which he perceives her; with that she has become different from any other being in the world, a unique and irreplaceable individual. In Hartmann's (1952) terms, this is the establishment of object constancy.

It is evident that this development starts with the inception of the reality principle. Furthermore, it is evident that the baby has to make considerable progress in applying this principle to achieve the above-mentioned results. The capacity to hold in suspense the gratification of the drive long enough to perceive and store the memory traces of the percept is indispensable. This means that he cannot give way simply and without concern either to his pleasure or to his unpleasure, but that he has to explore the percept, scan his memory traces, and recognize the person of the mother or reject the stranger.

With the achievement of object constancy we have arrived in the second half of the first year, at a level of structural development where we begin to discern important changes in the ego. During the first half year, what one could mainly observe of the ego was its equipment, which consists of what Hartmann calls "apparatuses" of the ego, that is, primary autonomy. In the course of development the ego apparatuses, which in the beginning were phylogenetically preformed innate ego nuclei, will acquire an archaic representation in the psyche.

We are speaking here of extremely elementary functions, for instance, that of prehension, of grasping. I have described and filmed its development elsewhere, beginning with forced grasping at birth and its progress to intentional grasping directed by volition.

In the second 6 months, we can see subordinate systems being formed within the structural organization of the ego, prototypes as well as precursors of psychological functioning, such as the defense mechanisms of the ego (Spitz, 1958, 1961). Prototypes appear to be innate somatic functions. Precursors, on the other hand, appear to be archaic psychological functions which in the beginning serve adaptation.

These archaic functions still take place in the conflict-free sphere of the ego, but toward the end of the first year a new form of adaptation will be set in motion. I am speaking of attempts to resolve intrapsychic conflict. It is at this point that the mechanisms of defense have their inception.

I intend to touch on only one of these mechanisms, the most obvious one and the one most widely used in the first year of life—the mechanism of identification. I wish to stress that until now, we defined identification as a process which takes place in the unconscious, hence is unconscious, and which consists in a certain redistribution of libidinal and aggressive cathexes. As a result of this redistribution a modification in the ego takes place.

Identification is the result of an unconscious process which takes place in the unconscious sector of the ego. It "represents a process of modifying the self-schema on the basis of a present or past perception of an object which is taken as model" (Sandler, 1960, p. 150). I have found this definition helpful because of its emphasis on the self.

While Freud used this term in discussing "self consciousness," "self observation," "self criticism," the concept "self"—as a counterpart of "object"—was introduced by Hartmann in 1950. Since then many authors have contributed to it (Jacobson, 1954, 1964; Spitz, 1957; Spiegel, 1959; Lichtenstein, 1963). I single out Jacobson's (1964) beautiful formulation: the sense of self or identity develops as "a process that builds up the ability to preserve the whole psychic organization . . . as a highly individualized but coherent entity which has direction and continuity at any stage of human development" (p. 27).

My own view of the self is: while the ego, one of the three psychic structures, is a theoretical construct, the self is a percept which stems from introspection, i.e., from our perception of ourselves.[4]

From my observations on infants and small children I have drawn the conclusion that the self is a product of awareness. Awareness in its turn is a function of the ego: like the ego, it develops. In the course of this process, the self develops as the cognitive precipitate of experience.

This cognitive precipitate, the self, begins to become manifest around the 15th month, about one year after the beginning of what I have called the awareness of the "non-I." The awareness of the "non-I" is achieved as a result of object relations in the feeding situation. The next stage will arrive when as a result of the infant's multifarious action exchanges with the "non-I" he becomes aware of his "I." These archaic relations and exchanges still remain within the somatic part of the personality. The exchanges themselves, the somatic relations with the "non-I," are invested with vast quantities of affect. For this reason these experiences are the first ones to mediate the perception of the surround.

In the course of the development which follows, the "I" will thus be perceived by the infant as a result of his perception of the "non-I." The inception of the self representation in its turn is the result of further affective exchanges experienced by the "I."

When after the 8th month the infant becomes the "executor" of his own wishes, he is also obliged to become his own "observer"; he becomes the observer of himself and as a result an observer of his self. Until then this was his mother's role, but now the child is obliged not only to observe his self, but also to judge it. This permits him to learn through experience in his attempts to understand, evaluate, and gauge the ever-changing tasks of daily living. This is a flexible, reality-adapted learning. It is quite different from the learning which preceded it, for up to that time changes in behavioral patterns were acquired thanks to the functioning of the law of effect and through

---

[4] In this context an interesting observation of Spiegel (1959) is worth mentioning. Staring fixedly at the regular interstices of a venetian blind, he noticed that when he moved his head from the vertical, the afterimage on the retina was modified by an angle corresponding to the inclination of his head. He explained this observation by distinguishing primary perception from the perception of the afterimage. *Primary perception* has as its frame of reference the external world and therefore remains constant. The afterimage belongs to the person, its frame is the body; that is, the images of the body which form the self. For this reason afterimages on the retina are variable.

the conditioned reflex. These two devices can elicit only reactive patterns, which are rigid in themselves; furthermore, being inflexible, they do not adapt themselves, or adapt only with difficulty, to changing reality during individual ontogenesis. The modification of such patterns can be acquired only in the course of phylogenesis, that is, over a long period, under the pressure of natural selection.

Conversely, those adaptive experiences which underlie learning take place in the course of reciprocal relations between the infant and environmental reality, be this alive or inanimate. Reciprocal relations and one-way relations involve either gratification or frustration or both, but the affective quality of gratification and frustration is of a much higher order in reciprocal relations than in one-way relations, and therefore more likely to lead to conflict.

Conflict in its turn expands, multiplies, and intensifies the relations themselves. This intensification then leads to the necessity of finding new methods of dealing with the situation. It seems to me that so many years after Freud had pointed out the seminal principle of conflict (and of defense against it), the creative role of conflict in development is still too little appreciated. We are ever inclined to stress its role in pathology and to neglect its positive side, namely, its vital role in the advancement of the individual and the species, its role in provoking the creation of adaptive devices. One of the great merits of Hartmann (1939) was his systematic research into this aspect of ego psychology.

In the case of the child the most important among such conflicts occurs when the child clashes with the will of the mother. Furthermore, conflicts with environmental reality (be it animate or inanimate) force the child to become conscious of his limitations. The limits of the self will thus be progressively restricted and narrowed down, while at the same time the feeling of omnipotence will decrease.

It follows that the self is in part constructed from the residues of magic omnipotence. The traces of this origin of the self will never disappear completely in the course of life. One can notice them even in the adult. However, the adult's return to the omnipotence of the self is inhibited by reality testing. On the other hand, sleep permits the suspension of reality testing because in this state perception and hence judgment are eliminated. The arrest of motility in sleep makes reality testing unnecessary.

The suspension of the function which has the task of reality testing opens the road which leads to a return to the origins of the self, that is, to magic omnipotence. With that, hallucination of need gratification becomes possible, in the form of dream activity. Similar processes operate in psychosis.

Coming back to the distinction between the self and the psychic representation of the self, I wish to stress once more that the self is a concept which has its place in the theoretical framework of psychoanalytic psychology; the *representation* of the self has perceptual and cognitive attributes and thus is something of which we are conscious. I believe that in the future development of psychoanalytic theory we shall have to consider the relation of the self in respect to the three psychic structures on the one hand and the metapsychological viewpoint on the other. It will become necessary to determine the place of the self from the topographic, the economic, and the structural viewpoints.

It will be apparent that I have omitted the genetic viewpoint, because the distinction between the self and the representation of the self becomes delicate. In speaking of the origins of the self, I have already stressed that it is subject to development.

In my observations of infants, I distinguished the following stages: (1) the infant's capacity to distinguish something beyond that which he feels; he achieves this between the 2nd and the 3rd month. It is the stage in which he becomes aware of the "non-I"; (2) the capacity to distinguish the "I" from the "non-I," which he achieves in the 3 months which follow the first stage; (3) the capacity to distinguish the libidinal object from any other person, a stage which he achieves in the course of the second half of the first year. In my concept the capacity to distinguish the object from the rest of the world marks the inception of the self in the psyche.

At this stage the infant becomes capable of experimenting with a host of new situations, behaviors, sensations. This change results from his increasing autonomy. At the same time, however, increasing independence also forces the infant to trace, or at least to retrace, the confines of his self representation. These confines were established in the course of experiences with the realities of the outside world. Now the child can no longer permit himself to act as he did before; hallucinatory experiences cannot satisfy him.

Actually, these hallucinatory experiences are hardly distinguishable from dream experiences; this confusion will continue for a while, and the difference between the two will not become definite even at an age as relatively advanced as the oedipal stage. There is no doubt that children of 5 to 6 years still confuse dream experience with reality. The best proof of this is the frequency of pavor nocturnus and the tendency to sleepwalking, which is much greater in the preschool child and even in the early latency child than in older subjects.

I described (1957) a number of phenomena which signal processes operating in the development of the self and its precursors. The first among these manifestations are certainly the so-called "experimental movements." They can be observed during the 4th month of life (approximately): the infant raises his hands to the level of his eyes and slowly moves his fingers and hands, following these movements attentively with his eyes. However, one should really say that he *seems* to follow them; for when I attempted an experiment, the result was somewhat disconcerting. I interposed a piece of cardboard between the child's eyes and his hands while he was performing "experimental movements"—thus making it impossible for him to see what he was doing with his fingers. In the majority of cases this did not stop the play of the fingers.

I conclude that this finger play contains an element which must be perceived by the infant in a coenesthetic manner. Recently I have learned from research conducted at the Hampstead Clinic that blind infants, though they are perfectly able to reach the stage of smiling, do not perform these so-called experimental movements.

It further follows that this behavior consists of two parts: (1) the coenesthetic sensations in fingers and hands; (2) a visual diacritic percept. One would be inclined to conclude that the visual percept of these movements represents a stimulus which triggers the repetition and that these are stimuli which the infant provides for himself, for his own enjoyment.

This finding has a parallel in the auditory sphere—the so-called babbling monologues, in the course of which the baby (beginning with the 5th month) imitates the sounds which he produces himself. Here again we encounter self stimulation—in a circuit requiring the hearing component to complete and elaborate the circuit. As mentioned previously, I would be inclined to accept such experiences and behaviors as precursors of the self.

Omitting the manifold developments which occur between the 8th and 15th month, we arrive at a much more advanced stage in the evolution of the self. This stage is marked by increased autonomy of the child, who now has acquired locomotion and the beginning of verbal communication.

Several behavior manifestations suggest that this is accompanied by a significant advance in the establishment of the self and of the self representation. I shall touch on only one of these, the negative head-shaking behavior, on which I have reported extensively elsewhere (1957). Around 15 months of life the child begins to use negative head-shaking for the purpose of expressing refusal and this signals an impressive progress in several dimensions. In the first place, this is probably the first abstraction of which the infant is capable and it takes place with the help of a series of drive displacements, drive modifications, and cathectic shifts. In the process a conspicuous role is played by the aggressive drive, the way in which it is manipulated, and the defense mechanism of identification with the aggressor.

In the second place, the infant has now acquired a semantic signal which will become the starting point for the development of the vast semantic system of language. The immediate consequences of this acquisition is that his dialogue, as I have called (1963, 1964, 1965b) the infant's preverbal transactions with his surround, will be enormously enriched.

Third, he has acquired an instrument with which to differentiate himself from his surround; by this very act, he imposes on himself a "becoming conscious" of his personality or, to be more exact, of his self. Furthermore, he has acquired a new path for the discharge of surplus energy, which previously had to be discharged through motor pathways.

Fourth, the child has acquired a new, completely different and much more effective way of conducting his relations with his surround; now he can replace motor action with discussion.

At this point I would situate the beginnings of an *organized* self and self representation. This should be distinguished from the inception of the unorganized self (mentioned earlier) which emerges in the second half of the first year. And this shadowy self is in its turn very different from what I have tentatively spoken of as possible precursors of the self, e.g., the "experimental movements."

I realize that in speaking of inception, I expose myself to two diametrically opposite objections. The first of these is that I do not situate the inception of the self early enough in development, that it should be pushed back to the 3rd month of life, and perhaps even earlier. That is the objection of those who take Jacobson's position; however, I believe that my previous discussion has sufficiently answered this objection.

The second objection could be raised by those who, following Erikson, place the establishment of the self (or identity) in adolescence or even later. I believe that in this case we are concerned mainly with semantics. It depends on what we call "the establishment" of the self, and what we mean by identity or self. No doubt, the self proceeds to incorporate and acquire additional and new dimensions throughout the individual's life history, hand in hand with the new acquisitions which his personality may achieve in the outside world, in relations with others (and also George Mead's "generalized other"), and in regard to the shifts and modifications taking place in his internal world.

It seems to me that as soon as the infant distinguishes objects from each other, and particularly as soon as he can choose and maintain in his memory his libidinal object, we should recognize the possibility and even the probability that the first rudiment of the self is also established. I am ready to concede that there are subsequent stations which will signal further progress in the organization of the self. In an earlier publication (1957), I mentioned, for instance, that around the 18th month one observes a phenomenon which reveals that a new step has been accomplished in the development of the self: the child begins to speak of himself in the first person or by using his own name. An interesting sidelight on this development can be found in Sanford Gifford's (1965) observation of a pair of monozygotic twins with different character formation.

Another particularly impressive example is that told by Clara and Wilhelm Stern, whose classic book on the language of the child was published at the beginning of this century. Peter, their son, in the second half of his second year, saw snow falling for the first time in his life. He became exceedingly excited and shouted: "Kiok, Kiok!" His parents told him: "No, Peter, this is called snow!" But the child insisted and declared firmly: "Peter, Kiok!" With this declaration, he stated his autonomy; he referred it to his own person by designating this person with his given name. In other words, he was saying to his parents: "I, by the grace of God. Peter, I myself will call it Kiok, whatever you may say!"

Those who have the opportunity to examine a series of photos taken of the same person at intervals of approximately one year, beginning with his first year until he is grown up, may be interested in the following observations: it is very impressive to see the face and expression of the subject change from one year to the next and assume a directed, oriented, and from then on consistently maintained expression. During the first year the facial expression is vague, undetermined, and slightly disoriented; the eyes look somewhat lost, as if in a daze. Even in the course of the second year the eyes assume from time to time this lost expression, particularly in unfamiliar situations.

After a person's expression has assumed consistency, it may remain unchanged in the course of all the vicissitudes of the subject's life, right into adulthood and beyond. An exception should be made for certain transitional periods in the course of puberty and at the inception of adolescence, where sometimes the face may again lose its clearly directed and oriented expression. I wish to stress this phenomenon which seems to me to confirm Anna Freud's statement (1936) that during puberty pregenital problems are once again revived before the final formation of personality. I would be inclined to say that a revision of the perception of the self takes place here in puberty before the final decision.

The fact that the first change in the indeterminate, vague, lost expression takes place suddenly from one year to the next (and according to my experience, during the preoedipal, perhaps I should say pregenital phase) permits one to assume the occurrence of an event which has forced the child to seek a new adaptation; it seems that the child has lived through a basic experience, which he had never encountered before. I would not go so far as to call this experience traumatic, but it is certainly a decisive one.

In a number of my analytic cases I discovered that this experience was the birth of a younger sibling, a competitor. Evidently, this is an event which demands a complete reorientation of the child, a new individuation, as it is called by Mahler (1957). Such a development implies an effort to acquire autonomy and independence, to acquire confidence in one's self, and a certain amount of self control, a certain mastery and security; all these are processes which lead to the becoming conscious of one's own self.

A report on a 5-year-old boy is illustrative; he was visiting his grandmother for a few days. On the first morning she came to take him to his bath and told him so; whereupon the boy replied in a peremptory tone: "I am I, and I wash myself!" One cannot, I believe, express at the age of 5 years one's awareness of the dignity of one's own self in a clearer manner. This is no longer merely a body self; this is the self of the total personality.

In conclusion, it should be realized that findings obtained through direct infant observation have numerous and far-reaching implications. These refer not only to the metapsychological viewpoint in its first formulation, but perhaps even more to the structural and genetic viewpoints, as well as to the problems presented by the introduction of the concept self. Clearly, only a very few aspects of these could be taken up here in detail. Furthermore, such factors as the adaptive viewpoint, substructures within the ego, the conflict-free sphere, were merely alluded to, while the important questions of primary versus secondary autonomy and primary ego energy and neutralization could not even be touched upon.

I mention them here as an ever-present concern in research on normal and pathological infant development. For the seeker, direct infant observation offers a huge mine of information, theoretical as well as clinical. The viewpoints I have discussed in my paper, and even more those which I mentioned above but was unable to deal with, provide the framework, the pointers, and the theoretical orientation in the new and fertile field of investigation of this *terra incognita*, the embryology of the psychic apparatus in man.

BIBLIOGRAPHY

Benjamin, J. D. (1961), The Innate and the Experiential. *Lectures in Experimental Psychiatry*, ed. H. W. Brosin. Pittsburgh: Univ. Pittsburgh Pr., 19-42.
de Ajuriaguerra, J. (1965), Paper presented at the XXmes Rencontres Internationales de Genève.
Eissler, K. R. (1962), On the Metapsychology of the Preconscious. *Psa. Study Ch.*, 17:9-41.
Erikson, E. H. (1950), *Childhood and Society*. NY: Norton.
Fenichel, O. (1945), *The Psychoanalytic Theory of Neurosis*. NY: Norton.
Freud, A. (1936), *The Ego and the Mechanisms of Defense*. NY: IUP, 1946.
Freud, S. (1895), Project for a Scientific Psychology. *The Origins of Psychoanalysis*. NY: Basic Books, 1954.
—— (1901), The Psychopathology of Everyday Life. *S.E.*, 6.
—— (1905), Three Essays on the Theory of Sexuality, *S.E.*, 7:125-245.
—— (1911), Formulations on the Two Principles of Mental Functioning. *S.E.*, 12: 213-226.

—— (1914), On Narcissism. *S.E.*, 14:67-102.
—— (1915), The Unconscious. *S.E.*, 14:159-215.
—— (1921), Group Psychology and the Analysis of the Ego. *S.E.*, 18:67-143.
—— (1925), Negation. *S.E.*, 19:235-239.
—— (1937), Analysis Terminable and Interminable. *S.E.*, 23:209-253.
Gifford, S. (1965), Individual Differentiation in Twins. Presented at the 24th International Psycho-Analytical Congress, Amsterdam.
Glover, E. (1930), Grades of Ego-Differentiation. *On the Early Development of Mind*. NY: IUP, 1956, 112-122.
—— (1932), A Psycho-Analytical Approach to the Classification of Mental Disorders. *On the Early Development of Mind*. NY: IUP. 1956, 161-186.
Greenacre, P. (1945), The Biologic Economy of Birth. *Psa. Study Ch.*, 1:31-51.
Harlow, H. F. (1958), The Nature of Love. *Amer. Psychologist*, 13:673-685.
—— (1959), Love in Infant Monkeys. *Sci. American*, 200:68-74.
Hartmann, H. (1929), Über genetische Charakterologie, insbesondere über psychoanalytische. *Jb. Charakterol.*, 6:73-96.
—— (1939), *Ego Psychology and the Problem of Adaptation*. NY: IUP, 1958.
—— (1948), Comments on the Psychoanalytic Theory of Instinctual Drives. *Essays*, 69-89.
—— (1950), Comments on the Psychoanalytic Theory of the Ego. *Essays*, 113-141.
—— (1952), The Mutual Influences in the Development of Ego and Id. *Essays*, 155-181.
—— & Kris, E. (1945), The Genetic Approach in Psychoanalysis. *Psa. Study Ch.*, 1:11-30.
—— —— & Loewenstein, R. M. (1946), Comments on the Formation of Psychic Structure. *Psa. Study Ch.*, 2:11-38.
Jacobson, E. (1954), The Self and the Object World. *Psa. Study Ch.*, 9:75-127.
—— (1964), *The Self and the Object World*. NY: IUP.
Lichtenstein, H. (1963), The Dilemma of Human Identity. *J. Am. Psa. Assn.*, 11:173-223.
Lipton, E. L., Steinschneider, A., & Richmond, J. B. (1965), Swaddling. *Pediatrics*, 35:521-567.
Mahler, M. S. (1957), In Panel: Problems of Identity, rep. D. Rubinfine. *J. Am. Psa. Assn.*, 6:131-142, 1958.
Maruyama, M. (1963), The Second Cybernetics. *Am. Scientist*, 51:2-3.
Mead, G. H. (1934), *Mind, Self and Society*. Chicago: Univ. Chicago Pr.
Montagu, M. F. A. (1953), The Sensory Influence of the Skin. *Texas Rep. Biol. & Med.*, II.
Nunberg, H. (1930), The Synthetic Function of the Ego. *Practice and Theory of Psychoanalysis*. NY: IUP, 1955, 120-136.
Rapaport, D. & Gill, M. M. (1959), The Points of View and Assumptions of Metapsychology. *Int. J. Psa.*, 40:153-162.
Riesen, A. H. (1965), Effects of Visual Deprivation on Perceptual Function and the Neural Substrate. *Symposium Bel-Air II Genève 1964. Déafférentation Expérimentale et Clinique*, ed. J. de Ajuriaguerra. Genève: Georg, 275-280.
Rubinow, O. & Frankl, L. (1934), Die erste Dingauffassung beim Säugling. *Z. Psychol.*, 133:1-72.
Sandler, J. (1960), On the Concept of Superego. *Psa. Study Ch.*, 15:128-162.
Spiegel, L. A. (1959), The Self, the Sense of Self, and Perception. *Psa. Study Ch.*, 14:81-109.
Spitz, R. A. (1945), Hospitalism. *Psa. Study Ch.*, 1:53-74.
—— (1946), Hospitalism: A Follow-up Report. *Psa. Study Ch.*, 2:113-117.
—— (1956), Countertransference. *J. Am. Assn.*, 4:256-265.
—— (1957), *No and Yes*. NY: IUP.
—— (1958), On the Genesis of Superego Components. *Psa. Study Ch.*, 13:375-404.

—— (1961), Some Early Prototypes of Ego Defenses. *J. Am. Psa. Assn.*, 9:626-651.
—— (1963), Life and the Dialogue. *Counterpoint*, ed. H. S. Gaskill. NY: IUP, 154-176.
—— (1964), The Derailment of Dialogue. *J. Am. Psa. Assn.*, 12:752-775.
—— (1965a), *The First Year of Life*. NY: IUP.
—— (1965b), The Evolution of Dialogue. *Drives, Affects, Behavior*, ed. M. Schur. NY: IUP, 2:170-190.
—— & Wolf, K. M. (1946a), The Smiling Response. *Genet. Psychol. Monogr.*, 34: 57-125.
—— —— (1946b), Anaclitic Depression. *Psa. Study Ch.*, 2:313-342.
Stern, C. & W. (1907), *Die Kindersprache*. Leipzig: Barth.
Tausk, V. (1919), On the Origin of the "Influencing Meachine" in Schizophrenia. *The Psa. Reader*, ed. R. Fliess. NY: IUP, 1948, 1:52-85.
Thorndike, E. L. (1913), *The Psychology of Learning*. NY: Teachers College, Columbia Univ.
Volkelt, H. (1929), Neue Untersuchungen über die kindliche Auffassung und Wiedergabe von Formen. *Berichte über den 4. Kongress für Heilpädagogik*. Berlin: Springer.
von Senden, M. (1932), *Space and Sight*. London: Methuen, 1960.
Waelder, R. (1930), The Principle of Multiple Function. *Psa. Q.*, 5:45-62, 1936.

Notes on the Development of Basic Moods

The Depressive Affect

MARGARET S. MAHLER, M.D.

One of the significant trends that has been inspired by Heinz Hartmann's classic work, *Ego Psychology and the Problem of Adaptation* (1939), has been the interest awakened in psychoanalytically oriented observational research into early psychic development.

Hartmann proposed that we adopt the term "conflict-free ego sphere" for "that ensemble of functions which at any given time exert their effects outside the region of mental conflicts" (p. 8f.). He then went on to say: "If we take seriously the claim of psychoanalysis to be a general theory of mental development, we must study this area of psychology too, from our points of view and with our methods, *both by analysis and by direct observation of infant development*" (p. 10f.; my italics).

Hartmann drew attention to the many aspects of human psychology that involve or are based upon nonconflictual adaptive processes in development, emphasizing that the description and definition of mental phenomena must include its reality-oriented and adaptation-facilitating characteristics and regulations: "Adaptation . . . involves both processes connected with conflict situations, and processes which pertain to the conflict-free sphere" (p. 10).

The most fruitful approach to the exploration of the conflict-free sphere would be direct and indirect observation of *undisturbed development* rather than the study of disturbed function.

From the Masters Children's Center, New York. This paper is based on research supported by the NIMH, USPHS, Bethesda, Maryland, Grant No. MH-08238.

Clinical Professor of Psychiatry, Albert Einstein College of Medicine; Director of Research, Masters Children's Center.

"The degree of adaptiveness can only be determined with reference to environmental situations (average expectable—i.e., typical—situations, or on the average not expectable—i.e., atypical—situations)" (Hartmann, 1939, p. 23).

Adaptation is in general a reciprocal relationship between the organism and its environment. One dimension of the latter that observational research into normal development might consider is "the average expectable environment." The infant's environment consists at first of the mother-infant dual unit, which coincides with Hoffer's (1955) "internal milieu,"[1] and which I believe has its "autistic" beginning before the "symbiotic phase." Adaptation may be regarded as beginning with the infant's fitting into his symbiotic environment. This adaptation is synonymous with his success in drawing his mother into his "internal milieu," i.e., with finding "good enough mothering" (Winnicott, 1965). As soon as this occurs, the infant passes from a brief "normal autistic phase" into the symbiotic phase, in which the mother functions both as the infant's (external) auxiliary executive ego (Spitz, 1951) and also as his "protective living shield," thereby complementing and replacing the "protective barrier or shield against stimuli" and rescuing him "with care" from potentially overwhelming, inundating inner tensions and outer excitations (Freud, 1926; Kris, 1956; Winnicott, 1956; Khan, 1964).

It is in the "dual-unity" sphere of preverbal intercommunication and interaction that cumulative (or, as I would rather say, with Kris, "strain") traumata may occur within the "average expectable environment."

The complexity and difficulty of mother-infant psychological development is compounded by the fact that "good enough" mothering necessarily falls far short of optimally adaptive mothering in our culture, a fact which should be emphasized.

Ernst Kris and his coworkers (Coleman et al., 1953) as well as Therese Benedek (1959) have drawn our attention to the fact that mothering is a developmental variable, with a succession of phases marked by varied and complex adaptive tasks that average mothers cannot be expected to meet with even gradations of success.

As workers in the field map out important landmarks of early psychic maturation and development, it is an important and interesting

[1] Claude Bernard: *milieu intérieur.*

task to study the circular mother-child interaction as a developmental process which shapes the personality of the young, but also shapes the personality of the adult maternal partner (Benedek, 1959). Hartmann (1939) says that "the task of man to adapt to man is present from the very beginning of life" (p. 31).

The task of man to adapt to man, as it has to do with the very beginning of individal life, is the topic of my present study of the "normal separation-individuation" process.

I came to the study of the normal separation-individuation phase from a study of symbiotic child psychosis, which had strongly suggested that childhood schizophrenia could be traced back to vicissitudes of personality development during the second part of the first year and particularly to the second year of life. During that period, the maternal partner of the dual unit for some reason could not be used by the infant-toddler either as auxiliary ego or as a "protective shield against stimuli," nor could she be used as "the beacon of orientation in the world of reality" (Mahler and Gosliner, 1955). Minute study of the separation-individuation phase—about which we know comparatively little, especially in so far as the ego's developmental tasks are concerned—would therefore help to understand better the genesis and the still entirely puzzling nature of schizophrenia.

It is my hypothesis that, in certain toddlers, the maturational spurt of locomotor and other autonomous ego functions, if it takes place concomitantly with a lag in their emotional readiness to function separately from the mother, produces organismic panic, the mental content of which is not readily discernible, because the child (being still in the preverbal stage) cannot communicate. Acute or insidious "organismic distress," with concomitant inability to utilize the mother as external organizer or auxiliary ego, arrests structuralization of the ego. The very fact that maturation proceeds while development does not, renders the rudimentary ego extremely brittle. Fragmentation may result, and the well-known clinical picture of infantile psychosis then ensues (Mahler, 1952).

The maturational spurt I referred to above presumably occurs within the age span after the infant "hatches" (if he hatches at all) from the symbiotic dual-unity stage with his mother.

As early as 1955, Gosliner and I suggested that there is a *normal* developmental phase of separation-individuation, which confronts *every* child with certain developmental tasks and is beset with potential crises. The normal separation-individuation process requires developmental readiness on the part of the infant-toddler to differentiate from the mother within the framework of the usual emotional availability of the mother (Mahler, 1961; Mahler and Furer, 1963), the most important factor of "the average expectable environment" (Hartmann, 1939, 1950).

Within the pilot phase of the separation-individuation research project (an observational study), we were able to distinguish the outline—the contour, as it were—of the main steps of the separation-individuation process. We conceptualized these in terms of four subphases (Mahler, 1965; Mahler and La Perriere, 1965).

The First 18 Months of Life

The first step, or "subphase" is *differentiation*, which begins with the hatching process, and which is conceptualized as the emergence of the infant's self representation from within the imaginary "symbiotic membrane" of the mother-child dual unity. In some infants a veritable hatching process may be seen, which has observable phenomenological characteristics. With this hatching process is ushered in the period of differentiation, which extends approximately into the 9th and 10th months.

The second step, or subphase, can be designated as the *practicing period par excellence*. It extends from about the 9th or 10th month to about the 16th to 18th month. This period, which coincides with what Phyllis Greenacre (1957) has termed the child's "love affair with the world," results in the "mastery" of certain locomotor skills, cognitive capacities, and other partial autonomous ego functions. These functions, during the practicing period, attract so much libido that the junior toddler is emotionally relatively independent of the love object and absorbed in his own narcissistic pleasures. Upon the attainment of mastery of some autonomous ego functions, however, he becomes increasingly aware of his separateness and *pari passu* very much aware of his need for his mother's acceptance and renewed participation.

The subphase in which renewed approach behavior can be observed usually extends from about the 16th or 18th month well into the third year of life. This period of *rapprochement* is very important for laying down the foundation of later mental health or psychopathology.

This very crucial period of development gradually goes over to the fourth subphase of separation-individuation in which a certain degree of *object constancy* will be attained: i.e., mental representations of the mother become intrapsychically available (Hartmann, 1952). The memory traces of the love object enable the child to remain away from the mother for some length of time and still function with emotional poise, provided he is in a fairly familiar environment. Presumably this is so because inner representations of the mother are available to him.

In our studies we came across unmistakable evidence for the belief that a basic mood is established during the separation-individuation process. This basic mood or individually characteristic affective responsiveness is not due solely to innate factors but seems, at least to some extent, to be accentuated experientially and to counteract the constitutional characteristics of the individual child. This characteristic "base line" of the child's emotional responsiveness seems to derive from the preponderance and perpetuation of one or the other general emotional colorings that we found to be characteristic of one or the other of the subphases of the separation-individuation process (the practicing period or the period of rapprochement).

The psychoanalytic literature has recently been filled with observations and discussions about separation anxiety, object loss, and depression. These concepts are intertwined both clinically and dynamically. It is not always clear in the literature, however, that what is referred to as object loss is, more often than not, not real object loss, but *intrapsychic* "loss" of an object. Thus, the questions of a predisposition to depressive moods and separation anxiety, as well as of the relationship of the latter to object loss, are badly in need of further clarification.

Real object loss—i.e., loss of a love object in reality—does not occur frequently enough to account for the widespread proclivity, especially on the part of women, toward depressive moods or depressive illness. It must be a loss in fantasy—that is to say, *intrapsychic conflict* of a particular type or constellation (more frequent than real object loss, if not perhaps actually ubiquitous)—which is the genetic cause for the occurrrence of depression as an affect, as a proclivity toward a basic mood. It might therefore be profitable to examine the nature of the *intrapsychic process* which seems to result in this *sense* or *feeling of loss*, and which seems to set in motion the affective reactions of helplessness, sadness, grief, and depression (Bibring, 1953; Mahler, 1961).

In our separation-individuation study, we could see the earliest behavioral, mimetic, vocal, and verbal manifestations of affective reactions in our subjects—in small children who were never actually separated, for any length of time, from their primary love object or objects. We observed depressive reactions as well as their opposites—moods of exhilaration—in our children. This "mood predisposition" seems as a rule to be related to the intrapsychic vicissitudes of their separation-individuation process, which seems to activate characteristically either relatively positive or relatively negative mood dispositions (Jacobson, 1957).

From the point of view of my main hypothesis, what we see in the toddlers' behavior is a reflection of their intrapsychic working through of that unavoidable, predetermined growing away from the previous state of "oneness" with the mother, which is entailed by maturational differentiation and individuation. This loss—the necessity for a more or less gradual relinquishing of claims upon the need-satisfying, symbiotic object—implies the gradual giving up of the more or less delusional fantasy of symbiotic omnipotence, although this is to some extent compensated for by increased secondary autonomy (Hartmann, 1952) and sound secondary narcissism.

The subphase of differentiation represents the first step of the individuation process. It begins at the peak of the symbiotic phase.

By the 5th or 6th month, the infant seems to recognize his mother as the object through which his gratifications are provided and his discomfort relieved. One can readily observe that, when his mother's face is near him, the 5- to 6-month-old will take the initiative to seek contact, even to force the mother to respond (Brody and Axelrad, 1966). This first subphase of the individuation process develops parallel with the maturational growth of locomotor partial functions, such as creeping, paddling along, climbing, standing up, etc. It also includes looking beyond the immediate visual field (scanning), as well as progress in hand, mouth, and eye coordination, the expression of active pleasure in the use of the entire body, a much more active interest in inanimate objects, active turning to the outside world for pleasure and stimulation, and much more successful efforts at self stimulation. It is a period in which peek-a-boo games, initiated by the mother, are taken over by the infant.

These functions are continually stimulated by close proximity to the mother, as can be seen in the greater vivacity and the longer-sustained activity of the infant when he is in the mother's proximity compared with his lower-keyed activity when he is at a distance from her.

What we learn from our observations about this first subphase of differentiation—and this is true of affective development in general—is that the momentum of libidinal responsiveness is greatly augmented by visual, tactile, and auditory contact and intercommunication—by the "dialogue" with the mother (Spitz, 1963).

With the infant's spurt in autonomous functions, especially upright locomotion, begins his "love affair with the world," as Phyllis Greenacre has characterized it. During those precious 6 to 8 months, from the 10th or 12th to the 16th or 18th month, the world seems to be the junior toddler's "oyster." Libidinal cathexis seems to shift so substantially into the service of the rapidly growing autonomous ego and its functions that, during this so-called practicing period, some children appear to be intoxicated with their own faculties and with the greatness of "their own world." At any time after the 10th month, which marks the onset of the reality-testing period *par excellence*, there begins a steadily increasing libidinal investment in practicing motor skills and in exploring the expanding environment, both human and inanimate. This is true whether the child has already started toddling by then, or is still in the process of developing a proficiency in crawling, righting himself, or paddling around rapidly with a "belly crawl" of his entire body.

Elation seems to be the phase-specific characteristic or basic mood during the second subphase of individuation (the "practicing period").

The chief characteristic of this practicing period is the child's great narcissistic investment in his own functions, as well as in the "objects and objectives" of his expanding reality. Along with this, we see a relatively great imperviousness to knocks and falls and other frustrations (Mahler, 1963, 1965; Mahler and La Perriere, 1965).

As the child, through the maturation of his locomotor apparatus, begins to venture further away from the mother's feet, he is often so absorbed in his own activities that for long periods of time he appears

to be oblivious to the mother's presence.[2] However, he returns periodically to the mother, seeming to need her physical presence from time
to time. We see 10-month-olds crawling to the mother, righting themselves on her leg or touching her in other ways, or just standing and
leaning against her for "emotional refueling." It is easy to observe and
to interpret how the wilting, fatigued infant "perks up" in the shortest
time upon such contact.

The practicing of locomotion culminates in the toddler's becoming
more sure-footed, and the freely walking infant is at the height of his
mood of elation. For some, this is an intermittent mood; for others,
an almost continual one.

During the second 18 months of life, however, very important
libido-economic shifts and changes take place. The little child who is
practicing his skills, perceiving and coping with expanding segments
of reality, appears to be largely preoccupied with his narcissistic
pleasures. He seems, at least intermittently, to be delighted and impressed by his own rapidly developing new skills and his growing
perceptual and cognitive capacities (which are presumably expanding
with equal rapidity).

Just around the time of mastery (of important partial ego functions), he reaches the high point of his mood of elation, which is
buttressed by his sense of *his own magic omnipotence*. This great pervasive secondary narcissism had as its precursor the delusion in the
symbiotic phase of the symbiotic omnipotence of the mother-infant
dual unit.

The Second 18 Months of Life

The period during which the junior toddler of 10 to 18 months grows
into the senior toddler of 18 to 24 months and beyond represents a
most important turning point. Now the toddler experiences, more
or less gradually and more or less keenly, the obstacles to his "conquest of the world."

The period of rapprochement demonstrates with particular clarity
that the intrapsychic separation-individuation process consists of two
distinct, yet intertwined and complementary lines of development:
one of these is "individuation"; the other, "separation." During the
practicing period, and during the period of mastery, which continues

[2] This apparent obliviousness seems to be in direct proportion to the mother's
emotional availability during that subphase.

well into the second half of the second year, individuation proceeds very rapidly, on the one hand, so that the child exercises independence "to the limit." On the other hand, along with the acquisition of primitive skills and perceptual cognitive faculties, there is a clearer and clearer differentiation of the intrapsychic representations of the love object and of the self. Along with the child's awareness of his separateness comes his realization of the very large number of obstacles that stand in the way of his own magic omnipotent wishes and fantasies. At the very height of mastery, toward the end of the practicing period, it dawns on the junior toddler that the world is not his "oyster," that he has to cope with it on his own, every so often as a relatively help-less, small, and lonesomely separate individual. No matter how in-sistently the toddler tries to coerce his mother, she and he no longer function effectively as a dual unit—that is to say, he cannot partake, either, in the delusion he still maintains of parental omnipotence. Verbal communication and secondary-process thinking thus become more and more necessary; gestural coercion on the part of the toddler or mutual preverbal empathy between mother and child will no longer suffice to bring him to his goal of satisfaction, of "narcissistic 'well-being' " (Sandler and Joffe, 1965).

In addition to this growing awareness of individual separateness, the junior toddler gradually comes to realize that his love objects (his parents) are also separate individuals; they seem to act on diversified interests, the focal points of which are less and less identical with his own. This realization is arrived at, however, at a time when the tod-dler's delusion about his parents' unlimited power still persists. As for his inability to recreate the "omnipotent unity" of his earlier life, no matter how insistently he coerces his mother, at this point he can only regard it as her *withholding* from him an omnipotence which she possesses, but which *he* is no longer permitted to share. It remains for him to recognize—much later, in the postoedipal period—that he is not the only one who is not omnipotent, but that his parents are by no means omnipotent either. Hence, they cannot either share with him or deny to him an omnipotence that they themselves do not have (Jacobson, 1947).

There are mother-child pairs in whom the child has already had to exert himself quite a bit during the practicing period in order to obtain from the love object the libidinal supplies—the refueling—that were necessary for him to maintain a basically contented emotional affective state. Such a deficit of emotional supplies, which may have gone unrecognized at the time, may later become compounded and manifest itself (after the child's relatively brief and low-keyed "love affair with the world") during the course of the rapprochement subphase.

It is the mother's love and acceptance of the toddler and even of his ambivalence which enable the toddler's ego to cathect his self representation with "neutralized energy."

If there is a significant lack of acceptance and "emotional understanding" by the mother during the rapprochement subphase (which is also the beginning of verbal communication); or, at any rate, if there is an absence of a higher level of "dialogue" (Spitz, 1963), this circumstance compounds the stress trauma that may have existed during the preverbal mother-infant interaction. This deficit in mothering has tended to result in a diminution of the child's self esteem and a consequent narcissistic vulnerability. Ambivalence in behavior (which I would call "ambitendency"), and especially aggressive repetitive coercion of the mother and sometimes the father as well, seem to be age-adequate phenomenological signs, along with the normal negativism of this phase of "separation," which characterizes the anal phase. But prolonged and increasing ambivalence is a sign of skewed emotional development, an indication of increase of unneutralized aggression and of disturbance of the child's progress toward object constancy.

Our reconstructive and observational data suggest that, in those small children who show the "basic depressive mood," not enough sound secondary narcissistic libido has remained available, beyond the period of mastery, to be vested in the "objects and objectives" of his expanding world, and particularly not enough to cathect his own self representations. Too great a portion of his unneutralized aggression (Hartmann, Kris, and Loewenstein, 1949) is being taken up by the mechanisms of splitting and projection—a potentially pathological combination of defense, which serves to ward off the child's hostility (aggression) and his fear of annihilating the love object by his aggressive ambivalent fantasies while he struggles to restore the state of oneness with the love object.

The mother's renewed acceptance and active support during the rapprochement phase is thus a necessary prerequisite for the toddler's gradual realization and acceptance of the unreality of his "omnipo-

tence"—a realization which will allow the secondary narcissistic investment in his own autonomy to take place gradually, thereby protecting
him against acute deflation of his "omnipotence" and preventing serious injury to his self esteem.

The phenomenological, behavioral signs of unusual conflict become evident in some cases in the form of an increased coercion and
perhaps an increased "shadowing" of the mother. Less often, we have
been able to observe (or receive reports of) an exaggerated form of
the game of darting away from the mother in order to provoke her
into pursuing him and scooping him up. This means to the child a
passive physical reunion with the mother, a symbolic and repeated
undoing, as it were, of the "separation."

The quality and measure of the toddler's wooing behavior during
the rapprochement subphase provide an important clue for the assessment of the normality of the child's individuation process. Some of
our children have stubbornly refused to accept substitute adults; even
though they had seemed to be continuously dissatisfied in their mothers'
absence, they nevertheless displayed a constant whining and demanding as soon as their mothers reappeared. There have also been severe
and protracted separation reactions to everyday routine separations,
with a surplus of unneutralized aggression expressing itself in temper
tantrums.

From the data collected thus far, I believe that the collapse of
the child's belief in his own omnipotence, with his uncertainty about
the emotional availability of the parents, creates the so-called "hostile
dependency" upon and ambivalence toward the parents. This ambivalence seems to call for the early pathological defense mechanisms
of splitting the good and bad mother images and of turning aggression
against the self; these result in a feeling of helplessness, which, as
Bibring (1953) has empasized, creates the basic depressive affect.
These libido-economic circumstances may become the basis for responding habitually with negative mood swings.

The two pillars of early infantile well-being and self esteem are
the child's belief in his own omnipotence and his belief in the parents'
omnipotence, of which he partakes; these beliefs can be replaced only
gradually by a realistic recognition of, belief in, and enjoyment of his
individual autonomy, and by the development of object constancy
(Hartmann, 1952).

We could frequently observe that the "confident expectation"

(Benedek, 1938) of those toddlers who were already, whether for extrinsic or intrinsic reasons, carrying over a deficit of emotional supplies from the previous subphases was more readily depleted during the second 18 months of life. They succumbed more easily than others to an increasingly angry mood, which was interpreted by Bowlby (1960) as "continual protest." In some instances, they seemed periodically to fall prey to a desperate feeling of helpless loss (from which, however, a child usually recovers intermittently, and with relative rapidity). The intrapsychic experience of loss is compounded by the affect-laden symbolic significance of toilet training, and by the advent of the castration anxiety of the phallic phase of psychosexual development. I believe—contrary to Weinberger (1964)—that, in those cases in which the birth of a sibling has coincided with these intrapsychic conflicts, the significance of that event, even though it was great, nevertheless lay primarily in the fact that it accentuated, dramatized, and compounded the basically negative mood predisposition of the child. It was not the original cardinal conflict, and it did not generate per se the depressive affective mood or the proclivity to depressive illness.

The negative affective responsiveness, the "depressive mood," may be represented predominantly by separation and grief reactions—perhaps following a dramatic struggle with the love object—marked by temper tantrums, continual attempts to woo or coerce the mother, and then giving up in despair for a while; or it may be revealed in impotent resignation and surrender (in some cases with marked masochistic coloring). On the other hand, discontentment and anger may persist after a shorter period of grief and sadness—which, I believe, had constituted or represented an abbreviated period of mourning for the "good," need-satisfying, symbiotic mother (Mahler, 1961). In all cases, there is an increased clinging to the mother (not necessarily physically), and a focusing of highly ambivalent cathexis on her. This, in turn, stands in the way of the development of object constancy.

It is by no means the rule—indeed, it seems to be the exception—that the autonomous functioning of the ego is impaired. If anything, children who are prone to affect-laden behavior in their immediate interaction with the mother may function beautifully in other, more neutral situations. As far as we can tell from the limited data of a still ongoing project and our limited follow-up impressions, in the average toddler this negative-depressive affective responsiveness or mood either persists or gives way to a premature earnestness, a kind of unchildlike concern which may possibly indicate a precocity of superego structuralization. Even though in this paper I cannot elaborate on this problem, I must emphasize the importance of the double trauma of toilet training and of the discovery (at a much earlier age than we have thought) of the anatomical sexual difference as contributory factors in the genesis of the propensity of girls to depressive moods.

Sadness with psychic content, i.e., sadness which has an ideational as well as an affective component, must be distinguished from earlier physiological reactions (somatopsychic, at best) of unpleasure and pain—such as transient reactions to weaning, or longer-lasting bodily distress, which the later depressive response may or may not compound.

We have seen at least one male child who was continually fretful, fitful, and unhappy up to the 9th month of age. Until then he suffered from an undetected inguinal hernia and recurrent severe bronchitis. His mother was quite inept at making her young babies comfortable and at reading and responding to their cues. Following the discovery of the inguinal hernia and its repair, however, there was a most favorable change in the libido-economic balance in the mother-child interaction as well as (and even more importantly) in the child's intrapsychic economy. The mutual cueing of mother and child, which till then had been perplexing to the partners as well as to the observers, became quite satisfactory, and the little boy resumed the process of separation-individuation at an emotionally higher level. His "love affair with the world" now proceeded in high gear at the beginning of and during the practicing period.

Among two scores of infants and toddlers whom we have studied intensively so far during the separation-individuation period, the depressive response—with or without a generally angry mood—has been observed in girls definitely more often than in boys. Their anger toward and disappointment with mother for not having given them the penis could be traced convincingly in several cases. In two girls, in both of whom we have observed the separation-individuation process from the 10th month onward, signs of conflict and manifestations of depressive reaction increased after the period of the normal psychological elation of autonomous mastery.

Let me cite one case in whom the elements of a basic depressive mood, or negative emotional responsiveness, could be observed to become patterned during the vicissitudes of the separation-individuation phase. Ann showed intensification of approach behavior as early as during her 9th and 10th months; this was the result of her mother's relative emotional unavailability and aloofness. This deficit of emotional availability of the "love object," the mother (even though she was physically present), blunted the "zest of life" that is generally so characteristic of the practicing period.

Gradual depletion of "confident expectation" produced great ambivalence and the deflation, without sufficient substitution, of Ann's waning "sense of magic omnipotence." This went parallel with a decrease in self esteem. The usual abandon at the beginning of the practicing period was almost completely canceled out in Ann's case by her increased need for "refueling." She was seen beseeching her mother constantly with her eyes, wordlessly appealing for emotional supplies. The "love affair with the world," which clearly took place during Ann's 14th and 15th months, was observable, nevertheless, but it was of short duration and rather subdued.

For a while, the mother's apparently increased interest, which was in fact based on the desire for her child to become toilet-trained, seemed to have offered, when Ann was 20 to 22 months old, a common ground for *rapprochement* between mother and daughter. However, the toilet training, which was initially successful in this respect, also became enmeshed in conflict. Concomitantly with the mother's narcissistic withdrawal because of her third pregnancy, it too became a battlefield between mother and child.

When sister Susie was born, Ann expressed her ambivalence, and her pregnancy and birth fantasies, in pernicious withholding of feces. The "baby-stool" equation seemed to be unequivocal in her behavior and in her verbal material. At the same time, material about penis envy (she had an older brother), and an intense coveting of gifts, particularly from her father, came to the fore. We heard Ann tell her mother, during a painful defecation, that her daddy had "a little piggy—no, not a piggy, a baby horse in his stomach." She verbalized in primary-process fashion many other fantasies, anxieties, and wishes.

I would like to describe one routine separation situation which showed with particular clarity the splitting of the mother image as a result of Ann's great ambivalence and her need to preserve the good object against her own rage and destructiveness. From about 30 months on, Ann was left, once in a while and routinely, at our Center with her familiar and usually most cherished "play teacher," along with two other playmates (both within one week of her exact age). Whereas the two other children parted easily from their mothers, Ann (even though she herself had difficulty parting from the Center) displayed all the signs of anxious-angry-ambivalent separation problems. She delayed her mother's leaving by pretending to have to go to the toilet and by many other subterfuges. After her mother left, she cried and stamped her feet and then clung to the play teacher, at the same time scolding the very adult to whom she was clinging bodily and saying, "You are bad, you are bad." Anybody who came in by the door of the nursery she ordered *out* with angry determination. I decided to verbalize to Ann that I could see that she did not want anybody but her mother to come into the room. After repeating this a few times, I then left the room and observed from the booth for a while. When I came back and unobtrusively sat down at a far corner of the large playroom, Ann glanced at me out of the corner of her eye, then gently and petulantly muttered, "I want my mommy, I want my mommy." She laid her head on her teacher's shoulder and cried softly. In other words, as a consequence of the interpretation, a longing, libidinal mood had gained the upper hand, enabling Ann to give up for a time the splitting of the good and bad mother images. For quite a while, my entrance or the entrance of any other less familiar female adult became the trigger for Ann's longing for her mother. It was quite instructive to observe, however, that the actual reunion with the mother, which Ann seemed to desire so much, was never an unambivalent, joyous affair. For both partners, it was a visible disappointment; in Ann's case, the disappointment was also freely verbalized.

Our observational data support Bibring's contention (1953) that the depressive response is "a basic affective reaction, very much as anxiety is." In some children during the course of the individuation process, the increased intensity and duration, the habitual and continual character of the depressive response seem to represent this habitual negative affective reaction, which eventually may create a proclivity to depression. I believe that the depletion of "confident expectation" and diminution of self esteem, with concomitant deficit in neutralized aggression, create the libido-economic basis for the depressive mood. It is a relatively great and sudden sense of helplessness, as Bibring (1953) emphasized in his analysis of the causation of depression, which results from depletion of "basic trust" (Erikson, 1950) and from the collapse of the child's belief in his own and, after the oedipal period, in his parents' omnipotence (Mahler, 1961; Jacobson, 1947). On the basis of identification with the "aggressor," the mother (A. Freud, 1936), we then observe a turning of aggression against the self (as the victim of the "aggressor")—all this, even before superego precursors are consolidated into a superego structure.

While the primary autonomous functions of the ego do not seem to be adversely affected during the time span that we have studied so far (4 to 36 months, and some follow-up to the 4th and 5th year), the amount of neutralized libido and deaggressivized aggression necessary for sound secondary narcissistic cathexis of the self, and for maintenance of structural harmony between the ego and the ego ideal, does not seem to be as readily available to these children as to those who have not suffered acute loss of self esteem and depletion of trust in the love objects, during the second 18 months of life. Disturbance in interstructural harmony and interference with the achievement of object constancy are signaled by severe separation anxiety, along with the other signs of increased ambivalence; or else what occurs is a masochistic surrender of the child's own individuality, precocious overidentification, pseudo self-sufficiency, and flattened affective reactivity.[3]

BIBLIOGRAPHY

Benedek, T. (1938), Adaptation to Realty in Early Infancy. Psa. Q., 7:200-215.
——— (1959), Parenthood as a Developmental Phase. J. Am. Psa. Assn., 7:389-417.
Bibring, E. (1953), The Mechanism of Depression. Affective Disorders, ed. P. Greenacre. NY: IUP, 13-48.
Bowlby, J. (1960), Grief and Mourning in Infancy and Early Childhood. Psa. Study Ch., 15:9-52.
Brody, S. & Axelrad, S. (1966), Anxiety and Ego Formation in Infancy (in press).
Coleman, R. W., Kris, E., & Provence, S. (1953), The Study of Variation of Early Parental Attitudes. Psa. Study Ch., 8:20-47.
Erikson, E. H. (1950), Childhood and Society. NY: Norton.

[3] The girl's fantasy of being castrated and its influence on the ensuing ambivalence toward the mother seem to account for the greater frequency of the early and later depressive responsiveness in the female.

Freud, A. (1936), *The Ego and the Mechanisms of Defense.* NY: IUP, 1946.

—— (1965), The Concept of Developmental Lines. *Normality and Pathology in Childhood.* NY: IUP, 62-92.

Freud, S. (1926), Inhibitions, Symptoms and Anxiety. *S.E.,* 20:77-174.

Greenacre, P. (1957), The Childhood of the Artist. *Psa. Study Ch.,* 12:47-72.

Hartmann, H. (1939), *Ego Psychology and the Problem of Adaptation.* NY: IUP, 1958.

—— (1950), Psychoanalysis and Developmental Psychology. *Essays,* 99-112.

—— (1952), The Mutual Influences in the Development of Ego and Id. *Essays,* 155-181.

—— & Kris, E. (1945), The Genetic Approach in Psychoanalysis. *Psa. Study Ch.,* 1:11-30.

—— —— & Loewenstein, R. M. (1946), Comments on the Formation of Psychic Structure. *Psa. Study Ch.,* 2:11-38.

—— —— —— (1949), Notes on the Theory of Aggression. *Psa. Study Ch.,* 3/4:9-36.

Hoffer, W. (1955), *Psychoanalysis.* Baltimore: Williams & Wilkins.

Jacobson, E. (1947), The Effect of Disappointment on Ego and Super-Ego Formation in Normal and Depressive Development. *Psa. Rev.,* 33:129-147.

—— (1957), Normal and Pathological Moods. *Psa. Study Ch.,* 12:83-113.

Khan, M. M. R. (1964), Ego Distortion, Cumulative Trauma, and the Role of Reconstruction in the Analytic Situation. *Int. J. Psa.,* 45:272-279.

Kris, E. (1956), The Recovery of Childhood Memories in Psychoanalysis. *Psa. Study Ch.,* 11:54-88.

Mahler, M. S. (1952), On Child Psychosis and Schizophrenia. *Psa. Study Ch.,* 7:286-305.

—— (1961), On Sadness and Grief in Infancy and Childhood. *Psa. Study Ch.,* 16:332-351.

—— (1963), Thoughts about Development and Individuation. *Psa. Study Ch.,* 18:307-324.

—— (1965), On the Significance of the Normal Separation-Individuation Phase. *Drives, Affects, Behavior,* ed. M. Schur. NY: IUP, 2:161-169.

—— & Furer, M. (1963), Certain Aspects of the Separation-Individuation Phase. *Psa. Q.,* 32:1-14.

—— & Gosliner, B. J. (1955), On Symbiotic Child Psychosis. *Psa. Study Ch.,* 10:195-212.

—— & La Perriere, K. (1965), Mother-Child Interaction during Separation-Individuation. *Psa. Q.,* 34:483-498.

Sandler, J. & Joffe, W. G. (1965), Notes on Childhood Depression. *Int. J. Psa.,* 46:88-96.

Spitz, R. A. (1951), The Psychogenic Diseases in Infancy. *Psa. Study Ch.,* 6:255-275.

—— (1963), Life and the Dialogue. *Counterpoint,* ed. H. S. Gaskill. NY: IUP, 154-176.

Weinberger, J. L. (1964), A Triad of Silence. *Int. J. Psa.,* 45:304-309.

Winnicott, D. W. (1956), On Transference. *Int. J. Psa.,* 37:386-388.

—— (1965), *The Maturational Processes and the Facilitating Environment.* NY: IUP.

Some Adaptive Functions of Aggressive Behavior

ALBERT J. SOLNIT, M.D.

> "The man who first flung a word of abuse at his enemy instead of a spear was the founder of civilization" (Freud, 1893).

Heinz Hartmann's contributions to the theory of aggression have clarified and explained pediatric and nursery school observations that are reported in this paper. In the first part I shall examine the role of aggressive behavior in a group of sick infants. In the second part I shall report on a group of nursery school children whose aggressive behavior has confronted teachers with one of the most difficult and threatening problems in early child education, especially in culturally deprived neighborhoods. Hartmann's viewpoint has enabled us to approach these common problems of pediatrics and education by asking: what is the adaptive function of this aggressive behavior?[1]

His clarification of the role of aggression in development and adaptation (Hartmann, Kris, and Loewenstein, 1949; Hartmann, 1950, 1952, 1953) provided explanatory formulations of pediatric observations of aggressive, irritable behavior in young children recovering from a life-threatening illness. The observations indicated that such behavior served adaptive functions. These adaptive maneuvers are assumed to involve countercathectic processes. The implica-

Some aspects of this paper were originally presented at The Eighth Sophia Mirviss Memorial Lecture in San Francisco on April 11, 1966.

Director, the Child Study Center, Yale University School of Medicine.

Parts of this work were supported by the Children's Bureau, U.S. Department of Health, Education, and Welfare and the Connecticut Department of Health.

[1] In this paper no attempt has been made to refer to the extensive literature on aggression.

tions of these studies are further examined in nursery school observations in which there is an association, perhaps a correlation, between aggressive behavior and learning in the nursery school.

Hartmann's proposal in 1939 sets the background for these studies:

> No instinctual drive in man guarantees adaptation in and of itself, yet on the average the whole ensemble of instinctual drives, ego functions, ego apparatuses, and the principles of regulation, as they meet the average expectable environmental conditions, do have survival value. Of these elements, the function of the ego apparatuses . . . is "objectively" the most purposive. The proposition that the external world "compels" the organism to adapt can be maintained only if one already takes man's survival tendencies and potentialities for granted [p. 46].

In 1950 Hartmann added a further explanation:

> Vis-à-vis an external danger an aggressive response is normal, while sexualization may lead to pathology. If the defensive reaction against danger from within is modeled after the one to danger from without, it is possible that the use of aggressive energy—in this case, more or less neutralized—is more regular than the use of desexualized libido. This might also mean that in the case of defense against an instinctual danger, a place for aggression would more easily be found in the defensive reaction of the ego itself (in countercathexis); while the energy of the libidinal strivings, which could not as easily be disposed of this way, would have to be repressed (or warded off in another way). To come back to an earlier point: I would assume that the use, in countercathexis, of energy withdrawn from the drives is more general if they are of an aggressive than if they are of a libidinal nature. I realize, of course, the sketchy character of this statement, and also that I am simplifying what is actually a highly intricate process. However, this hypothesis, though I would not dare to decide whether or not it will prove to be correct, might be helpful (if integrated with others on the subject that have already been accepted in our analytic thinking) toward explaining the etiological predominance of sexual over aggressive factors in neurosis [p. 134].

Later (1952) this explanatory formulation was extended:

> Internal control is one aspect of the problem of countercathexis, which Freud repeatedly tried to account for, and one fundamental aspect of ego-id differentiation. But the fundamental question, namely, in which way the original transformation of the primary energy distribu-

tion into that representing instinct control takes place, is still in need of further clarification. It might be . . . that those inhibitory apparatus serving postponement of discharge, which are gradually integrated into the ego and which are probably also precursors of later defense mechanisms, play a role in the change of one mode of energy into another one. One may ask what we can say about the nature of the drive energies whose mode is being changed in the process of the formation of countercathexis. Again, it seems hazardous at present to venture a hypothesis with respect to this aspect of the primordial or precursory steps of differentiation. For a later stage, I tried to find an answer in the synthesis of two of Freud's hypotheses: the one, mentioned above, which says that free aggression may be an important factor in the disposition to conflict; and the other, which assumes that the features of defense against instinctual drives are modeled after defense in situations of danger from without. Withdrawal of cathexis would correspond to flight, and countercathexis to fight. On the basis of these two hypotheses we may develop the assumption . . . that the ego's countercathexes against the drives are likely to be mostly fed by some shade of neutralized aggression, which nevertheless still retains some characteristics of the original drives (fight). This assumption may well carry us a few steps further also in the understanding of pathological development. I think that the failure to achieve stable defenses, a failure we see in various forms of child pathology and which is also a crucial problem in schizophrenia, is to a large extent due to an impairment of the capacity to neutralize aggressive energy. This hypothesis also implies a double correlation of stable defense with constant object relations, if what I said before is true: that the development of constant object relations on the one hand facilitates, but on the other also depends on, neutralization [p. 174f.].

Throughout this presentation it should be kept in mind that references to aggressive behavior imply varying degrees of fusion of libidinal and aggressive energies. Although I shall mainly speak of aggressive reactions, at times the reference could just as well be to sexualized aggressive behavior. It also should be kept in mind that Hartmann's questions—whether pathological development follows upon the failure to maintain a state of object constancy—is examined first in the hospitalized children and then from another point of view in deprived nursery school children whose constant objects are characteristically aggressive. In this instance the constant object relates more regularly and expectably through aggressive behavior than through soothing, calming libidinal behavior; and the deficiency of the capacity for involuntary delay of instinctual discharge, the lack of ability to delay, becomes an obstacle to learning in the nursery school.

I

The study of children recovering from postinfectious diarrhea was stimulated by the fatal course of an infant who died despite the successful physiological treatment of postinfectious diarrhea.[2] As it turned out later, we were correct in assuming that the diarrhea had been viral in origin. The infection had yielded to the classical treatment of relieving the gastrointestinal system of unnecessary stress while replacing the fluids and electrolytes that were being lost through the diarrhea and metabolic demands. But the baby died despite the biochemical replacements and despite the detailed attention to the child's physical needs. In reviewing the death of this unfortunate child, we hardly had time to ask the question "why" before four more infants were admitted to our hospital with the same condition; an infectious diarrhea in which the infection had yielded to the treatment but the child's diarrhea continued on its life-threatening course. Our review did not suggest alterations in the physiological-biochemical treatment, which included electrolyte replacements suggested by regular biochemical evaluations, including the determinations of sodium and potassium as well as other electrolytes. The review did suggest that hospitalization was accompanied by a severe deprivation of the expectable mothering, crucial libidinal supplies, that these children, 5 to 12 months of age, would have had at home at a time when the specific awareness of the mother made her a particularly significant object. Since a living-in arrangement for the mother was not feasible at that time, it was decided to arrange for the provision of substitute mothering for the four infants by arranging for a unit system of nursing to replace the functional system. Each of the four children had the same student nurse for each of the shifts, and each nurse had the time to provide total care, essential libidinal nutrients, for the children to whom she was assigned. The student nurses were encouraged to hold, cuddle, talk to, and be very visible to each of the children in this unit, and to offer suitable brightly colored toys in an appropriate manner. The judicious and vigorous physiological and biochemical

[2] San Francisco Hospital, 1948.

care remained the same. Each of these children made a complete recovery, and it was in the observations of their recovery that the role of aggressive activity appeared as a pathway to health.

Each of the infants was washed out, limp, apathetic, and vocally reduced to a whimper by the time they were admitted to our unit in the hospital. The infectious process had subsided, but the diarrhea persisted. In each case, the return of interest in sucking and in food was preceded by evidence of more body tone, kicking and flailing activities of the extremities, and the expression of a vigorous, angry or irritable cry. Soon after the interest in sucking and food appeared, the diarrhea began to abate, and the nurses would tell us that the child was recovering.

The washing-out effects of the diarrhea was heightened to an alarming degree by the child's reactions to the loss of mothering attention, a fusion of libidinal and aggressive investments. These children, 5, 6, 7, and 12 months of age, were being deprived of their relationship to a need-satisfying constant figure who had become specific in many significant and expectable ways as their mother. This vital relationship was seriously compromised by the hospitalization that was otherwise so crucial for the recognition and effective treatment of the life-threatening consequences of their infectious diarrhea. Initially, these children had been placed in isolation in the communicable disease unit and after the infection had been treated they were transferred to our pediatric ward because the continuing diarrhea, anorexia, and lack of responsiveness represented a life-threatening condition. Return to home was too risky because the children still depended on the intravenous replacements and other protective treatment designed to promote the healing and recovery of the insulted body. However, the capacity to use this treatment regime was seriously hampered by the accompanying effects of maternal deprivation. The individualized need-satisfying nursing care enabled each child to retain and benefit from the medical treatment replacements he was given. One could say that the critical libidinal nutriments were required before essential mineral and caloric replacements could be retained and assimilated.

Why did aggressive, irritable behavior appear first rather than behavior signifying satisfaction and contentment as the nurse played with and cared for her patient, as she provided him with libidinal supplies? Probably because the child felt irritable, fussy, and uncomfortable, but also because there was a need-satisfying object. The student nurse actively cared for the child and provided him with meaningful stimulation and with a target for his feelings and behavior. The student nurse coaxed the child to pay attention to her and was the person to whom the child could relate. She enabled the baby to feel loving attention and provided him with a person against whom to discharge those irritable forces that are the forerunners to later aggressive activity. One could say that otherwise such psychic energies remain attached to and directed against the self. In the infant, the bodily self and the body are one and the same until the second half of the first year of life; that is, in the first months of life the child's psychological functioning is represented by the child's physiology.

In these children, recovering from a postinfectious diarrhea, the physical illness compounded by the loss of the mother had a regressive influence on the processes of drive differentiation and the differentiation of the self and the body. This speculation further suggests that with the maternal deprivation caused by the hospitalization, i.e., with the deficit of the need-satisfying object who had begun to become a specific constant object the infant's instinctual drive elements remain relatively undifferentiated and unneutralized. They were contained by the body and directed against the child rather than being discharged in a health-promoting interaction toward the mother and other aspects of the child's environment.

Hartmann's views again point the way to a clearer understanding of these phenomena. He said:

Neutralization of energy is clearly to be postulated from the time at which the ego evolves as a more or less demarcated substructure of personality. And viewed from another angle, we might expect that the formation of constant object relationships presupposes some degree of neutralization. But it is not unlikely that the use of this form of energy starts much earlier and that already the primordial forms of postponement and inhibition of discharge are fed by energy that is partly neutralized. Some countercathectic energy distributions probably arise in infancy. Again, these and related phenomena seem easier to understand if one accepts the hypothesis of gradations of neutralization as just outlined [1952, p. 171f.].

[Earlier, Hartmann (1950) had declared:] To take again an example from the field of "narcissism": it is of paramount importance for our understanding of the various forms of "withdrawal of libido from reality," in terms of their effects on ego functions, to see clearly whether the part of the resulting self-cathexes localized in the ego is still close to sexuality or has undergone a thorough process of neutralization. An increase in the ego's neutralized cathexes is not likely to cause pathological phenomena; but its being swamped by insufficiently neutralized instinctual energy may have this effect (under certain conditions). In this connection, the ego's capacity for neutralization becomes relevant and, in the case of pathological development, the degree to which this capacity has been interfered with as a consequence of ego regression. What I just said about the bearing of neutralization on the outcome of libido withdrawal is equally true where not libidinal but aggressive cathexes are being turned back from the objects upon the self and in part upon the ego [p. 129f.].

These theory-building contributions of Hartmann add another link to our understanding of how these children reacted and recovered. We could say that biochemical replacements were not retained because the capacity of the body to respond to such infusions was impaired by the absence of the love object. The nurse, as a substitute love object, provided libidinal infusions enabling the child to retain the biochemical infusions. I would hypothesize that without the libidinal supplies infused by the nurse there would not be sufficient neutralized energy to permit the body to retain and assimilate the biochemical replacements. To put it crudely, the retention of biochemical replacements represents a degree of physiological inhibition that may be the equivalent of the psychological capacity to postpone or wait. This psychological capacity requires that there be a countercathexis directed against the instinctual drives pressing for immediate discharge. Just as a child who cannot wait cannot develop, a child who cannot retain physiological pressures may suffer from chronic diarrhea amongst other conditions. Hartmann's work suggests and elaborates the concept "that countercathexis widely uses one of those conditions of more or less neutralized aggressive energy . . . which still retain some characteristics of the original drive (fight, in this case). It seems not unlikely that such forms of energy—it is not necessary to assume that all countercathexes operate with the same degree of neutralization—contribute to countercathexis even if the warded-off drive was not of an aggressive nature" (1950, p. 132).

One could say that in these children the demands that the body made upon the central nervous system—the mind—went awry to the point where they ceased to respond to physiological pressures with active behavior. Similarly, under these circumstances, the children ceased to respond to those physical replacements that were represented by the biochemical, antibiotic, and other physiological medical treatments.

The relationship to the aggressive, loving maternal figure is, as studies of the marasmic, institutionalized, affect-deprived child have suggested, a vital and essential protective and nurturing influence on the young child. This formulation is now elaborated to suggest the further consideration that the child's irritable, aggressive reaction may be the first response of recovery, adaptation, in such a situation because the aggressive energies destructively contained within or directed against the self are now redirected to an external object as the influence of the libidinally invested nurse aggressively stimulates and cares for the ailing infant. The nurse as an auxiliary ego aided each child's capacity to neutralize instinctual energies to bring into effect the countercathexes and postponing, inhibiting capabilities so necessary for retaining stimulation and eventually for utilizing gratification as a discharging, soothing experience. In turn, these processes provide the conditions for continued object relatedness and neutralization of instinctual drive energies so necessary for ego development and functioning.

In life-threatening situations, the first defense against the external or internal danger is flight or fight. Since flight is not maturationally available, the capacity to fight or actively to express aggressive outer-directed behavior requires an object from whom care is received— and who as an auxiliary ego facilitates the neutralization of instinctual energies. This need-satisfying constant figure is also necessary as an object toward whom reactive discharge is invited. Thus, the child is encouraged to respond in an object-related manner which also is necessary if the child is to have available the viable alternatives of fight or flight or their infantile equivalents. The apathetic, affectless marasmic child, our postinfectious diarrhea patients, had lost those alternatives; aggression and libido were relatively defused; and aggression was deneutralized and destructively bound within. Thus, the maternal object provides to the helpless infant on the one hand those targets against which libidinal and aggressive drives can be directed, and on the other the neutralizing, countercathectic influences of the auxiliary ego.

The need-satisfying mothering object carries out those ego functions that provide the expectable or required adaptive influences necessary for preservation of life and promotion of growth and development. If one further assumes that one of the essential functions available to the ego is to modify instinctual drive derivatives so that a countercathectic force becomes available for curbing and transforming the demand the body makes on the psychic apparatus, it may be that the absence of this influence, as in maternal deprivation, leads to physiological states of inactivity, including a lack of interest in food and external stimuli. Eventually this course of events results in the marasmic state or a variant of this driveless, defenseless, responseless condition.

In the case of the hospitalized infants with postinfectious diarrhea and their characteristic recovery described above, it is assumed that with the replacement of the need-satisfying object and the biochemical deficits the child regained the capacity to complain, to demonstrate evidence of defensive behavior, and to retain that physiological and psychological tone compatible with adaptive responses.

The study of these infants recovering from diarrhea enables us to elaborate the hypothesis that aggressive behavior may be adaptive, and to suggest that the absence of aggressive behavior may be an alarming evidence of maladaptation. In this study the maladaptation is debilitating physical illness magnified by the persistent loss of the constant love object, an auxiliary ego. With this loss the infant may be said to lose the capacity to form countercathexes necessary for curbing and channeling the instinctual drives and their derivatives. The regressed helpless state of these infants suggests that the relatively unmodified drives are discharged within the body with the aggressive components unbound and destructive. This condition, also characterized by a critical deprivation of stimulating, soothing, and satisfying libidinal experiences, demonstrates the absence of countercathectic influences, which I assume are a precondition for the alloplastic discharge of drive derivatives away from the body through the channels and adaptive devices that include action and socialization.

II

Studies of underprivileged children in nursery schools further illuminate many of Hartmann's theory-building formulations about the role played by aggressive energies and countercathexes in the adaptation of the developing child.

A significant number of culturally deprived, disadvantaged children in nursery schools are identified as learning problems because of their disruptive, hyperactive behavior. They constitute a major teaching problem and a frustrating challenge. It is the thesis of this presentation that their aggressive behavior, directed toward the teacher, also represents an adaptation to the noxious environment in which they have been reared. This noxious environment is characterized by an unpredictable alternation of excessive stimulation, often of a violent nature, and of deprivation of soothing libidinal experiences so necessary for fusing aggressive energies. The deficit of soothing libidinal experiences is frequently also associated with object loss, especially in foster children who have been moved about a great deal.

In the study of infants recovering from diarrhea, I became aware of aggressive behavior as a pathway to the restoration of healthy or adaptive functioning. In the second study I became aware that a disadvantaged child's aggressive behavior in the nursery school often was a communication which remained ineffective and which the child did not perceive as having been understood until the teacher communicated her own counteraggressive responses in a manner compatible with educational aims and processes. The teacher's response indicated her ability to identify with the child, via libidinal interests, but in a counteraggressive way, which responded to the child's implied request for a familiar specificity in their alliance. These children are invariably described as likable and annoying—even infuriating— by the teachers who can work effectively with them.

In this second study involving collaborative work with nursery school educators and aggressively disruptive children from a disadvantaged background, it gradually became clear that there was a turning point in the alliance of teacher and student after which sustained learning was more evident and effective. Before discussing this turning point it will be helpful to describe these children in the nursery school. Characteristically, they are less verbal and less interested in the usual exploitation of blocks, puzzles, and painting than children without this impulse disorder; but they are highly interested in action play outdoors and show a great deal of running, climbing, throwing, scampering, and falling behavior that tends to keep the group excitable and disrupted. Often the outdoor play, in which the children and teachers could tolerate a great deal more of such aggressive activity, becomes the situation in which the teacher's attention to such a child is not so splintered and conflicted by the educational needs of the other children. In the outdoor situation, moreover, the aggressive interaction between child and teacher also was more steady and less eruptive. The child's identification with the curbing, interested teacher and the teacher's positive identification with the darting, energetic child could then take place with a toning down of the difference between the aggressor and the victim, the provocateur and the provoked. However, it should be emphasized that the turning point usually was reached only after teacher and student had been able to communicate, to make contact along lines of aggressive behavior—not punitive or cruel behavior. Such contact was implied when the teacher referred to "the fight" or "the time I blew my top" or the time "I really let her know how I felt" or the time "I decided he was going to shape up."

Frequently a teacher would describe a positive change in such a child's behavior and learning, though the old patterns of eruptive behavior were still evident to a lesser degree, and I would ask, "When did you have your big fight?" The teacher with varying degrees of surprise or discomfort would ask how I knew. Then we would discuss how the stage had been set, how the teacher retained her teaching role but also had permitted herself to be "directed" by the child's insistence on having an aggressive adult partner, and finally how the teacher began to guide and "direct" the child into the role of the student in whom play, the elaborated use of school materials and toys, functioning as a member of his class group, and verbalization and mental activity replaced the direct aggressive behavior. Of course, when a teacher lost control and regressed to punitive cruel behavior in response to the child's provocations, then the full sadomasochistic relationship craved by the child was evoked, and education could not proceed under such conditions of neurotic interaction and gratification. A full repetition of the past and present relationships and experiences at home blocked education.

We should bear in mind that in the nursery school, play and playful behavior are viewed as serving the aims of education. In "The Child's Estate," Eveline Omwake (1963) examines the young child's use of play as a primary learning activity. She states:

. . . play [is] a perceptual-motor experience in a broad sense. Its affective and cognitive elements appear in crude form in the play of the very young child but gradually are refined to become the problem-solving activities and concepts later associated with more formal learning experiences. This refinement is achieved as the animate and inanimate objects in the environment assume a relatively constant meaning for the child and as he becomes able to use the symbolic communication and abstract ideas that are used to influence him and the conduct of those around him [p. 578].

[Omwake further indicates the educator's point of view about the children I am discussing when she says:] There are other children who are socially active but whose participation in group activity is consistently destructive to themselves and the situation because of their hyperaggressive, hostile, or literally disorganizing behavior. . . . such children are, among other things, indicating that they have a learning problem, i.e., an obstacle to their cognitive development that may be initiated by a psychological disturbance or a neurological deficit. Such children lack the controls, tolerance, discrimination, language, knowledge, and ideas necessary to maintain a place in group play [p. 587].

The educator's focus emphasizes ego development, especially the cognitive functions. Our studies indicate that this focus should be broadened to take into account that such children may come to school from a background in which such hyperaggressive and disorganizing behavior represents a way of life in their families. The conditioning that leads to this kind of play and behavior is one that also has served adaptive aims under the slum conditions in which the child has been reared.

The reactions of teachers to such children has constituted an important aspect of this study. Omwake (1963) summarizes the nursery school teacher's role as follows, "It is important to stress in this connection that nursery school teachers are the professional individuals in the lives of children who are most concerned with play as a learning experience. "Educational" supervision is an art which requires that the adult know when and how to make suggestions; *when to take decisive action,* and when to let the child's own experience become the teacher" (p. 582).

I would add that this implies that there is a unique relationship between teacher and student which enables the teacher to influence the child as outlined above and which enables the child to influence the teacher in a pertinent manner. Further, if the child's behavior is experienced by the teacher as primarily aggressive, the question of how the teacher uses her own counteraggressive reactions is crucial in considering how to teach such a child so he can learn from what the school experience offers.

From our studies it has become clear that such a child's aggressive behavior represents not only an embedded, familiar way of discharging tension but also a request for a specific relationship that is a partial repetition of his prior experiences with the significant adult figures in his life. It also has become clear that this request is similar to that of a person in a strange land who does not speak the language of that culture and who says, "If you can prove that you understand me when I speak my language, I will then be able to try and follow you when you speak your language." A brief illustration may be useful in showing how this communication can be arranged.[3]

In the nursery school, Danny, $4\frac{1}{2}$ years old, was provocative, excitable, and easily distractible. Danny was a foster child, one of three foster children in a Negro family that also had three children of their own. Danny's mother had finally been unable to care for him after her boy friend deserted her when Danny was $1\frac{1}{2}$ years old. There was a background of violence and instability. After a series of foster homes Danny was placed at the age of $2\frac{1}{2}$ with the T. family. The mother still saw Danny from time to time, and hoped she would be able to have Danny back with her some day. For the first weeks of nursery school the teacher curbed Danny's behavior by physical intervention, by one-to-one attention, and by guiding him into structured aspects of the nursery school curriculum or by interesting him in the use of materials and toys that tended to organize his behavior, e.g., puzzles. Although these pedagogical maneuvers temporarily curbed Danny's wild behavior, there was no carry-over. After several months it was clear that Danny liked nursery school and that he was developing certain skills and a familiarity with a wide range of materials, toys, games, and perceptual experiences. However, there was no evidence that Danny's own capacity to curb his wild behavior was less dependent on the teacher's concrete behavior and physical presence. The teacher, after several months of nursery school, had to be just as physically involved, just as specifi-

[3] I am grateful to Mrs. Katherine Lustman for making her observations of Danny available to this study.

cally guiding and curbing as she had been in the first days of nursery school. One day Danny disappeared into the kitchen where the juice and crackers were kept. He closed the door as he returned to the nursery school play area. Twenty minutes later, the teacher noticed water seeping from the kitchen to the playroom. The kitchen was flooded because Danny had covered the kitchen sink drain and left the water running. The teacher mopped up angrily and let Danny know she was furious as she did. He asked her tentatively why she was smiling. She angrily told him that she was not smiling, that she was angry, and that he had been naughty. The teacher told him with great feeling that he shouldn't have done what he had or at least he should have told someone about it. At first he seemed frightened by his favorite teacher's anger, but as he found out she wasn't going to hit, hurt or endanger him, he was no longer frightened though he appeared to be quite sober. In the next few weeks he became able to sustain organized play; he became more versatile in his use of toys; and he used language more frequently and effectively.

Danny in his early behavior and development had given evidence of psychic functioning in which the aggressive and libidinal drive fusion had been out of balance. The educational experience gave promise of restoring that balance in a limited way.

It is well understood from psychoanalytic studies and theory that the loving relationship between mother and child ordinarily serves to bind the aggressive impulses. In a healthy mother-child relationship the predominance of a close, affectionate tie helps to channel the instinctual drives, sexual and aggressive, by means of the child's need for this love of the parent and later through an identification of the child with the mother. When the maternal figure is punitive, attacking, and unable to substitute verbal communication for physical activity in guiding, influencing, or restricting the child's behavior, the young child's identification with the parent will reflect this primarily aggressive relationship, but he will still strive for the relationship and not withdraw from it. He can identify with the aggressor (Anna Freud, 1936). In the nursery school, initially such a child relates primarily to the play of other children through attacking, disrupting, and distracting their activities. His own attention span is usually below par compared to other well-developing nursery school children. These children develop significant difficulties in their formal learning activities, becoming early underachievers and school failures.

Although their oedipal aspirations and conflicts are evident in a muted and tentative way, such children are mainly under the dominance of their pregenital, especially anally organized instinctual drive-ego relationships.

Characteristically, on coming into the nursery school these children respond initially to other children with regressive, excitable, darting, attacking behavior. To the teacher they initially present darting-away behavior, inviting the teacher to pursue them in order to control their impulsive behavior. As he provokes, the child is the aggressor. As he is stopped, he becomes the victim. This impulsive, aggressive behavior in each instance requires that there be an exclusive contact with the teacher before such behavior can be contained. This demand for exclusiveness includes not only the block to education but also the pathway to learning. Such one-to-one contact requires that the teacher be firm if she is to control the student since he is unable to control himself. The teacher will have to stay with the child for some time before verbal and visual communications can be substituted for physical contact as the major inhibiting, guiding influence.

Although each of these children has a unique background and development, most of them have in common severely traumatic, disruptive experiences from earliest childhood. The parents have been episodically violent and unable to organize or plan in a consistent manner. In such families the loss of parents, the complexity and confusion of the fluctuating extended family, and the alternating states of marriage and separation or divorce set the stage on which the child attempts to ward off the helpless state of the victim by identifying with the aggressor, the adult caretaker or parent. The child persists in his impulsive, provocative behavior which was set in motion and internalized by this pattern of earlier experiences.

The adaptive functions of such behavior are related to the child's avoidance of the helpless state and to his tendency to prefer specific adults for such aggressive interactional attachments. In the nursery school the child invites the aggressive interest of one teacher and contributes to the establishment of—at times the demand for—a one-to-one relationship. Initially and for quite a long time this demand is a test of whether the child can arouse the determined interest of one teacher, on the child's terms of aggressive exchange. From the observations of how these children latch on to one teacher and how a teacher works with such a disruptive child, it becomes clear that the child by his specificity in relating to one adult implies a repetition of his relationship with other important adults, especially parental figures. This achievement of a degree of object constancy, despite evidence of maternal deprivation and repeated traumatic experiences, suggests that the relative deficiency of a stable libidinal attachment and the relative predominance of an eruptive aggressive tie can lead to the achievement of a disturbed and limited object constancy and an identification with the aggressor.

Certain elements of object constancy—of predictable, specific, personal relationships—can be achieved in a relationship characterized more by aggressive interactions than by libidinal ties. This runs contrary to our usual assumptions that libidinal relationships predominate in the achievement of object constancy. However, observations of nursery school children from underprivileged backgrounds and psychoanalytic observations of young children who have established a sadomasochistic relationship with their parents provide a basis for seriously considering this formulation. The average expectable environment (Hartmann, 1939) for these children is characterized by aggressive interactions, impulsive physical contacts, and counteraggressive responses from this environment which is frequently found in underprivileged families and in many families in whom sadomasochistic relationships are predominant. This does not imply an absence of libidinal strivings, gratifications, and relationships; but it does imply that the repeated and expected discharge of aggressive impulses becomes a way of life that finds support from a type of social reality, such as that of an urban slum neighborhood. In these neighborhoods the economic, social, and educational deficits promote direct action and detract from the advantages of postponement and planning for viable alternatives. In the slum of a modern city what can one hope for, plan for or expect, but the monotony of marginal conditions? Why wait? For what?

With this in mind we can understand that the impulsive child's provocative behavior in the nursery school is an attempt to re-create his own average and expectable environment. The teacher who is selected and responds to this provocative invitation because the child is likable and because her professional skill is challenged has made an unwitting agreement with the child. In this contract in which the teacher is engaged, the student attempts to evoke the familiar aggressive behavior from the adult, and the teacher's response, if she is attuned to the child's communication, will contain counteraggressive elements that provide a partial gratification for the child.

In many family situations there is an eruption of violence by the adult that becomes the final link in a sadomasochistic pattern. The completion of this pattern in which aggression is sexualized presents the greatest danger. In the nursery school, ideally, the aroused, often angry teacher, becomes specific, dependable, and predictable as she conveys her anger in a nonviolent manner. However, the teacher's aggressive behavior may range from visual, to verbal, to physical contact with the child in the attempt to curb him, to tone down his mounting impulsivity, and finally to redirect his activity. Of course, this process is very gradual, involves a great deal of repetition, and usually requires a long time before it reaches the point at which the teacher's influence becomes partly internalized.

For the teacher this process is a physically and psychologically exhausting experience in which establishing the optimal distance between spontaneity, with regression in the service of the ego (Kris, 1950), and deliberate control is constantly challenged by the child's almost irresistible invitation to regress to anal sadomasochistic behavior. Accepting this invitation would, of course, lead to a clearing of the air, which then would promote a vicious repetitive fighting relationship that blocks education.

In essence, the teacher functions as an auxiliary ego containing the child's aggressive impulses, in this way strengthening or making more effective the countercathectic forces available to the child for dealing with his driven behavior. It is as though the auxiliary ego function of the teacher is effective if she relates to the child's aggressive behavior by coming to grips with it—to provide an aid to countercathectic influences. If she relates to the child only with accepting love and tolerance, the working educational alliance may fail to develop. Affectionate interest alone will not promote a new balance between aggression and libido if the child, unable to relate to this unfamiliar mode of communication, continues to provoke until there is an explosion that hinders the educational experience. The teacher meets the child's aggressive invitation by nonexplosive counteraggressive behavior in which libidinal and aggressive components are well fused and under the control of his ego so that education will be able to proceed at some point. Thus a teacher is sufficiently like the object to which the child is accustomed and able to relate, and sufficiently different to promote education rather than the establishment of a sadomasochistic relationship. The teacher permits the aggressive behavior toward her to be expressed, and she will respond in a controlling manner which permits the child to identify with the aggressor. The teacher as the "victim" does not permit a danger situation to develop, nor does she permit a gratification of the child aggressor.

The teacher's aggressivity, which includes her verbal expressions of anger, is constructive when it is controlled, clearly and firmly expressed, and devoid of regressive punitive or physically violent qualities. In this way the teacher serves as a model in which aggressive behavior is modified and becomes expressed under the domination of the ego. Of course, the teacher cannot succeed if her libidinal interests and expectations are not sustained and in the long run pre-eminent. The child who related predominantly through aggressive physical behavior and along the lines of an identification with the aggressor now relates similarly to the teacher. As the aggressor, the teacher may express appropriate aggression and anger, but in a non-violent and well-controlled manner, and with a substratum of tolerable friendliness and affectionate approval. When the child is able to relate to the teacher in this way his aggressive behavior can gradually be curbed and transformed into the mental substitutes for this behavior, associated with the availability of neutralized energy for the ego's functions. Among these functions are the adaptive counter-cathectic processes which permit the ego to stem drive impulses prior to transforming them into the neutralized energies necessary for the attending, observing, thinking activities of education. Under these influences, aggressive and libidinal instinctual drives can fuse in a more balanced and constructive manner.

To restate this formulation, children who relate primarily through aggressive activity have frequently been exposed to a combination of violent physical overstimulation, and the repeated loss of love objects, parental figures. In addition, they have lacked the opportunity to build from a solid foundation of those affectionate ties which enable the young child to explore the world of toys and inanimate objects—transitional objects (Winnicott, 1953)—invested as substitutes by the loved one. These part substitutes serve as essential transitions to the verbal and mental elaboration of the infantile physical experiences.

In these children the earliest physical experiences have often been associated with violence and pain rather than with pleasurable, soothing satisfaction. Despite the inconsistency of violence and loss, of overstimulation and maternal deprivation, a number of these children have achieved the capacity to relate, to differentiate, and to form predictable relationships with adults, i.e., to achieve a form of object constancy. While the latter is disturbed, it is also adaptive to the noxious environment in which they have been reared. Their instinctual "beasts" have not been domesticated, but have been alternately aroused and beaten or aroused and deserted without adequate safety and limits, thus matching the junglelike aspects of their outer life and inner life, adapted to each other in a sadomasochistic link which interferes with social and intellectual development. The noxious environment of the slum discourages the development of the capacity to postpone impulse discharge and to substitute age-appropriate, phase-specific gratifications for inappropriate infantile wishes; the process of planning, guided by such reality considerations as substituting long-term aims for short-term satisfactions, is markedly handicapped in a world of poverty and discrimination in which one can plan only for misery.

It should be emphasized that in the children I have described, children with a certain type of impulse disorder, education can neither treat nor cure them; education can only aim to promote learning despite what appears to be a condition which tends to block the constructive use of educational experiences. The correction of social disorders and of personal psychological impairment cannot depend on education alone; on the other hand, when education can carry out its mission, the efforts to correct social disorders and personal psychological deviations will be helped in an essential manner. Such efforts are often diluted to insignificance because education is also ineffectual.

We should recognize openly that this type of educational work requires a great deal of one-to-one contact. This challenge may not be so overwhelming if we take stock of the many needs that each nursery school has for one extra teacher to be available from time to time. There are other reasons to insist that the ratio of teacher to students be improved, not only in nursery schools but also in the higher grades; just as it is quite evident that the gains of the nursery school experiences will not be maintained if the higher grades fail to provide appropriate educational experiences. But this is still another chapter in the desired close collaboration of psychoanalysis with education, pediatrics, and the professions concerned with social welfare.

Summary

The studies I have reported on examine the destructive and constructive uses of aggression. The observational data are quite diverse, deriving from a group of hospitalized infants with postinfectious diarrhea and from nursery school children with disruptive aggressive behavior. The common elements are the adaptive functions of aggression (1) in the recovery of psychophysiological functioning in the sick infants and (2) in the learning functions of some underprivileged nursery school children. In both situations the remedy depended on sufficient one-to-one attention by individual adults whose skills permitted them to serve as auxiliary egos in quite specific ways. These adults provided libidinal supplies and served to modify the expression of instinctual drive derivatives in these children. In the first group it was the nurse who provided this care. In the second group the teacher became effective in promoting the education of such children.

I am fully aware that education will not cure the social disorders of our time, nor can it cure the child of his individual neurotic or impulse disorder. It is more in the spirit of prevention at all levels that the lessons learned from these studies can be applied. It is appropriate and critical in this period of man's astounding capacity for destruction and construction that we examine the ways in which man's aggressive behavior can be exploited for the benefit of mankind. I can think of no more fitting place for the scientific consideration of such problems as this volume in honor of Heinz Hartmann.

BIBLIOGRAPHY

Freud, A. (1936), *The Ego and the Mechanisms of Defense*. NY: IUP, 1946.
Freud, S. (1893), On the Psychical Mechanism of Hysterical Phenomena. *S.E.*, 3:25-39.
Hartmann, H. (1939), *Ego Psychology and the Problem of Adaptation*. NY: IUP, 1958.
——— (1950), Comments on the Psychoanalytic Theory of the Ego. *Essays*, 113-141.
——— (1952), The Mutual Influences in the Development of Ego and Id. *Essays*, 155-181.
——— (1953), Contribution to the Metapsychology of Schizophrenia. *Essays*, 182-206.
——— Kris, E., & Loewenstein, R. M. (1949), Notes on the Theory of Aggression. *Psa. Study Ch.*, 3/4:9-36.

Kris, E. (1950), On Preconscious Mental Processes. *Psychoanalytic Explorations in Art*. NY: IUP, 303-318.

Omwake, E. B. (1963), The Child's Estate. *Modern Perspectives in Child Development*, ed. A. J. Solnit & S. A. Provence. NY: IUP, 577-594.

Winnicott, D. W. (1953), Transitional Objects and Transitional Phenomena. *Int. J. Psa.*, 34:89-97.

Impulse Control, Structure, and the Synthetic Function

SEYMOUR L. LUSTMAN, M.D., Ph.D.

If one accepts the conceptual utility of a forced, somewhat fiction-alized dichotomy, it is possible to define two extremes of a continuum within psychoanalysis. On the one hand, analysis can be viewed as a theory and method of treatment of neurotic, intrapsychic conflict. On the other, it can be conceptualized as a broad theory of human development and behavior. The former yields a clinical theory of great utility, arising from and relating to data obtained in the classi-cal analytic treatment setting. The latter evolves ever more compli-cated and abstract theoretical propositions which are frequently at a considerable distance from treatment data. This position accepts and seeks other techniques and sources for the collection of data, and accepts and seeks responsibilities beyond the couch.

However, to theorize without a clinical dimension is to run the risk of irrelevance or an empty logician's game. The conceptual, methodological, and substantive richness of a happy merger of the two can be found in the impetus given psychoanalysis by Heinz Hartmann and Anna Freud and their many gifted collaborators and students.

At the present time, the United States has launched a far-reaching and historic program to offset the developmental deficiencies which accompany cultural deprivation. It is to the challenge of this that analysts can respond as a group of experts whose knowledge of children has applicability (A. Freud, 1965a, 1965b; A. Freud and Burlingham, 1943, 1944), but more than that as a group of develop-mental scientists who have available a rare opportunity for research.

From Yale University, Child Study Center and Department of Psychiatry.
I would like to express my appreciation to Dr. A. J. Solnit for his aid and interest.

From my own extensive observations of such children, I tend to divide them into at least three subgroups—a division based on their accessibility to an educational experience. Some children, with relatively intact development, will profit immediately from an enriched nursery school experience. In another group, the deprivations have been so great that the lack of ego development will make it impossible to use our current nursery school techniques. For convenience, I include in this group children with brain damage, autism, severe retardations as well as the extreme of the so-called maternal deprivation syndrome (A. Freud and Burlingham, 1943, 1944; Spitz, 1945, 1946; Provence and Lipton, 1962). By far the largest group falls somewhere in the middle; in these children development has proceeded but with marked distortions and gaps. It may well be, as Anny Katan (1965) suggested, that the latter two groups must be helped long before the preschool program. This will undoubtedly be true of many. However, at the moment we must consider the possibility that preschool programs may be profitable if they can be reconstructed to meet the needs of the middle group.

It is my distinct impression that the key to aiding this group lies in the understanding of the development of impulse control. I have made this the cornerstone of my thesis because it appears to be the fundamental defect which militates against any impact of the nursery school.

The ability to learn, to use a school experience, to relate to a teacher or a toy in a constructive way depends directly on the progressive ability to sit still (at least for short periods), to attend, to resist distraction (from within and without), and to invest in the task. In short, it depends on those aspects of secondary-process function put forth by Freud as delay, detour, binding, control of access to motility, regulation of discharge, and control of attention, all of which we attribute to the ego. It is precisely this developmental defect that makes school so unrewarding for these children and overwhelms their teachers.

It is quite likely that the cardinal issue involved in making this group a high-risk population for subsequent delinquency (Michaels, 1954, 1955; Greenacre, 1945; Rexford, 1963) lies in the relationship between impulse control and superego formation. Experiential and educational enrichment via nursery school programs is doomed to partial success or failure unless we can devise ways of enhancing the development of stable inner controls of impulse. In psychoanalytic terms, these functions must reach a state of secondary autonomy to free the child for optimal further development in the direction of health and adaptation.

This paper presents a preliminary report of one aspect of a series of studies on the normal development of impulse control. The data are drawn from two sources; one, the psychoanalytic treatment of an impulse-ridden, encopretic child; and the other, a quasi-experimental observational research conducted with 24 normal nursery school children.

Since the attempt to correlate material from two such disparate sources is not without hazard, I feel some methodological considerations are in order. Among his many methodological contributions, Heinz Hartmann has repeatedly referred to the relative utility of direct observational methods to supplement the psychoanalytic method as sources for data in psychoanalytic research.

The cautiously stated usefulness of this frame of reference is noted in Hartmann's insistence that any method of data collection implies a selection of data. Both Kris (1950) and Hartmann (1950b) point out that the research advantage of the psychoanalytic method lies primarily in the fact that it makes visible the sphere of conflict. More than that, it permits judgments concerning the relative importance of formative forces which minimize the tendency to what Hartmann (1955) termed "genetic fallacy," i.e., equating directly a function with its genetic past. It is from this frame of reference that he stresses the need for supplemental observational studies, but with a sober word of warning when he states, "A great number of childhood situations of incisive significance for the formation of adult personality have a low probability of direct manifestation" (1950b; see also A. Freud, 1965a).

Thus it would be naïve to assume that such disparate methods, yielding such essentially different levels or orders of data, could possibly address themselves to precisely the same problem. However, as envisioned by Freud, Anna Freud, Hartmann, Kris, Loewenstein, Mahler, Spitz, and many others, there is some gain from the loose complementarity of viewing the same developmental issue from two different vantage points—one, the study of pathology; and the other, the study of normalcy.

I feel that in one sense such an approach follows the historical methodological strategy of the biological sciences with which psychoanalysis has quite crucial formal relationships. From the classic ablation experiment of physiological research, we know that one can frequently best highlight the function of a structure by its absence. This was essentially the method Freud used in developing a nomothetic developmental theory from the psychoanalytic treatment of severe pathology. At present this technique is most clearly demonstrated in the analysis of the blind child to explore the impact of vision on development (Burlingham, 1961, 1964, 1965; Sandler, 1963; Fraiberg and Freedman, 1964).

In its positing a continuity between the "normal" and the "pathological" and in its basic interest in the underlying processes, psychoanalysis parallels the position of modern biology, about which Paul Weiss (1961) made the following lucid statement:

> ... changes in the standard pattern of formative processes lead to deviations from the standard form: deformations end up as "deformities." In this sense deformities become valuable clues to the inner workings of formative processes [p. 134]. Pathology and developmental biology must be reintegrated so that our understanding of "abnormal" will become but an extension of insight into the "normal," while, *pari passu*, the study of the "abnormal" will contribute to the deepening of that very insight [p. 150].

Analysis, too, in its observational studies, has turned to the study of the normal.

Developmental Postulates

At the outset, I would like to state my basic developmental postulate which will be quite familiar to child analysts and developmental researchers. Psychic development, like biological maturation, appears in some ways to have an intrinsic motor force of its own. Anna Freud (1965a) has called this the child's need to complete development. When we treat children analytically we may affect the direction, the content, and the speed, but the force of development, once started, has a momentum of its own. This can frequently be noted in analytic counseling of parents, where by holding a few things constant, the developmental momentum may be counted on to carry an oedipal child into latency rather than into the distorting direction of a prolonged oedipal phase. And yet, from the presence of arrested development (Provence and Lipton, 1962; Spitz, 1945, 1946, 1959), attention is drawn not only to those aspects which impede or possibly stop development, but to those elements which maintain or give fresh impetus to the momentum of development. One such instance would be adolescence in which organic factors contribute to this.

Following a thought of Ernst Kris, my thesis is that phase-specific crises form an integral part of this developmental process. I feel that child analysis is perhaps the richest place from which to view some of the underlying characteristics of this developmental pressure.

For the purposes of this paper, I cannot report the analysis in its entirety and must be quite selective in my choice of data. I do this with awareness of the danger of such selectivity. I am isolating phenomena *in spite* of my awareness of crucial interrelationships with other areas, and deliberately treating them as if they were separable; even separate. However, this too is a classic methodological problem in the study of complex systems. Simplification and the artifact of isolated phenomena are accepted and necessary scientific procedures. I remain acutely aware of the fact that to compartmentalize without destroying relevance is no easy task.

Nevertheless, I shall attempt to do so for the following reasons. First, discretion forces me to this position. Second, my major interest is not in the factors which produced the pathology, but in certain aspects of the development of control. Third, as implied above, I feel some attempt can be made to formulate certain characteristics of developmental forces apart from their immediate content, direction, and rate.

Analytic Data

Although I have seen a number of such children, I shall focus on the analysis of one. The child to be described was an only child and was brought to analysis at the age of five. The presenting complaints were persistent encopresis and sporadic enuresis in a behaviorally uncontrolled child. Tim was given to severe temper tantrums, could tolerate no frustration, would not accept any substitute gratifications, was violently destructive of all property, and could not be controlled by any form of parental prohibition or punishment. At the time he entered analysis, the symptom of fecal soiling had a quite clear-cut object-related aspect, in the sense that it directed severe aggression against the parents. As is usual with such a symptom, aggression and counteraggression characterized the familial interactions. Consider if you will the level of provocation in the following: the boy would shake stool out of his trouser leg, unmindful of whether it fell on the living room rug, and then continue his play, unmindful of whether he stepped in it or not—but always managing to step in it.

Attempts to make Tim responsible for cleansing himself and his clothing in the bathroom resulted in such disastrous smearing that they had to be given up by both parents. Attempts at controlling other aspects of his disruptive behavior by isolating him in his room resulted in his destroying the property of his room, including even the walls and the door. However, such focused violence should not mislead the reader to underestimate the chronic and omnipresent impulsivity which characterized this boy when violence was not a component of his behavior.

Within the treatment, the first few hours of the trial period were so chaotic and uncontrolled that one had to consider the possibility of a psychosis. Tim's motoric behavior was frenetic, and in short order he would succeed in getting all of the equipment of the playroom in one huge mess on the floor, at which point he would lie down in it and blatantly masturbate with both hands, one on his penis and the other rubbing his anus. The chaotic, disorganized quality of the first few hours was quickly modified, but control of impulse remained the central therapeutic and developmental issue. Fortunately, among his ego strengths was a rapidly emerging, unusually gifted intelligence and a great sensitivity to and capability of psychological insight.

In the course of his psychoanalysis, which lasted four years, the boy gained complete control of his intermittent enuresis and his life-long encopresis, and established sufficient control over other aspects of behavior and fantasy to permit him to become an outstanding student and a participating member of his peer group.

I have subsequently had occasion to see Tim during his adolescence. While his therapeutic gains have withstood the upheavals there was a quality of continuing impulsivity about him. One could still sense his chronic level of excitement, his periodic difficulty in restraint, and his propensity for violence. Interestingly enough, he retained a characteristic trait of "impulse buying," which had been noted during his childhood analysis. At that time and during his adolescence Tim would find it absolutely impossible to forestall the immediate spending of his allowance. This was characteristically done under the sway of his uncontrollable attraction for the object he bought; in fact, however, he had no regard for the object, which almost immediately became insignificant. Of greater import, however, was the fact that his wish to see me centered around the emergence of sadistic fantasies and his fear that he would not be able to control his desire to touch and provoke excited sexual fights with girls.

As stated above, within the limitation of this report I shall not analyze the genesis of his pathology. Instead I shall attempt to describe the rather unusual circumstances in which he achieved control in the treatment and concern myself primarily with the process by which this came about.

For a better part of a year, the treatment was contained—with great difficulty—within a playroom. Although the boy was quite verbal and played many different games, his uncontrolled abuse of the room and its contents—with the exception of the person of the analyst—was unabated. There were times when this was quite clearly related to transference issues, but by and large it had a momentum of its own, and was a constant background cacophony to the treatment. Tim continued to be hyperkinetic and frenetic, showing no demonstrable success in his own attempts to control himself either at home or in the treatment.

At one point during the analysis, due to much-needed repair and decoration of the playrooms, I was forced to move the sessions to my own office. The boy was visibly shocked, almost stunned, at the differences in the two rooms. In retrospect, although there had been a great deal of preparatory interpretive work around control, it had had no apparent effect. Yet it obviously prepared the way for the rather dramatic impact of this experience for the boy. At first, the change seemed to produce a sudden and conspicuous awareness of difference and of self. This, in turn, immediately seemed to precipitate the crystallization of an inner conflict which centered about "making a mess" or "controlling himself." Immediately following this, there was an externalization of the inner conflict, in that the boy quickly verbalized his conceptualization that the playroom was a place he would use to make a mess and the office was a place which had to be clean.

For the moment I shall leave aside the obvious transference and countertransference aspects of this situation, other than to state in all honesty that I was internally prepared to protect my property and that I have no doubt that my concern communicated itself to Tim in other than verbal ways. For although I was prepared to control his destructive behavior, it never became necessary for me to verbalize any prohibitions. However, it must be stated that my attitude toward destructiveness was not qualitatively (or consciously quantitatively) different in the playroom.

The playroom was quickly refurbished, and once again became available for our use. However, Tim seemed to have a need to use the dichotomy of the two different localities, and I decided to permit his use of this externalization. He would select, for reasons of his own, where he wanted to go for his hour. In the playroom his behavior continued exactly as before. When he chose the office, his inability to control himself permitted only very short periods at first, and he seemed to depend on the office itself to control him. What was noteworthy in this was his insistence that the office was responsible for his behavior. However, a recognition of his own lack of control was abundantly apparent in his frenzied and sometimes frantic plea to run down to the playroom. It had the urgency with which many children desperately seek a toilet at the very last moment. On all such occasions, he would erupt into his usual, markedly disorganized and disruptive way of "making a mess."

Although I mentioned above that Tim played games in the playroom, none of these ever went to completion, and his play was characterized by restlessness, difficulty in attention and concentration, constant and sometimes violent motoric discharge, and, whether planned or not, varying degrees of inevitable "mess."

On the other hand, when Tim felt controlled by the office, the first somewhat primitive, tentative attempts at controlling himself took the form of efforts just to sit still. He would then try to lie quietly on my couch. Ultimately he turned to play that most attention-demanding of games—chess. In the home and in the playroom, impulse always won the day. In my office, control became ever more pronounced and continuous. This quite dramatic and progressive change continued. With interpretive help, it became clear to him that he was controlling himself and not the office controlling him. It became possible for Tim—of his own choice—to tolerate longer and longer periods within the office, and to resort to fewer uses of

the playroom and motoric discharge. His restlessness and distractibility diminished, and, concomitantly, his ability to concentrate on
chess increased. As a matter of fact, in a relatively brief period of
time, the entire treatment was transfered to the office and, needless
to state, he became a remarkable chess player.

It would seem that the phenomenological aspects of this child's
behavior suggest the following theoretical conceptualization. As long
as the energy involved in his activity was fully instinctualized, this
not only disrupted intellectual development, but seemed to cripple
all ego functions. The strenuous efforts involved in early control give
one quite clearly the impression of such a heavy investment of the
limited attention cathexes available that for the moment all other
functioning was impoverished and blotted out. I am thinking particularly of the almost heroic efforts to just lie still or sit still. With the
sublimation there was an increased amount of energy available to the
ego. This is assumed from the clear emergence of ego functions such
as the availability of attention cathexes for longer periods of time,
organized learning, memory, thought, planning, etc.

Even in this brief vignette, one can see the continued utility of
such concepts as energy, neutralization, and secondary autonomy.
This is particularly so when one considers, phenomenologically, the
effort to sit still in contrast to the subsequently automatized activity
of sitting still for prolonged periods of time. At this point there was
sufficient energy freed in the form of attention to undertake such a
sublimated, high-level activity as chess. Prior to this achievement of
secondary autonomy, it had not been possible to engage in games,
talk, even noise, because of the intense effort at control; or to put it
another way, because all the available pyschic energy was used for
control.

There is one other facet which must be stressed. At no time was I
able to detect any evidence of shame or guilt related to his fecal soiling or to his destructive behavior at home or in the playroom. Nor
were his parents ever able to induce or recognize guilt or shame. It
was only in the office that Tim first began to experience an awareness
of his persistent odor. This was followed by some feeling of embarrassment and subsequently by shame about his symptom, and guilt
about his behavior, e.g., after he had broken a piece of equipment
(Piers and Singer, 1953; Jacobson, 1964).

The sequence of his play went from amorphous, restless, highly distractible, impulsive play, which was frequently the vehicle for making a mess, to highly organized, thoughtful, controlled planning such as is necessary for a good chess game. This became his favorite game and would on occasion take up the entire hour, with Tim sitting quietly for long periods, immersed in the intricate strategy of the game.[1]

As stated above, the sporadic enuresis and the encopresis yielded completely and never reappeared. Symptomatic aspects of Tim's improvement were demonstrable at home and at school, where, as stated before, he became the outstanding student in his grade. His outbursts and restlessness decreased at home, and although he periodically experienced an intense longing for excitement and violence, it became possible for him progressively to disengage himself more and more from the mutually shared and provoked excitement of quarrels with his parents.

One is tempted to conceptualize this split as an externalization of a conflict between the id and the ego—externalized to two different physical localities. In the one his behavior and thinking were dominated by primary-process mechanisms, and in the other, by secondary-process mechanisms. As treatment progressed, his aggression, curiosity, and the need for violent struggle underwent a sublimation into highly competitive scholarship and well-controlled, remarkable chess playing. The "messiness" was not controlled by any markedly prominent reaction formation, as might have been expected. To this day, he remains anything but an excessively clean or neat child. As stated above, the impulsive quality remains and his wish to see me in adolescence was motivated primarily by his fear of the strength of the instincts—which in his fantasy seem to remain fused into a sadistic sexuality.

However, there is more involved here than an id-ego conflict. I have described Tim in the early part of the treatment as a guiltless, impulse-ridden child, who felt no real discomfort either in terms of his symptoms or his behavior. There was no discernible shame or embarrassment in spite of the fact that his malodorous symptom was quite vehemently noted by his peers and his teachers—in addition to his family. I have also described how self awareness, embarrassment, and shame gradually appeared in his analytic material. From these

[1] This is, of course, no description of the complex course of treatment; it is merely a focus on my part on the limited concerns of this paper.

constituents emerged a sense of morality which became firmly established to the extent that such problems as cheating, intellectual dishonesty, fraudulence, or "taking sexual advantage" of a girl were handled by well-developed superego functions. He was now capable of conflicts which were characterized by guilt.

DISCUSSION

Before attempting any further theoretical conceptualizations, I must again apologize for this very limited vignette and for the compartmentalization of this issue of control. It is quite obvious that the particularly unique oedipal problems were crucial factors in both the pathology and its relative improvement. There can also be no doubt that primitive identification processes played a dominant role in the failure of controlling structures to emerge (Ritvo and Solnit, 1960; Lampl-de Groot, 1947; Reich, 1954) and that, in addition to insight, identification processes with the analyst likewise played a part in the subsequent emergence of such structures via internalization during the treatment. As stated above, I am trying to focus on the internalization process.

At present there exist several definitions of internalization. One is that of Hartmann (1947):

> In stressing the importance of such factors as anticipation, postponement of gratification, and the like, in the development of action, we at the same time give action its place in the general trend of human development, the trend toward a growing independence from the immediate impact of present stimuli. . . . This trend can also be described as one toward "internalization." . . . Trial activities with whose help we attempt to master a situation, to solve a problem, are gradually internalized: thinking is, in this sense, trial action with small quantities of psychic energy. . . . Finally, the internalizations that are essential to the formations of the superego lead to a growing independence from the outside world in so far as a process of inner regulation replaces the reactions and actions due to the fear of the social environment (social anxiety) [p. 40f.].

In a recent publication, Hartmann and Loewenstein (1962) have become even more specific: "We speak of *internalization* when regulations that have taken place in interaction with the outside world are replaced by inner regulations" (p. 48).

This statement focuses more on external than internal regulation as a source. Yet the success of this regulation depends on its being an integrant with structures of the ego and with other processes relating more directly to instinctual pressure. In the analysis of Tim, a number of defenses were observed to emerge and the instinctual elements seemed to have undergone a degree of sublimation apparent in his scholarship and well-controlled competitive chess playing. Further, the motoric equipmental factor seems to have drawn its emphatic hyperactivity from the strength of the uncontrolled instinct and, as instinctual energies were neutralized, became less prominent, though it was still present.

Since the central therapeutic and development issue of the analysis was internal control, it may be of value to focus on the process by which a significant part of this was accomplished. In a general way it may be stated that the therapeutic analysis mobilized processes which paralleled normal developmental processes. The structuralization of control (i.e., stable function highly resistant to change via regression or reinstinctualization) can be approached by any number of conceptualizations. I shall limit myself to two possibilities.

What seems to me of greatest interest (and what I shall refer to in the experimental part of this report) is the interlocking, reciprocating, and synergistic relationship between superego and ego components in structuralized delay. We ordinarily view delay and detour as functions of the ego. In particular circumstances, we speak of the superego siding with the ego; e.g., in utilizing the ego's defenses in those areas where a superego conflict characterized by guilt may emerge. The relationship between the mental structures may be described as antagonistic or collaborative under different circumstances.

This collaborative relationship requires more attention, as, for example, in the phenomenon of self observation which may or may not have a superego character.[2] In addressing themselves to this collaboration, Hartmann and Loewenstein (1962) speak of an optimal tension between the two agencies. They suggest that the synergistic alignment may be accomplished by such factors as the possible ego syntonicity of some superego demands, the possibility that an ego aim may borrow the force of a superego demand, or the coordination which results from the synthetic function of the ego (which would be involved in all of the above).

[2] See Loewenstein and Stein in this volume.

Theoretically, the major problem is integration. There is a clear need for central concepts which could take into account the complex synthesis of control as evidenced in the case of Tim. Although I shall not address myself to this issue in this paper, it can be identified as the difficulties inherent in applying the structural hypothesis to supra-structural phenomena.

The elements which have to be accounted for in this instance suggest the possibility of an excessively strong instinctual component about which one can only speculate. There can be no doubt of the significant equipmental factor of a hyperactive motoric type. There were moments when I felt that the activity type of this child might be hyperactive in the pathological sense suggested by Fries and Woolf (1953). There was a marked deficiency of ego structure, which was apparent in little or no internalized delaying or controlling substructures, and a fragmentation of other ego functions such as thinking. His unusual intellectual endowment was disorganized and disrupted by impulse and was not functioning in an adaptive way. In addition, there was the pronounced defect in superego formation.

It is logical to use the synthetic function of the ego as a point of departure. I have no doubt that something like a synthetic function is operative, but I have some difficulty in utilizing it as a concept because it was cast essentially in the form of instinct theory rather than ego theory.

Nunberg (1930) speaks of the tendency to unite, bind, to create, and the need for causality as attributed to a sublimated expression of the instinctual force of Eros.

> That which in the id appears as a tendency to unite and bind together two living beings manifests itself in the ego also as a tendency to unite and to bind—not objects, however, but thoughts, ideas and experiences. Thus, in the need for causality, the binding (synthetic) tendency of Eros reveals itself in a sublimated form in the ego [p. 123f.].

This puts the synthetic function of the ego on a level of abstract instinct theory of Eros that is not synonymous with libido theory.

I think there is a different way of conceptualizing this function, or functions, in ego theory, and it may have been similar considerations which led Hartmann (1947, 1948, 1950a) to speak of "organizing" or "integrative" functions. For example, in 1948 Hartmann said:

Self-regulation can be described on different levels; . . . there is one level of self-regulation which corresponds to what we usually call the synthetic function of the ego, or, as I would prefer to call it, its organizing function [see 1947]: it balances the psychic systems against each other and regulates the relationship between the individual and his environment. . . . The development of this organizing function seems to be part of a general biological trend toward internalization [p. 85f.].

Before further pursuing the conceptualizations of this ego function, I shall first consider some aspects of its development as suggested by the case of Tim.

In reviewing the analysis I am once again intrigued by the central position of the shock experienced by the child in shifting rooms. The crystallization which occurred seemed almost to have created a "shock wave" which set development in motion, gave it a specific direction and channeled the quality of momentum.[3] The speed and spread of development suggest to me the possibility of a "functional differentiation" within psychic-structure building similar to that in embryonic development. That is to say, as soon as a function becomes structuralized, i.e., as soon as it begins to function with a degree of stability, its further differentiation will tend to be modified by its own activity, in addition to other forces. The classic biological example of this is the circulatory system of the vertebrate embryo. As soon as the heart starts to beat, a momentum in development is established via the hydrostatic pressure and its effect on all of the blood vessels.

Further, this functional differentiation of one structure may very well act as an inducer to other structural development. I am led to these conceptualizations by the phenomenon observed in the analysis, particularly the sudden shock with its almost precipitous crystallization of awareness of difference, which in turn seemed of its own momentum to lead in the direction of self observation and awareness of conflict, followed by the externalization and subsequent reinternalization of that conflict. At the same time, it was this awareness and the subsequent externalization and internalization processes involved in the conflict solution which simultaneously seemed to lead in another direction—to embarrassment, shame, and guilt. What I am saying is that the appearance of certain consistent ego functions, e.g., self

---

[3] This is similar to the organizing impact of crises as postulated by E. Kris.

awareness, may have been the crucial "inducer" to superego formation. The content, the character, the rate of structure building were the result of the analytic treatment—but the induction and consequent structuralization seemed to come from an additional source: the internal impellant of development. I should think this occurred in much the same way as it occurs in normal development. Following Freud's proposition (1914), Hartmann and Loewenstein (1962) consider the capacity for self observation a precondition of superego development (see also Jacobson, 1964).

I would now return to the synthetic function and a possible conceptualization of its role in this process. As early as 1900 (Chapter VII) Freud spoke of a *hierarchy* of elements based on the *temporal* sequence of his first model of the psychic apparatus.[4] If we translate this *temporal* sequence from the model to a developmental or genetic sequence, we have the hierarchical structure of the ego. Freud (1901) was more specific on this point when he stated, "It may be surmised that *the architectonic principle of the mental apparatus lies in a stratification—a building up of superimposed agencies*" (p. 147). Such a hierarchy is itself synthetic and may be the *modus operandi* of that function as well as the recipient of its subsequent activity.

In the sense that it preserves relationships, such a hierarchy *itself* brings about a synthetic cohesion and must do so from the beginning of development. It is possible that much of the synthetic function of the ego derives from the hierarchical structure of the ego. Of central import is the time perspective since it is a progressively more mature organism which is involved. By functional differentiation, the synthetic aspects of this laminate structure (with its built-in relationships) may modify its own activity, so that further structure building has a cohesiveness and synthetic quality imposed by the nature of the already existing structure. This hierarchy is further implied in the relationship-preserving aspects of the primary and secondary processes, in which one does not *replace* the other, but *overlays* it.

From this view, a complex mental function such as impulse control is itself a *superordinate structure* involving a hierarchical stratification of drive derivatives, defenses, with both ego and superego elements having by temporal interaction intertwined on ever higher

----

[4] The conceptual utility of the hierarchical concept permeates the work of Rapaport (1960b) and Gill (1964).

levels. The highest level contains a complex stratification of *relation-ships* (not the least of which is man's ability to learn), which function in the control of man when he is at his most mature. Perhaps this can best be conceptualized as *patterning*, which by the temporal sequence and progressive maturational and developmental integrants bring about a synthetic function. This is customarily attributed to the ego elements involved. If disintegration or regression occur, lower levels of organization take over control at lower levels of integration, with behavior and thought more characteristic of primary-process function. This is most readily apparent in the rapid fluctuations found in some psychotic states (Pious, 1961). In many ways, this parallels Waelder's principle of multiple function (1930).

One other conceptualization should be stated. This is the proposition advanced by Loewald (1960, 1962, 1965) in which internalization is also the salient process. His concept of internalization differs from that of Hartmann, in that it is an organizational principle in which defensive processes (such as certain types of identification) may be a way station. Its utility lies primarily in the fact that it permits a unification of the underlying processes of the therapeutic action of psychoanalysis with some of the underlying processes of normal development. Loewald postulates enduring structures of ego and superego, but with subelements which are capable of relative reversibility, i.e., externalization, dissolution, and reinternalization on a markedly different and higher level of organization. The externalization process is quite different from that of projection as a defense, although there are projective elements in it. It is clearly referable to the transference phenomenon.

Loewald's conceptualization of externalization and reinternalization has particular relevance since it is primarily concerned with superego elements, some of which are then capable of moving into the ego core. It would seem to me that the basic process which I am describing in this child is that of externalization and reinternalization, a process which was both aided by and itself aided the addition of a superego component. It is this component which I feel contributed crucially to the construction of a higher level of organization.

On the whole I fear this has been a profound simplification. But I am in agreement with, and take comfort from, John Benjamin's (1959) discerning statement which, although formulated around the problem of predictions, has more general applicability:

Any theoretically minded psychoanalytic or psychiatric clinician who sets himself the task of formulating explicated predictions will be confronted with the problem of how to reconcile the complexity and variability of human functioning, as he sees it convincingly in his everyday work, with the relative simplicity of scientific formulation. For there is no doubt, in my opinion, that scientific progress often requires simplification, and that this holds particularly for work in complex systems. ... The distinction between productive simplification and grossly distorting over-simplification of another sort is of particular pertinence to psychoanalytic investigation [p. 71].

I hope this has not been "grossly distorting simplification of another sort."

Experimental Data

Having become interested in the structural control of impulse, it first seemed that a fruitful hypothesis would have to consider the relationship of equipmental givens. Although individual differences in drive endowment are extremely speculative, such equipmental factors as perceptual sensitivities, activity types, and the like are more readily available to empirical study. The hypothesis suggested was that drive endowment (Alpert et al., 1956) in close interaction with other equipmental factors could produce a quality of impulsivity of such a strong order that it would disrupt and impede ego control and result in impulse disorder. This limited hypothesis does not take into account superego factors, other than to imply that impulse disorder impedes and distorts their development.

My first difficulty occurred around the generalizability of such a hypothesis. Anyone who works with the so-called "culturally deprived" child of nursery school age, or who talks to the teachers who work with this group of children, readily becomes impressed with the prevalance of impulse disorders. It is neither logical nor statistically possible to conceptualize exceptional equipmental givens as a major component, or even a very significant component, in the production of such a high incidence of impulse control problems. Neonatal research seems to indicate that such congenital variations in endowment tend to fall in a normal distribution curve; statistically it is not conceivable that the problem of cultural deprivation has within it such a skewed element of the curve. While the hypothesis may still be of considerable value in individual cases, which under other circumstances can be thought of as hyperreactors, it is quite clear that the internalization process of structuralized regulation and the crucial quality of its underlying object relationships are the most significant factors.

As suggested above, such higher level structuralization which depends on internalizations is most frequently related to superego functions. The center of interest thus became the degree of interrelationship between the ego and the superego relative to impulse control. As stated elesewhere (1962), I agree with Loewald that one way of conceptualizing one aspect of this process is to assume superego elements internalized further into the ego core, where they may become ego characteristics.

METHOD

A sample of 24 normal nursery school children who ranged in age from 3 years and 7 months to 5 years were selected for study. To minimize anxiety as an independent variable, care was taken to plan this experiment so that it occurred within the normal nursery school experience of the child. Our nursery school has a room equipped with a one-way observation mirror. This room is a part of the usual nursery school space for the children, but can be sequestered off for studies such as these.

My assistant functioned as a nursery school teacher and was quite familiar to all the children before they became subjects in the study.[5] The design of the research was simple. The child was taken into this room to "play a game." He was presented with a large assortment of very attractive prizes, ranging from candy to toys, and given the following instructions:

> Here are some prizes. One of these is for you, for the game. We'll put the box here on the table. You will choose one for your own prize at the end of the game. Let's put the tray here while I show you the game.

The tray of prizes was then put in front of the child on his table, where it remained in full sight and easy reach for the duration of the experiment. The instructions continued as follows:

> Now here is a puzzle. And this is the game: you do the puzzle. You decide yourself when you are finished. You don't need to show the

5 I wish to express my appreciation to Mrs. I. Janis for her invaluable assistance.

puzzle to me. All you do is take the pieces *out* of the puzzle and put them all into this box. This is a special box to keep the pieces in. That's all there is to do with the puzzle. You'll be all finished when the pieces are back in the pieces box. And then you'll take your prize. *First* you do the puzzle; *second* you put all the pieces into the box. *Third* you take your prize. Now you tell me what you're supposed to do.

After the child repeated the instructions, the teacher said, "While you play the game, I'll be in this room next door, working on other things."

Each child had two sessions on separate days. The puzzles were selected so that they presented the child with one easy and one impossible task. The nursery school teacher would then, under the guise of other work, leave the room for a neighboring room where she could not see or be seen by the child; however, it was possible for them to communicate verbally. Thus the child was left alone with the task, in a state of relative temptation, with the possibility for cheating. I observed the experiment from the other side of the one-way mirror and dictated very precise notes of each session.

My thinking was that in the attempt to work with the puzzle, i.e., time spent working, concentration, degree of success, etc., one had some vague measure of ego function, at least in its relationship to work performance. It was hoped that the tempting prizes would throw into bold relief the struggle with delay and with detour in order to get to the gratification. It was not assumed that a tray of prizes would trigger off overwhelming instinctual drives, or that any conflict over delay with such temptation would in any way approach that experienced by a child under instinctual pressure. Thus this experimental situation represents no analogy to the kinds of real life situations one sees in treatment. It is simply an attempt to look at what hints one can find in the child's behavior which would indicate how he controls himself in such a temptation situation. In introducing the possibility of cheating, I hoped to include some aspect of morality, or at least to set the stage, so to speak, for cooperation or conflict between the delaying functions, if they were to emerge.

I must again emphasize the relative superficiality of such an observational technique, and the fact that it selects a superficial order of data as compared with the data obtained in psychoanalytic treatment. For one thing, this kind of observational material offers no possibility of reconstructing the genetic components of the behavior one observes;

while, on the other hand, it lends itself far too readily to the risk of overinterpretation. Moreover, such material yields no data on the basis of which predictions could be made. It merely illuminates one moment and what is in the ascendancy at that moment.

As to the data from the sessions, it must be stated that the experimental behavior of the child is not the only or even the most important field of observation. We can actually tell most from observing the *impact* of the experiment as revealed by the subsequent play of the child. One can here, following the psychoanalytic theory of play, assess if an existing conflict has been touched, and if so, the degree and strength of it. Thus the "experiment" is viewed as a *life experience* which will serve as the "seed" for subsequent play and will be related to it perhaps as the day residue affects the dream. It goes a long way toward answering the question: what is in the ascendancy for the individual child?

However, one must remain mindful of Hartmann and Kris's (1945) judicious warning: "details of behavior that in a cross-sectional analysis appear indistinguishable may clearly be differentiated by genetic investigation. Conversely, details of behavior that in cross-sectional analysis appear different and are actually opposite may have grown out of the same root, and may justify the same prognosis" (p. 18f.).

Observational data lend themselves to statistical analysis and to a different order of study. These will be reported in a future publication. Here, I would like to select only a few of these facets which relate to the concerns raised in the psychoanalysis of the encopretic child.

OBSERVATIONS

The individual differences in children were, of course, quite striking. However, by ranking them in terms of expert judgment of impulse control, there emerged a few who were excessively controlled, and a few who were excessively impulsive, with the majority in the middle. For example, the amount of time spent on trying to work the puzzles ranged from 30 seconds to 35 minutes. The majority gave ample evidence of controlling, delaying structures.

The most impulsive child, the purest example of an impulse disorder, was V., who was also the oldest child, aged 5. In both puzzle situations, he had a great deal of difficulty sitting still, was continually talking and asking questions about the prizes, handled the prizes, and was quite explosive and impulsive in manner. He had great difficulty in listening to the instructions and played with the box of prizes all the while. On both occasions, when asked to repeat the instructions, he lunged for a prize instead. It took a great deal of effort to get the instructions clear for him, and when he started work on the puzzles his performance was characterized by a very abrupt and almost spasmodic quality of handling the pieces. It should be noted that there was no neurological deficiency in any of these children.

It was clear that those ego functions subserving learning and work were markedly impaired in that he tried to force the puzzle pieces into place without regard to shape or color, winding up by throwing them back into the box and then trying another piece. His distractibility and poor concentration were apparent in the way his interests vacillated between the puzzle and the prizes. His movements became so fast that he was throwing some of the pieces on the floor, but he would pause long enough to pick them up. After only four minutes of the sort of work described above, he began to play with one of the toys and had to be encouraged to return to the puzzle. After 5½ minutes, he insisted, "I can't play the big puzzle" and threw a piece on the floor in anger. I noted that he was so impulsive in his movements that he kept knocking things over in the room. His puzzle work deteriorated into an aimless trial and error which had so little focus that he even took pieces out that had been correctly placed and tried to replace them with other pieces.

In an earlier session, with a very easy puzzle, V. demonstrated the same impulsivity, difficulty in restraint, distractibility, and wanting to grab prizes; on that occasion he gulped all of his chocolate prize and tried to talk the teacher into giving him toys and more chocolate. On the same occasion, about 15 minutes after completion of his session, while another child was working in the room, V. burst into the room, attempted to grab a Hershey bar, and had to be ejected.

V. had a severe impulse disorder. However, at no time did he show anything that could be related to morality. He seemed very straightforward in grabbing what he wanted, although extremely immature in his inability to delay. All the nursery school teachers agreed that there was in fact no sneakiness or deceitfulness in V.'s behavior. I would tentatively describe V. as having an impulse disorder, as a child in whom superego conflicts were not central, and in whom there was crucial delay in the emergence of superego structures. He would be considered the most immature because of the total absence of such phase-specific conflicts.

I would now like to contrast V.'s behavior with the performance of another child, S., aged 4 years 11 months. S. was a very controlled child, who sat quietly listening to the instructions, looked at the prizes but did not touch any of them, and almost immediately indicated some problem or conflict related to the situation. He did this by announcing that he did not want to eat any candy because it would give him cavities. This was not an infrequent comment from this group of middle-class children, and we assumed this was a parental prohibition which was usually prefaced with "My Mommy" or "My Daddy says. . . ."

S. worked the easy puzzle quite promptly and seemed a model of the secondary process in his work. That this was not yet structuralized in the sense of stable function became apparent when he was given the impossible puzzle. After a very great effort and increasing signs of frustration in the form of agitation, S. stole a piece of the puzzle by slipping it into his pocket, and then became calm.

Of all the children in the study, S. was the only child who stole a piece of the puzzle. His performance showed great conflict, enormous efforts of restraint in terms of the prizes, repeated references to parental prohibitions in his chatter while at work, and an attempt to use the nursery school teacher as a controlling force. He did not take a prize without completing the puzzle, but displacing a conflict, he stole a piece of the puzzle. There are obviously many more overdetermined aspects to this behavior, but to attempt to unravel these from this cross-sectional moment of behavior would be pure speculation.

It is interesting to note his usual nursery school behavior. The nursery school teachers described him as the child who seemed to have the greatest concerns about morality, frequently playing the policeman: he was the most vociferous advocate of following all the adult rules and regulations; yet he was also the sly instigator of getting other children into trouble. He was repeatedly referred to as the "conscience of the group," who was always telling who had done the wrong things. He also wanted to "help the law to stop bad boys," saying in addition, "I want the law to be nice and clean and straight." For S., issues of prohibition and morality had moved to dominance and assumed the proportions of a developmental crisis. Thus by virtue of the problem being dealt with developmentally, S. was much more mature than V. The primacy of the conflict was apparent in the fact that for weeks after this experience this child brought puzzles and prizes with him to school and "played the game" with other children in a classic passive to active attempt at mastery. He was the only child in this group who demonstrated such a need to master anxiety in this fashion.

A word of caution about predicting S.'s ultimate resolution and subsequent honesty. It is not possible—to do so would be to commit Hartmann's "genetic fallacy" and to ignore the possibility of reaction formation and change of function. Yet the intensity of the conflict seems to be one level of approach.

Another child, J., aged 4 years 5 months, did the following: after the departure of the teacher, he worked for about 3 minutes in a thrusting, spasmodic fashion, grabbing a piece, thrusting it in one direction, changing his mind and thrusting it in another direction, etc. After 3 minutes, he dumped all the pieces into the pieces box, informed the teacher he had finished with the whole thing, and while waiting for her to come into the room, leaned over and happily hugged the entire box of prizes.

This boy was given three trials with the impossible puzzle and with each behaved in the same way. He would start with a burst of activity, making no attempt to put the pieces in properly, just moving them about while looking at the prizes. He would then dump all the pieces, announce that he was finished, and pick up a prize.

Another child, A., aged 4 years 8 months, performed as follows: while listening to the instructions, he explored all the prizes in an attempt to choose what he wanted when he finished. After the teacher departed, he picked up one piece, put it in the puzzle form, shook his head as if to say it was impossible and put it back in the box, announcing in a loud voice that he was all through and he was going to leave. He picked up a prize and was halfway out the door, at which point he paused and then returned, apparently needing the teacher's permission to leave. The entire performance took less than 30 seconds. In discussion with the teacher, he insisted that he had completely worked the puzzle; in spite of her determined efforts, he insisted with equal determination to the very end that he had done the work properly.

DISCUSSION

This type of observational research can only be thought of as demon-strating one kind of cross-sectional situational behavior of a child. When placed in a situation which demanded work, but which also demanded the ability to delay gratification, and which presented the opportunity for cheating, their performance seemed to show the fol-lowing characteristics: with the exception of the impulsive children, all others were capable of restraining the impulse to take a prize. This varied from touching the prizes but continuing to work, to just occa-sionally looking at the prizes and continuing to work, to completely ignoring the prizes. The children seemed to be in different stages of development, the differences referable to whether the regulation was internal or external. This was particularly evident in those children who in their spontaneous verbalizations reported parental prohibitions, for example, the comment about eating candy and cavities (a common one), and who used the teacher's voice or presence in the other room as a restraining factor. For example, one child would look at the prizes and then walk over and look at the teacher through the door of the room in which she was sitting, and then return and go to work on the puzzle. This use of the teacher seems clearly to relate to the external regulation-internalization process.

Although the prizes must have presented greatly differing degrees of attractiveness to the children, that they were tempted was apparent. For the purposes of this paper, what impressed me was the significant degree of already existing moral prohibitions in these children. By that I do not mean to imply the existence of developed superego functions. I am referring only to the fact that aspects of morality which are later handled by the superego were already apparent, although they still function primarily as external regulations. I do not think that the use of parental prohibition or of the presence of the teacher is a conscious aid in controlling themselves. I think rather that it reflects a stage of identification, i.e., the attempt to be like the parental figure and do what the parental figure wants by accepting prohibitions (or by dis-placing them to other adults). Only when internalization (in Hart-mann's sense) is complete can one speak of superego. In this regard, it is interesting to note that all of the children who quoted their par-ents' prohibitions about eating candy in terms of cavities not only were quite clearly using this as a way of preventing themselves from taking the candy, but all ate candy in the presence of the teacher immediately after the puzzles. This is a classic example of the *use* of external control in delay. It is object-related, although the object is absent, and is a stage on the way to internalized control.

Some of the children were not capable of exercising sufficient control to address themselves to the task, but their attempts to do so seemed to lack any component of morality. Other children showed clear evidence of cheating and stealing. In still other children there was what I would call a precocious closure of prohibition, which led them to appear frozen, immobilized, even paralyzed. One such child just sat for many minutes staring stubbornly at a wall until I interrupted the experiment.

In a very general way it seems to me that in the majority of this middle-class sample of essentially oedipal children, restraint of impulse had an attendant quality of still external regulation and morality. I would postulate that the same reciprocating developmental processes which form ego and superego structures are in operation here and in the psychoanalysis reported. It is apparent that there is not yet a definite superego, but it is also clear that we are observing some aspects of the developmental process which sets the stage for subsequent superego crystallization. In some few children, this phase-specific developmental task was absent, and they presented the most impulsive-appearing behavior of the group. In a way analogous to the shock experienced by Tim, it is possible that the oedipal crisis functions as such a shock or crisis, impelling awareness, forcing crystallization, and giving momentum to both ego and superego development. Viewed economically, shock as a special instance of crisis mobilizes intra-psychic tensions of such magnitude that it imposes the need for resolution. Such crises may act as organizers around which functions are patterned (Kris).

Considering the disorganized family of the culturally deprived, the distortions and inability to enter into or to resolve oedipal conflicts may account for the failure of the superego development as an integrant in impulse control. It may be that the disorganization of the family does not permit the oedipal phase to reach the crisis intensity necessary to induce further ego and superego development. I here assume that under certain conditions crises (phase-specific as well as others) can act as inducers for further development. This occurs via the internalization, externalization, and reinternalization processes. In other circumstances crises can lead to pathology.

I would like to return for a moment to the issue of prediction of superego function from behavior such as this. As stated above, one cannot predict superego function from this kind of behavior because of the grave risk of a "genetic fallacy." As Hartmann defined it, essentially this is a striving for an oversimplified one-to-one relationship which ignores the psychoanalytically described phenomena of displacement, reaction formation, and change of function. In addition, development simply does not progress in this kind of mathematical linear relationship with simple accretions of bits of more mature behavior. Rather it is characterized by a discontinuity; e.g., there may be cheating which, with the resolution of the oedipal conflict, may rather precipitously undergo such a change of function as to appear externally as control on a completely different level of organization.

Summary

I have presented material from the psychoanalytic treatment of a child with an impulse disorder, and an observational research from a cross-sectional sample of middle-class children in the oedipal phase. The data obtained by the two techniques are strikingly different, yet seemed to illuminate some aspects of the same behavior. To maximize the utility of the cross-sectional research, it will be necessary to extend the groups to include a clearer genetic aspect by studying the phallic and the latency child. However, it seems to me that they both demonstrate that regulation of impulse is developmentally related to internalization processes and that this internalization builds restraining structures which are a stratification of both ego and superego components.

This is not to say that ego and superego are the same. On the contrary, it is of the greatest utility to maintain these sets of functions as very different. What it does suggest is shared boundaries, in that certain ego elements may induce the development of superego elements and can exist side by side, sharing common developmental roots and processes. Perhaps they can be conceived of as being separated by a permeable boundary which permits an optimal tension between them, as proposed by Hartmann and Loewenstein (1962). It is quite plausible that this boundary becomes noticeable only when it is the locus of the increased tension of conflict. Hartmann (1960) suggests that the transvaluation of values may be related to the integration of ego and superego aims. I do not feel that this is contradicted by a conceptualization which suggests that the hierarchy itself may prove a significant aspect of the synthesis rather than merely a product of it. Once the superego is established, drive restraint or control of impulse can no longer, or rarely, be assigned to the ego alone. I would feel that such structuralized delay is the result of very complex superordinate structures in which drive derivatives, ego defenses, and superego components are all integrates of such stratification as is implied in stable structure. Moreover, such integrates are altered by the whole of patterning and represent an "internal parallelogram of forces" (Waelder, 1960) that defies isolation. Psychoanalytic theorists must posit contextual units that make possible adjudication of variations in such complex behavior. This must occur on the level of concept formation. I suggest that it is more fruitful to define the synthetic functions of the ego in terms of levels of organization and of hierarchies rather than in terms of Freud's most abstract level of instinct theory.

Implications for Cultural Deprivation

Although American educators have sporadically expressed concerns about personality development, the educative process has focused almost exclusively on content. Teachers have become specialized according to grade and subjects within grade. As a result, cognitive development has been the major accomplishment, and perhaps appropriately so, since other aspects of development were presumed to be largely determined by, and the responsibility of, the home.

The plight of the culturally deprived child presents a complex challenge, made all the more perplexing because the problem abides by no middle-class standards. This population is deprived in a cognitive sense, but more important, it is deprived in almost all areas of personality development.

Because of its crucial central position, education must broaden its definition and scope to accept responsibility for more than content. The attempt must be made to aid educators to address themselves quite specifically to personality. This must not be done to the exclusion of concerns about cognitive development, but the primary emphasis must be placed on those aspects of development which lead to dropouts, delinquency, and psychopathology.

Although cognitive development and other aspects of personality development are related, there is no compelling evidence that the former has any significant correlation with the latter. Training in one cannot be expected to have a generalizing effect on the other—although many psychologists make this assumption. Going to my major concern, for an example, studies in the cognitive development of moral values and judgments (Piaget, 1932) have no direct correlation with moral behavior. As a matter of fact, there is an imposing body of clinical evidence which demonstrates convincingly that knowledge of rules and cognitive moral judgments in no way precludes psychopathy.

The ideal tools and techniques are not yet at hand. One way in which psychoanalysis can be of service to the educator is to bring its knowledge of normal and pathological development to bear on systematic research in the area. As I have suggested above, the point of departure must be in the area of impulse control and behavioral morality as a function of internalized psychic structure.

One must experiment with new ways of constructing the educational experience to mobilize and capitalize on the internal impetus to development. If one retains as his anchor the central relevant issues of dropouts, delinquency, and psychopathology, he is led to those aspects of development that are mediated through object-related experience. Predicated upon object constancy, this process produces and depends on periodic increases in intrapsychic tension which reaches an unbearable intensity, and thus imposes on the child the need for resolution. Via internalization processes, internal structures are built (which are characteristic for the specific object relationship) and enable the child to delay and control his impulsivity. These are crucial precursors of the moral development we attribute to the superego. Object constancy and developmental crises are, I suggest, the core prerequisites.

One of the most common characteristics of the culturally deprived population is the tenuous quality of its familial arrangements. It is clearly evident that the disorganized family offers no basis upon which to form the kind of object ties which would lead to the internal structure-building process suggested above.

Accordingly, it may be fruitful to think of reconstructing preschool and primary school education to overcome the principal object deprivation and to capitalize on the child's hunger for objects. This calls for a primary emphasis on object ties with the teacher rather than the existing emphasis on cognitive development.

Practically, this may call for a female teacher who stays with a small group of children from preschool through the primary grades—teaching *all* content herself. It may call for experimentation with periodic introduction of a male teacher, who shares specific functions. Thus the *same* teacher will be intimately involved with the child for perhaps eight or more years.

This is in sharp contrast to our current cognitively based educational patterns with their aforementioned specialization. At present, teachers are changed regularly so that the child is expected to relate to a large number of primary teachers and an infinite number of subject specialists.

I am suggesting that this is successful with children who have the usual family ties, and that it will be unsuccessful and conceivably harmful for those children who, by virtue of cultural deprivation, have been unable to invest in the few inconstant adults available.

This shift from emphasis on enhancing the child's cognitive development to an emphasis which maximizes object constancy may be viewed by some educators as regressive. To my mind it places first things first. Within this framework, a systematic research effort must be made to delineate the techniques by which the object tie to the teacher can be most rapidly and firmly enhanced. One possibility is artificially induced crises and rescue situations. One must investigate the many developmental processes with which psychoanalysis deals. For example, identification with the aggressor may be explored. By this I do not imply construction of a cruel environment, but rather a prolonged, consistent firmness, over many years, relating to the same adult.

Perhaps the basic scientific issue is that of the "critical phase" concept. In point of fact, this is by no means a settled issue, and it may be this very population that can muster evidence for or against the hypothesis.

However, if it is true that maximal development depends on emergence or structuralization at a critical period—then nursery school is already far too late and an insufficient device. If, on the other hand, some of these children have a sufficient degree of development so that this is not the overriding factor, then it may be possible to construct an environment (focused on object constancy and fostering intensity of relationship) which can mobilize developmental needs and processes in the child.

While focusing primarily on education, I am in no sense suggesting exclusion of the existing families, however disorganized. Quite the contrary is indicated—with vigorous research on techniques to aid the adults. What I mean is a primary focus on a maximal use of the teacher as a crucial object in the child's life. With the ability to make object ties as tenuous as they are in this group of children, frequent change of teacher will not enhance the possibility of intense relatedness, which psychoanalytic experience insists is the single most crucial variable in this problem.

BIBLIOGRAPHY

Alpert, A., Neubauer, P. B., & Weil, A. P. (1956), Unusual Variations in Drive Endowment. *Psa. Study Ch.*, 11:125-163.

Benjamin, J. D. (1959), Prediction and Psychopathologic Theory. In: *Dynamic Psychopathology in Childhood*, ed. L. Jessner & E. Pavenstedt. NY: Grune & Stratton, 6-77.

Beres, D. (1958), Vicissitudes of Superego Functions and Superego Precursors in Childhood. *Psa. Study Ch.*, 13:324-351.

Burlingham, D. T. (1961), Some Notes on the Development of the Blind. *Psa. Study Ch.*, 16:121-145.

—— (1964), Hearing and Its Role in the Development of the Blind. *Psa. Study Ch.*, 19:95-112.

—— (1965), Some Problems of Ego Development in Blind Children. *Psa. Study Ch.*, 20:194-208.

Fraiberg, S. & Freedman, D. A. (1964), Studies in the Ego Development of the Congenitally Blind Child. *Psa. Study Ch.*, 19:113-169.

Freud, A. (1965a), *Normality and Pathology in Childhood*. NY: IUP.

—— (1965b), Comments in J. Goldstein and J. Katz: *The Family and the Law*. NY: Free Press, 261-264; 959-962; 1051-1053.

—— & Burlingham, D. (1943), *War and Children*, NY: IUP.

—— —— (1944), *Infants Without Families*. NY: IUP.

Freud, S. (1900), The Interpretation of Dreams. *S.E.*, 4 & 5.

—— (1901), The Psychopathology of Everyday Life. *S.E.*, 6.

—— (1914), On Narcissism. *S.E.*, 14:67-102.

—— (1920), Beyond the Pleasure Principle. *S.E.*, 18:3-64.

—— (1937), Analysis Terminable and Interminable. *S.E.*, 23:209-253.

Fries, M. E. & Woolf, P. J. (1953), Some Hypotheses on the Role of the Congenital Activity Type in Personality Development. *Psa. Study Ch.*, 8:48-62.

Gill, M. M. (1964), *Topography and Systems in Psychoanalytic Theory. Psychol. Issues*, 10.

Greenacre, P. (1945), Conscience in the Psychopath. *Am. J. Orthopsychiat.*, 15:495-509.

Hammermann, S. (1965), Conceptions of Superego Development. *J. Am. Psa. Assn.*, 13:320-355.

Hartmann, H. (1939), *Ego Psychology and the Problem of Adaptation*. NY: IUP, 1958.

—— (1947), On Rational and Irrational Action. *Essays*, 37-68.

—— (1948), Comments on the Psychoanalytic Theory of Instinctual Drives. *Essays*, 69-89.

—— (1950a), Comments on the Psychoanalytic Theory of the Ego. *Essays*, 113-141.

—— (1950b), Psychoanalysis and Developmental Psychology. *Essays*, 99-112.

—— (1955), Notes on the Theory of Sublimation. *Essays*, 215-241.

—— (1960), *Psychoanalysis and Moral Values*. NY: IUP.

—— & Kris, E. (1945), The Genetic Approach in Psychoanalysis. *Psa. Study Ch.*, 1:11-30.

—— —— & Loewenstein, R. M. (1946), Comments on the Formation of Psychic Structure. *Psa. Study Ch.*, 2:11-38.

—— —— —— (1949), Notes on the Theory of Aggression. *Psa. Study Ch.*, 3/4:9-36.

—— & Loewenstein, R. M. (1962), Notes on the Superego. *Psa. Study Ch.*, 17:42-81.

Jacobson, E. (1964), *The Self and the Object World*. NY: IUP.

Katan, A. (1965), Some Nursery School Observations and Their Implications. Read at the Hillcrest Anniversary Program, Washington, D.C.

Kramer, P. (1958), Note on One of the Preoedipal Roots of the Superego. *J. Am. Psa. Assn.*, 6:38-46.

Kris, E. (1950), Notes on the Development and on Some Current Problems of Psychoanalytic Child Psychology. *Psa. Study Ch.*, 5:24-46.

—— (1956), The Recovery of Childhood Memories in Psychoanalysis. *Psa. Study Ch.*, 11:54-88.

—— (1962), Decline and Recovery in the Life of a Three-year-old. *Psa. Study Ch.*, 17:175-215.

Lampl-de Groot, J. (1947), On the Development of Ego and Superego. In: *The Development of the Mind*. NY: IUP, 1965, 114-125.

Loewald, H. W. (1960), On the Therapeutic Action of Psychoanalysis. *Int. J. Psa.*, 41:16-33.

—— (1962), Internalization, Separation, Mourning, and the Superego. *Psa. Q.*, 31:483-504.

—— (1965), On Internalization. Read before the Western New England Psychoanalytic Society.

Lustman, S. L. (1962), Defense, Symptom, and Character. *Psa. Study Ch.*, 17:216-244.

Michaels, J. J. (1954), Delinquency and Control. *Am. J. Orthopsychiat.*, 24:258-265.

—— (1955), *Disorders of Character*. Springfield, Ill.: Thomas.

Nunberg, H. (1930), The Synthetic Function of the Ego. *Practice and Theory of Psychoanalysis*. NY: IUP, 1955, 120-136.

Piaget, J. (1932), *The Moral Judgment of the Child*. Glencoe, Ill.: Free Press, 1948.

Piers, G. & Singer, M. (1953), *Shame and Guilt*. Springfield, Ill.: Thomas.

Pious, W. L. (1961), A Hypothesis about the Nature of Schizophrenic Behavior. *Psychotherapy of the Psychoses*, ed. A. Burton. NY: Basic Books, 43-68.

Provence, S. & Lipton, R. C. (1962), *Infants in Institutions*. NY: IUP.

Rapaport, D. (1960a), Psychoanalysis as a Developmental Psychology. *Perspectives in Psychological Theory*, ed. B. Kaplan & S. Wapner. NY: IUP, 209-255.

—— (1960b), *The Structure of Psychoanalytic Theory*. *Psychol. Issues*, 6.

Reich, A. (1954), Early Identifications as Archaic Elements in the Superego. *J. Am. Psa. Assn.*, 2:218-238.

Rexford, E. N. (1963), A Developmental Concept of the Problems of Acting Out. *J. Am. Acad. Ch. Psychiat.*, 2:6-16.

Ritvo, S. & Solnit, A. J. (1958), Influences of Early Mother-Child Interaction on Identification Processes. *Psa. Study Ch.*, 13:64-85.

—— —— (1960), The Relationship of Early Ego Identifications to Superego Formation. *Int. J. Psa.*, 41:295-300.

Sandler, A.-M. (1963), Aspects of Passivity and Ego Development in the Blind Infant. *Psa. Study Ch.*, 18:343-360.

Spitz, R. A. (1945), Hospitalism. *Psa. Study Ch.,* 1:53-74.
—— (1946), Hospitalism: A Follow-up Report. *Psa. Study Ch.,* 2:113-117.
—— (1959), *A Genetic Field Theory of Ego Formation.* NY: IUP.
—— (1965), *The First Year of Life.* NY: IUP.
Waelder, R. (1930). The Principle of Multiple Function. *Psa. Q.,* 5:45-62, 1936.
—— (1960), *Basic Theory of Psychoanalysis.* NY: IUP.
Weiss, P. (1961), Deformities as Cues to Understanding Development of Form. *Perspectives in Biology and Medicine,* 4:133-151.

The Normal Personality in Our Culture and the Nobel Prize Complex

HELEN H. TARTAKOFF, M.D.

If psychoanalysis is to fulfill its potential for becoming a general psychology of human motivation and behavior, this contingency will be due in large measure to the contributions of Heinz Hartmann. His paper *Ego Psychology and the Problem of Adaptation* (1939a), containing the germinal ideas for many of his later writings, is replete with challenges to the clinician as well as the theoretician and researcher. The following passage served as a stimulus for this paper:

> Adaption obviously involves both processes connected with conflict situations, and processes which pertain to the conflict-free sphere. . . . It would be . . . an enticing task to trace, in a concrete case, the interaction of those processes which assimilate the external and the internal stimuli and lead to average adaptiveness and normal adaptation, with those mechanisms which we know better and consider to be causes of developmental disturbances. It would be equally interesting to trace such interactions in many problems of character development, in that aspect of the personality which we call "ego interests" . . . For instance, the influence of special talents on the distribution of narcissistic, object-libidinal and aggressive energies, their role in facilitating certain forms of conflict solution and in determining the choice of preferred defenses, are clinically important but insufficiently studied problems [p. 10].

Although this paper touches tangentially on sociological issues, its virtual focus will be a psychoanalytic consideration of narcissism, ego interests and adaptation, with special reference to the gifted.

Source of the Psychoanalytic Data

The therapeutic scope of psychoanalysis has gradually broadened in the past 50 years to include conditions outside the circumscribed sphere of the "classical neuroses" and the closely related hysterical, compulsive, and phobic personality types. A substantial body of psychoanalytic literature documents this trend (Stone, 1954; et al.) as well as the modifications or, better, expansions of technique suitable for other conditions (Loewenstein, 1951; Kris, 1951; Hartmann, 1951; Glover, 1955; et al.). Among the new "types" encountered which have widened "the data of psychoanalytic observation,"[1] the so-called normal character has received considerably less attention than the more pathological states (Tartakoff, 1958). The fact that "normality" may take diverse forms not only from one culture to another but within the framework of a single culture greatly complicates the task of attempting to make a differential diagnosis between the normal and the neurotic personality.[2] So, too, do the multiple criteria which must be applied in any attempt to assess mental health[3] (Jones, 1931; Glover, 1932; Hartmann, 1939b).

Applicants for psychoanalytic training in Europe and England provided the initial impetus for the study of the "normal personality." During the Nazi regime and as a result of the subsequent sociopolitical upheaval precipitated by World War II, the center of psychoanalysis shifted to the United States. The widespread effects of this dislocation and of the climate of the American setting on the character of psychoanalytic training and practice have been discussed at length by Knight (1953), Lewin and Ross (1960), and Greenacre (1961). As a result of its infiltration into current thinking as well as other less subtle influences, during the 1940s psychoanalysis, as a body of knowledge and a method of treatment, grew in popularity and gained a measure of prestige in this country which it had not previously enjoyed here or abroad.[4] With its wider acceptance, this discipline had an impact on a number of related fields and on education in general. This trend was soon reflected in a marked increase in the number of applicants for psychoanalytic treatment, among them prospective patients from

[1] In their paper on "Culture and Personality" (1951), Hartmann, Kris, and Loewenstein discuss this subject at length in terms of the relation of psychoanalysis to the social sciences.

[2] No systematic attempt to do so will be made in this paper.

[3] See Marie Jahoda's monograph (1958) prepared for the Joint Commission on Mental Illness and Health for a comprehensive discussion of the problems involved and the criteria she recommends for assessing mental health.

[4] Talcott Parsons' publication (1964) *Social Structure and Personality* contains an illuminating sociological analysis of the reception of psychoanalysis in the United States.

other professions, from the academic sphere, and from the field of business. For the most part, these analysands had not experienced the crippling effects of the acute or chronic symptomatic neuroses; neither did the majority of them suffer from severe disorders of mental functioning bordering on the psychoses. Among them were a number of recognizable character types (Fenichel, 1945) and only if one takes the view that no one is normal since all men are subject to conflict and harbor neurotic mechanisms (Michaels, 1959), could these patients be categorized as neurotic.[5]

Some of the applicants from the fields of social work, psychology, sociology, and anthropology sought analysis overtly to broaden their knowledge for professional purposes. Few among this group recognized any underlying motivation for entering treatment. Others turned for help explicitly because of dissatisfaction with their personal lives. The majority of these aspirants for psychoanalytic treatment could be evaluated as "healthy" from the sociological point of view.[6] They functioned effectively, occupying roles appropriate to their age, sex, social status, and intellectual or other abilities. On the whole, they were able and ambitious, had utilized the opportunities for achievement offered by our society, and filled roles which won them respect and, in some instances, prominence. Prevalent among the complaints of the patients dissatisfied with their current life situations were difficulties arising from their competitive strivings, or competition on the part of their coworkers or other associates. Another source of dissatisfaction lay in disappointment in their intimate human relations, recognized in some cases to be due to their own failure to gratify the needs of their marital partners, children or friends. A more urgent problem motivated the request of a number of middle-aged applicants for psychoanalytic assistance: i.e., an intense feeling of disillusionment with life based on their conviction that they had neither fulfilled their "promise" nor received the objective acclaim to which they aspired. Although the majority of the "normal" types proved to be asymptomatic, in the last-mentioned group reactive depressions, anxiety at-

[5] If one rejects the concept of a statistical norm, as it seems one must, the alternative becomes equally untenable, i.e., a hypothetical "ideal" type. Nonetheless, we cannot abandon the concepts of health and illness and some working basis for what can be classified as normal remains implicit for purposes of analysis.

[6] Chapter 10 of Parsons' book (1964) is entitled "Definitions of Health and Illness in the Light of American Values and Social Structure."

tacks under stress, and psychosomatic symptoms were not uncommon.

Despite the diversity of personalities represented, with the exception of the disillusioned patients mentioned above, one unifying outlook on life appeared to be shared by the majority of these individuals: i.e., an optimistic anticipation that their virtues, their talents, or their achievements would be rewarded by success if they took appropriate steps to work toward this goal. In contrast to "those wrecked by success" (Freud, 1916), these patients had become remarkably dependent upon the fulfillment of their expectations of life and saw in therapy a means to this end.[7] Furthermore, the accomplishment of their goals, whatever direction or configuration they took, had become essential to the maintenance of their psychic harmony.[8]

Sociocultural Factors

In the instance of those who entered psychoanalysis for professional reasons, especially candidates in training whose anticipation of achievement lay in the future, a special constellation (to be discussed later) warded off any acute awareness of dissatisfaction, and therefore the dependence upon success did not become readily apparent. In his paper "Therapeutic Problems in the Analysis of the 'Normal' Candidate" (1954), Maxwell Gitelson maintained that "so-called normality" masks a character disorder which is promoted by our culture. He said: "The very fact that in the *narcissistic neurosis* the ego maintains its capacity to perceive and to deal 'adaptively' with external reality makes it possible for the intra-psychic conflict to be laid out on the framework presented by the environment, and to follow there a course which has the aspects of 'normality' " (p. 176; my italics).

Although the phenomenology on which Gitelson based his conclusions corresponds with my experience, the diagnosis of "narcissistic neurosis" leads to considerable confusion and does not seem warranted

---

[7] Of course superego conflicts over unresolved oedipal fantasies played a part in their efforts at self improvement, yet, as will be discussed below, narcissistic determinants from the preoedipal period and their subsequent reinforcement by society proved to be more important. Success in life frequently serves to ward off the negative self image, which is latent in the "normal" as well as the neurotic. Although a conscious sense of guilt was remarkably absent in many of these patients, unconscious self-destructive trends based on archaic fantasies often became activated when they met with frustration.

[8] Menninger et al. (1963) give a systematic presentation of the "principles" involved in maintaining "the vital balance."

in this context.[9] Still, as I shall demonstrate, narcissism may undergo a special fate in our social structure. Gitelson's remarks clearly take into account the influence of social factors on personality. The effect of the social system upon the individual and its relation to personality structure was considered in a number of connections by Freud. Hartmann (1944, 1950b) reviews some of the most salient among them and expresses his own views on the relation of psychoanalysis to social science.

Sociologists make a clear distinction between cultural goals and the available institutional means of achieving these goals. They state that, in so far as an integration between these two components of social structure is maintained, an equilibrium exists in the social structure. Merton (1957) finds a significant discrepancy between the "success-goals" which are emphasized and encouraged in contemporary American culture and the institutional means of reaching these goals. His comments on the cultural reinforcement and promotion of success, even in the face of frustration and failure, are relevant:

> The family, the school and the work place . . . join to provide the intensive disciplining required if an individual is to retain intact a goal that remains elusively beyond reach, if he is to be motivated by the promise of a gratification which is not redeemed. . . . Central to this process of disciplining people to maintain their unfulfilled expressions are the cultural prototypes of success, the living documents testifying that the American Dream can be realized if one but has the requisite abilities [p. 137].

Merton represents the point of view of a number of social scientists who consider that our social structure produces a strain toward "anomie and deviant behavior" (p. 158).[10]

---

[9] For example, the term "narcissism" was utilized in relation to normal, neurotic, and psychotic states in the period between 1910 and the introduction of the structural point of view. The diagnostic category of "narcissistic character," especially when further qualified by the term "disorder," continues to refer to pathology of a borderline psychotic type. This diagnostic confusion runs throughout the literature. No small part of the difficulty may be due to the manifold usages to which this concept has been put. As has been pointed out (Hartmann, 1950a; Glover, 1958; Jacobson, 1964), narcissism is a generic term which applies to different developmental stages, to different functions, and to varying degrees of self versus object cathexis. A series of papers which appeared in the *J. Am. Psa. Assn.*, Vol. 12 (1964) are addressed in part to this problem, clarify some aspects of it, and make certain new contributions.

[10] The social scientists, following Durkheim, use the term *anomie* to indicate alienation from social "norms." Although it is primarily a sociological concept, Merton points out that it has been utilized in describing the psychological component of "normlessness."

Parsons (1964) takes a different stand. In his discussion of what he calls the "spiritual malaise" in our time, he states that the processes of rapid social and cultural change account for this apparent instability. He emphasizes the more positive aspects of growth which the changes embody. One example of this growth is put forward in his searching consideration of the uniquely positive attitude which has developed in the United States toward the treatment of illness in general and mental illness in particular. In this context Parsons makes a number of arresting statements (p. 288f.). For one, he postulates that illness represents deviance and becomes a threat to conformity in a society which upholds achievements as a valued goal, whereas treatment is seen as "an opportunity for therapeutic achievement." He states that the "activistic" orientation in Western medicine to the problems of health and illness embodies one expression of the "activism" which constitutes a social norm. According to him, in America illness is considered to be not an inevitable aspect of the human condition but a state which is "intrinsically manageable and controllable." Furthermore, he applies this hypothesis to an analysis of the process of therapy. For example, Parsons refers to psychiatric treatment as an "opportunity" for constructive, therapeutic work for the therapist as well as for the patient. In emphasizing this point, however, he speaks of the therapeutic work done by the patient as an "active striving for recovery through 'cooperating' with the physician," thereby contrasting this "doctor-patient collectivity" with the traditional orientation which designated two types of individuals occupying widely differentiated roles: that of the competent authority figure who treats and that of the passive patient who depends upon the doctor for help.[11]

As will be discussed below, this same activism which is responsible for much of the optimism and success in this culture, and accounts for the readiness with which many Americans accept psychiatric treatment, can become a serious source of resistance in psychoanalysis. In their more extreme form, socially sponsored attitudes to the effect that all things are possible if one but tries hard enough (activism)

[11] Nunberg (1925) recognized the necessity for an active desire on the part of the patient, a will to recover, as an indispensable prerequisite for improvement. Wheelis (1950, 1956) has taken the position that the significance of both "action" and "will" on the part of the patient has received insufficient recognition by psychoanalysis. In a recent paper, Greenson (1965) discusses the "working transference," contrasting it with the transference neurosis per se and underlining its importance for the successful outcome of psychoanalytic treatment.

represent Utopian illusions, whether they be religious or scientific in content, which have a long history on the American scene.[12]

Clinical and Technical Observations

In keeping with the multiplicity of personality configurations included in this category, the resistance to psychoanalysis presented by the so-called normal finds diverse forms of expression. Despite the heterogeneity of the phenomena encountered, some general comments are applicable. It has frequently been observed that characteristic defensive measures constitute one essential aspect of ego function and structure in "normality" as well as in neurosis. In addition, defensive mechanisms and behavior patterns may serve adaptive purposes (A. Freud, 1936; Hartmann, 1939a; et al.). Those defensive behaviors which have proved most adaptive will present the first line of resistance toward psychoanalysis in the well-organized personality. Adaptational strivings toward action as a means of mastering the unique situation of psychoanalysis may be observed with considerable regularity in those patients who have achieved success in their life situation. "Active mastery"[13] will be expressed in characteristic ways. It may become apparent in "reversal" (from passivity to activity), it may take the familiar form of "intellectualization," or it may be expressed by "compliance." Moreover, all three of these adaptive-defensive measures may be present in the patient's effort to impress the analyst with his knowledge of psychoanalytic theory.

The fact that action may serve neurotic purposes has long been familiar to psychoanalysts. I refer, of course, to the well-known phenomenon of "acting out" of neurotic conflicts. Theoretically and clinically important as the discovery of this tendency to repeat infantile conflicts in current life situations (including "acting out in the transference") has proved to be, this focus has tended to obscure the highly adaptive aspects of action. As Leo Berman once commented, it is difficult to determine where "acting out" ends and "real living" begins. In this connection the concept of "social compliance," introduced by Hartmann (1939a), is cogent. To put it in his words (1944): "one could speak of a kind of social selection and understand this as the

[12] For a discussion of "active technique" in psychoanalytic treatment, see Glover (1955), Tartakoff (1956).

[13] Jahoda (1958) uses "active mastery" of the environment as one of the criteria for mental health.

displacements in the social environment which are accessible or forbidden to a given type of individual" (p. 29). The distinction between acting out (as a manifestation of unresolved intrapsychic conflict) and of social action (which serves as an outlet for individual needs in a form acceptable to the superego and in compliance with social opportunities and requirements) can best be explored in the clinical setting.

Active mastery both of the psychoanalytic situation and of the derivatives of the id which it stimulates finds expression in the analysis of the normal personality in a variety of opening "gambits" on the part of the patient. Close observation may indicate that these approaches to analysis (which is experienced as an adaptive task), in addition to circumventing free association, have narcissistic transference implications. They frequently convey the patients' unspoken expectation of evoking acceptance, argumentation (itself a response), or acclaim for their performance. Such behavior has most frequently been understood as primarily seductive, competitive, or as serving a defensive function. It is less often recognized that precursors of such behavior were acquired in the earliest mother-child relationship and continued throughout the socialization process, thereby assuming a highly adaptive purpose in terms of their current cultural referents. The behavior itself has become infinitely complex as a result of the many factors which have contributed to it over time; it has also become structuralized. Still, in essence, its genetic forerunner—the appeal for gratification initiated by action—remains a central motivating factor. In my opinion, this transference expectation of achieving a special position vis-à-vis the analyst repeats a highly significant segment of the child's past experience—a hypothesis which will be developed later. It appears that the patient is not only defending himself but adapting (or maladapting, since deviance may take precedence over conformity to the task at hand). In so doing, he is attempting (however unconsciously) to evoke a response which originated in the early mother-child situation and became reinforced by the active encouragement and overt rewards provided by early family, educational, and social influences.[14]

In my experience, expectations of recognition for achievement (in contrast to wishes for sexual gratification or fears of castration) as-

---

[14] The patient who experiences the treatment situation as a required "task" often associates it to his early school life and the analyst becomes identified with teachers from the primary school years.

sume a more insistent quality in the early phase of the analysis of the "normal" than is the case in the analysis of the symptom neurotic. Moreover, provocative behavior, which is geared toward active mastery, will often persist or become replaced by more "rational" (Hartmann, 1947) ego attitudes, e.g., externalization of conflicts may increase if the adaptive meaning is bypassed. On the other hand, if the patient's efforts to demonstrate his ability to master the situation are understood in the adaptive context and interpreted as repetition of a position which has previously met with success, another transference manifestation of preoedipal origin frequently declares itself: a re-externalization of the ego ideal may occur in the form of idealization of the analyst. This stance, the small child's reaction to the superiority of the parent whom he tries to emulate, becomes intensified with his growing recognition that he must comply with certain unfamiliar and unanticipated requirements—in the instance of the analysis, he must follow the basic rule. If he does so, the patient, like the child, expects a reward. Through conformity he expects to become endowed with ideal qualities in order to partake of that which he experiences as the omniscience and omnipotence of the analyst. Once this anticipation declares itself (however unconscious it may be), a perpetuation of this transference state is apt to continue until the appropriate interpretations have their impact. An indefinite deferment of the expression of aggression in the form of anger or rage at the frustration imposed by the analytic situation is one sign of such a "stalemate" (Glover, 1955). These patients often refer to analysis as a game.

In the handling of these cases, it is of the utmost importance for the analyst to recognize that adaptive manifestations of resistance demonstrated by achievement or other means of conformity utilize "institutionalized behavior" (Parsons, 1949; Hartmann, Kris, and Loewenstein, 1951).[15] "Institutionalized" and "noninstitutionalized

---

[15] Parsons (1949) defines "institutions" as systems of patterned expectations. He says: "the essential aspect of social structure lies in a system of patterned expectations defining the *proper* behavior of persons playing certain roles, enforced both by the incumbents' own positive motives for conformity and by the sanctions of others" (p. 35). Hartmann et al. (1951) adopt this terminology (using it in a somewhat wider sense to include practices of child care) and then differentiate between institutionalized and noninstitutionalized behavior. They say: "Psychoanalytic observation suggests that from a dynamic point of view they may differ considerably and in various ways." Here they point out these differences as they are reflected in problems of motivation and discharge. They continue: "The same institution may, in some persons, appeal most effectively to their ids; in others, to their superegos; in a third group, it may be used predominantly by their ego interests, etc. The influence of

behavior" coexist from early childhood. Some of the genetic determinants of both types of behavior and their confluence will be discussed later. For the present, it will suffice to point out that certain behavior patterns readily become "institutionalized in the transference," so to speak, and prevent the full development of other manifestations of the transference neurosis essential to a thorough analysis (Tartakoff, 1956). In addition to the light they throw on adaptation as it serves resistance, the above observations offer an opportunity to study regressive manifestations which, in the process of recapitulation in the transference, illuminate in reverse order the eventual fate of narcissism as it undergoes "secondary autonomy" (Hartmann, 1939a) in the course of development.[16]

Most psychoanalysts would agree that patients who have developmental defects of constitutional or very early experiential origin, in particular those which have interfered with the formation of "object constancy" (Hartmann, 1952) do not fulfill the essential criteria of analyzability. Clinical experience has, however, produced abundant evidence to the effect that varying degrees of narcissism from the stage of early mother-child interaction ("anaclitic" tendencies, "part-object" relations) continue to coexist with later developmental trends into adult life. The persistence of a "need-fulfilling" orientation clearly influences the nature of object relations but does not necessarily exclude the capacity to form a transference neurosis if later stages of libidinal development have been reached.[17]

To return to the effect of the psychoanalytic situation, a number of authors have documented ego aspects of the mother-child relationship which become reactivated in this unique atmosphere and consti-

---

institutions may relate to various developmental levels. It may affect personality formation. It may be set apart as the 'institutional' part [differentiating it] from the 'private' part of the personality, etc." (p. 110f.).

[16] Hartmann's application of the biological concept of "change of function" put forth in a number of his papers and his reintroduction of Freud's concept of "ego interests" (see, in particular, 1950a) deserve further study in this context.

[17] In his *Introductory Lectures* (1916/17, p. 420ff.) Freud categorized psychopathology into the "transference neuroses" and the "narcissistic neuroses," the latter designating severe mental illness which he considered to be intractable to psychoanalytic treatment. Although it is no longer adhered to in a strict sense, this diagnostic division may have had a deterring effect on the analysis of narcissism. Certainly, this emphasis bypassed its positive, adaptive aspects which had received considerable attention in Freud's original paper "On Narcissism" (1914). In *Civilization and Its Discontents* (1930), he not only viewed characterological manifestations of narcissism to be within the range of normal functioning but attributed many of man's cultural achievements to this tendency.

tute the "basic transference" (Macalpine, 1950; Greenacre, 1954; Ritvo and Solnit, 1958; and others). Relatively little emphasis has been placed on the accompanying infantile narcissistic fantasies which become activated in the course of analysis. This omission may be due to the fact that such fantasies often remain a silent source of resistance,[18] ubiquitous as they are known to be.[19] Expectations of rebirth, of a magical cure, and of the gratification of omnipotent fantasies (e.g., the wish to be the "chosen one" or to become the "powerful one") first find verbal expression in the second year of life. As I have indicated, factors in both the pyschoanalytic situation and process contribute to the regressive activation of these wishes. It has long been recognized that the two-person relationship revives and, to some extent, gratifies the narcissistically oriented desire to be the center of attention as well as stimulating object-directed libidinal longings.[20] In the analysis of the "normal," narcissism frequently becomes a second line of resistance. When the initial adaptive forms of resistance have been worked through, confirmatory evidence of a narcissistic orientation may be found in the conscious desire expressed by some patients to evoke admiration or acclaim from the analyst. Murray (1964) designates this expectation as a "narcissistic entitlement." Another version of this wish may be externalized in the form of the fantasy of being preferred to all other patients or, in some instances, it may become a temporarily entertained conviction of being the one and only love object of the analyst. Once insight has been gained into these wishes, they become less ego syntonic and their analysis can proceed.

Special Resistances in the Training Analysis

Some aspects of the resistance encountered in the "normal" can best be exemplified by the special situation of the training analysis. Training confronts us with an unusual set of circumstances which complicates the uncovering of narcissistically motivated resistance. Specifically,

[18] The unconscious motivations of the general practitioner and the psychotherapist were scrutinized by Edward Glover as early as 1929.

[19] See Loomie et al. (1958) for the passive fantasy of being "special," the "hero"; also note the relationship between the "discovery of talent" and the "family romance."

[20] Stone (1961) considers at length the role of the physician as a central factor in the establishment of trust on the part of the patient. The magical expectations of the patient are dealt with in this context. He also differentiates between the "primordial" transference and its more "mature" form and states that the two may coexist, the former often serving as an unverbalized source of resistance.

the candidate, who has opted for psychoanalysis as a career, has had his choice of profession sanctioned through his selection by a training institute. This reality lends a reinforcement not only to transference but to potential countertransference manifestations; consequently they may escape observation and analysis. Moreover, identification with the training analyst in question, which, as in every identification, involves a shift from object cathexis to self cathexis, assumes in this instance a crucial significance. Other considerations which influence the selection of our candidates, in particular the aptitudes, talents, and skills we establish as criteria for eligibility, may also lend validity to our candidates' anticipation of success in their chosen field and thereby promote adaptive solutions to intrapsychic conflicts which obscure their unconscious determinants.

Returning to the problem of narcissism and its possible vicissitudes, the resistance inherent in idealization of the training analyst has a critical effect with long-standing consequences if its interpretation is omitted or fails to result in insight. This is due in part to the fact that the reality of the training analyst's position as a representative of an institute, where he also serves as administrator and "judge," tends to increase the likelihood that he will be cast in the role of the protector, the omniscient or the omnipotent one. As Freud reminded us, quoting Anatole France, it is hard for a mortal who acquires power not to misuse it. In addition to its impact on the training analysis in question, countertransference involvement which permits the perpetuation of idealization of the analyst has an inevitable effect on future generations of patients. They in turn will attempt to resist the analysis of their conflicts by investing the analyst with the magic powers of the medicine man (behind whom lies the omnipotent parent), hoping to participate in this magic and thereby to promote their self interests as well as to gratify their instinctual wishes.

Reality factors introduced by the candidate's prospective career may likewise contribute to his resistance to analysis. The fact that the candidate has been selected for training, and expects to become a colleague of his analyst, reinforces the fantasy of being the patient with a special destiny. In view of this reality, the infantile origin of such a wish may elude analysis. Moreover, the training analyst may fortify magical and omnipotent fantasies, like the parent who tries to restore "his own lost narcissism" (Freud, 1914) by virtue of his unconsciously determined investment in the special worth or superiority of his candidate-child. The countertransference reaction may also constitute an interference if the analyst plays into the patient's tendency to institutionalize the student-teacher relationship. Either stance proves difficult for training committees to counteract. For this reason, some institutes separate the functions of training analyst and committee member who must pass official judgment.[21]

The·criteria we establish for our candidates not infrequently pose additional sources of resistance. Whatever their problems may be, our candidates have special aptitudes. To mention the most obvious, if we have selected them judiciously, they possess superior intelligence, psychological perceptiveness, and some of them have creative ability of an artistic, scholarly or scientific nature. A candidate's innate endowment, in interaction with developmental factors, will have had an influence on the solutions he has found, the defenses he has established and the adaptation he has made. Gifted men throughout the ages have contributed to the world and undoubtedly have gained considerable self satisfaction in the process. For example, a past history of superior intellectual achievement may have gratified instinctual tendencies, elevated self esteem, and facilitated the development of ego interests which have found an outlet in socially valued action. Normal as such reactions may be, we still must ask what effect psychoanalytic training may have on a person with a comparable history of success which has yielded such rewards.

Today we require that our candidates undergo as thorough a personal analysis as possible in order to achieve a breadth and depth of self understanding which will qualify them to understand others. To this end, we ask that they direct their attention over a prolonged period of time to the exploration of their own psychic operations; the "subject," in this instance, becomes the "object" of investigation and through introspection, among other factors, insight is gained. The fact that the training of the candidate has, as its explicit aim, the acquisition of self knowledge with the eventual goal of treating others —an object-directed pursuit *par excellence*—does not alter the means to this end. Two major obstacles to progress may arise in this regard. As noted above, action orientation may interfere with the capacity of candidates to tolerate conflict and sustain self observation. The fact

---

[21] Lewin and Ross (1960) in their comprehensive survey consider at length the complexity of the reality factors involved and indicate some of the problems they pose for the training analysis.

that they are engaged in a profession which offers abundant opportunity to take action at the same time that they are undergoing their "didactic" analysis increases this possibility. Or we may discover in the course of treatment that the facility for energic shifts from object to self cathexis (which, under favorable circumstances, can readily be reversed and heighten the capacity for psychological perceptivity) rests on a greater degree of self interest than is compatible with psychoanalysis as a career. In such instances, the personality of the training analyst, with whom the candidate identifies, may have a decisive effect on altering this orientation. Eventually, however, the outcome will also depend upon whether the candidate has attained an optimal degree of independence from the transference object as well as a relative freedom from self interest.

The foregoing manifestations of resistance to psychoanalysis were considered primarily in relation to those factors inherent in the situation and process which may reinforce narcissistically oriented attitudes in the form of self interests. The entire subject of ego interests reintroduced by Hartmann (1939a, 1944, 1947, 1950a, 1950b, 1956), including his discussion of their determinants, their aims, and the degree of neutralization of energy involved (1950a), is pertinent to this problem. If our observations of the adaptive patterns of the so-called normal character are meaningful, culturally sanctioned outlets for tensions offer neither a panacea nor the assurance that "objective" solutions are necessarily free of conflict. Were this the case, one would expect the individual to be more resilient to stress in the event that internalized expectations of success do not meet with the anticipated rewards.

As a result of the rapid advances which have taken place in the basic sciences, an additional source of conflict has arisen which has a tangential, if not a direct, bearing on our training programs. Today, more than at any period in the brief history of psychoanalysis, applicants for psychoanalytic training have developed a special interest in and have acquired considerable knowledge of cognate fields. In some instances, their involvement lies primarily in another, more "scientific" field: e.g., the pursuit of neurophysiology and biochemistry. The request for psychoanalytic training by applicants with a background in one of the above fields often entails the conscious or preconscious expectation that psychoanalysis will provide a key to the "secrets" of mental functioning (which they hope to acquire through training) and thereby will uniquely equip them to advancé knowledge through experimentation, utilizing the more precise methods of the basic sciences. In other cases, the interests of these applicants may be equally distribúted between psychoanalysis and a second field, leading to an impasse.

Adaptive as the efforts to encompass two or more disciplines may be—and thereby to achieve a hitherto unattained integration of separate fields of endeavor—such ambitious aims frequently give rise to a conflict of ego interests ("intrasystemic conflict") which reflect "intersystemic conflict" (Hartmann, 1950a, 1951). Moreover, experience in the training of such candidates demonstrates that the more fully their ambitions become reinforced by reality factors (culturally encouraged goals), the less accessible they are to the psychoanalytic method. This state of affairs confronts thoughtful analysts and education committees of institutes with a dilemma regarding the advisability of accepting these applicants for full training. Certain institutes—and, more recently, the American Psychoanalytic Association—have found solutions to this problem by offering partial training, exclusive of clinical work, or training for research purposes only, which permits of supervised clinical work.[22] Psychoanalysts are not unmindful of the importance of the advancement of knowledge. Therefore, as previously discussed, we accept the complications which the analysis of these candidates involves.

The "Nobel Prize Complex"

Experience gained over a number of years of psychiatric work with college students, teachers, research workers, and representatives of the professions, including our own discipline, have led me to introduce a new nosological entity, the Nobel Prize complex.[23] This subgroup may also be exemplified by individuals who entertain other ambitious goals: e.g., the wish to be President, to attain great wealth, to become a social leader or to win an "Oscar." The majority of patients so designated are intellectually or artistically gifted and evoke consid-

[22] The Boston Psychoanalytic Institute has been offering partial training to colleagues in allied fields for over two decades. In 1957 the American Psychoanalytic Association approved an exception to training standards which permits education committees to recommend especially qualified applicants to the Board on Professional Standards of the American Psychoanalytic Association for complete training for research purposes.

[23] This designation was not intended to apply to Nobel Laureates.

erable admiration from others, on whom they have a charismatic effect. In these cases, objective achievement becomes overshadowed and, often, inhibited by a preoccupation with acclaim. The goal of "all" or "nothing" which such persons entertain interferes with the effective expression of their potentialities.

The Nobel Prize complex has its genesis in infancy with pre-objectal, preoedipal, and oedipal determinants, as well as another distinguishing feature: precocious ego development. The majority of persons with this complex are first-born; many have, in fact, been the "one and only" child. Among the individuals in this category whom I have analyzed, the two previously mentioned fantasies have been present, frequently in varying combinations: (1) the active, omnipotent fantasy of being the "powerful one," with grandiose features; and (2) the passive fantasy of being the "special one," chosen by virtue of exceptional gifts.[24] Owing to a developmental imbalance (to be discussed later), the oedipal conflict undergoes an unusual fate in both instances. Its competitive component often takes precedence over its libidinal aspect in those persons who have been singled out from childhood as exceptionally "bright." In the individuals who have been recognized as extraordinarily beautiful as well as artistically gifted, the narcissistic libidinal component assumes undue importance.[25] In either instance, psychoanalysis reveals a circumvention of the resolution of oedipal conflict. A history of physical defects or traumata has not proved to be a decisive etiological factor in precipitating conflict and therefore the early lives of these persons cannot be compared to those of Freud's "exceptions" (1916).[26] Such patients do, however, become hypersensitive to minor disappointments in later life, in particular to lack of recognition. Because of their exceptional endowment and the precocity which accompanies it, these individuals have not found it necessary to seek the favor of others by the usual efforts to win love. Moreover, the corrective effect of reality confrontation on fantasy has been lacking because of their special fate. The attention they have attracted in the family situation is continued in the early

[24] Phyllis Greenacre's papers approach this subject from a different point of view. (See in particular 1957, 1958, 1962.)

[25] The highly perceptive papers by Annie Reich which consider the pathology of the ego ideal are relevant here (1953, 1960).

[26] Jacobson (1959) considers that not only persons with afflictions but those with extraordinary gifts reveal the psychology of "exceptions." She finds the common denominator in their narcissism.

school experience. The expectation of success becomes firmly established during the latency period when they continue to excel and win out over rivals, either through outstanding academic performance or by virtue of their other gifts. By late adolescence, the intellectually gifted frequently find that their superior performance has won them a position in the ranks of our new social status, the "meritocracy." In some ways, they resemble patients whose achievement has taken the form of physical prowess. Pleasure derived from achievement and the gratification attendant upon recognition by others have in all such cases interfered with a capacity to relate fully on an object-libidinal basis. The dependence of these patients appears to be focused primarily on evidence of success in the sphere of their ambitions. Only in the event of loss of love or support does the extent of their dependence on significant persons in their private lives become apparent to them.

The patients I refer to who manifest a Nobel Prize complex are neither borderline nor psychotic. On the whole, they are well integrated and although their experience of the outer world has, as previously noted, lacked the usual correctives emanating from confrontation with their limitations, their reality testing is not otherwise impaired. By and large, their expectations have been directed to goals which are culturally encouraged and their talents have found an outlet in highly adaptive activities which effectively utilize ego functions of primary and secondary autonomy. Yet their expectation of attaining a position of extraordinary power or of winning worldwide recognition, which would be the logical extension of their infantile wishes, has fallen short of fulfillment.[27] The "Dream of Glory" which these patients entertain has been reinforced by goals in our social structure. It is, in fact, the personal expression of the American Dream—a narcissistic fantasy which has become institutionalized. The unconscious determinants of the Dream have remained repressed; therefore, feelings of depletion, precipitated by a realistic or fantasied disappointment, be it on the level of love or work, lead quickly to a sense of failure, often accompanied by depression and psychosomatic symptoms

---

[27] There are, of course, some persons who do achieve such recognition and power, but realistic fulfillment is never commensurate with the infantile fantasies and it brings realistic burdens and responsibilities which the child cannot fathom. Jahoda (1958) in her discussion of the multiple criterion approach draws attention to the "psychological price" of mental health. Smith (1950) introduced the idea of optimum mental health which he considers to be a question for empirical research.

which influence some of these persons to seek treatment.[28] As would be expected, when they become patients they unconsciously look upon treatment as a magical cure. In some cases (as described earlier) the infantile basis of the illness can be analyzed as it is repeated in the transference and a new *modus vivendi* can be established. Others in this group recover only when their self-directed ego interests (Hartmann, 1950a), which lie close to their omnipotent fantasies, once again give promise of fulfillment in reality. The study of such cases proves highly instructive in so far as it throws light on the relation between so-called narcissistic phenomena, endowment, adaptation, and (from the point of view of the individual) maladaptive solutions in our particular culture (Hartmann, 1939a).

Modern Western culture, despite its realization of nuclear power, its conquest of space, and its partial mastery of the elements, is not more conducive to the development of fantasies of omnipotence than other cultures, either past or present, with their belief in magic and their reliance on mythology. Originating in the unconscious as they do, such fantasies are not bound by time or space. However, there is a difference in the values, goals, norms, and institutional means with which various sociocultural settings meet these wishes and expectations.

In the previously cited paper on the "normal" candidate, Gitelson (1954) defined the healthy personality as follows: "In the balanced operation of the personality we expect to find an emotionally 'open' system of communication between the various institutions of the mind, operating through a fluid process of checks and balances among the instinctual and defensive tendencies, so that none is fully isolated, self-operating and self-sustaining" (p. 175).

Psychoanalytic contact with the "normal" indicates that this "balanced operation" depends upon an "open" system of communication, not only between the various psychic systems but with the historical past and the sociocultural present which constitute his current experience.[29] If the particular society in which man lives both

---

[28] If these disturbances lead to decompensation, we no longer find adaptive behavior. When these patients do develop symptoms, they resemble "basic ego states" (E. Bibring, 1953), i.e., acute anxiety and depression or psychosomatic symptoms which again have basic physiological as well as psychological determinants (Schur, 1955, 1958).

[29] The most eloquent spokesman for this psychosocial point of view is Erikson. His elaboration of the concept of group identity (Freud, 1921) in terms of the relation of the individual to his historical position in time and space, as well as to the basic social and cultural processes which are communicated from generation to

supports and fosters unrealistic expectations which promote his infantile fantasies of supernatural powers, the necessary "checks and balances," which confrontation with reality lends, will be only partially effective. In the event that a person chooses a profession which, by its very nature, elicits magical expectations in others, his awakening to the reality may be further delayed. Eventually, however, confrontation must occur and will lead to a response commensurate with the discrepancy between fantasy and fact unless some pathological solution intervenes. Middle age appears to be the turning point.

Genetic Considerations

Although the Nobel Prize complex constitutes a preoccupation with acclaim which has specific cultural referents, it highlights certain aspects of normal development in a society geared to success. Sociocultural influences alone or in combination with child-rearing practices cannot account for the phenomena observed in the normal personality. The articulation and interaction of psychobiological and sociocultural factors, complex as they may be, must be considered in any effort to explicate our findings. At the risk of omitting a number of factors basic to maturation and growth, let us focus on some of the genetic determinants central to our thesis. To do so, we must return to the prehistory of the personality.

Psychoanalytic research based on the direct observation and testing of infants has offered some valuable correctives to psychoanalytic assumptions regarding infantile development and has given a firm foundation to others. Among those psychoanalytic propositions which have been strengthened is the centrality of the biologically based mother-infant interaction in the growth process. The unique position in the unfolding of the maturational-developmental sequence occupied by the mother has been validated by a number of investigators (Spitz, 1945, 1946; Escalona, 1953; Mahler and Gosliner, 1955; Ritvo and Solnit, 1958; Provence and Ritvo, 1961; Provence and Lipton, 1962).

Efforts to trace the genesis of man's illusions of omnipotence must remain speculative. It has been assumed by some authors that their earliest determinants lie in a state of tension (drive motivation); others

---

generation (1950), and his designation of stages of ego development in the "healthy personality" (1959), are of great significance for a general psychology. Their consideration goes beyond the scope of this paper.

have attributed their origin to the infant's need to seek and respond to external stimuli (the need to function). From both theoretical positions, the inference has been drawn that the forerunners of fantasies of omnipotence and causality have a common origin in the infant's own activity. Apocryphal though they may seem from our present standpoint, Ferenczi's (1913) conjectures regarding the relationship between the development of omnipotence and the sense of reality focused attention on the coincidental origin of these seemingly disparate phenomena. A number of years later Piaget (1937) expressed the opinion that the infant's own activity initiates that which he terms "magical-phenomenalistic causality." He postulated that, if the infant were conscious of a self independent of objects in the first sensorimotor stage of development, he would try to utilize this "omnipotence" to undertake "the conquest of the world" (p. 235). Approaching the subject from another point of view, Hendrick (1942) posited that the infant's effort to control the environment has its origin in rudimentary sensorimotor development. According to Spitz (1965), feelings of omnipotence arise after the infant has transcended the simple reflex stage, i.e., in the period of appeal which stimulates response on the part of the environment:

> In this achievement of enlisting the mother's help . . . through screaming, the human being experiences for the first time the *post hoc ergo propter hoc* in connection with his own action. . . . [This] principle will subsequently branch into two directions. One of them will remain in its crude form as a basic mode of functioning of the primary process. The other will be progressively refined until it becomes one of the most potent ideational tools of man in the form of the principle of determinism [p. 153f.].

This postulate, i.e., that omnipotence and the precursors of causality have a common origin in the infant's ability to evoke response through his own activity, may have a bearing on later adaptive behavior patterns which could help to explicate our findings.

As self and object gradually become differentiated, maturational and growth factors increase the adaptive activities at the infant's disposal to appeal to external objects for the gratification of his needs. Foremost among these means are the social smile, vocalizations, syllabic utterances and gestures, which have their precursors in the early weeks of life.[30] Because the infant remains passively dependent during this period, observers tend to minimize his increasing ability to influence and control others through his activity. Moreover, it has been assumed by a number of authors that, as the child becomes aware of this dependence, he invests the "powers" who gratify and frustrate his needs with omnipotence and simultaneously renounces his own feelings of power. The latter assumption—that the child renounces omnipotent feelings and thereafter evokes them only defensively to compensate for feelings of inferiority—requires reexamination. Direct observation as well as retrospective reconstruction support the assumption that projective and introjective mechanisms play a part in promoting both the child's omnipotence and his animistic view of his surroundings. In her discussion of these projective-introjective mechanisms during the preoedipal period Jacobson (1964) states: "At this stage the child displays submissive, clinging, following attitudes or behavior alternating with temporary grandiose ideas showing his 'magic participation' in the parents' omnipotence. There are erratic vacillations between attitudes of passive, helpless dependency on the omnipotent mother and active, aggressive strivings for self expansion and a powerful control over the love objects" (p. 44).

Jacobson postulates that a frequent merging of self and object images occurs not only during the preoedipal years but well into and even beyond the oedipal period, thereby lending the child's relationship to the mother "narcissistic qualities" which follow him through life. It is my impression that if the state of "magic participation" becomes prolonged and reinforced by conscious or unconscious maternal attitudes, the child's fantasies of omnipotence do not undergo a modification in keeping with reality. Instead, they tend to persist on an unconscious or preconscious basis along with the expectation that his narcissistically oriented needs will find the rewards in the outer world which he originally experienced through interaction with his mother. I shall return to this point in my discussion of the special constellation which obtains for the gifted.

During the second year of life, the normal child's development is characterized by a considerable array of motor skills as well as other ego functions, which give him an actual control over his environment.

---

[30] Empirical research on infants and neonates continues to shift the timetable of these forerunners closer to birth (Wolff, 1959, 1960).

As many authors have pointed out, the child's accomplishments at this age constitute gains never again to be equaled in so brief a time span. A growth spurt of such diversity and magnitude, which leads to increasing mastery, must also contribute to the consolidation of subjective feelings of power at the same time that it gratifies narcissistic needs and perpetuates magical thinking. Among a number of promising longitudinal projects, a systematic study of "separation-individuation" based on the observation of "average" mothers and "normal" children from 6 months to 3 years of age is now in progress (Mahler, 1963; Mahler and Furer, 1963; Mahler and La Perriere, 1965). In her 1963 paper Mahler says:

> It is interesting to note how, in general, by the time the toddler has mastered the ability to move from and to the mother, the balance dramatically shifts within the bipolar mother-toddler interaction from activity on the part of the mother to activity on the part of the child. Once the toddler has mastered locomotion and begins to learn manipulation, these important partial functions and every new skill become elements of a language weighted with a steady accretion of secondary and largely unconscious meaning—a wordless appeal for love and praise from the mother, an expression of longing, a search for meanings, a wish for sharing and for expansion. The mother, as the catalyst of the individuation process, must be able to read the toddler's primary-process language [p. 315].

With language development, active mastery becomes accelerated by the acquisition of the power of words and the child begins to express his longings for love and praise in phase-specific terms and to reveal the egocentricity of his wishes. As was true earlier, his growing capacity for mastery alternates with frustration and failure both in terms of instinctual and ego control. His successes and failures are now accompanied by efforts to please, by verbal demands for attention, and by negative responses which elicit parental encouragement, rewards, and punishment in kind.

As evidence of the sense of self becomes increasingly manifest in the child, we observe a growing object constancy (Hartmann, 1952) and a more constant attitude toward sustained activity. For progressively longer periods, the child invests both objects and activities with interest. Nonetheless, these interests remain primarily self-directed and the accompanying verbalizations have a narcissistic orientation even when they refer to other persons. The fact that considerable organization of mental representations has occurred is revealed by the spontaneous expression of fantasies and wishes by the child at this stage, yet the content of these ideational representations would be looked upon as grandiose or presumptuous in the adult. The effect of maternal influence in perpetuating narcissistic fantasies by praise of an exaggerated nature (vis-à-vis the child's actual performance), thereby revealing her concordance with the child's narcissistic wishes, can readily be documented. Anna Freud (1936) commented on the readiness with which parents participate in the child's denial of reality in play and upon the functions of playthings in furthering the child's fantasy of controlling the world (p. 90f.).

When more complex cognitive functioning becomes available, further neutralization of instinctual drives leads to secondary autonomy and the capacity for autonomous functioning becomes increasingly structuralized (Hartmann, 1950a). Socially sanctioned expectations conveyed by the parents have a greater impact at this point. The centrality of the dynamic interaction of mother and child in the early stages of socialization has been documented by sociologists.[31] Less attention has been paid by psychoanalysts to the process of early ego identification than to the consideration of forerunners of superego formation. In our child-centered culture, the effective pedagogical method of directing the small child's abundant energy into his budding ego interests,[32] with the implicit or explicit promise of rewards for his accomplishments, is a secret every mother knows. Thereby, "pathways of discharge" (Hartmann et al., 1951) are opened up for the child as alternative outlets for the instinctual pleasures he is expected to relinquish. Whereas these developing ego interests, sponsored by the parents, continue to remain largely self-centered at this stage, they also serve as forerunners of genuine ego identifications as well as of the ego ideal.

Parental praise, which fosters the child's emergent abilities, indelibly impresses upon him the "causal" relationship: autonomous activity leads to pleasurable internal sensations as well as to external

[31] Parsons et al. (1954) and Parsons (1964) consider at length the mother-child "interdependence" in the socialization process. Pursuing the implications of Freud's comments on the impact of environmental factors on man, Parsons speaks of the "interpenetration" of the personality and the social system.

[32] White (1963) emphasizes the effect on later life experience of independent activity and achievement in childhood.

response and admiration. Since the child's development has not progressed beyond the phase of egocentricity at this period, either success or failure may continue to promote magical fantasies and contribute to idealization of the parents. These trends coexist with the small child's gradual objectification of his "world," which has little relation to the scientist's "reality" at this time (Hartmann, 1947; see also Erikson's [1964] distinction between "actuality" and "reality").[33] Eventually, the emphasis upon success, fostered by our society and conveyed by the parents, becomes internalized in the form of true identifications. One might conclude that, from this time onward, the wish of the small child to alter the world in keeping with his fantasies falls upon fertile soil.

A sociocultural setting which emphasizes the goal of success may perpetuate narcissistic and omnipotent fantasies of being the "chosen" one, the "powerful" one, into the oedipal years and color this phase in a manner which complicates object-libidinal development. Space does not permit a detailed consideration of the outcome of the oedipal conflict under these circumstances. However, in so far as object relations remain primarily self-oriented and active mastery is encouraged, the child's wishes may become readily externalized into channels both inside and outside the family setting which offer an adaptive outlet for competitive strivings and elicit the desired response and admiration. As a result, phase-specific anxieties are apt to be minimized and the unrealizable nature of oedipal fantasies can more easily be denied. Helene Deutsch (1964) refers in this context to an "ego-ideal unit." However, the inevitable but crucial disappointment becomes postponed and may lead to a break-through in adolescence or, in certain cases, to dissatisfaction with one's fate in later life.

The above circumstances may also help to account for the lack of conscious feelings of guilt in many so-called normal persons in our culture. It is possible that superego development which, according to psychoanalytic theory, is based on identification, becomes aborted when the oedipal wishes are "laid out on the framework presented by the environment" (Gitelson, 1954, p. 176), and there-

---

[33] For the small child the "impossible" does not exist. A 2-year-old believes he can fly like a bird or, more accurately, in the animistic stage of his development, he and the bird have the same potentialities. Considerably later he speaks of making the "biggest" and the "bestest" rocket to fly to the moon. Characteristically, the moon is at this stage conceived of (anthropomorphically) as something put there in space by man or as a "man" who protects or threatens the child.

fore do not meet with a definitive phase-specific solution. Clinical experience offers evidence to the effect that the regulation and control of behavior remain unduly dependent on external "laws" in many otherwise well-functioning personalities. One is also impressed by the wide discrepancy between the high standards to which many persons give lip service and their dependence upon permission and acceptance by significant authority figures in order to maintain their self regard. On the other hand, psychoanalytic treatment reveals an unconscious, archaic superego with "omnipotent powers" at work in the majority of so-called normals.

We must now ask how the foregoing observations relate to development in the instance of the unusually gifted. A child endowed with exceptional cognitive abilities, talents, or physical attributes may have a subjective reaction to his own adaptive abilities which accelerates individuation at the same time that it reinforces early feelings of omnipotence. In addition, he will have an advantage over his siblings and playmates. If we also take into account a unique response on the part of adults, especially the parents whose narcissistic involvement in their progeny was recognized early by Freud (1914), it is understandable that the gifted child may meet with a unique fate. The effect of silent adoration or verbal acclaim in the face of precocious development must, at a very early age, affirm the growing child's fantasy that he is "the center of the world" and therefore destined to share the omnipotence which he projected onto the parents and they reflected back onto him, thereby confirming his own feelings that a special destiny awaits him. As previously noted, the wish that one's performance be applauded by others is further confirmed by the institutions which support such expectations. In this psychosocial climate, wishes readily give way to beliefs, and the triad of autonomy, achievement, and acclaim may become firmly rooted.

In the case of the gifted individual, such a constellation may lead to success if preoccupation with achievement does not take precedence over the capacity to utilize one's gifts in keeping with realistic goals. Of course, the reality limits of these goals become more difficult to assess in an age in which science fiction verges on fact. Nonetheless, whenever autonomous functioning remains irrevocably associated with grandiose narcissistic fantasies fostered in childhood, true antonomy may not be achieved no matter how great the individual's potentialities. In this instance, one is reminded of an addiction which is characterized by an insatiable desire to recover an infantile state of gratification which can never be fulfilled in reality. Disillusionment in such instances may not occur until middle age, when recognition and reward on an ascending scale are no longer forthcoming.

Not all normal or gifted children in our social structure meet with the same destiny. Some will adapt to goals well within their reach. Among the gifted, a few will find worldwide renown, as previously noted. In others, the interaction of constitutional, emotional, social, and economic factors may lead to neurosis, psychosis, or alienation. Pathological and maladaptive forms of behavior have been more intensively studied than the so-called normal personality and therefore have not been the focus of this paper.

Before concluding we should once again question the validity of the use of a normative concept. Perhaps one begs the question in focusing on what is "normal" when a considerable part of one's sample has been comprised of persons who have sought the atypical experience of undergoing psychoanalytic treatment.[34] Another objection to designating the phenomena observed as "normal" may well be raised since the sample from which the following tentative conclusions are drawn consists of persons with special aptitudes, many of whom have exceptional talents. Moreover, the correlations presented in this paper are based primarily on my observations. Further psychoanalytic investigation as well as empirical research with similar and different types of normal personalities is clearly indicated.[35]

Summary and Conclusions

In consonance with "the activism" which constitutes a social norm and the success goals fostered in our culture, the so-called normal

[34] Some corrective regarding the latter objection may be found in my participation in the Harvard Student Study, a research project under the auspices of the Harvard University Health Services (supported by the National Institute of Mental Health, Grant #5R12MH09151). This project offers a unique opportunity to observe changes over a four-year college period in late adolescents with special aptitudes. In addition to the test instruments on 250 subjects, the data consist of intensive interviews of 40 students conducted by team members other than the psychoanalysts involved. The problems raised in this paper regarding the determinants and aims of ego interests, as well as the relation of narcissism and its vicissitudes to mental functioning and to adaptation in general, constitute one focus of this project.

[35] A research project conducted by Grinker et al. (1962) at George Williams College studied a very different population and led to inferences which applied to one type of mental health. According to the authors, it will be necessary to conduct research on "many kinds" of population in order to delineate other types of normality" (p. 452).

(represented by a diversity of types) approaches psychoanalysis as an adaptive task to be mastered. Characteristic defensive behavior which serves adaptive purposes, coupled with the expectation of receiving recognition for achievement, presents the first line of resistance in these cases. When such behavior is understood in the adaptational context and interpreted as a repetition of earlier behavior patterns which have been rewarded with success, a second line of resistance frequently declares itself. It takes the form of idealization or of aggrandizement of the analyst. By a magical cure, the patient expects to become endowed with ideal qualities or to participate in the "omnipotence" projected onto the analyst. Derivatives of omnipotence in the form of narcissistic fantasies become conscious when interpretation of this primordial transference has its impact. If unrecognized, either form of resistance tends to become institutionalized, thereby obstructing the full development and resolution of the transference neurosis. Some special problems which the above types of resistance may present in the training analysis are discussed. The Nobel Prize complex, a new nosological entity which has specific cultural referents, is described and its etiology outlined.

An attempt is made to relate dependence upon success and magical expectations, so common in our culture, to the early history of the individual and the subsequent process of socialization with which it articulates. It has previously been postulated that the infant's own activity, which prompts the environment to respond to his needs, stimulates the first feelings of omnipotence and creates the earliest basis for the experience of causality. The child's subsequent recognition of his dependence, occurring in the course of differentiation of self from object, has been assumed to result in an aggrandizement of parental power with a simultaneous renunciation of his own sense of omnipotence. The renunciation hypothesis is questioned in the light of the preoedipal child's capacity to introject the "omnipotent" parent and to merge magical self and object images. It has been generally accepted that a longing to recapture the "lost narcissism" leads to the eventual formation of the ego ideal and that the regulation of self esteem is thereafter largely dependent upon this internal agency. The degree of dependence on external recognition observed in the normal adult and the facility with which he reinvests narcissistic fantasies at the expense of object relations cannot be accounted for by the above. It is proposed that some determinants from the separation-individuation phase be considered in this context: the relationship between the rapid maturation of ego functions and activities, the narcissistic orientation characteristic of this period, and the influence of the mother during this developmental phase.

A number of interrelated hypotheses are presented. In this child-centered culture, the mother-child interactions, which occur before true causality has been established, have a number of potential consequences not previously emphasized. They may lay the foundation for the child's expectation of receiving recognition and reward for his adaptive achievements. They tend to perpetuate derivatives of omnipotence in the form of narcissistic fantasies, the latter coexisting with other derivatives of narcissism which undergo secondary autonomy. This narcissistic orientation complicates the establishment of object relations and the resolution of the oedipal conflict. Consequently, self-directed ego interests may occur at the expense of mature object love and other object-directed ego interests. During the latency period, expectations of achievement conveyed by family and school become institutionalized in the process of socialization. Henceforth, rewards are offered for success which lend a reality basis to the gifted child's wishes. Our social structure continues to reinforce narcissistically oriented attitudes throughout adolescence and into adulthood. It does so without adequate consideration for the limited institutional means of fulfilling such wishes. Moreover, preoccupation with admiration and acclaim may lead to an inhibition of the individual's capacity to function. As a consequence, dissatisfaction and disillusionment may ensue when life does not fulfill the infantile "promise."

BIBLIOGRAPHY

Bibring, E. (1953), The Mechanism of Depression. *Affective Disorders*, ed. P. Greenacre. NY: IUP, 13-48.

Deutsch, H. (1964), Some Clinical Considerations of the Ego Ideal. *J. Am. Psa. Assn.*, 12:512-516.

Erikson, E. H. (1950), *Childhood and Society*. NY: Norton.

—— (1959), *Identity and the Life Cycle. Psychological Issues*, 1.

—— (1964), Psychological Reality and Historical Actuality. *Insight and Responsibility*. NY: Norton, 159-216.

Escalona, S. (1953), Emotional Development in the First Year of Life. *Problems of Infancy and Childhood*, ed. M. J. E. Senn. NY: Josiah Macy Jr. Foundation, 11-92.

Fenichel, O. (1945), *The Psychoanalytic Theory of Neurosis*. NY: Norton.

Ferenczi, S. (1913), Stages in the Development of the Sense of Reality. *Sex and Psychoanalysis*. NY: Basic Books, 1950, 213-239.

Freud, A. (1936), *The Ego and the Mechanisms of Defense*. NY: IUP, 1946.

Freud, S. (1914), On Narcissism. *S.E.*, 14:67-102.

—— (1916), Some Character Types Met with in Psycho-Analytic Work. *S.E.*, 14:309-333.

—— (1916/17), Introductory Lectures on Psycho-Analysis. *S.E.*, 16.

—— (1921), Group Psychology and the Analysis of the Ego. *S.E.*, 18:67-143.

—— (1930), Civilization and Its Discontents. *S.E.*, 21:59-145.

Gitelson, M. (1954), Therapeutic Problems in the Analysis of the 'Normal' Candidate. *Int. J. Psa.*, 35:174-183.

Glover, E. (1929), The Psychology of the Psychotherapeutist. *On the Early Development of Mind*. NY: IUP, 1956, 91-107.

—— (1932), Medico-Psychological Aspects of Normality. *On the Early Development of Mind*. NY: IUP, 1956, 235-251.

—— (1955), *The Technique of Psycho-Analysis*. NY: IUP.

—— (1958), Ego Distortion. *Int. J. Psa.*, 39:261-264.

Greenacre, P. (1954), The Role of Transference. *J. Am. Psa. Assn.*, 2:671-684.

—— (1957), The Childhood of the Artist. *Psa. Study Ch.*, 12:47-72.

—— (1958), The Family Romance of the Artist. *Psa. Study Ch.*, 13:9-43.

—— (1961), A Critical Digest of the Literature on Selection of Candidates for Psychoanalytic Training. *Psa. Q.*, 30:28-55.

—— (1962), The Early Years of the Gifted Child. *1962 Yearbook of Education*. NY: Harcourt, Brace & World.

Greenson, R. R. (1965), The Working Alliance and the Transference Neurosis. *Psa. Q.*, 34:155-181.

Grinker, R. R. Sr., Grinker, R. R. Jr., & Timberlake, J. (1962), Mentally Healthy Young Males (The Homoclites). *Arch. Gen. Psychiat.*, 6:405-453.

Hartmann, H. (1939a), *Ego Psychology and the Problem of Adaptation*. NY: IUP, 1958.

—— (1939b), Psychoanalysis and the Concept of Health. *Essays*, 1-18.

—— (1944), Psychoanalysis and Sociology. *Essays*, 19-36.

—— (1947), On Rational and Irrational Action. *Essays*, 37-68.

—— (1948), Comments on the Psychoanalytic Theory of Instinctual Drives. *Essays*, 69-89.

—— (1950a), Comments on the Psychoanalytic Theory of the Ego. *Essays*, 113-141.

—— (1950b), The Application of Psychoanalytic Concepts to Sociology. *Essays*, 90-98.

—— (1951), Technical Implications of Ego Psychology. *Essays*, 142-154.

—— (1952), The Mutual Influences in the Development of Ego and Id. *Essays*, 155-181.

—— (1956), The Development of the Ego Concept in Freud's Works. *Essays*, 268-296.

—— Kris, E., & Loewenstein, R. M. (1951), Some Psychoanalytic Comments on "Culture and Personality." *Psychological Issues*, 14:86-116, 1964.

Hendrick, I. (1942), Instinct and the Ego during Infancy. *Psa. Q.*, 11:33-58.

Jacobson, E. (1959), The "Exceptions." *Psa. Study Ch.*, 14:135-154.

—— (1964), *The Self and the Object World*. NY: IUP.

Jahoda, M. (1958), *Current Concepts of Positive Mental Health*. NY: Basic Books.

Jones, E. (1931), The Concept of a Normal Mind. *Papers on Psycho-Analysis*. London: Baillière Tindall & Cox, 5th ed., 1948, 201-216.

—— (1953), *The Life and Work of Sigmund Freud*, I. NY: Basic Books.

Knight, R. P. (1953), The Present Status of Organized Psychoanalysis in the United States. *J. Am. Psa. Assn.*, 1:197-221.

Kris, E. (1951), Ego Psychology and Interpretation in Psychoanalytic Therapy. *Psa. Q.*, 20:15-30.

Lewin, B. D. & Ross, H. (1960), *Psychoanalytic Education in the United States*. NY: Norton.

Loewenstein, R. M. (1951), The Problem of Interpretation. *Psa. Q.*, 20:1-14.

Loomie, L. S., Rosen, V. H., & Stein, M. H. (1958). Ernst Kris and the Gifted Adolescent Project. *Psa. Study Ch.*, 13:44-63.

Macalpine, I. (1950), The Development of Transference. *Psa. Q.*, 19:501-539.

Mahler, M. S. (1957), On Two Crucial Phases of Integration Concerning Problems of Identity. In Panel: Problems of Identity, rep. D. Rubinfine. *J. Am. Psa. Assn.*, 6:131-142, 1958.

—— (1963), Thoughts about Development and Individuation. *Psa. Study Ch.*, 18:307-324.

—— & Furer, M. (1963), Certain Aspects of the Separation-Individuation Phase. *Psa. Q.*, 32:1-14.

—— & Gosliner, B. J. (1955), On Symbiotic Child Psychosis. *Psa. Study Ch.*, 10:195-212.

—— & La Perriere, K. (1965), Mother-Child Interaction during Separation-Individuation. *Psa. Q.*, 34:483-498.

Menninger, K. A., Mayman, M., & Pruyser, P. (1963), *The Vital Balance*. NY: Viking Pr.

Merton, K. R. (1957), *Social Theory and Social Structure*. Glencoe: Free Pr.

Michaels, J. J. (1959), Character Structure and Character Disorders. *American Handbook of Psychiatry*, 1:353-377. NY: Basic Books.

Murray, J. M. (1964), Narcissism and the Ego Ideal. *J. Am. Psa. Assn.*, 12:477-511.

Nunberg, H. (1925), The Will to Recovery. *Practice and Theory of Psychoanalysis*, 1:75-88. NY: IUP, 1956.

Parsons, T. (1949), *Essays on Sociological Theory*. NY: Free Pr. of Glencoe.

—— (1964), *Social Structure and Personality*. NY: Free Pr. of Glencoe.

—— et al. (1954), *Family, Socialization and Interaction Process*. NY: Free Pr. of Glencoe.

Piaget, J. (1937), *The Construction of Reality in the Child*. NY: Basic Books, 1954.

Provence, S. & Lipton, R. C. (1962), *Infants in Institutions*. NY: IUP.

—— & Ritvo, S. (1961), Effects of Deprivation on Institutionalized Infants. *Psa. Study Ch.*, 16:189-205.

Reich, A. (1953), Narcissistic Object Choice in Women. *J. Am. Psa. Assn.*, 1:22-44.

—— (1960), Pathologic Forms of Self-Esteem Regulation. *Psa. Study Ch.*, 15:215-232.

Ritvo, S. & Solnit, A. J. (1958), Influences of Early Mother-Child Interaction on Identification Processes. *Psa. Study Ch.*, 13:64-91.

Schur, M. (1955), Comments on the Metapsychology of Somatization. *Psa. Study Ch.*, 10:119-164.

—— (1958), The Ego and the Id in Anxiety. *Psa. Study Ch.*, 13:190-220.

Smith, M. B. (1950), Optima of Mental Health. *Psychiatry*, 13:503-510.

Spitz, R. A. (1945), Hospitalism. *Psa. Study Ch.*, 1:53-74.

—— (1946), Hospitalism: A Follow-up Report. *Psa. Study Ch.*, 2:113-117.

—— & Cobliner, W. G. (1965), *The First Year of Life*. NY: IUP.

Stone, L. (1954), The Widening Scope of Indications for Psychoanalysis. *J. Am. Psa. Assn.*, 2:567-594.

—— (1961), *The Psychoanalytic Situation*. NY: IUP.

Tartakoff, H. (1956), Recent Books on Psychoanalytic Technique. *J. Am. Psa. Assn.*, 4:318-343.

—— (1958), Introduction to Panel: The Psychoanalytic Concept of Character, rep. A. Valenstein. *J. Am. Psa. Assn.*, 6:567-575.

Wheelis, A. (1950), The Place of Action in Personality Change. *Psychiatry*, 13:135-
148.
——— (1956), Will and Psychoanalysis. *J. Am. Psa. Assn.*, 4:285-303.
White, R. (1963), *Ego and Reality in Psychoanalytic Theory. Psychol. Issues*, 11.
Wolff, P. H. (1959), Observations on Newborn Infants. *Psychosom. Med.*, 21:110-
118.
——— (1960), *The Developmental Psychologies of Jean Piaget and Psychoanalysis.
Psychol. Issues*, 5.

Old Age: Its Liabilities and Its Assets

A Psychobiological Discourse

GRETE L. BIBRING, M.D.

> "The old gray mare she ain't what she used to be many long years ago." *Da capo ad libitum.*
> *—American folk song*

> "If a family has in its midst an old person it possesses a jewel."
> *—Chinese proverb*

> ". . . Sans teeth, sans eyes, sans taste, sans everything."
> *—As You Like It*
> Act II, Scene 7
> Shakespeare

> "Wisdom is with the aged and understanding in length of days."
> *—Job 12:12*

In the course of the last twenty years I had the opportunity to work, in a general hospital[1] as well as in private practice, with an increasing number of elderly patients with neuroses, character disorders, acute anxiety states or patients under the stress of organic illness. I saw them under a variety of circumstances, as an observer or consultant, in psychotherapy or psychoanalysis. The impressions which I gathered and some of the conclusions at which I arrived over time brought me ever so often into conflict with concepts which were widely in use among psychoanalysts and to which I too adhered initially, expecting to find them corroborated without much doubt. It proved

[1] Beth Israel Hospital, Boston, Massachusetts.

that this was not always the case. I plan to discuss here some of the questions that seem to lack adequate answers within the current psychology of aging and to suggest some modifications which proved useful to me for a fuller understanding of this process.[2]

For a considerable time the psychology of old age has not been a central area of investigation for psychoanalysts, and especially not in so far as it relates to the process of normal and healthy aging. Only a few authors have concerned themselves with this topic (Helene Deutsch, 1945; Erikson, 1950; Benedek, 1950).

As early as 1898 Freud expressed pessimism regarding psychoanalysis as the appropriate technique for the aged: "Psycho-analytic therapy is not at present applicable to all cases. It . . . fails with people who are very advanced in years, because, owing to the accumulation of material in them, it would take up so much time that by the end of the treatment they would have reached a period of life in which value is no longer attached to nervous health" (p. 282). Later, Freud listed among further difficulties especially the rigidity of character configuration and defense and the increasing complications of adverse circumstances and reality constellations at this late phase of life. It was to a large extent due to Freud's cautioning that many psychoanalysts avoided intensive therapy with elderly patients. Although much of Freud's concern has retained its validity, and some of the very same problems still present sizable obstacles to treatment, his warning resulted in excessive reluctance in undertaking psychoanalytic therapy of the elderly. This in turn led to a paucity of clinical observations, leaving certain areas in the psychology of old age vague or even silent. They either escaped our attention or were explained on the basis of analogies and approximations. Only relatively few papers relating to this subject were published before 1950. Abraham (1919) was the first author who twenty years after Freud's article qualified the by then generally accepted point of view that elderly patients are of necessity poor therapeutic risks.

As time went on, psychoanalysts, aware of the mounting size and needs of the aged population, found themselves increasingly committed to work therapeutically with older people, though not yet to the same extent to which this has become the concern of general

---

[2] I regret that within the framework of this article I shall have to restrict myself to an outline of what seem to me the important issues. The detailed discussion as well as the particular case material will have to await later publication.

psychiatrists and psychologists in the field of mental health and a focus of investigation for biologists and physiologists.

The psychoanalytic writings on old age relate predominantly to the frequent and rather severe pathology of this period and to the special problems of therapy with the elderly patient (Kaufman, 1937; Gitelson, 1948; Grotjahn, 1955; Goldfarb, 1955/56; Gillespie, 1963; Levin, 1963). Only quite recently has the interest in normal aging taken a more central position. There now exist several studies of those aspects of aging which are related to the changes in gonadal function and their influence on the libidinal process as well as of the ensuing disturbances of a previously reached equilibrium between instinctual drives, modes of release of tension and inhibitions. The most frequently discussed problems are narcissistic and object-libidinal losses, fear of death, and the far-reaching instinctual regression.

Considering the multitude of specific conflicts and traumata in late life, it does not seem too surprising that this period is frequently perceived as one of disintegration or, at best, of stagnation. This impression may further be reinforced by our individual reactions toward aging and death, especially as they touch on, or are related by us to, our own future fate—a rather disconcerting topic for most people. And last but not least, working with elderly people taxes our therapeutic zeal which seeks worth-while success more through help given to the young than to the old who have in all probability only a limited span of time at their disposal.

The feelings evoked by the theme of death were impressed upon me by an episode which occurred during my student days. My involvement and serious interest in psychoanalysis gained momentum when I had the privilege to attend a few of the meetings of the Vienna Psychoanalytic Society. On one of these occasions Schilder mentioned his intention to work with dying patients in order to gain more insight into attitudes and reactions to death. I fully remember the uneasy silence which followed this daring and, as I recall it subjectively, almost sacrilegious statement, which fortunately did not deter Schilder from pursuing his interest (Schilder, 1927; Bromberg and Schilder, 1933).

Yet there are valid reasons to approach the topic of aging from a different direction, from the vantage point of life, development, and maturation. It may be necessary to justify this proposition on objective grounds, in order to avoid replacing a somewhat pessimistic prejudice by its antithetical overoptimistic counterpart. If we define development as a regular process of change in form, size, and function of the organism, then senescence has to be termed a developmental phase; its changes proceed in an orderly fashion, not in a random, individually variable form, and they follow a genetically given pathway through which control is introduced into the changes (Birren, 1959).

It may prove more difficult to answer the next question, that of maturation as a characteristic of old age. This dilemma, I believe, is predominantly due to a value judgment, rather generally attached to the concept of maturation. There exists a tendency to consider most steps forward in the life cycle as something slightly better than what has been before, and the word "maturing" holds implicitly an element of approval—until the cessation of the procreative function is reached. Yet in the human species, different from the salmon, the genetically given pattern does not end at this juncture, and longevity of man, safeguarded by medical progress, might reveal some intrinsic characteristics for which the term maturation—or, if this seems preferable, the term ripening—is appropriate. To understand this more adequately, we have to revise our tendency to perceive maturation exclusively in terms of a set system of values and have to introduce a more realistic and appropriate perspective. It seems that all those events in life in which intense new adjustments are necessary, forced by concomitant radical shifts in the somatic as well as in the psychological functions, like puberty, pregnancy, and menopause, represent a special, critical challenge for the individual (Benedek, 1950; G. Bibring, 1959; G. Bibring et al., 1961). Ever so often, if this psychosomatic crisis is not solved adequately, it may lead to neurosis, character disorder, and even psychosis. Such disappointing failures occur relatively frequently in the process of aging, yet they have to be understood as an equivalent of the postpuberty and postpregnancy disturbances and not as phenomena specific for old age. Furthermore, if the new tasks of this period are mastered well and adaptation to the changing inner and outer conditions has been achieved successfully, old age like every other developmental move has its gains as well as its losses, compared with the preceding period.

Rather than pursuing the pathology of aging, I shall attempt to concentrate on the special tasks which confront the aging person, and on the losses and gains which occur normally and characteristically in this phase. Or, in other words, we have to separate those achievements of previous developmental phases that are affected by restrictive factors in old age from those which continue unabatedly —barring diseases and traumata—and then raise the question whether there are distinctive functions under the changed conditions of late life which deserve our attention as representing an age-related special form of achievement.

As far as the problems are concerned which have to be met and solved, we cannot help but be impressed by the amount and variety of difficulties which occur almost regularly at this time of life. There is first and foremost the biological fact of termination of the reproductive function, an event that taxes severely the man's self esteem, so intimately related to his virile strength, and that of the woman, derived from her feminine attractiveness and female function.

Not biologically but culturally determined is a second crucial factor in the life of the majority of individuals in our society: the termination of a person's employment, his retirement. This again is to some extent of particular psychological importance for the man whose work achievements symbolize indirectly his contribution as the male; the woman's "retirement" problem, though equally serious, consists mainly in the separation from her children, at first through their greater independence as they grow up and finally through their marriage and establishment of their own home. In both men and women this leads to a disruption of contacts, a loosening or loss of object ties which had persisted through many years, and with it to some degree of isolation and emotional frustration. The termination of regular and essential work creates additional problems for other reasons. As much as we may complain about the burden of our work load, it fulfills for the human being a most important function in channeling some of his primitive impulses and needs toward sublimation. Aggression, greed, self centeredness, envy, etc.—they all may be used successfully in the service of professional and social activities, finding expression in the striving for achievements, for success, for leadership, for rewards, etc. To close this valuable outlet increases the inner pressure and tension, the feelings of helplessness and uselessness, and may turn loose aggression or produce depressive reactions (E. Bibring, 1953).

Other specific problems and traumata which invariably have to be met by the aging person are physical illness, frequently with

ensuing disability or chronic conditions, lessening of visual and auditory acuity, and the loss of the highly valued attractiveness of appearance and excellence of physical performance.

One of the most drastic assaults on the psychic equilibrium is the
unavoidable loss of friends and relatives which accompanies the late
years and which renders the aging person increasingly lonely, isolating him further from objects of high emotional value.

And finally, death as the inevitable outcome gains at this time a
significant position in the concept of one's self, in the relation to life
and to one's future. It is a well-known phenomenon that in most
healthy individuals the certainty of death which exists throughout
life is easily disregarded for many years; whereas the normal aging
person is bound to give it at least some attention. In studying attitudes
toward death in different individuals we are impressed with the
variety of quite dissimilar notions (Freud, 1913a; F. Deutsch, 1935;
Anthony, 1940; Bonaparte, 1951; Eissler, 1955; Payne, 1964; Weisman, 1965). This diversity may well be due to the fact that fantasy
cannot be corrected by direct experience; for the closest each of us
can come to a realization of the concept is through experiencing the
death of a person to whom we are strongly attached. Everything
beyond this is left to our individual imagination, which differs considerably from person to person. We therefore find in our clinical
work a wide spectrum of specific and often diametrically opposed
fears of death in different patients. It is my impression that the origin
of these varied forms of apprehension is determined quite regularly
by each patient's leading unconscious childhood anxieties. Accordingly, death may be feared as retaliation for one's own destructive
impulses, or it may represent the dangerous realization of masochistic
fantasies of complete surrender. It may provoke claustrophobic anxieties of being closed in or covered by a closeness that is deeply desired
and has to be warded off. Or death may stand for castration anxiety,
for fear of being annihilated, swallowed by the unknown; it may
revive old fears of being abandoned and deserted in the darkness—
there are probably as many variations as there are unconscious forms
of childhood conflicts, all of which we then summarize under the
term: fear of death.

It has been stated repeatedly that fear of death is a ubiquitous
factor. When it appears to be absent, the explanation likely to be
given is that it is warded off by denial. Clinical evidence does not

uphold this position. Although it is to be expected that death, with its unique peculiarity of being the crisis *par excellence*, and yet remaining unknown, alien, and inevitable, may well touch on the most central areas of our concerns: it represents the loss of one's self as the main recipient of narcissistic investment, the loss of all objects by being lost to them; and it evokes the earliest anxieties which are prone to gather around an idea that is presented from childhood on as the greatest disaster that can happen; and children are taught to avoid it at any price. Yet to assume that there is only one way of dealing with this perplexity simplifies unduly the manifold possibilities at our disposal. On the same basis on which we have to acknowledge the variety of concepts of death, I believe that we also have to consider a variety of specific and individual ways of dealing with its threat. For instance, there are people who genuinely have no deep grievance against dying, even though we often observe that as they come closer to this event, periods of alarm can set in, which may have to be assuaged by transient defensive emergency measures. This does not yet justify the assumption that a state of equilibrium at the thought of death cannot be genuine but is achieved only by its denial. In general we have to remember that each individual will deal with this issue according to the special circumstances and according to his habitual mechanisms of defense, and it becomes clear that this too will cover a wide range of effective methods.

To illustrate the diversity encountered, we have only to compare two well-known examples from the literature. In a paper on the psychological reactions to extreme and sudden dangers of mountain-climbing accidents, Pfister (1930) reports cases which deal with this experience by complete denial of the oncoming catastrophe and by turning it into its glorious, rosy opposite. A markedly different position is presented by Freud (1915), who summarizes his deliberations as follows: "We recall the old saying: *Si vis pacem, para bellum.* If you want to preserve peace, arm for war. It would be in keeping with the times to alter it: *Si vis vitam, para mortem.* If you want to endure life, prepare yourself for death" (p. 300).[3] This implies that

---

[3] It does not escape our attention that Freud's translation of his paraphrased version: *Si vis vitam, para mortem* is not exactly verbatim. It would have to read: "If you want to preserve life, prepare [yourself] for death." However, to contemplate Freud's modification further would lead us into complicated detours which are neither appropriate at this point, nor would they affect the over-all meaning which I inferred from the quotation.

awareness of and readiness to face and enter the uncanny unknown are the key to coping successfully with its otherwise disruptive effect on our life. To add one rather succinct manner of treating this subject: Senator Theodore F. Greene of Rhode Island was asked by an interviewer how it felt to have one's ninetieth birthday. He answered laconically: "Better than its alternative."

In summary, all the accumulated experiences which have been enumerated so far represent in their regularity and in their characteristic combination what we consider to be the tasks of old age. Whether they are dealt with successfully depends to a large extent on the psychological condition in which an individual enters this critical period. If he is not already afflicted with a neurosis or with a neurotic predisposition toward specific aspects of aging, he may well become unsettled and deeply distressed at certain periods and under certain trying circumstances, but we can expect him to be able to surmount these difficulties in time and adjust to the changing conditions. The decisive roles in the resolution are played by a variety of factors: by a life that had its measure of instinctual gratification, by an ability to tolerate narcissistic injuries without serious regressive reactions, and by a superego structure that is sufficiently flexible and tolerant to permit some unavoidable modifications in the standards of the preceding years.[4] It then can be shown that the receding sexual drive does not of necessity lead to intense anxiety or depression, nor does retirement objectively represent demotion and abandonment; an emotionally resilient person, furthermore, can accept and integrate the limiting and disabling physical conditions without breaking down. All these experiences, taxing as they may be—especially the loss of beloved people, which represents the most intensive challenge to a person's inner resources—all lie within the limit of human adaptability. But once these adversities have been mastered and the crisis subsides, we may discover that there is an unexpected linkage between the very same events which were the cause of such intense distress and the further developmental moves in old age. For by the same token of emotional losses and ensuing withdrawal and detachment, by the decrease of the intensity of instinctual drives, by the cooling off of the libidinal involvement, by the easing of the heavy

---

[4] In a most stimulating paper Kurt Eissler (1963) discussed his interesting theory about the function of the superego in old age.

burden of rigid work commitments, old age can provide a freedom from outer and inner pressure which in this form may never have existed before.

Considering the intensive realignment which has to take place in the libidinal economy and in the redistribution of psychic energy, we may ask whether there are sufficient resources and sufficient impetus left which can be put to use in maintaining adequately the interest in living and functioning under these changed conditions. It is a generally accepted assumption that, as the genital sexual strivings decline, earlier, pregenital impulses and their derivatives take their place. This then accounts for the usually increasing appreciation of certain pleasures, like food and physical comfort, people's care and attention, or for the inclination toward the observance of minute habits and the insistence on regularity of daily events. There is, furthermore, in many cases a desire to take up old interests which had been given up in early adolescence, brushed aside as nonessentials in the heavy commitments of adult life; and if there is a genuine capacity of deriving satisfaction from the subtler pleasures of an aesthetic or intellectual nature, the aging person may well turn back to them after many years.

This process of establishing a positive adjustment to a new phase of life deserves some reconsideration and requires partial revision of the term regression, which is without exception included in the psychoanalytic theory of old age. The term is applied so generally and almost taken for granted in the literature, as if it represented a basic feature of the vicissitudes of instincts in the aging. It is employed without further differentiation from the concept we ordinarily have in mind when we use this term: i.e., regression as an essential factor in the neurotic process, a means of dealing with intense unconscious conflicts, leading to recathexis of earlier libidinal positions, to reaction formation against the re-emerging pregenital impulses, and finally to symptom formation produced by the compromise between the two opposing forces. There is no convincing reason to assume that this mechanism, pertaining to psychopathology, underlies all the changes which take place in the instinctual manifestations of the aged—provided that we do not yield to the implicit bias that pathology is a constant admixture to the aging process. This distinction is important, although sometimes difficult to maintain, in

view of the fact that neurotic regression also occurs, and quite frequently, at this critical juncture.[5]

There is another form of regression which reinforces the over-all
tendency toward libidinal withdrawal—this is regression in the service
of the ego (Kris, 1934), the protective and adaptive modes which
are employed in situations of stress outside of neurotic conflicts (Hartmann, 1947; A. Freud, 1951, 1963, 1965). They too may well play
an important role for the elderly person, facilitating and sustaining
the necessary acts of resignation and renunciation. However, the
main course of the instinctual shift which I discussed before, as closely
as it may resemble other, actively regressive moves, is not to be seen
as reaction to conflicts or stresses, but is part of a sequence of psychobiological events, initiated by the progressive involution of the gonads.
As they are the source of the mature sexual drive, their receding
functions result in the decrease of the intensity of drive. And what
had been achieved under the impact of endocrine development in
puberty, the primacy of the genital organization over the instinctual
components, will now lose its powerful position under the reversed
endocrine conditions of later life. It seems in keeping with clinical
observations made on the normal aging individual to explain in this
way the signs of undisturbed and undisturbing pregenital trends
(Berezin, 1963; Linden, 1963; Zinberg, 1963). In an earlier discussion
(1965), I used as an analogue the diurnal changes in the sky: the
stars are present all through the day, but they become visible only
at sundown. Similarly, needs and wishes of early years, which were
present but played a minor role for many decades, regain their importance when the urgency of the intensive drives of an active goal
and object-directed life diminishes. These needs and wishes then
come to our attention as the special concerns and peculiarities of the
aged, and they play a significant role in providing him with a variety

[5] It may be of interest to note that in contrast to the axiomatic position which the
theory of regression in old age holds in the psychoanalytic literature, there is a
marked absence of studies investigating or corroborating this thesis further. In an
attempt to trace the origin of the theory I found only two papers which concern
themselves with the issue: Freud's essay on "The Disposition to Obsessional Neurosis"
(1913b) and Ferenczi's article, "Psychoneuroses in the Age of Involution" (1921). In
both papers the conclusions were based on case material from disturbed patients—
and then were discussed as a possible explanation of the frequently observed post-
climacteric character changes in older women. At no point was it stated that this
refers to a regular occurrence and, as a matter of fact, the picture drawn by both
authors was more representative of a character neurosis than of a normal elderly
woman.

of satisfactions. The lowered level of intensity on which pressures and discharge of drives operate under the new conditions corresponds well to the diminishing strength and resilience of the whole organism (Shock, 1962), and thus a balanced state of equilibrium can be established.

In the preceding pages I have limited myself to a discussion of the psychological phenomena related to the alterations of an instinctual nature, based on endocrine involution, and to the specific life experiences which are characteristic of the normal course of aging.

Aging, however, is not restricted to the instinctual life, but involves the whole organism and its performance. Therefore, it is of particular interest for us to broaden our field of investigation and to turn our attention to the ego and ego functions and to ask how far these may be influenced by the aging process in the central nervous system, i.e., the organ that represents their somatic substratum.

From the earliest beginnings of his discoveries and throughout all his years of exploration, Freud held firmly to the conviction and the hope that his psychological findings and the contributions of biology would meet in the future, establishing a comprehensive foundation for the theory of man (1895, 1940).

Psychoanalysts are keenly aware of the basic biological orientation underlying our psychological system, at least as far as it relates to the theory of instincts and to id psychology. However, for many this does not quite include the field of ego psychology, and it is Hartmann's merit to have corrected, whenever possible, this misunderstanding and to have explicated those factors which clarify the ego's relatedness to the biological concepts of psychoanalysis (1939, 1950). As early as 1927 Hartmann introduced in his writings the question of the interdependence between psychoanalysis and the natural and social sciences. He, like Freud, foresees significant scientific gains in the rapprochement between our field and that of biology and physiology. At the same time he expresses concern lest we might be tempted to make use of their scientific methods, models, and terms, which seem considerably more exact than ours, before they prove to be adequate for the special conditions of our own science (1958).

These cautioning remarks are certainly called for, considering the various attempts to streamline the complex system of psychoanalysis —even if it has to be at the expense of essential content—in order to facilitate communication and to keep up with the physical science.

At the same time this should not be misunderstood as condoning a disregard for advances made in related fields. Critical attention and the willingness to give careful thought to achievements which promise to contribute to our own endeavor are part of our scientific commitment.

Some interesting beginnings have been made with regard to ego development in early childhood. Bronson (1963) approached this problem by relating neurophysiological findings to psychoanalytic concepts of ego functions in infancy. Other authors have studied the correlations between early personality development and the conditions of the sensory or neuromuscular apparatus (Bergman and Escalona, 1949; Wolff, 1960).

If we broaden our approach to include physiological data, there are reasons to expect that old age, like infancy, may yield further insight into ego-psychological mechanisms such as thought processes, perception, memory, all of which are subject to the changes peculiar to this late phase of life.

My own interest in this problem developed in the course of studying the contrasting images of the aged among different cultures (Simmons, 1946; Parsons, 1948; Chandler, 1949). We know that in many primitive societies the oldest members are believed to have great, even superhuman, power, vast knowledge, and are revered as magicians, priests, and prophets. We find a somewhat similar situation in highly developed cultures with strong family ties and with religious systems and philosophies that value tranquility, tolerance, and wisdom, in cultures that do not idealize ambition, intense activity, and worldly achievements: there the old person by far surpasses the young in esteem and in stature as the mentor and teacher. In contrast, in cultures in which youth and strength and the ability to change to new ways and to dare and venture are the traditionally admired ideal, the slow-moving, conservative, aged individual may be tolerated and treated kindly at best, but he has little or no significant function or value. This implicitly fosters the general opinion that he is not only physically but also intellectually not quite competent. What then are the objective facts? This was the question that intrigued me. Where does the main distortion lie—in the overidealization of the intellectual capacity of their elders in some cultures or in the depreciation of their mental functions in others?

I shall not present here the tortuous ways I had to pursue in this inquiry, but record briefly the main sources which I found helpful and the conclusions which I drew tentatively; those will finally lead me back to the main thesis of this paper.

If we again concern ourselves exclusively with the healthy older person who does not show any signs of distinctive mental pathology, two questions are foremost. The first refers to the characteristic impairment of memory for recent events; the second is a similarly frequent absentmindedness or slight confusion with a tendency toward parapraxes in writing, speech, and actions. We are inclined to resolve these problems by utilizing the concept of repression, so familiar to psychoanalysts: conflicts—between wishful fantasies, which serve to replace the painful and disappointing present, and superego prohibitions—are warded off, permitting an escape from this distressing dilemma as well as from disenchanting reality testing. The actual events are shut out, whereas episodes from earlier, better days are kept alive and admitted to recall. Here, as in our discussion of regression, full credit has to be given to the importance of these psychological findings which can be confirmed in a great number of cases. But here, as before, there should be some recognition of the physiological changes which occur at this time and which may contribute to a fuller appreciation of the total process.

The rapid development in the fields of biochemistry, molecular biology, and neurophysiology indicates that many of the heretofore unexplained phenomena of aging might come closer within our reach. Two of the salient recent advances have bearing on our questions. First, the research done on memory coding, following the work of Watson and Crick (1953) on DNA (deoxyribonucleic acid) and the subsequent studies on messenger RNA (ribonucleic acid), produced a number of interesting investigations concerned with RNA as the carrier of memory engrams, with their distribution over the central nervous system, and their storage place in the brain (Hyden, 1960; McConnel et al., 1959; Corning and John, 1961; Penfield, 1959; Penfield and Milner, 1958; Magoun, 1958). Further studies indicated that the content of RNA in the nerve cells increases significantly between the ages of 3 and 40 and declines rapidly after 60 (Hyden, 1961). Although there is still the controversy going on whether the genetic molecules, DNA and RNA, are the exclusively important factors in the coding of memory, or only one, though essential, element among others, the import of the basic conception has been acknowledged widely (Dingman and Sporn, 1964; Schmitt, 1965). In summary, it suggests that memory loss in senescence is somatically conditioned and that stored memory deposits are not, or at least less, affected by the aging process in the brain than are recent memories.[6]

A second source of relevant data comes from neuroelectrical and neurophysiological research on the transmission of nerve impulses from one neuron to the next. In the course of the later years, this process is found to develop irregularities which affect perception in specific ways. The nerve impulse, which is identified as an electric change, normally progresses from one neuron to the next by way of chemical modifications at the locus of transmission (synapse) (Brazier, 1961; Eccles, 1965). Chemical deviations have been discovered in the synaptic area of the old individual and it is hypothesized that these are responsible for disorganizing the process of transmission. These factors interfere with the synchronous firing of nerve impulses which guarantees the smooth progress of the wave of excitation over the length of its pathway; instead they create spontaneous, disrupting, random firing.

In order to evaluate the kind and intensity of disturbances in the

[6] If I may be permitted to indulge in further conjectures—knowing perfectly well that this whole area of investigation is still in a highly experimental stage—a rather captivating sequel can be imagined. DNA has been identified by Watson and Crick as the molecular basis for the genetic replication between the parent organisms and their progeny. RNA furthermore is considered by a large group of research workers as the basis for the formation and preservation of memory. But at the same time experiments are now pursued which claim that memory of learned skills can be transferred from one flatworm (planarian) to another, by the latter's ingestion of the former's RNA content (McConnel, 1962). I do not lose sight of the doubts which have been evoked by these experiments, nor do I overestimate my competence to form an opinion of my own. Yet I find it rather intriguing to link these present efforts in solving the enigma of heredity and memory with two early theoretical speculations:

One is Semon's *Die Mneme*, the psychophysiological system that attempts to connect the phenomena of memory engrams and heredity (1904). The present investigations may provide some biological foundation for this theory which never had any real influence on contemporary scientific thinking. The other refers to one of Freud's imaginative speculations on hereditary memory (1939): "When we study the reactions to early traumas, we are quite often surprised to find that they are not strictly limited to what the subject himself has really experienced but diverge from it in a way which fits in much better with the model of a phylogenetic event and, in general, can only be explained by such an influence. . . . Its evidential value seems to me strong enough for me to venture on a further step and to posit the assertion that the archaic heritage of human beings comprises not only dispositions but also subject-matter—memory-traces of the experience of earlier generations. . . . My position, no doubt, is made more difficult by the present attitude of biological science, which refuses to hear of the inheritance of acquired characters by succeeding generations. I must, however, in all modesty confess that nevertheless I cannot do without this factor in biological evolution" (p. 99f.).

mental functioning of the later years of life a number of psychological tests have been carried out, comparing the performance of older age groups (55 and above) with groups of younger persons (20 and above) (Lorge, 1939). They demonstrate that under average conditions the test scores show a ratio clearly in favor of the younger group. However, careful analysis of the details of performance led to the following interesting conclusions. There is a definite slowing down of the perceptual process in the old person. He is less able to scan the incoming stimuli and to evaluate them in optimal time, i.e., as quickly as the young person does. He therefore is also less able to react to and manipulate the incoming stimuli in optimal time. This is ascribed to the synaptic changes causing volleys of impulses that interfere with signal detection and decoding. Though the responses are slower, it appears that they are not less discriminating than in the sample of young individuals. Other drawbacks are due to the difficulty in retaining recent impressions, i.e., to the decline in memory that has been discussed above.[7] Finally, there is a reduced capacity to withstand stress, as part of the general loss of resilience; this is greatly taxed in the test situation by the impact of constantly varying stimuli which cannot be processed adequately and thus lead to a kind of overloading of the afferent channels. However, when the time limit is lifted in testing both groups, then the scores of the older persons improve markedly and they even show some advantage over the younger individuals, with especially high results in the area of organized, stored information. In contrast to the performance under laboratory conditions, the elderly are able in real life to compensate for their defects; they retain their ability for strategic organization of their tasks and as workers they proved more responsible, have fewer accidents, spoil less, need less supervision, and their output is equal to that of younger men (Welford, 1959).

If we now take these findings back to our earlier summary, to the characteristics of the aging person who has come to terms with his object-lidibinal and narcissistic losses and with the incisive changes in the intensity and quality of his instinctual drives, then we become aware of a rather impressive configuration. The changes which occur at this time in the ego as well as in the instinctual drives correspond mutually in significant ways, and in their combination they not only

[7] George Klein's paper (see this volume, pp. 377-389) contributes significantly to the understanding of the different aspects of memory.

represent the limitations of this last developmental phase but they also contribute to its special style and to its achievements. In the light of this, what then are the relevant characteristics of the aged person? He is slowed down in his motor activities and cannot keep up with the pace of life around him. He is less dominated by his instinctual drives than is the young person, less emotionally involved in people and issues, less enthused about their virtues, and more tolerant of their shortcomings. He is forgetful and avoids as far as possible the barrage of incoming stimuli which renders him inattentive, but he is also less distracted and influenced by them. He is altogether more inner-directed than before, inclined to reminisce and to meditate. Whatever knowledge and experience he has acquired over many years and his command of intelligent task solution remain with him for indeterminate time.

There are marked variations in the libidinal as well as in the ego-psychological organization of different individuals, in their endowment which enables them to deal with some factors better than with others, in their history which may have prepared them well or left them unequipped to meet the challenge of this new pattern of life. There are also marked differences to be found in the chronology of the somatic changes and in the intensity with which these changes take place. At the same time we can be certain that all forms of aging have in common some of the basic features outlined above, either singly or in combination, explicitly or in modified form. They therefore permit us to sketch in rough outlines the essential weakness and strength of the aging person. His limitations lie in his increasing failure to remain an equal partner in the world of active striving, in his withdrawn and self-contained inclinations, and in his lack of interest, attention, and memory for outside signals and communications. In a world where "Go-Go!" is the password, he easily appears to be an obstacle and at times a burden.

I see the assets of the aging in the primacy of his thinking process which, drawing on accumulated knowledge and experience, is relatively free from emotional involvement and bias, and relatively closed against the interference of immediate perceptual distraction. In the mythical elaboration of primitive societies this has given rise to the image of the magician, the priest, and the prophet. In more rationally oriented cultures the equivalent role of choice is that of the counselor, the arbiter, the elder statesman.

This was expressed in his witty way by Aristide Briand who was asked to explain why the French show such preference for octogenarians in the most responsible government positions. To which he answered, "Because there are too few ninety-year-old men around."[8]

BIBLIOGRAPHY

Abraham, K. (1919), The Applicability of Psycho-Analytic Treatment to Patients at an Advanced Age. *Selected Papers on Psycho-Analysis.* London: Hogarth, 1948, 312-317.
Anthony, S. (1940), *The Child's Discovery of Death.* NY: Harcourt, Brace.
Benedek, T. (1950), Climacterium. *Psa. Q.,* 21:1-27.
Berezin, M. A. (1963), Some Intrapsychic Aspects of Aging. In Zinberg & Kaufman (1963), 93-117.
Bergman, P. & Escalona, S. K. (1949), Unusual Sensitivities in Very Young Children. *Psa. Study Ch.,* 3/4:333-352.
Bibring, E. (1953), The Mechanism of Depression. *Affective Disorders,* ed. P. Greenacre. NY: IUP, 13-48.
Bibring, G. L. (1959), Some Considerations of the Psychological Processes in Pregnancy. *Psa. Study Ch.,* 14:113-121.
——— (1965), Discussion of: A Transference Reaction in a Sixty-six-year-old Woman, by M. Gitelson. *Geriatric Psychiatry,* ed. M. A. Berezin & S. H. Cath. NY: IUP, 187-194.
——— et al. (1961), A Study of the Psychological Processes in Pregnancy and of the Earliest Mother-Child Relationship: I & II. *Psa. Study Ch.,* 16:9-72.
Birren, J. E. (1959), Principles of Research on Aging. *Handbook of Aging and the Individual,* ed. J. E. Birren. Chicago: Univ. Chicago Pr., 3-42.
Bonaparte, M. (1951), *Monologues devant la Vie et la Mort.* Paris: Presses Universitaires de France.
Brazier, M. A. B. (1961), *A History of the Electrical Activity of the Brain.* London: Pitman.
Bromberg, W. & Schilder, P. (1933), Death and Dying. *Psa. Rev.,* 20:133-135.
Bronson, G. (1963), A Neurological Perspective on Ego Development in Infancy. *J. Am. Psa. Assn.,* 11:55-65.
Chandler, A. R. (1949), The Traditional Chinese Attitude towards Old Age. *J. Geront.,* 4:239-243.
Corning, W. C. & John, E. R. (1961), Effect of Ribonuclease on Retention of Conditioned Response in Regenerated Planarians. *Science,* 134:1363-1365.
Deutsch, F. (1935), Euthanasia. *Psa. Q.,* 5:347-368, 1936.
Deutsch, H. (1945), *The Psychology of Women,* 2. NY: Grune & Stratton.
Dingman, W. & Sporn, M. B. (1964), Molecular Theories of Memory. *Science,* 144:26-29.
Eccles, J. C. (1965), The Synapse. *Sci. Amer.,* 212:56-66.
Eissler, K. R. (1955), *The Psychiatrist and the Dying Patient.* NY: IUP.
——— (1963), Preliminary Remarks on the Psychology of Dementia Senilis. Abst. in: *J. Am. Psa. Assn.,* 12:151-159, 1964.
Erikson, E. H. (1950), *Childhood and Society.* NY: Norton.
Ferenczi, S. (*c.* 1921), A Contribution to the Understanding of the Psychoneuroses of the Age of Involution. *Final Contributions to the Problems and Methods of Psycho-Analysis.* London: Hogarth, 1955, 205-212.

---

[8] Personal communication from Marie Bonaparte.

Freud, A. (1951), Observations on Child Development. *Psa. Study Ch.*, 6:18-30.
────── (1963), Regression as a Principle in Mental Development. *Bull. Menninger Clin.*, 27:126-139.
────── (1965), *Normality and Pathology in Childhood.* NY: IUP.
Freud, S. (1895), Project for a Scientific Psychology. *The Origins of Psychoanalysis.* NY: Basic Books, 1954, 347-445.
────── (1898), Sexuality in the Aetiology of the Neuroses, *S.E.*, 3:261-285.
──────·(1913a), The Theme of the Three Caskets. *S.E.*, 12:289-301.
────── (1913b), The Disposition to Obsessional Neurosis. *S.E.*, 12:311-326.
────── (1915), Thoughts for the Times on War and Death. *S.E.*, 14:273-302.
────── (1939), Moses and Monotheism. *S.E.*, 23:3-137.
────── (1940), An Outline of Psycho-Analysis. *S.E.*, 23:141-207.
Gillespie, G. W. (1963), Some Regressive Phenomena in Old Age. *Brit. J. Med. Psychol.*, 36:203-209.
Gitelson, M. (1948), The Emotional Problems of Elderly People. *Geriatrics*, 3:135-150.
Goldfarb, G. A. (1955/56), Psychotherapy of Aged Persons. *Psa. Rev.*, 42:180-187; 43:68-81.
Grotjahn, M. (1955), Analytic Psychotherapy with the Elderly. *Psa. Rev.*, 42:419-427.
Hartmann, H. (1927), *Die Grundlagen der Psychoanalyse.* Leipzig: Georg Thieme.
────── (1939), *Ego Psychology and the Problem of Adaptation.* NY: IUP, 1958.
────── (1947), On Rational and Irrational Action, *Essays*, 37-68.
────── (1950), Comments on the Psychoanalytic Theory of the Ego. *Essays*, 113-141.
────── (1958), Comments on the Scientific Aspects of Psychoanalysis. *Essays*, 297-317.
Hyden, H. (1960), The Neuron. *The Cell*, 5:215-323, ed. J. Brachet & A. E. Mirsky. NY: Academic Pr.
────── (1961), Satellite Cells in the Nervous System. *Sci. Amer.*, 205:62-70.
Kaufman, M. R. (1937), Psychoanalysis in Late-Life Depressions. *Psa. Q.*, 6:308-335.
Kris, E. (1934), The Psychology of Caricature. *Psychoanalytic Explorations in Art.* NY: IUP, 1952, 173-188.
Levin, S. (1963), Depression in the Aged. *Geriatrics*, 18:302-307.
Linden, M. E. (1963), Regression and Recession in the Psychoses of the Aging. In Zinberg & Kaufman (1963), 125-142.
Lorge, I. (1939), Psychometry. *Amer. J. Orthopsychiat.*, 10:56-57, 1940.
McConnell, J. V. (1962), Memory Transfer through Cannibalism in Planarians. *J. Neuropsychiat.*, 3:S42-S48 (Supplement #1).
────── Jacobson, A. L., & Kimble, D. P. (1959), The Effects of Regeneration upon Retention of a Conditioned Response in the Planarian. *J. Comp. Physiol. Psychol.*, 52:1-5.
Magoun, H. W. (1958), *The Waking Brain.* Springfield, Ill.: Thomas.
Parsons, T. (1948), Age and Sex in the Social Structure of the United States. *Personality in Nature, Society and Culture*, ed. C. Kluckhohn, H. A. Murray, & D. M. Schneider. NY: Knopf, 363-375.
Payne, E. C. (1964), Teaching Medical Psychotherapy in Special Clinic Settings. *Psychiatry and Medical Practice in a General Hospital*, ed. N. E. Zinberg. NY: IUP, 135-168.
Penfield, W. (1959), The Interpretive Cortex. *Science*, 129:1719-1725.
────── & Milner, B. (1958), Memory Deficit Produced by Bilateral Lesions in the Hippocampal Zone. *AMA Arch. Neurol. Psychiat.*, 79:475-497.
Pfister, O. (1930), Schockdenken und Schockphantasien bei höchster Todesgefahr. *Int. Z. Psa.*, 16:430-455.
Schilder, P. (1927), Über Stellungnahme Todkranker. *Med. Klin.*, 27:784-786.
Schmitt, F. O. (1965), The Physical Basis of Life and Learning. *Science*, 149:931-936.
Semon, R. (1904), *Die Mneme.* Leipzig: Engelmann.
Shock, N. W. (1962), The Physiology of Aging. *Sci. Amer.*, 206:100-111.
Simmons, L. W. (1946), Attitudes toward Aging and the Aged. *J. Geront.*, 1:72-95.

Watson, J. D. & Crick, F. H. C. (1953), Genetical Implications of the Structure of Deoxyribonucleic Acid. *Nature*, 171:964-967.

Weisman, A. D. (1965), *The Existential Core of Psychoanalysis*. Boston: Little, Brown.

Welford, A. T. (1959), Psychomotor Performance. *Handbook of Aging and the Individual*, ed. J. E. Birren. Chicago: Univ. Chicago Pr.

Wolff, P. H. (1960), *The Developmental Psychologies of Jean Piaget and Psychoanalysis. Psychol. Issues, 5*.

Zinberg, N. E. (1963), The Relationship of Regressive Phenomena to the Aging Process. In Zinberg & Kaufman (1963), 143-159.

———— & Kaufman, I., eds. (1963), *Normal Psychology of the Aging Process*. NY: IUP.

IV

Contributions to
Psychoanalytic Theory

Self Observation, Reality, and the Superego

MARTIN H. STEIN, M.D.

My thesis is the following. First: self observation is an essential element in the process of reality testing. Second: self observation and self evaluation are inextricably linked, and are intimately involved with superego functions. Therefore, the superego functions play an essential, if indirect, role in reality testing and reality adaptation.

I

I should prefer to distinguish between the terms "reality testing" and "reality function," using the former as a special case of the latter, generic term. Thus reality testing, as used here, would consist of the examination whether a sense impression is a genuine perception of objective reality, a distorted perception, or a hallucination.

Freud's simplest description of reality testing is to be found in "A Metapsychological Supplement to the Theory of Dreams" (1917), defining it as the "function of orientating the individual in the world by discrimination between what is internal and what is external . . . [via that] which determines whether the perception can be made to disappear or whether it proves resistant. Reality-testing need be nothing more than this contrivance." He ascribed it to "the system *Cs.* (*Pcpt.*) alone" (p. 233). Later, this should have placed it clearly in the ego, but it underwent a number of vicissitudes before and since in Freud's writings, and for good reasons.

The above definition did not quite cover the ground, for it failed to account sufficiently for the very "reality" in which Freud was interested, namely, that which is determined by the inspection of one's own mental processes. In his later writings he recognized this inadequacy, as well as the complications which accompanied a more inclusive definition. The latter was most clearly expressed by Hartmann (1956): "In a broader sense, reality testing also refers to the ability to discern subjective and objective elements in our judgments on reality" (p. 256).

It is reasonable to assume that reality testing as applied to the outer world, and that which is directed toward one's own mental processes, are interdependent. I am of the opinion that self observation plays a ubiquitous role in reality testing. The latter would be subject to serious limitations or impairment were there not a constant flow of stimuli from the inner world and were the capacity lacking to perceive and evaluate these inner stimuli.

This is, after all, one of the basic assumptions underlying the theory of psychoanalytic therapy. We do expect, at least implicitly, that as a result of analysis our patients will see the world more clearly and deal with it more efficiently. Our approach differs from other psychotherapies in that we explicitly *avoid* reality testing—at least in the usual sense. We need not tell our patients that they have misjudged a life situation, nor do we as a rule give in to the temptation to correct a misapprehension of some analytic event. Instead, we attempt to correct, by analysis, those distortions of self observation which become evident in the analytic situation. By attaining a clearer vision of his own mental processes, by unsparing honesty with himself, we hope that our patient's distortions of perception of the outer world will be reduced to a minimum.

Defects in self observation are not solely responsible for the misinterpretation of perceptions; lack of adequate data, unfamiliarity, disturbances of the perceptive apparatus, defective intellectual capacity may all impair reality testing. But I would maintain that self observation is a *necessary*, although not a sufficient or sole determining factor in the adequate evaluation of reality.

Not only does defective capacity for self observation result in impairment of reality testing; reciprocally, assaults from outside may impair the accuracy of perception of one's inner world. Sensory deprivation experiments and solitary confinement often result in serious disturbances of the capacity to distinguish inner from outer stimuli. So-called brainwashing, in which a mass of incongruous stimuli is supplied, may again lead to distortions of one's self image. Overwhelming external stimuli (such as exposure to prolonged combat conditions, or intractable pain) may produce similar disturbances. It is evident that some flow of more or less familiar perceptual stimuli readily capable of integration into one's past experience is necessary for the maintenance of adequate self observation and evaluation.

Ordinarily in the healthy adult we see the most marked shifts in the function of reality testing in connection with sleep and dreaming. The waking process, in fact, constitutes a crisis with respect to one's attitude toward the outer world. The chief task of one who wakes from sleep is to determine that he is *awake;* that what occupied him before, the thoughts, perceptions, and affects of his dreams, were indeed part of the dream; that they came from within and from the past, not from the outside and the immediate present.

This process of waking has been described most vividly by Marcel Proust (1920), who seems to have spent much of his life making observations for which the rest of us have neither the introspective capacity nor the leisure:

> That kind of sleep is called "sleeping like lead", and it seems as though one has become, oneself, and remains for a few moments after such a sleep is ended, simply a leaden image. *One is no longer a person.* How then, seeking for one's mind, one's personality, as one seeks for a thing that is lost, does one recover one's own self rather than any other? Why, when one begins again to think, is it not another personality than yesterday's that is incarnate in one? One fails to see what can dictate the choice, or why, among the millions of human beings any one of whom one might be, it is on him who one was overnight that unerringly one lays one's hand? What is it that guides us, when there has been an actual interruption—whether it be that our unconsciousness has been complete or our dreams entirely different from ourself? There has indeed been death, as when the heart has ceased to beat and a rhythmical friction of the tongue revives us. No doubt the room, even if we have seen it only once before, awakens memories to which other, older memories cling. Or were some memories also asleep in us of which we now become conscious? The resurrection at our awakening—*after that healing attack of mental alienation which is sleep*—must after all be similar to what occurs when we recapture a name, a line, a refrain that we had forgotten. And perhaps the resurrection of the soul after death is to be conceived as a phenomenon of memory [my italics].

To the child who awakens from a nightmare, we say (after turning on the light): "There was no tiger, you are safe, it was only a dream." In effect we advise him to test reality by looking about him, to recognize that his experience was not based on external perception.

In urging him to admit: "It was only a dream," we hope to start another important mental operation. Now he is to inspect his own psychic processes, and to decide that what he experienced came from *within* and does not have the same significance as that which might have come from outside. This need not always be so. If we had said, "The tiger is gone now," we should have reassured him perhaps, but discouraged investigation of the internal source of the tiger in his room. But if we say, "There was no tiger, it was only a dream," we are urging him to look for the sources of the tiger within himself; inviting him, so to speak, to do a little bit of introspection. Here we urge more active self observation in order to strengthen the function of reality testing.

This experience is not confined to children. Many of us may remember episodes of awakening from a vivid dream and for a few interminable moments being unsure that the dream had really been only that, and not a part of the world's reality.

II

To what extent is the superego involved in this process? There has never been widespread agreement on this question, and Freud does not seem to have been altogether sure of the answer.

In 1921, he stated: "The fact that the ego experiences in a *dream-like* way whatever he [the hypnotist] may request or assert reminds us that we omitted to mention among the functions of the *ego ideal* the business of testing the reality of things" (p. 114; my italics). The "omission" was a significant one, for reality testing was definitely attributed to the ego two years later (1923).

This shift inevitably followed the formulation of the structural hypothesis, since the ego was granted exclusive jurisdiction over transactions with the "external" world. Nevertheless, this did not settle the problem entirely for Freud (see 1933). He was not at all certain which structures, ego or superego or both, were responsible for the evaluation of the psychic processes themselves, and it seems likely that he was never satisfied with the answer.

Over thirty years ago, Waelder (1934) declared, "This function of the superego, self observation, with its perception of inner events, makes a contribution to the distinction between inner and outer world, between fantasy and reality. . . . The intactness of the super-ego function is therefore a necessary condition of proper reality testing."

A similar attitude is implicit in Isakower's (1939, 1954) work, and he is in general agreement with the point of view that the superego must play an important role in self observation (personal communication).

Gitelson (1964), in his last major statement, described reality testing as "not simply a solipsistic ego function, but . . . also a manifestation of social validations internalized in the superego" (p. 452).

With the progress of ego psychology, however, more and more functions have been ascribed to the ego portion of the mental apparatus. This has led to the development of a consistent and workable body of theory, thanks especially to Hartmann and to his collaborators, Kris and Loewenstein. It has reached a point of development which allows us to direct to it a great number of questions, with the expectation that it will be more or less successful in answering them.

In general, the implications of Hartmann's closely reasoned work are that self observation becomes, with progress toward maturity, more and more an ego rather than a superego function.

There is agreement, at any rate, that regardless of how it operates, reality testing is *influenced* by the superego. Hartmann's (1956) statement may be taken as representative: the superego "among other and partly opposite results . . . [may bring about] some degree of narrowing or distortion of the child's knowledge of inner reality . . . it may occasionally influence even the testing of outer reality" (p. 256).

Generally, it is stated that the superego's role in reality testing need not be a negative one, that it does not *necessarily* interfere with the efficient operation of this function. Nevertheless, it is often cast in the role of a nuisance, if not an actual obstacle to reality testing. Freud (1933) had suggested that the ego ought to become "more independent" of the superego, a puzzling statement in the context of some of his other ideas, and especially so in the light of his own character structure. Hartmann's (1960) suggestion that what is needed is "autonomy" of ego and superego functions is undoubtedly an improvement, emphasizing as it does the integration of functions.

Jacobson (1964), regarding self perception as an ego function exclusively, believes self evaluation to be shared by both ego and superego (p. 130). At the same time she concludes that "the super-ego introduces a safety device of the highest order, which protects the self from dangerous internal instinctual stimuli, *from dangerous external stimuli*, and hence from narcissistic harm" (p. 133; my italics).

Hartmann and Loewenstein (1962), while assigning perception of one's own mental processes to the superego as well as to the ego, are inclined to emphasize the "negative" influence of the former, its capacity to distort the ego's function of reality testing. But this argument by no means rules out the possibility that the superego, under certain conditions, may have an adaptive function.

But to relegate self observation exclusively to the ego makes it very difficult to describe with any precision the role of the superego, if any, in adaptation to external reality, nor can we be very clear how "self evaluation" occurs.

In deciding where we wish to place self observation in the psychic apparatus, we are faced with an uncomfortable dilemma. The ego must include the apparatus which regulates the drives, as well as that which is responsible for interchanges with the outside world. The power to regulate implies, of necessity, the power to register, to observe and discriminate. On the other hand, to the superego has been assigned the task of "keeping a watch over the actions and intentions of the ego and judging them, in exercising a censorship" (Freud, 1930, p. 136). In contemporary language, it is the self, or part of the self, which is observed, and therefore we may describe this superego function as self observation. If the superego is responsible for at least some vital aspects of self evaluation, but not for self observation, how is the latter function performed? If the superego portion of the mental apparatus is fed information about the self by the ego (a reasonable assumption), should it then be thought of as evaluating without *observing* that information about the self? This would not make sense.

III

Reality testing and the other reality functions (those functions of the psychic apparatus having to do with direct adaptation to external reality) should be relatively easy to observe, and we ought to be able to postulate whether, and to what extent, superego functions are related to them.

An attempt to bring forward clinical and other observations which would allow us to trace more precisely the role of the superego in this field is by no means an easy task. While one can cite numerous adaptive aspects of superego function, of a general nature (Hartmann, 1960; Schafer, 1960; Waelder, 1960; Jacobson, 1964), to do so in the field of reality testing is another matter. Yet we must first try to answer the question whether the superego, like an ideal policeman (as it is so often represented in dreams), ever "prompts" the ego in the direction of *more* adequate reality testing, as well as the reverse.

But let us begin with a familiar example from clinical practice, in which the superego function is if anything an apparent nuisance. A patient is presented with an interpretation dealing with a bit of behavior. For example, he is told that a certain action of his seems to be determined, at least partly, by his need to express some aspect of an unconscious fantasy and to induce a particular reaction (not necessarily aggressive) in me.

The patient responds immediately, or a bit later, with the assertion that he has been *accused* by me, and that he now recognizes how much I disapprove of his behavior. Actually, I may not have disapproved in the slightest. The behavior itself may have consisted of something so overtly benign as coming to the session a bit early, or removing his wet shoes to avoid soiling the couch. We may assume, therefore, that the disapproval experienced by the patient is a projection of his own guilt.

But why the guilt? Current theory presents us with two available explanations, neither excluding the other. First, the interpretation has facilitated (in a way still obscure to us) the emergence of a drive manifestation, since it has interfered, at least temporarily, with some relatively stable defense. The superego responds to a threatened defiance of its prohibitions, by the id, or id and ego combined, and tension is produced between superego and ego, resulting in guilt. This in turn is projected onto the analyst.

Second, the patient may be thought of as defending himself against the interpretation by distorting it, turning it into a hostile attack which must be met by a counterattack. Thus he obscures the clarifying function of the interpretation, and protects himself from the anxiety or guilt which might have been aroused by it. Which of these we would favor might depend on whether or not we could detect very much evidence of guilt in his response.

Other layers of meaning could be adduced. For example, the patient may have the desire to be an object of attack as a passive victim, but this is less pertinent in the context which interests us here.

In general such a reaction as the one described is most common when one interprets behavior, as opposed to a dream, for example, and when the interpretation is pertinent ("correct") if not necessarily ideal in its timing.

In any case we are dealing with a manifestation of resistance, a hindrance to communication between patient and analyst and (implicitly) between the self-observing functions of the patient's psyche and his other mental processes. As such, it interferes with that portion of the reality function which is at the heart of the analytic process, namely, the capacity for useful observation and evaluation of one's inner life.

Beyond that, the resistance also affects the accuracy of the patient's judgment of the "external" world—at least so far as he tries to determine for himself what really went on between him and his analyst. We do know that a premature attempt by the latter to deny the punitive role the patient assigns to him may result in quite absurd arguments, which serve only to fix the patient's belief in his analyst's disapproval of him.

On the other hand, it is not at all uncommon for the patient, on leaving the office at the end of the session, to recognize that his analyst was not at all disapproving. If this happens, it is generally possible to continue on the original path of analysis which began with the interpretation, including the resistance to it.

But let us try to go beyond this and to explain to our own satisfaction why he experienced manifestations of guilt, and how this was accompanied by distortions of his perceptions of both inner and outer world, the latter represented by the analytic situation. This is not so easily demonstrated in conventional structural language.[1]

There are fortunately other sets of observations which raise questions about the role of the superego in reality testing. Isakower's (1939, 1954) writings, previously cited, treat problems of consciousness as central, and have much to do with my interest in the subject;

---

[1] Would things have gone more smoothly if guilt (and the superego) had not entered the picture? At first glance, we should say yes, but when we remember that such resistances may lead to very useful bits of analytic work, we are not so sure that even here, in the long run, reality testing may not have been "prompted" by superego function. But I fear that this presents us with a paradox which cannot be resolved in these terms and had better be left in a footnote for the present.

but recent studies on superego function have placed little emphasis on sleep and the dream.

It seems very odd that phenomena which have been matters of common belief for centuries, and which are part of the personal experiences of most people, should have received so little attention from us. Who would deny that much insomnia is stimulated by the conscience? Why did Lady Macbeth pace the halls of her castle, if not out of guilt? And why do some of us awaken all too early in the morning with a vague discomfort which prevents our returning to sleep? Is it not often a sense of guilt, not anxiety alone, over an incomplete task? (Such as a scientific paper still unwritten!)

John Keats expressed most eloquently the plea of the insomniac: he addresses his words to Sleep, "soft embalmer of the still midnight . . .":

> Then save me, save me, or the passed day will shine
> Upon my pillow, breeding many woes,
> Save me, save me from curious
> Conscience that still lords
> Its strength for darkness, burrowing like a mole,
> Turn the key deftly in the oiled wards,
> And seal the hushed Casket of my Soul.

We need not rely on poetic evidence alone, and can bolster our argument by citing clinical observations. Here the evidence is overwhelming that guilt, the conscience, the functions of the superego, have a pronounced effect on sleep.

In clinical depressions and often in milder transitory depressive states, in which the superego plays a crucial role, sleep disturbances are extremely common. Insomnia, particularly early waking, is typical. And while we need not doubt the accompanying ego disturbance, one could not describe such phenomena adequately without reference to the superego and its hyperactivity, relative or absolute.

This implies no oversimplification. But the regression, which overtakes the superego as well as the ego in sleep, results in phenomena which may well make sleep intolerable and waken the sleeper. An "internal" danger may be experienced as if it were an external one, whether that internal danger be a bodily sensation or a more truly "internal" drive manifestation. What is it here which rouses the sleeper? Is it the result of ego or of superego function? Or is it rather derived from a phase in which these apparatuses were poorly, if at all, differentiated? The danger signal is often marked by a good deal of guilty affect—a reliable sign of superego involvement.

We may return now to our analytic patient who felt accused. What is the central task of the treatment itself, if it is not to help the patient to distinguish "inside" from "outside," "fantasy" from "reality"? To do this, we must help him to recognize, to understand, and to evaluate his own mental processes. In this instance, we help him to see that his idea of the analyst's disapproval is fantasy, not fact; and we do this not by the usual kind of reality testing, which might degenerate into persuasion, but rather by allowing him to understand that he has confused "inner" and "outer." (The "reality ego" [Freud, 1915].)

The analogy may be made closer and more pertinent by applying Lewin's (1955) concept of the analytic situation. Lewin demonstrated to what extent analysis retains its links with the hypnotic state out of which it developed, and how usefully it may be formulated in the language of sleep and dream psychology. The analyst "soothes" the patient into some state of awareness which has dreamlike characteristics, then acts to wake the "dreamer" by a confrontation or an interpretation, or merely by ending the session. I have suggested elsewhere (1965) that this approach may be useful in explaining why interpretations are often treated by the patient as if they had a "superego tinge." (See Isakower, 1939, 1954.)

In states of consciousness generally considered "regressive" (e.g., the analytic session, sleep, psychopathological states such as the psychoses) the differentiation between ego and superego functions becomes blurred, if not entirely lost (Freud, 1933). It is interesting that when Freud (1921) originally placed reality testing in the ego ideal, it was in the context of the "dreamlike" hypnotic trance.

But the problem is still not solved, for "intrusions" of superego functions do not seem to be limited to regressive states, or even to parapraxes, such as Freud's (1936) on the Acropolis. I refer to the everyday conflict over telling the truth, an activity generally recognized as having close connections with conscience and moral values, and thereby necessarily with the superego as well as the ego.

As analysts we are impressed with the very clear dependence of "truth telling" on "truth knowing," and therefore on reality testing

—the need to know what is fantasy and what is fact, or what is "inner" and what is "outer."

Ordinarily if one tells an untruth out of ignorance, there should be no moral taint attached. Yet for young children this is not so. They feel a lie is a lie and should be punished, whether one has access to the facts or not. What becomes clear to the older child and adult, had not been evident to the prelatency child (Piaget, 1932).

When we proceed from the problem of telling the truth to other people to that of telling it to ourselves, we come closer to the child's point of view. Many of us willy-nilly regard self deception as highly undesirable, not only in a utilitarian, but even more strongly in a moral sense, and we are likely to react with guilt whenever we catch ourselves in a serious lapse. As analysts we possess, and attempt to inculcate in our patients, an attitude of telling oneself "the truth" which has the qualities of a moral imperative. We are anything but neutral on this subject!

Hartmann's (1960) discussion of this problem in *Psychoanalysis and Moral Values* is one of the best, for he demonstrates with the greatest skill both the elegance and the depth of ego psychology, along with its inevitable limitations. He comments on Freud's "self-control and discipline that had taught him to face reality at all costs" (p. 16), and on the moral factor implied by such intellectual integrity. For Hartmann, the ego "tests" moral values, interprets them and decides on their "genuineness" or "authenticity" (p. 50f.).

But can truth telling, especially to oneself, be explained adequately in terms of ego-superego tension? In terms of the structural hypothesis, it appears to be the best available brief statement. Yet if we attempt to apply it on the level of clinical observation and theory, we experience some serious difficulties. For example, if we examine the way people learn to tell the truth, we get the impression that the moral and punitive factors (those which will enter into superego) play a leading role in this area of childhood training. Moral teaching and reality testing are hardly to be distinguished by the young child. It takes a long time for him to be impressed with the unfortunate results of self deception and lying to others, if he ever is.

He is taught that lies are bad and forbidden, and only later that they are likely to carry penalties other than parental disapproval. While the first such lessons are interpreted morally (and generally so presented explicitly by the parents), the final stabilization of a well-structured rejection of self deception will depend on an advanced phase of ego development as well. But would the latter, alone, be a sufficient condition?

In the adult, while both ego and superego functions are involved in "telling the truth," it seems reasonable to suppose that the *first* automatic control of the tendency to lie is a well-internalized response in which superego function is dominant. It may be considered relatively archaic, although developmentally it would be traced chiefly to the oedipal or postoedipal period—that is, the phases in which superego precursors are being organized into an integrated structure.

Usually it is only after a fraction of a second has passed that one reacts to the (ego) assertion, "Honesty is the best policy." And so often, how weak is this voice compared with the earlier ringing commandment, "Thou shalt not lie." Here the first automatic superego-impelled response is more often than not adaptive in its effects, if not entirely rational in its sources. While it may not involve reality testing directly, it has much to do with its efficiency.[2] Are we therefore justified in regarding it now exclusively or nearly exclusively as an ego function?

We may go further, and examine how a child learns a piece of reality testing which is not ordinarily associated with ethical stand-

---

[2] Hartmann (1956) suggests a reason why many adults (some philosophers among them) cannot accept the logical difference between a moral imperative and a factual statement. He says, "The child is constantly confronted with value judgments which cannot be validated objectively but which are presented to him as statements of fact. 'This is good' and 'that is bad' are often presented to him in the same way as 'this is red' and 'that is green.' Such presentations also become part of 'socialized reality' " (p. 258). Such a childhood experience is certainly dependent on the early stage of ego development at which the experience occurs. I should like to modify Hartmann's statement in only one respect, to admit that we are by no means sure that we can do better than the philosophers in this respect—and that perhaps most of the difficulty we encounter in differentiating superego and ego function arises from having been exposed to this experience as children, and never having recovered from it entirely.

Piaget's (1932) work on *The Moral Judgment of the Child* does nothing to encourage making sharp distinctions between moral judgment and other types, even in children of six or seven. He states, aphoristically, "Everyone is aware of the kinship between moral and ethical norms. Logic is the morality of thought, just as morality is the logic of action."

Isakower (1939) has pointed out that in a number of languages including English the terms "right" and "wrong" may be applied both to moral questions and to those of fact.

The logical differentiation between moral imperative and factual statement can be approached only asymptotically—ever coming closer to the line but destined never to reach it.

ards. Every city child must be taught quite early how to cross a street, as a matter of safety, not morals.

When he makes his first impulsive dash for the curb (often at 18 months, or earlier), he is restrained physically, and generally told "no" very firmly. With further attempts, he will be talked to rather sharply. If he has to be snatched from under the wheels of cars very often, he may even experience his parents' anger, by scolding or physical restraint which may go beyond what legal authorities call "necessary force."

He can hardly ignore the fact that his parents are prohibiting, and perhaps angry. No matter what words they use, their tone and gestures will carry *that* message more readily than the knowledge that the action must be inhibited for other reasons (Spitz, 1958). Only later does he know that one avoids running into the roadway because the *cars* are dangerous to life. For in this period of the child's life (his reality testing being poorly developed), the primary danger is experienced as coming from the parents—idealized as they are.

Let us now try to trace the future of this bit of childhood experience. It depends for a time on the parents' real or imagined presence. Eventually, it may be internalized, and to the extent that it retains a morally tinged imperative (that it is *bad* to run into the street) it becomes a nucleus[3] within the developing superego. It may therefore run parallel to another bit of learning (that it is *physically* dangerous to run into the street) which may be thought of as a nuclear element within the ego.

If today we approach a crossing, and are faced by a red light, which psychic agencies are involved in our behavior? Very often, if we have been well trained in childhood, we experience a quick hesitation, after which we pause to consider whether or not the signal may be safely disobeyed. The second, less automatic reaction, in which the risks are calculated and action is taken accordingly, is one in which ego function dominates, and we need not consider it further here.

The initial response of hesitation is not so simply explained. If it is derived, as I maintain, from the original prohibitions of the parents, and if it may be expressed by an internal voice, "Thou shalt not run into the street!" it would be directly related to those early parental

[3] Or a "microstructure" (Gill, 1963).

prohibitions, described above. As such, it would be related genetically to the experiences which we regard as destined to enter into the function of the superego.

We may infer that the superego, even in adult life, has "prompted" the ego in a situation in which there is no longer a true moral issue, but in which such an issue had been raised in childhood. While archaic in origin, this operation appears to have become "reality syntonic" or adaptive.

Hartmann (1955) has very properly pointed out that genesis and function are not identical, that in essence what may be derived in a superego fashion, so to speak, need not become or remain a part of the superego. The residues of an experience, however derived, may ultimately be incorporated into the ego in such a way as to ensure certain automatic responses. But the question remains, how often and how completely do such responses lose the marks of their origin? How often do they depend more or less permanently on relatively archaic mechanisms in which ego and superego functions are inextricably joined?[4]

In his paper "A Tribute to Heinz Hartmann," Solnit (1964) emphasizes Hartmann's contribution to the idea that the pleasure principle is related to reality testing, via the approval of the love object; "if the child is not capable of coöperating with the love object or the love object with the child, early learning mechanisms may be jeopardized. These would include those mechanisms through which the ego's functions become experienced as pleasurable when they are harmonious with the directions and influences of the parental figure. A paucity of such early learning mechanisms interferes with the ego's ability to develop unpleasure in the face of danger and the child is then less well protected from the necessary—and desirable—risks of the average expectable environment" (p. 480).

To how great an extent this interference with learning to avoid danger enters into and becomes part of a superego as well as an ego disturbance is the kernel of the problem which we are trying to solve.

Another set of data is pertinent in this regard.

Greenacre's (1948) work on sexual differences in superego development, based on empirical observation and clinical theory, has

---

[4] See Reich (1954).

not yet been adequately incorporated into the body of superego theory on a metapsychological level.

This was based on Freud's (1925) discussion of the effects of anatomical differences on the resolution of the oedipus complex. He stated that "for women the level of what is ethically normal is different from what it is in men. Their super-ego is never so inexorable, so impersonal, so independent of its emotional origins as we require it to be in men" (p. 257).

Greenacre, accepting this point of view, goes further, and establishes even more direct and earlier links between body sensations and superego development. About the formation of ideals she says, "the boy has a more intact body image in which all his senses concur, while the girl has a mysterious, partly silent, unseen, and not directly palpable area of which she is dimly but not clearly aware and which stimulates her imagination without much chance for reality testing" (p. 164).

She ascribes to girls, on the basis of information from the most diverse sources, "less readiness to submit to the necessities of life . . . more bias . . . an unreliability as to facts; i.e., a tendency to lie" (p. 158f.). (This is not a value judgment by the author. I have chosen, out of context, those elements which have the closest relation to reality testing and superego function.)

The importance of her findings does not lie solely in the demonstration that men and women treat certain kinds of reality differently because of superego differences; rather it is significant on genetic grounds, since it furnishes us with an aspect of the superego concept which is rooted directly in perceptive experience, and which may be susceptible to being traced through later developmental phases. While the chief effects of the perceptions of different body parts will be in the formation of the ego, there will also be more or less direct influences on the development of the superego. Genetically, at least, the latter is close to external reality. Again, to what extent will genesis permanently influence function?

Nunberg's (1951) observation, "conscious perceptions of the ego must be sanctioned by the superego in order to acquire qualities of full, uncontested reality" (p. 8) is pertinent to the analytic situation (see above), and deals with still another aspect of the superego's relation to reality. It has a broad application to problems of derealization, depersonalization, and the like, in which the superego appears to play an important part (Oberndorf, 1934, 1939; Jacobson, 1959).[5]

The superego not only affects the sense of reality; it plays an essential role in giving permission to *know*.[6] When curiosity and the acquisition of knowledge are impaired, we generally look for a super-ego element in the disturbance. When, on the contrary, investigation and learning are active and efficient, we tend to ignore the role of the superego, as if it were operative only in a negative direction, forgetting both the permissive elements of the conscience and the positive influence of the ego ideals.[7]

The following clinical example illustrates the point. A patient had troublesome problems in study, particularly in ease of reading. Any attempt to learn matters connected with his work, or even to read for pleasure, required undue effort and time, and was often accompanied by feelings of guilt. This could be traced to his child-hood experience in attempting to investigate the circumstances of his own very traumatic birth. His efforts had been met with silence, evasion, or frank disapproval.

Once after a particularly successful day, in which he had learned a good deal from a skillful teacher, he expressed the fantasy that I would show him that he was deceiving himself, that he had not really been so successful in learning. He was aware that his guilt was pro-jected—but why the guilt? Then he said, "You know, I've noticed that I can read the magazines in your waiting room with great pleas-ure, and I never feel guilty about that!" It was because the magazines carried my sanction, implicit in their location.

---

[5] The superego's relation to problems of identity may be illustrated briefly by a case described by M. H. Horowitz (personal communication). His patient, who suf-fered from a profound identity disturbance, was capable in an elated state of working rapidly and well. "He was in consonance with his aggrandized ego ideal. The *external* reality was *clear;* the cost was to the *internal* reality of his identity." When he felt differently about himself (ugly and inferior), "everything was fuzzy and work was impossible . . . visual perceptions were distorted."

Here, with the ego-superego fusion of the elated state (Lewin, 1950), "external" reality testing was more acute than usual. In addition, the superego sanction seems to have given an increased conviction to the patient's sense of the reality of his ex-perience, even though distortions of "internal" reality persisted. When depressed, however, all reality testing suffered and he experienced something akin to derealiza-tion.

[6] I am grateful to Eli Marcovitz and Robert Waelder, who highlighted some of this material in their discussion of an earlier draft of this paper.

[7] Nor do I see any substantial justification for considering the ego ideal to be sep-arate from the superego—a concept which adds more difficulties than it resolves.

In the analysis, my permission was necessary to allow him to investigate the circumstances of his birth and childhood. In a previous analysis, he had never done so, in spite of the obvious importance of the issue in the genesis of his neurosis; he never felt permission had been given, and such investigation was therefore still forbidden. In this case the superego first *forbade,* and later *permitted,* the ego to be curious and to know a vital piece of reality.

The role of such superego sanction in the investigation of forbidden secrets is well known, although it has been insufficiently stressed. Everything of importance in science, from Freud's investigation of childhood sexuality to the astronomers' search for the secrets of the universe, has had a forbidden quality and often enough has been met with savage reprisals by the elders of society. Innately we place the "integrity" of the scientist, a character trait heavily dependent on the intactness of the superego, in a position even higher than his intelligence. Freud was of course the model of the scientist, who employed self observation (and self criticism) most explicitly, although the example of Darwin should also be cited.

I cannot omit one last example of the superego's connection with reality—humor. Freud's (1927) paper on the subject deals primarily with irony, that variety which depends above all on the capacity to observe oneself and one's own psychic processes. The superego, Freud says, repudiates reality and serves an illusion. Yet we may join him in regarding such humor as "a rare and precious gift."

This superego influence on reality testing again appeared at first sight to be a negative, interfering one. Yet irony implies a capacity for detachment, for sharpened recognition of the psychic processes, and for an evaluation of the latter which bespeaks not only the persistence of the parents' influence, but even more, the employment of that influence for the most highly developed uses. Irony is generally held to be a sign of maturity, and appears later in children than puns and other jokes.

Here the evaluation of "external" reality suffers only apparently. The evaluation of "internal" reality benefits, if anything; while on balance, the capacity to recognize and deal with all spheres of reality gains by this dynamic event (see also Waelder, 1934; Rosen, 1963).

The use of irony is not so very different from what happens in the "ideal" analytic situation, in which a temporary inhibition of attention to external reality is accepted as a condition for increased acuity of self observation (Stein, 1965).

IV

If we deny the superego a clear role in self observation and relegate this function entirely to the ego (an extreme view), we acquire the merit of internal consistency, so long as we confine our considerations to the ego. But this reduces the superego, after all, to the status of a very tenuous structure, without clear connections with either ego or drives.

This is no easy dilemma. As noted previously, Freud (1933) gave as one of the primary objects of analysis the achievement of independence of the ego from the superego. Yet in the same lecture he had included among the superego's functions those of self observation, conscience and the holding up of ideals (p. 66). Unless we assume a deliberate paradox, which we have no right to do, we must assume that "independence" was meant in a very limited sense.

Among the attempts to solve this problem, the most prominent and probably the most systematic and consistent is Hartmann's, which has been described in a series of papers, most of which were written in collaboration with Kris and Loewenstein. His concept of the developed superego is narrower than Freud's (1933) description, although it has close logical connections with *The Ego and the Id* (1923) and other Freud papers.

Hartmann regards the superego as a structure formed under ego and drive influence, whose adaptive functions, at least, are taken over more and more by the ego during the individual's progress toward maturity. The mature conscience, "healthy" ideals, depend on ego functions, on which the superego exerts some influence, often silent. Mental health, particularly with regard to ethical problems, is a function of adequate integration of ego and superego function.

It would be inappropriate to describe Hartmann's conceptual system in detail; it is widely accepted as the most highly developed point of view in contemporary metapsychology, and most authors regard it as the standard by which alternative hypotheses must be measured. As a theoretical structure it has the virtues of great sophistication, elegance, and consistency.[8]

---

[8] Schafer (1960), in a discussion of the superego in energic terms (see also Beres, 1958; Jacobson, 1964), establishes a link between the use of aggressive energy by the

Even so, Hartmann's work leaves some questions unanswered, and there are still serious gaps in our theory. Rapaport (1960b), in one of his last works, attempted to deal with the "perplexities" which have plagued our attempts to achieve an adequate working definition of the superego, especially in terms of ego-superego differentiation. "The differentiation of the ego and the id is not sharp but progressive. It reaches a definitive crystallization with those defense identifications which arise as a solution of the oedipal conflicts. This point is a separating line between the integrates passive and those active in relation to the drive-tension. The former attain a dominant integration by the superego, the latter a dominant integration by the ego, though these dominances and this separating line are, however, relative."

Rapaport's explicit attempt to clarify the relative and incomplete differentiation between superego and ego is analogous to Gill's (1963) treatment of ego and id differentiation (see also Rapaport, 1960a). It is in accord with Freud's (1933) statement: "We cannot do justice to the characteristics of the mind by linear outlines like those in a drawing or in primitive painting, but rather by areas of colour melting into one another as they are presented by modern artists. After making the separation we must allow what we have separated to merge together once more. You must not judge too harshly a first attempt at giving a pictorial representation of something so intangible as psychical processes. It is highly probable that the development of these divisions is subject to great variations in different individuals; it is possible that in the course of actual functioning they may change and go through a temporary phase of involution. Particularly in the case of what is phylogenetically the last and most delicate of these divisions—the differentiation between the ego and the super-ego—something of the sort seems to be true" (p. 79).

Rapaport himself lists the adaptive aspect of superego theory as one of those which are still to be clarified. Yet it is this, along with the genetic, which is closest to clinical observation and therefore

---

superego and its adaptive function. One is reminded here that aggressive energy, in the early days before *Beyond the Pleasure Principle* (1920), was self-preservative. To some extent the dual instinct theory may have led to a situation in which the superego, being associated largely with aggressive energy, became more and more identified with punitive and even maladaptive functions—a situation which could be reversed only by assuming the neutralization of such energies, and leaving energic hypotheses of superego function in a quite uncertain state.

should be most capable of being tested in the light of clinical theory.

Clinical observations do generally support that aspect of superego theory which allows for a blurred and readily permeable border between superego and ego. This is most evident in such regressive states as sleep and the analytic situation, in which superego-ego differentiation is reversed, a process similar to but not identical with that which occurs in mania.

The metapsychological concept of the superego's "closeness" to the drives, and its "passivity" with respect to them (Rapaport, 1960b), offers greater difficulties in terms of clinical theory. The same is true to some extent of its investment with aggressive energy. These aspects of the theory cannot be replaced or dispensed with readily, for historical and other reasons. Moreover, they account quite adequately for some genetic observations, and are readily applicable to pathological conditions in which the punitive aspects of the conscience play a destructive, even catastrophic, role.

But it would seem that we have not yet been able to state clearly enough the role of the superego functions, such as the conscience, in "normal" adaptive behavior; and we are in a scarcely better situation with regard to such considerations as the maintenance of ideals and standards, and the upholding of traditions. Even such brittle reeds as "good manners," the inculcation of *noblesse oblige*, the doctrines of chivalrous behavior, all heavily dependent on superego function, have had an important, if somewhat unreliable, role in dealing with reality problems as well as with the drives.[9] We must find some way of accounting for remnants of moral teaching which persist in everyday life, for humor, for superego functions in waking, and for sexual differences in ideals.

If we were to relegate self observation to the ego, excluding the role of the superego, it would be difficult to avoid treating self evaluation similarly as an ego function. It is far too difficult to separate these two mental operations with any precision. Logically, excluding both self observation and self evaluation from the superego would lead to a concept of the latter as a vestigial structure, whose functions are to be taken over by the maturing ego. In the healthy adult, the superego would be active only under abnormal conditions; its per-

---

[9] Horowitz (personal communication) reminded me that it is the psychopath who is often most concerned with "politeness," as if he needed this superficial code to hide the absence of an efficient inner mechanism.

sistent operations could be regarded as evidence of imperfect ego function, of psychopathology, or immaturity at least.

On the other hand, we might choose to regard the superego as a permanent and integral part of the psychic apparatus of the adult. A concept of the superego which includes self observation as a functional component, and which allows it some role, however indirect, in the handling of reality, would appear to be much more useful in accounting for our clinical and developmental data. And it might even reverse the trend toward what Sandler (1960) has called "conceptual dissolution" of the superego.

To consider reality testing as the manifest resultant of several components, namely, ego and superego (and the drives as well), is ultimately only an application of the principle of multiple function (Waelder, 1936). It is not too much to expect that other manifest operations, which are observable or can be inferred at levels of clinical generalizations or clinical theory (Waelder, 1962), may be treated similarly: as resultants of components representing all the major structures of the personality, rather than being treated as if they were a function of one alone—usually, although not invariably, the ego. We might speak then of "structural" rather than "ego" psychology.

It should not be a matter for surprise, or even for regret, that our theory on the highest level of abstraction does not correspond precisely to that which is closest to clinical observation. Metapsychology and clinical theory employ somewhat different methods of approach; and while they may use the same terms, we should not expect these terms to bear exactly the same meanings in different contexts. True, we must strive for unity and consistency which will apply to all levels of abstraction. But we should be under no illusion that such a state of affairs can be attained without major changes in our theory— which will in turn bring about new and difficult inconsistencies. We should welcome such disturbances as signs of the continued growth of a major scientific discipline.

BIBLIOGRAPHY

Beres, D. (1958), Vicissitudes of Superego Functions and Superego Precursors in Childhood. *Psa. Study Ch.*, 13:324-351.
Freud, S. (1914), On Narcissism. *S.E.*, 14:73-102.
———— (1915), Instincts and Their Vicissitudes. *S.E.*, 14:117-140.

—— (1917), A Metapsychological Supplement to the Theory of Dreams, *S.E.*, 14:222-235.
—— (1920), Beyond the Pleasure Principle. *S.E.*, 18:7-64.
—— (1921), Group Psychology and the Analysis of the Ego. *S.E.*, 18:69-143.
—— (1923), The Ego and the Id. *S.E.*, 19:12-59.
—— (1925), Some Psychical Consequences of the Anatomical Distinction between the Sexes. *S.E.*, 19:248-258.
—— (1927), Humour. *S.E.*, 21:159-166.
—— (1930), Civilization and Its Discontents. *S.E.*, 21:64-145.
—— (1933), New Introductory Lectures on Psycho-Analysis. *S.E.*, 22:3-82.
—— (1936), A Disturbance of Memory on the Acropolis. *S.E.*, 22:239-248.
Gill, M. M. (1963), *Topography and Systems in Psychoanalytic Theory. Psychol. Issues*, 10.
Gitelson, M. (1964), On the Identity Crisis in American Psychoanalysis. *J. Am. Psa. Assn.*, 12:451-476.
Greenacre, P. (1948), Anatomical Structure and Superego Development. *Trauma, Growth and Personality*. NY: Norton, 1952, 149-164.
Hartmann, H. (1955), Notes on the Theory of Sublimation. *Essays*, 215-240.
—— (1956), Notes on the Reality Principle. *Essays*, 241-267.
—— (1960), *Psychoanalysis and Moral Values*. NY: IUP.
—— & Loewenstein, R. M. (1962), Notes on the Superego. *Psa. Study Ch.*, 17:42-81.
Isakower, O. (1939), On the Exceptional Position of the Auditory Sphere. *Int. J. Psa.*, 20:340-348.
—— (1954), Spoken Words in Dreams. *Psa. Q.*, 23:1-6.
Jacobson, E. (1954), The Self and the Object World. *Psa. Study Ch.*, 9:75-127.
—— (1959), Depersonalization. *J. Am. Psa. Assn.*, 7:581-610.
—— (1964), *The Self and the Object World*. NY: IUP.
Lampl-de Groot, J. (1962), Ego Ideal and Superego. *Psa. Study Ch.*, 17:94-106.
Lewin, B. D. (1950), *The Psychoanalysis of Elation*. NY: Norton.
—— (1955), Dream Psychology and the Analytic Situation. *Psa. Q.*, 24:169-199.
Loewald, H. W. (1951), Ego and Reality. *Int. J. Psa.*, 32:10-18.
Nunberg, H. (1951), Transference and Reality. *Int. J. Psa.*, 32:1-9.
Oberndorf, C. P. (1934), Depersonalization in Relation to Erotization of Thought. *Int. J. Psa.*, 15:271-295.
—— (1939), On Retaining the Sense of Reality in States of Depersonalization. *Int. J. Psa.*, 20:137-147.
Piaget, J. (1932), *The Moral Judgment of the Child*. NY: Collier, 1962.
Proust, M. (1920), The Guermantes Way, I. *Remembrance of Things Past*. London: Chatto & Windus, 1960.
Rapaport, D. (1960a), *The Structure of Psychoanalytic Theory. Psychol. Issues*, 6.
—— (1960b), A Theoretical Analysis of the Superego Concept (third version). Unpublished manuscript.
Reich, A. (1954), Early Identifications as Archaic Elements in the Superego. *J. Am. Psa. Assn.*, 2:218-238.
Rosen, V. H. (1963), Variants of Comic Caricature and Their Relationship to Obsessive-Compulsive Phenomena. *J. Am. Psa. Assn.*, 11:704-724.
Sandler, J. (1960), On the Concept of the Superego. *Psa. Study Ch.*, 15:128-162.
—— & Rosenblatt, B. (1962), The Concept of the Representational World. *Psa. Study Ch.*, 17:128-145.
Schafer, R. (1960), The Loving and Beloved Superego in Freud's Structural Theory. *Psa. Study Ch.*, 15:163-188.
Solnit, A. J. (1964), A Tribute to Heinz Hartmann. *Psa. Q.*, 33:475-484.
Spitz, R. A. (1958), On the Genesis of Superego Components. *Psa. Study Ch.*, 13:375-404.
Stein, M. (1965), States of Consciousness in the Analytic Situation. *Drives, Affects, Behavior*, ed. M. Schur. NY: IUP, 2:60-86.

Waelder, R. (1934), Ätiologie und Verlauf der Massenpsychosen. *Imago*, 21:67-91, 1935.
——— (1936), The Principle of Multiple Function. *Psa. Q.*, 5:45-62.
——— (1960), *Basic Theory of Psychoanalysis*. NY: IUP.
——— (1962), Psychoanalysis, Scientific Method and Philosophy. *J. Am. Psa. Assn.*, 10:617-637.

On the Theory of the Superego:
A Discussion

RUDOLPH M. LOEWENSTEIN, M.D.

In recent years several authors have expressed the opinion that the theory of the superego is in need of reevaluation.[1] The main reason advanced for this view was that some analysts found it difficult to distinguish conceptually between functions of the superego and those of ego or id when they attempted to apply the theory to clinical situations. Some have even voiced a doubt whether it is altogether justified and fruitful to maintain the concept of an independent psychic system superego. Questions of another kind have likewise been raised, not concerning the concept itself, but dealing with particular points of the theory.

In this paper I shall not attempt to convince the reader of the validity of the superego concept. Assuming its value, I propose to clarify a few questions which arise when the theory is confronted with clinical observations. I hope that this attempt will contribute to a more precise conceptualization as well as to a better understanding of concrete clinical phenomena.

I

From the beginning of his clinical studies, Freud (1896) pointed to the active participation of warded-off self reproaches and self-punitive tendencies in the symptoms of psychosis and neurosis. His early descriptions conveyed the notion that these tendencies were uncon-

The general approach of this discussion is based on a paper written jointly with Heinz Hartmann (Hartmann and Loewenstein, 1962).

[1] Among them Martin H. Stein as Chairman of a panel on the "Current Status of the Theory of the Superego" at the May, 1964 meeting of the American Psychoanalytic Association (see Goodman, 1965).

scious and were important determinants of his patients' behavior. In his later study of obsessive-compulsive neurosis (1909), he pointed to the important role played by guilt feelings. He stressed that intense conscious guilt feelings were present in these patients, but that the true motives of these guilt feelings as well as their role in the patients' symptomatology remained unconscious. Since Freud's paper on " 'Wild' Psycho-Analysis" (1910), we are familiar with the existence of neurotic disorders determined by the patients' reactions to such sexual gratifications which they cannot tolerate. Freud (1916) also described those who break down, wrecked by success, and those who become criminals from a sense of guilt.

Clinical experience, since then, has confirmed these observations in numerous cases presenting these symptoms either in obvious and severe forms or in less clear-cut and less damaging manifestations. Many patients are affected by potency disorders, frigidity or other neurotic symptoms determined partly by unconscious, warded-off moral qualms.

In some later writings Freud (1914, 1917, 1921) described normal and pathological phenomena which led him to separate a part of the ego, "a differentiating grade in the ego," whose function it is to observe and to criticize, approve, disapprove or punish the ego (or the self, as we would say today).

Freud's formulations in *The Ego and the Id* (1923) represented a profound change in the conceptual framework of psychoanalysis. Before then, the unconscious had been loosely equated with the repressed drives, and the preconscious and conscious with the ego. From 1923 on, Freud chose to regard functional differences as more important criteria for the conceptualization of the psychic apparatus than the qualities of consciousness and unconsciousness. Due consideration was henceforward given to the unconscious character of resistances and defenses: an unconscious part of the ego was described by him. The clinical observations briefly mentioned above, of unconscious moral demands, were likewise given their due place: together with the conscious moral exigencies of man, they have since then been called the superego.

In introducing this concept Freud described, as if to add more weight to it, a type of patient (by now well known) who presents a *negative therapeutic reaction*, who becomes and remains ill due to a need for punishment. This latter term is more significant than that

of unconscious guilt feelings. It points to the fact that what we deal
with in these patients is not alone a feeling, but a powerful and tenacious, although unconscious, force which counteracts the instinctual
drives as well as the most essential aims and interests of the ego. Such
cases of negative therapeutic reaction are but extreme forms of the
innumerable neurotic disorders in which self punishment plays a more
or less malignant role.

One characteristic of the superego is today often neglected:
namely, the fact that most of its activity is unconscious, not only
descriptively but also dynamically; that its contents and functioning
often differ widely from the consciously adopted moral code of the
individual; moreover, that its demands are often tenaciously warded
off by the ego, in ways which are similar to the ego's defenses against
instinctual drives.

The cases of patients presenting negative therapeutic reactions
superficially appear not to be very different from ordinary types of
neurotic disorders. While their life histories may reveal the particular importance of self-punitive tendencies, the unconscious guilt feelings become clearly observable only in the course of analysis. One
might say that in all these cases the symptomatology is determined
not only by the pathogenic conflict between drives and ego, but also
by a third independent variable: the unconscious "moral forces," the
superego. Indeed we must assume that this third variable always
exists in adults (it may be different in young children), but that its
impact is of varying intensity.

II

Many parents have observed the following scene: With a still un-
steady walk a child of about two approaches an interesting object,
while saying out loud: "Don't touch it." After a visible struggle, he
stops short of the forbidden action and finally turns around to play
with something else. This phenomenon is interesting, for it shows the
inhibiting power of parental words on the child's wishes. It shows
that by repeating them exactly, he begins the internalization of prohibitions—based, we presume, on the mechanism of identification
with his parents.

To these identifications we ascribe the innumerable acquisitions
which bring about the child's gradual socialization. In most cases
we can only infer their existence, not observe them; and we might

regard as a moot question whether these acquisitions are developments of the child's innate potentialities or results of identifications. It seems most convincing to assume a complex interaction between both.

Hartmann (1939) has pointed out that the newborn is equipped with primitive apparatuses which have an inhibiting character, and that these apparatuses will later be under the control of the ego when it has gradually differentiated from the common matrix called the "undifferentiated stage" of psychic development (Hartmann, Kris, Loewenstein, 1946). The "oughtness" mentioned by Jones (1947)[2] is probably based on such inborn givens, characteristic of the human species, although it may manifest itself only some time after birth and through an identification with the parents. Like any other animal species, man has at his disposal, as part of his inborn equipment, apparatuses which enable him gradually to understand his specific environment and to learn from it the behavior patterns required in socialization.

Why then do we say, with Freud, that the superego is formed only later, as the heir of the oedipus complex or at its expense, as a corollary of its dissolution? Do not children, before that age, display internalization of prohibitions? We must understand that the development of ideals, or feelings of guilt and shame, and of self-punitive reactions is a gradual process. There is an enormous difference between children in the phallic phase and in the seventh year of life. The instinctual drives manifest themselves differently in the beginning of latency. The instinctual attitudes toward the parents have changed profoundly. The moral prohibitions have become much more independent of external pressures. What is most significant are precisely the phenomena subsumed under the term "dissolution of the oedipus complex." In the latency period the incestuous and competitive strivings of the oedipal conflicts are to a great extent being replaced by aim-inhibited relations with the parents. Although many adults remember some of their childhood sexuality, hardly anyone recalls the actual oedipal strivings. But for this state of affairs, mankind would not have needed the discoveries of psychoanalysis, nor would each individual patient need the drawn-out process of analysis to discover these conflicts in himself.

The early latency period is also characterized by a decisive advance

[2] Heinz Lichtenstein mentioned this factor in the panel cited above.

in the development of the ego, which enables the child to go to school
and learn to read and write. He acquires more knowledge about the
world outside the family, and the authority of the parents henceforth
is partly replaced by that of teachers and to some extent of classmates.
The world of the infant is centered mainly on human beings, and the
child first comes to know reality in terms of his human objects. It
takes years of development to learn to distinguish an inanimate from
the human object. In fact, no human being completely loses some
remnants of anthropomorphic beliefs and reactions to the world.

A somewhat similar state of affairs obtains for the gradual development of the superego from its early genetic determinants. There can
be no doubt that a certain degree of ego development is a precondition
for the formation of the superego (Hartmann, Kris, Loewenstein,
1946; Hartmann and Loewenstein, 1962). When we speak of the
formation of the superego we imply that from then on a number of
childhood conflicts between ego and environment, between ego and
drives, and within the ego, are being solved in a somewhat different
way. For instance, the child learns from then on to separate moral
conflicts more clearly from other conflicts. A younger child does not
distinguish sharply between them: a prohibition to cross the street
has moral undertones for him. The clear separation between what is
dangerous and what is "evil" is the result of superego formation. To
pursue the analogy with the ego: we are never completely free of this
early equation of danger with "evil." We see here that ego and superego mutually further each other's development.

Nevertheless, it is important to maintain a clear distinction between preconditions and early genetic determinants of the superego
on the one hand, and the formed system superego on the other (Hartmann and Loewenstein 1962). We call superego that organization
within the mental apparatus which becomes a systematic third independent variable in the intrapsychic conflicts, and which exercises
control over drives and some essential tendencies and functions of the
ego, e.g., individual self interest and even self preservation.

We do not conceive of the superego as having been formed merely
out of an identification with the parental prohibitions, introjected like
a foreign body. Sandler (1960) proposed to reserve the term introjection for the type of identifications leading to superego formation.[3]

[3] See the discussion of the use of the terms identification and introjection in
Hartmann and Loewenstein (1962).

However, the superego develops not only as the result of introjection, important as this mechanism may have been for its formation. The superego also has at its disposal instinctual forces that were involved in the oedipal conflicts. The child also identifies with the superego of the parents; that is to say, these identifications or introjections enable him to take over not only the contents but the very functions of the system superego from his parents. However, the superego has also been formed within the child's mental apparatus as a "differentiating grade" in his ego; it is endowed with aggressive forces directed against the ego; it is an inner organization consistently centered around conscious and unconscious moral demands of the individual, his family, and society.

III

The functions of the superego were only gradually delineated by Freud. Moreover, in the course of time he used two terms to designate this structure: ego ideal and superego. Even now we distinguish two subgroups of superego functions: the ego ideal and the superego in the narrow sense. These two terms not only represent the remnants of a historical development of ideas; they refer to two types of functioning—two aspects—of the system superego, which are genetically and clinically recognizable to some extent.

The functions of the superego are closely tied to some motives for defense, whereas the mechanisms of defense are functions we ascribe to the ego itself. Obviously, this division cannot be applied to early childhood. There exists a gradually evolving sequence of motives for defense (Freud, 1926), a sequence of what is perceived as outer and inner danger that triggers signal anxiety and hence defense. The sequence is well known: fear of loss of the object, fear of loss of the object's love, fear of castration (punishment), and, finally, superego anxiety. It is only at this latter stage of development that one can speak of the superego—internalized moral standards—as motive for defense.

Yet the preceding developmental stages here mentioned form building blocks which ultimately enter into the contents and functions of superego anxiety. Therefore the ego is influenced by the superego in ways that can be roughly divided into two categories: influences of the ego ideal and of conscience. The demands of the ego ideal can be approximately translated as follows: "I ought to behave and be like the person I want to be, so as to be liked by him," whereas the demands of conscience usually have the connotation: "I should not behave or be as I would wish." These "translations" of the "inner voice" representing the superego are obviously mere approximations. In reality a great variety of wordings can be observed. Most often, the commands and prohibitions are implicitly present together; e.g., "you ought not to do this," implying "but you ought to do that," and vice versa. Dr. Charles B. David (personal communication) drew my attention to the fact that the Ten Commandments contain both prohibitions and commands. While considerable agreement exists among analysts regarding the functions of the prohibiting superego and its origin in the dissolution of the oedipus complex, there is far less agreement concerning the ego ideal. Indeed, genetically the latter is not as directly traceable to oedipal conflicts, but is rather connected with the ontogenesis of narcissism on the one hand and with idealizations of the parents on the other (Jacobson, 1964). The value for clinical work of distinguishing the development and activity of the ego ideal, as opposed to the prohibiting superego, is obvious. However, to regard the ego ideal and the superego as two distinct structures is no more justified than to view aggression and libido as separate systems, rather than as two parts of the id.

Some authors, e.g., Novey (1955), and Sandler et al. (1963), consider that the genetic factors in the formation of the ego ideal, its relation to narcissism, present a difficulty in viewing it as part of the system superego. They cannot reconcile the early formulations of Freud (1914), according to which the ego ideal is the substitute for the lost infantile narcissism, with his later proposition that the parents are taken as models for the child's ego ideal.

Freud (1923) modified his theory of narcissism. In introducing the structural theory, he stated: "At the very beginning, all the libido is accumulated in the id. . . . The id sends part of this libido out into erotic object-cathexes, whereupon the ego, now grown stronger, tries to get hold of the object-libido and to force itself on the id as a love-object. The narcissism of the ego is thus a secondary one, which has been withdrawn from objects" (p. 46).[4]

This shift in the concept of primary narcissism reflects views which not only fit better the over-all concept of the mental apparatus,

_____

[4] It has been pointed out that narcissism refers to the libidinal cathexis of the self and not of the system ego (Hartmann, 1950; Loewenstein, 1940).

but which point to the extreme difficulty of stating clearly what happens in the mind of a child in the first few months of life. For that earliest period, neither reconstructions from later analyses nor direct observations will yield definite answers to questions regarding the interaction between primary and secondary narcissism. Primary narcissism can mean a more or less continuous state of quiescent satisfaction, and possibly a feeling of omnipotence based on hallucinatory satisfactions. However, if self idealization is referred to, one is more likely to imagine a state of affairs in line with Freud's later formulation; i.e., self idealization based on an overvaluation or idealization of parental objects which is secondarily "withdrawn from them" onto the self. In view of the complex interplay, at various stages, between identifications with idealized parental images, projections of omnipotence onto the latter, and subsequent reidentifications and reprojections, it is hardly possible to circumscribe the respective roles, at a given age, of narcissistic and object cathexes in the ontogenesis of the ego ideal.

Pertinent in this context is the following statement by Hartmann and Loewenstein (1962): "In the development of the ego ideal both self-idealization and the idealization of the parents play a role. These two processes gradually become integrated . . . , but certainly not always completely integrated. The degree to which the ego ideal is determined more by early self-idealization or more by idealization of the object later becomes more important for both normal and pathological development. Of significance for future pathological development might also be the persistence of early forms of self-aggrandizement or of overvaluation of parents that may stand in the way of the formation of later types of idealizations" (p. 61). Valuable observations of this type of neuroses were described by Reich (1954, 1960) and Murray (1964).

The function of idealizing oneself or the parents starts very early in life. However, to quote Hartmann, Kris, and Loewenstein (1946, p. 33), "it seems that at the pre-phallic stage, idealization is predominantly concerned with the area of puissance: the child aggrandizes the parents in order magically to partake in their protection and power."[5] But gradually the moral idealization increases in importance:

[5] This does not mean that even in that period the child does not strive to be like the "good" parents or to become the "good child" whom the parents want him to be, as Sandler (1960) has pointed out.

the child "identifies not only with the parents as they are, but with the idealized parents, i.e. the child purifies their conduct in his mind, and the identification proceeds as if they were consistently true to the principles they explicitly profess or aspire to observe. Hence Freud's formulation, the child identifies with the superego of the parents." And it is only toward the end of the phallic phase, under the impact of castration anxiety, that idealization concerns predominantly moral behavior.

Overvaluation, aggrandizement, and idealization do not stop with the formation of the superego. Moreover, the enrichment and development of the superego continue in latency, in adolescence, and—to a lesser extent—in adulthood. And the other kind of overvaluations of self or of others also continues at the same periods of life. It is often not difficult to distinguish moral ideals from those other ideals that will hardly accrete to the superego; for example, the wish to become a great football player or a *femme fatale*. But there are some ideals which lie in between, as it were. Such are the four "cardinal virtues" of classic Greece: justice, prudence, courage, and temperance. They are not all moral, strictly speaking, as we understand morality today, yet they are "ideals of perfection" which we include among the aims set by the ego ideal. It is important to distinguish the "wishful concept of the self" (Jacobson, 1954), from those ideals which represent "the aim-setting function of the ego ideal," as Hartmann and Loewenstein (1962) defined it.[6]

IV

The superego as a system is a construct, as are the id and the ego. Yet there exists a group of phenomena, of functions that have some characteristics in common, to which we refer as the superego. The mental phenomena we actually observe, however, partake of the whole human mind; and it is for the sake of scientific description, and of distinguishing them from other groups of phenomena, that we divide them into three centers or substructures of functioning. Such division raises many problems, particularly with respect to the interaction between superego and ego functions, depending on the conditions under which

---

[6] Sandler et al. (1963) have proposed to replace the term "ego ideal" by "ideal self." The latter might be more in harmony with some present-day terminology, but unfortunately the authors fail to distinguish between these various types of ideals and the concept of ideal self and thus make it difficult to use the term.

behavior is observed: whether in an analytic setting or in a nursery school class, for example.

Before discussing some of these problems, let us recall certain unusual situations in human life. Under the impact of powerful libidinal or aggressive drives, some individuals may disregard any consideration of morality, or of personal safety, to attain gratification. One might say that at these moments the superego and most ego functions, except those necessary for the satisfaction of the drives, are silenced. In such instances, whatever is left of reality testing is at the service of the id. Yet we would not maintain that reality testing is an id function. Is not much of our work concerned with disorders in which the ego subserves instinctual and moral demands? Nevertheless, we maintain that it is of value for the scientific understanding of these phenomena to distinguish between them.

The same is true when we observe extreme situations of the opposite kind, e.g., serious danger to a person's life and safety. Here the libidinal drives as well as any kind of superego function may seem to have vanished. At other times one may have the impression that all there is to a human being is his conscious ego, yet we do not assume that the id and the superego no longer exist in him at such times.

Temporary suspensions of superego functions are well known. Gustave Le Bon (1895) described the loss of moral controls of individuals under the influence of the "group mind." In *Group Psychology and the Analysis of the Ego*, Freud (1921) explains some of these phenomena by the identification between members of a group and a surrender of the individual's superego in favor of the group leader, whose will and decisions henceforth take over the superego functions of each member of such group. Love for the leader and awesome dread of him, as well as identification with the fellow group members, can achieve this momentous change in a person's psychic structure. The libidinal factor in the dependence on the leader confirms the significance of the libidinal forces at work, side by side with aggression, in the relation between ego and superego (Nunberg, 1932; Schafer, 1960).

If we compare an individual's behavior in adolescence with his behavior in latency or in adulthood, we can see that the various areas of functioning or the modes of behavior regulation may be completely upset by shifts in the relative strength of id and ego; and the role of the superego functions in adolescence seems at times to be completely absent and at other times to be overwhelmingly powerful. Even in the more or less stabilized life of an adult, regulation of some behavior may be predominantly influenced at times by instinctual drives or moral demands or by the exigencies of the ego, and each may or may not be in conflict with the others.

Although the functions serving survival pertain mainly to the ego, one would not be able to survive in a social environment without the existence of instinctual drives and moral functions. Viewed from this angle, both id and superego have a survival value. For instance, while we ascribe reality testing entirely to the ego, both id and superego can contribute to this function. The resonance of one's own id allows one's ego better to perceive and evaluate instinctual manifestations in others as well as in oneself. An analogous situation seems to obtain with regard to the superego in the perception of "moral" or "immoral" behavior of others, and the superego always plays a role in the evaluation of such behavior in oneself. In this sense, the superego may partake of certain areas of reality testing.

When Freud (1923) first introduced the idea of an "unconscious conscience," an unconscious morality, he remarked that psychoanalysis had been accused of representing people as "worse" than they were and now would be accused of describing them as "better" than they were. The fact was, he added, that people were both better and worse than they appeared to be, and that psychoanalysis merely was discovering more about them than had been known thus far.

Analytic experience confirms the opinion of some philosophers that many moral actions have an admixture of instinctual or selfish motives. However, psychoanalysis also discovered that unconscious superego motives may codetermine behavior which seems to lack any moral goal, e.g., criminal acts due to a sense of guilt. We know that unconscious participation by all three substructures of the mind is always present in human behavior. However, the relative importance of id, ego, and superego influences varies greatly from one situation to another in a given individual. Even the same behavior may be determined in him at one time mainly by superego motives, at another time (e.g., under changed political or social conditions) predominantly by ego interests. We also know that there are great differences between individuals in this respect.

To illustrate the interaction between ego and superego functions,[7] I should like here to discuss an interesting and controversial problem, namely, the phenomena subsumed under the heading of self observation. One can distinguish between two kinds of self observation:

1. Varying degrees of awareness of inner psychic processes, such as affects, thoughts, sensations of the pleasure-pain continuum, etc. I believe there is general agreement that self observations of this kind are attributable to the ego.

2. A reflective observation of inner processes, when awareness comprises both object and subject of observation. I suppose this second kind is referred to when self observation is considered to be a superego function. In some pathological and occasionally in some normal cases, it takes the form of self watching, self criticizing, as if by an inner observer. Psychoanalytic experience teaches us that such critical introspection may also remain preconscious, or even unconscious, and come to the fore only in the guise of a symptom. Freud (1933) based the concept of an unconscious system superego on certain mental phenomena. One of them was the delusion of being observed, and he therefore attributed the function of self observation to the superego. In this instance, the self observation is projected onto the hallucinated voice of an imaginary observer. Such projections represent a breakdown of normal superego functioning. There is clinical evidence that in normal or neurotic persons, self observation may have self-disparaging or self-punitive motives and can lead to self deception based on guilt feelings (Hartmann and Loewenstein, 1962). If all self observations contained self-deceptive elements, one would unquestionably have to attribute self observation to the system superego. However, this is not the case. From every favorable analytic experience we learn that toward the end of analysis, patients are capable of objective self observation untainted by self deprecation or self deception.

We may now try to define more precisely which is the part of the superego in self observation and which the part of the ego. The superego, whose role it is to demand truthfulness,[8] helps to maintain objectivity, but not rarely impairs self observation due to self-critical

---

[7] I am of course aware that no formulation about this interaction can completely avoid the semantic defect of anthropomorphic presentation.

[8] Because of its moral connotation and significance the demand for truthfulness is attributable to the activity of the superego.

or self-punitive tendencies. The essential elements, however, the perception of what really is observable within oneself, and its observation, are functions attributable to the ego, albeit often standing in the service of the superego.

The interrelation between superego and ego functions is frequently more intricate than this example showed. Superego formation presupposes a sufficient degree of maturation and development of the ego. Once the superego has been formed, there is continuous further interaction between the two structures. The systematic teaching of religious and ethical principles, from latency on, certainly enlarges the scope and strengthens the functioning of the newly formed superego (Hartmann, Kris, Loewenstein, 1946; Loewenstein, 1951), while the superego's role in the search for truth sharpens and enhances ego functioning. On the other hand, the further development of id and ego in adolescence and adulthood often leads to a progressive limitation of some areas of superego regulation; e.g., sexual gratifications become not only permissible and imperative, but even socially desirable. Some other superego regulations are gradually replaced by concern for reality, for social responsibilities and expediency, and for ego interests. These changes represent not a complete elimination of the previous superego regulations, but a subordination of superego demands in these areas to demands of the ego. Clinical experience often shows that such subordination of superego demands is only apparent and is achieved by means of defensive mechanisms. One might say that in these cases, the repressed superego demands "return" in the form of neurotic symptoms and inhibitions.

The complexity of interactions between superego and ego is particularly pronounced when we consider the limits within which superego regulations are, or remain, internalized. I referred before to Freud's (1921) remarks concerning the members of organized groups, who may relinquish their superego to a variable degree in favor of a leader. An attenuated and temporary form of this mechanism can be observed during analytic treatment. Patients go through periods when their transference reactions, such as fear of disapproval or of punishment on the part of the analyst, reveal the projection of some of their superego functions onto the analyst. This projection is never complete, the core of the superego remaining internalized inasmuch as the oedipal conflicts remain repressed until they may gradually be unearthed by the analytic process. Nevertheless, it is remarkable that these phenomena appear so regularly and consistently. One might see in them an indication that some parts of moral behavior regulation never are completely internalized, that the do's and don't's are never the concern of the superego alone. This is not surprising if we remember the role of social anxiety—an ego function—in the regulation of behavior. When patients fear disapproval or punishment on the part of the analyst, one can often clearly distinguish whether they project earlier anxieties or superego anxiety onto the analytic situation. But this distinction is not always easy. In some, the danger represented by the superego takes regressively the form of earlier threats, e.g., danger of separation. Such regressions are possible, in turn, because the superego anxiety never completely loses its roots in earlier danger situations (Freud, 1926; Schur, 1953, 1958).

Our task of distinguishing a projected superego anxiety from social anxiety is frequently fraught with similar difficulties. If in some cases the part of each can be clearly discerned, in others the distinction remains uncertain. Such uncertainty may be due to an incomplete differentiation of superego from ego regulation in some areas, the "shaded area" of which Freud spoke. This hypothesis seems to find confirmation in several types of observations.

When human beings behave "morally," they do so not only at the behest of the internalized superego but also from fear of law-enforcing agencies and because of social anxiety—i.e., fear of public opinion. Apparently, the superego of the average citizen needs the support of his ego, cautioning against unpleasant consequences of his acts. Man, especially while young, is always in need of real objects with whom he can identify, and whom he can admire and take as the models of an ideal or as his measure of what distinguishes right from wrong. In this respect, part of a woman's superego might be replaced more easily by the actual person of the beloved man than a man's superego by the person of a loved woman.

For the formation and functioning of the superego, both the auditory and the visual spheres are important. Remembering the wrathful face or eyes of an idealized person is a reflection of guilt feeling. Imagining the victim of one's aggression, particularly his suffering expression or his reproachful gaze, can indicate intense remorse. In some people, however, the guilt may be quite tolerable so long as they do not actually see the victim of their aggression. A patient of mine once remarked that he would not commit a hostile act against a friend because he would have to look him in the eye, whereas he might well act in that particular way if he were sure of never seeing the friend again.

When Freud (1923) first introduced the concept of a superego, he described its formation as a result of the child's identification with the parents. Later (1930) he modified this theory, so as to take into account the frequent discrepancies between actual parental behavior and characteristics of the child's superego. (For example, lenient behavior of the parents may stand in contrast to a particularly severe superego in the child.) He drew the conclusion that the child identifies not with the parents' actual behavior but with their superego, when his own is being formed. The clinical observations here reported would seem to indicate that both Freud's earlier and his later theory were correct: that both refer to observable data. The actual behavior of the parents in "moral" matters combines with their superegos, their "purified" images, to become the prototype for the identifications forming the superego of their child.[9]

It seems fitting to close this discussion with a brief note on the interrelations that obtain between ego and superego as a result of the psychoanalytic process.

We do not expect the superego's functions and demands to become replaced by those of the ego. However, the psychoanalytic treatment leads often to an increased influence of the ego in areas pertaining to the superego, as is also often the case in the domain of instinctual drives. This increased influence of the ego can be attributed to its role in the awareness of internal and external reality, and its ability to confront past, present, and future reality. The analysand is expected to become aware of unconscious demands of his superego, to trace them back to their genetic antecedents, and to confront them with his conscious moral code. He is also expected to foresee the consequences of his behavior for himself and others. For example, the patient may become aware of the unconscious motives behind self-punitive tendencies depriving him of some important aims in life. The action of his ego then may be to allow more gratification than certain unconscious superego demands would permit; or the ego may recognize the wisdom of effacing itself and letting some superego exigencies prevail.

[9] However, without a reconstruction of the parents' actual behavior in this area, we cannot know how the two kinds of identification are intertwined in a given case.

In addition, with the help of the analytic process, the ego may be able to modify the functions of the superego in some ways; e.g., it may weaken the self-punitive function and give more power to the warning role of the superego. Insignificant as such cathectic shifts may appear, they can represent the difference between neurosis and mental health.

BIBLIOGRAPHY

Beres, D. (1958), Vicissitudes of Superego Functions and Superego Precursors in Childhood. *Psa. Study Ch.*, 13:324-351.
David, C. B. Personal communication.
Freud, S. (1896), Further Remarks on the Neuro-Psychoses of Defence. *S.E.*, 3:162-185.
——— (1909), Notes upon a Case of Obsessional Neurosis. *S.E.*, 10:153-249.
——— (1910), 'Wild' Psycho-Analysis. *S.E.*, 11:221-227.
——— (1914), On Narcissism. *S.E.*, 14:73-102.
——— (1916), Some Character-Types Met with in Psycho-Analytic Work. *S.E.*, 14:309-333.
——— (1917), Introductory Lectures on Psycho-Analysis. *S.E.*, 16:412-430.
——— (1921), Group Psychology and the Analysis of the Ego. *S.E.*, 18:69-143.
——— (1923), The Ego and the Id. *S.E.*, 19:12-59.
——— (1926), Inhibitions, Symptoms and Anxiety. *S.E.*, 20:87-174.
——— (1930), Civilization and Its Discontents. *S.E.*, 21:64-145.
——— (1933), New Introductory Lectures on Psycho-Analysis. *S.E.*, 22:5-182.
Goodman, S. (1965), Report on Panel: Current Status of the Theory of the Superego. *J. Am. Psa. Assn.*, 13:172-180.
Hartmann, H. (1939), *Ego Psychology and the Problem of Adaptation.* NY: IUP, 1958.
——— (1950), Comments on the Psychoanalytic Theory of the Ego. *Essays*, 113-141.
——— (1960), *Psychoanalysis and Moral Values.* NY: IUP.
——— Kris, E., & Loewenstein, R. M. (1946), Comments on the Formation of Psychic Structure. *Psa. Study Ch.*, 2:11-38.
——— ——— ——— (1951), Some Psychoanalytic Comments on "Culture and Personality." *Psychoanalysis and Culture*, ed. G. B. Wilbur & W. Muensterberger. NY: IUP, 3-31.
——— & Loewenstein, R. M. (1962), Notes on the Superego. *Psa. Study Ch.*, 17:42-81.
Jacobson, E. (1954), The Self and the Object World. *Psa. Study Ch.*, 9:75-127.
——— (1964), *The Self and the Object World.* NY: IUP.
Jones, E. (1947), The Genesis of the Super-Ego. *Papers on Psycho-Analysis.* London: Baillière, Tindall & Cox, 5th ed., 1948, 145-152.
Lampl-de Groot, J. (1947), On the Development of the Ego and Super-Ego. *Int. J. Psa.*, 28:7-11.
——— (1962), Ego Ideal and Superego. *Psa. Study Ch.*, 17:94-106.
Le Bon, G. (1895), *Psychologie des Foules.* Paris: Flammarion.
Loewenstein, R. M. (1940), The Vital and Somatic Instincts. *Int. J. Psa.*, 21:377-400.
——— (1951), *Christians and Jews.* NY: IUP.
Murray, J. M. (1964), Narcissism and the Ego Ideal. *J. Am. Psa. Assn.*, 12:477-511.
Novey, S. (1955), The Role of the Superego and Ego-Ideal in Character Formation. *Int. J. Psa.*, 36:254-259.
Nunberg, H. (1932), *Principles of Psychoanalysis.* NY: IUP, 1956.
Piers, G. & Singer, M. B. (1953), *Shame and Guilt.* Springfield, Ill.: Thomas.

Reich, A. (1954), Early Identification as Archaic Elements in the Superego. *J. Am. Psa. Assn.*, 2:218-238.

———— (1960), Pathologic Forms of Self-Esteem Regulation. *Psa. Study Ch.*, 15:215-232.

Ritvo, S. & Solnit, A. J. (1960), The Relationship of Early Ego Identifications to Superego Formation. *Int. J. Psa.*, 41:295-300.

Sandler, J. (1960), On the Concept of the Superego. *Psa. Study Ch.*, 15:128-162.

———— Holder, A., & Meers, D. (1963), The Ego Ideal and the Ideal Self. *Psa. Study Ch.*, 18:139-158.

Schafer, R. (1960), The Loving and Beloved Superego in Freud's Structural Theory. *Psa. Study Ch.*, 15:163-188.

Schur, M. (1953), The Ego in Anxiety. *Drives, Affects, Behavior*, ed. R. M. Loewenstein. NY: IUP, 1:67-103.

———— (1958), The Ego and the Id in Anxiety. *Psa. Study Ch.*, 13:190-220.

Spitz, R. A. (1958), On the Genesis of Superego Components. *Psa. Study Ch.*, 13:375-404.

Superego and the Function of Anticipation with Comments on "Anticipatory Anxiety"

LEO A. SPIEGEL, M.D.

We owe to Heinz Hartmann our steadily increasing absorption in those functions subsumed under the convenient heading of ego. Among the ego functions which Hartmann has investigated and the one to which he has particularly drawn our attention is that of adaptation (1939). By virtue of its dual perceptive surface and its control of the discharge system, the ego functions as the adaptive organ of the psychic apparatus.

Among the functions devoted to achieving the ego's over-all goal of adaptation, one is pre-eminent—that of anticipation—a function which Hartmann (1939) has also emphasized. This paper will be devoted primarily, but not exclusively, to the function of anticipation in regard to the demands of the id and to its progressive refinement during the course of individual development. The emphasis on what I term internal anticipation rather than on anticipation of external events was stimulated by technical difficulties encountered in the analysis of certain patients. Therefore, this paper is written with a focus on anticipation as it is seen in the analytic session.

My main thesis is that the "final" perfecting of the function of "internal" anticipation is tied to the establishment of the superego. To put it schematically at this point: the superego, when "finally" established, significantly assists, perhaps (partially) replaces, the ego as the chief internal sensory organ of the mental apparatus. Furthermore, I believe that this assistance results in a finer calibration of the function of anticipation than has existed before. Generally, as a sensory organ, the superego has a protective function vis-à-vis the id (Freud, 1895).

315

The idea of the superego protecting the ego through internal anticipation (in another connection, e.g., obsessional neurosis, the superego paradoxically "harassing" the ego through the same protective function, will be discussed) naturally brings to mind the important and corrective paper of Schafer (1960) on the loving and protective aspects of the superego in addition to its punitive side. However, the use of such terms in our discussion of the superego has, I believe, made many of us uncomfortable, a discomfort rarely made explicit. The loving, the hating, the severe, the forbidding, applied to the superego, are all terms in a sense illegitimately borrowed from the discourse of object relations just as if a parent were being discussed. Yet such terms are clinically justifiable since they do refer to the functioning of the patient in and out of analysis.

On the other hand, discussion of the superego in these anomalous terms has led to proposing questions of dubious reality; for example, whether in a given case the superego is sadistic or the ego masochistic. It is rarely possible to answer this question. But when the same question is applied to the *whole* individual we can usually say whether he is sadistic or masochistic or both, with considerable conviction. Therefore, while such terms (and related ones, such as harsh, etc.) are applicable to individuals, it is questionable whether they can usefully be applied to the institutions of the mind.[1]

For example, the patients under consideration in this paper might be seen by some analysts as suffering from a harsh superego. Yet my point will be that the patients' suffering was due primarily not to an overactivity of the superego but, on the contrary, to a relative failure of superego activity. This view has been concretely helpful to me in envisaging and ordering complex analytic material. Therefore, an attempt is made in this paper to formulate an aspect of the superego in terms other than harsh, severe, or loving.

This view assumes that the increasing acquisition of the function of anticipation as an (assumed) aspect of the superego may be observable during the course of analysis. And as the analyst consciously directs his attention to this growth, the previously mentioned phenomena may become intelligibly connected in a way that would not

[1] Naturally the formulations of the superego in nonparental terms have also received considerable attention, recently in papers by Hartmann and Loewenstein (1962), Jacobson (1964), Hammerman (1965), Schafer (1960), Sandler (1960), Stein (see Goodman, 1965), and previously by Beres (1958), Spitz (1957), Reich (1954), Jacobson (1954), and Weissman (1954), as well as others.

have been possible without drawing on the function of anticipation as an aspect of the superego. The detailed application of this viewpoint to the complexities of analytic material is at present an ongoing study of which a few clinical illustrations will be noted in this paper.

The essence of what I propose follows: the developed superego in its sensory aspects functions along two closely interwoven paths, a finely calibrated type of internal perception of the id and a protection of the ego against the traumatic effect of large amounts of drive energy. In these ways it functions analogously to the protective barrier against external stimuli (Freud, 1895, 1920); it represents an effort toward minimization of quantity[2] and toward equilibrium. Quantity (and quality) as they occur in various works of Freud have been presented and discussed by Gill (1963) in his enlightening monograph. I am also indebted to Bauer for a summary of the "Project" (Freud, 1895) which has facilitated my understanding of it.

Section I of this paper will develop the clinical material from which the formulations concerning the function of anticipation and the superego are drawn. The formulations themselves will be presented in the second section. The clinical material in the first section offers etiological and technical questions of interest, but these will not be pursued to any extent. Rather, the clinical material will be sifted primarily for its relevance to the function of anticipation.

I. The "Traumatic Syndrome"

GENERAL CLINICAL DESCRIPTION

In this paper I have gathered together a number of clinical analytic observations which I found difficult to understand and to meet technically. As I contemplated these observations (a contemplation imposed by the therapeutic problems), a similarity to certain aspects of the traumatic neurosis became apparent. The term "traumatic syndrome" was coined to indicate similarities of certain patients to the patient suffering from the true traumatic neurosis; on the other hand, it is enclosed by quotation marks to indicate that no recent trauma has occurred such as occurs regularly in the genesis of a true traumatic neurosis.

---

[2] The term quantity of instinctual energy in the id will be employed to cover not only absolute quantities but also those quantitative conditions (rate of discharge in a given unit of time) which presumably govern conditions of pleasure and unpleasure in the id.

What was striking and puzzling about these patients was their *behavior in the analytic session*. This was quite different from that of the usual patient. Especially impressive in the *analytic behavior* of these patients was the enormous extent to which their peculiar functioning in the session opposed the analytic processes. Consequently, only a small fraction of the session was truly analytic in the usual sense of free association and adequate responsiveness to interpretation.

A quick enumeration of five features of these patients as revealed in the analytic session will give a picture of their style of analytic functioning. First, a high level of diffuse tension was nearly always present during the analytic sessions. This showed itself in speech which at times approached a kind of strangled utterance, a manifestation of the struggle against the resistance of hypertonic laryngeal muscles. Either spontaneously or on questioning it became clear that the body musculature was extremely rigid and that the anal sphincter too was tightly contracted. The second feature was especially curious and, indeed, disappointing. Rarely did the analytic session reduce the patient's tension; on the contrary, it left the tension unaffected or even increased it to what seemed an intolerable bursting point. Third, anxiety marked each session without, or nearly without, exception. While noting it and complaining about it, *the patient seemed more tolerant of the anxiety than is usually the case with the average analytic patient*. Fourth, the patient, after announcing his anxiety did relatively little about it analytically. It did not serve as a *signal* to direct his analytic efforts to it in order to make himself more comfortable. As a consequence the analysis proceeded at a chronically high level of painfulness. Fifth, investigation revealed a chronic, low-grade sexual excitation, or better, sexual irritability, during the analytic session (i.e., mild genital sensations).

The above group of findings in the *analytic session* will be referred to as the "traumatic syndrome" to differentiate it from the true traumatic neurosis in which a recent trauma has occurred. These five features also existed to a certain extent outside of the analytic session; they were merely brought to a more exquisite flowering in the session. (It should be noted that these features did not prevent these patients, in contrast to the patients suffering from a traumatic neurosis, from carrying on the ordinary activities of life, impaired as they might appear to be under analytic scrutiny.)

If we disregard etiology, the clinical pictures of the "actual" neuroses and the traumatic neuroses coincide; therefore no objection exists to ranging the clinical material of this paper under either heading. However, taken strictly, the actual neuroses of neurasthenia and anxiety presuppose, as etiology, current interference with the natural unfolding of sexual activity. I would be disinclined to ascribe the clinical picture presented by these patients (especially as seen in the analytic session) to such an agent alone. Furthermore, doubts have been raised concerning the real existence of the "actual" neuroses (Brenner, 1953) (see also Blau [1952] in support of anxiety neurosis). Rather than sidetrack the development of the paper onto this controversial issue, the term "traumatic syndrome" has been chosen. This choice has an additional advantage; it implies that trauma did at one time play a part in the genesis of the "traumatic syndrome."

Since the characteristics of this state appear in the analytic session itself, the temptation presents itself to dismiss it as transference. That transference, loosely speaking, plays a role in this syndrome cannot be denied, but it is important to note the unique feature of this transference which marks it off from the transference of the classical neurosis. It is rigid, unvarying, inflexible, monotonously the same from session to session, in contrast to the variable transference of the classical neurosis. Therefore, transference does not so much explain the "traumatic syndrome" as it needs to be drawn into the understanding of the syndrome as a whole; it itself requires explanation.

NATURE OF ANXIETY IN THE "TRAUMATIC SYNDROME"

Initially, the average analysand's untrained response to the analytic process is to follow the pleasure principle. As unpleasure situations potentially productive of anxiety or of pain *threaten* to appear in the analytic session, free associations shift, become shallow, skip around, and finally cease. We identify this phenomenon as resistance, consider it to be a manifestation of the ego's response to conditions of unpleasure in the id, i.e., mobilization of the defense mechanisms and the affect of anxiety or of pain. As the benefits of analysis become apparent to the analysand, he gradually learns to tolerate these unpleasure situations because he anticipates future gain and he therefore continues his associative work for some time despite the unpleasure generated by it. In this way, his analytic ego comes more and more under the sway of the reality principle—another way of formulating his increase in ego strength. Clearly, the dominion of this principle always remains incomplete. The ego shifts now toward the reality principle, now toward the pleasure principle.

In the case of the "traumatic syndrome," however, neither the pleasure principle nor the reality principle appears to govern the *analytic hour*. This difference first came to my attention through the patients' curious response to their own anxiety (right from the beginning of each session). It was not only apparent that they were tense and anxious, but they also spoke about it. However, this painful state and its verbalization did not serve as a signal to induce them to analyze anxiety so as to obtain relief from the discomfort. In fact, each session followed the other in identical fashion with practically no analysis of their anxiety attempted by them.

After many repeated but futile attempts to stimulate analytic work toward understanding each anxiety state as it arose, I was slowly compelled to acknowledge that the anxiety was something special and different from that usually encountered in analysis. It became clear that this anxiety could not be viewed as a signal, for the patients simply *tolerated* the anxiety during the session but did not analyze it. They certainly did not tolerate it because they *anticipated* a future gain through analyzing it and then modifying conditions of unpleasure in the id; this would have been following the reality principle. Nor did their anxiety serve as a signal announcing flight from conditions of unpleasure in the id and thus making them temporarily more comfortable, for the anxiety persisted throughout the session. This would have been following the example of the classical neurotic who, as just described, follows the pleasure principle, at least in the beginning of his analysis.

These considerations lead to the hypothesis that *this* anxiety is a discharge phenomenon, i.e., is automatic. In this case, since the ego confronted by conditions of unpleasure in the id does not produce a signal of anxiety and initiate defenses against unpleasure conditions stemming from the id, it can be considered as having lost or not attained the *function of anticipation* in the "traumatic syndrome." It is generally recognized that the anxiety in the true traumatic neuroses is likewise a discharge phenomenon without signal significance. Because of this similarity between the two conditions it is natural to consider an underlying relation between them. Such a belief can be corroborated or refuted by ranging the clinical symptomatology of the one against the clinical symptomatology of the other.

DYNAMIC-ECONOMIC COMPARISON OF THE
"TRAUMATIC SYNDROME" TO THE TRUE TRAUMATIC NEUROSIS

The symptoms of the true traumatic neurosis are usually divided, broadly speaking, into those of *discharge* (i.e., drive discharge)— chronic anxiety, tension of the muscular system, gastrointestinal and cardiovascular irritability—and those of *inhibition and blocking*— morbid fatigue and mental torpidity (Fenichel, 1945). This symptomatology is explicable on the basis of an excessive influx of stimuli over a given period of time (constituting in psychoanalysis the definition of trauma). "Excessive" is used to indicate that the ego did not find it possible at the time of the traumatic occurrence to discharge, bind, and distribute energies liberated by the stimuli. The *discharge* phenomena are then viewed as belated attempts at mastery of these energies, while the *inhibitory* symptoms represent the ego's blocking of *new* influx of stimuli because it is already overburdened. Both aspects then are part of the over-all goal of the psychic apparatus to keep the quantity of psychic energy at a minimum.

Let us now turn to the special group of patients who present, primarily in the *analytic session*, the symptomatology of the "classical" traumatic neurosis, i.e., the "traumatic syndrome," to see if the features of this syndrome fall naturally into the same categories. I shall begin with the second group of symptoms, the inhibitory and blocking phenomena. We encounter them in the analysand's response to the most significant *external* stimulus of the analytic session—*the interventions of the analyst, which are regularly and relentlessly negated, destroyed, rendered innocuous.* The ego thus performs the essential function of minimizing the inflow of stimuli in the *session* by blocking them, but at the cost of *adaptation* to the important external stimuli of the session—namely, the interventions of the analyst.

When one sees in the "traumatic syndrome" the relentless annihilation of each and every interpretation, regardless of its meaning (through misinterpretation, neglect, distortion), and when one sees that each analytic session begins *de novo* as if no analysis (I am of course schematizing for purpose of clarity) had taken place in all the preceding sessions, one finally comes to the conclusion that an additional force beyond that found in the usual classical analysis is at work. One comes to the conclusion that in the "traumatic syndrome" the ego treats every interpretation as a burdensome, additional stimulus which must be blocked off regardless of its meaning. Because the "traumatic ego" responds to interpretations as if they were burdensome stimuli to be blocked off, they cannot fulfill their essential function, in analytic cure, of conveying content.

Therefore, one rarely discerns a beneficial relaxing effect from a good interpretation in these patients. On the contrary, as previously noted, following an interpretation, one observes an increased tension participated in by the skeletal and the laryngeal muscles. The anal sphincter too is contracted, and mild genital sensations may develop in the effort to discharge tension. After each interpretation the patient may even reach a pitch of acutely uncomfortable tension, which can be understood as a primitive response to the impact of increased stimuli.

Those analysts who prefer a content interpretation will emphasize both a permanent negative transference and a chronic rage against the analyst. That these patients have their teeth set in a permanent, stubborn rage against the analyst is true, as it is also true that they cling to him by way of the medium of this destructive rage. As a description of fact, no objection at all can be made to this formulation, but it is important to note that both the monotonously negative transference and the rage require explanation and are not in themselves explanatory. As stated before, a permanently negative transference and a chronically destructive rage which always gain the upper hand over the adaptive functions of the ego in the analytic session are themselves puzzling phenomena.

While the negation of the analyst's interpretations represents the blocking of the chief external stimuli of an analytic session, the widespread body tension, together with the chronic anxiety of these patients, obviously represents the *first* group of traumatic symptoms— that of drive *discharge*. It can be seen that such a widespread drive discharge simultaneously increases the depth of the protective barrier and thus tends to fend off quantities of external stimuli (Freud, 1920). Thus the discharge symptoms also aid the inhibitory ones in reducing the input of stimuli, essentially those emanating from the analyst. The "traumatic ego" is evidently striving toward rigid stability and is not concerned with adapting itself to the analytic session.

However, a number of symptoms of the true traumatic neurosis are not found either regularly or with sufficient intensity to impair the daily extra-analytic functioning of the patients included under the heading of "traumatic syndrome." Repetitive traumatic dreams, recall of the trauma in the daytime, intense emotional spells, and pronounced somatic symptoms (previously described) do not form an essential part of the picture. In the true traumatic neurosis, the ego is struggling to attain an equilibrium in the face of the disturbing quantity of libidinal and aggressive energies liberated by a relatively recent (with regard to onset of symptoms) event—the trauma.

The ego of the "traumatic syndrome" in the analytic session is responding *as if* a recent trauma had occurred and *as if* it therefore also had to master quantities of liberated instinctual energies. The mystifying question then presents itself: why does the ego of the "traumatic syndrome" function in certain circumstances (e.g., in the analytic session) *as if a recent trauma had occurred which had liberated quantities of instinctual energy when none in fact had recently taken place?*

II. *The Function of Anticipation and Superego*

SUPEREGO AND AVOIDANCE OF QUANTITY

This question has led me to propose the following two answers. I begin by ascribing an anticipatory function to the normal ego. A failure of the superego to anticipate the emergence of a quantity of instinctual energy in the id confronts the ego of the "traumatic syndrome" with the task of meeting internal quantity. It then essays to achieve this task through blocking of external input and discharge of internal input.

However, understanding the "traumatic syndrome" itself is peripheral to my main interest, which is understanding the anticipatory function of the superego. The "traumatic syndrome" serves only as a means of dissecting out of the complex of functions assigned to the superego the hidden one of anticipation and its place in the "machinery" of the mind.[3]

Let us return now to the point of departure, the functioning of the ego in the "traumatic syndrome." It is useful to describe more precisely the problem that confronts it. The issue is not so much that the ego of the "traumatic syndrome" meets quantity of stimuli in

[3] For this reason, the genetic material bearing on the origin of the "analyst as traumatic agent" will not be gone into.

primitive ways but that it has to meet quantity at all. Behind this statement lies the idea that the ego of the normal person as well as large segments of the ego of the classical psychoneurotic does not have to meet internal quantity at all because the intact function of anticipation which is here ascribed to the superego works to prevent quantity of inner stimuli *from making their appearance at all.* But when quantity does make its appearance, the primitive ego functions of nonspecific blocking and nonspecific discharge must also reappear.

The development of the mental apparatus with the proliferation of thought processes goes of course in the opposite direction, toward utilization of minimal quantity. However, in regressive conditions when quantity is released—adolescence, inception of psychotic episodes, in traumatic neurosis as a result of an external event, in the "traumatic syndrome" as a result of an assumed failure of the superego in its function of anticipation—the primitive ego functions of blocking and discharge must then reappear.

ANTICIPATION AND THE TWO PRINCIPLES OF MENTAL FUNCTIONING

The elements which constitute the process "anticipation" are: perception and then a reaction to the percept, a reaction which in turn is determined by the goal of adaptation of a general or specific nature. While separating the process "anticipation" into its three constituents, it is obviously a connected whole, a Gestalt with three elements: perception, reaction, goal.

Perception as an aspect of anticipation is usually thought of in connection with perception of external reality, but perception of the internal milieu (*innere Wahrnehmung*) can also be thought of in connection with the function of anticipation.

In our laboratory, the analytic session, a situation exists in which perception of external reality is extremely narrow, limited primarily to perception of the analyst. Consequently perception of internal events becomes facilitated. From the viewpoint of perception, we can formulate the analytic process as a study of the effect of one external stimulus, the analyst, on perception of internal events. The analysand, given the directive of free association, can be compared to the subject of an experiment in external perception who is given another kind of directive.

The ego of the "successful" analysand tolerates the unpleasure generated or about to be generated by his free associations because he anticipates a future gain. His ego, operating under the reality principle, employs the function of anticipation to attain the goal of cure through analysis. This is usually the only kind of anticipation that is considered—*anticipation in the service of the reality principle*, i.e., anticipation of a future gain.

Is there not a primitive precursor observable in the analytic session, out of which this reality-tied function of anticipation has developed?

Again, recourse to observation of the patient on the couch shows that he will occasionally follow the pleasure principle. He will avoid continuing the unpleasure generated by his free associations through a variety of defensive maneuvers. This avoidance will become evident in the style and content of his free associations.

What has initiated these defensive maneuvers and caused the ego to regress to the pleasure principle? Presumably, the ego and superego sense processes in the id which could lead to a discomfort experienced as overwhelming (potential traumatic situation); intimations of anxiety and pain appear (signal anxiety and pain); the drives in the id are then inhibited by the ego. The essence of this situation is the *anticipation* of further significant unpleasures emanating from the inner world and their avoidance. Here the *function of anticipation is in the service of the pleasure principle*, not in the service of the reality principle.

We naturally assume that the reality-tied function of anticipation has evolved out of an earlier one, which functions under the pleasure principle. How could such an evolution have taken place? It is possible to envision the development of the reality-tied function of anticipation by way of the development of permanent objects ("constant" objects in Hartmann's terminology [1952]). Signal anxiety and pain caused by the disappearance of the transient object may be appeased when the permanent object presentation is established in the mind, even though the external object is in reality absent. The infant would then correctly *anticipate* the return of the external object—reality anticipation. This endogenous growth (development of permanent object presentation) would enable the ego to tolerate the unpleasure of the moment—the disappearance of the object. A complete *psychoanalytic* theory of anticipation in the service of reality would attempt to trace the development of the function of anticipation from this point on to its widening and sophisticated use in the external world of real dangers where specific object loss is not obviously involved. However, this is not the focus of my paper, and I return to the anticipation of internal events and the superego.

CLOSER FORMULATION OF THE CONCEPT OF ANTICIPATION WITH SPECIAL REFERENCE TO ANTICIPATION OF INTERNAL EVENTS AND THE SUPEREGO

In addition to the usual emphasis on the signal activity of the ego in a consideration of anticipation, two other constituents of a fully developed function of anticipation are also involved. One element is subsumed under mental conditions resulting from the *inception* of conditions of unpleasure in the id. The second is subsumed under mental reactions to the *consequences* of acts, physical or mental, associated with conditions of unpleasure.

I shall begin with the first and consider in this connection the child who has burned his hand by putting it in the fire. It is said that "the burned child dreads the fire," which obviously means that by virtue of the development of thought, the child is able to imagine the consequences of repeating the act. He no longer needs to put his hand in the fire for even a moment in order to convince himself of its inadvisability. He need not even bring his hand in safe proximity to the fire to feel its warmth, a signal, and then withdraw it. We can now see that perfected anticipation of external events aims at preventing even the *inception* of conditions of unpleasure in the external world. I am speaking of the mental apparatus when it is governed by the pleasure principle and not by the reality principle. (In this example, both happen to coincide.)

Let us turn now from perfected anticipation in the external world (e.g., the already burned child who performs a mental experiment and does not need to touch the fire in order to stay away from it) to the internal world. The condition of unpleasure in the id corresponding to the fire could be, for example, a "dammed-up state"—a quantity of undischarged and unbound instinctual energy. The ego under the pleasure principle may respond to the condition of unpleasure in the id with anxiety and by attempting to alter this condition in the id through its defense mechanisms.

While it is true that in this way the ego utilizes the affect of anxiety in preventing *further* development of conditions of unpleasure in the id through its defense mechanisms, this can hardly be thought of as perfected anticipation. Granted that a state of maximum unpleasure is thereby avoided, a certain amount of unpleasure in the shape of affective signals of anxiety is nonetheless experienced. Thus, a perfected function of internal anticipation must have as an ingredient some kind of act of thought which will prevent the appearance of the affect signal and substitute a thought signal. This seems present in the unconscious thoughtlike consideration given to consequences of id wishes.

Let us take an example from the external world where the consequence of an action is not as immediately painful as in the case of the hand in the fire—that of walking in the rain without rubbers. In this case, we recognize that the parents' own function of anticipation with its accompanying concern for consequences results in a parental injunction to wear the rubbers, and the child is thus protected. We also recognize that when wearing rubbers in the rain is finally initiated by the child himself, it is at first a result of a superego dictate, not of an ego function. The child will wear this article in obedience to the internalized commands of the parent. The consequences of such an act appear to be considered first along lines of the consequences of obedience and of disobedience, of whether the act is good or bad. Originally the act is not considered in relation to reality. It is as if the child first said to himself: "I am bad not to wear rubbers and in order to avoid being bad I must wear them." It is not as if the child said to himself: "I don't want to catch a cold and therefore I will put on my rubbers."

This original dominance of the pleasure principle over the reality principle with regard to the concern for consequences can also be observed in exaggerated form in the rituals of the obsessive-compulsive. The "if, then" such as "if you step on the crack, then you'll break your mother's back," to mention one approaching the normal of these rituals, represents a concern for consequences. While the ritual is permeated with magical thinking, it nonetheless represents thinking of the consequence of an action. Our knowledge of the important role of the superego in the formation of rituals hints therefore at the significance of the superego for the perfected function of anticipation.

The injunctions of the parents to the child constitute an enormous stimulus for the "if, then" concern for consequence. For the "do this" and "don't do that" of the parent mean explicitly or implicitly "because," such as "because it's good for you" or "because it is the right

thing to do." It seems likely therefore that the concern for consequences, which is an important constituent of the function of anticipation, becomes introjected and becomes a component of the superego.

In the course of development, the concern for consequences may
become an ego function, i.e., be carried out with regard to reality, be
regulated by the reality principle. Originally, however, it appears to
be an internalization of the parent's own concern for consequences,
a superego function carried out under the pleasure principle as are
all superego functions (the implications of this view for the erratic
functioning of psychopaths are obvious; see Greenacre, 1945).

In teasing out two important constituents of the total function of
anticipation—prevention of inception of conditions of unpleasure and
concern for consequences—an artificial separation between them has
been created. It is obvious that the first element can be realized only
by virtue of the second.

The point of the examples of the hand in the fire and the rubbers
in the rain is to underline the fundamental difference between even
minimal experiencing of unpleasure (anxiety signals) and an attempted avoidance of all unpleasure, of even the inception of conditions of unpleasure—not putting the hand in the fire even momentarily, putting on rubbers before getting slightly wet.

In the examples given, an act of thought—an experiment which
carries out the "if, then" in the mind only—was found to be the
agent which prevents the experience of even a slight unpleasure. This
type of act of thought belongs to the general area of *intentions* (acts
contemplated but not yet fulfilled), and one can think of it actively
as *intending*.

Can mental activity which refers to external events such as "hand
in the fire" and "rubbers and rain" be applied to incipient events in
the id? The following working hypothesis is suggested. The superego inspects[4] the id continuously, registers its state, i.e., "senses" the
id, and then performs an act of thought on its registrations, transforming them into something which, were it to originate in the system Cs.,
would correspond to *intentions*. They are then transmitted to the ego,
but they do not appear in consciousness as *intentions* in the ordinary

---

[4] The inspection of the id by the superego is not considered in this paper to be
synonymous with self observation. The latter is viewed as a complex function, of
which superego inspection of the id is but one component.

sense of the word. They are experienced as anxieties in accord with the pleasure principle which governs information from the interior.

It will now be asked: But what is the phenomenological difference in consciousness between these anxieties which arise from the super-ego's thoughtlike anticipatory function vis-à-vis the id (sensing and intentioning) and those anxieties which arise directly in the ego from the significant increase of instinctual pressure from the id. The first type of anxiety, I suggest, possesses a thoughtlike, causallike concern for consequences. This concern can be discerned more easily when statements pertaining to this type of anxiety are made explicit, thus: "*If* I go out, *then* the horse will bite me," "*If* I argue with my husband, *then* he will make a scene." The *form* of this anxiety (not necessarily its content) is ascribed in the view presented to the sensing, *intentioning* activity (anticipatory function) of the superego.[5]

The neologism *intentioning* has been coined in order to denote the thoughtlike working over of id derivatives by the superego in contrast to the ego's broader and more inclusive intending function.

The intending function of the ego is influenced, but not completely determined, by the intentioning activity of the superego. If the ego is subservient to the id (i.e., if its goals are determined by the id as in certain acting-out characters), then the intending of the ego and the intentioning of the superego coincide. More often, however, they do not coincide since the ego frequently has goals of its own.

The concept of the ego's intending is contiguous with a number of related ideas. It is related to willed action, as opposed to accidental action, to a desired action, and finally to goal. These three contiguous ideas imply a considerable complexity in the function of intending.

The ego's "final" intending is very much influenced by a number of factors beside that of superego intentioning. The external input which it possesses via its own perceptual apparatus is an important factor. Another is the goal the ego sets itself; a third, its store of recollections. All of these together with superego intentioning are submitted to the synthesizing activity of the ego. The final resultant is represented by an intention of the ego.

[5] According to this view, the appearance of psychoneurotic phobias at the stage of the consolidating superego (e.g., little Hans) is not accidental, nor is their disappearance with its consolidation (e.g., Little Hans). For the relation of phobia to superego, see Deutsch (1928), Alexander (1930), Bornstein (1949), Rangell (1952), Wangh (1959), Ruddick (1961).

It may appear incongruous to assign a thoughtlike activity to the superego in view of its wild and primitive nature, but we have only to remember the stimulus given to superego formation by the *words* of the parent and the "exceptional position of the auditory sphere" (Isakower, 1939, 1954) to consider the association of thought and superego as acceptable. And we may express this origin of the superego in parental words by saying that its anticipatory activity is carried out by means of adding words to the id drives. Thus there emerges the typical anxiety thought in words: "I am afraid that or because. . . ." But when the anxiety results from the direct impingement of quantities of instinctual energy on the ego, it is much more of a direct, affective, wordless experience. The separation of the anxiety response into an affective process and into a thought process was cogently formulated by Schur in 1953.[6]

During analysis the analysand's anxious preoccupations and anxiety symptoms—all of which usually have a thought and word quality—may assume the shape of early childhood's direct, affective response to quantity in the id. This presents the ego with a puzzling situation. It has become accustomed to dealing with unpleasure conditions in the id through using the words supplied to it by the superego and attaching them to possible events in the external world.

In addition to the thought and word structure of the second, superego type of anxiety, two subjective features mark it off from the first type. These are the qualities of time and space. The anxiety deriving from the direct impingement of quantities of energy on the ego always has a directly present-tense, experiential quality. Anxiety deriving from the anticipatory function of the superego necessarily has a quality of futurity attached to it. It may take the ordinary normal form of general concern about the future. Indeed, a mild degree of such anxiety—usually termed concern—seems an inevitable result of superego development. This anticipatory function of the superego may also result (given other concomitant factors) in more pathological forms with identical emphasis on the future—a sense of *impending* disaster, or a phobia with its implicit "I am afraid that the horse *will* bite me."

---

[6] Schur's views on signal anxiety and my views on anticipatory anxiety generated by the thoughtlike intentioning function of the superego differ from each other. Since anxiety is but one aspect of this paper, the consideration of our differing views is reserved for another paper devoted to anxiety alone.

The second feature which distinguishes the two anxieties is the subjective experience of internal and external. The first type which is predominantly bodily and affective may be observed as being experienced inside of one; the second, outside of one. The "internality" of the first appears linked to the characteristics of a discharge phenomenon; the "externality" of the second to being a thoughtlike process.

Normal concern about the external world, diffuse anxiety about happenings in this world, phobic anxiety concerning it find expression in words—and words are experienced as external. "The part played by word-presentations now becomes perfectly clear. By their interposition internal thought-processes are made into perceptions. It is like a demonstration of the theorem that all knowledge has its origin in external perception. When a hypercathexis of the process of thinking takes place, thoughts are *actually* perceived—as if they came from without—and are consequently held to be true" (Freud, 1923, p. 23).

If the superego is an internal sensory organ, then it too acts, like external sensory ones, through its thoughtlike activities as a screen or barrier—but in this case against energies from the id. We can now return momentarily to the "traumatic syndrome" and to the question which led to this paper: why the ego of the "traumatic syndrome" responds in the analytic session as if the mental apparatus had experienced a real, external trauma. We have only to assume that the superego has lost (or never achieved) the function of anticipation. Then the ego would not receive this support from the superego in screening energic quantities of the id. In the true traumatic neurosis, excessive quantities are released by a trauma; in the "traumatic syndrome," they are "released" by the failure of the superego to anticipate quantities in the id and through its thoughtlike activity to prevent them from impinging on the ego, which then must respond by blocking and discharge.

The hypothesis that the superego acts by way of thoughtlike *intentioning* as a protective barrier for the ego against the drive energies of the id appears to throw light on otherwise puzzling anxiety attacks. The sporadic anxiety attacks of the psychopath can be understood by ascribing them to his defective superego. Thus in some cases we arrive at what can be considered a paradoxical conclusion, or one contrary to our usual thinking. It is not the severity of the superego which initiates certain anxieties, but on the contrary a deficiency in its activity.

The exaggerations wrought by pathology appear to corroborate the hypothesis that, with the development of the superego, certain functions of internal perception are taken over by it. Speaking of the ego's puzzlement about its feeling of guilt in obsessional neurosis even when it knows itself to be innocent, Freud (1926) says: "The superego behaves as though repression had not occurred and as though it knew the real wording and full affective character of the aggressive impulse, and it treats the ego accordingly" (p. 11).

According to the hypothesis presented here, of the monopoly of the superego on internal perception, the words "as though" in the above quotation would have to be omitted. For we would find it quite as it should be that the superego should "know" the id, and the ego be in ignorance of it.

And further, it is quite correct for the superego to "treat the ego accordingly," or to put it another way, for it to inform the ego of the aggressive urges of the id. For due to the obsessional neurotic's libidinal regression to anal sadism, this transmitted superego information corresponds to a certain psychic reality. As Freud points out in the succeeding paragraph, even further pathology would ensue were the ego to bar the path to such communications from the superego.

However, in the event that conditions in the id are predominantly normal and have reached the genital level, the superego will then report genital intentions to the ego. The effect of such a report will be some kind of pleasurable feeling, in contrast to the feeling of guilt in the obsessional case just discussed. In the obsessional neurosis with its anal-sadistic libidinal level we are accustomed to speak of a harsh superego. In the case of a genital organization of the libido, we can also speak of a benevolent superego (Schafer, 1960), although we are not accustomed to do so. But in the view presented here of the superego's anticipatory functions, a less anthropomorphized way of describing its activity and of avoiding, at least in some cases, such terms as harsh and benevolent becomes apparent. In the one case, the superego senses and reports to the ego anal-sadistic wishes; and in the other, genital wishes of the id.

Many references have been made in the literature to Freud's guess that the ego's hurrying ahead of the libido in its development constitutes a predisposition to obsessional neurosis (1913), but it has been difficult to describe the mechanics of the apparently disturbing effect of such a disharmony between a precocious ego and a regressive id. The hypothesis advanced here makes it possible to take a step in the direction of such a description. If the child's ego has "unified" itself, perhaps at the expense of excessively excluding fantasy (as a result of anxiety), its grasp of reality will be relatively correct and devoid of contamination by fantasy. The information that this ego then receives from the external world is very different from the information transmitted to it by the superego about the id. The task of synthesizing these conflicting sets of information is much greater than it would be were the ego more primitive in its perception of the external world. A corroborating step in the application of this view would consist in showing the necessary connection of this dynamic conflict between two sets of information, external and internal, and the development of obsessional character and symptoms, e.g., isolation. As mentioned previously, this is a long step requiring the observation of more clinical material.

We have imperceptibly moved into the field of intrasystemic conflict (Hartmann, 1950), of a potential conflict in the ego as a result of two disparate inputs. The likelihood of a high frequency of such conflicts within the ego appears great because of the following considerations.

The conscious and preconscious anticipation of external events appears to be regulated at first by the pleasure principle. Feelings of guilt, discomfort, anxiety appear when a forbidden action is intended. The action may not then be carried out. Later on, reality factors in the broadest sense (Hartmann, 1947) may become decisive, and we then speak of the dominance of the reality principle in ego functioning.

It appears most unlikely, however, that the reality principle makes any impression on the anticipation of purely internal events. For the reaction of the ego to the sensing and intentioning of the internal events of the id by the superego can be only to interfere with processes in the id through its defense mechanisms, which usually run off automatically under the pleasure principle. (To a mild extent, an exception to the dominance of the pleasure principle in these internal transactions is to be found in the willed, strict adherence to the fundamental rule in analysis.) The external anticipatory activity of the ego guided by the reality principle and the internal anticipatory activity of the superego guided by the pleasure principle appear bound to collide frequently.

Clearly, the division of anticipation into internal and external is artificial. No intended act of any significance can exist without simultaneously arousing external and internal anticipation. However, the transference situation, when crystallized into the transference neurosis, is ideally arranged for the predominance of internal anticipations. Perception of the analyst as an external object results primarily in internal response (in so far as displacements to the external world do not occur). The superego can register the state of the id wishes toward the analyst, transmit them in the form of unconscious intentions, experienced as anxieties containing a thought quality—a connected causal ("because, then") quality. It is this thought quality which enables the analysand to describe his thoughts and feelings toward the analyst. This quality, I believe, is an important ingredient of "analyzability." When the chief resistance to analysis lies in the associative process itself and when this resistance remains unchanged from session to session despite changes in analytic material, then the source of the resistance may reside in anomalies in the structure of the superego.

A lack of aptitude for being truly "psychological" in analytic sessions can be seen in patients who act out punishment needs. In them, punishment *follows* guilt in an unending cycle; *anticipation* of guilt feeling in forestalling guilt-laden action does not occur or is ineffective.

When beneficial changes occur in the associative process or in the effective anticipation of guilt feelings, I would ascribe them in part to an improvement in the superego's "sensory" function vis-à-vis the id. I would correlate this functional change in the superego to the working through of anomalies within the superego itself, springing from complicated identifications. Behind these issues shimmers the deep problem of the common roots of responsibility for moral action (Hartmann, 1960; Beres, 1965) and for self observation. A consideration of this problem leads in turn to the study of the correlation between therapeutic analysis and emerging moral values.

Further clinical observation will be necessary to determine whether the concept of the superego as an internal sensing and anticipating organ throws any new light on the differentiation of anxieties, the need for punishment, the lack of psychological aptitude in certain analysands, and perhaps the form of some neuroses.

Summary

The function of anticipation can be conveniently envisaged as evolving through stages; from the first, in which it is not yet present, to the second in which an approximation to anticipation appears in the response of an ego governed by the pleasure principle, to the third in which a true thoughtlike function of anticipation as an aspect of the superego appears.

The first stage is one in which the ego primarily attends to the quantitative aspect of stimuli, external and internal, and neglects their meaning. In its striving toward equilibrium, the ego blocks input indiscriminately (regardless of its meaning) and discharges instinctual energies regardless of psychic wishes. One might then say that at this stage there is a tendency of the psychic apparatus to be guided in its perceptual and discharge activity by the repetition compulsion. The normal model is to be found in earliest infancy, which shows some of these features.

The second stage, in which an approximation to anticipation appears, is one in which the pleasure principle and not the repetition compulsion is dominant. The ego receives intimations, commonly called signals, of anxiety as a result of conditions of unpleasure in the id. It intervenes in these id processes through its defense mechanisms and strives to alter the conditions of unpleasure in the id to a less unfavorable state. If one introduces a finalistic note by saying that the ego strives to alter the condition of unpleasure in order to avoid a traumatic state, then one can speak of a function of anticipation existing at this point of development. The protective action of anticipation at this stage consists in permitting a small amount of painfulness (anxiety) to occur but preventing a greater amount.

Perfected anticipation appears in the third stage with the consolidation of the superego and the introduction of a thought and intentioning process by the superego, possessing a resemblance to the logical "if, then." The superego inspects the id continually and transmits the information obtained by its thought process to the ego in the form of anxiety, which is different from earlier signals. It possesses the thought form of "I am afraid because," or "I am afraid that" or "if, then." A mild degree of anticipatory anxiety seems to be a necessary consequence of the establishment of the protective, anticipatory activity of the superego. It is suggested that some forms of pathology may be understood in terms of conflict within the ego, between two sets of disparate inputs—internal and external.

The achievement of the third stage of anticipation results in increased specialization in the mental apparatus. The superego becomes the internal "sense" organ with a thoughtlike activity functioning as a stimulus barrier against the id and the ego, an external sense organ combined with thinking. In the former the thoughtlike activity is governed by the pleasure principle (in mature individuals); in the latter, by the reality principle.

The patient who does not reach this stage of superego development (because of specific early events, especially deceptions) presents a more or less typical picture in the analytic session which has been described under the heading of "traumatic syndrome." Behind this picture lies first the central fact that the ego's intention in the session is no more than a rationalized version of the raw instinctual aims of the id. And behind this subservience of the ego to the id (i.e., it *consistently* fails to follow the reality goals of analysis in each session) lies the real *inability* of the superego to add words to the aims of the id. Such a contribution from the superego (which normally exists) would *enable* the ego to enter into a struggle between its reality goals and the aims of the id. Without this contribution from the superego, the ego is exposed to the raw energies of the id and is compelled to attempt blocking and discharge at any cost ("traumatic syndrome").

For a long time these patients appear unanalyzable because true free association is conspicuously absent. Clinical experiences seem to indicate that the same superego deficiency which accounts for the appearance of the "traumatic syndrome" also accounts for this lack of free association. The knowledge of this connection between superego deficit and trouble in free association is helpful. It signals the analyst to attend to superego deficiencies in the analytic session, if the capacity for free association and therapeutic gain is to increase. Obviously one must also work backward in time, especially toward early, *real* parental deceptions which, becoming revitalized in the session, dynamically modulate and distort the associative process.

BIBLIOGRAPHY

Alexander, F. (1930), *The Psychoanalysis of Total Personality.* NY: Nerv. & Ment. Dis.
Bauer, S. Unpublished manuscript.

Beres, D. (1958), Vicissitudes of Superego Functions and Superego Precursors in Childhood. *Psa. Study Ch.*, 13:324-351.

—— (1965), Psychoanalytic Notes on the History of Morality. *J. Am. Psa. Assn.*, 13:3-37.

Blau, A. (1952), In Support of Freud's Syndrome of "Actual" Anxiety Neurosis. *Int. J. Psa.*, 33:363-372.

Bornstein, B. (1949), The Analysis of a Phobic Child. *Psa. Study Ch.*, 3/4:181-226.

Brenner, C. (1953), An Addendum to Freud's Theory of Anxiety. *Int. J. Psa.*, 34:18-24.

Deutsch, H. (1928), Agoraphobia. *Neurosis and Character Types*. NY: IUP, 1965, 97-116.

Fenichel, O. (1945), *The Psychoanalytic Theory of Neurosis*. NY: Norton.

Freud, S. (1895), Project for a Scientific Psychology. *The Origins of Psychoanalysis*. NY: Basic Books, 1954.

—— (1909), The Analysis of a Phobia in a Five-year-old Boy. *S.E.*, 10:3-149.

—— (1913), The Disposition to Obsessional Neurosis. *S.E.*, 12:311-326.

—— (1920), Beyond the Pleasure Principle. *S.E.*, 18:7-64.

—— (1923), The Ego and the Id. *S.E.*, 19:3-66.

—— (1926), Inhibitions, Symptoms and Anxiety. *S.E.*, 20:77-174.

Gill, M. M. (1963), *Topography and Systems in Psychoanalytic Theory. Psychol. Issues*, 10.

Goodman, S. (1965), Panel Report: Current Status of the Theory of the Superego. *J. Am. Psa. Assn.*, 13:172-180.

Greenacre, P. (1945), Conscience in the Psychopath. *Trauma, Growth and Personality*. NY: Norton, 1952, 165-187.

Hammerman, S. (1965), Conceptions of Superego Development. *J. Am. Psa. Assn.*, 13:320-355.

Hartmann, H. (1939), *Ego Psychology and the Problem of Adaptation*. NY: IUP, 1958.

—— (1947), On Rational and Irrational Action. *Essays*, 37-68.

—— (1950), Comments on the Psychoanalytic Theory of the Ego. *Essays*, 113-141.

—— (1952), The Mutual Influences in the Development of Ego and Id. *Essays*, 155-181.

—— (1960), *Psychoanalysis and Moral Values*. NY: IUP.

—— & Loewenstein, R. M. (1962), Notes on the Superego. *Psa. Study Ch.*, 17:42-81.

Isakower, O. (1939), On the Exceptional Position of the Auditory Sphere. *Int. J. Psa.*, 20:340-348.

—— (1954), Spoken Words in Dreams. *Psa. Q.*, 23:1-6.

Jacobson, E. (1954), Contribution to the Metapsychology of Psychotic Identifications. *J. Am. Psa. Assn.*, 2:239-262.

—— (1964), *The Self and the Object World*. NY: IUP.

Rangell, L. (1952), The Analysis of a Doll Phobia. *Int. J. Psa.*, 33:43-53.

Reich, A. (1954), Early Identifications as Archaic Elements in the Superego. *J. Am. Psa. Assn.*, 2:218-238.

Ruddick, B. (1961), Agoraphobia. *Int. J. Psa.*, 42:537-543.

Sandler, J. (1960), On the Concept of Superego. *Psa. Study Ch.*, 15:128-162.

Schafer, R. (1960), The Loving and Beloved Superego in Freud's Structural Theory. *Psa. Study Ch.*, 15:163-188.

Schur, M. (1953a), The Ego and the Id in Anxiety. *Psa. Study Ch.*, 13:190-220.

—— (1953b), The Ego in Anxiety. *Drives, Affects, Behavior*, ed. R. M. Loewenstein. NY: IUP, 1:67-103.

Spiegel, L. A. (1959), The Self, the Sense of Self, and Perception. *Psa. Study Ch.*, 14:81-109.

Spitz, R. A. (1957), *No and Yes*. NY: IUP.

Wangh, M. (1959), Structural Determinants of Phobia. *J. Am. Psa. Assn.*, 7:675-695.

Weissman, P. (1954), Ego and Superego in Obsessional Character and Neurosis. *Psa. Q.*, 23:529-543.

Some Thoughts on Adaptation and Conformism

JEANNE LAMPL-DE GROOT, M.D.

If we wish to distinguish between adaptive and conforming behavior, it is advisable to define the concepts "adaptation" and "conformism" as clearly as possible. In ordinary usage, these terms are often equated. Adaptive behavior is often viewed merely as surrendering to environmental demands and as completely in line with existing social laws, norms, and values. However, I believe that we should reserve the term "conformism" for this kind of compliant conduct.

In certain circumstances adaptive behavior does coincide with conforming to social demands. However, the concept of adaptation comprises much more than conformism and I shall try to define it in more exact terms later on in this paper. I shall begin my discussion by considering both adaptation and conformism as they apply to a person's behavior as a reaction to his environment.

The concept of adaptation originated in biology. Living organisms "adapt" themselves to the environment. If they do not, they cannot survive, either individually or as a species. In animals adaptation to the environment can occur through changes in the individual; e.g., in fur-bearing animals the thickness of the fur varies with the degree of heat and cold; in many amphibian species the color of the skin changes according to the coloration of the environment, etc. However, adaptation can also be achieved by changing the environment, by searching for and finding more suitable surroundings; e.g., migratory birds travel south in the winter to exchange their cold homeland for warmer countries; fish swim up a river to propagate in an environment suitable for their offspring; certain species of game migrate every year in order to find water and proper food, etc.

In human beings we encounter even more complex forms of adaptation. Freud speaks of autoplastic and alloplastic adaptation. In contrast to animals, human beings, by virtue of having evolved a differentiated mental life, have gradually changed their natural outer world into a complicated social environment. Therefore, they must "adapt" not only to guarantee survival and to protect their offspring; they must adjust to the society which generations of their ancestors have created and in which they are living.

As far as I know, Heinz Hartmann was the first analyst who systematically applied the concept of adaptation to psychological phenomena. He describes (1939) three forms of adjustment: (1) a change in the individual, i.e., a passive acceptance of the demands, norms, and laws of the environment; (2) a change of the environment by actively influencing it; and (3) a search for another environment where the norms and demands are more acceptable to the individual. The second and third forms could be described as active or creative adaptational processes, while in the first instance, the passive acceptance of social norms, the individual "conforms" to the environment.

While there is a limited parallel between psychological phenomena and biological processes, the complexity of man's mental life requires that the psychological concept of adaptation be extended to include the differentiated inner processes. The concept covers modes of behavior and is *not* merely a mental mechanism, in which sense it is sometimes used. Human "adaptation" comprises passive and active (creative) adjustment to the outer world as well as a synthesis of the forces at work in the different functional parts of the structured mind. It is well known that during growth, conflicts between id, ego, and superego functions arise and their solution involves a number of mental mechanisms. *Inner* adaptation requires a harmonious balance between instinctual and emotional needs, ego activities, and the person's moral system. I shall first deal with outer adaptation.

Outer Adaptation

Whether a passive, conforming or an active, creative adaptation to the social milieu emerges is determined by a wealth of factors difficult to unravel. I shall try to highlight some aspects of the complicated processes involved.

Isaac-Edersheim (1965) states that "adaptation" is ego *and* ego-ideal syntonic, whereas conforming conduct is ego syntonic but impairs the ego ideal.

Hartmann (1960), in describing how the ego's tendency to master inner conflicts can be curtailed by danger threatening from the environment, writes: the ego's "adaptive function will often overstep its integrative capacities. Thus in an environment where there is a high premium on conformism, the ego, still as a mediator, may well enforce the neglect or the suppression of personal moral valuation, even if they have, for the individual, a considerable integrative function. In such instances, social anxiety might have proved stronger than the demands of the personal moral system" (p. 32f.). This is certainly true of people who have been able to build up "a personal moral system"; that is, it is true of people who have grown up in a milieu which was not too authoritarian and which allowed some freedom at the time the child's superego was being established by introjection of parental norms and values. However, in cases where the integrative function is really overlaid with social anxiety, should we not speak of conforming behavior? We become aware of the necessity to distinguish between the *mechanism* of adaptation as a mental tool and adaptation indicating a behavioral attitude. Here I shall use adaptation in the second meaning.

Most children of parents who demand complete obedience and conformity do not acquire a nonconforming superego. Only exceptionally strong and gifted children can sometimes succeed in building up norms of their own which deviate from those of their parents. An impressive example of such an exception is described by Irving Stone (1961) in his novel about Michelangelo. Young Michelangelo was an obedient son to his authoritative father. At the age of 13, however, the boy, driven by an irresistible urge to become a sculptor, opposed his father's normative conviction that the Buonarroti were "noble burghers" and that labor and "work with the hands" were beneath their dignity. Michelangelo did not resist his father and uncle when they beat him severely, but he pursued his goal, becoming an apprentice first to the painter Ghirlandaio and later to the sculptor Bertoldo. His four younger brothers conformed to their father's demands. They all ended up as good-for-nothings, dependent upon the financial support of Michelangelo. It is interesting to note that Michelangelo's nonconformism led to a full unfolding of his forcefully driving talent and to his becoming one of the greatest sculptors of the Renaissance. He nevertheless paid for his disobedience to his father with a strong inner struggle and guilt feelings that forced him to live in poverty in order to meet the financial demands of his family.

There are, of course, less gifted persons with authoritarian parents who quietly develop nonconforming norms in childhood. However, their oppositional ideas often acquire a compulsive character very similar to those of the conformist, and this results in inhibition or paralysis of creative activities. Vladimir Nabokov, in *The Real Life of Sebastian Knight*, writes: "Well did he know that to flaunt one's contempt for a moral code was but smuggled smugness and prejudice turned inside out."

Throughout the history of man there have been periods when people lived and children were brought up under the pressure of authoritarian rulers and ruling classes, when conforming behavior was demanded on penalty of cruel punishment and on pain of death. In recent times the experiences in Nazi concentration camps during World War II are probably among the most striking examples. Many of the concentration camp victims had formed their norms and moral codes while living in freedom in democratic countries. When they were exposed to the most cruel and threatening authorities in the concentration camps, many of them could not adjust at all and soon died. A few of them managed to survive in spite of hunger, disease, exhaustion, and torture. Were these people able to conform only by ignoring or "suppressing" their personal moral values? There were undoubtedly many different individual solutions to this problem, but I would like to cite E. de Wind (1965), who is one of the very few survivors of the Auschwitz gas chambers. In a most impressive article he describes how a kind of adjustment took place by a "reversal of values." The high valuation of life, usually so common among human beings, had to be completely abandoned. The only thing to look forward to was death. The only "value" that mattered was how to escape or minimize the cruel treatment, how to die in the least painful way. The word "liberation" no longer meant being rescued from the Nazis; it meant "going the road through the chimney of the gas chambers" (de Wind, 1965). Persons who could not accept this new "norm" were felt to be threatening and they became outcasts. When rumors of German defeats began to circulate, the idea of a possible "real" liberation was confusing and even dangerous.

The general devaluation of life applied to the lives of everyone— one's own life and also the lives of wives, husbands, children, companions. "Compassion" for others had only one form: to smooth their way to death. Nevertheless, there must have been a deep unconscious clinging to life. It is possible that in these exceptional circumstances the paradox became true that a passive surrender to the idea of death was the only way to survive.

An even more difficult question to answer is whether and how the survivors of the concentration camps managed to readjust to their environments after their liberation. It is well known that some of them did not succeed, having become mentally or physically crippled personalities. Others did succeed, although the road from forced conformism and reversal of values to active (creative) adaptation was extremely difficult.[1]

However, people who live in more favorable circumstances, in a social milieu which allows for some kind of individual moral code, are also confronted with the problem of conformism versus creative adaptation, though in a different way. I shall describe two examples of conforming behavior and one example of nonconforming behavior.

1. *Conformism in persons with defective superego development.* In some persons the superego as an inner agency, an inner voice of conscience and value judgment, has not been fully established. These persons will easily conform to outer demands and let their behavior be guided by them. The causes for this may be a deficiency in the mechanisms of introjection and identification and unstable parental images, though several other factors may also be responsible (Freud, 1923, 1930).

2. *Conformism in persons with strong inner anxiety.* Some persons have developed a superego and nevertheless feel impelled to conform to a nonauthoritarian "social milieu." In this case we can assume that their "social anxiety" is due not so much to reality factors as to *inner* (neurotic) anxiety projected upon the outer world. Their conformism is used as a defense against their unsolved inner conflicts. Inner anxiety may have many sources, e.g., a clash between instinctual impulses and the ego organization. In delinquents the id tendencies have to some extent overwhelmed the ego which then has to "conform" to the id, thus causing these persons to oppose the environment.

---

[1] Isaac-Ederheim (1965) describes similar situations in concentration camps in a slightly different context.

More often the outcome of the conflict is a neurotic condition in which the inner anxiety, under the guise of social anxiety, leads to conformism with the environment.

I would like to mention a special case which we often encounter in our analytic work. I am referring to persons with great ambitions and a strong competitive urge who are not gifted enough to realize most of their ambitions. This failure often mobilizes intense aggression toward rivals and in turn may lead to strong anxiety. Here again, conforming to outer demands may be used to cover up the inner fears and neurotic inhibitions, and eventually result in symptom formation. When patients suffer from their inability to live up to their personal moral code, we try to help them solve their neurotic conflicts and re-establish their own norms and values. A "healthy" development into harmonious personality requires the capacity to integrate instinctual needs, moral and value codes, ego activities and talents, in interaction with the inevitable demands of the special social milieu. I have previously (1949, 1962, 1963) dealt with these complex processes, and Hartmann (1939, 1956, 1960) has contributed extensive and valuable propositions in regard to these problems.

3. *Nonconformism in persons with a strict and rigid superego.* During the structuralization of the mind, the superego, emerging in childhood as an inner deposit of infantile parental object relations, often retains the rigidity of primitive archaic processes. While some ego functions develop in the conflict-free sphere and are flexible enough to profit from new experiences, the superego functions often retain their original rigidity in spite of changes in content. This is particularly true when, at the time of the superego's emergence, aggression is turned inward and invested in the superego, a process that may be induced by, and ward off, anxiety provoked by aggressiveness. In order to keep this aggression under control, the superego must be very strict and often cruel in its demands. The person then experiences his individual moral code as a universal law and for this reason is intolerant of persons whose moral codes deviate from his.

People in authority sometimes use their fixed personal convictions to influence weaker persons to recruit followers and to keep them in obedience. The decision as to which norms and codes are indispensable to the maintenance and growth of a given society and which can be left to individual preference is a very difficult one. It is a question that belongs as much to the realm of sociology as to that of psychology. From the psychological side I would like to stress that this is a problem for both the ruler and the ruled. People in authority *can be* authoritarian, but it is *not necessary* that they demand unconditional surrender. They could try to encourage individual opinions and value judgments. This is desirable not only in sociopolitical fields but also in all areas of education. For instance, a scientist with a very wide knowledge of his field may either try to force his opinions on his students or he may stimulate the development of original thinking in them. The different outcomes will depend on the interaction of the personalities of teacher and students.

In summary, we may say that in general an individual who has been able to acquire some kind of a personal moral code will conform to his environment under the following conditions.

a. When the rulers are authoritarian and possess the material power to enforce complete obedience, the subjects may have to conform but they secretly retain their personal values. However, under extreme conditions such as occur in countries under dictatorships and in concentration camps, individuals must not only conform but also change and possibly reverse their moral systems. Here "social anxiety" is the response to *real* dangers.

b. When the leaders are nonauthoritarian and permissive in regard to differences of personal opinions and norms and the individual is an unharmonious (mentally disturbed) person who has projected his fears onto the environment, the individual usually changes his personal moral system according to what he thinks is expected of him. His original norms and ideals that are not completely in accord with expected environmental demands are either repressed or warded off, or they are more or less destroyed. Here "social anxiety" is a response to *psychic reality*, though from a *social* point of view the anxiety is *unrealistic*.

What I have described thus far are extreme positions. Actually, we often encounter mixed situations, e.g., milieus that are dictatorial in some respects and permissive in others; in these situations individuals are subject to a number of fears leading to conformism in some areas, but they retain a limited amount of freedom of personal judgment in other areas. It would be interesting to study the different outcomes of the various interactions (Mitscherlich, 1963).

Inner Adaptation

In addition to the necessity for some kind of adaptation (active or passive) to the environment, the individual maturing under the impact of internal conflict must bring into equilibrium the various tendencies emerging from the different structures of the mind. The synthesis required for a "healthy" outcome is one of the functions of the ego organization. In order to achieve inner harmony, a number of other ego functions must remain unimpaired, e.g., the capacity to distinguish between inner and outer worlds, sound reality testing, and an undisturbed awareness of inner processes and faculties. To put it in other words: if a person is able to grant himself satisfaction of his instinctual and emotional needs to such an extent that it does not lead to an impairment of ego interests and his moral system, if he succeeds in developing his personal qualities and talents freely, and if his values and norms are shaped in such a way that they can be respected, we may speak of a well-balanced personality, in whom the process of "inner" adaptation has been carried out in a fortunate way. This description of the harmonious interaction of the functions of the different structured parts of the mental personality is an ideal picture. It presupposes the presence of an ego organization which can develop all of its potential faculties and talents, which has the instinctual and emotional impulses completely under control, and which is able to shape the moral system in accordance with those faculties and impulses. A person's inner harmony depends upon the intactness of the ego's basic functions of mediation and synthesis. This ideal picture is seldom realized. If it *is* realized, we can speak of an active adaptational process in the psychic inner world. If, on the other hand, the ego *fails* to master the id impulses (drives and affects)—the case with which we are only too familiar—the ego's defensive measures are accompanied and followed by inhibitions, ego impairments, and neurotic symptoms as compromises between id tendencies and ego interests. Furthermore, if the ego proves to be too weak to influence the moral system, it frequently surrenders to the superego demands, which results in similar restrictions and distortions of the person's faculties. In both cases we may speak of a passive adaptational process, which in these forms belongs to the realm of pathology. The threat of being overwhelmed by strong instinctual impulses or of being punished by a severe or cruel superego arouses anxiety that paralyzes some ego functions and forces the ego to give in to compromise formations. Sometimes both id and superego work together in endangering the autonomy of the ego organization, e.g., if the superego is secondarily sexualized and especially if the latter is invested with a great amount of aggression turned inward. However, passive adaptation is not always a pathological process. In certain circumstances it may promote inner balance and optimal functioning, especially if it alternates with active, creative adaptation. There is a really significant difference between a person who can *choose* to act in accordance with id and superego demands in order to achieve an optimum of unfolding faculties and of inner harmony and a person who out of fear must surrender to them with the consequence of impairment of capacities and equilibrium.

Returning to my proposal to distinguish between adaptation to and conformism with the environment, I would now like to suggest the extension of these definitions to the inner mental processes as well. *Inner* adaptation, then, could be defined as a creative process that brings forth a harmony between the various interests and needs of the different areas in the personality. A well-balanced mixture of their acceptance and their change will result in a synthesis and lead to an optimal functioning of the total personality. Conformism could be defined as a passive surrender to inner needs and demands—a surrender motivated by fear and resulting in impairment and restriction of the person's achievements.

Thus far I have presented some ideas on adaptive behavior (1) in regard to the outer world and (2) as a process of "inner" adaptation. This separation is, however, an artifact. In reality there is constant interaction between behavior directed toward the environment and processes mediating between the various tendencies of the inner world. Fear of the instinctual impulses is highly dependent upon prohibitions from outside. Fear of the superego has developed from parental demands and is still influenced by authorities and social norms. However, the more a person has achieved inner equilibrium by mediating and by creative adaptation to the different needs and demands from the inner world, the more he will be able to balance passive and active (creative) adjustment to the outer world.

I have already described situations of oppression in which an active adjustment cannot be achieved. Here the "creativity" must take refuge in inner changes, e.g., the reversal of ideals. The longing to be rescued was reversed into a craving to be "liberated" by death.

If one can subscribe to a common idea that the striving for survival is a "natural" and therefore a "normal" process, we must consider conformism to be the most "normal" attitude in a totalitarian society, although it greatly restricts the individual's mental growth. In a free and democratic society, the chances for creative adaptive behavior are considerable, and so are the possibilities for an unfolding of psychic faculties.

I must now point out another simplification I have made use of. In speaking of the ego organization I have not differentiated between the multiple ego functions which *may*, but very often *do not*, act together in the process of active adjustment. Some faculties and talents may function as an impetus to creative action, whereas other ego characteristics may act in an opposite way, restricting the person's free functioning. An example would be rigid character traits that developed as a result of conflicts, reaction formations, and defensive measures (Hartmann, 1956, 1960).

Finally, I would like to underline that the acquisition of inner and outer harmony of reality-directed creative inner and outer adaptation is dependent upon a multitude of complicated and vulnerable mental processes and is achieved only in rare cases. The ego organization must have special capacities to deal with a very strong drive endowment and with a moral system that may have become very rigid in the course of generations transmitting their norms and demands. The outcome will depend on the ego's consistency, on its faculties, and especially on its ability to neutralize energy and to use it for constructive activities.

Conclusion

1. A distinction should be made between adaptation as a mental mechanism and adaptation as a pattern of behavior.

2. A further distinction should be made between adaptation and conforming behavior.

3. Conformism should be defined as behavior characterized by passive surrender to inner and outer demands and norms and motivated by inner anxieties or social anxiety.

4. Adaptation should be defined as behavior directed by a crea-

tive assessment of inner and outer factors and leading to equilibrium
and constructive action.

BIBLIOGRAPHY

de Wind, E. (1965), Voor wie aan Auschwitz ontkwam gaat de Bevrijding door.
    Nieuwe Rotterdamse Courant, January 23.
Freud, S. (1923), The Ego and the Id. *S.E.*, 19:3-66.
——— (1930), Civilization and Its Discontents. *S.E.*, 21:59-145.
Hartmann, H. (1939), *Ego Psychology and the Problem of Adaptation*. NY: IUP,
    1958.
——— (1956), Notes on the Reality Principle. *Essays*, 241-267.
——— (1960), *Psychoanalysis and Moral Values*. NY: IUP.
Isaac-Edersheim, E. (1965), MS.
Lampl-de Groot, J. (1949), Neurotics, Delinquents and Ideal-Formation. *Searchlights
    on Delinquency*, ed. K. R. Eissler. NY: IUP, 246-255.
——— (1962), Ego Ideal and Superego. *Psa. Study Ch.*, 17:94-106.
——— (1963), Symptom Formation and Character Formation. *Int. J. Psa.*, 44:1-11.
Mitscherlich, A. (1963), *Auf dem Weg zur vaterlosen Gesellschaft*. München: Piper.
Nabokov, V. (1941), *The Real Life of Sebastian Knight*. Norfolk, Conn.: New
    Directions, 1959.
Stone, I. (1961), *The Agony and the Ecstasy*. NY: Doubleday.

A Note on Reality Constancy

JOHN FROSCH, M.D.

The establishment of love object constancy[1] is considered most essential for the achievement of mature love object and reality relations (A. Freud, 1952, 1963; Hartmann, 1952; Spitz and Wolf, 1949). As a corollary to love object constancy I should like to suggest the concept of "reality constancy" which is as necessary as the former for the development of a mature reality adaptation. Reality constancy is a psychic structure,[2] which arises in conjunction with the estab-

A condensed version of this paper was presented before the New York Psychoanalytic Society on October 12, 1965. I am grateful to the discussants of this paper, many of whose comments I have incorporated in the paper. I am especially indebted to Nathaniel Ross and William Frosch for their aid in the preparation of the manuscript.

From the Department of Psychiatry, Division of Psychoanalytic Education, State University of New York, Downstate Medical Center, New York.

[1] Whenever the term "object constancy" is used we must keep in mind that it refers to "love object constancy," to delineate more sharply the difference from reality constancy.

[2] The word structure is used in its generic sense. The question whether one can refer to reality constancy as a psychic structure is allied to the question of how one refers to object constancy. The latter question was discussed by Bernard Fine before a meeting of the New York Psychoanalytic Society in May, 1965. This discussion grew out of considerations on the subject of separation anxiety, held by the Kris Study Group under Rudolph Loewenstein. Is object constancy an ego function, a process, a structure, or a psychic organization? Cogent arguments were presented for all these viewpoints. The same considerations also apply to the question how one should designate reality constancy. Edith Jacobson, in her discussion of this paper, felt that it should be considered a quality which characterizes ego functions concerned with reality. Rudolph Loewenstein, in his discussion, stated that in order to describe a psychic structure and to distinguish it from other such structures, it is useful to characterize it by the psychic functions or the process by which it manifests itself. In his opinion, a further heuristic advantage of describing reality constancy, in terms of the autonomous functions involved in it, is that it encourages one to look for the details of the narrow phenomena and processes which we put under the

lishment of stabilized internal representations of the environment. Reality constancy evolves out of a concatenation of environmental experiences, memories, perceptions, ideas, etc., deriving from cathectic relationships with the human and nonhuman environment. Its existence is reflected in the autonomous operation of the ego functions concerned with the environment—for instance, those involved in contact with reality, feeling of reality, testing of reality, etc. It lends to these functions a stability and continuity which enables the individual to preserve his identity and to tolerate alterations and changes in the environment without psychic disruptions or adaptational dysfunctions. Genetically, reality constancy is, in the earliest stages of its development, intimately interwoven with the development of object constancy, and to a considerable extent evolves out of the latter. However, subsequent development makes it pertinent and heuristically valid to view reality constancy as a more encompassing structure than object constancy, and it may ultimately even include the latter.

Object Constancy

Anna Freud (1963, 1965) traced the development of object constancy from the earliest periods of the biological unity between infant and mother to its firm establishment. For this, as many writers have emphasized, consistency in the behavior of the primary love object is necessary; it facilitates the formation of an object representation which can remain constant in time and space and consistent with itself in spite of subsequent alterations and changes in the object relations of the developing individual (Spitz and Wolf, 1949, p. 110). When these features characterize object representation, we have object constancy. Its establishment facilitates the tolerance of temporary separation from the love object as well as the ability to tolerate ambivalence toward the love object without fear of the impact of such ambivalence upon the latter (Anna Freud, 1965, p. 65).

It should be made clear that the psychoanalytic concept of object constancy is not to be confused with the concept of the "stable

---

heading of reality constancy. However, I am in agreement with Hartmann (1955), Hartmann, Kris, Loewenstein (1946), Rapaport and Gill (1959), and others that any psychic phenomenon which achieves some degree of stability, continuity, and organization could correctly be referred to as a psychic structure in the generic sense of the term.

object" in academic psychology (Hartmann, 1952). The latter evolves out of external perceptual experiences and does not take into sufficient account important intrapsychic and interpsychic processes. The development of object constancy proceeds under the impact, not only of external stimuli, but also of those derived from the internal environment. Furthermore, the nature of the energy and the extent to which cathectic flux plays a role in the development of object constancy are not taken into sufficient account by academic psychologists, some of whose views derive from Piaget's contributions. As Hartmann (1952) indicated, "This constancy probably presupposes on the side of the ego a certain degree of neutralization of aggressive as well as libidinal energy . . . and on the other hand it might well be that it promotes neutralization. That is, 'satisfactory object relation' can only be assessed if we also consider what it means in terms of ego development" (p. 163). It is perhaps because he does not take these factors into consideration that Robert White (1963) has made the assumption that inanimate objects are more important than the maternal object in the development of stable object relations.

In animals the impact of strong emotional experiences and arousal in relation to objects during so-called "critical periods" has been indicated by Scott (1962) as taletelling in the development of strong and lasting attachments to such objects. Punishment, for instance, did not inhibit the formation of a social bond. Somewhat analogous are observations in humans. But close as it is, this type of relationship does not necessarily mean that object constancy has been established.

A patient, Mrs. A., to whom I shall subsequently refer in more detail, had a physically close but extremely ambivalent contact with a very sadistic, cruel, and from what I could tell almost psychotic mother. At the age of 43 Mrs. A. was incapable of tolerating separation, while changes in object contact provoked anxiety. The unresolved ambivalence did not permit the development of object constancy in spite of the continuous, but highly charged physical contact with the mother.

An interesting illustration of the fact that continuous physical presence was not the determining factor in the development of object constancy was provided by William Niederland (Discussion Group, 1964). He described the experiences of a patient who, as a child, was forced by Nazi persecution to live in secrecy with his parents in a very small room in the home of some benefactors. The ever-present possibility of discovery and the constant attempts of the parents to prevent the child from making noises which might betray their presence contributed to disturbances in the development of object and reality constancy, in spite of the continued actual presence of the parents in what was a limited and constricted, seemingly "unchanging" physical environment.

It must therefore be re-emphasized that the continuous physical presence of an object does not itself result in the development of constancy. The reciprocal interaction between ego functions and object makes it clear that the psychoanalytic concept of object constancy goes far beyond strictly sensorial perceptual experiences in relation to physically "stable" objects, and that the totality of psychic operations contributes a great deal to the development of object constancy. Many of these considerations will prove relevant to the concept of reality constancy to be discussed in this paper.

Reality

It is important at this point to establish a frame of reference for the use of the term "reality." Hartmann (1956), in one of the definitive papers on this subject, defines objective external reality as one which can be validated by certain methods. Intersubjectivity may play a role in this validation, since opinions and reactions of others to a given phenomenon may be taken into consideration as objective data. However, he points out that there is also a conventional or socialized knowledge which is intersubjectively accepted without validation (see also Freud, 1927, p. 25f.). In discussing internal reality, Hartmann says, "In speaking here of 'inner reality,' I am referring to the fact that in a sense all mental functions, tendencies, contents are 'real'; fantasy activity also is real, though not realistic. That is, to recognize that a fantasy is, as a mental act, real does not mean that its contents reproduce reality" (p. 265f.).

In elaborating upon these remarks, I would suggest that the external world, that is, external reality (environment), consists of material objective reality, which stimulates the sense organs, as well as of nonmaterial reality, such as conventionally accepted knowledge. But external reality also has its mental representations. Internal reality (internal environment)—and I am proposing this in a rather broad sense—includes on the psychic side memories, fantasies, impulses, desires, affects, thoughts, the body image, identity, self representation, etc. Furthermore, it includes the correlate of material objective reality, namely, material internal reality, such as various somatic phenomena which may be derived from explicable or inexplicable processes. These may include somatic sensations of various sorts—pain, heart rhythm, etc. These are generally not included in the concept of the internal world, which is usually construed as psychic. However, the mental representations of these phenomena are generally involved in psychic processes.

The development of concepts of reality, as well as those of the ego functions involved with reality, is very much dependent upon the human object (Hartmann, 1956, p. 255f.). Most writers have considered libidinal gratification and frustration, and the libidinal shifts accompanying these experiences, crucial in the building up of reality. To Glover (1932, p. 179f.), reality is a need-gratifying object or its subsequent variants. White (1963) has denigrated the role of instinct-gratifying or frustrating objects in the development of reality. However, I doubt if there would be much disagreement with the concept that in the early stages of psychic development the self and the love object represent reality, and the retention of reality involves the preservation of the love object, which is equated with survival of the self. For that matter, the genetic development of self, ego, object, and reality is closely interwoven, as was aptly expressed by Fenichel (1937, p. 29).

Genetic Considerations

In the building up of reality, through the interactions of the organism with the human and nonhuman environment, there is a developmental course in the evolving of reality constancy just as there are lines of development in the evolving of love object constancy (Anna Freud, 1963, 1965). It is, however, a developmental course influenced by stimuli and experiences deriving from other than the love object. In early development, reality is generally interpreted in terms of the self experience. However, ultimately this exclusive dependence on self experience has to be abandoned if reality adaptation is to develop independent of instinctual needs. In the building up of reality, forces ultimately deriving from the environment other than the self and the love object assert themselves to augment the over-all process of internalization, which eventually results in the stable representation of reality. A mature capacity for environmental adaptation makes it imperative that reality evolve beyond the self and the love object as the frame of reference.

This becomes clear when we evaluate the influence of stimuli upon psychic development. It has been pointed out that not only deprivation of stimulation, but also overstimulation can produce severe distortions in psychic development (Greenacre, 1941, 1952, 1954; Bergman and Escalona, 1949; Spitz, 1964). As Greenacre (1954) indicated, "when very prolonged, severe stimulation or when multiplicity of simultaneous stimulations occurs which results in a flooding of the organism with excitation, then all channels of discharge are utilized and there may be a state of confusion, with loss of specificity of response to stimulus which is repeated later in life in states of stress" (p. 22f.).

Perhaps the crucial factor is not so much insufficient stimulation or overstimulation, as nonphase-related and inappropriate stimuli. Greenacre (1952) summarized this view in the following statement: "It appears that in evaluating the effect of trauma in the young developing organism, it is important to consider not only the maturational phase at which the trauma occurs, whether the specific nature of the trauma is one which tends to reinforce the libidinization of the dominant phase or to reinstate an already developed phase, either by direct stimulation or by encouraging regression for adequate satisfaction; but further whether the specific nature of the stimulating trauma calls for a response in accordance with a phase which is close to maturity or as yet quite immature. In addition to the specific nature of the trauma in terms of its relation to the timetable of libidinal development, the severity and the duration of traumatic conditions are most important in shaping the results" (p. 294f.). This aspect of the problem, the impact that traumata have on psychic development, served as a focus for discussion at the Arden House meetings at which Anna Freud (1954) and Greenacre (1954) again underlined the importance of relating the traumatizing effect of stimulation to the developmental phase. Goldfarb (1963) has suggested that "the so-called hypersensitive child is one who is living in a family environment which is specifically hyperstimulating for *him* and beyond *his* capacity to cope with perceptually" (p. 54).

It is clear, therefore, that there are stages in psychic development in which restriction of stimulation by the environment is appropriate or in which certain kinds of stimuli may be phase-related, while in other stages more active and different kinds of stimulation may be needed for furthering psychic development. It is the dysphasic nature, as well as other experiences surrounding such stimulation, which may be crucial. The child may experience painful external and internal stimuli which are quieted by the ministrations of the mother, so that mothering tends to reduce the intensity of stimulation and facilitates the maturational development of the stimulus barrier. This was most succinctly brought out by Benjamin (1961), who said, "We have reason to hypothesize from our own small sample within the range of so-called normal mother-child relationships that the absence of adequate tension reduction during this 'critical period' has important results in helping to create an increased predisposition to anxiety" (p. 27).

On the other hand, the child's reactions to the environment in the process of need gratification indicate amply that there seems to be a reaching out and seeking out, in addition to a responsiveness to these experiences and stimuli. At a certain stage this reaching out goes beyond the process of need gratification—for instance, playful movements in response to sound, reaching out for the presented rattle, after feeding, etc. This environment-directed seeking out reflects the active role the ego plays in the building up of reality and ultimately in contributing to reality constancy.

Many of the stimuli impinging upon the child are obviously derived from other than the maternal object. In the earliest psychic stages, it is probable that all stimuli, even those derived from the nonhuman environment, fall within the global experience of the infant-mother relationship. They become associated with the mother and are encompassed in the early memory traces of the latter and in representations of the love object. As such they play a role in the development of object constancy. However, this is different in later stages of psychic development. With the gradual development of differentiation of self from external reality, there begins to evolve a capacity to discriminate between the quality and the source of stimuli, and the capacity to differentiate an experience as deriving from the love object and other human objects, as well as from the nonhuman environment.

Although not referring to reality constancy as such, Goldfarb (1963) alludes to its development as follows: "In the process of evolving a clear differentiation of the whole self from the whole environment, it is clear that there must be a consciousness of the environment as a constant source of stimulation, shifting and yet permanent and continuous in time and space" (p. 51f.). He refers to schizophrenic children in whom deviant motility did not permit this constancy to develop and says, "The most obvious result of such environmental kaleidoscopic inconstancy is the above-mentioned disorientation with regard to the crucial concepts of time, place and person. Clinical manifestations of the disorientation to the outer world are manifold. What is most significant is the impact of such confusion on the child, an impact which includes a sense of environmental fluidity, temporariness, and unfamiliarity, whether in reference to things or humans. Objects are not conceived as unitary and permanent, particularly if they are absent from direct sensory contact" (p. 52).

Just as individuation and separation, self and nonself discrimination are essential for the development of object constancy (Hartmann, Kris, Loewenstein, 1946, p. 20; Mahler, 1963, p. 309f.), so does the capacity to differentiate self from the environment facilitate the development of reality constancy. The latter in turn ultimately supports the preservation of differentiation between the self and the environment. Reality constancy appears and grows to the accompaniment of separation and individuation, the development of the reality principle,[3] and concurrently with environmental differentiation.

In many borderline patients this differentiation has not been clearly developed, and the nonhuman environment is still instinctualized and animistic. The symbolic meaning of the inanimate and nonhuman environment takes on pathogenic proportions in the defective reality constancy seen in borderline and psychotic patients. The environment has not reached its full reality significance and is frequently quite alive for such patients. I have in previous communications (Frosch, 1959, 1964a, 1964b) discussed the clinical manifestations of this disturbance in a number of patients with psychotic character. During an especially phobic period, one such female patient said, "You know, Dr. Frosch, everything around me is alive, the lamp, the book, the pillow, everything." These objects were all capable of feel-

---

[3] Within that domain governed by the reality principle, and even contributing to its operations, is reality constancy. Just as the development of the reality principle is dependent upon the evolution of ego functions concerned with reality, so is it related to the development of reality constancy which is itself an expression of the operations of the reality principle. Schur, in his discussion, suggested that reality constancy is the more or less permanent result of the functioning of reality testing (as well as other ego functions concerned with reality) extended over a prolonged period of maturation and development, under the dominance of the reality principle.

ing and of having affect. At one point the patient indicated that if things around her were alive, she could also feel and be alive.[4]

It is important in the process of differentiation between self and environment that the ego functions concerned with the latter develop so that they may operate relatively conflict free and with relatively neutral energy, thus facilitating the mastery of environmental experiences. In the same way as ambivalence in relation to the object impedes the development of object constancy, so must the relationship to the environment be fairly free of ambivalence and drive instinctualization for reality constancy to develop. In a sense the development of reality constancy is supported by the neutralization of energy used by those ego functions concerned with environmental mastery, and subsequently reality constancy also facilitates the preservation of neutralized energy used in these functions.

In the earliest stages of psychic development the factors entering into the development of object constancy are interwoven with those facilitating the development of reality constancy.[5] Disturbances in development of the former may interfere with development of the latter. For instance, traumatic experiences at the hands of the love object may interfere with drive neutralization, as a consequence of which there may be a pervasion of the nonhuman environment with unneutralized drive energy. This may interfere with the internalization and building up of stable representation of the environment and therefore of stable reality constancy. Nonetheless I believe that it is

[4] In discussing this subject Loewenstein suggested that "A well-developed reality constancy could also be characterized in terms of emancipation from animistic or anthropomorphic reactions to inanimate or nonhuman reality. It is not necessary to assume that the maximum independence of it is always optimal. An optimal in some people, for instance, writers, poets, painters, is to preserve remnants of a somewhat anthropomorphic view of nonhuman nature. It is possible that for some descriptive biologists the same might be true; whereas in other people, the remoteness from an animistic view of nature goes beyond the usual. They like to think of and understand nature in terms of abstract concepts, as far as possible removed from an experiential approach to nature. All these various types of approach to nature should not be considered as pervading the whole of the personality; for instance, a theoretical physicist might nevertheless possess a very animistic approach to some aspects of reality, and, conversely, an artist, painter or poet may have perfectly well-developed functions of reality constancy."

[5] John McDevitt in discussing this point said, "Possibly a more fruitful way to look at the matter would be to think of both object constancy and reality constancy slowly developing as a consequence of the multiple interactions between the infant (with his maturing drive and autonomous ego functions) and the environment (both animate and inanimate). A consistent positive relationship with the libidinal object— the mother—would be crucial in this step-by-step acquisition of both object constancy and reality constancy."

important to be aware that some of the disturbance in ego functions concerned with reality may derive from environmental experiences not directly related to the love object alone. It is furthermore my belief that reality constancy is *not* identical with object constancy. The operation of reality constancy ultimately achieves an autonomy, which has its own special qualities.[6]

On the other hand, it would be hard to say in the face of well-established object constancy to what extent environmental experiential factors may interfere with the development of stable reality constancy.[7] A corollary to this question is whether sound reality constancy can ultimately develop despite defects in object constancy. In recent years I have had occasion to see in consultation many highly successful industrial executives. They showed an excellent capacity to test reality, revealed no perceptual or other distortions in the ego functions concerned with reality, but many of them revealed marked disturbances in object relationships. Many lacked the capacity to form sustained human relationships. In others, these were highly contaminated and ambivalent. In still others, it was very clear that they felt unsure of themselves in close interpersonal relations and constantly sought the reassurance of being loved by others.

Some twenty years ago, I had the opportunity to analyze Mr. Z., a man whose case I believe illustrates this problem. Unfortunately, my thinking with regard to the concepts discussed in this paper had not yet crystallized and at the time I was working with this patient I did not have these concepts as a frame of reference. Nonetheless, it may be worth while to discuss some aspects of this case. Mr. Z. entered treatment, at the age of 45, for what was apparently an aggravation of a lifelong depression, beginning impotence, and fear that his second

---

[6] McDevitt in his comments on this paper suggested, "There is not a one-to-one relationship between the development of object constancy and reality constancy. The two overlap, each contributing in its own way to the other. Object constancy is easily disrupted by poorly neutralized sexual and aggressive impulses directed toward the object, whereas reality constancy has additional determinants and results primarily from the operations of autonomous ego functions utilizing more neutralized energy."

[7] Nathaniel Ross in a personal communication suggested that this could be the case in children who experience repeated and protracted febrile illnesses, at critical periods in development—i.e., before stable representations of the environment were established. In such instances the perceptual distortions which not infrequently accompany high fevers could, if persistent, contribute to the impairment in the development of reality constancy even though the development of object constancy may not have been disturbed.

marriage would fail. In the course of the analysis, apart from the usual transference distortions and occasional acting out, he showed no patent disturbance in the ego functions concerned with reality, and continued to conduct his business affairs in a highly successful manner. Mr. Z. yearned to be loved and was very much attached to his second wife in an almost childlike way. It turned out that his fear of losing her was based not only on his impotence but on his inordinate need for her affection, love, and support, which his wife found quite disturbing.

Mr. Z.'s early life was replete with highly charged exposure to cruel, cold, punitive, and rejecting parents. During the analysis there was a constant outpouring of sheer unmitigated hatred toward both parents. The only salutary human experience was his contact with a rather warm, loving, and encompassing older female cousin, of whom he continued to speak with affection. From early life he had to fend for himself in order literally to survive. Lack of food was not an infrequent experience. His relation to human objects was anxiety-ridden. He needed constant evidence and reassurance that he was loved and wanted. When love was offered he was never sure that it was real, meant for him as a person, and given without an ulterior motive.

I could understand the genetic aspects of the poor object relations quite well, but I could not understand at that time why in the face of the severely disturbed object relations and what I would in retro-spect consider poorly developed object constancy, there seemed to be no gross disturbance in the ego functions concerned with everyday reality and the environment. In other words, reality constancy seemed well established. Perhaps this was to some extent accounted for by the fact that in contrast to the exceedingly traumatic relations with early significant objects, Mr. Z. received a great deal of support and grati-fication from the successful mastery of environmental and work situ-ations. But I do not really know why he developed what I believe to be good reality constancy.[8]

Some consideration ought to be given at this point to the role that constitutional factors may play in the development of reality con-

---

[8] In her discussion of this paper, Edith Jacobson also referred to cases in which reality constancy seemed to have developed although object constancy was defective. She felt that what accounted for this was that reality constancy rested on a some-what different basis from object constancy in that the mastery of reality—i.e., of the inanimate object world—allows more room for aggressive drives, ambitions, and narcissistic gratifications.

stancy. Bak (1964) indicated that the factors entering into the capacity to establish object relations may in some instances be constitutionally defective. If this is so it would be clear that the development of object constancy would be impaired. I have on a previous occasion (1964b) called attention to the inherent push toward differentiation which facilitates reality contact. Perhaps this is one of the many features of preadaptiveness (Hartmann, 1939) which ultimately facilitates the fitting in of the organism with the "average expectable—i.e., typical— situations, or on the average not expectable—i.e., atypical—situations" (p. 23). Hartmann (1956) in commenting on this said, "the child is born with a certain degree of preadaptiveness; that is to say, the apparatus of perception, memory, motility, etc., which help us to deal with reality are, in a primitive form, already present at birth; later they will mature and develop in constant interaction, of course, with experience" (p. 246). The fate of the interaction between the innate apparatuses for preadaptiveness and environmental experiences is probably important for the development of reality constancy. Rather than speak of inherent defects in reality constancy, it might be more appropriate to speak of inherent defects in those autonomous ego functions which form a part of preadaptiveness. Such defects make it difficult for reality constancy to develop. Schur illustrated the interplay between constitutional and experiential factors as it may affect reality constancy.[9] He referred to a research chemist who, although quite brilliant, had some marked deficiencies in certain aspects of everyday reality. This was reflected, among many other aspects, in confusion between right and left, east and west, and a host of household information of a trivial nature. When this patient went to school it became evident that he had serious reading difficulties with perceptual distortions and other findings pointing to a constitutional abnormality. There were many early traumatic experiences and Schur indicated that a good deal of analytic material "confirmed the hypothesis that this deficiency of an important apparatus for primary autonomy contributed to the preference for denial as a defense mechanism. This was applied not only to inner conflict but to many aspects of external reality as well. In correlation with the failure to develop object constancy and the pathology of instinctual and ego development, the consequences of an innate abnormality contributed to a deficiency of reality constancy."

[9] In his discussion of this paper.

Ego Functions and Reality Constancy

I shall now turn to a more detailed consideration of the mutual influence between many ego functions and the development and operation of reality constancy. Ego functions such as reality testing, perception, delay, anticipation, intentionality, predictability, etc., are interwoven with the development of reality constancy as well as with its operations. The hierarchical development of reality constancy goes hand in hand with the hierarchical development of these ego functions. This is seen especially in the function of reality testing.

Freud (1925) stated that the first aim of reality testing "is, not to *find* an object in real perception which corresponds to the one presented, but to *refind* such an object, to convince oneself that it is still there" (p. 237f.). There is of course some question as to what Freud meant. In a footnote to this discussion, Rapaport (1951) says, "Freud apparently refers to the distinction between verification of the existence of the referent of a memory image in reality (rediscovery) and the successful search for a reality referent of an invention of creative imagination (discovery)" (p. 346).

It is probably true that reality testing involves some previous experiences with an object, or something similar enough to the object, so that a representation is established which can be matched with a subsequently appearing real material object, in order to test the reality of the latter. However, it is the previous mastery of an environmental experience and the successful employment of the ego functions involved in doing so which achieve representation as well. Among other factors, we are dealing with past experiences in realized or fulfilled anticipation, an important factor in the building up of reality constancy. The representations of such experiences bring about the development of reality constancy, which ultimately makes possible good reality testing.

We must take into consideration different layers, aspects, and modes of reality testing as well as a hierarchy in its development (Hartmann, 1956). These are closely related to the genetic development of reality constancy. The use of muscular activity, body sensations and functions, somatic self experiences, touching, tasting, smelling, introjective-projective techniques—all represent earlier modes of reality testing. Furthermore, intersubjective acceptance without validation plays an important role in the testing of reality during the child's early development when he is under the influence of early significant objects. The child needs the external support of the parent in his attempts at testing reality (Hartmann, 1956, p. 257f.). The influence of the superego upon reality testing was alluded to, with varying emphasis, by many authors (Freud, 1921, 1923, 1936; Balint, 1942; Hartmann and Loewenstein, 1962; Nunberg, 1951). Nunberg (1951) states that "conscious perceptions of the ego must be sanctioned by the superego in order to acquire qualities of full, uncontested reality. This assumption could be helpful in understanding why . . . changes in the patient's superego also enhance the reality-testing faculty of the ego" (p. 8).

In the course of its development, the mature functioning of reality testing requires the diminution of those influences which originally played a role in shaping it, and the earlier modes of testing reality must give way to more autonomous ones. In connection with the building up of the self and realistic testing, Jacobson (1964) points out that the establishment of reality, object, and self representations depends to a large extent on the maturation of perception and self-perceptive functions—that is, on reality testing, at the expense of the projective and introjective mechanisms which are more characteristic of earlier modes of reality testing (p. 91). In the course of psychic development, reality testing becomes more and more internalized. This goes hand in hand with the evolution of reality constancy, which is correlated with the stabilization of internalized images of the external environment and its qualities, and constitutes a more reliable frame of reference for reality testing. It is clear that the more advanced the modes of reality testing are, the more firmly is reality constancy established, and vice versa.

Among the many ego functions interwoven with the development of reality constancy is that of perception. Goldfarb (1963) views the process as follows: "There is an active cognitive process intermediate between percept and action which stores the multitude of diverse and disparate percepts in the form of essences, regularities, universals, constants, and predictables. On this basis, the ego is able to formulate suitable representations of the environment and plans for managing it" (p. 59). In Goldfarb's opinion, the building up of "constancy" and "universality" of the environment is facilitated by distance perception—i.e., visual and auditory ones. This is not possible with proximal receptors (p. 58). The capacity for discriminatory perception facilitates the development of object constancy and reality constancy, but is also dependent upon the existence of these structures.[10]

Where poor reality constancy exists, trust in one's own perception is impaired. This requires a reinforcement by strong stimuli from the external environment or constant external reaffirmation. In such instances parental imagos continue to exert an active influence upon the ego in reality testing. I have previously (1964a) described a patient who, while lying on the couch, saw the lights dim. Mr. Y. did not trust his own perception and needed my reassurance that the lights had actually dimmed. Gustav Bychowski (Discussion Group, 1964) described a hallucinating patient who insisted that his mother stay with him constantly to tell him whether the voices were real. In order to encourage internalization of reality testing, therapists must among other things reinforce the patient's trust in his own perception. Trust in one's perception is closely related to another ego function, anticipation.

Defects in the development of anticipation may in some instances contribute to the subsequent appearance of unreality feelings. It might therefore be relevant at this point to present some thoughts on the phenomenon of unreality feelings, a common disturbance in patients who suffer from a defect in reality constancy. Although it is possible, within the framework of the hypotheses hitherto proposed to explain this phenomenon, to delineate some of the processes which facilitate feelings of unreality, it is not yet clear whether there are prototypic experiences which eventuate in feelings of unreality or depersonalization, and, if so, what these are. It is therefore difficult to speak of regression to those periods where these phenomena are phase-related. Nonetheless, some further scrutiny of the genetic aspects of the ego functions involved might be indicated. I would like to make it clear that I am talking of prototypic processes which may subsequently be used in the service of psychic needs, rather than the specific experiential content to which these processes are related.

[10] Mahler (1960) indicated that early traumatic experiences may contribute to a failure in the perceptual integrative capacity of the ego. This defect will potentiate dedifferentiation to the point where primal discrimination between living and inanimate is lost. In essence Mahler looks upon dehumanization and reanimation as a regressive adaptation when the ego's perceptual integrative capacity fails. Yet it is the latter defect which facilitates the reanimation of the nonhuman environment. I also wonder what role defects in the development of reality constancy plays in facilitating this dedifferentiation.

That renunciation and frustration play an important role in the building up of the reality principle and reality testing is by now generally accepted. This is most clearly expressed by Jacobson (1964), who says, "The total effect of his [the child's] disheartening experience is a 'disillusionment' . . . which normally has a beneficial, double influence. Promoting the child's testing of external and of his own internal reality, it assists him . . . in gradually relinquishing his illusions, i.e., his magic fantasies about his love objects and himself. At the same time, however, it is the main incentive for the child's increasing idealization of his parents, because it stimulates . . . strong, reactive libidinal strivings. . . . In general, if the hostility released by such experiences can be sufficiently absorbed and utilized by the ego, the function of reality testing profits greatly. Critical and self-critical functions are stimulated, the realistic perceptions of the world and of the self expand and sharpen, and the ability of the ego to tone down illusory concepts and expectations becomes reinforced in turn" (p. 105f.).

I believe that these considerations are equally applicable to the development of reality constancy. Painful and unpleasant experiences have to be considered, mastered, accepted, and incorporated into the representation of reality. This ultimately contributes to the establishment of reality constancy, which in turn facilitates the acceptance and the recognition of unpleasant ideas and experiences as part of the environment, as well as the need to "reckon with it" as Ferenczi (1926, p. 378) put it. In this process of "reckoning" we must realize that reality constancy occupies an important and central role. It enables the ego to deal with unpleasant reality, rather than to deny it, for instance, by taking refuge in psychosis.

On the other hand, I wish to re-emphasize the expectation and the experiencing of gratification as very important ingredients in the building up of reality, the ego functions concerned with reality, and therefore, in my opinion, in the development of reality constancy.[11] Although I have underscored the importance of accepting the unpleasant in reality in the development of reality constancy, it should also

---

[11] Freud (1900) had early alluded to the role of the experience of satisfaction in the building up of reality (p. 566). Hartmann, Kris, and Loewenstein (1946) also alluded to the important role that drive gratification plays in facilitating self-nonself differentiation as well as in the development of object constancy and the ego function of anticipation. "That distinction [differentiation], however, seems to become impossible unless a certain amount of gratification is allowed for" (p. 20).

be stressed that this goes hand in hand with the expectation of the pleasant. For anticipation to operate effectively in the service of the reality principle, there must be a reasonable expectation of gratification, an expectation which must have been fulfilled at some time. Therese Benedek (1938) re-emphasized the importance of gratification in the building up of reality, maintaining that physiological satisfactions facilitate periods of preoccupation with the environment and that this widens the horizons of reality (p. 202). The development of confidence and positive anticipation, in her opinion, is built up by gratification rather than frustration. Repeated frustration without ultimate gratification or the anxiety generated by undue delay, result in impairment of ego development (p. 205).

The expectation that a given set of circumstances, or an object, etc., may within time gratify one's needs makes one willing to accept its reality. If an external source of need gratification does not fulfill its function, in time, following repeated disappointment of anticipation, it is no longer considered a part of reality. If a child is repeatedly offered a toy, reaches out for it, but is not permitted to get it, he will after a while give up his attempts to reach for it. He may lie and look at it, or even become apathetic and unresponsive to the stimulus, which one can assume is still acting upon the sense organs, but the object is not accepted as a *bona fide* stimulus containing within it the expectation and anticipation of gratification and mastery. Even if the external source later presents itself, it may be regarded as unreal because the element of expectation and anticipation has atrophied.

Mrs. A., a patient with psychotic character would in analysis develop periods of detachment which, upon closer examination, assumed aspects of depersonalization and feelings of unreality. This was frequently accompanied by perceptual distortions in the treatment situation in which the room itself began to take on different form. The sequence of her experiences had a repetitive cycle: she would quite unrealistically glorify and overexaggerate the attractiveness of a given person or situation; then would follow the inevitable disillusionment, rage, depression and detachment. The withdrawal and depersonalization were not only related to a denial and repression of the rage, but represented an identification with a near-psychotic mother who had had what appears to have been depressive withdrawals. The mother repeatedly frustrated and disappointed the child with aloofness and traumatic rejections, to which Mrs. A. frequently alluded. "My mother, in kissing me, always held her body away from me. I don't remember her ever holding me." She described her mother as being "out of this world" and, without relating the two, she also spoke of her detached feelings as having an out-of-this-world quality. Further exploration of the detached periods found them accompanied by a lack of trust in her environment, and generally a feeling of cynicism and hopelessness about people's intentions. They were "really playing a game; didn't really mean it; it was not for real," etc. Once, when Mrs. A. went to a party and was complimented on her appearance, she began to feel very uncomfortable, things around her had an unreal yet familiar quality. It was the feeling she had had about her mother, who would on rare occasions say something complimentary, but who more often had repeatedly betrayed and disappointed her. Mrs. A. would frequently experience feelings of unreality and depersonalization after the failure of a project she had undertaken, at first with great enthusiasm, followed by disillusionment. This was not unlike earlier experiences, "when I lived in a dream world," which was related to the inability to cope with and master environmental experiences, such as work at school. She was incapable of sustained effort and would become discouraged very easily. This is a patient who, at an early age, had been exposed to a real environmental disintegrative experience in which the very world around her fell apart and whose whole life was characterized by transience. The external environment could no longer be depended upon, just like her mother. She could not count on physical structures being where she thought they should be, etc. Reality constancy was impaired. For some time following these experiences, and the subsequent transience of her homes, nothing seemed quite solid. She could not be sure of things; in fact, her memories of this period and even of recent events were quite vague.

Still another patient, Mrs. B., described how everything assumed an appearance of unreality when she went to a party with her husband. The people did not look quite clear. She was terribly frightened because she was afraid of losing her hold on reality. She felt a little guilty because her mother was coming to her house and she had not prepared anything to eat for her, or, at least what she had prepared were just hamburgers. Somehow she felt she ought to be with her mother, to feed her. Again, she spoke of the fear of losing reality; possibly she would then lose her mother. At this point she asked her husband for a drink; for some reason he paid no attention to her and did not get it. The feelings of unreality became quite marked, she became quite panicky, feared being unreal, and again spoke of losing her mother. The denial of all gratification and the frustration were clearly seen as related to the feeling of unreality, but here again it was not only a denial of rage or a killing off of the people that played a role in the depersonalization and feeling of unreality. As the material unfolded, it became very clear that disappointment in the lack of gratification led her to feel that the object was frustrating, depriving, and that she could expect nothing from it. She herself felt guilty when she could not feed her mother, in the same way that she felt rejected when her mother disappointed her. Throughout work with this patient, material relating to her extreme expectation of gratification from the mother and disappointment in this, accompanied by feelings of unreality, pointed up the fact that the element of the lack of anticipation of gratification played an important role in the feelings of unreality.

I therefore wonder whether feelings of unreality, whatever other contributants there may be, may in some instances derive from the prototypic feeling which may be experienced with recurrent frustration and disappointment of the anticipation of wish gratification, or the unsuccessful attempts at mastery of environmental experiences. Experiences with the nonhuman environment (see the case of Mrs. A.) may also contribute to such feelings. The repeated disappointments may result in a disbelief in the reality of a need-gratifying object or situation even when this ultimately presents itself. In other words, there is a refusal to accept what is recognized as a perception as conveying a feeling of unreality, a lack of belief in one's perceptions. The feelings of unreality may in some instances ward off the pain of disillusionment which was previously experienced in situations of repeated frustrated anticipation and failure of mastery. It is therefore likely that in addition to the many factors playing a role in feelings of unreality, in some cases the function of anticipation is impaired, and that in such instances reality constancy is impaired. These considerations underline the importance of need gratification in widening the scope of the child's world of reality and in establishing reality constancy.

I wish to call attention to predictability as a correlate of anticipation. The element of delay introduces the idea of the future and consequently predictability. Predictability—the confident expectation of finding things in the future—is contingent upon reality constancy.

Reality testing relies on comparing current experiences with and re-affirming the past, but reality experiences must have an element of predictability which also enters into the process of reality testing. Firmly established reality constancy supports confidence in the function of prediction which is involved in reality testing. Thus, I anticipate that if I go to 34th Street and Fifth Avenue, the Empire State Building will be there.

The correlative genetic development of reality constancy, with many ego functions concerned with reality, implies that when disturbances of the former exist we find regressive modes of relating to reality and the use of earlier ego functions. Firmly developed reality constancy will tend to support the use of mature ego functions, combat regressions, and contribute to "ego strength" (ego autonomy). On the other hand, it will permit the individual to tolerate regressive experiences without fear of loss of reality contact.

Clinical Considerations

It is clear from the above discussion that poorly developed object and reality constancy will bring many disturbances in their wake. This is especially the case in borderline patients, who demonstrate most distinctly the importance of both for the preservation of love object and reality relations. Of course, in such cases it is especially difficult to make a clear distinction between disturbances in the environmental adaptation, which exist because of a failure of the development of object constancy, and disturbances which are related to impairments in the development of reality constancy. In borderline cases we find impairment of both.

This was brought out in a patient whom I have described in more detail elsewhere (Frosch, 1964b), and to whom I alluded above. Mrs. A. had numerous fantasies of world disintegration. Exploration revealed the close relationship between the poorly developed object constancy and the world disintegration fantasy which also reflected her own inner sense of disintegratoin. The poorly developed object constancy was further threatened by the destructive hostility which automatically brought in its wake the possibility of her own disintegration because of self-nonself confusion. Her very world, so to speak, would disintegrate with the destruction of the love object. The world destruction fantasy was also related to a faulty development of reality constancy, which, although influenced by the poorly developed object constancy, was also in my opinion, among other experiences, derived from exposure to a natural catastrophic experience at the age of four, during which she had actually seen the environment disintegrate around her. Fire, buildings collapsing and disintegrating, people dying and dead, the whole physical environment in chaos—all had a tremendous traumatic impact upon her.

The background of this patient was replete with shifting environments, human and nonhuman. She had lived in so many different places that in a good portion of the analysis these could only be recalled when equated with certain significant events. "Oh, that was when I lived on X Street," or a particularly unpleasant color was associated with a given place. This was also true of her adult life, which, because of the nature of her employment, was characterized by transience and inconsistency. At times there was a vagueness and blurring of places she had been to and lived in, with a few significant islands standing out. This was equally true of more recent experiences. In the course of her analysis, this patient frequently had feelings of unreality, depersonalization, and uncertainty about her environment as well as of her own identity. Her dreams frequently involved world destruction and disintegration. For example, she had a marked flight phobia and, when she had to fly, there would be recurring dreams of world destruction—fires, etc. World destruction scenes in conjunction with repeated episodes of vagueness, confusion, unreality, etc., would recur in one form or another in association to the shifting of world events. There were marked feelings of inadequacy as well as actual inability to cope with and master ordinary environmental situations, e.g., orienting herself when traveling. Any sharp dividing line between this patient's poor object constancy and defective reality constancy would be difficult to establish. Nonetheless, the impact of an ever-changing or highly charged environment in bringing about poor development of reality constancy, in addition to the influence of poor object constancy, should not be minimized.

The inability of many borderline patients to tolerate changes in the human and nonhuman environment and in their receptivity and adaptation to new experiences is related to defects in the establishment of both object and reality constancy. Mrs. A. was in subsequent years quite uncomfortable in new and unfamiliar settings. She had difficulty in orienting herself to such situations and restricted her field of operations, devoting herself with almost obsessive fixity to the familiar tasks of housekeeping duties rather than embark on newer and more venturesome prospects, which had been part of her professional life in the past.

Spitz and Wolf (1949) in discussing this problem said, "It is the original experience with the libidinal object which creates an expectancy pattern. Where that is lacking each single object will have to be approached as an experiment, as an adventure, and as a peril" (p. 110). I would say that this is equally true in meeting new environmental experiences when there is deficient development of reality constancy. The latter facilitates, for instance, the transition from the analytic situation to reality. Patients with defective reality constancy have repeated difficulty in reorienting themselves to the external environment after an analytic session. They have difficulty in preserving their identity to physical changes taking place in the office. I have called attention on another occasion (1959, 1964a) to the anxiety evoked in a patient with psychotic character when I moved my office. She knew who she was in my old office, she knew "who" (sic) my old office was. My new office was a stranger, she could not orient herself to it. Everything in it looked so big, so threatening, and at times unreal. Such reactions may also be experienced in relation to the changing appearance of the analyst.

Abraham Freedman (Discussion Group, 1964) presented an experience in which he felt psychotic transference reactions developed. He had grown a beard over a vacation period and observed the effect of his changed visage on the transference situation. All the patients noticed the beard and reacted to it in some way, but the effect on the transference situation in the patients was quite different. The disturbed reactions were especially observed in borderline patients, who were in some instances quite markedly shaken and upset. Freedman felt that his neurotic patients, in whom the ego functions concerned with reality contact were preserved, could deal with their fantasies about the analyst and always recognized the analyst as a separate realistic being. This was not always true of the borderline and psychotic patients.

In many borderline patients there is deficient stabilization of internalized images of the external environment, which goes with the development of reality constancy, and reality representation is not fused or correlated with material reality. To correlate the two, such persons need the constant reaffirmation by material reality. They could in many instances hold on to material reality quite well, but the hold on representations was quite insecure. I have described (1964a) a patient who had a great deal of difficulty in buying clothes for her children when the latter were not physically present. She could not visualize how big they were, whether they were thin or fat, etc. She also had difficulty in buying things for the house (e.g., curtains), because she was never quite sure what the house really looked like when she did not see it. This is one of the consequences of a tenuous reality constancy, and brings into play regressive modes of relating to reality.

When reality constancy is not established, there is resort to earlier modes of testing reality as seen, for instance, in the need for support from the object in order to confirm reality as well as the use of earlier sensory modalities. Attention has repeatedly been called to the observation that many psychotic and borderline patients have a need for stimuli in order to maintain a hold on reality. During analysis, such patients, who have faulty reality constancy, need the continuous perception of their surroundings to maintain contact. They become quite anxious when placed on the couch, especially during earlier stages of treatment. However, I have found that in later stages of treatment even with fairly severe regressive ego states I could still continue to work with such patients on the couch, provided I allowed ample opportunity for perceptual contact with their surroundings. This is reminiscent of the stage before object constancy has developed, when the child is unable to tolerate the nighttime separation from the mother (A. Freud, 1952, 1965). The need for the light to be on, the repeated requests for the rereading of a story, the endless calls for a drink of water—all operate in the interest of nullifying separation.

The need to preserve contact with reality will, in some adults with tenuous object and reality constancy, lead to their clinging to transitional objects and phenomena (Winnicott, 1953). An illustration of this is the person who at night turns on the radio, ostensibly to hear the news. He falls asleep with the sound of the radio droning in his ears and turns it off only much later while still practically asleep. Such a person cannot permit himself the degree of regression which is required to fall asleep; he must preserve some tie to the environment via a transitional object—the radio. In such instances, we see the result of deficient development of object and reality constancy.

Frequently, in borderline patients, the outer world as well as their own bodies have to be especially stimulus rich in order to emphasize and maintain contact with reality. They sometimes require strong stimuli to convince themselves of their own reality as well as that of the external environment. A patient reported that he had to have repeated orgasms in the course of a night in order to experience strong sensations which made him feel alive and in contact with reality. One of my patients remarked that I might construe her nail biting as having sexual significance, but, she said, "That's only sometimes." She really bit her nails to feel herself—to know who she was —to feel alive.

My own observations of disturbances in reality constancy have in the main been on adult patients. Goldfarb (1963) and McDevitt described manifestations of defects in reality constancy in severely disturbed children. McDevitt[12] referred to institutionalized children, psychotic children, or those with organic brain disease, many of whom showed disturbances similar to those in adults with defective reality constancy. They revealed an inability to see objects in predictable ways, disturbances in time-space relations, disorientation with regard to the outer world, magical thinking, and animation of the inanimate world, etc.

Most of my remarks about reality constancy have been concerned with the external environment. There are many indications that this concept may be equally applicable to some aspects of the internal environment, especially to internal material reality, which consists of somatic phenomena derived from explicable and inexplicable processes. Under ordinary circumstances there is an automatic awareness that there is a body unity and a rhythm, and integration to the operations of this internal reality. There is an element of predictability and automatic awareness of the interrelatedness between body sensations and body functions and body parts. We take for granted that a sensation in the bowel relates to evacuation, that the heart is beating, the lungs are breathing, that the head, arms and legs are part of the body, etc. Reality constancy is a factor in the maintenance of this unity of the processes of the internal environment.

Disturbances in reality constancy may be reflected in undue heightened perception and awareness of the ordinary body operations

---

[12] In his discussion of this paper.

as well as lessening in the feeling of reality about one's body parts as seen in depersonalization, for instance. I have in other communications (1959, 1964a, 1964b) presented some examples illustrating severe disturbances of the body image, expressed, for instance, in fragmentation and disconnection of one part of the body from another as well as in marked distortions of bodily appearance. One such patient with psychotic character grew a beard to keep his head attached to his body. Diarrhea was viewed by him as the action of a hostile and foreign object "who" would not let him alone. Goldfarb (1963) has called attention to the difficulty that schizophrenic children have in "consciously recognizing and assigning meaning and predictability to inner body processes, even when these are rhythmically recurrent and daily in occurrence" (p. 50). However, further studies are required in order to understand many aspects of reality constancy as applied to the internal environment.

The above-described examples are but a few of the clinical manifestations which may derive from the faulty development of both object and reality constancy. Although, as I have indicated, it is difficult in borderline cases to delineate sharply which manifestations derive from defects in the former and which from the latter, there are, I believe, sufficient indications that the concept of reality constancy offers a useful frame of reference with which to approach and gain understanding of some manifestations of disturbances with reality.

Concluding Remarks

The concept of reality constancy evolved out of an attempt to establish a frame of reference within which to comprehend certain clinical observations as well as an attempt to understand what we may be trying to achieve in certain problems. Clinical experience with patients suffering from psychotic character repeatedly called attention to the impairment of the ego functions concerned with reality. In order to study these disturbances more effectively, I proposed in previous studies (1959, 1964a) that the position of the ego and its functions toward reality be more specifically delineated. To achieve this purpose I suggested that we scrutinize separately the relationship with reality, the feeling of reality, and the capacity to test reality. It became necessary, however, to evolve a frame of reference within which to view the interrelationship of these areas as well as the impact they had upon one another. In some of my patients, the development of trust in their perceptions frequently went hand in hand with a diminution of perceptual distortions and improvement in reality testing. It became apparent that there was some unifying factor that provided a degree of cohesion, continuity, and stability to these functions. When we confront a patient with reality and help him test reality and develop trust in his own perceptions, we facilitate the development of reality constancy. The very stability of the analytic setting is also an aid in doing so.

Among the many problems of Mr. Y., the patient who did not trust his own perceptions, were marijuana smoking and the association with questionable characters such as drug pushers, etc. He had an allegiance and loyalty to them which frequently brought him to the verge of antisocial activities, although he never did become involved. His capacity for evaluating and testing reality was at times so disturbed that on one occasion he walked by a police car smoking a marijuana cigarette. This was not simply a reflection of a rebellious attitude toward authority, but he actually could not quite grasp the reality implications of his act. As treatment progressed, the perceptual distortions diminished and he developed a greater trust in his own perceptual capacities as well as an improvement in testing reality. Near the end of treatment he was going to get married and quite spontaneously indicated he was not planning to invite his former questionable friends to his wedding or to his house. What if the police had them under surveillance and began to implicate him, his wife, and his family? The achievement of this degree of capacity to evaluate and test reality concurrently with improvement in the other ego functions concerned with reality, in a person in whom these areas had shown such marked impairment, reflected the development of a degree of reality constancy which augured well for the future.

Summary

The concept of reality constancy is proposed as a psychic structure which facilitates the operations of the ego functions concerned with the environment. Its existence lends to these functions a stability and unity which enables the organism to preserve its identity and orientation amidst alterations and changes in the environment without appreciable psychic disruption or adaptational dysfunction.

Reality constancy arises in conjunction with the internalization and stabilization of environmental images. Although genetically and in its operations reality constancy is closely interwoven with object constancy, I believe that in the light of its subsequent development and functioning it is valid to view reality constancy as evolving beyond the limits of love object constancy. Environmental experiences in addition to those deriving from the love object play an important role in its evolution.

The operations of anticipation, predictability, perception, reality testing, and other ego functions are facilitated by reality constancy. Defects in reality constancy play a role in contributing to the development of feelings of unreality, difficulty in experiencing new and experimental situations, and the preservation of reality contacts.

Reality constancy enables the ego functions concerned with the environment to operate at a mature level. It combats regressive modes of operation and yet under appropriate circumstances permits the ego to tolerate regression. As such it contributes to ego autonomy and ego strength.

BIBLIOGRAPHY

Bak, R. (1964), Comments on Object Relations in Schizophrenia and Perversion. A. A. Brill Address, New York Psa. Soc.

Balint, M. (1942), Reality Testing during Schizophrenic Hallucination. *Brit. J. Med. Psychol.*, 19:201-214.

Benedek, T. (1938), Adaptation to Reality in Early Infancy. *Psa. Q.*, 7:200-214.

Benjamin, J. D. (1961), The Innate and the Experiential in Child Development. *Lectures on Experimental Psychiatry*, ed. H. W. Brosin. Pittsburgh: Univ. Pittsburgh Pr., 19-42.

Bergman, P. & Escalona, S. K. (1949), Unusual Sensitivities in Very Young Children. *Psa. Study Ch.*, 3/4:333-352.

Discussion Group (1964), The Nature of the Psychotic Process. Am. Psa. Assn.

Fenichel, O. (1937), Early Stages of Ego Development. *C.P.* 2:25-48. NY: Norton, 1954.

Ferenczi, S. (1926), The Problem of Acceptance of Unpleasant Ideas. *Further Contributions to the Theory and Technique of Psychoanalysis*. NY: Boni & Liveright, 1927, 366-378.

Freud, A, (1952), The Mutual Influences in the Development of Ego and Id. *Psa. Study Ch.*, 7:42-50.

―――― (1954), In: Problems of Infantile Neurosis: A Discussion. *Psa. Study Ch.*, 9:16-71.

―――― (1963), The Concept of Developmental Lines. *Psa. Study Ch.*, 18:245-265.

―――― (1965), *Normality and Pathology in Childhood*. NY: IUP.

Freud, S. (1900), The Interpretation of Dreams. *S.E.*, 5:565-566.

―――― (1921), Group Psychology and the Analysis of the Ego. *S.E.*, 18:67-143.

―――― (1923), The Ego and the Id. *S.E.*, 19:3-66.

―――― (1925), Negation, *S.E.*, 19:235-239.

―――― (1927), The Future of an Illusion. *S.E.*, 21:3-56.

―――― (1936), A Disturbance of Memory on the Acropolis. *S.E.*, 22:239-248.

Frosch, J. (1959), The Psychotic Character: Psychoanalytic Considerations. Abst. in
    J. Am. Psa. Assn., 8:544-548, 1960.
—— (1964a), The Psychotic Character: Clinical Psychiatric Considerations. *Psychiat. Q.*, 38:81-96.
—— (1964b), Delusional Fixity, Sense of Conviction and the Nature of the Psychotic Conflict. Abst. in *Psa. Q.*, 23:617-618.
Glover, E. (1932), A Psycho-analytical Approach to the Classification of Mental
    Disorders. *On the Early Development of Mind*. NY: IUP, 1956, 161-186.
Goldfarb, W. (1963), Self-Awareness in Schizophrenic Children. *Arch. Gen. Psychiat.*, 8:47-60.
Greenacre, P. (1941), The Predisposition to Anxiety: I & II. *Psa. Q.*, 10:66-94;
    610-638.
—— (1952), Some Factors Producing Different Types of Genital and Pregenital
    Organization. *Trauma, Growth and Personality*. NY: Norton, 293-302.
—— (1954), In: Problems of Infantile Neurosis: A Discussion. *Psa. Study Ch.*,
    9:16-71.
Hartmann, H. (1939), *Ego Psychology and the Problem of Adaptation*. NY: IUP,
    1958.
—— (1952), The Mutual Influences in the Development of Ego and Id. *Essays*,
    155-181.
—— (1955), Notes on the Theory of Sublimation. *Essays*, 215-240.
—— (1956), Notes on the Reality Principle. *Essays*, 241-267.
—— Kris, E., & Loewenstein, R. M. (1946), Comments on the Formation of Psychic
    Structure. *Psa. Study Ch.*, 2:11-38.
—— & Loewenstein, R. M. (1962), Notes on the Superego. *Psa. Study Ch.*, 17:42-81.
Jacobson, E. (1964), *The Self and the Object World*. NY: IUP.
Mahler, M. S. (1960), Perceptual De-Differentiation and Psychotic 'Object Relationship.' *Int. J. Psa.*, 41:548-553.
—— (1963), Thoughts about Development and Individuation. *Psa. Study Ch.*,
    18:307-324.
Nunberg, H. (1951), Transference and Reality. *Int. J. Psa.*, 32:1-9.
Rapaport, D., ed. & tr. (1951), *Organization and Pathology of Thought*. NY: Columbia Univ. Pr., 338-348.
—— & Gill, M. M. (1959), The Points of View and Assumptions of Metapsychology. *Int. J. Psa.*, 40:153-162.
Scott, J. P. (1962), Critical Periods in Behavioral Development. *Science*, 138:949-958.
Spitz, R. A. (1964), The Derailment of Dialogue. *J. Am. Psa. Assn.*, 12:752-775.
—— & Wolf, K. M. (1949), Autoerotism. *Psa. Study Ch.*, 3/4:85-120.
White, R. W. (1963), *Ego and Reality in Psychoanalytic Theory. Psychol. Issues*, 11.
Winnicott, D. W. (1953), Transitional Objects and Transitional Phenomena. *Int. J.
    Psa.*, 34:89-97.

The Several Grades of Memory

GEORGE S. KLEIN, Ph.D.

For psychoanalysts the problem of memory has crystallized mainly around a concern with forgetting, and with forgetting explained from the vantage point of repression. By forgetting I mean memory loss—a failure of retrieval or the inaccessibility of experience residues to awareness. The positive sides of memory processes—perceptual registration, coding, and consolidation, and qualities that distinguish the remembering experience from other modes—have generally not attracted interest, except for Freud's earlier speculative models of how traces are established and retained which he put forward in the "Project for a Scientific Psychology" (1895), in *The Interpretation of Dreams* (1900), and much later in "The Mystic Writing-Pad" (1925). With few exceptions (Lewy and Rapaport, 1944; Rapaport, 1942, 1951b; Kris, 1956; Schwartz and Rouse, 1961; Luborsky, 1964), these suggestions of Freud remain unexplored.

The tendency of psychoanalytic writers to view memory in terms of forgetting and loss and almost entirely from the vantage point of repression is not contradicted by the reminder that the conscious revival of the forgotten is, after all, a critical objective of psychoanalytic therapy. This was, of course, one of Freud's important concerns, as, for instance, when he experimented with devices for eliciting forgotten memories (see his early papers on hysteria, e.g., 1893/95). But Freud's focus on remembering proceeded not so much from questions of how traces are established (the learning and perceptual

From the Research Center for Mental Health, New York University. Presented at the Panel on Memory and Repression, 1964. Preparation of this paper was aided by a Research Career Award grant K6-MH-19728 of the National Institutes of Health.

processes involved) and the processes of storage, as from the question of how to make stored events available to conscious reflection. Freud seems not to have made much of the possibility that modes of acquisition and of storage might themselves have bearing on techniques of inducing remembering and of reconstruction. He did in scattered instances offer hints on these matters, particularly in the early papers; he alluded, for instance, to the importance of state of consciousness and of its affective concomitants in trace formation, especially in accounting for the formation of a repression and for its peculiarly persistent and tenacious effects on behavior. But there have been few attempts as yet to make systematic capital of this in a theory of memory. Generally, it has never seemed as important to ask how traces of experience are *established* and what is the nature of such traces as it has been to ask why an allegedly stored event has been forgotten, what has happened to the forgotten (repressed) memory, and how the long-forgotten can be resuscitated. The events of memory that are susceptible to the "pull of repression" tend to be regarded as vaguely passive processes, loosely referred to as the "memory function."

It is easy to see how the narrow view of memory as forgetting and of forgetting itself as almost entirely an outcome of repression proper came to prevail in psychoanalytic conceptions. The equation of forgetting and repression was etched into clinical practice by the early, and since tarnished, assumption that the key factor in neurotic disturbance is a memory of an actual event—an experience residue isolated through repression, which by virtue of that repression acquires pre-emptive power over behavior. In this assumption, the forgotten event is the troublemaker, and to divest it of its force it is necessary to alter its status of "forgotten." By the rules of clinical inference which govern the psychoanalytic session, what is repressed and why it is repressed take precedence, and this dictum is no less true today than heretofore.

Moreover, the equation of forgetting and repression is probably endemic to the therapeutic situation generally. Forgetting as it appears in the psychoanalytic situation is, in fact, most of the time of interest only in its nonadaptive aspects, for when a connection is not verbalizable or when an experience remains unacknowledged as a memory, it is not easy to deal with it therapeutically. Forgetting is a nuisance in therapy. Schlesinger has aptly pointed out that normal forgetting is not necessarily negative and inadaptive (Panel, 1964). It is even an important factor in the continuing efficiency of memory schemata, since it is often "the normal result of the organizing process of memory which works through the continuous development of memory schemata." While in this sense forgetting is not necessarily enemy to memory, in the psychoanalytic situation it is too often enemy to therapeutic progress. It is therefore not surprising that at this late date Schlesinger's reminder that not all instances of forgetting should be viewed as repressions can be a pertinent observation for a psychoanalytic audience.

The persistent hold of repression upon memory theory is especially interesting when we take note of the fact that the theory of repression is itself no longer confined to memory phenomena alone. Today the scope of repression is acknowledged to extend beyond simply the isolation of early traumatic experiences; nor, for that matter, is it identified only with the "memory function." We speak of repressed impulses, repressed fantasy, repressed perceptions, also, and probably in contrast to Freud, of repressed affects (e.g., guilt feelings), resistance to awareness of causes and connections—these are not matters simply of forgetting and of memory. But while the regions in which repression can operate are now acknowledged to extend beyond the "memory function" alone, the earlier link of memory with forgetting through repression is still prominent.

In this light, it is important to ask in what ways a more detailed concern with the adaptive side of memory functioning—remembering in its positive aspects—can alter and deepen our perspective to memory phenomena generally and to clinically observable ones in particular. As an example of the possible fruitfulness of reversing the emphasis on "forgetting" to one upon "remembering," take the matter of recall of dreams. Freud titled a section of his *Interpretation of Dreams*, "Why Dreams Are Forgotten after Waking." This is generally the more popular question about dream recall, and it is reasonable in therapeutic practice to make this emphasis; certainly a forgotten dream is not as useful as a remembered one. But perhaps a fresh perspective can be gained to understanding the function of dreams if we were to say: Far from forgetting being a dynamically central event, *remembering* a dream is the exceptional event. Assuming, then, that forgetting dreams is the natural event, the interesting question becomes: how is it possible that we remember dreams at all, and what is the function of recall? Possibly dreaming and the *recall* of dreams have different functions; possibly recall depends on factors other than its function. It may be more useful to *have* a dream than to *recall* it, in so far as fulfilling the dream's function of drive discharge is concerned. This would then make it meaningful to inquire about the special aims and causes of *dream recall*.

Contemporary ego psychology forces upon us a broader and at the same time more differentiated regard for the activity of remembering—a process quite independent of, yet subject to, repressive influences. Hartmann (1939) has written: "memory, associations, and so on, are functions which cannot possibly be derived from the ego's relationships to instinctual drives or love-objects, but are rather *prerequisites* of our conception of these and of their development" (p. 15). If we take Hartmann's statement seriously, then the older idea of memory as simply the storage of traces which remain immutable is no longer an acceptable model to work with. Even putting to the side Lashley's (1950) rueful remark that he spent thirty years looking for the memory trace, only to discover that it is everywhere and nowhere, the model allows neither for a developmental conception of changes in memory functioning nor for the possibility that memory may function adaptively in a variety of ways. Regarding remembering from the standpoint of its nondrive aspects, we are alerted to the possibility that a *variety* of functions are hidden beneath the enigmatic reference to "the memory function," and its implicit assumption that there is little else to memory than storage, and little else to memory activity than erasure.

Considering memory from its aspect of contributing to environment-adequate and drive-adequate behavior—its adaptive aspects—contemporary experimental psychology provides a more differentiated picture of memory functions than is implied by the familiar psychoanalytic assumption of a unitary memory function. From a structural viewpoint, these functions may be viewed as a succession of threshold levels, the surmounting of which is the condition for the occurrence of each function:

1. *Registration.* An essential condition of retention is a modality-mediated activation (auditory, visual, etc.) produced by an encounter or an event. Registration refers to an aftereffect or excitatory effect of such encounter, extending to an associative structure or schema, which outlasts the duration of the stimulus. Not all inputs register in

this sense, i.e., produce an excitatory effect, and not all that register achieve the status of a trace or structured residue. Registration is thus a distinctive aspect of the process of remembering. Freud touched on the distinction in the "Project for a Scientific Psychology" (1895):

> Any psychological theory deserving consideration must provide an explanation of memory. Now any such explanation comes up against the difficulty that . . . after an excitation neurones are permanently different from what they were before, while, on the other hand, it cannot be denied that, in general, fresh excitations meet with the same conditions of reception as did the earlier ones. Thus the neurones would appear to be both influenced and also unaltered—"unprepossessed". We cannot off-hand imagine an apparatus capable of such complicated functioning [p. 359f.].

The phenomenon of registration has received particular attention in experimental studies of the differences between stimulation capable of eliciting awareness or "report" on the one hand and nonreportable excitatory effects of stimulation on the other (Pine, 1960; Fisher, 1960; Klein and Holt, 1960).

2. A second aspect of remembering involves not only registration of an encounter, but that of *storage* or retention. However, experimental studies have disclosed that this itself has two fairly independent aspects—*short-term* storage and *long-term* storage (Broadbent, 1958). Conditions adequate for short-term retention of impressions do not insure retention for longer periods. The experimental work that has developed around this distinction is a complex story (Sperling, 1963; Mackworth, 1963; Postman, 1964; Waugh and Norman, 1965).

3. A third aspect of remembering has to do with what has been variously termed *coding, categorization,* or *location within schemata.* Here organization of retained impressions within existing schemata of meaning is crucial to the continued utilization of stored experience.[1]

4. Finally, a critical aspect of remembering concerns processes of *retrieval* and *reconstruction.* A retrieved memory refers to the condition of a former state of affairs that is acting in the present. A retrieved memory is not necessarily *remembered. Remembering* in-

---

[1] E.g., Lashley: "Fixation in memory is generally possible only when the remembered material forms part of a dominant system. . . . We remember the content of a book, not in the author's words, but in meanings which fit into previous knowledge of the subject" (1950, p. 7f.).

cludes, in addition, a re-enactment of the awareness which the re-
memberer had of that fact on the occasion of its occurrence. Only if
an image is accompanied by some awareness that "this is something
like what I felt then" or that "this is the way something looked then"
can it be called remembering. (Many experimental studies of memory
are not necessarily studies of remembering in this sense, since remembering as a mode of *experience* is rarely a focus of inquiry.)

On this basis, there are two aspects of the retrieval problem that
should be distinguished: the *experiential* mode in which a memory is
retrieved and the *state of consciousness* which frames the context of
retrieval. Here we are indebted to Rapaport's insistence upon the distinction between states of consciousness and varieties of modes of
awareness, and to the importance he gave to these neglected facets
of thought organization for a proper accounting of cognitive organization (1951b, 1952). The distinction is often obscured in discussions
of memory which are mainly absorbed by the substantive issue of
memory contents.

Retrieval may take forms other than that of actually experiencing
a retrieved content as an act of remembering. It is not necessary for
a memory or stored event to be recalled in order for it to influence
present behavior. Memories unaccompanied by recall may be experienced as reconstructions—i.e., aroused *beliefs* about past events, while
actual *recall* involves the experience of an event in the mode of remembering. We also *act out* our memories as well as experiencing
them *qua* memories. Thus, the varieties of forms in which retained
experience intrudes upon behavior, and the processes involved in con-
verting what is stored to memory experience specifically are distinctive facets of memory functioning, with memory experience only one
aspect of retrieval or of the behavioral impact of stored experiences.

These distinctions among the modes in which memories are experienced are important because they have much to do with the way
in which the retrieved event is acted upon. Modes of conscious experience are associated with different grades of "realness" and these
are closely interrelated with judgment and reality testing, i.e., with
how we behave adaptively in relation to the retrieved event. The
possible actions that can be triggered by a cognized event will differ
according to whether it is perceived, imagined, remembered. To perceive a chair is more likely to elicit an actual movement toward the

chair and to sit on it than is an imaginal experience of the chair, or a remembered chair.

Failures of reality testing have often to do with inappropriateness of experiences rather than with forgetting or actual failures of retrieval. Not only may a memory be responded to without an accompanying sense that one is *remembering* and without, therefore, the grade of reality belief associated with such an experience; it may also happen, as clinical experience shows, that an imagined event can be mis-experienced in the distinctive cast of a *remembered* experience —and responded to accordingly (see, e.g., Arlow, 1959).[2]

An important consideration in the problem of retrieval is the organismic state—*"state of consciousness"* (Rapaport, 1951b, 1952, 1957; Klein, 1959) or *"ego state"* (Niederland in Panel, 1964; Rubinfine, 1965)—that accompanies both acquisition of a memory in the first place and its later re-emergence in retrieved form. Besides the mode in which the stored event is specifically experienced, there seems good reason to believe that different states of consciousness, e.g., alert wakefulness, reverie, etc., provide differing opportunities of activation of stored events, in differing forms and transformations, and in varying experiential guise. In Rubinfine's summary: "As one moves on the continuum from the cathectic organization of full waking consciousness and its schemas which are conceptually organized and typified by secondary process and close relationship to the reality principle toward more dreamlike states, there is a regressive revival (cathexis) of more archaic schemas of ego functioning. These more archaic schemas are drive-organized and typified by the operation of primary processes as well as reduction in self-awareness, and with

---

[2] The question touched on here is the extent to which vividness of experienced recall can be taken to be a valid indicator of remembering, a question dating back to Freud's early belief that the repressed ideational contents of hysterical disorders were those of actual environmental happenings. Later he discovered that such contents are more often fantasied constructions which, in coming to light with affective intensity, are felt *as if* they were being re-experienced. Thus, it could not be assumed that the freshness of a re-presented idea reflects qualities associated only with remembering. Such an idea may owe its "wonderful freshness," as Freud put it, not to memory, but to the repressive power itself. That is, vividness and affective intensity may be qualities sustained and even implemented by the repressive process. (For example, a sense of "familiarity" is likely to be attached to derivatives of the most deeply repressed ideas.) Therefore, it is often more to the point to speak of a repressed idea than of a repressed memory; not only a memory, but a fantasy (or rather, the schema that serves as a basis for a fantasy) can be repressed. It may be noted that related issues have been raised by Penfield's reports of the experiences which subjects have under temporal lobe stimulation.

their revival the distinction of self and nonself becomes hazier." The importance of such states for acquisition of memories is largely an unexplored issue, although it was early suggested (Breuer and Freud, 1893/95; Ferenczi and Rank, 1925) that the peculiar intensity of repressed memories, of traumatic and affect-ridden memories owe their qualities to the state of consciousness that initially accompanied acquisition. Conversely, reconstruction and retrieval may be contingent upon revival of the same state, a condition prescribed by Freud as an associative setting most conducive to the recollection of a dream (1900, p. 101f.). Rubinfine (1965) and Niederland (Panel, 1964) offer clinical examples of remembering occurring in the context of such changes of "ego state."

Taking, then, as a vantage point to memory the view that it comprises adaptive processes that convert experience to residues having momentary, short-term and long-term usefulness in behavior, retrievable in various guises (of which memory *experience* is only one) and in different "ego states" or "states of consciousness"—all this complicates the accustomed reference to the "memory function." However, it is a needed beginning to implement, on the one hand, the concept of autonomous ego functioning and, on the other hand, such concepts as "recall" and "working through" in the psychoanalytic situation.

Some Implications

1. If remembering is conceived in terms of classes of function (tracemaking or registration; storage or retention; and retrieval), it is clear that *forgetting* need not itself be regarded as a unitary process; its behavioral meaning will be different in relation to each phase of the remembering process. In regard to retrieval, forgetting may mean loss of the *remembering experience* of a retrieved event, without implying that the memory is eliminated from storage or that retrieval through other modalities of experience, e.g., imagery, gesture, or somatic displacements, is impossible. By the same token, forgetting may occur in the sense of an erasure that prevents long-term storage without loss of short-term utility. However, forgetting in the sense of erasure is entirely different from forgetting in the sense of transformation within or assimilation to existing schemata. Finally, from the vantage point of memory in its positive structural aspects, certain questions about forgetting become quite meaningless and even absurd

which before seemed sensible within the simple conception of a unitary memory function. One such question is: can everything once remembered be forgotten? The question is meaningless if no specification is made of the memory function in respect to which forgetting is presumed to occur.

2. With memory viewed as comprising several functions, the effects of repression on memory are now seen to take on various forms according to the function implicated.

It becomes reasonable to expect repression to operate in respect to some, but not all, aspects of memory functions. It is possible to conceive of repression at a *perceptual* level—that is, at the very process of registration or trace-making. For instance, repression of perceptual registration could conceivably involve the actual desensitization of a receptor via downflow inhibitory circuits from the cortex to receptor surfaces. Contemporary neurophysiological developments offer encouragement to such an assumption, and thereby open an exciting prospect of a meaningful extension of the psychoanalytic concept of repression (Granit, 1955; Eccles, 1964; Diamond et al., 1963). Such experiments have suggested that stimulus inputs presumably coded in the neocortex can induce a temporary corticofugal or downflow inhibition of the receptor temporarily restricting input from this modality. This would prevent the type of reverberating playback that is necessary for registrations to acquire persistence for short-term or long-term storage.

Repression can also occur in relation to already registered stimuli. This would imply that a repressive erasure process could prevent the consolidation of a registration beyond short-term storage in the memory system. Or, repression can apply to transformations within the consolidation process of long-term storage itself. Freud (1901) once suggested that normal forgetting takes place by way of condensation, and that "Repression makes use of the mechanism of condensation and produces a confusion with other cases" (p. 134).

Rapaport (1951a) has proposed that memory storage can occur in terms of *drive-organized* and *conceptual* (nondrive) organizations (residues of adaptive encounters with the environment). Thus, a further aspect of repression in this phase of the memory process would have to do with its effects on either or both of these classes of stored events.

And finally, repression may affect the *retrieval* function in distinctive ways. It may produce *total* inaccessibility of a memory to behavior, or only its *partial* occlusion in the sense of disallowing identification of a memory as a *memory experience* ("my memory of. . ."; "my experience of. . ."). The latter is the traditionally familiar effect of a repression. However, retrieval in other forms may still be evident in the form, say, of *images* or of *actions* whose significance is not apparent to consciousness.

These considerations shift emphasis away from memory as a single function which is uniformly affected by repression, to a more detailed regard upon *where* in the remembering process the force of repression is being exerted. It makes a difference whether repression is effective at one or another side of memory; the behavioral effects of repression will vary according to the phase of the memory process that is captured by it.

3. I have tried to emphasize memory in its *adaptive* aspects—as a multiple-sided process combining registration, coding, and storage, schema assimilation and retrieval processes. One implication of this emphasis is that memory functioning may reflect different styles of adaptive strategy—what I have termed elsewhere styles of secondary-process functioning (1954, 1958). It seems reasonable to assume that memory functions are enlisted in implementing such styles. This viewpoint attaches importance to individual differences in remembering behaviors and tries to understand them in terms of the generalized modes of control that characterize a person's ego system—his typical ways of processing inner and outer stimuli, and his means of arriving at adaptive solutions to his encounters with stimulation. Following Hartmann (1939, 1964), we find it essential to speak nowadays of conflict-free, autonomous thought functions. But conflict-free adaptations need not all be identical. At least in the laboratory where we have studied the problem, under conditions where behavior is not easily referred to conflict or defense, people respond in characteristically selective ways to stimulation. Differences among people in these experimental perceptual and memory tasks are produced by equally adaptive and equally effective modes of resolving the tasks. It is as if secondary-process functions are themselves organized in terms of rules of economy—adaptive economy—which are independent of conflict, perhaps even of defense, and specifically of repression.

One such mode of adaptive control which we have had experience with in the laboratory is termed *importing*—a concept originated by my colleague Irving Paul (1959) to describe a characteristic style in which once-learned verbal material is remembered. Attention to importing as a strategy of remembering came up when Paul found that some subjects regularly introduce explicatory or gap-filling material when they are confronted with the task of recalling stored material. Among subjects who rarely show such imported gap-filling elements, some show instead a tendency to widen gaps by stripping away; they *skeletonize* in remembering. The tendencies to import or skeletonize are reliably measured, and studies increasingly show that the importing tendency is a substantially general one for those who show it, appearing in a variety of verbal materials and in different memory tasks. Studies now in progress are exploring the ways in which the importing style of remembering may signify a more general principle of ego control and whether it may coincide with certain defensive dispositions.

It is, of course, a major issue whether an apparently cohesive style of secondary-process behavior such as the importing tendency in remembering has itself originated in defensive solution to conflict invoked in childhood which has since crystallized into an autonomous characterological tendency. The reverse possibility is also, however, to be entertained: that the choice of defense may itself be predicated on a predisposition for certain modes of arriving at adaptive solutions (Gardner et al., 1959). In this regard recent findings that importers seem to show characteristics more closely associated with hysterical dispositions than with obsessive compulsive ones take on interest. Counterphobic and repressive tendencies seem to appear more frequently in diagnostic assessments of the importers (Paul, 1965).

I would also like to mention that the styles of importing and skeletonizing illustrate how forgetting and remembering can have either adaptive or nonadaptive significance. Forgetting need not be instigated by repression. In the skeletonizing tendency, it contributes to efficiency of selection. The difference between importing and skeletonizing is mainly in respect to the means by which elements of memory are sharpened, in the one case by embellishments, an introduction of redundancies, in the other case by an active forgetting process which strips away the less relevant. Thus from the standpoint of memory behavior as a reflection of cognitive style, forgetting is seen as an ego process which may assist in the processes of storage and retrieval, and serve as one means of consolidating organization of recalled material.

Most of my remarks have been aimed at the necessity of viewing clinical phenomena of memory loss, remembering experience, and modes of retrieval within a broad perspective to memory conceived as comprising a variety of adaptive functions. A further objective in the development of psychoanalytic conceptions of memory deserves at least brief mention—that of bridging clinical observations and non-clinical experimental studies of memory processes. A difficulty in accommodating psychoanalytic theory to proliferating experimental data on memory is that what contemporary psychoanalysis likes to call the "structural point of view" is actually explanation in functional rather than in causal-process terms. Explanation in terms of function is, of course, central to the psychoanalytic enterprise, even perhaps its unique contribution compared to other psychological theories. Yet, it is important to realize that when we speak of "forgetting" or of "repression," we are implying more than function; we are also implying structures behaving in characteristic ways, and beyond that, a model of the actual processes of memory. To speak of the adaptive properties of memory is to speak of functions carried out by structures, but description of function is a long way from postulating the operational rules of the structures that subsume it. The "structural point of view" of contemporary psychoanalytic theory does not in itself constitute structural models in this sense. An eventual systematic theory would have to encompass the functional attributes of memory in their adaptive and inadaptive aspects, which psychoanalytic theory alerts us to, within a general conception of the structures of memory processes. The data of forgetting and repression of the psychoanalytic situation will come to have a coordinate place alongside those from experimental laboratories when attempts are made to translate the functional explanations that are the proper concern of psychoanalytic considerations, to a general theory of memory *process*, and to explicit structural models of how these functions are actually carried out.

BIBLIOGRAPHY

Arlow, J. A. (1959), The Structure of the *Déjà Vu* Experience. *J. Am. Psa. Assn.*, 7:611-631.
Breuer, J. & Freud, S. (1893/95), Studies on Hysteria. *S.E.*, 2.
Broadbent, D. E. (1958), *Perception and Communication*. NY: Pergamon Pr.
Diamond, S., Balvin, R. S., & Diamond, F. R. (1963), *Inhibition and Choice*. NY: Harper & Row.
Eccles, J. C. (1964), *The Physiology of Synapses*. Berlin: Springer.

Ferenczi, S. & Rank, O. (1925), *The Development of Psychoanalysis*. NY: Nerv. Ment. Dis. Monogr. 40.

Fisher, C. (1960), Introduction to *Preconscious Stimulation in Dreams, Associations, and Images. Psychol. Issues*, 7:1-40.

Freud, S. (1895), Project for a Scientific Psychology. *The Origins of Psychoanalysis.* NY: Basic Books, 1954.

—— (1900), The Interpretation of Dreams, *S.E.*, 5.

—— (1901), The Psychopathology of Everyday Life. *S.E.*, 6.

—— (1925), A Note upon the 'Mystic Writing-Pad.' *S.E.*, 19:227-232.

Gardner, R. W., Holzman, P. S., Klein, G. S., Linton, H., & Spence, D. P. (1959), *Cognitive Control. Psychol. Issues* 4.

Granit, R. (1955), *Receptors and Sensory Perception*. New Haven: Yale Univ. Pr.

Hartmann, H. (1939), *Ego Psychology and the Problem of Adaptation*. NY: IUP, 1958.

—— (1964), *Essays on Ego Psychology*. NY: IUP.

Klein, G. S. (1954), Need and Regulation. *Nebraska Symposium on Motivation*, ed. M. R. Jones. Lincoln: Univ. Nebraska Pr., 224-274.

—— (1958), Cognitive Control and Motivation. *Assessment of Human Motives*, ed. G. Lindzey. NY: Rinehart, 87-118.

—— (1959), Consciousness in Psychoanalytic Theory. *J. Am. Psa. Assn.*, 7:5-34.

—— & Holt, R. R. (1960), Problems and Issues in Current Studies of Subliminal Activation. *Festschrift for Gardner Murphy*, ed. J. G. Peatman & E. L. Hartley. NY: Harper, 75-93.

Kris, E. (1956), The Recovery of Childhood Memories in Psychoanalysis. *Psa. Study Ch.*, 11:54-88.

Lashley, K. S. (1950), In Search of the Engram. *The Neuropsychology of Lashley*, ed. F. A. Beach et al. NY: McGraw-Hill, 1960, 478-543.

Lewy, E. & Rapaport, D. (1944), The Psychoanalytic Concept of Memory and Its Relation to Recent Memory Theories. *Psa. Q.*, 13:16-41.

Luborsky, L. (1964), A Psychoanalytic Research on Momentary Forgetting during Free Association. *Bull. Phila. Assn. Psa.*, 14:119-137.

Mackworth, J. D. (1963), The Relation between the Visual Image and Postperceptual Immediate Memory. *J. Verb. Learn. & Verb. Behav.*, 2:75-85.

Panel (1964), Memory and Repression, rep. W. G. Niederland. *J. Am. Psa. Assn.*, 13:619-633, 1965.

Paul, I. H. (1959), *Studies in Remembering. Psychol. Issues*, 2.

—— (1964), The Effects of a Drug-induced Alteration in State of Consciousness on Retention of Drive-related Verbal Material. *J. Nerv. & Ment. Dis.*, 138:1-25.

—— (1965), The Personality Correlates of a Remembering Style. MS.

Pine, F. (1960), Incidental Stimulation. *J. Abn. Soc. Psychol.*, 60:68-75.

Postman, L. (1964), Short-Term Memory and Incidental Learning. *Categories of Human Learning*, ed. A. W. Melton. NY: Academic Pr., 145-201.

Rapaport, D. (1942), *Emotions and Memory*. NY: IUP, 2nd ed., 1950.

—— ed. (1951a), *The Organization and Pathology of Thought*. NY: Columbia Univ. Pr.

—— (1951b), Consciousness. *Problems of Consciousness*. NY: Josiah Macy, Jr. Foundation, 18-57.

—— (1952), Projective Techniques and the Theory of Thinking. *J. Proj. Tech.*, 16:269-275.

—— (1957), Cognitive Structures. *Contemporary Approaches to Cognition*. Cambridge: Harvard Univ. Pr., 157-200.

Rubinfine, D. (1965), Notes on a Theory of Reconstruction. MS.

Schwartz, R. & Rouse, R. (1961), *The Activation and Recovery of Associations. Psychol. Issues*, 9.

Sperling, G. (1963), A Model for Visual Memory Tasks. *Hum. Factors*, 5:19-31.

Waugh, N. C. & Norman, D. A. (1965), Primary Memory. *Psychol. Rev.*, 72:89-104.

The Mechanism of Repression

CHARLES BRENNER, M.D.

For psychoanalysts defenses and their mechanisms of operation are an important part of ego psychology. It is to be expected, therefore, that they are a topic which Heinz Hartmann has discussed on more than one occasion, and to which he has made important contributions. As an example of the way in which he has enlarged our knowledge of this subject one may mention the suggestion that the energy at the disposal of the defenses may typically derive from the aggressive drives (Hartmann, 1964, ch. 7, 9, 10). Closely related is his proposition that in schizophrenics the instability and the inadequacy of many aspects of their defensive functioning may be attributed to the insufficient neutralization of the aggressive energies utilized by their defenses (ch. 10).

The present paper is an expanded version of a presentation at a recent panel discussion on "Memory and Repression" which took place at the December, 1964 meeting of the American Psychoanalytic Association (see Niederland, 1965). Though not directly an outgrowth of Hartmann's contributions to the theory of defense, it owes much to both their spirit and their content.

The principal and definitive discussion of repression is contained in Freud's many references to the subject, which occupied his interest in a major degree for more than thirty years. Most other references to the subject are little more than excerpts from Freud's ideas or synopses of them. Since a comprehensive review of Freud's writings on repression is available in the recent literature (Brenner, 1957), it will not be repeated here. It will suffice to quote from the 1957 review the following summary of the final stage of the development of Freud's concept of repression.

Repression is one of the several defense mechanisms which the ego may employ against an instinctual drive which is the source of anxiety. Thus the *occasion* or *motive* for repression is anxiety, usually anxiety aroused by a derivative of an instinctual drive. The *target* of repression is ordinarily a libidinal drive, but it is possible that repression may also be employed on occasion against an aggressive or destructive drive (Freud, 1930) and it certainly may be so employed against a superego demand (Freud, 1923).

The *mechanism* of repression consists in the establishment of a countercathexis by the ego. Repression is thus possible only after a substantial degree of ego development has taken place. The mechanism of the earliest, infantile repressions is the same as that of later ones, i.e., the establishment of a countercathexis by the ego. However, the infantile repressions are the basic ones. Later repressions are by and large repetitions or consequences of the infantile ones. The adult ego represses something only to the extent that, and only in those areas where it is still infantile as a consequence of infantile repression, or other similar, infantile defenses. With these exceptions it can deal with instinctual demands and with external stimuli in other ways, e.g., in the case of the former by judgmental repudiation, in the case of the latter by adaptive behavior of some kind.

The source of the energy of the countercathexis in repression is uncertain. Perhaps it comes from the pool of neutralized libidinal energy which is generally at the disposal of the ego for the purpose of carrying out its various functions (1923). In any case an equilibrium is established between the repressed drive and the countercathexis of the ego which is relatively stable, but which may shift in one direction or another under circumstances to be described below.

The *effects* of repression are twofold. In the first place, the drive and its derivatives are excluded from the ego and are consigned to the id, which means that as long as the repression is maintained the repressed drive has no access to consciousness, produces no emotional consequences, and does not give rise to any motor activity aimed at gratification of the drive. However, the repressed drive persists in the id and exerts a persistent pressure in the direction of emergence into consciousness and of gratification. Consequently, there is a tendency for derivatives of the repressed drive to intrude into the functions of the ego and to reach consciousness in dreams, jokes, fantasies, slips, neurotic symptoms, and other similar psychic manifestations which in general may be described as compromise formations.

Such compromise formations are referred to as instances of a *return of the repressed*. The return of the repressed implies a failure of repression, a failure which may be either temporary or prolonged, either so direct as to be unmistakable or so disguised as to be hardly perceptible, and either of such slight practical importance in the life of the individual as to pass quite unnoticed or of such great importance as to be decisive for the whole future course of his life. There are three general conditions under which a return of the repressed may occur: (1) a weakening of the defenses of the ego, as by illness or sleep; (2) a strengthening of the drives, as in puberty or as the result of long continued frustration; (3) a correspondence between the content of current experience and of the repressed drive. To these should be added the influence of current seduction, which presumably corresponds in part to each of the three conditions just mentioned [p. 43ff.].

What I wish to focus attention on is the following. In the classic view, just summarized, compromise formations in which repressed drive derivatives reach consciousness and affect behavior are considered to be failures of repression. The view is that in so far as repression is successful, whatever mental elements have been repressed are effectively barred from access to consciousness (conscious recall of memories, emotional expression) and to conscious behavior. It is only when there is a *return of the repressed* (failure of repression) that disguised and distorted derivatives of what has been repressed appear in conscious mental life. The first instances of the sort which came to Freud's attention were neurotic symptoms. Soon thereafter he recognized the same kind of compromise formation in the dream work and in the psychological processes responsible for the slips and errors of daily life (everyday psychopathology) and for jokes and joking.

With the development of ego psychology which followed the publication of *The Ego and the Id* (1923) there has come a much fuller understanding of the importance of compromise formation in mental functioning (Waelder, 1930), normal as well as pathological. The ideas basic to this understanding are usually subsumed under the heading: the principle of multiple function, as Waelder suggested. The application of this principle to the theory of repression in an explicit way is a principal objective of this paper.

If one follows the line of thought which Freud first stated explicitly in his monograph on Jensen's *Gradiva* (1907), repressed mental elements, e.g., repressed instinctual derivatives, are conceived of as constantly striving for expression in conscious mental life when one is awake no less than when one is asleep. The tendency to strive for expression in this way is attributed to the cathexis of mental energy which invests the repressed elements. We assume that the energy in question constantly presses toward discharge, in consonance with the pleasure principle. According to the principle of multiple function, a strongly cathected mental element, even though repressed, i.e., opposed by a countercathexis, will tend to influence conscious mental life and behavior to some degree. Put in another way, the phenomena of our daily mental life, whether fantasies, thoughts, plans, or actions, are compromises among id, ego, and superego forces and tendencies. This, we may assume, is something that holds true in general for mental functioning; it is not to be thought of as true only in those relatively atypical cases called neurotic symptoms. Compromise formation is a general tendency of the mind, not an exceptional one. Id impulses, even repressed ones, exert an influence on conscious mental functioning and behavior, although their tendency to do so is inhibited or counteracted more or less thoroughly by the ego's defenses (countercathexes).

What evidence is available for such a theory of repression? To what extent do the observable data of thought and behavior support it?

The most convincing evidence would appear to be that available in clinical practice from the application of the psychoanalytic method. To the extent that a patient is able to relax his tendency to direct and edit his thoughts consciously, unconscious strivings will find expression in his conscious mental life as he reports it to his analyst. Among these unconscious strivings are repressed id impulses (instinctual derivatives) and superego demands (self-punitive and self-destructive trends). In other words, when a patient follows the fundamental rule of analysis, it becomes readily obvious that his conscious thoughts are compromise formations in which repressed mental elements play a significant role. We know from clinical experience that deeply repressed mental elements are represented in the patient's thoughts, and hence in what he tells us as he lies on the couch. What he says may, for example, represent more or less clearly a parricidal or an incestuous wish, or one or another perverse instinctual desire. In this context the words "more or less clearly" are the index of the degree of disguise and distortion imposed upon the warded-off instinctual derivative by the ego's defenses and superego prohibitions. A patient's unconscious, incestuous wishes toward his sister may be readily apparent as one of the determinants of his associations if he speaks about Lord Byron, or about the marriage customs of the Egyptian Pharaohs; it will be much less, or not at all apparent, if his associations have to do only with his study of poetry or ancient history in high school, or if he talks at length and with indignation about the sorry state of current drama and about the tendency of dramatists to write plays dealing with sexual perversions to the exclusion of any sort of normal and healthy sexuality. In other words, in one compromise formation derivatives of a repressed, instinctual wish may be more clearly apparent than in another. Nevertheless, our clinical experience justifies the assertion that repressed mental elements are not simply barred from access to conscious mental life. On the contrary, a powerfully cathected mental element, even though repressed, exerts an influence on conscious mental life. It plays its part, whether that part be obvious or obscure, in the creation of those compromise formations which are the stuff of conscious mental life and action.

There are other available data which point in the same direction as the clinical evidence just cited. Freud (1915) explicitly noted that repressed mental elements might at times find expression and satisfaction in normal, waking, mental life; that is, under circumstances other than dreaming on the one hand, or the mechanism of a return of the repressed on the other hand which is characteristic of neurotic symptom formation and of the psychopathologic manifestations of everyday life. "Special techniques have been evolved, with the purpose of bringing about such changes in the play of mental forces that . . . the repression of an instinctual representative which would otherwise be repudiated is removed. These techniques have till now only been studied in any detail in jokes" (Freud, 1915). It will be recalled that the special technique which Freud (1905) particularly emphasized in his monograph on the subject was what he called the "fore-pleasure principle." By this he meant that the childish pleasure of playing with words, which is associated with assonance, rhyming, neologisms, etc., is a sufficient pleasure premium to overcome the repressive forces which ordinarily bar sexual or aggressive trends from consciousness. The pleasure premium, he assumed, permits the repressed wishes to emerge into consciousness, even though for a brief time only, and to contribute their share of pleasure to joker and listeners. In fact, as Freud (1905) emphasized, the economy of the mind being what it is, the *major* source of pleasure in sexual and aggressive jokes comes from the gratification of repressed instinctual impulses, even though it is the childish pleasure in playing with words that makes this possible in the first place.

It will be noted that the "special technique" for lifting repression in normal, waking life which Freud described with reference to jokes is an example of what Kris (1952) proposed to call regression in the service of the ego. Whenever such regression is marked, whether it be in joking, in intellectual or artistic creativity, in the enjoyment of works of art, in religious activities, in less exalted forms of play and pleasure-seeking behavior, etc., there is a tendency for what has been repressed (or otherwise defended against) to become increasingly conspicuous in conscious thought and action. To put the same idea in terms of the principle of multiple function, any substantial degree of regression in the service of the ego is likely to cause a relative increase in the role of repressed mental elements in determining conscious thought and action and a corresponding decrease in the role of the forces aimed at barring from consciousness what has been repressed. Regression in the service of the ego is by definition an aspect of normal mental life. Consequently the data derived from the observation of such aspects of mental functioning may be added to those derived from clinical observations to support the conclusion that repressed mental elements are not simply barred from access to conscious mental life. On the contrary, as I have already stated, repressed elements of the mind normally play their part along with other mental forces in determining conscious thoughts and actions.

Indeed, the more precise knowledge of many aspects of normal psychology, which has been one of the important consequences of the introduction by Freud (1923) of the so-called structural theory of the mind (ego psychology), has underlined the importance of the relationship between what has been repressed (or otherwise defended against) in childhood and adult goals, ambitions, and character traits. For example, any individual's choice of a love object or choice of profession is certain to be profoundly influenced by repressed mental elements, the best known of which are those related to the oedipal complex. These are statements the correctness of which should be immediately apparent to any analyst both on the basis of personal and of clinical experience, and it should be emphasized that they are only two examples from among many to illustrate how repressed mental elements enter into the organization of the conscious aspect of mental life in accordance with the principle of multiple function.

Another important aspect of the mechanism of repression is that the balance of forces which determines it varies from time to time. Repression represents a dynamic rather than a static equilibrium between the forces striving toward conscious expression ("the repressed") and the counterforces (countercathexes) which oppose them. The shifting nature of the balance is obivous in jokes, for example, and indeed Freud (1915) himself remarked in that connection that "as a rule the repression is only temporarily removed and is promptly reinstated." Even more immediate and convincing evidence is afforded by clinical analytic experience. It often happens in the course of treatment that a patient will recall a previously repressed childhood memory or wish, only to forget ("re-repress") it by the next hour. Closely related are instances of momentary forgetting during an analytic session, a subject recently studied by Luborsky (1964). Luborsky's findings are thoroughly consistent with a concept of the mechanism of repression as a dynamic balance among opposing forces. Fenichel (1934) likewise formulated this concept in the following emphatic way: "The dynamic conception views the psyche as a continuous struggle between mental trends which seek discharge and the defensive and selective forces of the ego, between the instinctual cathexes and the anti-cathexes of the ego." It should perhaps be noted that although in the passage just quoted Fenichel omitted from consideration conflicts between ego and superego, as well as the role of the superego in conflicts between ego and id, the omission was merely in the interest of simplicity of expression. In fact, Fenichel often drew particular attention to the role played by the superego in various intrapsychic conflicts. For example, he emphasized the importance of analyzing ego-superego conflicts in obsessional patients.

All of these considerations suggest that the classic concept of repression, expressed in the extensive quotation at the beginning of this article (Brenner, 1957) should be somewhat revised. The classic concept emphasizes the idea that repression bars certain mental elements from access to conscious mental life and action, except in those instances of failure of repression which Freud referred to as "return of the repressed." Such failures are, generally speaking, classed as pathological in waking life (neurotic symptom formation, everyday psychopathology), though they occur normally as part of dreaming.

What is proposed as an alternative to this classic concept is one which emphasizes rather that repression results from an interplay of forces within the mind in which the balance is predominantly in favor of those forces which seek to bar one or several mental representations from expression in conscious mental life, usually with limited success. In other words, repressed mental elements usually play a part, in accordance with the principle of multiple function, in the phenomena of conscious mental life. How large a part they play is different from instance to instance. I wish to emphasize also that the balance among the opposing forces involved in repression is a dynamic one. It may and does constantly shift. It is often different during sleep (dreaming) from what it is during waking life, and it varies frequently in waking life itself, as, for example, in joking and the many other mental activities referred to as regression in the service of the ego.

It is possible to advance an explanation of the observable shifts in repression on the basis of our current theory of anxiety and its relation to defense. Following a suggestion made by Wangh (1964) with respect to jokes, we may formulate the matter in the following way. Repression and other defenses are instituted and maintained by the ego in order to prevent, or at least to minimize the development of anxiety, guilt, etc. In the case of repression, for example, were it not for the ego's defenses, the id or superego element in question would emerge into consciousness to the accompaniment of intense anxiety. If some way can be found to avoid the development of anxiety other than by the institution of repressive countercathexes, then the element in question can be tolerated in consciousness, and can even, in the case of an instinctual derivative, give rise to pleasure.

Thus, for example, an incestuous fantasy in a work of fiction can be a source of pleasure to individuals in whom incestuous wishes would, under other circumstances, give rise to guilt and anxiety, or would be opposed by one or another familiar defense. As Sachs (1942) pointed out, under the special circumstance of being part of a literary or artistic audience, one can enjoy what is otherwise forbidden and frightening. In such a situation guilt is avoided, or diminished, by being shared. It is as though each individual said to himself, "It's all right to enjoy this. Everyone is doing it, so it's perfectly permissible." It will be noted that the mechanism of sharing guilt just described resembles the changes in superego functioning described by Freud (1921) in his monograph on group psychology.

In the example just given, in which an otherwise abhorrent incestuous fantasy is consciously pleasurable when it is part of a work of
fiction, the attitude, "It's only make-believe. It's not real," likewise
assists both author and audience to diminish the countercathexis of
repression without anxiety. The realistic knowledge that something
is unreal with respect to a work of art seems akin to the mechanisms
of denial and isolation with which we are familiar in our clinical work.
When it comes to obscene or aggressive jokes, the attitude, "It's just
a joke; not to be taken seriously," produces a similar alteration in the
functioning of the superego in the direction of less strictness and
more permissiveness. Every storyteller knows how risky it is to tell
a joke without making sure that his audience knows that what he is
about to say is intended to be funny. When one does so, there is
always the danger that one's audience will take one seriously and will
react with disgust, unpleasure, or anger, instead of laughter.

These few indications of the ways in which anxiety may be normally sufficiently avoided or reduced to result in a significant though
temporary weakening of repression must suffice for the present. Any
thoroughgoing discussion of the subject would be beyond the proper
bounds of the present paper; it belongs rather to a more general study
of anxiety and defense mechanisms. I shall conclude with a few remarks on the concept of return of the repressed and its relation to
symptom formation.

According to the classic theory of repression, the appearance of a
neurotic symptom is caused by a failure of repression with a return
of the repressed. The considerations brought forward in the present
paper suggest a somewhat different formulation, which would run
as follows. Repression signifies a dynamic equilibrium between forces
striving for discharge (e.g., an instinctual derivative) and other, opposing forces (defenses, superego prohibitions). If something happens to
shift the balance among these forces in a direction which is unfavorable to the ego's defenses, the result will be an increased emergence
into conscious mental life and action of the previously repressed instinctual derivative. If the shift is long continued, and if the emergence of
the instinctual derivative is felt to be dangerous (arouses signal anxiety), the compromise which results will be of the nature of a neurotic
symptom or character trait. By the same token, a shift in the equilibrium which is favorable to the defensive forces, and which diminishes a patient's tendency to react with anxiety to an instinctual

derivative which has given rise to a neurotic symptom, will result in the symptom disappearing or becoming less severe.

In other words, instead of referring the appearance or disappearance of a neurotic symptom to a failure of repression with a return of the repressed, and to a successful re-establishment of repression, respectively, I suggest that these clinically observable phenomena are better explained as consequences of shifts in the balance among opposing forces within the mind. The first explanation, as noted earlier, tends to view repression as a static equilibrium, in so far as it is successful, i.e., in so far as an individual is mentally healthy. The second explanation conceives of repression as the result of a dynamic balance, of an interplay of forces within the mind, which may shift from time to time, either normally or pathologically. When repression is called successful, the balance is predominantly in favor of those forces which we call defenses and which, in the case of repression, act to bar from conscious awareness, from control of motility, and from emotional expression the derivatives of the instinctual drives or other mental representations to which we refer as "the repressed."

BIBLIOGRAPHY

Brenner, C. (1957), The Nature and Development of the Concept of Repression in Freud's Writings. *Psa. Study Ch.*, 12:19-46.

Fenichel, O. (1934), Concerning the Theory of Psychoanalytic Technique. *C.P.*, 1:332-348. NY: Norton, 1953.

Freud, S. (1905), Jokes and Their Relation to the Unconscious. *S.E.*, 8; see especially 134-138.

―――― (1907), Delusions and Dreams in Jensen's *Gradiva*. *S.E.*, 9:7-95.

―――― (1915), Repression. *S.E.*, 14:146-158.

―――― (1921), Group Psychology and the Analysis of the Ego. *S.E.*, 18:67-143.

―――― (1923), The Ego and the Id. *S.E.*, 19:12-59.

Hartmann, H. (1964), *Essays*, NY: IUP.

Kris, E. (1952), *Psychoanalytic Explorations in Art*. NY: IUP, 177.

Luborsky, L. (1964), A Psychoanalytic Research on Momentary Forgetting during Free Association. *Bull. Phila. Assn. Psa.*, 14:119-137.

Niederland, W. G. (1965), Report on Panel: Memory and Repression. *J. Am. Psa. Assn.*, 13:619-633.

Sachs, H. (1942), The Community of Daydreams. *The Creative Unconscious*. Cambridge, Mass.: Sci-Art Pub., 11-54.

Waelder, R. (1930), The Principle of Multiple Function. *Psa. Q.*, 5:45-62, 1936.

Wangh, M. (1964), Personal communication.

Psychoanalysis As an Exact Science

DANIEL LAGACHE, M.D.

Overture: A Story Such As This

A few months ago I found myself on a committee which includes representatives of the various psychological sciences, among them two psychoanalysts. A representative of the "scientific" trend asked that psychology be classed among the exact sciences; he employed various arguments, some of a doctrinal, others of a tactical order. I was stimulated—even provoked—by this suggestion and I answered that if the tactical advantages were to be considered, even though they are problematical, the basic question was this: not whether or not psychology was an exact science, but rather whether it was a masculine or a feminine science (it is a fact that in France, more than in other countries, the proportion of female psychologists would perhaps be considerable if many of them did not abandon psychology for marriage and motherhood). My interruption gave rise to laughter; nothing more was seen in it than a reply from the famous Byzantine controversy over the sex of angels. It provoked, however, some serious remarks: that exactitude in psychology involved not only numbers but also, e.g., experimental methodology.

Psychoanalysis was not mentioned. Certainly its position in France has markedly changed in the last 20 years. It is nonetheless true that even today many physicians and psychologists consider it a "wicked science" bordering on fantasy and magic. However, in spite of its humorous form, my intervention was serious; only analysts know the echo which abstract ideas, clear and distinct, can find in the unconscious fantasies. This occasion gave rise to or revived in me the question whether psychoanalysis is a conjectural or an exact science. The purpose of this essay is to show, with the help of sufficiently rich and varied clinical material, in what way and in what measure psychoanalysis is an exact science.

My intention is not to look for exactness elsewhere than in the psychoanalytic technique itself. I am certainly aware that psychoanalysis has been able to find confirmation by recourse to nonpsychoanalytic techniques. I myself have made statistical studies which led to the precise definition of statistical unities extracted from the integral relations of the patient's sayings (1947). On the other hand, nonanalytic methods have been used to obtain experimental confirmation of psychoanalytic concepts (Sears, 1943). Neal Miller, starting from postulates borrowed from psychoanalysis and learning theory, and basing himself on experiments, gave an admirable hypothetico-deductive exposé (in Hunt, 1944). I could also mention the experimental work on the repetition compulsion by Mowrer (1950). More than 10 years ago I founded a Laboratory for Social Psychology which can claim to figure today among the very first in France and perhaps in Europe. However, I shall leave all this to one side, and pose the question concerning the scientific exactness of psychoanalysis strictly with respect to its methods of investigation and proof.

It is nothing new to recall here the analogy which exists between experiment and management in psychoanalysis. In the latter we try to maintain constant the conditions of investigation, such as introducing into the psychoanalytic field only one change at a time, whether it is an interpretation or a material modification, in order to be in a better position to discern its effects and to avoid the confused situations which many simultaneous changes regularly bring about. Thus the basic rules of psychoanalysis—the rule of free-floating attention, the rule of abstinence, and the rule of the minimum—make up the most favorable arrangement for exploring the fantasmatic[1] unconscious, the structure of the psychic apparatus, the topology of the inner world, and so on.

The impersonality of the analyst, the effacement of his individual peculiarities, his anonymity and silence likewise bring him nearer to the experimentalist. He approximates "the man without qualities" of Musil's novel, Der Mann ohne Eigenschaften, "without for that matter losing the fully fresh and vigorous impulse which deserves our

[1] Fantasmatic is a form of mental creativity to be distinguished from imagination or fantasy.

admiration and gives to the individual his flavor and his price" (Hermann Hesse, *Das Glasperlenspiel*).

This impersonality is a matter of contention. The demands of patients lead to certain technical deviations which sometimes result in making the therapist too special a man. Certain Jungians have told me that they do not practice psychotherapy differently from Freudians. However, it is in the Jungian doctrine of psychotherapy that one finds the most highly developed form of the personalization of psychotherapy. Not that the direct confrontation, the exposition of the countertransference, cannot be indicated at certain junctures in psychoanalysis; but "flexibility" ceases to be suppleness when it is applied uniformly to all cases. It becomes a systematic and rigid flexibility. Some years ago I heard a lady in treatment with a Jungian express alarm at the approach of vacation time. Her therapist had confided to her his own distress: "It is not for myself that I am afraid but for him." How much more do we prefer the reply of Ella Sharpe (1937) to a patient who, on the threshold, told her of his horror before the weekend: "Calm yourself, I shall be quite all right." This reply, full of humor and slightly sarcastic, nevertheless also contained an interpretation.

Similarly, the spirit of the principles of psychoanalysis involves a limitation to impersonality. Impersonality is not the ideal of the robot psychoanalyst but rather the fruit of a sublimation. The excess of an affected and put-on impersonality makes him in the end a very personal eccentric. The impersonality of the analyst is not that of a robot. It is much rather an accomplishment beyond the ground rules of transference and countertransference, beyond his narcissistic and sadomasochistic intentions, not through a destruction of his "fantasy" but through its reasoned exploitation. Classic management and elegance of technique aim at an economy of means, at the elimination of seduction and suggestion, but the guiding rules comprising it are amended until they turn to or threaten to turn to obstacles to the progress of treatment. Leaving to one side "borderline" cases in which these improvements may be justified, the rule of the minimum, according to the formula of Hanns Sachs, happily tempers the rule of abstinence on condition that the satisfactions afforded the patient touch on nothing crucial and that they always leave a margin between what is asked for and what is given. More than by "benevolent neutrality," a formula which Freud borrowed, not without humor, from the language of diplomacy and which to that extent is somewhat marked by formalism, the inner attitude of the analyst might be defined by the term "affectionate distance." For my part I do not see how the analyst could do otherwise in the case of sometimes irritating, demanding, and, at certain times, disturbing patients.

The sound rule, however, remains impersonality and the dedication of the analyst to his technical and therapeutic role. The distance could not become too affectionate without having confidential and emotional revelations interfere with the development of the transference neurosis, with the ever clearer expression of fantasies and special demands. The personalization of analysis proceeds from a contemporary myth which places the accent on individuality at the expense of the subject. In a certain political context, the "cult of personality" has been denounced, but personality has also invaded psychological theory and practice. One can only be grateful to Freud for having most frequently, except in his last writings (1940), spoken of the *psychic apparatus*. Such a formula reminds us that personality is a construct, a theoretical model, and that the human being is a complex network of structures, processes, and relations.

This does not mean that analysts harbor the illusion in this respect that the efficiency of investigation and treatment depends on the mechanical application of technical rules which can foresee all eventualities. Analysts begin to realize, for example, that their personal reactions are not limited to a countertransference response to the patient's transference. The analyst also makes a transference onto the analysand and, as a result of this fact, the analysand's transference is more or less widely a countertransference. The absence of any attempt to seduce is, in many cases, a means of seduction. The analyst is a "participant observer"; *objectivity excludes objectivism*, that is, the misunderstanding of the role of the observer in the production, observation, and interpretation of phenomena. This is true even in certain branches of physics.

It is in this way that psychoanalysis has played a considerable role in the methodological refinement of the psychological and social sciences. Its role has been not only to make known facts and ideas. For example, psychoanalysis has certainly contributed to the understanding of the complexity of the "cognitive factor," a concept widely used by psychologists. Less visible though more essential has been its drawing attention to the role of the man of science, of his character, in the orientation, development, and efficiency of his research. Gaston Bachelard (1947), for example, very relevantly showed the infiltration of oral, anal, and genital fantasies in obsolete forms of physics. Yet, what is the status of physics today, whatever our admiration for its discoveries and its efficiency? Physicists are less inclined than is believed to deceive themselves about the exactness of their science, and they are more likely to surrender to fantasy when they risk entering the human field. Many sociologists and ethnologists demand or invoke a psychoanalytic basis. In animal experimentation, the best psychologists have taken into consideration the framework of the laboratory and the person of the experimentalist (Liddell, in Hunt, 1944). For these reasons psychoanalysis plays the role of a pilot discipline in modern science; few scientific disciplines have played a comparable role in the development and refinement of scientific observation.

On the Transference Neurosis: Overdetermination, Inner Consistency, and Validations (Enny's History)

The principal reason why psychoanalysis has functioned as a pilot science, though it has not been recognized as such, is its discovery of the unconscious and fantasmatic the implications of what goes on in the "psychoanalytic field,"[2] above all, the discovery of transferences and countertransferences as much on the analyst's side as on that of the analysand. For the sake of greater precision, I shall speak here of the "transference neurosis." "Transference" is a psychological concept. It is only by abbreviation that analysts speak of transference. It is rather the transference neurosis which concerns them; that is, the "artificial illness" born of the interaction of the disposition to transference and the management of the analysis, the latter functioning as a "precipitating factor" in the transference neurosis (Freud, 1911/15). The transference neurosis is not only an automatic repetition; it is an attempt at restitution, a new effort to pose and resolve unconscious conflicts which have not been resolved. The distinction made by Edward Bibring (1943) between the repetitive tendency and the restitutive tendency, the Zeigarnik effect, whose experimental study (1927) and projective exploitation (Murray et al., 1938) proceed from psychoanalysis and complement each other, contribute to

[2] I call the "psychoanalytic field" the field of communication between the analyst and the analysand.

our understanding that the defeat of infantile sexuality and the narcissistic injury connected with it do not prevent the transference repetition but rather motivate it.

It is frequently difficult to follow its route, difficult for the patient as well as for the analyst, and above all for the beginner who only slowly becomes capable of long-range prediction. I shall give only a few examples, the first, that of an analysis pursued for 6 years. Its great difficulty, the slowness of its development, renders more striking the light which brought the attention to the transference neurosis.

Enny was 28 years old at the time of our first interview. From the age of 17 on, she suffered from very painful obsessions, some of long duration, the others transient. After a difficult early childhood, she suffered, from about 6 years of age, from phobic fears, various ceremonials concerning principally dressing and defecation. Hysteria did not appear to be the core of the obsessional neurosis. Her character was a mixture of such traits as a strong disposition to emotion and passion which gave to her obsessions something dramatic, even theatrical. She was very close to the idea that her obsessions were a defense against emotion. The obsession, she said, is what bars, what interrupts, what prevents contact and life. Not less than her intelligence, her capacity for emotion and passion, the liveliness of her complaints, and her desire to live fully augured favorably for her capacity to change, however great her fear of any change was. She belonged to a middle-class family not free of neurosis, and was a highly specialized technician. This profession had been the object of a sudden, impulsive choice completely baffling to her, and the analysis of this showed much later that it had been determined by dominating fantasies. In the conjunction made up by the profession itself and her employer, she had found a counterpoint for most of the fantasmatic structures[3] which dominated her unconscious: union with parents themselves united, envy of and desire for a penis, return into her mother's body.

The choice of an analyst made her enter at first into the transference neurosis. She had already been treated, about 10 years before, first by a sorcerer's apprentice, then by a new and inexperienced analyst who had the caution to apply what he had been taught. But more wisdom and art were required: too rigid a technique resulted, after

[3] Fantasmatic structures can be either unconscious or preconscious, but not conscious. They can be investigated by means of constructions.

about 2 years, in a state of great hostility and blockage. Subsequently she consulted many analysts. Not one accepted her; or, more probably, she accepted none of them. She accepted me because, among other reasons, the colleague who sent her to me was a woman. This circumstance had provisionally removed a difficulty—the fear of inhibition and interruption; from the first year of the treatment onward, many dreams—the very first dream itself—revealed a woman interposing herself aggressively between Enny and the father figure she sought to join.

Another transference manifestation arose before the beginning of the treatment. It seemed to her radically incompatible to go into analysis and to remain at her factory. With the same impulsiveness with which she had chosen her profession, she quit the job she had held for many years and to which she was strongly attached. For a rather long time, she continued to work as a specialist in another factory under conditions which were doubtless less favorable. After many attempts, she finally quit her job again, giving up the profession she loved so much to become a billing clerk. She very strongly resented the mediocrity, even the abjection, in her eyes at least, of this new position. It was for her analysis, for the analyst, that she made this sacrifice, thus setting herself up as the poor victim of a monster with exorbitant demands, but seeking at the same time to inculpate the analyst. In fact, she had done no more than go to the end, but in an opposite sense, of the obsessional incompatibility, which she had resented from the beginning, between the exercise of her profession and the psychoanalytic treatment.

Very soon also appeared anxiety and inhibition so that, after the first meetings, I allowed her to leave the couch. Thus the analysis continued with Enny sitting up and facing me, and without my trying to force her difficulty in speaking, without my taking refuge in too radical a silence. Because of the very fact of her ambivalence, she was forced to idealize the analyst. For a long time, she spoke of the "perfection of the transference." Then she abandoned that term. The analogy between her attitude toward her mother and her attitude toward the analyst was so striking that she could admit it was "transference love" only by conceding that her love for the analyst was not "being love" ("*amour-être*"), a term she invented to distinguish it from the "object-love" ("*amour d' objet*"),[4] according to her less

---

[4] This terminology was her own one and in no way the psychoanalytic one.

profound, which she had been able to experience or which she happened afterward to feel for other men. This love appeared to be in contradiction, if not with her demands and claims, with her phases of opposition and moments of violence. That hostility she wanted only to attribute to the transference, more easily to the father transference, finding then in the idea of transference a defense against the present and actual reality of her hostility and her sadomasochistic fantasies.[5] Little by little, a dominant fantasmatic structure emerged: the lively apprehension of an interruption during reciprocal union with the loved object. Obsession was what interrupted "contact," that is, emotional communication not only with people but with her inarticulate environment, nature, certain sights whose fascination for her she did not understand. Masturbation, which she finally came to talk about, was also a thing she experienced in the fear of interruption, exclusively in dreams, not when she masturbated awake. The day she spoke of this for the first time, she lived through the session in the anxious fear of an interruption, noticing the slightest noise, whereas she knew from experience that our meetings were never interrupted. To tell the truth, she was rarely alone with her analyst, fantasying the presence of witnesses, especially of the "chorus of ladies of the family," whatever prevented her unconscious desire to masturbate before the analyst, and the analyst from masturbating before her, although in a dream her mother would have been there as a witness.

As the analysis progressed, the hold of the separation anxiety became less constraining, although it developed later into a form more threatening to the treatment. Enny took up the idea of seeing, in the frame of her Parisian life, her mother, various members of her family, all living in the "provinces," whereas, during the first years of her independent life in Paris she had established a rigorous isolation which she alone had the right to break by visiting her relatives. It was thus her claims on and her movements of hostility toward the analyst which helped her approach her old place of work and her former employer, which at first showed itself in dreams in the clearest fashion when she was dissatisfied with her analyst. The interpretation of this material brought out nostalgia, the desire to return to something which had been a replica of her childhood, of her union with her

---

[5] A piece of daydreaming was the fantasy of eating the analyst, first the hair and finally the toes.

united parents, but which the incompatibility between love for the father and love for the mother had disturbed. In fact, she sharply reproached herself for her father's death, which occurred when she was 17. This death was closely followed by a dream of consummated incest which she had never been able to confess to her mother.[6] From that time on, she had felt a weight on her breast. Without doubt that had been the principal precipitating factor of the adult neurosis; in the first obsession the incompatibility had been displaced onto a story about some books which were given to her: four when she wanted only one.

The incompatibility apparently continued to diminish. Enny resumed friendly relations with her former employer, but he did not rehire her. He did not raise the question, and Enny did not dare to ask him, attributing the reticence of her former employer to the interference of "the big one," that is, his wife. Then she began to look for other employment in her specialty with little enough conviction, always finding obstacles, usually real difficulties of distance and schedule onto which she displaced the fantasmatic incompatibility of analysis and profession. Finally, she accepted a position in a sound enterprise. She had known its director in the first factory where she worked. She again found enthusiastically the profession which she loved so much. However, something was lacking: the presence of her former employer. She herself perceived the movement by which she displaced this lack onto a great obsession; she was all the more uncomfortable because she was in direct touch with the realistic controls which she had to deal with. Patient and minute analytic labor left no doubt about it: her obsession made her find anew the primal scene she did not realize she was seeking—union with her parents united to each other, the fantasy of being inside her mother's body.

However precise these interpretations were, they appeared to change nothing in the current great obsession. Enny understood. It was so logical that she could not deny it. She herself provided unexpected confirmation, but, she said, she felt nothing and remembered nothing. Logically, yet to the astonishment of the analyst, the obsession disappeared as it had come. Just as Enny had displaced onto her

[6] During the treatment an exact replica of this dream recurred: the sexual partner was the father himself.

work the sorrow she experienced because of the absence of her former employer, so also the obsession disappeared as she began to become attached to her new employer. He was a good, intelligent man, a bachelor, in some way a mysogynist. He watched closely over Enny's work, talked with her, frequently took her to town since the factory was rather far from Paris. But how was she to reconcile this growing attachment with her feeling for the analyst, a feeling which Enny obstinately maintained had not changed in any way? Once again Enny got out of the difficulty by isolation: her feeling for the analyst was "being-love"; her attachment for her employer was only "object-love." Since, however, she found "contact" in this relationship, that is, intellectual and emotional communication, the impression of living to which she clung above all else, the contact was upset by her tension over her obsessions, interrupted by these obsessions and, most of all, by "flash-ideas" (or "arrow-ideas"), above all by the untimely return of a surname which had once been given to her employer and which implied a doubt about his sexual orientation. Thus Enny, without knowing it, sought to avoid competition with a woman as she did to elevate the role of the penis in the lovers' relations. Several dreams left no doubt about the soundness of this interpretation.

But the more friendly her relationship with the new employer became and the more Enny became attached to him, the more pronounced became the incompatibility and the more active the anxiety over interruption. Then things began all over again. Enny could not give up her work and her employer. Here she found "contact" and pleasure in living, though with some limitations. The fantasy of interruption was projected onto analysis; it was the analyst who was the interrupting agent and it was the analysis which she had, actively, to interrupt.

This time, however, she was in analysis and analysis helped her to self criticism. If Enny *felt* that she had to interrupt the analysis, she *judged*—and probably felt to a small extent—that she could not do so, that it was "her only lifesaver." Enny asked to interrupt her treatment for 2 months, but this was something like a legal fiction. It would be decided that we would stop for 2 months but we would begin again in 2 days. Enny herself smiled at this deceit. Moreover, two occasional interruptions of the analysis, one because of a short vacation she took, the other on account of a short but distant mission on the analyst's part, made her reflect. In the course of these interruptions of the analysis, both of which involved her missing two or three sessions, Enny realized that the temporary but effective interruption of the analysis in no way stopped the obsessional interruption either of the "contact" or of the pleasure she found in the activities which she preferred. It was therefore from her and her alone that the interruption came.

Abandoned for a short time, the idea of interrupting her analysis reappeared very quickly when her employer's attitude, while remaining within the bounds of friendship, became more affectionate and intimate. Enny felt a lively sexual emotion. Then again she thought eagerly about interrupting the treatment, for her "destiny" was certainly to "live" what brought her existence and to live it fully, not in tension and the watchfulness required to repulse every obsessional interference.

I let things go along patiently without taking her at her word when she spoke of stopping and I did not try to keep her. Finally, Enny seemed to realize that she could neither give up her work nor interrupt her analysis. Her "destiny" was not to give herself entirely, in so far as her obsessions allowed, to the opportunities life offered her but rather to confront this mysterious incompatibility between her work and analysis, an incompatibility which she solved, at the beginning of the treatment, by giving up her job and her first employer. To interrupt the analysis would only be to repeat, to "begin again," but this time in the opposite direction.

There we are, after 6 years of regular analysis, in spite of considerable material, in spite of resistances and silences to which I shall return shortly. Not all this material can be deciphered, but the main lines of the analytic route can be disengaged. Rather soon, during the course of the 2nd year, I had realized the dominant character of the fantasy of being interrupted in reciprocal fusion with the love object. Continuation of the analysis showed how basic was the "fantasmatic" of interruption. It was also expressed in the major phases of the transference neurosis. It was made evident by the incompatibility between "work *plus* employer" on the one hand and "analysis *plus* analyst" on the other. At the outset, Enny tried to escape from this incompatibility by giving up her work and her employer. As the incompatibility and the fear of interruption grew weaker, she drew little by little closer to "work *plus* employer"; she drew so very close that it was then the "analysis *plus* analyst" which she thought of withdrawing from. She is today fighting with the conflict and, it would seem, is in a position to face up to it.

What is at the root of the problem? Without doubt, the choice between the mother and the father and oral-sadistic fantasies concerned with the penis. In this respect, "work *plus* employer" had been found to offer a symbolic expression of intimate union with father and mother united to each other. This was also what made analysis possible, since a woman had sent Enny to me; but the "analysis *plus* analyst" did not have the same incantatory force as the first. The consenting woman was effaced in favor of the woman as obstacle, in favor of the wife of the analyst, of whose existence Enny was aware and whom she had occasionally seen.[7] To the impossibility of choosing between father and mother were connected the complications of masculine and feminine identifications, of phallic and castrated positions, and, more deeply, of penis envy and the desire for a penis. Enough data have been collected to form the hypothesis of work from an infantile sexual theory reflecting sadomasochistic and oral intentions pointing toward the paternal or maternal penis. But just as one obsession can serve on occasion as a defense against another obsession and diminish the pressure of the latter, so also obsessions, above all, great obsessions, remain a defense against the "unknown crime" which distressed Enny more than incest and which had been vouched for only by dreams of heterosexual coitus whose sadomasochistic tonality was only indicated (the difficulty in penetrating of too large a penis). The "unknown crime" no doubt was the "original wording" (*Wortlaut*) of the obsession.

A Psychoanalytic Session: The History of Puff

Our progressive steps lead us (after having talked of the management of analysis and its course as the transference neurosis reveals them) to the detailed recital of an analytic session. I shall take it from the history of a patient in the course of his 2nd year of analysis. He is a relatively untalkative subject—and we shall later discover the reason why. This circumstance leads me to intervene rather often to mark the stages of a discourse which is sufficiently clear analytically. Another gain here lies in not overweighting and slowing up our exposition by the details of too abundant material.

[7] Certain data which I cannot cite show that the second employer, the object of her passion, represented at once both the analyst and the analyst's wife.

Puff was a man about 40 years old. It is of some importance that he was sent to me by one of his friends, my former patient, who, after a difficult adolescence, had entered upon a brilliant, successful professional career. Puff was a well-built person, tall and thin, with excellent manners, a bit formal and shy, with an intelligent and keen if not vigorous and fertile mind. He belonged to an upper-class family in which he was the third and last son. He did not lack money and his relatives had helped him find a social position, but he was stagnating in a subordinate role and not earning very much. There was a reason for this since he turned up his nose at his studies and, at one point, at an attractive job, but one as little remunerative as it was likely to satisfy his family. Then he set himself in order, married, had several children. The first interviews were enough to make it clear that what he resented as mediocrity and defeat centered about an ambivalent conflict with his father, an important and rich businessman, then very old. On the surface, Puff could not abide his father. He blamed him for not having loved or esteemed him; for instance, for not having complimented and encouraged him on the occasion of certain scholastic successes which the father had, on the contrary, belittled. In fact, what Puff was looking for was his father's love and consideration. He came so that, thanks to another father, he might develop and improve himself, cease to be a little boy and become a man, rise socially, and earn a great deal of money. Although he was very sensible, what he expected from the analyst was a miracle. The treatment developed as might have been foreseen, that is, by his defense against a transference love such as I have rarely observed among male patients. The existence of homosexual fantasies was not in question; for instance, he brought up a dream in which one of his business connections, an older man, sucked his penis. In another, there were the analyst's advances against which he had to defend himself. The session to be reported occurred about 16 months after the beginning of the treatment; an abstract of it was made as soon as the patient left.

As usual, Puff begins by being silent for a rather long time. He cannot expose himself to direct talk with the analyst but only "by delay," simultaneously inhibited and sustained by the thought that he must *interest* the analyst.

Puff: . . . I feel that I shall have nothing to say today.
I: How do we know?

Puff: If I had done something bad, I could not talk to you about it because I want you to maintain your sympathy and esteem for me. I know very well, however, that you will say nothing and will not criticize at all.

I: But you are not sure of what I shall think even if I say nothing?

Puff: . . . Not you especially but respectable people, for instance, one of my directors, the one I find *interesting* . . . my superior, just above me, I detest him and he doesn't *interest* me. It's indifferent to me what he thinks. . . .

I: You mention only men as likely to judge you badly.

Puff: Not only men. It could also be women, but respectable women. . . . Well, women who would be a little like men. . . .

I: In fact, you are trying to drown the fish and suppress the fact that it is with respect to the psychoanalyst that you felt yourself in the wrong at the very time when this action was taking place. . . .

Puff: . . . No. If I had committed a sexual act it would be anybody. . . . In fact, it is a sexual action. I have deceived my wife without feeling at all guilty, but while doing it, I thought I wouldn't tell you about it.

I: That is why, at the beginning of the session, you had the impression that you would have nothing to tell me today.

Puff: I do not feel guilty. It's more complicated. I think that the psychoanalyst thinks that I think that the psychoanalyst might think that I think he is jealous of me. It's crazy.

I: Crazy or not, perhaps it means something just the same.

Puff: I don't know. I think that you are *interested* in me, that you don't want me to think of anything except the analysis; for instance, like deceiving my wife. . . .

I: Even before analysis you had escapades. Three months ago when you told me of a new adventure, you didn't think of the analyst.

Puff: That's not the same thing. Besides, to tell the truth, I've never deceived my wife. Those were never affairs, just passing fancies. . . .

I: And this time it's not a passing fancy?

Puff: Yes.

I: Now, you do not feel greater guilt toward your wife?

Puff: No, it's with respect to you.

I: If you had an affair with a woman whom you wanted, you would not feel unfaithful to your wife but to your mistress. You have the idea that I might be jealous, that I expect you to be faithful to me. Your analysis is for your unconscious an extramarital affair, the partner in which is your analyst. You protect yourself from such an idea. But in fact you love the analyst and you want to be loved by him. That is why you feel guilty for having deceived him.

The movement of the session is remarkably clear; it is easy to reconstruct it:

—Initial defense by a reticence sustained by resistance properly so called: fantasmatic and criticized fear of being badly judged by the analyst.

—Abatement of the defense by an interpretation.

—An attempt to weaken resistance, to deprive it of specificity (fantasmatic and criticized fear of being badly judged by the analyst).

—Interpretation of the defense by the weakening of guilt in the eyes of all "respectable people."

—Defense maintained but attenuated allows the patient to confess the nature of his self reproach: a sexual action.

—Interpretation of the initial defense.

—Admission of the fantasy of the analyst's jealousy, rationalization of the fantasy.

—The analyst notices that the sexual action in question is not fantasied as a fault except in the analyst's eyes.

—Denial of unfaithfulness with respect to the wife (the distinction between an affair and a passing fancy). Recognition of guilt with respect to the analyst.

—Final intrepretation: analysis fantasied as an extramarital affair with the analyst.

Someone will say perhaps that this is too easy, superficial, even that it is not "psychoanalytic." I do not think so: such a session is centered about the chief demand of the patient and its fantasmatic basis: to be lovingly and passionately loved by the father, a passive, homosexual, and feminine position, against which the patient protects himself. The analyst's method aims at bringing to light as precisely as possible the patient's unconscious desire, the defense which this desire gives rise to, the obstacle which this conflict between desire and defense constitutes with respect to the progress of the treatment and, as we shall see in a moment, the application of the fundamental rule.

A Very Ordinary Word, "Interesting." Return to the Respective Histories of Puff and Enny

In the account of a session borrowed from Puff's analysis, I have several times underlined Puff's use of the verb "to interest," and to its derivations. Interest, to interest, to be interested, interesting, to make oneself interesting—these are all ordinary terms. They cease being so by the unusual frequency with which Puff had recourse to them. The context reveals their hidden sense. Other analyses demonstrate the generality of the phenomenon. Passing from the analytic session to the details of the material, we turn to the language of the analysand and the vocabulary he uses. I return to some aspects of Puff's history.

For a long time, Puff was at first "a good little boy." The youngest of three sons, he had no opportunity to learn the difference between the sexes and there is no logical difficulty in admitting that, for him, implicitly, the possession of a penis by women and little girls was never in doubt. In his 6th or 7th year, he was seduced by a grown man in the following manner: it was one of his grandfather's employees in a huge country house. This man was popular with children. Things remained within bounds until one day he unbuttoned his trousers and exhibited before Puff a penis which seemed immense to the little boy, and he masturbated. The demonstration completed, Puff began to masturbate with a good deal of pleasure, most often alone, but also with boys his own age or slightly older. As for girls, having discovered that they had no penis and thus, as he believed, no possibility of pleasure, he began to despise them. They were not *interesting* or, rather, *amusing*, for, if he knew the word "interesting," it was "a word for grownups" and he did not yet have the right to use it. After a delayed puberty and a prolonged adolescence he had rare homosexual adventures in which he played the passive role typical of the ephebe. But he was also solicited by women. He liked them young, pretty, and seductive, but above all, with something masculine in their physical type, the cut of their hair, their character, even their first names. He suffered from no impotence either in satisfying himself or them in the most ordinary way, but his preferences did not lie here. What he liked above all, what, in analysis, he declared he would never give up, was to seduce a woman, preferably a young girl or an innocent young woman, to lead her gently to the point of masturbating in front of him while he at the same time masturbated in front of her. The thing remained *interesting* so long as it remained within the limits of a "stage setting." It ceased to be so when the woman, getting into the act, let herself go, thus causing an irruption in the stage setting of his fantasy, no longer the actress whose role he had defined but a beast of pleasure, independent of him. Thus, although Puff no longer had any sexual relations with men, although he got along well with his wife and occasionally with other women, woman was *"interesting"* only in so far as the sight of her clitoral masturbation made her a replica of a man masturbating.

But matters did not stop there. Though Puff no longer had homosexual relations, he continued to be interested in men, or at least in certain men. They were "older" men, not necessarily chronologically, but superior intellectually, men with knowledge and degrees, secure in high social position but also courteous, likable men, without arrogance, in whose eyes he himself could pass as interesting. One rarely sees, I believe, the homosexual fantasy transposed with such precision into social feelings.

The analyst was also an interesting man; everything he said was important and one had to interest him. Thus it is that Puff's homosexual position with respect to the analyst was transposed into his difficulty in speaking; he could not say just anything at all. He had to say *interesting* things. This unreasonable demand relative to speech, which brings to light its phallic echo, leads back to Enny's history.

With Enny the speech difficulty obviously concerned the fundamental rule, a difficulty very common in obsessives. The most classic defensive conflict was perfectly conscious. What was in her mind was stupid, displaced, without interest. She felt ashamed or guilty at having such thoughts. If she told them, the analyst would no longer love her. He would ridicule her or become irritated.[8] The analyst therefore had to question her, extort replies, open her up. Sometimes she announced that it would suddenly happen some day like a load which she had to get rid of by vomiting or by an enormous defecation. More often, she compared her difficulty to what might pass intimately between a man and a woman. Preliminaries were necessary. The man could not at the outset throw the woman on a bed and possess her. This sexual significance of speech permitted us to return with more precision to Enny's sexual position.

Consciously, Enny assumed a feminine position. She had desires, she would have liked to make love with a man and conceive a child by him, provided she loved the child's father. But, according to her, she

---

[8] Enny sought to explain rationally the discomfort which obsessions introduced into her communication with her friends: if her obsession made it difficult for *her* to talk, her own discomfort upset her interlocutor and the conversation stopped. But that was not the true explanation. Very early, she believed strongly that if she had a bad thought, that is, an obsessive idea, automatically, without knowing anything about it, and as a result of the fact of the magical power she attributed to thought, her interlocutor ceased to love her.

was incapable of giving pleasure as a woman, of becoming the object of a man's love and desire. Moreover, she did not like women and did not want to be like them. Women were futile, lugubrious, vengeful, sticky, *"casse-pied."* She certainly had some women friends, but her true friends were men. She herself dressed, if not in a masculine fashion, at least soberly, even poorly. She wanted nothing to do with any clothing which revealed her shape and it was only after several years of analysis that she introduced into her dress more care and imagination, which, in her eyes, was daring. She never wore jewelry; she used no makeup. She wore flat shoes except on special occasions.

Her unconscious position was dominated by her desolation at having, in place of a penis, a hole which sometimes seemed the fearsome crater of a volcano. Her penis envy was allied to the sadomasochistic fantasy of being raped and killed by a man. Her overestimation of the phallus was such that when she became attached to her second employer, beginning with certain rumors which had formerly been current and not only to protect herself from the idea of a rival, "flash-ideas" which disturbed her so much expressed neatly the homosexuality which her unconscious fantasy lent to this employer; so that, in her dreams, the rival appeared several times as a man. The homosexual relations which her dreams attributed to her employer consisted of an oral-sadistic aggression of the penis which left traces of bloody saliva on the pillow. This was a symptom which she had initially experienced in her own case and which she had associated with the theory of sexual relations, a fantasy which she subsequently eliminated by substituting for it the reasonable explanation of gingivitis.

This feminine demand which she disapproved of she acted out on the couch without in the least realizing that she was developing attitudes to the analyst which she condemned in women. But she protected herself against the idea that the analyst could love and desire her. That would be as if a *street sweeper* had declared his love to the Queen of England. More often and not without obstinacy, penis envy, transparent in the metaphor of the street sweeper, expressed itself in a comparison with Simone de Beauvoir. Simone de Beauvoir would have been able to declare herself to the analyst. She was a graduate in philosophy, she was a famous writer. Enny herself had no degree, was ignorant, she had nothing, she was nothing. Often her fantasies of being castrated turned against the analyst: she would have liked him to be as miserable as she was, abandoned, deprived of everything.

It is in the context of the phallic-castrated opposition that Enny's inability or refusal to observe the fundamental rule is rooted. To utter everything which came to her mind would have been to utter nonsense, uninteresting things, as women do. The analyst could only ridicule her, even become annoyed, that is, castrate her or confirm an already accomplished castration. She therefore had to choose what was important and to say only interesting things, things which men expect; that is to say, show herself to the analyst not as castrated but as phallic. She triumphed on the day when her second employer confided to her that women for him were only a means of relief, not even of pleasure, and that he had no way of conversing with them, which recalls a French proverb: "Be beautiful and be quiet."

I could multiply examples. With women in analysis, I have often observed a concern to interest the analyst in conjunction with castration anxiety and the phallic demand. When the patient demands the right to conduct her analysis herself and choose the material which appears important to her, the contribution of this material may be fantasied as a bomb which the patient throws into the analytic field. In a complementary fashion, the analyst's speech is often fantasied as fertilizing speech. The patient, grappling with a resistance, tries to persuade the analyst to talk. He has only to say a word and it will be the germ which she will make fruitful in the same way in which, when the employer throws out an idea, it is his secretary who makes something of that idea.

The same fantasies are observable in men, even those of fecundation in connection with an unconscious feminine position. I shall cite only one case because the word "interesting" appears here in a slightly different way. He was an intelligent, keen, educated man. His problems centered around the same phallic-castrated opposition. If he happened to show himself intelligent, energetic, and efficient, he ran the risk of symbolically castrating the analyst, which he feared above all, for he needed to believe in the latter's strength. It remained for him to castrate himself by casting doubt on the interest of what he had accomplished and discussed. Through the progress of an analysis in which his recantations did not cease to slow up the outcome in a more articulated fantasy, he arrived, however, at situating very exactly certain aspects of his behavior on the day when he said "that it no longer interested him to play at being interesting," which meant that his castration no longer caused him enough anxiety so that he had to exhibit himself as symbolically phallic.

In current speech, "interesting" is an overworked and common word. This is not the case in analytic investigation. Its ties with the phallic fantasy, whether in its direct sexual form or in a sublimated and social form, leave no doubt. Its semantic relationship with terms such as "investment" and "cathexis" opens a theoretical problem which would be beyond the scope of this essay.

On the clinical and technical level, the study of the word "interesting" shows the attention which the analyst must bring to the language of his patients and the precision with which he can determine the fantasied meaning of terms which seem on first analysis abstract and banal. Words are for the most part worn-out pictures whose abstract and objective sense appears only in ordinary conversation. It becomes the analyst's business to prick up his ears when recourse to a certain word seems too frequent or too odd. Through the lever of that word, it happens that *what is thought unconsciously* slips into what the analysand *thinks consciously* and wants to say, as is the case with slips of the tongue and puns in dreams. A valuable practice, so long as it does not go to the length of systematically sacrificing the *signified* for the *signifying*, an excess in which it is the theoretical presuppositions and the fantasies of the analyst himself which are revealed.

I shall complete this study of the word "interesting" by a personal story, both old and recent, which will introduce us to new questions.

One summer day my wife, who is also an analyst, and I went to dine in a restaurant, the almost complete emptiness of which created a strange atmosphere. This impression was reinforced in that, through the window, we could follow the maneuvers of a streetwalker (in French slang, *une clocharde*) so accomplished that she had the aura of having been disguised and of inventing her role for a film. We decided to spend the early part of the afternoon at the cinema and to see Ingmar Bergman's *Silence*, which our patients had not allowed us to ignore.

The story takes place in a few days. With remarkable ease, Bergman condenses in that time most of the themes of the analytic fantasy. The author seems to have had recourse to all the techniques of what I call the "panoply of condensed psychoanalysis." One hears only the talking, shouting, crying, even pleasurable moaning, of two hysterical sisters, one homosexual and jealous of her younger sister, the other

deliberately and defensively attracted to men. The father appears as
a superior valet in a dress coat and black tie whose obliging, benevolent, even affectionate interventions prevent the worst and moderate
the outbursts of these ladies. Not that there is not an attempt at the
seduction by this valet of the most silent of the characters, a little boy
of 6 or 7 years of age. An event to which he is doubtless no stranger
helps him escape as it does from the attempt of a troop of dwarfs who
at one point dress him up in a pretty, billowing gown which reaches
to his feet. The little boy is silent: he sees everything, understands
everything, knows everything, and says nothing except to speak on
occasion in the manner of the little boy in Andersen's story who
destroys the adults' illusion by declaring, "The emperor has nothing
on." Through the long corridors of a large hotel, he walks on cat's
feet, his toy pistol in his hand. Occasionally he frightens the men
there, for example, surprising a Turk on a ladder in the act of polish-
ing a chandelier.

On returning to our home, we talked about the film, not without
criticizing it. I no longer know by what bypaths I came to tell a story
of my youth. In my 20th year, I was often invited by an uncle who
had married a singer and who lived grandly. It was a small dinner for
four, in evening dress. The guest of honor was a rather old musician
who had once been famous as a composer and conductor. He had the
air of stepping right out of the *Belle Epoque* (and it is from that
period that my uncle's style of living derived). The man was in formal
dress with white tie. His still rather abundant white hair, arranged
with a part, fell in a manner at once negligent and studied. His mus-
tache also fell, as did the monocle he wore, hanging from a ribbon of
black watered silk. After a delicious meal with good wines, after the
liqueurs, he retired early and a little disarrayed. Saying good-bye to
me, he pressed my hand in his and spoke: "You *interest me* very much,
my child." Once the door closed, my aunt laughed: "You understood?" she asked. I answered phlegmatically: "Of course."

When I told my wife this story, she did not frown. The intervention in daily life of frequently wild analytic interpretations might
be considered a childish disease of analysts if one did not all too often
see the habit persist in experienced analysts with whom, after all, it is
not impossible that it expresses the "mind of childhood" but not in
what the latter may possess, which is estimable, lovable, and exquisite.
My wife and I adhere to the principle of not using analytic interpreta-

tions in our personal conversation, especially if there is some disagreement between us. But this time there was no disagreement. After a period of silent reflection, she said to me, using the very terms of my aunt in the story I had told her, "You understood?" Silent in my turn, I replied a moment later: "Of course. The valet in full dress in Bergman's film was the old musician and I saw myself in the little boy."

"Figments,"[9] *Memories, Fantasmatic Structures, and Mnemic Structures. Concerning Outer Confirmation. Figments in the Shape of a Bell*

The isomorphism of my youthful memory and the attempted seduction of the little boy by the valet had unconsciously led me to relate the youthful memory to my wife. This isomorphism thus introduces us to the last part of this study: certain relations of our figments and memories with fantasmatic and mnemic structures. It also takes another path. The material which I shall set forth concerns figments in the shape of a bell. The bell shape is presented at least twice in Bergman's *Silence;* once when the dwarfs clothe the little boy in a long and billowing court dress, and again when the little boy shoots his gun at the Turk on the ladder while he is cleaning a chandelier hanging from the ceiling and more or less swaying like the clapper of a bell. Moreover, during the luncheon which preceded the film, a luncheon which the small number of patrons and the maneuvers of the streetwalker had enveloped in an odd atmosphere, out of key but not disconcerting, the shape of the bell had already been evoked not only by the single word *clocharde,* but also because this streetwalker was dressed in a sort of overcoat I had never seen before which fell to the ground, widening gradually toward its base. I shall precede the exposition of the material with a few general remarks.

"Constructions in Analysis" is not only one of the last writings of Freud (1937), it is one of his most exact and decisive on the nature and the extent of psychoanalytic investigation. Freud there gives evidence of the relative failure of the recall of childhood experiences in the course of treatment and of the prevalence of construction as compared to interpretation. In psychoanalytic investigation we always

---

[9] "Figment" translates the French *fiction.* It designates the productions of fantasmatic activity, derivatives of the unconscious mental activity in thought, speech or action, whether accompanied by belief (dream or delusion) or acted out, revealing unconscious wishes.

reconstruct. The analyst proceeds by inference. What he interprets or constructs is behind what is explicitly formulated by the patient. But our constructions or reconstructions are located on two levels. We grasp in *statu nascendi* the movement of unconscious thought or of the process of fantasies, starting with limited material. This is the proper time for reconstructive interpretations, which are not really constructions. The construction *regroups* a series of partial and confluent interpretations; however, it deals not with the movement of the unconscious thoughts or with the "fantasy process," but with the structures of the dominant fantasies and their interlocking in a whole. Our desire to link constructs to actual experiences of childhood and to obtain the recall of the latter is often frustrated or, as Freud points out, the evoked memories bear on what is incidental, not on what is central. This is not to say that such a goal is never reached. For instance, many patients never arrive at any memory of childhood or adolescent masturbation, and we have no way of proving that they are wrong when they assert that they have never practiced it. But on many occasions, usually in connection with a dream, the analyst succeeds in reconstructing the equivalents of childhood masturbation, in making the patient again find the diffuse pleasure which accompanied the representations in question: forgetfulness of time, sadomasochistic, sexual impregnation fantasies which accompanied forepleasure. These fantasies are often acted out, mixed with the fear of being discovered, followed by a diffuse uneasiness colored by shame or guilt. In Enny's case, e.g., the type of ecstasy which she experienced in her childhood when confronted with certain enigmatic sights or natural sights (the contemplation of a beautiful tree) was regularly accompanied by the fear of being discovered and interrupted. In other, rarer cases, we receive external confirmation from childhood witnesses and this permits us to consider the object of constructions as a structure both fantasmatic and mnemic. Such is the point I should like to develop: the extremely precocious character of mnemic experiences and structures which construction can arrive at. The material will be borrowed from my own analysis, that is, my didactic analysis, the first one.

I had chosen Dr. Rudolph M. Loewenstein, basing my choice on his reputation and on the advice of a friend. My analysis took place from 1933 until the end of 1936, with a single interruption of a few weeks.

My father had been a prestigious and powerful person to me.

Always dressed in a black frock coat and wearing a top hat as was then the custom for men of a somewhat prominent position, he inculcated in me "the best feelings" which were his own: honor and fatherland, "Long Live the Army," protection of the widow and orphan (he was a lawyer), heroism (I was still only a child when he recited long passages of Corneille's *Le Cid* to me). He loved me very much, perhaps too much, sometimes allowing himself to criticize my mother and then using overly tender words with me, which left me amazed and silent. He had a long illness which somewhat depressed me, during my prepuberty years, and I resented him for dying too soon and abandoning me. My mother was a devoted mother, especially when I was ill. Although she always defended herself against my teasing on the subject, she preferred her other son, my junior by less than a year, who remained for a longer period her little boy and was more tender to her. I found compensation through a nurse who was proud of me and for whom I remained solicitous after she had left us. My maternal grandmother also preferred me, was also proud of me and of my scholastic success. For her I was the reincarnation of her husband, whom I did not remember at all but whom a photograph showed in school uniform, his arms loaded with prizes. These circumstances eased the management of my rivalry with my brother, to whom I abandoned my mother like an indulgent husband who, busy with "*interesting*" things, allows his wife to become impassioned over their child. Very soon, I had other interests: studies, games of soldiers, and building, design and painting, music, reading, verses. I liked to play with my companions, gladly commanding those of my own age, protecting the younger, especially those entrusted to me, above all, little girls with whom I discouraged a few rare and naïve attempts at seduction with gentle firmness, but not without some flames which brought about daydreams like that in which a total destruction of humanity and culture left me alone with one of them, in an artificial grotto, having saved, from all books, only a geometry text. When my father died, I reinforced my firm attitude: I became the protector of the widow and of the orphan, which means that I identified myself more strongly with the ideal father, who was considered to be, because of his profession, "the protector of the widow and of the orphan."

In my analysis, Loewenstein seems to have been for me less a father than an older brother, thus returning to the fraternal situation which had been mine. He behaved like a protective older brother, only in a negative way, that is, by being conciliatory, not seeking to compete with me in the ingenuity of interpretations of which he was very sparing. Rivalry was compensated for by the fact that if he was much farther advanced than I in psychoanalysis, I was farther along in a medical career. However, I looked for his weak points, suspecting him of napping during sessions, criticizing his taste for detective stories (he had left some lying about on a worktable)—with some hypocrisy since I was far from scorning such reading matter. The fraternal character of this rivalry does not seem doubtful to me. In the course of this analysis, I had a dream which took me to a beach to which my oldest memories are attached. I was going to bathe; I met my mother and reassured her. She was terribly worried, believing that my brother had been carried off by the tide. This rivalry expressed itself clearly in the transference. I envied my analyst for certain social and professional relationships.

I accepted my analyst's decision when he suggested the termination of my analysis, after a dream in which I had identified myself with Freud. I was fully alive, I was happy, everything was going smoothly, and I derived great pleasure from the reception which my analyst and other colleagues accorded to the presentation of my first psycho-analytic papers in 1937.

Although the analysis was interrupted, I nonetheless reproached my analyst for having given me up, for taking another patient in my place, perhaps as I had likewise reproached my father, perhaps as I had likewise reproached my mother. Then the friendly sharing of the same professional life, the serious events which we both encountered separately but which sustained us when circumstances brought us together again, created other links between us.

I have thus traced out the large outlines of the memory I retain of my training analysis, perhaps with some complacency. Without less complacency, I excuse myself by saying that it is rare for an analyst to give evidence from his own analysis. And I come to that with respect to which the sketch of this analysis was only an intro-duction, namely, fantasies, or better, figments in the shape of a bell. They show that the analysis had gone further than I had realized. Loewenstein was enough struck by it to suggest to me that I find a way of publishing these results, something he could not do himself. Until now I have never done so. I did not clearly understand their range. I did not consider the thing as interesting as research I had then under-taken. Or I did not like to talk about myself even in a disguised form. It was still too near or else it displeased me to take for myself what I wanted Loewenstein to look upon as a common possession. After hav-ing thought that he had forgotten these bell-shaped fantasies, I was satisfied when he remembered them. If I were to risk a hypothesis, I would say that the insistent return of bell-shaped figments in my analysis, my pleasure in reporting them, in finding new expressions of them and new origins, was for me a way of forcing my analyst to *interest himself* in something which had played a role in my most distant past.

It is today impossible for me to reconstruct the multiple and varied material, dreams, daydreams, flash-ideas, through which I struggled to break my analyst's silent listening, to find again and again the fascinating bell shape.

One thing was certain, which is that it referred to my father, whose penis I had once had occasion to observe. Much later, in the course of my medical studies, I was struck by the expression "a rod (penis) like a bell-clapper" (*une verge "en battant de cloche"*), even more struck when I observed this phenomenon among some of my patients or the medically different but morphologically similar phe-nomenon of paraphimosis.

The maternal reference was equally clear: very early enlightened by certain prayers, I had refuted the fables of the birth of children, fables which I had believed in strongly enough to tear up a cabbage patch (in France one used to tell children that boys were born in cabbages, girls in roses). I had no idea of the relations between the sexes, even though I had perhaps been a witness of the relations be-tween my parents. I had no motion either of the anatomical difference between the sexes to the point that when a girl cousin (10 years younger) was born, I peremptorily declared that her "little faucet" had not yet grown. I did not doubt that my mother had a large penis: I had been convinced when very small by overhearing her urinate, and I had added to the loud and prolonged noise the vague picture of a large penis. The whole of this experience again easily leads to the bell shape.

The importance of the fantasy of the phallic mother was con-firmed by a dream. In the dream, I saw a girl cousin of my age stretched on a bed, her skirts raised, her legs slightly apart, exhibiting a nice pair of testicles and a large, erect penis.

The homosexual references were not doubtful: I associated the person in the dream to a youthful comrade, somewhat feminine, whose name, by an unforced play on words, could be understood as designating the *muliebria*. I found myself in competition with him over two comrades, in no way homosexual though they formed a kind of couple or closed group admitting to intimacy only chosen friends.

But most of the associations of ideas concerned the very person of the dream. She was a cousin almost exactly my age whom I had met only rarely. Circumstances brought it about that I saw much more of her from our 15th year on. She was said to resemble my mother. My mother herself resembled an aunt, this cousin's grandmother, and the resemblance is striking in a family portrait which this cousin still possesses. My cousin was said to resemble me to the point that peasants who did not know us well took us for brother and sister; and I myself was said to resemble my mother. As for me, I found my cousin much prettier, with her no doubt ambiguous face which bore an astonishing resemblance to that which Leonardo da Vinci gave to his Bacchus and his Mona Lisa, with the famous "Vincean smile": *un certain sourire*. My cousin had a beautiful, joyful contralto voice. She liked to tease me in various ways, especially by hiding with my brother to whom I had quite given up my mother but to whom I did not intend to abandon this cousin. We were full of interest in and affection for each other. Unlike my mother, she admired me and showed me that she did. Later on, somewhat older, we went out together, which displeased and upset my mother. Various circumstances, my studies and hers, my determination not to marry soon, which had never been a question between us, spaced out our meetings. Only analysis made me understand the small incident that had been decisive. She thought she had made me spend too much in the course of a walk, which was untrue because, although my resources were limited, the expense had been modest. In fact, what had annoyed me was the red hat she wore, a *cloche* hat such as they wore in the 1920s. I found confirmation of this in the fact that exactly the same incident had put a stop to my going out with a female fellow student some years later. In both cases, it was hats the shape and red color of which displeased me. I associated the fact with another circumstance: when I was still a child, I used to choose my mother's hats, since she was generally of an indecisive character. From the moment that I saw less of my cousin, my mother saw more of her. My career and World War II kept me away from Paris for 10 years. We found each other again, still friendly and trusting. Placed in similar, if not identical, circumstances in which my mother had found herself, my cousin proved to have both character and judgment. At the time of my analysis, we hardly ever met, each one being taken up by his family and professional commitments. Nothing explained to me why I had dreamed of her if not the correspondence which existed between her image and the fantasy of a phallic and more discreetly castrating mother than my own mother.

Yet I did not succeed in satisfying myself with the fantasy of the phallic mother as the explanation of all these fictions in bell shape. The explanation was "ready made." Other memories led me back to my father. I have said that my oldest memories date from the 4th year, from vacations we passed on a beach in lower Normandy. These memories are numerous and precise. One of them follows. One day my father took me fishing with his friends. They fished with rod and line in the port. I see myself clearly, returning at nightfall from fishing with all the men armed with fishing poles. It must have rained a little, because my father was sheltering me beneath his wide cape, a family institution which we called the *collet*.[10] I looked among the oldest photographs dating from my 1st year, approximately 9 months old, therefore earlier than my brother's birth and contemporary with my mother's second pregnancy. One shows me seated on my father's right knee, he holding me with his right arm while he raises the left to shake a *rattle*. But the other shows me in my nurse's arms, naked, sitting straight up, and in my serious face, black eyes, a perplexed and attentive expression. She appears as a rather tall, thin young woman with a thin face, black eyes, a gentle smile, watching me tenderly. It was on this occasion that she declared to my mother: "Well, Madame, our son is beautiful," a reflection which my mother, when she recounted it much later, made apparent she had not appreciated.

I did not find what I was looking for, but it seemed to me that I was getting "warmer." What was I looking for? I would be led to suppose today that it was an explanation which would allow me not to bring either my father or my mother into question and, safeguarding the fantasy of the phallic mother, to eliminate that of castration.

10 In French, a synonym for *pèlerine*.

It is probable in any case that the libidinal charge of the bell shape caused me to continue. I recall very exactly the circumstances in which something new appeared. I was in my study, about to get up to go to dinner, standing precisely against the left-hand drawers of my desk. Like lightning, the idea struck me that the first concrete object which had had the bell shape was nothing other than my cradle, that is, a cradle such as was made at the beginning of this century, topped by a staff around which floated ample muslin curtains. Chance brought it about that my mother was dining with us that evening. She confirmed the exactness of my thought. In addition, I had a precise memory of this cradle because it had later served for a rather long time for my brother. She added spontaneously and without trying to please (because she distrusted the questions I happened to ask her at this time about my early childhood), no doubt motivated by the obscure notion of a similarity between the two shapes: "Your first plaything was a *folie*. You must have been 6 months old." It is perhaps useful to recall that a *folie* is a sort of doll which has no legs and which is mounted on a staff one holds and shakes by hand. The doll has a clown's costume, a little saw-toothed skirt, a pointed hat, and, at the tip of the hat, as on each tooth of the skirt, a bell. I shall add that my nurse used to sing me songs, especially in the evening, which much annoyed my mother, and that, being a Northerner, she could not fail to have sung "Le Petit Quinquin," in which comical "Polichinelle" and the "pointed hat" have a prominent place as gifts which Petit Quinquin's mother promises her little boy if he is good. Thus the cradle and the toy, both bell-shaped objects, had made up an important part of my childhood surroundings. The private world where I rested was bell-shaped. My first toy was bell-shaped. It is likely that the toy was first shaken in front of me and that, a little later, when maturation made me capable of sensorimotor coordination and more efficient manipulation, I shook it myself. Probably it was left with me in the cradle as is common with a child's first toy. These are plausible hypotheses. I shall not risk supposing that the name of my first toy suffices to make of me, almost 20 years later and by an almost sudden decision, contrasting with the projects I was contemplating but not without continuity with earlier projects, a specialist in madness (*folie*). That would be to overestimate the determining power of "words." Moreover, it is possible that the toy had disappeared from my universe when language entered it. I have, however, retained a special taste for this word and its various uses, as for designating, in the eighteenth century, little country houses where one had a good time; but "little houses" were then also madhouses (*les petites maisons*) and some of them, with their pointed roofs, still had a shape close to that of a bell 30 years ago.

To all this one can object only that the strong libidinal investment of the bell shape provoked, toward the end of my analysis, an abundant projection of bell-shaped figments and the obstinate search for a memory which took them into account; no more than to my efforts, which were not entirely fruitless, to interest my analyst and to make of the bell an object which tied us to each other. One can think that the obstinacy of my search betrayed a resistance to giving up the fantasy of the phallic mother and admitting castration, the insistence on substituting things for people, that is, for my father and mother. But things, at first animate, are substitutes for people, "transitional objects," before becoming truly things. Moreover, the toy had surely been shown to me by my father, my mother, and my nurse before being given into my own hands. And one of my nurse's songs promised me Punchinello's gift and a pointed hat. From the point of view of administering proof, even if the explanation is not complete, it seems "radical" in the proper sense of that term. Its exactness is confirmed by the sudden, unexpected way in which the idea of the cradle (and one can add, the memory of the cradle) crossed my mind, coinciding with the external testimony of my mother who, with the *folie*, introduced into the story of my 1st year an object isomorphic both as to the cradle and the maternal phallus, with the difference that the cradle enclosed me whereas the *folie* was outside me and a means of exchange.

The isomorphism of mnemic and fantasmatic structures in respect to figments ensuing by way of unconscious, preconscious, and conscious fantasy is at the basis of these acted and thought figments. It also enables the analyst to trace these figments back to the unconscious formation that had structured them "for better or for worse." Acted or thought figments can be delusory, but they can also lead to truth in judgment and efficacy in action. These latter do not lose all resonance in the unconscious fantasy, even though they are not determined by it. They are of the order of "sublimation in action": in one case as in the other, repetition and symbolization are combined.

Even today, by the choice of bell-shaped figments and by some insistence on interesting my analyst in them, I repeat what appears toward the end of my didactic analysis. This transferential repetition had itself been the return of the first objects, cradle and toy, which from the beginning of my life and at the very least in the course of my 1st year, had structured my surroundings and given "shape" to very old experiences of communication and exchange.

Such facts seem to show that the fantasmatic structures which determine fantasies and figments are mnemic structures, although recall and external testimony do not corroborate in every case, even in the majority of cases, their experiential and mnemic origin. This in no way eliminates the hypothesis of primary fantasies, of *a priori* structures of fantasy, but it does show that if such *a priori* structures exist, they need a concrete material in order to be actualized (Lagache, 1964).

Finale

Homage to him who, throughout a long career, has tried to bring to light the foundations of psychoanalysis and to establish its status as a scientific discipline (Hartmann, 1927, 1958, 1959; Hartmann, Kris, and Loewenstein, 1953), this essay had as its purpose to answer the question, futile or fundamental, whether psychoanalysis is a conjectural or an exact science. Daring yet prudent, the answer is that psychoanalysis is exact in some portions of its results, whether isolated or taken together. A methodical although incomplete review of the problems has shown that arguments are not lacking. But the real question—I mean the psychoanalytic, therefore, fantasmatic question —was to know if it was masculine or feminine, phallic or castrated. In this perspective, the thesis sustained can be said to express a narcissistic and phallic demand; the analyst need not feel himself in a lesser and guilty position with respect to the specialists in other sciences from mathematics to the social sciences. It would be much rather to castrate himself to give up pertinent methods of investigation and proof, to alienate himself in a hazardous way in servile imitation of sciences whose operating methods do not correspond to what we are looking for.

Setting aside bad work and the confusion of the material in certain cases, the appearance of inexactness in psychoanalysis arises from many factors. Not the least is the enormity of the material. The analyst is like the physicist who must deal with tons of ore in order to extract a few milligrams of radium. The fantastic also is at issue here; it can be overestimated. This is the case with "wild" interpretations and with presumptuous confidence in the most piercing intuitions. Yet the analyst must not underestimate the fantastic or shut himself up in a sterile rationalism. Operationally, all the material which the fundamental rule brings is to be considered as a series of figments issuing from mnemic structures and from unconscious fantasy, including the most obstinate defenses and rationalizations. This is an essential condition of the fecundity and the exactness of psychoanalytic investigation (Lagache, 1964).

For exactness we shall find neither by fantasy nor by logic alone but rather by their complementary interplay and our ease in moving from one to the other. We may here recall the epigram of Thomas Edison concerning genius: 5 per cent inspiration, 95 per cent perspiration. Let us transpose it, not without noting the mythical illusion which would make of figures alone the guarantee of exactness: psychoanalysis is made up of 5 per cent fantasy and 95 per cent logic. But what would the other sciences be, even mathematics and mathematical physics, if sometimes a strange idea did not set deductions in motion? Moreover, scientific discoveries and technical inventions often seem fantastic in the common man's eyes as it happened with what had been called "the scandal" of psychoanalysis.

More fundamentally, psychoanalysis can be exact because unconscious thought is not as inexact as one likes to say it is. It is much rather the defensive maneuvers of the conscious and unconscious ego which confuse it. The "fantasmatic" has its reasons which reason does not know,[11] which fantasy does not know either, and which reason alone can recognize, provided it does not shut its eyes irrationally to the fantastic. Being as fond of the clinic as of theory, I shall supply another example.

A few months ago I saw an English film, with one of my children, which has had some success. It was *Tom Jones*, inspired by Fielding's novel. It is the colored description of the English countryside of the eighteenth century, above all of the "squires" whose life was divided between caring for their lands, the hunt, feasting, and lewdness, at least if one accepts the film's account. A gallant squire one evening finds a baby in his bed, a beautiful little boy, of parents unknown. He

[11] Based on Pascal's aphorism, "The heart has its reasons which reason does not know."

decides to raise the baby as his son and to call him Tom Jones. The baby grows up, very quickly in the film. He becomes a handsome young man, not of the most serious kind, and a great skirtchaser. He would have been hanged for an unsuccessful plot if at the last moment the squire, who leads an idle and disorderly life but who is a very honorable man, did not arrive on his horse at a gallop to cut the rope from which Tom Jones is already hanging and to give him the hand of his daughter. Happy ending!

At this time I was preoccupied with an annoying business. I dreamed the following night that I found myself in eighteenth-century surroundings and on the point of being hanged or of having my head cut off, for the apparatus intended for this execution was a *croissant*, a garden tool meant for cutting the upper branches of trees, an ambiguous tool since the cutting edge is operated by a long cord. I was without anxiety and everything was arranged. Happy ending!

I omit most of what the interpretation of the dream provided me. That I had taken the story of Tom Jones for my own use is obvious. One point had held me: why had the squire called the baby Tom Jones with so much decisiveness? In the course of this auto-analysis, the name of Jelly Roll Morton, a jazz pioneer, came curiously to mind, but I did not neglect this unforeseen intrusion. There was present to my mind the meaning of Jelly Roll in American folklore. Almost immediately, I recalled the meaning of John Thomas in English folklore. It was easy to reconstruct the permutations through which John Thomas had become Tom Jones probably through a deliberate confusion of Fielding's. Had not the associations of ideas played their role very well in making me think of Jelly Roll while I was questioning myself about Tom Jones?

The exactness of psychoanalysis is therefore not *the ambitious myth of minds misled by the fantastic*. It is the rational use of the psychoanalyst's fantasy to decipher the fantasy of the analysand. I could multiply examples of this. Simultaneously, this knowing and simple game of fantasy and logic is the condition of the fecundity of psychoanalytic investigation and its exactness. It is also a protection against doubtful adventures. If the analyst knows how to combine fantasy and logic, the discoveries at which he arrives are satisfactory enough to temper his zeal, to make him patient, to encourage him to persevere and to wait until whatever could not be clarified at the time is clarified later. The pleasure he finds in the exactness of research and discovery is not the least of the reasons which make the art of the analyst, as I have sought to show elsewhere, a "sublimation in action" (Lagache, 1962/64). Need we recall that the exactness of our interpretations and our constructions, better than any mysterious mechanisms, contributes to realizing the progress of investigation as do long-term and lasting clinical changes in a process in which the efficacy of research is subordinated to the search for truth? Exactitude is another source of the analyst's pleasure; he deprives himself of it when he does not know how to wait.

Summary

To envisage psychoanalysis as an exact science is a way of replying to two errors, the objectivist myth which makes of psychoanalysis a "wicked science" and the obscurantist myth of the zealots of unreason. After having compared the management of psychoanalytic investigation and experiment, analysis deals on the basis of clinical material consecutively with the transference neurosis, the developments within the psychoanalytic session, the patient's vocabulary, and, finally, the relations between the clinical material and the unconscious fantasy and mnemic structures based on early infantile experiences. The conclusions are as follows: pyschoanalysis is an exact science, at least in isolated or unified portions of its results; the appearance of inexactitude derives principally from the enormity of the material to be treated, from overestimation and underestimation of the fantastic. Psychoanalytic exactitude proceeds from the fact that the processes of unconscious thought are not so much false as confused by the equally unconscious defensive maneuvers of the ego. Finally, the satisfaction that the analyst finds in exactness is a protection against sterile, even dangerous, adventures and a guarantee of therapeutic efficacy. This satisfaction is one of the characteristics which make the exercise of psychoanalysis a "sublimation in action."

BIBLIOGRAPHY

Bachelard, G. (1947), *La Formation de l'Esprit Scientifique*. Paris: Vrin.
Bibring, E. (1943), The Conception of the Repetition Compulsion. *Psa. Q.*, 12:486-519.
Freud, S. (1911/15), Papers on Technique, *S.E.*, 12:85-173.
——— (1937), Constructions in Analysis. *S.E.*, 23:257-269.
——— (1940), An Outline of Psycho-Analysis. *S.E.*, 23:141-207.

Hartmann, H. (1927), *Die Grundlagen der Psychoanalyse*. Leipzig: Thieme.
—— (1958), Comments on the Scientific Aspects of Psychoanalysis. *Essays*, 297-317.
—— (1959), Psychoanalysis as a Scientific Theory. *Essays*, 318-350.
—— Kris, E., & Loewenstein, R. M. (1953), The Function of Theory in Psychoanalysis. *Drives, Affects, Behavior*, ed. R. M. Loewenstein. 1:13-37. NY: IUP.
Hunt, J. McV., ed. (1944), *Personality and the Behavior Disorders*. NY: Ronald Pr.
Jourdan, P. (1958), Mythes et Réalités du Chirugien. *Les Temps Modernes*, Mai-juin, 2267-2278.
Lagache, D. (1947), *La Jalousie Amoureuse*. Paris: Presses Universitaires de France.
—— (1951), Some Aspects of Transference. *Int. J. Psa.*, 34:1-10, 1953.
—— (1952), Le Problème du Transfert. *Rev. Franç. Psa.*, 16:5-115.
—— (1962/64), La psychanalyse comme sublimation (in press).
—— (1964), Fantasy, Reality, and Truth. *Int. J. Psa.*, 45:180-189.
Mowrer, O. H. (1950), *Learning Theory and Personality Dynamics*. NY: Ronald Pr.
Murray, H. A. et al. (1938), *Explorations in Personality*. NY: Oxford Univ. Pr.
Sears, R. R. (1943), *Survey of Objective Studies of Psychoanalytic Concepts*. NY: Soc. Sci. Res. Council.
Sharpe, E. F. (1937), *Dream Analysis*. London: Hogarth Pr.
Zeigarnik, B. (1927), On Finished and Unfinished Tasks. *A Source Book of Gestalt Psychology*, ed. W. D. Ellis. NY: Harcourt, Brace, 1938.

V

Clinical Problems

Posttraumatic Amnesias and Their Adaptive Function

HELENE DEUTSCH, M.D.

This paper is a tribute to Heinz Hartmann's great contribution to scientific progress in psychoanalytic theory.

Reviewing his numerous writings (published in part in collaboration with Ernst Kris and Rudolph Loewenstein), one is very impressed by his highly developed capacity for theoretical thinking, a product of his erudition in the philosophical and biological disciplines and of his deep knowledge of the genetic aspect of psychoanalysis. Using this background he has led the way in creating a "unifying theory" and in establishing a solid psychoanalytic ego psychology. Hartmann's statement (1952) that concept formation in analysis does not differ in principle from concept formation in science in general is certainly valid, but we must not forget that these concepts are based on clinical observation in which the intuitive approach plays a much greater part than it does in purely scientific endeavors. Freud's work, which "owes much to his supreme capacity of observation and to his unflinching objectivity vis-à-vis new facts" (Hartmann, 1952, p. 180), also owes much to a quality of his genius which transcends his capacity of observation.

The purpose of psychoanalytic work with individuals is to correct their impaired ability to function and to achieve a certain degree of psychic integration and harmony. How much the application of Hartmann's fruitful and stimulating theoretical ideas to technical measures will contribute to practical results is yet to be seen. A "classical" analyst will have no difficulty in recognizing the new elements as closely related to what he has learned and experienced before.

In this paper emphasis will be put on the problem of adaptation. The data presented are substantiated by objective and direct observation and, according to my interpretations, are pertinent to Hartmann's theoretical ideas.

The clinical material deals with certain forms of amnesia. Since amnesia is closely related to preconscious mental processes, I would like to refer to them not in their far-reaching theoretical implications but only in so far as they constitute a frame of reference for the clinical problems involved.

Freud's (1915) definition includes the statement: preconscious is unconscious in the sense of being latent and easily made conscious. In general terms, the condition for transforming "preconscious" to "conscious" is provided by the analytic process and consists in a successful lifting of defenses. If we want to apply this definition to the clinical observations presented here, it should be expanded to read: "easily made conscious under *specific* (individually varying) conditions."

Everyday analytic observations confront us with the interplay between preconscious processes and amnesia. To name only two examples: some patients claim that they do not remember anything, or that they remember only very little, from their long and successful analysis. Their conscious memory, temporarily dormant, can be easily revived when the patient finds himself in analysis again, because the material was preserved in the preconscious.

We frequently encounter another manifestation of the preconscious: what was successfully raised from the unconscious through hard analytic labor was, according to the patient's subjective feelings, "always conscious." I think that this phenomenon is due to the fact that what we considered "unconscious" was often preconscious, hidden under the blocking effect of secondary defenses.

Perhaps we can generalize and say that the greatest part of the unconscious brought to light through analysis was always stored in the "preconscious," and that the deeply buried experiences of childhood, the confrontation with old historical events, are only reconstructions. During analysis one may discover patches of amnesia for single events or even for some periods of life which completely escaped the awareness of both the analyst and the patient.[1] These

---

[1] In his paper "The Personal Myth" (1956) Kris discusses a patient who "lost two years of his life." This amnesia was brought about by the patient's need to maintain his "autobiographical screen" in accord with his fantasies.

events never had an evident traumatic effect and their presence in the psychic life of the patient did not interrupt the stream of life or interfere with the course of analysis. Amnesia may manifest itself in many ways; moreover, it may serve various functions.[2]

One patient in analysis discovered an "amnestic patch" which had never been apparent in his initial analysis with a very competent and experienced therapist; nor had it appeared throughout the preceding year of analysis with me. The amnesia could be clearly demarcated in regard to time; it extended from June to October of a certain year and embraced the period between the end of graduate school and the start of his professional career.

I shall briefly outline the patient's life history and his experiences preceding the amnesia.

Mr. Jones came to analysis after two years of a not very successful treatment with a male analyst, who decided that the patient might do better with a female therapist. Clinically he presented a great variety of psychosomatic symptoms, fluctuating and unspecific attacks of anxiety and mild depressions. In the period preceding the beginning of the new analysis, he complained about feelings of *depersonalization*. His professional duties made it necessary to interrupt his analysis from time to time.

He was the youngest child and the only boy in a family of four children. His father had deserted the home when the boy was about four years old. As the only "man" of the family the patient was the center of attention of four adoring women and the great hope for the future of the family. Paradoxically, although brilliant and studious, he was a passive, effeminate sickly boy. Unfortunately for him, no masculine figure was available for identification. His memory of his father was of a pejorative character.

Such a family situation presents two great dangers: (1) the reinforcement of the oedipal situation, the gratifying "I am the only man," owing to the absence of the father; and (2) the lack of an adequate object for identification and for ego development. The first of the dangers (oedipal) expressed itself in neurotic sufferings and, as we shall see, in the patient's love life; the second, in the deficiency of his ego development.

He never went through the adolescent turmoil of "identification

---

[2] Eissler (1955), for example, presented a case in which amnesia served the gratification of an aggressive impulse.

crises"; he was kind and helpful to others and was liked by many, but there was nobody in his past, boy or girl, who interested him for any length of time or exclusively.

In his first year at college he met Mrs. X, a 36-year-old mother of three girls (!) and wife of a businessman, "not a very impressive personality" according to the patient's conception of him. Mrs. X became pregnant in the first year of their affair and gave birth to a boy. There was no doubt for the lovers that the child was theirs, but they did not consider it advisable to deprive the child of legitimacy and conceded him to Mrs. X's husband. The patient never showed the slightest interest in the little boy.

About eight years later, the patient decided to break up this adolescent love relationship. During the previous year, he had already reached a degree of maturity that made him recognize that this relationship would be unfavorable to his development, to his new goals in life, his ideals, etc. Shortly thereafter, he ended the affair during his last semester at graduate school. There were some meetings, a long correspondence with Mrs. X, and the break was undramatic. It was evident that both partners had had enough of this abnormal liaison. Soon after this break he married a very young girl and had a little daughter with her; shortly afterwards the wife suffered a miscarriage (also a girl). She again became pregnant at the beginning of the last period of the patient's analytic treatment. After the wife gave birth to a boy the situation in analysis changed. The patient was in a state of joyful excitement, neglected all his activities, and stayed at home most of the time to take care of his boy, lest something happen to him. On the whole his behavior was like that of a young boy who, having received his first recognition, uses it as an incentive for his fantasies. The main tone of these fantasies was: the little boy is a "genius" and will fulfill all his father's frustrated ambitions.

The patient's analysis—for a long time unproductive—was now making progress and it was in this period that we discovered his amnesia. Little by little, the details of the forgotten past were recollected; they revealed events leading to the successful dissolution of the affair. The lovers met in another country, spent the time traveling, not as lovers but only as friends, without regrets, without resentment, and without grief. The patient remembered that only once was there an emotional upheaval: when Mrs. X told him that their son was unusual and wonderful, a boy genius, he reacted with great anger and anxiety.

Because the definitive separation was but the last act of a longer, preparatory period in which all forces of ambivalence, of resentments against the woman, all guilty feelings, etc., were well managed and discharged, relief from the anticipated loss reactions was achieved to a great extent. One can only assume that even in the last encounter the atmosphere of loss followed the couple to the peaks of Swiss hills which they climbed together in good friendship.

So far the enigma of amnesia could not be solved, but it seems that the solution may be found in the patient's emotional upset when Mrs. X described the boy genius. More hope for clarification came from a more recent event, the birth of his son, which undoubtedly started the process of recollection.

Insight into the whole situation makes it evident that the patient was not able to harvest the fruits of victory over his actual oedipal involvement, because regressive turmoil within his ego interfered with the successful use of his newly gained freedom. We may assume that the weakness of the progressive forces and their defensive use accounted for the fact that the process of maturation was not quite what one could have expected. "We have to face the fact that what is adaptive in one respect may interfere with adaptation in another" (Hartmann, 1956, p. 254).

In the case of Mr. Jones, the control of instinctual drives involved in the oedipal situation proved efficient, but full adaptation to reality was impossible. The synthetic forces in the ego failed because simultaneously with the solution of the oedipal conflict a regression to the preoedipal situation took place.

In the process of breaking up his adolescent love affair, the patient's old grandiose fantasies were regressively revived. The awareness of the existence of a boy genius, who would now take his place in the mother's admiration; the nostalgic identification with the boy who is now what he once was; the despair because he is again forced to give up the glorious self adoration; "the narcissistic blow" coming simultaneously with the loss of the object—all this was more than his injured and regressed ego could take. In this specific case the regression was facilitated because he never experienced the identification crisis of adolescence, his father was never his ideal, and his relationship to his mother was infiltrated by her admiration of him.

He managed the situation without any pathological reactions; his adjustment to his new role as a "mature" husband of a young wife was quite satisfactory.

Since my conception of this patient's psychological problems led me to his preadolescence, my interest in this developmental phase of boys was renewed. My previous work with girls of this age incited in me the urge for comparison, but I evidently needed direct confrontation with a patient's specific problems to formulate the psychological riddles of preadolescent boys more precisely.

We have recently learned a great deal about adolescence. The literature in the years after the publication of Anna Freud's basic book (1936) contains many valuable contributions to the problems of adolescence (Spiegel, 1958). This period, with its typical and, at the same time, rich and manifold manifestations has incited the interest of psychoanalysts more than any other developmental period.

Much less attention has been paid to the period immediately preceding the shift to adolescence.[3] I do not intend to deal here with all aspects of preadolescence, but shall discuss only those problems that are relevant to our understanding of Mr. Jones.

Comparing boys with girls of the same age (10 to 13) as a starting point, one arrives at a definite conception of analogies and differences, which are far-reaching, interesting, and illuminating.

Both sexes have in common a decreasing capacity for object relationship, the incipient dissolution of childhood attachments, and the energetic turning toward one's own ego with the preadolescent increase of narcissism.[4] Common to both sexes is a certain paradox of psychological elements: on the one hand, there are the typically increased "turn to reality" and the reinforcement of the process of adaptation; on the other, simultaneously with the increase of narcissism, there is the intensification of fantasy life.

That a "thrust toward activity," while characteristic of both sexes, will be stronger in boys is to be expected. But some boys, for example, Mr. Jones, disclose even in this period more passive-feminine traits, whereas girls much too often enjoy being "tomboys."

There are also differences in the increase of "turning to reality" versus the intensification of fantasy first mentioned. We would expect

---

[3] See, however, the very important work by Blos (1958, 1962, 1965).

[4] I am using the term "narcissism" for simplification, but I consider Hartmann's preferred term "narcissistic ego cathexis" scientifically more correct.

the first to be predominant in boys; the second, in girls. This again was not quite true in the case of my patient.

In the character of fantasies, there is a definite and general difference between the sexes.

The central task of the preadolescent boy is his search for an ego ideal. In this immensely important task he may be deprived of an object for a solid identification. In preadolescence the devaluation of one's father is, even in a favorable environment, a normal process, and the choice of a substitute seems to be difficult, considering the extremely high demands. Whereas the adolescent is much more active in his attempts to reach the ideal in the external world by activity, the preadolescent boy to a very large degree gratifies his need in fantasy. The image of himself may be a conglomeration of traits taken from various objects, but it definitely is the expression of a narcissistic aggrandizement: "that is how I want to be, how I am." The persistence of this narcissistic condition can easily become dangerous.[5]

The importance of preserving an external ideal lies in the fact that the ideal represents a continuity of the child's libidinal attachments so decisive for his emotional adjustment in the future. If the integrity of the boy's ego is to be preserved, he has to accept a certain degree of disillusionment without giving up the object of identification.

The most important external object for both boys and girls in this period is a friend of the same sex—"a boy like me" (or "a girl like me"). When one keeps the increase of narcissism in mind, one understands this kind of object choice better.[6]

In a two-boy relationship the emphasis is more on the ego ideal, on the uniqueness and splendor gratified in fantasy. The boy's frequently poor performance in reality seldom spoils this fantasy, but only helps to reinforce it or to postpone fulfillment in the future. Observing the activities of two boys, one can see how the most primitive games become great technical inventions; simple cut-out stars, astronomical wonders, etc.

Of course, there are individual differences in all these "typical features" not only in the two sexes but also in the predominance of one or another component in an individual irrespective of his sex.

After this limited review of these particular developmental prob-

[5] Hendrick (1964) emphasizes the danger of severe pathology when the ego ideal is traumatized in prepuberty.
[6] For further comparisons, see the chapter on "Prepuberty" (Deutsch, 1944).

lems, let us return to Mr. Jones. We learned that the important role of the little boy in the traumatic situation was determined by the patient's past—specifically by the "glorious" past of the never fully relinquished fantasy world. Losing this boy—now forever, when he broke with his mother—was like losing his own, never relinquished identity as a 10-year-old "genius" which he had once dreamed of being. It is not possible to bring analytic material in the framework of this paper. But the re-emergence of the son born in reality—a new and suitable object for the lost identification—and the importance of this re-emergence in the psychic recovery of the patient can convince us sufficiently of the validity of the interpretation.

We have seen that Mr. Jones's amnesia cleared up after the birth of his legitimate son. There was no doubt that with this event the glorious image of his own preadolescent ego could be reinstated, and in this way the main factor in the previous traumatization was eliminated.

In addition, the newly born boy not only was an adequate object for the patient's own narcissistic fantasies, but the boy also provided an opportunity to bring to life the patient's deficient object relationship.

We have seen that it was not the therapy but a real event which, through gratification supplied by the external world, achieved a better functioning of the patient's ego and, by a detour, a more harmonious relationship with the environment. "The inner world and its functions make possible an adaptation process which consists of two steps: withdrawal from the external world [here partially in amnesia] and return to it with improved mastery" (Hartmann, 1939, p. 58).

It is doubtful whether the effect of trauma is forever removed with the recovery of an amnesia. Every traumatization creates—or increases—a disposition to repetition. Every traumatic reaction is a miniature of a traumatic neurosis; its traces can be more or less revived by a suitable provocation. A new traumatic experience, especially one identical with (or similar to) the previous one, can easily act as an *agent provocateur* for identical reasons.

Whether there exists a real "completion" of an internal process, which once taxed the individual beyond his capacity, is questionable. I do not believe that any "catharsis" is able to achieve a full return to the *status quo ante* or that assimilation, adaptation, etc., can successfully end a traumatic process.

The patient under discussion had an opportunity to meet his unresolved inner situation with the most favorable solution; fulfillment in reality of a certain inner goal which proved unattainable in the situation that had led to the traumatic reaction.

The gratifying new role of the "father of a boy genius" had, as we have seen, a very positive effect on the patient's pathology; the amnesia cleared up and the symptom of depersonalization subsided. When such direct compensation in an external situation is not available, the work of restitution depends more on the inherent adaptive capacities of the ego, on the strength of defenses, etc. In a dynamic sense, amnesia also served our patient's attempt toward adaptation by way of evasion. In this endeavor the simplest way was to deny the whole experience—"it did not happen"—keeping in consciousness only the wished-for end result, the break with the beloved.

With the change of the reality situation, amnesia as a form of adaptation was no longer necessary. The birth of his legitimate son had a direct affinity to the traumatic situation. It is to be assumed that the revival and assimilation of the traumatic events which led to the amnesia were of great importance. His mastery of fatherhood needed this revival as an emotional experience and, regressive as it may have been, in this way it also served adaptive forces.

The validity of the patient's solution of his conflicts remains questionable. In regard to his gross pathology the result was very positive: the amnesia cleared up and the symptom of depersonalization subsided.

We are impressed with the influence exerted by therapy on this symptom, which is considered grave in regard to the integration of the ego. Evidently in Mr. Jones, this symptom of depersonalization was a manifestation of defensive forces resulting in a shift of his inner tensions to feelings of change of his personality, sensations of estrangement, etc. As freedom from these tensions was regained, this form of defense could be dispensed with.

This patient seems to me an adequate clinical illustration of Hartmann's (1939) important statement regarding "progressive and regressive adaptation." He refers to adaptation as progressive when its direction coincides with that of development. But there are adaptations—successful ones—which use pathways of regression, i.e., "detour through regression." This patient's love and marriage represented a progressive adaptation, while the therapeutically effective fatherhood, which was based on the preadolescent boy's fantasy, was a regressive adaptation.

Another patient, Mr. Smith, disclosed during his analysis that a certain event in his life was and always had been submerged in amnesia. In contrast to Mr. Jones, Mr. Smith had always been aware of this amnesia; what was particularly striking, however, was his complete lack of concern about this lapse.

Mr. Smith came from a wealthy Scandinavian family who emigrated to the United States because of the father's business affiliations. The patient was born in America and always considered himself an American. The mother, a former high school teacher, was stern, active, demanding, and very devoted to the education of her children. The father was easygoing and humorous, more of a playmate for his sons than a figure of authority. Mr. Smith refused to enter his father's business and chose engineering as his profession, in which he was very successful. His marriage and family life were quite satisfactory. His neurotic problems were minor; some personality difficulties brought him to analysis.

One brother was born when the patient was 5 years old and another when he was 10. Later, during his 14th and 15th years, two sisters were born—without any evident emotional reactions on his part. The birth of a sibling is always, under all conditions, a traumatic event. The trauma can be mild, or it can be strong; the child's reaction can take a pathological form, or his mastery of the situaion can obliterate all traumatic traces.

In the case of Mr. Smith, there was no overt pathology, but certain characteristics of his personality, dreams, etc., gave ample evidence of a traumatic reaction. The trauma became linked with the birth of his first brother, Joe, and affected his instinctual life. His intense jealousy of the newborn brought a regressive reinforcement of orality and an erotic cathexis of the female breast, a reaction to his excitement at observing the infant being nursed. This cathexis remained a permanent part of his love life. His identification with his mother after his brother's birth had a very feminine character and resulted in the passive-feminine components of his whole personality. He spent a lot of energy in an effort to overcome this passivity, and many of his overly masculine activities were due to reaction formations.

His phallic interest did not suffer in this competition-laden atmosphere because he definitely felt a victor: his penis proved to be larger than those of his brothers. This phallic superiority continued in his "big-brother" feelings.

He was able to discharge his tension in an emotional—even a

dramatic—acting-out maneuver to unburden the excitation created by the trauma. The acting-out episode was like an illustration of the well-known rescue fantasy (I do not remember whether this acting out was after or before his mother returned home with a "blue package"). He suddenly disappeared from home, got lost. This episode was very vividly remembered and reported in analysis: the poor, helpless boy wandering around, not in the jungle, but in the brush in a distant neighborhood until finally—as in a fairy tale—he was found and brought home to his distressed parents. The joy over his return was supposed to overshadow his parents' interest in the newborn baby.

The symbolic meaning of the lost and rescued boy illustrates not only his competition with the baby, but also his aggressive impulses and reactive guilt feelings. On the whole, he assimilated the birth well, and it was only in the structure of his libido and personality that one could see the impact of the traumatic event. His reactions, though regressive, were in accord with his developmental period. A 5-year-old boy is on the verge of entering the latency period. Since this latency is a rather theoretical concept, however, one assumes that there are still very strong residua of previous developments to be conquered, the oedipal problems to be brought to some solution, etc. Of course, trauma will reinforce the instinctual confusion and may distort the oedipal situation (as in this patient's identification with the oedipal mother).

The amnesia mentioned previously was related to the birth of his second brother, Henry, when the patient was 10 years old. He did not remember his mother's pregnancy, delivery, or the newborn infant, and he even had the impression that all the events of life during this period were nonexistent or very hazy.

On the other hand, all details connected with the birth of his first brother, Joe, were extremely vivid in his memory, and he was always ready to report on them "with pleasure." This "with pleasure" could be taken literally, because he was always glad, even enthusiastic, whenever he was given the opportunity to speak about it. He was especially eager to interest me in the first birth when I pressed him to speak about the second. In analysis we are familiar with situations in which a highly cathected event is replaced by another one which has associative connection with it. Such replacement usually serves some form of resistance.

But this attitude of Mr. Smith was very impressive. He spoke again and again about the birth of Joe. He remembered "everything," and the very richness of the reproduced memories frequently created the impression that they were a kind of "screen memories" (Freud, 1899), aiding his amnesia for the birth of Henry.

When we compare the two traumatic events (when he was 5 and then 10 years old), we realize that the second event occurred when he was in the difficult preadolescent phase of development.

For the purpose of clarity I wish to repeat briefly the previously presented description of preadolescence: identification with a person in the external world is the guiding spirit in the inner situation. The ego ideal is now gradually undergoing internalization and assimilation. In this process overvaluation of the external object is very important. Everything that weakens the demanded standard constitutes a trauma to the ego. One can assume that at other times no more than the usual adaptive forces could cope with a trauma. However, when the same trauma occurs at this very moment of ego development, as it did in the case of Mr. Smith, the situation is different.

Mr. Smith's ego ideal was formed by identification with his mother —due to a somewhat complicated family constellation. Unfortunately the birth of a child at this time was not very favorable. The event in itself was conceived as sexual; it revealed the mother as a sexual object and tended to debase her image. The regressive trend mobilized by the event was reinforced by the residuum of the previous trauma. We remember that whenever Mr. Smith approached the event of the birth of Henry in his analysis, memories of the birth of Joe almost always appeared.[7] This proved two factors: (1) a certain identity of emotional responses to the two births; and (2) the resistance to recalling the second event, the very existence of which was denied (amnesia).

I have emphasized that the old situation contributed regressive elements to the new one. Moreover, reactions differed according to the stages of development. It may happen that an event which in a previous stage of development was highly traumatic loses most of its traumatic force at a later stage.

[7] A hardly believable episode occurred after Henry's birth: Joe, now 5 years old, disappeared from home in exactly the same manner as his older brother (the patient) had after Joe's birth. Joe ran away and had to be "rescued." Our patient took a very active part in the expedition, now in the role of rescuer. What after the birth of Joe he had experienced *passively* (the lost boy), he now re-enacted *actively*. It impresses us as a nice fantasy! But Mr. Smith, who did not remember anything, had reliable information from his environment: this event really took place. We suspect that the "big brother" in some way inspired the younger one in this act of repetition!

Generally, traumatization means that every trauma—even when it is managed well—leaves a residuum which constitutes a disposition. Later reactions will depend on the quantity and quality of defenses, on the capacity for neutralization, etc., developed during the time elapsed between the traumas.

It may even happen that the consolidation of the inner world reaches a point at which a new traumatic event not only seems ineffective, but even proves fruitful and of positive value for further development. "What was true this time need not be true on another occasion, with a person changed by the very experience" (Waelder, 1963, p. 40).

If we assume that Mr. Smith's development in the five years intervening between the first and second trauma had proceeded according to the developmental schedule, we would expect Waelder's statement to be applicable. It was *not* applicable because the new traumatic situation provoked the ominous devaluation of the mother.

The following, built on analytic material, seems to illustrate the boy's desperate need to rehabilitate his mother's image:

In a family consisting of two boys it is commonly expected that the third child will be a girl. The image of his parents which Mr. Smith conveyed to me made me assume that they were convinced that it would be a girl. This was not a "symbol," it was a wish, an expected fact, a promise on the part of the mother. I suspected that all the preparations were made for the arrival of a girl—an assumption which was later confirmed.

When a boy was born (we can assume in an atmosphere filled with the patient's doubts about his mother), it was a blow to her omnipotence, to the reliability of her promises. The foundations of the 10-year-old boy's beliefs were again shaken. In his use of denial and undoing, in all his attempts to create the illusion that his mother was powerful and always right, he did not resort to a kind of negative hallucination and pretense that the infant was a girl, that it had no penis (such hallucinatory experiences are not unusual), but he acknowledged and accepted the reality of the baby's penis. Nevertheless, he did not fully accept that the child was not a girl. Since these events remained under amnesia during the whole period of analysis, this statement is a mere speculation on my part based on a conviction gained indirectly by reconstruction of the following analytic material:

In the first weeks of analysis the patient recalled that he once had

had the opportunity to see a girl's genitalia: when he was quite young, he had observed a girl at close range so that every detail of her body had been distinct. He had seen her penis, her legs, etc. The impression was so strong that he was still able to describe the whole visual situation: the building in front of which she was standing, the polka-dot dress she wore, etc.

The second episode happened much later and occurred in the back of a garage. The exhibition was no longer so innocent, it was like an intended seduction on the part of the girl. He had seen her genitalia, including her penis, very clearly.

He did not immediately understand my question: "You really saw their penises?" Only after my insistent questioning did he acknowledge, while laughing, that his visual recollection could not be correct because a girl does not have a penis. But until this call to reality he had never doubted his version of these experiences.

The denial of the fact that a woman has no penis is a very well-known maneuver to counteract castration fear, and it is an everyday experience in analysis to see patients who adhere to the fear (and the hope) that the penis may be hidden somewhere. But this absolute feeling of reality, this lack of correction, this astonishment when confronted with his mistake, are possible only when the experience was a reality: he *had* seen a girl with a penis, and this was the little brother who his mother had promised would be a girl.

As interesting as this observation may be, I would not consider it relevant to my topic if it did not support the thesis that the amnesia in this patient served a specific function: his desperate attempt to rescue his mother as an ideal and an adequate object of constructive identification.

We gain a better understanding of the psychological forces behind the *amnesia* if we view it as an attempt to save the image of the mother as an ego ideal. The action, the denial of the whole traumatic event—"it did not happen"—were followed by definite results. There was noticeable progress in the boy's development: one can say there was an energetic push in adaptation. This adaptation had a very definite character—a turn toward reality, a submission to the reality principle. It was certainly used to counter the dangers of his fantasy life, but in a sense it also restored his relationship with his mother. Adjustment to reality had been strongly emphasized and applied very early in the mother's education of her children.

Even if we consider this kind of adaptation a good resolution of the trauma, we must concede that the repression restricted his capacity to sublimate. His intellectual curiosity, for example, which had been present since early childhood, was too close to its instinctual sources; it had a voyeuristic character and was the offshoot of that particular period of his life in which secrets concerning the parental bedroom and above all the mysteries of his mother's body were the center of his investigations. This curiosity was to some degree replaced by the mature inquisitive mind of the scientist he had always wanted to be. Although his ambitions were built on good mental qualities, he lacked the creative effort which usually does not go with a strongly reality-oriented mind. One might even say that certain inner values were not easily available to him, because his adaptive forces were sufficient for his attainment of great success in professional activities, social prestige, family life, etc. His amnesia was an ally to these forces, but henceforth also an enemy to reach higher goals. His ego was in a closed room with only one exit: adaptive forces turned toward reality.

This efficient, good, but restrictive function of his amnesia can be compared with a government which takes good care of the immediate needs of the population and so prevents the revolutionary forces from coming into action.

As a safety valve the amnesia cooperates with that part of the ego which in a given situation is ego syntonic, and it excludes those elements which in a specific stage of development are dangerous for the ego.

The repression of those instinctual drives which normally contribute to the development of imagination (Kris, 1952) also resulted in a restriction of Mr. Smith's development. In his "turn toward reality" there was not much room left for fantasies. Looking at his life, from a general point of view, we can say that he was a satisfied, even happy person. He did not exchange one life principle for another because he was a perfect example of Hartmann's (1956) statement: "One cannot state in a general way that reality-syntonic behavior curtails pleasure . . . there is also the fact that the activities of the functions that constitute the reality principle can be pleasurable in themselves" (p. 244).

Returning to the problem of amnesia, I wish to stress again that the patient was always aware of it, but in a peculiarly unemotional manner. He was not astonished, frightened, or curious, and there was no evidence of a wish to conquer the amnesia. Only when he saw my interest and, above all, when he felt threatened by the possibility that this omission might prolong the analytic procedure, did he start to make an effort to recall the missing elements. He achieved no more than to refresh the information given to him indirectly and later by members of his family. I had to give up my own efforts and "finish" the analysis, disregarding the amnestic gap.

We have seen that in the case of Mr. Smith the amnesia was a defense against a definite trauma. The psychic reactions to the traumatic event were very threatening to the process of further maturation and consolidation of the ego. An amnesia for the entire event, which was repressed and declared to be "nonexistent," seemed to be the only—or the best—form of defense.

Since the circumstances of the amnesia were such that one can rightly consider the repressed material to have been conserved in the preconscious, the persistence and rigidity of the amnesia are baffling. We have seen that in the case of Mr. Jones the amnesia disappeared when certain conditions were changed.

In the case of Mr. Smith one would think that his satisfactory adaptation created an appropriate condition to make the amnesia unnecessary. How can one explain that this did not take place even with the help of analysis? What counterforces made the amnesia irreversible? Perhaps analytic insight can aid in clarification.

During analysis Mr. Smith was often in contact with his mother. He was in a position of great responsibility, a father figure for students and workers on big architectural projects, a consultant in important decisions. He always acted without any neurotic problems. But somehow—as a kind of gesture of filial respect—he managed it so that in all decisions his dependency on his mother was evident. It was discreet, tactful, hidden.

On the other side, behind love and devotion were his doubts about his mother's reliability, her truthfulness, her sexual life, etc. It was clear that his relationship to his mother—mature as it seemed—was still overshadowed by his childhood experience.

Another source of information was the transference. His fantasies regarding me were intensely and consciously sexual. Disregarding my old age, he identified me in his fantasies not with his mother, but with a notoriously dirty, debased, mentally abnormal, erotomanic cleaning woman whom he had known as a child. At other times he reinstated me to my important role as analyst and planned, in an irrational way, to give up his profession and to become an analyst like me. This dual evaluation expressed itself also in his relationship to analysis as such. He vacillated between enthusiastic acceptance and devaluating disbelief. On occasion he accused me of being dishonest, insincere.

Even without much speculation we can understand the persistence of Mr. Smith's amnesia: mature, responsible, successful in all aspects of life reality, Mr. Smith was still the 10-year-old boy fighting against the effects of the trauma. As in his youth, values important to his ego were still endangered, and the never-relinquished childhood dependency on his mother called for the defensive help of amnesia.

This statement seems paradoxical when one recalls that the defensive function of the amnesia was connected with a specific developmental stage of the ego. The ego of the adult is an independent, mature unit, able to function on its own, but still restricted by forces of the past. Resolved as his old identification with his mother appears to be, analytic insight revealed that this identification and the tendency to devalue her still persisted. And as long as these old forces had a representation in his inner life, he could not give up the defensive amnesia.

Summary

Two cases of amnesia are presented. They serve as a clinical demonstration of certain ego-psychological processes.

Both patients reacted with amnesia to traumatic events, using denial of the existence of these events as a defense. In both, this defense served individual goals: in the first case (Mr. Jones), the denial of an intolerable narcissistic blow; in the second (Mr. Smith), the saving of the ego ideal endangered by devaluation of the object of identification.

Remarkable in the first patient, whose amnesia developed in his adult life, was the fact that the "trauma" and the consecutive amnesia were due to a regressive process in the ego during a period of progress in his libidinal life. This patient was not aware of his amnesia; he discovered (and then eliminated) the deficiency in memory only when certain conditions in reality led to a corrective gratification of the repressed injury to his narcissism.

The second patient (Mr. Smith) covered by amnesia a trauma which occurred when he was 10 years old. Even in analysis he was not able to recover the memory of the traumatic events. This patient had always been aware of the amnestic gap, but he was not aware of the results of the trauma. All his achievements were harmoniously combined in a perfect adjustment to reality: profession, marriage, sex, etc. How much of these achievements was due to the autonomous (synthetic) function of the ego and how much to its defensive forces could not be unraveled. Only to the analytic observer was it evident that far-reaching restrictions existed in his functioning (for example, lack of creative imagination). These indicated a certain degree of ego impairment, which also manifested itself in the persistence of his amnesia. I tried to explain this persistence with the help of analytic material not directly related to the amnesia.

In both cases we can speak of "ego weakness" in the traumatic situation: in Mr. Jones, the pathogenic event regressively mobilized a revival of preadolescence with its demands and frustrations; Mr. Smith was actually in this critical period of development when the trauma occurred, and his pathology was the result of his emotional fixation at this period.

Since our knowledge of the chronological development of defense mechanisms is not sufficient, it is impossible to say whether the kind of amnesia my two patients demonstrated correlates with the particular phase of ego development in which both of them were at the time of the trauma. As we have seen, the avoidance of certain dangers to the ego and the achievement of better adaptation were the objectives which, to a certain degree, were obtained by the amnesia.

BIBLIOGRAPHY

Blos, P. (1958), Preadolescent Drive Organization. *J. Am. Psa. Assn.*, 6:47-56.
——— (1962), Preadolescence. *On Adolescence*. NY: Free Pr. of Glencoe, 57-75.
——— (1965), The Initial Stage of Male Adolescence. *Psa. Study Ch.*, 20:145-164.
Deutsch, H. (1944), *The Psychology of Women*, 1. NY: Grune & Stratton.
Eissler, K. R. (1955), An Unusual Function of an Amnesia. *Psa. Study Ch.*, 10:75-82.
Freud, A. (1936), *The Ego and the Mechanisms of Defense*. NY: IUP, 1946.
Freud, S. (1899), Screen Memories. *S.E.*, 3:301-322.
——— (1915), The Unconscious. *S.E.*, 14:159-215.
Hartmann, H. (1939), *Ego Psychology and the Problem of Adaptation*. NY: IUP, 1958.
——— (1952), The Mutual Influences in the Development of Ego and Id. *Essays*, 155-181.
——— (1956), Notes on the Reality Principle. *Essays*, 241-267.

Hendrick, I. (1964), Narcissism and the Prepuberty Ego Ideal. *J. Am. Psa. Assn.*, 12:522-528.

Kris, E. (1952), *Psychoanalytic Explorations in Art*. NY: IUP.

——— (1956), The Personal Myth. *J. Am. Psa. Assn.*, 4:653-681.

Spiegel, L. A. (1958), Comments on the Psychoanalytic Psychology of Adolescence. *Psa. Study Ch.*, 13:296-308.

Waelder, R. (1963), Psychic Determinism and the Possibility of Predictions. *Psa. Q.*, 32:15-42.

Depersonalization and Derealization

JACOB A. ARLOW, M.D.

In his writings, Hartmann (1950) emphasized repeatedly how the various functions of the ego which ordinarily operate in an integrated fashion may undergo separate transformations in the course of the defensive process. The purpose of this communication is to apply this concept to the phenomena of depersonalization and derealization. In previous studies I have used this approach to elucidate certain aspects of the *déjà vu* experience (1959a) and of distortions of the sense of time (1957). It is my thesis that depersonalization and derealization may be understood as representing a dissociation of the function of immediate experiencing from the function of self observation. In addition, I hope to demonstrate that this split occurs as a result of an attempt of the ego to ward off anxiety. As in the case of *déjà vu*, depersonalization reflects a breakdown of the integrative capacity of the ego operating through the medium of fantasy. Both wish fulfillment and defense contribute to the phenomena of depersonalization and derealization. A similar approach in this direction was made by Hartmann in 1922.

To concentrate first on depersonalization, any analysis of this phenomenon must be correlated with the clinical features characteristic of this abnormal mental state. The most common elements of depersonalization that one encounters clinically are the following. The patient reports a feeling of being split. He feels as if he were two selves at the same time. One self appears to be standing off at a distance in a detached and relatively objective manner observing another

Faculty, New York Psychoanalytic Institute, and Clinical Professor of Psychiatry, State University of New York, College of Medicine.

representation of the self in action. To the observing self the latter appears separate and estranged. Stated in terms of ego function, this state represents a sudden, dramatic dissociation of two functions of the ego which ordinarily operate in a harmonious and unified fashion. These functions represent two aspects of the sense of self, the sense of immediate participation and the awareness of observing oneself in action, i.e., self observation. Expressed in terms of self representation, depersonalization may be said to constitute a split between the participating self and the observing self. In depersonalization the sense of estrangement applies particularly to the participating self, and there is a concomitant accentuation of the function of the observing self. In spite of the fact that the participating self is treated as an object, the alienation of these two sets of functions is never complete. As the patient reports it, the observing self continues to maintain a sense of connection, however tenuous, with the participating self. The purpose of this paper is to indicate the defensive and wish-fulfilling meanings of this dissociation and to offer some suggestions concerning the origin of the predisposition of the ego functions to split in the manner indicated above.[1]

Survey of the Literature on Depersonalization

The literature on depersonalization may be divided into three broad categories from the point of view of the explanatory concepts employed by various authors. These concepts emphasize primarily: (a) the role of defense; (b) shifts in libidinal cathexis; and (c) conflicting identifications in the ego or superego.

Freud (1936) regards depersonalization as an example of the outcome of the ego's attempt to keep certain drive derivatives in repression. Bergler and Eidelberg (1935, 1950) made the concept of defense more specific in that they connected this function with the need to ward off anal exhibitionistic wishes. In this situation the ego effects a transposition of drive representation. The anal exhibitionism is converted into voyeurism, and the self is taken as the object of the voyeuristic wishes. As a concomitant defense, the mechanism of denial was stressed. Blank (1954) also emphasized the defensive use of

---

[1] Reich (1960) stressed the connection between exhibitionism and self consciousness in narcissistic personalities. The narcissistic imbalance shifts cathexis to the self from ego activities which are ordinarily neutral. This may lead to depersonalization. Bellak (1964) emphasized depersonalization as a variant of self awareness.

depersonalization against the threatened irruption of id derivatives and pointed out that the feelings of anxiety accompanying the attacks of depersonalization (from which the patients suffer) represent evidence of the failure of defense, which permits the precipitating anxiety to be experienced consciously. Fisher and Joseph (1949) studied related states, namely, fugue with awareness of loss of personal identity, and demonstrated how these dreamlike experiences could be understood from the point of view of the ego defending itself against derivatives of aggressive and erotic drives which it experiences as dangerous.

Fenichel (1945) and Nunberg (1955) both emphasized the narcissistic conflict in states of depersonalization. They explain the clinical phenomena by the concept of massive shifts of libidinal cathexis from investment in several objects (Fenichel) or one specific object (Nunberg) to the ego. "In states of estrangement, an increased narcissistic cathexis of the body is countered by defensive reactions; in depersonalization, an increased narcissistic cathexis of mental processes is handled in the same way. In depersonalization, overcharged feelings or conceptions are repressed. . . . The experiences of estrangement and depersonalization are due to a special type of defense, namely, to a countercathexis against one's own feelings which had been altered and intensified by a preceding increase in narcissism. . . . The results of this increase are perceived as unpleasant by the ego which therefore undertakes defensive measures against them" (Fenichel, 1945, p. 419). This approach essentially tries to utilize quantitative concepts concerning shifts of cathexis in order to account for feelings of unreality. The model employed follows that used by Freud (1914) in explaining the loss of the sense of reality which takes place in schizophrenia.

Nunberg (1955) also uses quantitative models as explanatory concepts: "The perception of the loss of a love object or the lowering of libido quantities is accompanied by the feeling that the reality of the perceptions and sensations of the ego has been lost. . . . the feelings of estrangement are the direct result of the *sudden* transposition of the libido from the object to the ego" (p. 134).

Stamm (1962) correlates the state of depersonalization with a regression to a primitive, oral, undifferentiated state (in which one of the main features is a withdrawal of cathexis from external objects) in pursuit of a wish for erotic fusion and for loss of differentiation between self and object. This state is characteristic of the fulfillment of the triad of oral wishes. In addition, he stressed the relationship between depersonalization and dreamlike states.

Sarlin (1962) states that the mechanism of depersonalization is an ego defense against powerful id drives. Depersonalization operates by withdrawal of cathexis from the self representation and results in feelings of estrangement from the self.

Oberndorf (1939, 1950), Jacobson (1954, 1959), and Sarlin (1962) analyze depersonalization from the point of view of conflicting identities. According to Oberndorf, there is a precise correlation between depersonalization and an inharmonious relationship between the major identification in the superego and the actual body ego (e.g., a feminine superego identification in a man). In the presence of such a sexual conflict one aspect of the self has to be repudiated. Jacobson's main point is that depersonalization eventuates from conflicting identifications in the ego itself. One identity is unacceptable to the other, and the repudiation of one may lead to feelings of depersonalization. In a similar vein, Sarlin maintains that depersonalization may result when the conflict between the parents becomes internalized within the ego of the child. In the struggle between simultaneous hostile identifications with both parents, the identity of the individual is lost.

As indicated, my approach coincides with the view that depersonalization represents the outcome of an intrapsychic conflict in which the ego utilizes, in a more or less unsuccessful way, various defenses against anxiety. The split in the ego which results in the dissociation between the experiencing self and the observing self takes place in the interest of defense. Explanations which utilize the concept of quantitative cathectic shifts to account for the phenomena of depersonalization are actually describing the phenomenon in different terms. In addition, such explanations do not make clear which functions of the ego are cathected or decathected, nor do they explain why depersonalization rather than grandiosity or hypochondriasis results from the shifts in cathexis. Explanations of depersonalization on the basis of conflicting identifications within the ego are actually explanations based on intersystemic conflicts, although they do not indicate this explicitly. The ego is built up of many identifications. Conflicts of identifications within the ego become dynamically significant only when the specific identifications represent derivatives of an id or of a superego demand (Arlow, 1963). In addition, these explanations do not account for the choice of defense by the ego.

Clinical Data

My own clinical experience with the analysis of patients who had attacks of depersonalization established the following points:

1. Depersonalization may occur in patients with very mild as well as very severe psychopathology.

2. Depersonalization and derealization are usually found together, although one or the other may be more prominent.

3. Almost all patients commented on the dreamlike nature of the experience.

4. All the patients, in their reports of the experience, stressed the subjective sensation of being split into two centers of awareness, a feeling of two selves, each operating in a different fashion. There was a self which seemed to be off in the distance involved in some realistic activity; at the same time, another portion of the self was experienced as observing the rest of the self as if it were an object. The major sense of identity was with the observing self; the participating self was not experienced with the same full sense of reality. There was nonetheless a sense of connection, however distant, with the participating self.

5. Experiences of depersonalization occurred in the context of severe intrapsychic conflict. Derivatives of the aggressive drive were especially prominent in these conflicts.

6. In those cases which were studied intensively, it was possible to trace the genesis of the defensive split of the ego in depersonalization. Disturbances in identity and the use of isolation, denial, and displacement were significant. It was striking, however, that for the most part the sense of personal identity was unaffected during the attacks of depersonalization.

The following clinical data constitute the main steps of my insight into depersonalization.[2]

CASE 1

The first patient described explicitly and dramatically the splitting of the sense of self which takes place in depersonalization. He was a

_____
[2] I am indebted to Dr. M. Furer for one of these cases.

14-year-old boy who was treated because of sensations of change in his body and recurrent attacks of depersonalization. When asked what was wrong, he complained, "Things are phony. I don't feel real. I don't feel myself." This patient was treated psychotherapeutically with the help of finger painting. He took the initiative in incorporating finger painting into the therapeutic process. While trying unsuccessfully to explain how he felt during an attack, he turned and reached for the painting he had made a few minutes earlier. In pale yellow, he had drawn two indistinct figures at opposite ends of a road. He pointed to the more distant one and said, "I am this person, but during an attack I feel that I may be this one [pointing to the opposite figure]. Or I'm here and sometimes I feel that I am there. During an attack I don't know who I am or where I am" (Arlow and Kadis, 1946).

This patient's conflict centered around his aggressive wishes toward his younger brother. His character structure was based upon a reactive combination of kindliness and tenderness toward his sibling. In situations which unconsciously represented to him the possibility of fulfilling his wish to destroy his brother, he would become depersonalized. Depersonalization represented an attempt to repudiate his undesirable, aggressive wishes. It had its origin in an experience in the country when the patient was 7 years old. He had pushed the younger brother out of a tree. The brother fell only a short distance, but had the wind knocked out of him and lay motionless on the ground. In the short interval of time before the brother's breath returned, the patient had the thought, "I've killed him." This was followed by the opposing thought, "It cannot be true." At that moment the patient experienced his first attack of depersonalization and derealization. In effect during the attack of depersonalization the patient's unspoken defense could be expressed in the following words, "I do not have to feel guilty for what is happening. I have nothing to do with it. I am only an observer. The whole thing is not real anyway." This same combination of defenses was used by the patient in associating to many finger paintings in which a rabbit or some other small animal symbolizing his younger brother was killed.

Sixteen years after the completion of this patient's treatment, he returned for consultation in order to discuss whether he should give up his job and move back to Brooklyn from an outlying section of Long Island. What had happened was that his father had died and his younger brother, who had remained unmarried, had moved back into his mother's apartment. During his conflict whether or not to move, the patient experienced once again mild attacks of depersonalization. There was a characteristic pallor which would sweep over the patient's face when he became depersonalized. During the more recent series of interviews this pallor and the accompanying depersonalization recurred whenever the patient talked about his brother. As on previous occasions, the depersonalization disappeared when the patient was able to recognize his hostile wishes toward his brother.

CASE 2

A 25-year-old woman who was seen for only a short period of time was suffering from depersonalization and derealization accompanied by states which may be described as midway between fugues and somnambulism. In the description of her complaints, she demonstrated the splitting of the sense of self into a participating and observing portion. When she had attacks of depersonalization, she felt quite alien from "the person" whom she observed involved in actual experience. This was accompanied by certain sensations of perceptual distortion in which the light seemed to be growing dimmer or brighter or in which the participating self seemed to be receding more and more from the observing self. On the other hand, in her somnambulistic, fuguelike states, she would become wholly immersed in the hallucinatory dream images. During such periods, she would become completely unaware of herself in relationship to the environment. The function of self observation was reduced to a minimum. Contrariwise, the function of experiencing was enhanced. On one occasion, immersed in her daydreams, she traversed a distance of half a mile along a busy street in mid-town New York, completely oblivious of what was happening to her in relationship to the environment. Only after she came out of the trance and reoriented herself in time and place was she aware of the fact that she had covered a certain distance of space and that she had lived through a certain period of time. Obviously she had maintained sufficient orientation toward reality to avoid being struck by automobiles while crossing the street, but no awareness of this portion of her mental activity could be recalled. She stated that she had been completely oblivious of herself as an entity functioning in the environment. The only awareness she could recollect was concerned with participating in her hallucinatory daydream.

This case is introduced to demonstrate the dissociation of the function of the observing self from the experiencing self. Hysterical hallucinosis is in a sense the opposite of depersonalization. In hysterical hallucinosis there is maximal investment in the function of immediate experience and an almost complete obliteration of the function of self observation. In depersonalization the opposite situation holds true. Self awareness is heightened and the sense of participation in action is minimized or alienated.

CASE 3

A 30-year-old male suffering from anxiety hysteria had two attacks of depersonalization. In order to understand the significance of these attacks, the following pertinent material is given. The patient was one of a set of identical twins. His brother died during college years under circumstances which led the patient to consider himself responsible. The patient reacted to his brother's death by patterns of denial and isolation. Upon retiring, he would say good night to the twin bed. When someone who did not know of the brother's death inquired after the brother, he would say, "He is all right." In his mind there were two opposing attitudes toward his brother's death. He both acknowledged it and denied it. He would never pronounce the words, "My brother is dead."

The typical "twinning reaction" took place between the patient and his brother. As children they liked to confuse people through their similarity. In his memories, the patient was often unsure whether something had happened to him or his brother. For example, he recalled an incident in which one of them had been struck in the head by a stone, but he was not sure whether it had happened to him or to his brother. When his brother was alive and he discussed the incident with him, his brother also recalled the incident, but he too was not sure who had been hit by the stone.

During his illness, which was characterized by claustrophobia and agoraphobia, the typical mechanism of the "protector under protection" could be discerned. When the patient was caught in traffic on a bridge or in a tunnel and became anxious, he would look at the driver of the car alongside of him and conclude, "If he is all right, so I must be all right too." The patient said that when his brother was still alive and he wanted to know whether the hair at the back of his head was properly groomed, he would look at the back of his brother's head. He used his brother instead of a mirror. In a sense, therefore, his brother could be used as an external self representation.

This patient had two attacks of depersonalization. The first took place at the beginning of his illness. This followed an experience in which the trauma of his brother's death was symbolically re-enacted. The patient had to make a decision whether or not to move a desperately sick uncle to the hospital. He decided to go with his uncle to the hospital by ambulance. The uncle, who represented to this patient a hated rival of the oedipal phase, expired in the patient's arms. The patient blamed himself for the uncle's death. A few nights later, the patient had a dream in which he saw himself split into two images. With one image he had a very strong sense of identification. The other image seemed to be floating upward toward the ceiling. He felt overwhelming anxiety and experienced a compelling need to grasp the aberrant image of himself and to bring it back to his body to re-establish his unity. Otherwise he felt he would lose his identity and split into two persons. He awoke from this dream in great anxiety with feelings of depersonalization and some derealization. These feelings did not leave him for four to five hours.

The second experience of depersonalization took place on the couch during the analysis. For months we had been analyzing the magical nature of his denial of the brother's death, especially his magical belief that as long as he did not pronounce any statement affirming that his brother was dead he could continue to believe that his brother was alive. Finally, the patient decided to face his fear. He said, "My brother is dead." As he said the words he felt extremely sick, turned pale, sat up on the couch, held his head in his hands, and felt completely estranged.

In both instances the experience of depersonalization served to buttress the denial of the reality of his brother's death. The patient had the unconscious fantasy of carrying within him an introject of his brother's. The abdominal pains which he experienced represented evidence that his brother was alive within him, that in effect he had not killed him. To forget his brother, to lose his introject was tantamount to an act of murder. By pronouncing the words, "My brother is dead," the patient had undone the denial which he had maintained for so long a time. The feelings of depersonalization and derealization which followed represented an attempt to repudiate what he had just done. In effect he was saying, "What I have just said is not real.

My brother *is* alive and therefore I do not have to feel guilty or fear retaliation."

CASE 4

The patient was a 31-year-old housewife who came to treatment with many complaints. Outstanding among these were severe attacks of depersonalization and anxiety. Ordinarily she was a quiet, rather obsequious woman, but when she *heard herself*, as she described it, shouting at her children and *observed herself* losing control, she felt she needed help. During treatment it was discovered that the attacks of depersonalization occurred under the following conditions: in association with scenes of violence, when the patient experienced the surging of violent impulses or when she was in a situation of overhearing or being overheard in private activity.

The patient, an articulate woman, was able to give a very precise description of her subjective mental state during an attack of depersonalization. She said she felt as if she were suddenly split into two persons, one person who was experiencing and another person who was standing off at a distance observing her own self in action. She felt involved with the "observing self" and dissociated from the "experiencing self." The analysis demonstrated that by this type of splitting during attacks of depersonalization the ego was able to repudiate to a degree the emergent id impulse which threatened to break through the barrier of repression. In effect, during an attack of depersonalization, the patient's unspoken defense could be expressed in the following words, "I do not have to feel threatened or guilty. What is happening has nothing to do with me. I am only an observer."

The conflicts from which the patient was suffering were the outgrowth of a disappointing marriage to a cold, detached man. She felt that the marriage had been a grievous mistake, but she could not admit to her parents that she had "made a mess" of her life. Instead she became anxious and withdrawn, unconsciously involved in fantasies related to her oedipal period. These fantasies centered on the wish to replace her mother in relation to her father and were connected with two experiences of witnessing the primal scene which she interpreted in a typical sadomasochistic fashion. She had reacted to them with mild depersonalization. By splitting into a participating and an observing self she repudiated the masochistic and retaliatory dangers which might follow from her identifying with her mother in fantasy. The fears of overhearing and being overheard were actually anal representations of oedipal wishes associated with the primal scene (Arlow, 1961).

The tendency to render alien certain portions of her experience was soon well documented. Her true feelings about her husband were not voiced by the patient herself. They became apparent from the analysis of a number of short stories which the patient had prepared for a class in creative writing. Even in this class, the patient did not behave as the other students did. She had to dissociate herself from her own product. Unlike the other students, she could not read her own creations. Someone else read her story for her while she behaved like an observer in the class. She had severe social anxiety and was afraid of criticism. She feared loss of control.

The danger of losing control reminded the patient of two proto-typical situations involving splitting of the ego into an observing and participating self. On the first day of kindergarten, the patient had an "accident." She lost control of her bladder and made a puddle in the classroom. The unsympathetic teacher gave the patient a cloth and made her clean up while the rest of the class stood around jeering and laughing. At first the patient felt overwhelmingly humiliated, but she mastered her embarrassment in the following manner. Suddenly she felt that she was one of the group of her classmates, laughing and jeering at the unfortunate little girl in the center of the circle. While identifying with the aggressors, she now felt no sense of identification with "the unfortunate little girl" at all. She had become an observer and by repudiating the humiliated self, who was busy mopping up the urine, she no longer felt ashamed.

The model for this type of splitting and for repudiating a portion of the self had been established during the period of bowel training. The mother was a peculiar person whose life revolved around her own and her children's bowel habits. She foisted many of her own bathroom rituals upon the children, examined their stools, established regimens of mineral water, enemas, etc. She insisted upon cleanliness and control and would repudiate and humiliate any child who made a mess. The patient learned how to manage the situation when she had an "accident." She would walk away from the stool and would come upon it a few minutes later with a feeling of complete dissociation. The stool no longer had any connection with herself. She completely repudiated her own product. What a few moments before had been within her own body and identified as part of her own self, had now become ego alien and foreign. This method of denying a portion of herself and of her experience the patient employed later in connection with her menarche. Her first period began during her sleep. The patient awoke and discovered she was menstruating and that she had stained the bed. She promptly went to sleep again having the thought that when she would awake she would discover that it was all untrue and that she had not begun to menstruate at all.

CASE 5

This material from the analysis of a 50-year-old business man concerns one attack of depersonalization which the patient had in a critical situation while he was in analysis. What is striking about the analysis of this attack is the fact that depersonalization served not only to ward off anxiety but actually enhanced the patient's capacity to deal with a difficult situation. It had, accordingly, an adaptive function.

The patient suffered from anxiety hysteria characterized by recurrent attacks of anxiety, fear of death, and globus hystericus. His symptoms were based upon typical castration anxiety associated with conflicts of the oedipal phase. This patient was inhibited in direct competition. His fear of retaliation led him to hide behind a "false front" of altered identity. The defensive use of splitting of the self representation is elucidated by the following material.

The patient was the fourth of five children. Three daughters had been born to his parents. These were followed by two boys who died in infancy. The mother, a superstitious peasant woman in a Baltic country, was determined that the patient should live. She bent her primitive magic to that end. At birth, the patient was given several names. When he was 2½ years old, according to the family legend, the patient took seriously ill. It was thought that he was going to die. His mother changed his name on that occasion in order to confuse the Angel of Death. According to the primitive beliefs of that region, God gives the Angel of Death a decree to take the life of a certain individual. If the individual's name is changed before the Angel can fulfill his mission, it is possible to confuse the Angel of Death who will not be able to track down and identify his victim.

The link between his defenses against the danger of castration and his identity disturbance was analyzed in connection with a dream. Part of the manifest content of this dream was the word *"shibboleth."* This word was associated with the story in the Book of Judges in which the members of a clan of an Israelite tribe were put to the sword. The members of the clan went into hiding, but their true identity became known when they were asked to pronounce the word *"shibboleth."* It was characteristic of the members of this clan to pronounce the word *"sibboleth."* The inability to pronounce properly betrayed the true identity of the individual and meant that he had to die. This material demonstrated that the patient unconsciously needed to conceal his identity in order to avoid punishment.

The attack of depersonalization occurred in a situation of direct confrontation which the patient had with his junior partners. Because of certain contractual obligations, a renegotiation of the arrangements among the partners became necessary. Several of the junior partners banded together in an obvious attempt to undermine the patient's position, if not to dislodge him altogether from his leadership in the firm. The patient was very anxious in this situation. He understood the efforts of his junior partners in terms of a group of siblings organized to destroy the authority of the father. This experience revived the patient's castration fears. While consciously he saw himself in the father role in relationship to his junior partners, unconsciously he felt himself to be in the position of the child who was threatened with castration by the oedipal father (cf. Rangell, 1955).

Eventually the patient could no longer evade a showdown meeting with his junior partners. Although he experienced great anxiety in anticipation of the meeting, he managed the actual confrontation very successfully. From his report it was clear that he had been depersonalized throughout the meeting. He said that he felt unreal, that he was not himself during the negotiations. He could observe himself as from a great distance, talking and maneuvering. The part of himself which was actually involved in the negotiations seemed unreal, distant, and unconnected to him. Even the sound of his voice seemed strange and alien. He reported that he felt safe and unperturbed because it seemed to him that he was not at all involved in the proceedings. The night after the negotiations, however, he had an anxiety dream which related to his oedipal conflict.

This material illustrates how depersonalization served to master castration anxiety. This fear of castration was stimulated by a realistic difficulty which reactivated infantile, oedipal conflicts. The patient became conscious of the fact that depersonalization represented a form of reassurance when he said he could feel safe and unperturbed because he was not at all involved in what was taking place. This method of reassurance was concretely represented in the experience of depersonalization by the splitting of the self representation into two separate components in a manner similar to that in the previous cases. The use of this method of defense was facilitated by previous experiences in which danger situations were magically averted by assuming a false identity.

CASE 6

The following clinical material demonstrates the origin of an attack of depersonalization in the context of fear of retaliation from rivals. The patient is a 46-year-old woman who suffered from guilt over hostile competitiveness toward her mother and sister. When she became pregnant she had a dream which expressed feelings of triumph over her mother and her sister. The sister had recently had a miscarriage which had aroused in the patient thoughts that the sister might die. On the day following the dream she was supposed to visit her mother. She complained about being very busy and had no time to feel anything but the unpleasant burden of being pregnant. The happy sensation of triumph had been pushed aside. She then added that she had been having an odd sensation during the day as though the pregnancy was happening to her and yet at the same time as if she were not really involved. She had the feeling as if she were a little, flat-chested, hairless child standing off and observing the pregnant woman. She said, "Perhaps there is some pleasure in being pregnant, but I am scared and I have the feeling that I don't deserve this, that it couldn't possibly be happening to me." The patient went on to add that as a result, she felt that everything was unreal, not only the pregnancy, but everything in her life.

Depersonalization and derealization appear in situations of realistic, external danger. In such instances these states are not pathological. Up to a certain point they may be adaptive. Jacobson (1959) mentions political prisoners who developed depersonalization during interviews with their captors. During these interviews the prisoners were able to handle themselves and their interrogators quite effectively if they felt detached from the situation. I would add that they avoided panic and maintained control by acting as if the situation were unreal, as if they actually were not involved, as if, in fact, they were only interested spectators, sympathetic but not completely identified with the hapless captive. The depersonalization which the business man (case 5) developed during negotiations with his junior partners also had an adaptive effect. It helped him master his anxiety in a situation of direct confrontation and thus spared him the damaging consequences which might have ensued had he lapsed back into his characteristic defense of pseudo imbecility.

CASE 7

The use of depersonalization and derealization to deny realistic danger may be observed most convincingly in people who have survived serious dangers. A patient who had twice been involved in automobile accidents experienced depersonalization and derealization on both occasions. During the first accident he felt like a detached, unconcerned observer. His life did not seem to be threatened at all in spite of the fact that he was clearly aware, at the time, that he was in mortal danger. During the second accident, while his car was careening out of control, he experienced a narrowing of the field of vision and found himself reflecting calmly on his own reactions. He thought to himself that this is how aviators must feel before they crash. Finally, as the car was about to strike an embankment, he made the following judgment. "This is all very foolish. I have a wife and two children at home. This can't be real. It can't be happening to me." In a fantasy which portrayed him as omnipotently invulnerable, he detached himself from the threatening danger and surveyed with calm objectivity another representation of himself which stood in danger of being killed.

Discussion

Clinical material demonstrates that depersonalization may appear when the ego is confronted by a danger which it cannot master. The danger may be a realistic, external one, in which instance depersonalization, up to a certain point, may serve an adaptive function. The states of depersonalization and derealization which are of significance in clinical practice, however, are those which arise out of internal danger. By a process of denial in fantasy, and displacement, the internal danger may be treated as congruent with the perceptions of the external world. The perceptions of the external world are taken as representatives of the internal danger and, accordingly, are repudiated. This is the mechanism involved in that portion of the patient's experience in which the world about him seems estranged and not quite real. The sense of reality is impaired while reality testing remains intact. There is no loss of the sense of identity.

Depersonalization serves a defensive function in the face of inner danger. Like *déjà vu* and distortions of time sense, depersonalization is an example of a regressive ego state which serves a reassuring function in the face of danger. The reassurance might be stated in the following words: "I don't have to worry. I don't have to be afraid. This danger is not real; besides, it is not happening to me." This reassurance is not entirely successful because the denial involved is only partial, not complete. Some awareness of the danger persists.

The method used in analyzing the structure of the experience of depersonalization is based upon three elements: (1) Technically, the experience of depersonalization is treated in the same manner as the manifest content of a dream or any other event. (2) The background of the preferred mechanisms of defense employed by the ego is investigated genetically. (3) The regression of certain functions of the ego is viewed in the context of defense mobilized by anxiety.

1. Several years ago Lewin (1952) demonstrated how phobias may be analyzed by treating them as if they were the manifest content of a dream. The text of the symptom, the patient's description of the phobia, is placed in the context of the patient's conflicts, and each element is treated like an element of the manifest content of a dream. Following this suggestion, I applied this method to the analysis of the *déjà vu* phenomenon and to distortions of the sense of time. Two factors should be underscored in this method. First, as in the case of the dream, the comments which the patient makes describing the experience must be treated as part of what one wishes the patient to associate to. Thus, if the patient characterizes a dream as being "vivid" or "eerie" or "interesting," etc., each one of these adjectives is treated as part of the dream and associations to them are elicited. The same is done with characterizations of the depersonalization experience such as, "I felt unreal. It was as if in a dream. I seemed a stranger to myself," or "I observed myself as from a distance," etc. One can obtain the patient's verbal account of his experience and encourage him to associate to the various elements of his account, bearing in

mind that every detail, every turn of phrase, every chance comment is in fact unconsciously determined and may throw light on the unconscious determinants of the patient's symptom or altered ego state.

The basis of this approach was established by Freud (1908) when he called attention to the connection between hysterical symptoms and unconscious fantasies. In general, hysterical symptoms allude to, or are part of, an unconscious fantasy expressed in body language or in physical action. The content of unconscious fantasies varies from patient to patient and from symptom to symptom, but a relation between conscious symptom and unconscious fantasy is present in each case.

A similar relationship may be demonstrated between altered ego states and unconscious fantasy. This applies to depersonalization and derealization. In these states the fantasy seems to be primarily a defensive one which can be expressed by the words, "This isn't happening to me. I'm just an onlooker," in the case of depersonalization, and by, "All of this isn't real. It's just a harmless dream, or make-believe," in the case of derealization. The fantasy, however, and especially the reassurance it conveys, does not become conscious *as a fantasy*. Instead the patient either *experiences* a feeling of estrangement from his surroundings or his surroundings appear unreal to him, or both. The unconscious fantasy gives rise to a conscious experience which the patient perceives as real, a process which in this respect is entirely analogous to the one which Freud demonstrated in hysterical symptom formation.

In the analysis of depersonalization or derealization a further element relates to the affect accompanying the experience of depersonalization. In this connection the analogy to the typical examination anxiety dream is especially valuable. In the examination anxiety dream, the patient is anxious not because he is dreaming that he is failing an examination. Actually the patient dreams he is failing an examination because he is anxious. The reassuring component of the dream which is contained in the manifest content of failing an examination (one which in reality he has already passed) proves insufficient to master the anxiety. Similarly, in depersonalization, the patient is not anxious because he feels depersonalized; he feels depersonalized because he wishes to ward off an anxiety-arousing danger.

2. Since the introduction of ego psychology, the problem of the choice of neurosis has been examined with emphasis on the influences

affecting the choice of defense employed by the ego. Fenichel (1939) stated the criteria which are essential for an adequate understanding of the genesis of a defense mechanism in his study of counterphobic attitudes. Hartmann (1950), Greenacre (1952), and Kris (1950) have studied the biological, developmental, and maturational factors which influence the nature and the function of ego defenses. More recently, Wangh (1959), in a careful study of ego development in a patient with phobias, elucidated how early object relationships, identifications, and the vicissitudes of the instinctual drives combined to fashion the functioning of the ego and superego in such a manner that the development of phobias was practically a predictable outcome of the patient's intrapsychic conflicts. In the analysis of the material presented earlier in this paper, I have attempted to follow this line of investigation and to demonstrate which experiences in the life of the patient disposed the ego to utilize a defensive splitting of the self representation, displacement, isolation, and denial as preferred methods of defense.

3. The structure of depersonalization and derealization typifies the regression of ego functions in the context of intrapsychic conflict. Studies of schizophrenia and psychosis, in particular, have demonstrated how certain functions of the ego may regress to more primitive modes of operations in the interest of warding off anxiety (Arlow and Brenner, 1964). Such regressions, however, are not confined to the psychoses. They may be observed transitorily in the neuroses as well as in the psychopathology of everyday life. Prominent among the functions which tend to regress in this fashion are perception, thinking, and reality testing (i.e., the ability to distinguish between fantasy and perceptions of the external world). In the case of *déjà vu* experience, the misperception of sensory data serves an ego need (defense) by asserting that the current danger is insignificant because it had already been mastered on an earlier occasion. In the case of certain distortions in the sense of time, the incorrect apperception of overly extended time duration may have the reassuring significance that the danger situation is unimportant because it is still in the distant future.[3] In the case of depersonalization, the altered perception of the self representation and the related change of feeling tone serve the ego's need to

---

[3] Distortions of time sense demonstrate how wish-fulfilling and defensive fantasies may intrude into the realm of the ego and alter its functioning.

ward off anxiety by assuring the individual that the danger is unreal (derealization) and that it actually does not involve him (depersonization).

To recapitulate, the essential ego alteration in the state of depersonalization is a dissociation of two ego functions which ordinarily operate in an integrated fashion, the function of self observation and the function of experiencing or participating. In depersonalization, this is felt as a split into two self representations, a participating self and an observing self. The participating self is partially, not completely, repudiated. A tenuous sense of connection, some feeling of identification, is still maintained with this self representation. The instinctual wishes which threaten to return from repression are displaced to the participating self or to the external world or to both. An attempt is made to repudiate these wishes by dissociating oneself from the self representation or from reality, or by considering the participating self or reality alien and estranged or both.

There are several primitive phases of ego development or functioning which may be regressively activated in the institution of this complex set of defensive maneuvers. These earlier modes of ego functioning have some of the features which appear later in states of depersonalization. Regressive reactivation of function from four early phases of ego activity seems genetically significant for depersonalization.

1. Many patients who experience depersonalization state that they feel unreal or as if in a dream. The experience of dreaming, is, of course, a regular and normal form of regression. In dreaming, two of the characteristics of depersonalization are very prominent. The dream is sensed as being unreal and there is a split in the sense of self into two self representations, an observing self and a participating self.

The reassuring awareness that what one is perceiving during sleep is only a dream is apparently a constant element in dreaming (Freud, 1900). In this aspect, it resembles the reassurance furnished by the sense of immobility during sleep. When the instinctual derivatives threaten to rupture the barriers of repression, the dream may become a nightmare. Under such circumstances the ego renders reassurance in the form of the reminder, "This is only a dream. This is not at all real" (Arlow and Brenner, 1964).

The split of the self into an observing and experiencing portion is one of the most characteristic features of dreaming, as it is of depersonalization. Sometimes in dreams the self is actually represented by two different people.

The psychology of sleep and dreaming serves to elucidate some of the specific features of depersonalization, specifically those features which pertain to the sense of estrangement or alienation of one or another of the organs of the body. Isakower (1938) described phenomena of the hypnagogic state in which some of the organs of the body are experienced as ego alien. Arlow (1949) and Beres (personal communication) have reported dream material from which the structure of organ alienation or estrangement could be deduced. In both instances the ego tried to repudiate certain forbidden anal wishes by "repudiating" the organ, by attempting to place it or its representative "at a distance" outside of the body image.

2. The phase of the transitional object, the phase during which the limits of the self and the nonself are not yet clearly demarcated (Winnicott, 1953; Jacobson, 1954), may be a prototype of the splitting of the self representation observed in depersonalization. Regression to this phase could possibly serve as the basis for the type of splitting observed in depersonalization. Data from my clinical experience do not contain evidence of a regressive reactivation of modes of ego function from this very early period of life. It would seem, however, that the findings reported by Stamm (1962) and by Jacobson (1959) could be conceptualized in terms of such a regression.

3. The relation of the child to its own fecal matter during the anal phase served as the prototype for the defensive split in the self in a very striking manner in one of the cases reported. During the anal phase the child has a very close narcissistic relationship to the fecal matter. Within the body, the fecal mass is considered part of the self. Freshly extruded, the fecal mass is experienced as existing in the external world, outside of the body, but retaining, nonetheless, a sense of connection with the self. Such experiences of the anal phase may serve as a model predisposing the child to repudiate a portion of himself in situations of conflict. The process of extrusion of the fecal mass, therefore, also contains the prototype for later mechanisms of denial and dissociation. In certain obsessional patients, all objects which have passed through the individual's experience are, in a regressive way, endowed with this quality of the sense of self which at one time pertained to the freshly extruded fecal mass (Fenichel, 1945). Objects are treated like food which, having passed through the body,

has been endowed with a sense of self. Subsequently, existing in the external world, they may be experienced by the individual either as belonging to the self or as alien. Oral and anal phase correlates of perception and mental activity form the basis upon which dissociation and alienation of the self may be built—mechanisms which are so important in depersonalization.

4. There is another phase of development in which there is a split between the experiencing and the observing self, or at least in which the self image may be treated as an object existing in the external world. This is the phase of the discovery of one's self before the mirror (Elkisch, 1957). Burlingham (1952) has demonstrated that the child at first regards his mirror image as another person, not himself. Only later is the connection made between the external sensory perceptions and the self. The split in the sense of self observed in depersonalization has its prototype in the experience before the mirror. This is a characteristic feature in the psychology of twins and in the narcissistic object choice. In the phenomena known as "the double" and the "imaginary companion," there is a similar defensive splitting. The ego in these instances tries to ward off the danger situation with the reassurance that not the self but the mirror image, the double, is the one who is threatened. Similarly, by the device of the imaginary companion, it is another portion of the self, a portion which one can observe, describe, and even criticize, that is vulnerable to anxiety and punishment. This type of mechanism was the basis of the defensive tendency to split the self representation in cases 3 and 5.

Summary

In this communication I have proposed that the phenomena of depersonalization may be understood in terms of a specific set of reactions of the ego in the face of danger. These reactions consist of a split in the self representation into a participating self and an observing self. The danger situation is experienced as pertaining to the participating self. The rest of the self is dissociated from the participating self. The latter is experienced as estranged. By a process of displacement, the warded-off impulses are connected with the participating self. In the act of repudiating these impulses the rest of the ego dissociates itself from the participating self through a defensive denial in fantasy. This results in a feeling of estrangement or depersonalization. Essentially the ego treats as real a fantasy in which the danger is conceived as involving a stranger, not the self.

These phenomena were studied by treating the experiences of depersonalization and derealization as one would a fantasy or a dream. The alteration of the ego state is explained in terms of a defensive regression to more primitive modes of ego functioning. This regression forms the background for the tendency to split the self into observing and participating parts. The primitive modes of ego functioning which are regressively reactivated are related to dreaming, the phase of the transitional object, the infantile relationship to the fecal mass, and the experience before the mirror. All of these may affect the experiencing of the self. My material does not make it possible to state whether any one of these phases is more significant than the others in establishing the tendency for the self representation to split. There may be individual differences depending upon the vicissitudes of development in each patient. From my material it also does not appear that there is any characteristic phase specificity to depersonalization and derealization. Depersonalization and derealization are examples of altered ego states instigated by defense and dominated by regressive distortion of certain ego functions. They may appear in connection with many different nosological or diagnostic entities. They do not seem to be typically related to conflicts emanating from a particular phase of psychosexual development.

BIBLIOGRAPHY

Arlow, J. A. (1949), Anal Sensations and Feelings of Persecution. *Psa. Q.*, 18:79-84.
——— (1957), A Contribution to the Psychology of Time. Read at the Los Angeles Psychoanalytic Society.
——— (1959a), The Structure of the *Déjà Vu* Experience. *J. Am. Psa. Assn.*, 7:611-631.
——— (1959b), The Concept of Repression. Read at the International Psycho-Analytical Congress, Copenhagen.
——— (1961), A Typical Dream. *J. Hillside Hosp.*, 10:154-158.
——— (1963), Conflict, Regression, and Symptom Formation. *Int. J. Psa.*, 44:12-22.
——— & Brenner, C. (1964), *Psychoanalytic Concepts and the Structural Theory.* NY: IUP.
——— & Kadis, A. (1946), Finger Painting in the Psychotherapy of Children. *Am. J. Orthopsychiat.*, 16:134-146.
Bellak, L. (1964), *Unfinished Tasks in the Behavioral Sciences.* Baltimore: Williams & Wilkins.
Bergler, E. (1950), Further Studies on Depersonalization. *Psa. Q.*, 24:268-277.
——— & Eidelberg, L. (1935), Der Mechanismus der Depersonalisation. *Int. Z. Psa.*, 21:258-286.

Blank, H. R. (1954), Depression, Hypomania, and Depersonalization. *Psa. Q.*, 23:20-37.

Burlingham, D. T. (1952), *Twins.* NY: IUP.

Elkisch, P. (1957), The Psychological Significance of the Mirror. *J. Am. Psa. Assn.*, 5:235-244.

Fenichel, O. (1939), The Counter-Phobic Attitude. *C.P.*, 2:163-173. NY: Norton, 1954.

—— (1945), *The Psychoanalytic Theory of Neurosis.* NY: Norton.

Fisher, C. & Joseph, E. D. (1949), Fugue with Awareness of Loss of Personal Identity. *Psa. Q.*, 18:480-493.

Freud, A. (1951), Observations on Child Development. *Psa. Study Ch.*, 6:18-30.

Freud, S. (1900), The Interpretation of Dreams. *S.E.*, 4 & 5.

—— (1908), Hysterical Phantasies and Their Relation to Bisexuality. *S.E.*, 9:155-166.

—— (1914), On Narcissism. *S.E.*, 14:67-102.

—— (1936), A Disturbance of Memory on the Acropolis. *S.E.*, 22:239-248.

Greenacre, P. (1952), Pregenital Patterning. *Int. J. Psa.*, 33:410-415.

Hartmann, H. (1922), Ein Fall von Depersonalization. *Z. Neurol. Psychiat.*, 74:593-601.

—— (1950), Comments on the Psychoanalytic Theory of the Ego. *Essays*, 113-141.

Isakower, O. (1938), A Contribution to the Pathopsychology of Phenomena Associated with Falling Asleep. *Int. J. Psa.*, 19:331-345.

Jacobson, E. (1954), The Self and the Object World. *Psa. Study Ch.*, 9:75-127.

—— (1959), Depersonalization. *J. Am. Psa. Assn.*, 7:581-610.

Kris, E. (1934), The Psychology of Caricature. *Psychoanalytic Explorations in Art.* NY: IUP, 1952, 173-188.

—— (1950), Notes on the Development and on Some Current Problems of Psychoanalytic Child Psychology. *Psa. Study Ch.*, 5:24-46.

Lewin, B. D. (1952), Phobic Symptoms and Dream Interpretation. *Psa. Q.*, 21:295-322.

Nunberg, H. (1955), *Principles of Psychoanalysis.* NY: IUP.

Oberndorf, C. P. (1933), A Theory of Depersonalization. *Trans. Am. Neurol. Assn.*, 59:150-151.

—— (1939), On Retaining the Sense of Reality in States of Depersonalization. *Int. J. Psa.*, 20:137-147.

—— (1950), The Role of Anxiety in Depersonalization. *Int. J. Psa.*, 31:1-5.

Rangell, L. (1955), The Role of the Parent in the Oedipus Complex. *Bull. Menninger Clin.*, 19:9-15.

Reich, A. (1960), Pathologic Forms of Self-Esteem Regulation. *Psa. Study Ch.*, 15:215-232.

Sarlin, C. N. (1962), Depersonalization and Derealization. *J. Am. Psa. Assn.*, 10:784-804.

Stamm, J. L. (1962), Altered Ego States Allied to Depersonalization *J. Am. Psa. Assn.*, 10:762-783.

Wangh, M. (1959), Structural Determinants of Phobia. *J. Am. Psa. Assn.*, 7:675-695.

Winnicott, D. W. (1953), Transitional Objects and Transitional Phenomena. *Int. J. Psa.*, 34:89-97.

Superego and Depression

DAVID BERES, M.D.

In the A. A. Brill Lecture, "On the Scientific Aspects of Psycho-analysis," Heinz Hartmann (1958, p. 305), said that " 'good theory' cannot be written without broad clinical experience and that every clinical understanding presupposes knowledge in theory." At the same time he pointed up the danger of confusing what is observed and what is hypothesized, that "the hypotheses may interpenetrate with fact finding in such a way that their hypothetical character is not always clearly recognized" (p. 305).[1] With these thoughts in mind I propose to consider several questions relating to superego and depression and to correlate clinical data and theoretical concepts. My questions fall into two categories.

1. Shall we separate from depression other affective states such as sadness, apathy, grief, and unhappiness, especially in terms of psychodynamic differences?

2. What is the role of superego function in depression and what is the relation of guilt to superego function and depression? As part of this question I also ask, can we differentiate guilt from allied affects such as remorse and shame?

I attempt, further, among the complex elements that enter into the clinical picture of depression, to separate the predisposing factors and the accompanying manifestations of depression from what I suggest is the basic, ever-present determinant. It is unfortunate that the

I wish to thank the participants in the Kris Study Group on Depression which 'met at the New York Psychoanalytic Institute in 1961-1963 and with whom I had the opportunity to discuss many aspects of this topic. The responsibility for the contents of this paper is, however, entirely my own.
[1] See also Hartmann, Kris, and Loewenstein (1953).

technical vocabulary of psychoanalysis includes terms that are in common usage. This applies to both "depression" and "guilt." It becomes imperative to clarify the scientific use of these terms in our work and to distinguish this from the loose use of such terms in everyday discourse.

I shall not review the extensive literature on depression except to note that most authors have recognized that depression as an affective state may occur in any pathological condition as well as in normal persons. This transient manifestation of depression is to be distinguished from depressive illness in which depression is the predominant clinical manifestation.

Freud (1917) described melancholia (which was his designation for depressive illness) as follows: "a profoundly painful dejection, cessation of interest in the outside world, loss of the capacity to love, inhibition of all activity, and a lowering of the self-regarding feelings to a degree that finds utterance in self-reproaches and self-revilings, and culminates in a delusional expectation of punishment" (p. 244). Freud related melancholia to the ambivalence associated with the loss of the loved object and distinguished it from grief and mourning.

Depression, whether a fleeting manifestation or part of a depressive illness, is an affective state. The patient may recognize this and report that he "feels depressed"; or he may not recognize his depression and express it indirectly, as, for example, by seeking out punishment. But shall we always agree with the patient when he states, "I am depressed"? May not closer examination reveal an allied affect, perhaps sadness, discouragement, unhappiness, or grief? This may seem to be a semantic problem, and some authors speak of different kinds of depressions. It is my opinion, however, that it would be more advantageous to separate depression from these other allied affects.

A frequent clinical finding in depression is the loss of an object, which may be the loss of a person, the loss of love, or the loss of a symbolic object which represents a loved person or ideal. Some authors have made such loss the primary basis of depression.[2] But does the loss of the object or the loss of love always result in depression? Clinical observation indicates that this is not so. Freud (1917, p. 250f.)

---

[2] For instance, Nacht and Racamier (1960, p. 484) maintain that "the loss of love is the fundamentally depressive situation . . . and the breaking of a close and mutual bond of love is at the base of every state of depression."

clearly demonstrates that an additional factor is necessary for the bereaved person to develop melancholia instead of a normal mourning reaction. What then determines whether, when there is a loss of an object, there will be anxiety, grief, sadness, or depression?

In observations of children the response to object loss can be studied *in statu nascendi*. The child's response differs in different phases of his development. The earliest phase, when the infant is in the stage of need satisfaction before object constancy is established, is characterized by a catastrophic reaction to the failure of gratification, the loss of the need-satisfying object. It is the reaction of "organismic distress" described by Margaret Mahler (1952, p. 286) with its "affectomotor storm-rage reactions." In a later phase, when object constancy has been established, and when separation of self and nonself is in progress, the reaction is sadness or grief if there is a disturbance in the relationship with the constant object, either by deprivation or separation. In this stage of his development a child's reaction to object loss or narcissistic injury does not have the quality of depression.[3]

Descriptive definitions of depression, though important in phenomenological studies, are of limited usefulness in establishing psychodynamic distinctions. Hartmann (1958, p. 309) has said on this point "that elements of behavior, similar in a descriptive sense, may be considered dynamically or genetically as rather different, and vice versa." Our search would then be for the distinctive underlying psychodynamic factors that enter into the depressive picture as distinct from those of other allied affects.

The familiar triad of "depressed moods, inhibition of thinking, and psychomotor retardation" is a definition which contains within it the term which we are trying to define and so fails as a definition. As a matter of fact, in the many books and articles on depression one finds that the authors usually take for granted the term itself and plunge directly into explanations of the factors that are advanced as the causes of depression, whether it be loss of object, narcissistic injury, loss of self esteem, helplessness, or hopelessness. I shall attempt to illustrate the difference between depression and other affects by clinical examples.

A young woman, 25, began the session by saying, "I feel de-

[3] Rochlin (1959) offers cogent clinical evidence to support this conclusion. I shall discuss this point further later.

pressed." On closer questioning she said that she did not feel blue, she did not feel like crying; "it is just that I do not like to get up in the morning; I feel down in the dumps." The patient was usually seen in the afternoon but this time came for an early morning session. Her complaint was that she missed the warmth of her bed, that she felt this way every morning when she had to get up. Even as she was talking her mood lifted and the so-called "depression" disappeared. This patient was an infantile character, very dependent on her mother; in fact, she came into analysis because of a postpartum depression. Yet I do not consider the episode I described as indicating a depressive reaction. Rather it seems like the hurt, disappointed feeling of a small child who does not get what she wants at the time when she wants it.

The patient's presenting symptom was of a different order. Her infant was 3 months old, a first-born child. She felt completely at a loss about the simplest matters concerning the care of her child. To this her mother had contributed by overprotecting her throughout her own childhood, fostering her dependence, and reminding her constantly that she was incapable of any sustained activity. The pregnancy itself had been without incident. There was evidence of marked oral fixation and strong penis envy. The explanation that the postpartum depression was a reaction to the narcissistic loss—the child being equated with the penis—suggested itself and was indeed a factor, but was not central in the patient's associations. What did appear to predominate was that the patient had strong aggressive and ambivalent feelings directed toward her child, toward her husband, and toward her mother, and that she felt guilty about these aggressive and ambivalent feelings.

The affective state which marked the presenting illness was quite different from the passing episode which I first described. In the former, she had an intense feeling of worthlessness, self degradation, and a conscious sense of guilt, as well as psychomotor retardation and anxiety; in the latter, there was only a feeling of apathy and resentment.

Another patient in whom the transition from one affective state to another could be noted in one session was a woman of 35, also with considerable oral fixation, who was talking about her dependency wishes which she had realized in the course of the analysis she must renounce. She expressed a feeling of sadness, which, however, she said was not painful. As her associations led to the death of her father which had occurred some years before when it was found that he had left a modest fortune although he had kept the family in a state of economic deprivation, she became angry and at the same time the feeling of sadness without pain was replaced by a feeling of painful dejection, which she recognized was the result of the guilt evoked by the anger against her dead father.

Even when the patient's reactions and the analyst's empathic response indicate a true state of depression, the analyst must question the patient's explanation of his mood, which may be a rationalization. A man of 35 appeared at his session looking distraught, with a sad, long face, and dragging out his words in a monotone slightly above a whisper. The empathic impression was indeed that of a depressive state. He explained his mood as "a general reaction"; he was disappointed in his accomplishments at his work. He expressed a feeling of hopelessness and fantasies of being killed. We may take the thought of self injury as an indication of guilt, but still there is the question: what is making the man guilty? I would maintain that the general feeling of failure in his work is not enough to explain his mood. It may even be that he feels inadequate as the result of a feeling of guilt.

Further associations revealed the source of the guilt to be competitive fantasies in the transference; these, in turn, were related to his ambivalent relationship to his father whom he had surpassed in professional achievement. His disappointment in his father covered a sense of triumph over him, and about this he felt guilty. In this instance the sense of inadequacy, the fall in self esteem, the hopelessness, the apathy, the disappointment were what I earlier spoke of as the accompanying manifestations of the depressive state. The determining factor in this case, as in those of the other patients I described, was guilt. If I had accepted the patient's first rationalization that his mood was the result of his feeling of inadequacy in his work, we would not have discovered the oedipal guilt behind the manifestation. I should also add that the sense of inadequacy in his work was itself a rationalization and quite unrealistic. It was the expression of a transference hostility and jealousy related to his competitive feeling toward me.

The depression which accompanies success is a familiar clinical finding described by Freud (1916) in "those wrecked by success." A striking example is a successful professional woman who had outstripped her husband in an allied profession, and who cried when she spoke of her success. This, it turned out, was because her accomplishment was a triumph, a reliving of the infantile jealousy of her older brother; and with the recognition of her envy, her aggression, and her hostility, her reaction was one of guilt and depression. It was, she said, "bitter fruit."

My thesis, as these cases illustrate, is that an essential determinant of true depression, whether as a transient manifestation or as part of depressive illness, is a sense of guilt which carries with it the assumption of a structured superego and an internalized conflict. I would maintain that without the sense of guilt and the structured superego we do not have what I would consider to be true depression. Where there is no guilt and in the so-called depressions of childhood before the superego is formed, I suggest that we are dealing with other affects such as sadness, apathy, or disappointment. These affects may and do to a considerable degree enter into and are part of true depression. Where there is helplessness, narcissistic injury, or loss of object, these factors can be resolved further to demonstrate the underlying guilt. Nor does the guilt stem directly from the helplessness, the narcissistic injury, or the object loss, but from the unconscious fantasies evoked by the experience, whether related to preoedipal or oedipal conflicts.

Other authors have advanced as causative factors of depression what I believe to be its accompanying manifestations. Bibring (1953), for example, emphasizes the state of helplessness and powerlessness of the ego and the decrease of self esteem, and he considers aggression and orality to be secondary factors. Jacobson (1953) also places narcissistic injury in the foreground of depression. She writes: "The central psychological problem in depression appears to be the narcissistic breakdown of the depressed person: his loss of self-esteem, . . . his feelings of impoverishment, helplessness, weakness, and inferiority; or, in the melancholic type, of moral worthlessness and even sinfulness" (p. 53).

I do not know how we can prove, as Bibring (1953) maintains, that the turning of aggression against the self is secondary to the lowering of self esteem. It is equally tenable that the guilt evoked by aggression may bring on lowering of self esteem. Jacobson (1953) in fact notes that, "The incessant complaints and self-accusations of the melancholic, his exhibition of his helplessness and his moral worthlessness, are both a denial and a confession of guilt: of the crime of having destroyed the valuable love-object" (p. 80).

The demonstration of guilt in a patient is not always a simple matter. Even a patient's statement that he is guilty does not necessarily mean that his affect corresponds to our dynamic understanding of guilt. He may simply be aware of wrongdoing, be remorseful, afraid of punishment, or even ready to confess in order to gain absolution. Nor does self punishment always indicate guilt. The turning of aggression on the self in childhood as well as in adult life is a familiar phenomenon and not necessarily associated with guilt.[4] There is the additional difficulty which stems from the concept of an unconscious sense of guilt. In our clinical work we assume the existence of guilt where there is self accusation or self revilement. This may be accompanied by a disturbance in the sense of reality and assume psychotic proportions of self blame. We also assume the existence of guilt in the cases of moral masochism which are familiar to us in the fate neuroses, patients whose lives seem to take on a pattern of repeated injuries and self-destructive activity. In the therapeutic situation we recognize the sense of guilt in the negative therapeutic reaction, although there may be other reasons for this response. There are more complex manifestations of the sense of guilt; e.g., the criminal who acts out of a sense of guilt and whose criminal behavior is the expression of a conflict in which the lesser crime is committed in order to cover up the more dangerous unconscious crime. Guilt does not necessarily lead to depression. The sense of guilt, whether conscious or unconscious, may mobilize ego defenses which result in other psychic manifestations such as obsessive character structure or obsessive-compulsive psychoneurosis (see Freud, 1909).

Freud (1930, p. 137) spoke of two strata of the sense of guilt, one coming from the fear of external authority, the other from fear of the internal authority. He also referred to "the bad conscience" of the individual who is afraid of external authority, but, Freud added, this does not deserve the name conscience, "for at this stage the sense of guilt is clearly only a fear of loss of love, 'social' anxiety. In small children it can never be anything else" (p. 125).

We are, of course, familiar with the psychoanalytic concept according to which the sense of guilt indicates an intrapsychic conflict

[4] In this connection see Anna Freud (1949, p. 39; 1965, p. 76), Beres (1952, p. 246), and Loewenstein (1957, p. 214).

dependent on internalization of superego functions. Freud makes this point in his description of the development from "social" anxiety to superego formation. He says: "A great change takes place only when the authority is internalized through the establishment of a super-ego. The phenomena of conscience then reach a higher stage. Actually, it is not until now that we should speak of conscience or a sense of guilt" (1930, p. 125). It needs no emphasis that the sense of guilt in the psychoanalytic frame of reference should not be equated with the dictionary definition of guilt: "the having committed a specified or implied offence." The sense of guilt, as the psychoanalyst sees it, can be the response to a fantasy, often an unconscious fantasy, as well as the response to an actual deed.

Unfortunately Freud was not consistent in his formulations on this subject. A few pages after he expresses the opinion that we should not speak of a sense of guilt until the internalization of the external authority, the establishment of a superego, he speaks of the two *strata* of the sense of guilt (see above), and adds, "As to a sense of guilt, we must admit that it is in existence before the super-ego, and therefore before conscience, too. At that time it is the immediate expression of fear of the external authority, a recognition of the tension between the ego and that authority" (1930, p. 136). The two statements are not compatible and I would follow Freud, in the interest of clinical and theoretical clearness, only in his suggestion that the sense of guilt be limited to superego activity, "the tension between the harsh super-ego and the ego that is subjected to it" (1930, p. 123).

These considerations raise the question whether guilt can be distinguished from other responses to wrongdoing, and whether this distinction can be made on the basis of the determining conflict being an internal or an external one. This applies especially to the distinction between shame and guilt.

A common clinical example of the distinction between shame and guilt is seen in patients who masturbate compulsively—even to the point of preferring it to intercourse, which often results in ejaculatio praecox. They rationalize their masturbation and state that they feel no guilt about it. When their masturbatory activities are analyzed, they react only with a feeling of shame and a concern that the analyst will disapprove of them. However, about their sexual inadequacy they usually express a feeling of guilt. Their obsessional character structure makes it possible for them to isolate in their masturbation their incestuous fantasies from the mechanical act of masturbation. This they cannot do in sexual relations with their partners because the incestuous fantasies then present themselves more forcefully and interfere with their sexual function. The relationship with a real person does not permit them to exercise the defense of isolation. When they talk about their sexual inadequacy they are self-accusatory and self-reviling. When they talk about their masturbation they are defiant, though ashamed.

I would suggest from such clinical observations that the determining factor which distinguishes guilt from shame is that the former stems from an internalized conflict and the latter from conflict with an external authority. There is not universal agreement on this point. Hartmann and Loewenstein (1962) question that one can distinguish between shame and guilt in terms of outer or inner sanctions. They "are reluctant to overemphasize the separateness of the ego ideal from the other parts of the superego, and it is, partly, the question of separateness on which the structural opposition of guilt and shame hinges" (p. 67). They are here examining the hypothesis proposed by Piers and Singer (1953) that "shame arises out of a tension between the ego and the ego-ideal, not between ego and superego as in guilt" (p. 11). I also would question this hypothesis, but at the same time I do not accept that it follows that shame and guilt cannot be differentiated in terms of outer and inner sanctions. I do not agree with Piers and Singer when they assume that shame is related to immature, infantile elements alone; that shame accompanies failure and guilt transgression. It is conceivable that failure also may evoke a fantasy which stimulates guilt rather than shame. Superego functions are involved in the maintenance of ideals, and the failure to live up to these ideals may evoke guilt as part of an intrapsychic conflict.

Freud (1905, p. 194) notes the role of shame in the child's gradual control of infantile sexual activities. Jacobson (1964) states that shame arises early in "reaction to pregenital (oral and especially anal) and to phallic-exhibitionistic strivings" (p. 143). Clinical evidence supports her statement that "shame and likewise inferiority feelings and feelings of humiliation have much more elementary narcissistic-exhibitionistic implications" than do guilt feelings which "seem to have a particular reference to hostility and harm to others, and in general to the quality of our object relations" (p. 146).

The moot question is whether this difference depends on the

nature of the conflict or on the degree of internalization of critical attitudes toward unacceptable behavior at different phases of development. In the young child in whom conflicts are essentially around pregenital drives and internalization has not yet developed, one would expect shame and not guilt to be the manifest response. Similarly, in older persons with regression of superego function and externalization of this function one would expect shame to replace guilt. It also follows that a conflict around infantile sexuality promotes regression with externalization of superego functions, and thus results in a shame reaction rather than a guilt reaction.

The factor of internalization is crucial in determining the different responses. It is necessary to consider this in some greater detail as my thesis depends on the formulation that the existence of a sense of guilt assumes the internalization of the functions ascribed to the super-ego and, in turn, that depression, whether as an affective state or as an illness, occurs only with the capacity to experience guilt (Beres, 1966). I would maintain, further, that the depressive mechanism, whether in a normal person with a transient depressive reaction, in a neurotic depression, or even in a psychotic depression, is similar; and that there are not different kinds of depressions but only different clinical manifestations of this unitary mechanism.

Freud (1940) states that about the age of 5 an important change has taken place in the child's psychic development: "A portion of the external world has, at least partially, been abandoned as an object and has instead, by identification, been taken into the ego and thus become an integral part of the internal world" (p. 205). Identification is an essential process for the establishment of internalization, but identification is not the same as internalization. There may be identification of a transitory nature, such as is characteristic in the young child or the "as if" character in adult life, without internalization. Identification precedes internalization. The term incorporation also needs to be more carefully defined in this context, although some authors use these three terms interchangeably, which I believe is incorrect. I shall digress briefly.

We recognize in human psychic activity, in children as well as adults, the response to perceptual stimuli by which what was in the external world is represented in the mind, in the internal world that Freud speaks of. The analogy to the instinctual process of "taking in" leads us to name this psychic process *incorporation*. The capacity of the human mind to create symbols transforms the incorporated perceptions into mental representations, what Freud called *"Vorstellungen."* The mental representation is built up on memory traces and both are theoretical constructs which must be distinguished from each other. Mental registration, which is essential for memory, occurs in animals as well as in man. In the human the imaginative faculty goes on to form the mental representation (Beres, 1960, 1965). Incorporation may be expressed as a fantasy of *introjection* and the product of this fantasy is the *introject.*

Introjects thus are mental representations and may be either self or object representations. The capacity to separate self representations from object representations must be attained before the child can separate self from nonself. As the child takes on the attributes of the incorporated object we recognize the process of *identification.* At first the self and object representations are merged, but as individuation progresses the attributes of the object become his own. He has become a separate individual, in time aware of his separateness and with functioning ego and superego.[5] Jacobson (1954) discusses the essential difference between ego identifications[6] and early infantile identification mechanisms: "The first are realistic in so far as they result in lasting changes of the ego which justify the feeling to be at least partially *like* the love objects. The latter are magic in nature; they represent only a temporary—partial or total—blending of magic self- and object images, founded on fantasies or even the temporary belief of being one with or of *becoming* the object, regardless of reality" (p. 243, my italics). Sandler (1960) also distinguishes these two phases of identification which he calls primary and secondary identification, the former being characterized by fusion of self and object (p. 150).

The final step in this process is *internalization* when the attributes

[5] Sandler (1960) in a detailed study of the superego deals with this problem. He says: "One can neither identify with nor introject aspects of another person unless one's ego has previously constructed some sort of mental model of that person" (p. 146). Sandler does not define "mental model." If this includes memory schemas which precede the formation of mental representations, I would agree.

[6] I must add at this point my opinion that it is confusing to speak of different kinds of identification, for instance, "ego identifications," "superego identifications," "preoedipal identifications," etc. The basic mechanism of identification is, I believe, the same in all instances. What determines the different end products of the process of identification are secondary factors—the phase of development, coexisting ego capacities, the nature of the characteristics with which the individual identifies, and, to a great extent, the theoretical orientation of the observer (Beres, 1958, p. 336).

of the object with which the child has identified become his own. It is a difficult concept to define. Even Freud's statement, which I have quoted, is only a description of the end product of a complex of activities involving memory, self representation, object representation, self and nonself separation, and the organizing function of the ego. We cannot see internalization. We can only see the end results of the entire process, the manifest derivatives in the thought processes, actions, and affective responses of the individual. Hartmann and Loewenstein (1962) also offer a descriptive definition: "We would speak of *internalization* when regulations that have taken place in interaction with the outside world are replaced by inner regulations" (p. 48).[7]

Ritvo and Solnit (1960) describe superego formation in three children observed in a longitudinal study. They focus on the role of early ego identifications and the process of internalization. I quote their conclusions in support of my thesis: "We use the term internalization to describe that process by which the ego forms inner or psychic representations of objects that had originally influenced the child from without. This process is a continuum from perception, to imitation, to taking over a characteristic of an object in an ego identification" (p. 255), and "Then, this ego identification can become available as a forerunner to the prohibiting, moralizing, socializing superego and its extensions, the ego ideal and conscience" (p. 299).

With internalization we assume a structured superego; but as we also assume that the superego develops gradually, we must postulate precursors of superego function. We find that before the superego has developed as an internalized psychic structure, certain drive manifestations and certain ego defensive measures are available to the child to deal with conflict situations. These include reaction formation, reversal, and turning on the self. An important clinical observation in young patients in latency or early adolescence, where there may be a good deal of acting out of delinquent behavior with evidence of minimal internalization and inadequate superego control, is the spoken and unspoken demand by these children for external controls.

---

[7] They also call incorporation an instinctual activity, a genetic precursor of identification. They note that clinically one often finds "incorporation fantasies" (p. 49). I spoke above of the latter as introjects, and of introjection as a fantasy of incorporation.

The bearing of these considerations on the problems of depression may be illustrated by two groups of patients who, though externally entirely different, suffer a similar psychopathological disturbance. The one group consists of patients brought up by parents who themselves have severe superego inadequacy, parents who expose their children to antisocial behavior or even to overt incestuous activity. The second group consists of patients who have received a strict religious upbringing and who from earliest childhood on have had their moral behavior determined by the external sanctions imposed upon them, the fear of punishment by divine authority. In both groups there is little opportunity for adequate internalization of appropriate superego functions. The similarity between the two groups appears clinically as the child approaches adulthood and is faced with the temptations of instinctual drive impulses without the support of external controls. This occurs in the patients brought up with strict religious training when they attempt to break away from their religious background. There is in both groups, characteristically, a period of phobic defense which may be followed by acting out or severe character disorder. My experience with patients of this sort is that they do not suffer actual guilt or depression; they manifest social anxiety or remorse. An example of such a patient was a 34-year-old virgin with a parochial background, who after a long period of phobic avoidance of any relationship with men found herself approaching a sexual relationship. Her anxiety expressed itself in the fear that her mother would find out, that the neighbors would see her, but she did not experience an inner guilt reaction. This patient suffered a great deal of unhappiness, but she did not demonstrate a significant depressive reaction. It remains to be seen whether her later response will be that of remorse or guilt. In the course of analysis such patients begin to internalize moral attitudes, thus undergoing a delayed development of superego. One can then observe an increasing expression of guilt and depressive reactions where before there had been only social anxiety and unhappiness.

The question of childhood depression arises in this connection. If I am correct in assuming that without a structured superego there cannot be either guilt or depression, how can we account for the published reports of depressions in children, when presumably an internalized superego has not yet developed? There are Spitz and Wolf's (1946) descriptions of "anaclitic depression" in children deprived of their mothers in early infancy; and there is the unusual case of an infant with a gastric fistula who developed what Engel and Reichsman (1956) called a "depression-withdrawal reaction," which "typically occurred when the infant was confronted alone by a stranger and was characterized by muscular inactivity, hypotonia, and sad facial expression, decreased gastric secretion, and eventually a sleep state. It vanished as soon as the baby was reunited with a familiar person" (p. 428f.). The authors' detailed clinical observations and the experimental evocation of the "depression-withdrawal reaction" are most impressive, but the reasons for calling it a depression are not convincing. They say: "First and foremost was the impact on the observer of the facial expression, posture, and inactivity, all of which called to mind a mood of dejection, sadness, or depression. There was a striking similarity between this appearance and that which we are accustomed to associate in the adult with comparable affects, whether part of normal grief or depression" (p. 438f.). However, precisely because in cases of this sort responses appear to be similar but may differ in their basic psychodynamics, it is important to distinguish sadness, unhappiness, or apathy from depression.

In a recent paper on childhood depression Sandler and Joffe (1965) also assume the existence of a "depressive reaction" in children. They see it as "a specific mode of affective reaction rather than a syndrome or an illness in itself" (p. 90), and they find it "in circumstances in which the child was faced with a specific type of threat to his well-being. An essential aspect of this is the feeling of having lost, or of being unable to attain, something which was essential to his narcissistic integrity. Coupled with this was the feeling of being helpless and unable to undo the loss" (p. 91). The authors note the similarity of their view to that of Bibring which I discussed above. The questions I raised about the latter apply as well to the former. The authors say: "There are, of course, many different ways in which the child can react to painful experiences of this sort [loss of well-being], and we cannot equate all varieties of unhappiness with the depressive reaction. If, however, his response is characterized by a feeling of helplessness, and he shows passive resignation in his behaviour, we can consider him to be depressed" (p. 92). The first part of this statement is the theme of my paper and I agree fully; the second part calls for further clinical validation and a clarification of the concept and definition of depression.

I shall not discuss the Kleinian concept of the "depressive position" in early infancy, because this would lead into a theoretical digression which is beyond the scope of this paper. The recognition of the significance of the child's growing awareness of and concern for the mother along with the need to control his aggressive drives is not unique to Kleinian theory. The introduction of the term "depressive" to denote this phenomenon does not contribute to its clinical understanding.

There are a number of investigators who question the existence of depression in children as I do. Rochlin (1959) speaks of a "loss complex" in the deprived child, rather than of a depression. He gives several clinical examples of object loss in children who "may become sad or grieve or appear briefly depressed over their object losses and revile themselves" but, he adds, "these reactions in childhood do not lead, as they do in later development, to depressive states which in the adult is essentially a cleavage between the criticizing faculty of the ego and the ego as altered by identification" (p. 300). He suggests: "For the clinical manifestations of pathological mourning and melancholia to take place presupposes that certain phases of psychic development have occurred" (p. 314). These phases, I suggest, are the development of an internalized superego and the capacity to experience guilt. Rochlin says further: "It is misleading and confusing to regard children who suffer severely and react by withdrawal from living objects as clinically depressed or suffering melancholia" (p. 303).

Mahler (1961) also maintains: "It has been conclusively established that the immature personality structure of the infant or older child is not capable of producing a state of depression such as that seen in the adult" (p. 342). She gives clinical illustrations to demonstrate that the young child who suffers the loss of an object may experience grief but not depression. Zetzel (1960) stresses the importance of developmental factors in the manifestation of depression. She questions the tendency to postulate infantile prototypes of adult depressive illness and considers rather the influence of infantile experiences on ego and superego development which may predispose the adult to depression (p. 497).

My own experience (1958) supports the conclusions of Rochlin and Mahler. The children described by Spitz and by Engel are apathetic and listless, but there is no evidence of the mood reaction associated with depression. Even in adults one may see withdrawal from the object which may be explained as decathexis of the mental representation of the external object with apathy and loss of interest but not necessarily depression. In the few instances in which I have seen a true depressive illness in a child this has occurred in latency at the earliest and in children who experienced premature identifications with a severe, dominating parent, who was lost to the child either by death or rejection. The child who reacts to the loss of an object or to narcissistic injury with sadness or apathy will more readily be relieved of his sadness when the object is restored or a satisfactory substitute becomes available, in the case of object loss, or if the narcissistic injury is undone and a substitute compensation is supplied. In the adult the reaction to narcissistic injury likewise will more readily disappear when the injury is undone, whereas the depression may not be affected by a change in the external circumstances surrounding the individual. I believe that when a person reacts to an object loss or narcissistic injury such as humiliation, defeat, or a failure with depression, we shall, on close examination, find that the injury has evoked deeper unconscious fantasies and conflicts associated with guilt.

A man of 30 with a severe character disorder manifested an infantile response to disappointment, object loss, and narcissistic injury. He was in his early years the center of an adoring group of aunts as well as his mother and grandmother. He lost this favored position at the age of 4 when his parents moved away from the rest of the family. He had a great deal of respiratory illness in childhood and at the age of 10 was sent to a warmer climate by himself for about 6 months. He insisted that his mother had not visited him during the entire period and his father only once when he had been passing through the area on a business trip. His relation to his parents was one of overt hostility mixed with dependence and submission. His aggressive impulses were central to his difficulties. As a child he bit himself and created open sores on his hands. He tortured animals. His fantasies were wildly sadistic. As an adult he partly expressed his aggression in verbal sarcasm and cynicism and partly turned it on himself—at one time he lost part of his finger by playing with a circular saw. In addition there were marked reaction formations. His outstanding complaint was his profound unhappiness. He had a sentimental sadness which he expressed in fantasies of being a poetic genius. He attributed this sadness to his having to give up his infantile wishes and to his inability to win the love and admiration which he sought not only from the people about him but also in the transference. He even obtained some exhibitionistic gratification from the display of sadness. Guilt reactions were hardly noticeable, and clinically I would not consider him to be a depressed person, despite his great unhappiness.

I noted at the beginning of this paper the importance of separating the essential determinant of the depressive mechanism from other factors which enter into the development of depression, factors which may be spoken of as predisposing to depression. In the analytic exploration of patients with depression we find a number of recurrent factors, which include: (1) a tendency to identification—an object relationship characterized more by merging with the object than by individuation; (2) aggression and ambivalence; (3) masochistic manifestations; (4) regression, both in libidinal drive manifestations and ego functions, that is, libidinally to oral and anal manifestations, and with regard to ego functions especially regression of reality function and object relationships; (5) disturbances of self esteem; (6) object loss; and (7) an ego state of helplessness. I consider all these factors secondary to the primary mechanism which is superego conflict with the evocation of guilt.

Although a study of depression should discuss these points in detail, it is not feasible in this paper to give more than a brief comment which may also serve as a summary of my thesis.

1. The prominence of the narcissistic and dependent nature of the object relationships of patients who tend toward depressive illness is well established clinically and appears in their tendency toward identification and oral fixations. It seems to me that these are factors which facilitate the sensitivity to frustration with resultant aggressive fantasies and superego response with guilt and depression.

2. Freud (1917) and Abraham (1924) have demonstrated the role of ambivalence in the development of depression. Jacobson (1964) also questions whether there can be depression without an aggressive conflict, the assumption being that the aggression has to be turned inward and thus operate in the sense of guilt. I do not believe that the turning inward of aggression plays as decisive a role in superego development as some authors maintain, but I would rather say

that aggression mobilizes guilt in an already functioning superego. That the superego utilizes aggressive drive energies in its activities is a valuable theoretical hypothesis.[8]

3. It has been observed clinically that masochism and depression may alternate in a patient who becomes depressed when he is unable to gratify his masochistic impulses. Here again the masochism is not the cause of the depression but an expression of the underlying guilt with the accompanying sexualization.

4. The prominence of regression in depression is an indication of the fixations which result from preoedipal traumata and predispose the individual to the frustrations which in turn may lead to depression. The regression may also be looked upon as a defensive effort on the part of the ego, though not a successful one. In this view a psychotic depression indicates a severe regressive response to the superego conflict and not that the basic psychodynamics are different from those in psychoneurotic depression or depressive reactions in normal persons.[9]

5. I also question the formulation that loss of self esteem is a cause of depression. Loss of self esteem may occur without depression; and when they appear together, we must ask what may be the causative relationship. Loss of self esteem may result from a superego conflict, the response of the ego to an internalized fantasy of judgment and punishment for a forbidden instinctual wish. There would be, along with the loss of self esteem, other evidence of inner conflict and guilt. The loss of self esteem would then be an accompaniment of the depression, not the cause of the depression. I would maintain that the loss of self esteem resulting entirely from a narcissistic injury— if this ever does happen—would be accompanied by sadness or disappointment and would swiftly disappear with the return of external approval.[10]

[8] On this point see Freud (1930, p. 123ff.) and Hartmann and Loewenstein (1962, p. 54f.).

[9] See in this connection Jacobson (1954), who writes: "In manic-depressives the regressive, magic identifications appear to reflect their fixation at the stage of magic participation of the child in the power and value of the idealized parents" (p. 257). Zetzel (1960) also emphasizes the clinical importance of regressive manifestations in depression. See also Freud (1917, p. 249) who points out the tendency to narcissistic regression as a precondition for depressive response to object loss.

[10] See Reich (1960): "It is obvious that the oscillations of self-esteem in compensatory narcissism bear similarities to cyclothymic states, but there are considerable differences. . . . Most noticeable is the difference of the role played by the superego. The sadistic intolerance of the superego, so predominant in the depressive phase of cyclothymia, is absent in the cases here described. The phase of lowered self-esteem is characterized preponderantly by anxiety and feelings of annihilation, not by guilt feelings" (p. 231).

6. I have already discussed object loss at length. Here I shall merely repeat that object loss leads to depression only when it is accompanied by ambivalence toward the lost object and subsequent guilt.

7. Bibring (1953) has made the ego state of helplessness the central causative factor in depression. Without going into any detail I would say at this point only that in every instance which he describes in his paper it is possible to postulate an underlying guilt reaction and it becomes very difficult to prove which is the primary disturbance.

I hope that I have made it evident that the questions I have raised are of more than theoretical significance. It makes a great deal of difference in our therapeutic approach to a patient whether the conflict is an internal one between different structures of the psyche or whether we are dealing with a person whose conflict is with outer forces. The latter situation is characteristically the one that we see in children; and when we find it in an adult patient, our therapeutic approach must be quite different from that to a patient with an intrapsychic conflict.

My conclusions are tentative. Whether they are valid or not can be established only by further clinical observation. This is the only solid foundation of psychoanalytic theory.

BIBLIOGRAPHY

Abraham, K. (1924), A Short Study of the Development of the Libido. *Selected Papers on Psycho-Analysis.* London: Hogarth Pr., 1927, 418-501.
Beres, D. (1952), Clinical Notes on Aggression in Children. *Psa. Study Ch.,* 7:241-263.
—— (1958), Vicissitudes of Superego Functions and Superego Precursors in Childhood. *Psa. Study Ch.,* 13:324-351.
—— (1960), The Psychoanalytic Psychology of Imagination. *J. Am. Psa. Assn.,* 8:252-269.
—— (1965), Symbol and Object. *Bull. Menninger Clin.,* 29:3-23.
—— (1966), The Functions of the Superego. *Psychoanalysis in the Americas,* ed. R. E. Litman. NY: IUP (in press).
Bibring, E. (1953), The Mechanism of Depression. *Affective Disorders,* ed. P. Greenacre. NY: IUP, 13-48.
Engel, G. L. & Reichsman, F. (1956), Spontaneous and Experimentally Induced Depressions in an Infant with a Gastric Fistula. *J. Am. Psa. Assn.,* 4:428-452.
Freud, A. (1949), Aggression in Relation to Emotional Development. *Psa. Study Ch.,* 3/4:37-42.
—— (1965), *Normality and Pathology in Childhood.* NY: IUP.
Freud, S. (1905), Three Essays on the Theory of Sexuality. *S.E.,* 7:125-243.
—— (1909), Notes upon a Case of Obsessional Neurosis. *S.E.,* 10:153-318.
—— (1916), Some Character-Types Met with in Psycho-Analytic Work. *S.E.,* 14:311-333.
—— (1917), Mourning and Melancholia. *S.E.,* 14:239-258.
—— (1930), Civilization and Its Discontents. *S.E.,* 21:57-145.

—— (1940), An Outline of Psycho-Analysis. *S.E.*, 23:141-207.

Hartmann, H. (1958), Comments on the Scientific Aspects of Psychoanalysis. *Essays,* 297-317.

—— Kris, E., & Loewenstein, R. M. (1953), The Function of Theory in Psycho-analysis. *Drives, Affects, Behavior,* 1:13-47, ed. R. M. Loewenstein. NY: IUP.

—— & Loewenstein, R. M. (1962), Notes on the Superego. *Psa. Study Ch.,* 17:42-81.

Jacobson, E. (1953), Contribution to the Metapsychology of Cyclothymic Depression. *Affective Disorders,* ed. P. Greenacre. NY: IUP, 49-83.

—— (1954), Contribution to the Metapsychology of Psychotic Identifications. *J. Am. Psa. Assn.,* 2:239-262.

—— (1964), *The Self and the Object World.* NY: IUP.

Loewenstein, R. M. (1957), A Contribution to the Psychoanlytic Theory of Masochism, *J. Am. Psa. Assn.,* 5:197-234.

Mahler, M. S. (1952), On Child Psychosis and Schizophrenia. *Psa. Study Ch.,* 7:286-305.

—— (1961), On Sadness and Grief in Infancy and Childhood. *Psa. Study Ch.,* 16:332-351.

Nacht, S. & Racamier, P. C. (1960), Depressive States. *Int. J. Psa.,* 41:481-496.

Piers, G. & Singer, M. B. (1953), *Shame and Guilt.* Springfield: Thomas.

Reich, A. (1960), Pathologic Forms of Self-Esteem Regulation. *Psa. Study Ch.,* 15:215-232.

Ritvo, S. & Solnit, A. J. (1960), The Relationship of Early Ego Identifications to Superego Formation. *Int. J. Psa.,* 41:295-300.

Rochlin, G. (1959), The Loss Complex. *J. Am. Psa. Assn.,* 7:299-316.

Sandler, J. (1960), On the Concept of Superego. *Psa. Study Ch.,* 15:128-162.

—— & Joffe, W. G. (1965), Notes on Childhood Depression. *Int. J. Psa.,* 46:88-96.

Spitz, R. A. & Wolf, K. M. (1946), Anaclitic Depression. *Psa. Study Ch.,* 2:313-342.

Zetzel, E. R. (1960), Symposium on 'Depressive Illness': Introduction. *Int. J. Psa.,* 41:476-480.

Problems in the Differentiation Between Schizophrenic and Melancholic States of Depression

EDITH JACOBSON, M.D.

Depressive states can develop in the course of any psychotic or neurotic illness. However, not only the symptoms but the conflicts underlying the depression and the mechanisms involved in it differ a great deal. Thus, attempts to discriminate more carefully between different kinds of depression (Asch, 1964; Grinker, 1961) are most desirable, provided differential diagnostic considerations are not neglected. The disregard for nosological distinctions may cause us to ignore significant aspects of the depressive picture, in which the specific illness may find a characteristic symptomatic expression.

Unfortunately, in severe states of depression it may be very difficult to make a clear-cut differential diagnosis, although this may be very important from the prognostic and therapeutic points of view. In many cases, it is not easy to decide whether we are dealing with a neurotic or a psychotic depression and, if the patient is psychotic, whether he suffers from a melancholic or a schizophrenic type of depression.

We know that patients belonging to the manic-depressive group may show features indicative of a schizophrenic depression; in turn, schizophrenic depressions may sometimes present the picture of a typical melancholia. These difficulties increase in the case of schizophrenic disorders which show a circular course. Many patients originally diagnosed as manic-depressives finally develop clearly schizophrenic manifestations. In view of the problems which such patients present, I should like to call attention to some characteristic differences in the psychopathology of schizophrenic and melancholic types of depression. These differences may easily escape the clinical ob-

499

server, but may be of great help in a correct diagnostic evaluation and understanding of such cases and in our therapeutic approach to them. I must emphasize that my paper will merely be an elaboration of ideas which I have briefly discussed earlier (1964), although in a different frame of reference.

Great clinical psychiatrists of the past, e.g., Kraepelin, Bleuler, and Lange, have thoroughly described the phenomenology of these various groups of psychoses. Lange (1928), for instance, says that we encounter "greatest difficulties in the distinction of melancholic versus schizophrenic depressions. . . . There are evidently clinical pictures which in the current episode as in the course of quite a series of attacks do not in any way make us think of a schizophrenic process in the future. Here only a schizophrenic heredity may arouse such a suspicion. On the other hand, we must not forget that cases which doubtlessly are circular melancholias can manifest ample additional catatonic features" (p. 198; my tr.).

Bleuler (1911), too, refers to "the periodic and cyclic forms of melancholic and manic moods seen in schizophrenia" (p. 207). He emphasizes that "chronic as well as acute depressions are found more frequently in the beginning of an outspoken [schizophrenic] illness than any other syndromes" (p. 254). "Yet, we do find genuine states of melancholic depression even in schizophrenics of long standing." However, he points to "the typical schizophrenic stiffness, super-ficiality, and exaggeratedness," and to the "extreme form of monoide-ism which, in contrast to that seen in simple melancholias, may here be almost absolute." He also mentions that "Delusions and especially hallucinations are rarely absent [in schizophrenia]." Bleuler believes that "The 'hypochondriacal melancholia' of other authors is usually a schizophrenic melancholia" and that ideas of grandeur "may exist side by side with the most appalling fears and terrors" (p. 209f.).

Kraepelin (1913) presents criteria similar to those which Bleuler regarded as significant for the differential diagnosis between melancholic and schizophrenic depressive states. But he, too, points out that "it may be impossible to distinguish it [the depressive psychomotor retardation] from the lack of mental agility and of the will power, such as is characteristic of dementia praecox. In the beginning of a dementia praecox . . . one hears from them statements quite similar to those of manic-depressive patients" (p. 951, my tr.).

Interestingly enough, we find an excellent and appreciative brief review of Freud's paper on "Mourning and Melancholia" only in Lange's monograph (1928). Although Lange wondered whether Freud had not thrown melancholic and hysterical cases together, he criticized not Freud but Jaspers for his psychological approach, for instance, to the manic states.[1]

I have deliberately quoted a series of outstanding psychiatrists of the past, all of them brilliant observers, who, with the exception of Bleuler, regarded any psychological approach, especially the psychoanalytic one, as scientifically questionable because they assumed an endogenous etiology of the psychotic diseases. To be sure, the hospitalized patients who were the predominant subjects of these authors' observations are likely to support this opinion, whereas ambulant psychotics or borderline patients, who may desire psychotherapy or even analytic treatment and be accessible to it, are apt to show the significant role of psychogenic factors in the development of both neuroses and psychoses.[2]

Yet in these milder ambulant cases that we so frequently see in our private practice, even more difficult differential diagnostic problems arise, since we may have doubts regarding the neurotic or psychotic, either manic-depressive or schizophrenic nature of the illness. In certain mild schizophrenic-hypochondriacal or cyclothymic patients who show a predominance of somatic autonomous (Campbell, 1953, pp. 52-81) disturbances over affective ones, a correct diagnosis can frequently not be established, because these patients may not even come into the orbit of a psychiatrist. Certain seemingly neurotic but actually mildly psychotic or prepsychotic (borderline) patients, who do come for psychotherapeutic treatment, may in its course suddenly develop a psychotic episode. Such experiences lend themselves to views which tend to blur the sharp lines of nosological dis-

[1] This is rather ironical, since Jaspers has been not only utterly disdainful but also amazingly uninformed about Freud's conceptions and their development.

[2] In this connection, it may be noted that in Bleuler's *Lehrbuch der Psychiatrie* (1949), in an annex to the part on the causes of mental diseases, H. Luxemburger (the author), without reference to Freud, applied the concept of the supplementary series of pathogenic factors to the psychoses as well. While emphasizing the constitutional factors, which he carefully distinguishes from the hereditary ones, he makes it very clear that the environmental influences must not be disregarded and that not all people who are constitutionally predisposed to a psychosis develop a psychotic illness.

tinction, not only between the two major groups of psychoses but even between psychotic and neurotic illness.[3]

I believe that far from helping us to re-evaluate and improve our old classifications, these trends of thinking prevent us from gaining clearer insight into the specific nature of the various types of psychoses and from adapting our modes of treatment and our psychotherapeutic or psychoanalytic technique to the particular kind of illness with which we are dealing.

Case Presentation

I shall present some pertinent case material that will permit me to point to certain features which distinguish this schizophrenic-melancholic condition from similar depressive states belonging to the manic-depressive group of disorders. For my purpose, the case of "Janet," a schizophrenic woman in her 40s, seems especially suitable, since I have been able to observe her during her childhood and again from the age of 30 until now, i.e., for a period of about forty years.

There was no evidence of a psychotic heredity in Janet's family. Her father consulted me for the first time when she was 7 years old. His wife was a beautiful, but very erratic, acting-out, narcissistic, and infantile woman. From the pathogenic point of view, it was significant that she had already had an affair with Janet's father while still being married to her first husband, his best friend. The latter was a highly intellectual man, who suffered from impotence. When she finally obtained a divorce, he shot himself, after telling the couple he hoped to ruin their happiness forever. Possibly, Janet's mother had already been pregnant by her second husband at that time. She certainly never ceased to feel guilty and to take out on this first child her hostility toward Janet's father, who had forced the divorce and later on turned out to be an eternal philanderer. The mother treated her daughter very cruelly, and never gave her any of the tenderness and affection which she showered on her second child, a son born three years later. Very early the little girl developed multiple phobic anxieties, especially about insect bites. Her anxiety had a panicky quality that I have hardly ever observed in neurotic children. I saw

---

[3] As we know, Freud (1924a, 1924b) sharply distinguished the pathology of psychoses from that of neuroses, and the different groups of neuroses and psychoses from each other. Heinz Hartmann (1953) and other psychoanalytic authors (Hendrick, 1951) interested in the study of psychoses clearly adhered to this point of view.

her tremble with fear when her mother yelled at her like a Prussian sergeant. From Janet's infancy on, her father took over the maternal role. But his behavior toward this lovely girl was and remained extremely seductive. As a result of her mother's cruelty and disciplinary behavior, Janet began to show compulsive traits as early as in the preoedipal period. She became overobedient, dutiful, conscientious, and overconcerned with her possessions. She never played with her dolls and toys lest she ruin them. At the beginning of latency, Janet developed a compulsive ritual before going to bed, which caused her father to consult me. Janet had always been a beautiful girl of more than average intelligence, but even as a child she showed a suspicious remoteness, stiffness, emotional emptiness and lifelessness, had a reading and learning block, and complained of continuous "boredom." At that time, the quality of her affective disturbance already made me think of a potential future schizophrenic psychosis. In spite of Janet's conspicuous symptoms, her mother rejected my suggestions for immediate treatment so stubbornly that the father was unable to achieve it. When Janet was 14 years of age, the family was forced to leave Germany for Belgium. Janet was sent first to Paris, then to a boarding school in England. Her father, who brought her there, immediately took her to the apartment of his mistress in London, sending Janet alone to the hairdresser while he made love to his girl friend. Soon after this incident, which Janet never forgot or forgave, she developed a severe depression.

A psychoanalyst—the late Kate Friedlander—was consulted. She diagnosed Janet's condition as a psychotic depression—possibly a beginning schizophrenia. Janet was taken home to Belgium, where she experienced the German invasion and was hidden away on a farm. In the following years she is said to have gone alternately into melancholic-depressive and manic-excited states, with healthy intervals of up to one year's duration. Because of the cyclic course, Janet was diagnosed as manic-depressive by some Belgian psychiatrists. In these years I did not see her. Her father told me after the war that since the beginning of Janet's illness the mother had become all too closely tied up with her. However, this seemed only to have increased their mutual hostility. I also heard that Janet had once been hospitalized in Switzerland and had received shock treatments, and that lately she had had longer more or less healthy intervals between her attacks. When Janet was not depressed, she led a rather promiscuous sexual life and once, with her father's help, had an abortion. He approved of her sexual freedom, and told her that "being so sick she should get whatever pleasure she could out of life." All her affairs ended with her being deserted.

At the age of 30, a short time after she had lost her father, Janet came to the United States. This was when I saw her again. She told me that her current lover, a married American man, had promised to obtain a divorce and to marry her. As could be expected, this affair also broke up. Some weeks later, Janet became depressed. She lost weight, suffered from insomnia and anorexia, withdrew from her relatives and friends, developed ideas of unworthiness, and had to give up her work because of her thinking block and her severe psycho-motor retardation. After several months of depression, Janet suddenly went into a state of severe catatonic excitement, with disorientation, confusion, bizarre behavior, and delusional ideas, mainly of poisoning. The whole episode, whose nature left no diagnostic doubts, lasted about a year. She needed several months of hospitalization, and had shock treatments followed by psychotherapy. Although her mother tried repeatedly to interfere, Janet accepted my therapeutic suggestion, and tenaciously continued her treatment with the same psychiatrist, Dr. David Milrod, for about fifteen years.[4] She is still seeing him from time to time, and has never had another episode. He worked with her very patiently and skillfully, and achieved an amazing success. In the course of her treatment, Janet managed to obtain a very appropriate job, which she is still holding. Moreover, in her late 30s she married a very suitable partner and has made an admirable adjustment to him. Nobody can predict whether she will have relapses in the future, but so far her recovery has been surprisingly good. Incidentally, her compulsiveness and most of her early childhood phobias have hardly subsided.

Discussion

Janet was one of those schizophrenic patients who, because of the cyclic course of her illness, had first been diagnosed manic-depressive (I could not find out what diagnosis had been made in the Swiss hospital). The depression with which her last episode started certainly resembled very much a simple not delusional melancholic state.

---

[4] I wish to express my gratitude to Dr. Milrod for discussing this case with me.

Only a careful psychoanalytic observer would have suspected that this was the beginning phase of a severe schizophrenic episode. Janet's ambivalence conflicts revolved about her father and her previous lovers—evidently father substitutes—who had all first seduced and then abandoned her. However, her most profound conflicts arose from her masochistic dependency on her narcissistic, sadistically domineering, and interfering mother, and from her futile efforts to liberate herself from this woman. The intensity and quality of her homosexual struggle with her mother, which had always been predominant in her conscious conflicts, made me most suspicious. There was an additional feature which did not fit in with the picture of a melancholic: not only in the initial stage but during the whole period of depression Janet's repetitious "record" of self accusations would often quite suddenly be interrupted by cold, sharply critical, and derogative remarks, especially about her mother, but also about her father, her previous lovers, her relatives and friends. The frozen expression on Janet's face, which never changed in accord with the content of her reproaches or self reproaches, was likewise conspicuous. Her hostility at that time did not show any delusional paranoid features. However, in her frankly hostile comments she revealed excessively greedy, crude, and rather absurd demands, which she wanted to impose on these persons. Such comments were followed by bitter complaints about her inability to assert herself and attain the fulfillment of her pregenital sadistic wishes.

This leads me to significant features in Janet's disturbances of self esteem, which differed from what we commonly see in melancholics, including paranoid or agitated depressive types. Her ideas of worthlessness revolved about her inability to work and to make a living—traits characteristic of her mother—or her inability to read and to pursue intellectual and artistic interests—deficiencies for which her mother had always blamed her father. Except for self reproaches of this kind, Janet expressed hardly any guilt feelings. Even during her depression, she spoke quite matter-of-factly of her previous promiscuous sexual life, of her affairs with married men, and of her past abortion. In other words, Janet did not suffer from feelings of "sinfulness," as melancholics commonly do; nor did she complain about her lack of feelings for others, about her inability to love. On the contrary, she blamed herself for being unable to make men "spoil" her, to be aggressive and retaliate against her past lovers by getting out of them whatever she wanted, e.g., expensive dresses and the like, and to attain dominance over them, over her mother, and people in general. Janet's frank demands, her open cold hostility, and her feelings of shame and inferiority about her failure to be a "successful mistress" not only played an outstanding role during her depression, but survived her acute episode for some years.

During that later period, it also became clearer that the core of her narcissistic conflicts were actually her identity conflicts. She felt that she would remain a complete "nonentity," unless she could aggressively assert her dominance over others. In contrast to her general integrity, decency, and generosity, and her compulsive concern with her work, these attitudes and ideas made at that time an even more absurd impression. Janet's ambitions to be a "successful mistress" had their origin in her parents' attitudes, especially her father's seductive behavior, who had encouraged her to permit herself complete sexual freedom and to get out of life all she wanted. In her childhood he had already called her his "princess" and promised her a wealthy husband, who would give her everything that was due to her loveliness. The father's interest in beautiful women and his loud praise of his daughter's beauty accounted for Janet's unusual vanity and her overconcern with her physical appearance, which during her period of depression acquired a hypochondriacal quality. For instance, Janet sometimes made quite bizarre remarks about the hair on her body and legs, or about her ugly eyes that looked like "jet buttons." She told me that she did not sweat from within to without, as other ordinary people do, but from without to within. Evidently, such ideas also expressed her wish to establish an identity of her own.

The strange mixture of Janet's compulsive character traits with impulsive behavior and ambitions to become a successful beautiful mistress reflected her identifications with her immoral father, the successful philanderer, with his values, with his mistresses, and also with her beautiful mother, and were expressive of the confused parental standards and of the contradictory parental attitudes toward her.

Very early Janet had learned about her parents' past. At a children's party, at the age of about 8 or earlier, she had overheard some ladies' gossip about her mother's affair with her father, the divorce, the first husband's suicide, and the like. Janet had not fully understood the story, but remembered having then developed the belief that her mother's first husband had actually been her father, and that her mother and the second husband had caused his death. This belief, which not only "made her different from other children" but also served to protect her from guilt feelings about the close incestuous ties between her and her father, developed into a paranoid delusion during her illness in Switzerland. When her father brought her to the hospital, she jumped out of the car and ran away, crying frantically: "You are not my father, you are a murderer! Help, help, he is going to kill me!" (The father was actually held by the police and arrested.) I may add that Janet's panicky and paranoid reactions to her father seemed to screen her underlying fears of her cruel mother and her masochistic surrender to her. Her father had actually tried to protect her from her mother's murderous hostility.

We can now draw an approximate picture of those features in Janet's depressive syndrome which were characteristic of a schizophrenic rather than a melancholic type of depression. Her history reveals the special environmental factors which influenced the vicissitudes of her object relations and identifications and of her instinctual and narcissistic conflicts and which played a significant role in the development of her psychotic illness. The mother's complete neglect of her daughter during the child's infancy, her cruel disciplinary behavior, and, later on, her narcissistic ties to Janet fixated the child on a sadomasochistic, pregenital, narcissistic level and led first to the early development of severe phobias, and later to a compulsion neurosis. They also prevented the establishment of a normal sense of identity and of a satisfactory regulation of self esteem in the little girl. In addition, her father's overindulgence, his seductiveness, and recurrent abandonments precluded a renunciation of her incestuous desires and the establishment of solid defenses in the ego. These confusing narcissistic parental attitudes, moreover, kept her from building up affectionate stable object relations and successful sublimations. Feeling neglected, deserted, and deprived of true tenderness by both parents, Janet no doubt already developed depressive states in early childhood, which even then showed schizoid emotional qualities and were expressive of a terrible lonesomeness. This early history is quite different from what we hear from melancholics, who frequently recall an early phase of parental overindulgence, followed by experiences of disillusionment and abandonment. In addition to this, Janet was severely traumatized in her beginning latency by overhearing and misunderstanding gossip about her parents' past history. I emphasized its effect on her childhood fantasies and on her future paranoid delusions. I also spoke of the traumatic influence of her emigration and the German invasion, and mentioned the event in London that precipitated her first breakdown. I believe that in the history of cyclothymics, such an accumulation of traumatic experiences is not commonly observed.

Of particular interest is the fact that the specific superego and ego pathology, which I described above, also made its appearance during the depressive phase of Janet's episode and was conspicuous enough to permit a correct differential diagnosis at that time. In spite of her severely retarded state, Janet would find a mode of frankly and coldly expressing her hostile attitudes and intentions, although only by virtue of complaining about her inability to gratify her aggressive demands and achieve her ruthless goals. This type of self reproach pointed to her complete inability to recognize the immorality of these goals. It revealed the defectiveness and deterioration of her superego, and the partial retransformation of her intersystemic conflicts between ego and superego demands into an intrasystemic struggle between her sadistic and masochistic strivings (Hartmann, 1950, p. 138). Hence, what Janet actually complained about during her depression was her masochistic surrender to her mother and to male or female substitute objects—a surrender which had been victorious over her wishes for revengeful, sadistic self assertion and dominance over these objects. I may add that the depressive clinging to objects also looked different in Janet from that of melancholics, who commonly complain that they have to depend on others. Janet simply tried not only to lean on other persons, but to exploit the services of those who attempted to help her. Evidently, she derived some satisfaction from the feeling that at least in this passive-indirect way she could achieve some dominance over them. Later on, when her paranoid delusions developed, she accused the same helpful persons of stealing her most precious possessions and of trying to poison her.

In spite of similarities in the main syndrome, the structure of Janet's depressive conflict is quite different from the superego-ego conflicts in melancholics, whose superego is excessively strict and cruel but not defective and deteriorated. The differences underline not only the failure of neutralization (Hartmann, 1953, p. 192) and the intensity of the destructive drives but also the particular vicissitudes they have undergone in the development of schizophrenic-depressive pathology.

SUMMARY OF ESSENTIAL POINTS

In cases of psychotic depression which present differential diagnostic problems, a thorough psychoanalytically oriented genetic exploration of the developmental history and past pathology, etc., is of greatest value for the establishment of a correct diagnosis. We may need many interviews with members of the patient's family; in these we must make particular efforts to understand the parental attitudes in the past and present, and their effect on the patient's emotional, instinctual, and intellectual development and behavior, and on the building up of his object relations, his identifications, his sublimations.

Furthermore, I tried to show how attempts at a reconstruction of the patient's history on the basis of such data obtained by the patient and his family may call attention to more or less subtle but significant symptomatic features, which reveal the specific structure of the underlying depressive conflicts, and thus may permit a correct diagnosis. In Janet's case, I emphasized the early onset of conspicuous affective disturbances, of her terrors, her emotional emptiness, her stiffness, her boredom, and of her severe compulsiveness. Regarding her current state, I pointed particularly to the content of her ideas of worthlessness, which superficially sounded like the usual "record" of melancholics' self accusations but actually were of quite a different nature. I discussed the conspicuous lack of feelings of "sinfulness," which are usually so predominant in manic-depressive melancholics, and spoke of the frank display of her ambitions to become a rather exploitative mistress, and her feelings of inferiority due to her failure to live up to these glorified ambitions. Finally, from these special disturbances of self esteem, I drew certain inferences with regard to the structure of this patient's narcissistic conflicts as compared with those of melancholics, and hence with regard to the differences in their superego and ego pathology.

The question arises how far these observations made in Janet's case are characteristic of schizophrenic depressions in general. With regard to the early onset of her affective disturbances, Janet reminded me of another female patient, whom I had also seen frequently during her latency years. At the age of 21, this patient developed a severe schizophrenic process that rapidly led to a complete deterioration.

Even as a child this patient, too, seemed to have been in a chronic state of depression. The utterly bland quality of her affects, her emptiness and "stupidity," and her inability to relate, frequently provoked her playmates and teachers to give her beatings, which she accepted silently though with signs of terror.

However, except for the patients who already show signs of a manifest psychosis in childhood, the early onset of such a conspicuous affective disturbance is by no means characteristic of schizophrenics in general, or of those who later on develop severe states of depression. More commonly, outspoken emotional pathology develops only later, with the onset or in the course of their manifest psychotic disorder, although its forerunners may become apparent in the entire emotional and personality development of these patients.

SUPEREGO PATHOLOGY AND DISTURBANCES OF SELF ESTEEM IN
SCHIZOPHRENIC DEPRESSIVES

The absence of feelings of moral worthlessness, which I described in Janet's case, is characteristic of many but by no means all schizophrenic melancholics. Among them we also find patients who, at least at certain stages of their illness, suffer from feelings or even from delusions of sinfulness, as melancholics commonly do. These cases present particularly difficult differential diagnostic problems. In some cases, the ideas of "sinfulness" may later on give way to feelings of inferiority and of being a "nonentity," such as I dicussed above. Sometimes they may even combine with complaints about the inability to pursue certain glorified aggressive goals, such as, in Janet's case, the ambition to be a "successful ruthless mistress." These absurd complaints may then be completely disconnected from concomitant ideas of moral worthlessness.

At this point I should like to refer to the last chapter in my book on *The Self and the Object World* (1964), where I briefly discussed the disturbances of ego and superego development and of identifications in schizophrenics, and compared them with those in melancholics (pp. 208-210). I also described "the type of schizophrenics in whose states of depression the guilt conflicts may be absent or recede in favor of paranoid fears of exposure, while feelings of shame and inferiority, self consciousness and fears or feelings of loss of identity frequently appear as a characteristic triad of symptoms" (p. 198). In the same chapter, I spoke of "a sadistic-criminal or a glamorous-grandiose pseudo ideal which . . . certain acting-out paranoid psychotic patients" may develop (p. 210). Two of my brief case examples in this chapter are pertinent to my current discussion, because these two male schizophrenic patients suffered from intermittent paranoid depressive and agitated states, which in the first case finally led to suicide. These patients did not present differential diagnostic problems. However, in the context of this paper, I want to emphasize that Janet's ambition to be a successful mistress was the counterpart of the sadistic types of gangster ideal which both these male patients had developed. In them, it was likewise maintained during their states of depression, in the form of wishful fantasies and of feelings of inferiority about their inability to pursue these aims. In contrast to Janet's symptoms, these manifestations were combined with paranoid fears of exposure or mild delusions of persecution.

The lack of paranoid delusions during the depressive period may, to some extent, account for the diagnostic difficulties in cases like Janet's (Jacobson, 1954). I may mention here that in some obsessional-compulsive neurotics, especially those with paranoid trends, we also find such a glorification of complete instinctual freedom and ruthlessness. However, in these patients such attitudes are expressive of their rebellion against the restrictions imposed on their ego by their compulsiveness; they are not ego syntonic and arouse severe guilt feelings.

THE DIFFERENCES BETWEEN THE PARANOID FEATURES IN
MELANCHOLIC AND SCHIZOPHRENIC DEPRESSIVES

Both may manifest ideas of reference and of persecution and corresponding hallucinations. However, as Kraepelin (1913) already pointed out, in contrast to paranoid schizophrenics, the cyclothymic paranoid depressives feel they ought to be persecuted. They deserve the persecution because of their "sins." This underscores the lack of conscious guilt feelings which paranoid depressive schizophrenics commonly show, at least at a more advanced stage of their illness. This has not only diagnostic but also important therapeutic implications. In a paranoid depressive schizophrenic, an untimely hint at the denial of guilt conflicts may arouse a sudden paranoid rage attack. Such a patient, a woman who suffered from circular depressive and hypomanic states, once during a severe depression told me a dream which clearly evidenced her guilt conflict about having neglected her little boy. When I pointed this out to her, she flew into a violent rage, denied having any guilt feelings or any reasons for them, and spoke in a grandiose way about her outstandingly high ethical standards and behavior. At the same time, she blamed me, her family, and others for our lack of integrity, and told ugly, distorted stories about her acquaintances. This patient also showed a rather parasitical behavior during her depressions—much more, indeed, than Janet did—and with a grandiose attitude, as though what others did for her was due to her outstanding personality. All these attitudes, which I described above, helped me to solve the differential diagnostic problem posed by this woman, who had likewise been regarded as a manic-depressive with paranoid trends.

Even more grandiose parasitic-psychopathic was the behavior of a young schizophrenic man, whose recurrent attacks of catatonic excitement always started with states of paralyzing depression that frequently made him unable to get out of bed. This patient would then expect to be treated at home without payment by "the best psychiatrists of New York." He would lie and cheat to get money and to obtain unbelievable amounts of drugs from many physicians. Exploiting everybody around him, he would justify his parasitism by pointing to the severity of his depression. As long as this patient could walk around, he would turn up at any time of the day and want to stay as long as he "needed" it.

This seems to be characteristic of the type of paranoid schizophrenic depressives who show frankly grandiose attitudes and behavior even during periods of depression. Because of their psychomotor retardation, melancholics may also have difficulties in keeping appointments, being punctual, and leaving when a session is finished. But I have never seen any melancholics, including paranoid types, impose themselves on their therapist, their friends, and their family, as this type of schizophrenic does during periods of severe depression.

DIFFERENTIAL DIAGNOSTIC PROBLEMS IN BORDERLINE PATIENTS

A certain group of these patients do not show manifestations of a psychotic depression but seek treatment because they suffer from recurring severe depressive states, sometimes alternating with hypomanic conditions. In these patients, we may have difficulty in deciding whether they are neurotics or mild psychotics and, in the latter case, whether they belong to the cyclothymic or schizophrenic group of .disorders. In impulsive, acting-out patients, who show predominantly hysterical attitudes and behavior, we can usually exclude at least an affective disorder. In manic-depressives, hysterical traits need not be absent, but they never predominate in the clinical picture. It is frequently more difficult to decide whether such patients are pregenitally fixated, impulse-ridden, hysterical neurotics or acting-out schizophrenics with hysterical features. In the first case, they often are accessible and responsive to psychoanalytic treatment conducted in a slow, careful, patient way, while this type of schizophrenic is commonly unable to tolerate an analytic situation. I may add that in Janet as well as in other schizophrenics, I could sometimes observe pseudo-hysterical behavior, which was actually expressive of the inappropriateness of their affects. In both schizophrenic and melancholic depressives the physical symptoms are mostly psychosomatic rather than hysterical, but in schizophrenics, in whom such symptoms may very rapidly appear and vanish, they combine more frequently with hypochondriacal fears and complaints.

COMPULSIVE TRAITS IN DEPRESSION AND SCHIZOPHRENIA

In my experience, certain compulsive depressives present even greater differential diagnostic problems, especially those with paranoid features who show a conspicuous emotional detachment. However, if they are obsessional-compulsive neurotics, their affective disturbances are likely to yield to a consistent analysis of their defenses, especially of their isolation mechanisms. In those who actually suffer from an affective disorder, we observe emotional withdrawal during times of depression; but, in spite of their compulsive traits, their capacity for warm affectionate relationships usually returns as soon as the depressive period has ended. This description coincides with earlier observations; e.g., Campbell (1953) quotes Kretschmer as saying, "the average cycloid . . . has a sociable, friendly, realistic and accommodating feeling about him. Because his temperament swings, with that of the milieu, there is for him . . . no tragically exacerbated conflict, but a life in things themselves . . . a capacity for living, feeling and suffering with the surroundings" (p. 33).

What characterizes the schizophrenic's compulsiveness is the opposite: a cool formality and politeness, stiffness and affectation, a remoteness and lack of emotional warmth, of spontaneity. In Janet's case, these suspicious traits and emotional qualities had already appeared in her childhood. They have markedly improved but are still in evidence.

In manic-depressives, moreover, I have never found a childhood history of such terrors, of such early and severe compulsive symptoms as in Janet and other schizophrenic cases, although during latency cyclothymics may begin to show compulsive character traits. In the latter, there are, furthermore, no such bizarre combinations or rapid alternations between compulsive and impulsive attitudes and behavior (except for the uncontrolled behavior during manic attacks), between sexual promiscuity and puritanism, between decency, altruism, and frank, aggressive selfishness and greed.

In seemingly compulsive paranoid depressive patients who are actually mild latent schizophrenics, the basic emotional pathology commonly also survives the depression and the treatment, although the latter may greatly improve the patient's ability to relate. This is the type of patient who may first seem to be accessible to analytic treatment but in its course suddenly develop a manifest psychotic episode, if they are not very cautiously treated. In such cases, a thorough study of the patients' psychopathology, particularly their specific superego-ego pathology, the quality of their object relations and the nature of the instinctual conflicts may offer sufficient criteria for a correct differential diagnosis.

THE NATURE OF CONFLICTS IN DEPRESSION AND SCHIZOPHRENIA

I shall once more define the differences between the depressive conflicts of the schizophrenic and of the melancholic from the dynamic and structural points of view.[5]

During the initial stage of a melancholic depression and likewise in the case of a "simple depression," the manic-depressive patient may be very irritable and frankly express his dissatisfaction with himself as well as with his love objects and with the whole world. However, as his ambivalence conflict increases, his destructive drive impulses tend to become completely absorbed by the superego and then turned against the self—a process which protects the ego from a discharge of hostility onto the external world.

Evidently, the intensity of the destructive forces and the defectiveness and deterioration of the superego and of the defense system prevent even severely depressive schizophrenics from turning their aggres-

[5] I must emphasize that my comparison does not extend to schizophrenic and manic-depressive psychoses in general, but is limited to schizophrenic and melancholic depressions.

sion consistently against their own selves (except when they are in a state of catatonic stupor). Despite their psychomotor retardation and their ideas of unworthiness, their hostility thus tends to break through to the surface and to erupt in some form, though devoid of a strong feeling tone and frequently screened by a glorification, rationalization, or idealization of aggressive goals, the true nature of which is denied.[6] This may lend conspicuously absurd qualities to the ideas of unworthiness of such patients.

To put it in structural terms: the melancholic suffers from a conflict between the superego and the ego, an intersystemic conflict (Hartmann, 1950) that reflects the discrepancy between his ego ideal, i.e., his overly high moral standards, and the pathologically distorted "sinful" image of his own self.

In the schizophrenic depressive, only a part of the conflict is between the superego and the ego; the other part is intrasystemic (Hartmann, 1950), i.e., within the ego. The partial regressive retransformation of the ego ideal into glorified wishful images of a powerful, ruthless, sadistic self permits aggressive fantasies and goals to enter the realm of the ego and to attain consciousness. As a result of these pathological processes, the conflict of the schizophrenic depressive is in part an expression of the discrepancy between such pregenital-sadistic ambitions and the image of his weak, helpless, masochistic self.

I am aware that for reasons of clarification my description of the structural differences between the melancholic and the schizophrenic depressive conflicts oversimplifies matters and thus does not do justice to the variety and complexity of individual cases, or to the different stages of illness. What I wished to underscore is the fact that schizophrenics tend to discharge their instinctual drive impulses, and especially their destructive ones, simultaneously or in rapid alternation on external objects and on the self. This tendency finds a symptomatic expression even during states of severe depression. It helps us to understand that schizophrenics, unless they are in a paralyzing depression, may easily alternate between suicidal and homicidal impulses and actions.

The dynamic and structural differences which I defined above

---

[6] Lange (1928) also mentions such sudden unexpected impulsive actions with inappropriate affect as characteristic of seemingly melancholic schizophrenic depressions (p. 198).

reflect the differences in the object relations and the primitive (narcissistic) identifications of melancholic and schizophrenic depressives
(Jacobson, 1954). In schizophrenic depressives, we may find a deficiency of object and self constancy, and a tendency to fusions between
self and object images resulting in a complex mixture of early types
of projective and introjective identification, or a rapid vacillation between them. The patient's opposing sadistic and masochistic strivings
may be split up and projectively attached to different object images,
and then, by virtue of introjective processes, set up in the patient's
opposing images of his own self. As paranoid trends color or change
the depressive picture or gain the upper hand, the "ruthless"-sadistic
self images are likely to become reprojected and reattached to external
objects, which then turn into threatening, hateful, persecutory figures
—such as in the one episode in which Janet's real father turned into
the "murderer." At that stage, the deterioration of the ego and the
processes of deneutralization (Hartmann, 1953) may advance to the
point where the ego is overwhelmed by destructive forces, and
the patient, going from a depressive into an excited catatonic state,
becomes manifestly homicidal or suicidal, or both.

THERAPEUTIC IMPLICATIONS

I believe, indeed, that a comparative study of melancholic and schizophrenic types of depression is of value not only for diagnostic and
prognostic reasons but also from the therapeutic point of view.

A clearer clinical and theoretical understanding of the different
psychopathology, the different conflicts and mechanisms involved in
these two groups of disorders, is exceedingly helpful in the treatment
of mild or latent psychotic (borderline) cases as well as in the case
of patients who suffer from florid psychotic episodes. Whatever treatment method we choose in the individual case, the results will not be
satsifactory unless we recognize the nature of the illness and understand the specific id, ego, and superego pathology with which we are
dealing.

This becomes particularly evident in the rare type of psychotic
patient who recovers from a schizophrenic episode with his ego sufficiently intact to permit him to undergo a more or less modified
analytic treatment. In such cases, the emotional responses and the
therapeutic effect of correct interpretations are sometimes amazing,

and may enable the patient to conclude his treatment successfully after several years.

Usually, psychotic patients, including latent psychotic or border-line cases, do best in a consistent treatment of very long duration, such as in Janet's case. (Periods of interruption are sometimes advisable, and may at times be necessitated by temporary hospitalizations.)

This seems to be especially valid in the case of manic-depressives and of schizophrenics who suffer from recurring severe states of depression. Those who at the end of a depressive period go into hypomanic states tend to stop treatment at that time, but promptly return when another depression sets in. However, manic-depressives, including paranoid types, usually want to stay with the same therapist, and should do so, since they are apt to develop an ambivalent but intense personal attachment to him. Schizophrenics, whose object relations are on a more regressive level, commonly show in rapid vacillation clinging, remote, and hostile attitudes toward their therapist. For this reason, and because of their severe superego and ego pathology and their lack of object and self constancy, they may stop treatment even during a period of depression, or run to another therapist when a new depression sets in. The tendency to change therapists seems to be especially characteristic of paranoid depressive schizophrenics. In some such patients, a change of therapist may even be advisable, for reasons outside the scope of this paper.

The differences in the transference of melancholic and schizophrenic depressives point to the different kinds of counterattitudes that the therapist must develop in these two groups of disorders. Because of their libidinal impoverishment, all psychotics and especially those who are in a state of depression need some degree of emotional warmth on the part of the therapist, but above all they need a great deal of patience. However, whereas melancholics require mainly gentleness, respect, and encouragement, even in severely depressive and anxious schizophrenics we must sometimes be very firm, or even strict, e.g., when they suddenly want to stop treatment, or behave in an excessively parasitical manner. Setting limits to such attitudes in the patient actually means lending him our ego and superego. Thus, such strictness does not imply that the therapist may not temporarily permit such patients to lean on his ego and "borrow" its strength. Discussions and interpretations of these attitudes do not in general become meaningful or effective before recovery from the depression or the whole psychotic episode. In suitable cases it may lead to a search for the infantile origin of the patient's instinctual and narcissistic conflicts, and of the past maldevelopment of his object relations and identifications. These patients need a long time before they can admit and understand the defects and contradictions in their value systems, and the corresponding pathological ego attitudes. I mentioned above the paranoid rage which a female paranoid depressive-schizophrenic patient developed when I made an untimely remark on her guilt conflicts. On the other hand, we must very cautiously wait before we can directly approach the melancholic's hostility conflicts.

My brief comments on the different problems arising in the treatment of melancholic and schizophrenic depressive patients were intended to underscore our need for a better understanding of the differences in their psychopathology, differences which determine the correct method of approaching them therapeutically.

BIBLIOGRAPHY

Asch, S. (1964), Depression. Abstr. in *Psa. Q.*, 23:463-465.
Bleuler, E. (1911), *Dementia Praecox or the Group of Schizophrenias*. NY: IUP, 1950.
———— (1949), *Lehrbuch der Psychiatrie*, 8th ed. (ed. M. Bleuler). Berlin: Springer.
Campbell, J. D. (1953), *Manic-Depressive Disease*. Philadelphia: Lippincott.
Freud, S. (1917), Mourning and Melancholia. *S.E.*, 14:237-260.
———— (1924a), Neurosis and Psychosis. *S.E.*, 19:149-153.
———— (1924b), The Loss of Reality in Neurosis and Psychosis. *S.E.*, 19:183-187.
Grinker, R., Sr., et al. (1961), *The Phenomena of Depressions*. NY: Hoeber.
Hartmann, H. (1950), Comments on the Psychoanalytic Theory of the Ego. *Essays*, 113-141.
———— (1953), Contribution to the Metapsychology of Schizophrenia. *Essays*, 182-206.
Hendrick, I. (1951), Early Development of the Ego. *Psa. Q.*, 20:44-61.
Jacobson, E. (1954), Contribution to the Metapsychology of Psychotic Identification. *J. Am. Psa. Assn.*, 2:239-262.
———— (1964), *The Self and the Object World*. NY: IUP.
Kraepelin, E. (1913), *Ein Lehrbuch für Studierende und Ärzte* [Band III, Klinische Psychiatrie, 2. Teil], 8th ed. Leipzig: Barth.
Lange, J. (1928), *Handbuch der Geisteskrankheiten* [Band VI, Spezieller Teil II, pp. 1-231, Die endogenen und reaktiven Gemütskrankheiten und die manisch-depressive Konstitution]. Berlin: Springer.

VI

Correlations and Applications
of Psychoanalysis

The Psychophysiology of Free Will

An Example of Vertical Research

ERNEST HARTMANN, M.D.

It is impossible for a scientist at present to believe in absolute free will. This statement looks excessively categorical at first glance, and perhaps requires clarification: By "it is impossible for a scientist," I mean only that this is impossible for one who acknowledges what science increasingly reveals about the orderliness of nature, and who accepts, as an operating rule at least, Occam's razor: Let there be no unnecessary postulates. By "absolute free will" I mean an exception to the laws of nature implying that certain actions are initiated *ex nihilo* by an act of volition rather than forming part of a continuing chain of causes and effects.

Ontologic determinism is almost universally accepted as a basis for science; however, there is much less agreement about epistemic determinism. In other words, if we indeed knew exactly the mass, velocity, and position of every particle in a given system, we could then predict exactly the future course of that system; however, we are far from being able to determine these quantities exactly, and many physicists argue that even theoretically it is impossible for us ever to determine them simultaneously. Yet Heisenberg himself, the foremost proponent of this view, states that his uncertainty principle affects only the latter, epistemic viewpoint, that he has no quarrel with ontologic determinism. This subject is well reviewed by Bradley (1962). Thus even if we accept the view that we can never learn everything about a system, that no matter how much we learn we shall still have to make certain statements in statistical, probabilistic form rather than in old-fashioned mechanistic form, this would nonetheless describe a lawful universe; there would still be no room whatever for an "exception" such as absolute free will. In other words, in so far as we are scientists, we must regard ourselves as part of nature and subject to her laws.

Yet, although we consider it established that there is no free will in an absolute sense, we must note that the *feeling* of free will exists in the normal human being as an empirical fact; I have the feeling, nay the certainty, for that is the quality of this particular feeling, that I am at this moment entirely free to continue writing, to stop, to take a nap, or a walk, and furthermore this feeling is not in the least diminished by reading the preceding paragraphs. (I have no qualms about using the word "fact" to describe a subjective state,[1] but perhaps a behaviorally oriented psychologist would feel happier with the "fact" that a statistically significant portion of a random sample of human beings, if asked whether they feel free to choose either of two simple equivalent alternatives, will answer "yes.") Thus any series of human actions can be seen by a disinterested observer as the determined outcome of the interaction of various organic systems, dependent principally perhaps on electron and ion movements within the central nervous systems of the participants, but at the same time each of the persons involved will feel a greater or lesser degree of free will, of choice, involved in his actions. Furthermore, this feeling of free will cannot be dismissed lightly by the scientist, for all our schools, our governments, and our sciences themselves appear to us to be founded on it, founded on the feeling that our actions matter, that we are free to change the world and ourselves. This all-important feeling, then, should itself be an object of study.

We have established that the feeling of free will does not correspond to an absolute free will. How, then, shall we consider this feeling? One way is to formulate and examine such questions as: What conditions are necessary for its presence or absence? What conditions increase or decrease it? These are now psychological and physiological questions which can perhaps be answered empirically, but only after we have established a framework for answering such questions. What is involved is of course the ancient and tantalizing "mind-body" problem; space does not permit a discussion of all the approaches that have been tried at one time or another; a simple framework for considering mind-body problems will be presented, purely on the ground that it

[1] A PSI state; see below.

has proved useful to me and others in thinking about these problems, since I do not believe we have any basis for speaking of the truth or falsehood of such a framework. Basically this is a framework of psychophysical parallelism (schematized in Figure 1):

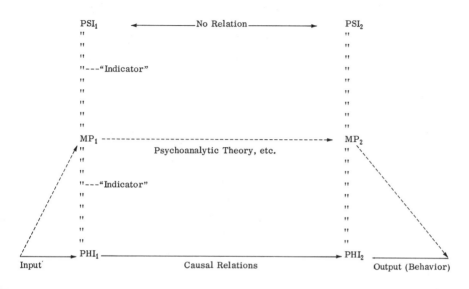

FIGURE 1

1. Consider mental functioning as well as its input and output under three systems: PHI, MP, and PSI. Consider all states of the brain and body to be "PHI states" and all events occurring in the brain or body as PHI events. (This includes input events, such as "light of a certain frequency strikes A's retina" and output events, such as "A walks to the door.") Consider as PSI states only the subject's consciousness and all its contents. ("A feels depressed." "A is aware of seeing a green field.") MP will be dealt with further on.

2. Causal relations exist between PHI states. (Causal is used in the physical sense involving a difference in time, a transfer of energy, and a necessary chain of events of some sort.)

3. No causal relations exist between PSI states.

4. No causal relations exist between a PHI state and a PSI state. The relationship is that defined by Hughlings Jackson as "concomitance" or what could be called functionally an "indicator" relationship. Thus there is no direct influence of PHI on PSI, or PSI on PHI. In studying a PHI system, a PSI state (or, more accurately, the subject's report of a PSI state) can be used only as an *indicator* to what PHI events might be occurring. We are used to hearing such statements as "His anxiety caused his ulcer." However, I do not believe this can usefully be taken to mean: the PSI event—feeling of anxiety —directly caused the physical event—his ulcer. Rather it means: the PSI event was concomitant with, or "indicated," a PHI state which caused a later PHI state that included the presence of an ulcer.

5. For every PHI state, there exists either one concomitant PSI state or no concomitant PSI states. (Any PHI state of a comatose, or sleeping, but not-dreaming subject, for instance, would probably have no concomitant PSI state.) For every PSI state there is one concomitant PHI state. (Or more than one in the sense that for a given PSI state there is presumably one PHI state of the brain or a certain portion of the brain, but this may be associated with variations of some other portion of PHI: position of the subject's body, for instance.)

6. It is clear from the above that PSI states cannot be studied directly, cannot be objectively observed, but are useful as "indicators" of PHI states which can be studied.

7. Although it is quite possible for psychological theories to restrict themselves to the system PHI including input and output (Pavlovian psychology does this; classical behaviorism goes further, and only considers the input and output portions of PHI), most psychological theories attempt to relate input and output through a system MP, connecting various postulated states of the mind (MP states) (see Figure 1).

I use the term "MP" since psychoanalysis, which has developed the most inclusive system of this sort, calls its psychological system "metapsychology." However, most other psychologies also employ a system of such "MP states." Heinz Hartmann (1939) has said: "At present we no longer doubt that psychoanalysis can claim to be a general psychology in the broadest sense of the word." In the present framework this would imply that all MP states, involving all aspects of mental functioning, can be described or expressed in psychoanalytic terms.

The term MP state refers to a conceptualization of the state of a subject's mind (psyche) at a given moment, or "what is really going on." (Whether or not the subject also is aware of a PSI state or event at that moment.) In the psychoanalytic model the MP state includes a description of all that is going on unconsciously. Perhaps ideally, from a theoretical viewpoint, it might be possible to describe the MP state in terms of the state of the subject's id, ego, and superego, the condition and strength of his drives and defenses, the placement of cathexes, etc. In practice such a description is usually not possible and in the clinical situation would perhaps not even be useful. At present, in place of such a "pure" structural, dynamic, and economic description, we employ a variety of less pure descriptions, which nonetheless clearly refer to the MP state. Thus, "Unconscious anger is present" does not describe a PSI state but is a rough "clinical" description of an MP state; in the simplest case it may mean an MP state, in this subject, which we have come to recognize as one which always precedes or leads to the MP state concomitant with the PSI state: I feel angry. Or more commonly it means an MP state followed by behavior, or accompanied by bodily signs, which one would expect from an MP state concomitant with a PSI feeling of anger, although in this particular case the PSI feeling is absent. In other words, "unconscious anger" is a rough formulation of an MP state based on similarity to another better known MP state—the one concomitant with conscious anger.

8. Relationships may be postulated between MP states, including relationships in causal form, although they will not be causal in the sense of physical energy transfer. No causal relations exist between an MP state and a PHI state or a PSI state. Again, the relationship between systems is functionally an "indicator" relationship. Thus a PSI state ("He is depressed") may indicate to the psychoanalyst an MP state (perhaps "he has turned his aggression inward") and this MP state, or relationships between two MP states, may hopefully indicate a PHI state. (Certain events are occurring in certain parts of his nervous system.)

9. For every MP state there exists either one or no concomitant PSI state. For every PSI state, there is at least one concomitant MP state.

10. Speaking very roughly, we could characterize the three systems as follows: PSI is what the (ideally naïve) subject thinks is going on in himself; MP is what the (ideally sophisticated) psychoanalyst thinks is going on; and PHI is what the (ideally sophisticated) physiologist thinks is going on.

11. Although all three types of vertical links can be used functionally, and heuristically, as indicator links, it should be pointed out that theoretically the link between systems MP and PHI is different from the other links. No true "mind-body" gap intervenes here, and quite probably as more is learned about the relevant aspects of PHI, and as MP concepts are refined, it will turn out that MP concepts, or at least the more valid MP concepts, are shorthand descriptions of PHI entities or PHI states.

In this framework it is possible to consider two kinds of research or investigation which, using Figure 1, will be referred to as *Horizontal and Vertical research*. Horizontal research can be carried out in MP or in PHI, but not according to our definitions in PSI. It involves investigating relationships, making and testing hypotheses within the system. Most psychoanalytic research involves horizontal research in system MP, and most physiological or biochemical research involves horizontal research in system PHI. In horizontal research the criterion for acceptability of a new concept or relationship is *cohesion* with the rest of the system, or its better established portions. This sort of investigation can be very fruitful, but obviously there are pitfalls in relying too heavily on cohesion if the other concepts of the system are not firmly established.

Vertical research is the investigation of relationships between systems PSI, MP, and PHI. In other words, it is the study of concomitance, the study of "indicators." Vertical research has been used relatively little in the past and certainly not to the full extent of its possibilities. There have of course been studies of relationships between PSI and MP, asking such questions as "What is going on in MP when a patient feels depressed?" There have been relatively few studies of what is going on in PHI (especially the most relevant, neurophysiological, parts of PHI) during a given PSI state or event, or of what is going on in PHI during a given MP state or event. Such studies, if well formulated, could be very fruitful to further horizontal research in both MP and PHI. By choosing a well-established relationship in MP, such as the difference between primary- and secondary-process thinking, it should be possible to direct horizontal PHI research to look for certain PHI relationships. On the other hand, well-established PHI events and relationships in the central nervous system should be used to suggest MP relationships and also as a check on existing MP theory, for probably those MP terms which turn out to refer directly or indirectly to central PHI events or states will be the most lasting and meaningful. One area studied in this way will be referred to later.

Having established this rough framework for our thinking, we can return to the problem of free will. The feeling of free will I have spoken of is obviously a PSI state and evidently a very prevalent one.[2] My investigation of this feeling will be an example of vertical investigation, and I shall consider two principal questions—the psychological question: What does the presence of the feeling of free will indicate in the system MP? (What are its MP concomitants?) and the physiological question: What does the presence of this feeling indicate in system PHI? (What are its PHI concomitants?)

First of all it is to be noted that the feeling I am investigating is not a feeling in the same sense as is a sudden stab of pain or feeling of anger. It is rather a mild and almost ubiquitous feeling, perhaps comparable to a feeling of quiet satisfaction, which is noticed chiefly when it is challenged or diminished. Therefore, rather than seeking specific MP or PHI occurrences concomitant with the feeling, we must rather look for prevalent MP and PHI states. Perhaps we can highlight such states by first asking what conditions are associated with changes in the feeling of free will. Decreases appear much easier to discuss than increases. We can immediately begin to list conditions which in our own experience or our experience with patients tend to be associated with a decrease or absence of the feeling of free will:

(a) Death, coma, dreamless sleep; these are obvious, but useless, since they are associated with the absence not only of the PSI state we are investigating, but of all PSI states.

(b) Confusional states, deliria, all states of clouded consciousness.

(c) Acute schizophrenic states, in which the patient often feels himself in the grip of forces too strong for him, and may feel quite

---

[2] This view has been expressed by Knight (1946): "Free will is a subjective feeling which is better called a sense of inner freedom."

unable to choose his own actions. This is true to a much smaller extent for chronic schizophrenic states.

(d) Severe depressive states. Here the affect is quite different from the case above, yet again the PSI state involves a diminished feeling of free will; the depressed patient usually describes feeling too burdened, too weighted down, too guilty, to summon up the "energy" to make even a simple decision.

(e) States of extreme hunger or thirst. (States dominated by a physical need.) Extreme fatigue could be considered here too.

(f) States dominated by sexual or aggressive drives, such as the last moments before an orgasm, or during a "blind" rage, when even a normal individual may feel himself to be in the grip of stronger forces that keep him from choosing his course of action, that deprive him of the feeling of free will.

(g) Certain neurotic states. For instance, a compulsion to say certain words, perform certain acts, or think certain thoughts; likewise a phobia. In these cases, there is a diminished feeling of free will only at particular times or in particular situations.

(h) Hypnosis and other states of increased suggestibility may represent a state of temporarily decreased free will.

(i) Certain medicated states must be included in this list. Drugs inducing sleep or drowsiness are obvious but again useless examples. However, I believe certain psychotomimetics may induce a state including a decreased feeling of free will: I have heard subjects reporting on experiences with LSD speak of feeling that they somehow "had to follow" a certain train of thought or even that they had to get up and walk around, do certain things, without having any choice in the matter.

(j) Possibly early childhood is associated with less feeling of free will; this is speculative, since we are speaking of a stage in which the subject cannot generally be expected to report his PSI states intelligibly; certainly many authors speak of early childhood in this way. For instance, Rapaport (1960) writes: "Observation shows that peremptory forms of behavior predominate in the early phases of human development, while voluntary ones predominate in later phases."

(k) Again, speculatively, it is possible that primitive man or man living in very primitive societies experiences less feeling of free will. Anthropologists generally report a life dominated by socially imposed actions, rituals, and taboos (compulsions and phobias) designed to placate the great mystic forces of the universe. Thus Lévy-Bruhl (1923), speaking of a number of primitive societies, frequently makes such statements as "Primitives are totally in the grip of various mystic forces"; or "Such alternatives or questions, natural for us, do not arise in the mind of the primitive." But perhaps this is leading us too far afield.

(1) Returning to the normal adult, there is one other condition, perhaps the most common one of all, which is associated with a lack of the feeling of free will, namely, the dream. In our dreams we participate in a range of actions as great as or even greater than in waking life, and we are capable of a considerable range of feeling, but as far as I can tell from the experiencing, perusal, and discussion of a large number of dreams, we are never aware of a feeling of free will. Certainly, there are some dreams in which decisions are made, or have to be made, but the dreamer's feeling is, "it just seemed to happen" or "apparently I decided to do such and such"; he sees himself making a choice occasionally, but does not have the experience (PSI state) of freedom to choose. There are certain persons who claim the ability to dream a dream over again at will, or to stop a dream voluntarily and give it a different ending; I have had only limited experience with this phenomenon, but it appears that the choice or decision is made before, after, or somehow outside the dream, quite likely during a body movement and very brief awakening such as usually accompanies a major "break" or change of scene in a dream.

What do all these conditions associated with a diminished or absent feeling of free will have in common? First, considering them in terms of the MP states involved, it is evident that from the standpoint of psychoanalytic theory these conditions have a great deal in common. They all appear to be associated with a relative "weakness" of the ego, and especially with a relative "weakness" of secondary-process thinking. This is brought about in a variety of ways (direct damage to the nerve cells, encroachment by the superego, encroachment by the id and the drives, immaturity of the ego). The neuroses do not represent a totally "weakened" ego or a clear-cut encroachment by the id except in so far as the specific symptoms represent a compromise formation with the id; but, in fact, in the neuroses there is also no clear-cut loss of the feeling of free will except when the specific symptoms are present. I shall assume, then, that the MP state concomitant with a decreased feeling of free will involves a "weak" ego, and the prevalence of primary-process thinking, in so far as there is thinking at all.

If we now refer to the psychoanalytic literature, we find that the connection I have made is clearly implied, though seldom emphasized, in many of the descriptions and definitions of primary-process thinking. Rapaport (1951) in his definition of primary process speaks of its "imperative" quality; Paul Schilder (1954) calls it "peremptory"; similarly Kurt Goldstein (1944), describing the "concrete thinking" in schizophrenics, emphasizes "lack of intentional activity" in its definition.

Let us examine the same question from a slightly different viewpoint, and notice what happens in a commonplace siutation when we gradually relinquish or lose our feeling of free will. We are all capable of summoning up a number of memories or pictures for ourselves, and we can often make valuable use of our ability to sit down and choose a picture, imagine a scene, examine a situation in fantasy. However, after choosing a particular memory or image and examining it critically in our minds, it often happens that we grow a little tired. At this point we relinquish some of our voluntary control over the fantasy and it begins gradually to take on a life of its own. We are capable of quite a range of fantasy, from directed abstract thought, to directed fantasy, to more undirected and more visual fantasy, and finally pure fantasy (or daydream) that appears to continue entirely without our direction. And as we relinquish control, as we lose the feeling that we can choose or direct the fantasy voluntarily, very strikingly the fantasy is taken over by primitive or primary-process thinking, involving improbable situations, condensations, displacements, and above all wish fulfillment. (More accurately, the form of thinking changes from secondary process toward prevalence of primary process, while the path to the goal changes strikingly from the longer reality-principle path to the pleasure-principle shortcut of immediate wish fulfillment.) Again a reduction of the feeling of free will appears to be associated with an MP state characterized by primary-process thinking.

Conversely, are there states we might examine characterized by an increase in the feeling of free will? This is difficult to decide. Certainly a more or less normal alert waking state involving an absence of the limiting factors listed above seems to be associated with as much feeling of free will as most of us experience. However, a few other possibilities might be considered: perhaps a state of emerging-into-health, for instance, after severe organic illness, or after escaping from a life-threatening accident, or a sudden emergence from one of the restrictive, low-free-will situations might be associated with a greater feeling of free will, representing a sort of rebound phenomenon. Likewise the feeling following problem solving, scientific discovery, or artistic achievement may include increased free will. And possibly another state, hypomania, might qualify; it is hard to be certain, but in so far as I can tell from my own experience and the reports of patients and others, a state of hypomania or euphoria may well be associated with an increased feeling of free will. How can this condition be conceptualized in MP terms? The state of mania involves, in one sense, a "weak" ego, which is often at the mercy of the drives, using chiefly the primitive and maladaptive defense mechanism of denial, and is quite defective in its functions of reality testing and relating to objects. However, mania, at least in its early phases, is also seen as a state of "strengthened" ego in the sense that it has conquered the superego; or, as Freud (1921) put it, the division between ego and superego disappears and the energy previously tied up in the struggle between them is placed at the ego's disposal; this latter view is more meaningful in considering an early phase of mania or the change from depression to mania than in conceptualizing a full-blown manic illness. If hypomania is considered merely a less blatant mania in both of the above senses, it lends no support to my thesis, but it is possible that there is a kind of euphoria or hypomania in which the early phase, liberation of the ego from the superego, is by far the stronger—following a depression, following the removal of some great worry, or following the understanding and working through of guilt in psychoanalysis. And I suspect that it is this sort of euphoria that is associated with an increased feeling of free will.

So, although we cannot study directly a state associated purely with the feeling of free will and have studied instead conditions associated with an increase or decrease in this feeling, we can conclude from these considerations that the MP state concomitant with the PSI state "feeling of free will" involves a "strong" ego, not encroached on by id or superego, and the dominance of secondary-process thinking.

The MP state we have characterized is of considerable importance, since it represents the major portion of what is often called
psychological health, and all psychiatric therapies in one way or
another aim for this MP state, accompanied, of course, by a greater
feeling of free will. The therapist deals with and thinks in terms of
the various factors involved in the patient's MP state, but a good
result will usually be signaled, "indicated," by a PSI state of increased
feeling of free will.

Can we say anything about our other question, about the PHI
state concomitant with the feeling of free will? Not very much at
this time, although there are promising leads. We can begin by re-
examining the various conditions associated with a decreased feeling
of free will, but we find we know little about most of them in system
PHI. Some of the first ones appear to involve a nonspecific poisoning
or destruction of the central nervous system. There are slight hints
that severe depressions may be associated with altered amine levels
and distributions in the brain. Schizophrenia has not been solidly
identified with any physiological or biochemical abnormality, despite
numerous attempts. The only consistent finding has been the great
variability of schizophrenic patients on a wide variety of physiological measures, so that there tend to be more extreme values among
schizophrenics than among comparable groups of nonschizophrenics,
even though the mean values for the two groups are the same.

Thus, as a first approximation we might see the PHI state we are
looking for as one characterized by homeostasis: a *milieu intérieur*
with certain physiological and biochemical boundaries such that
changes beyond those boundaries may result in a state concomitant
with decreased free will. Certainly infants are known to have poor
homeostatic mechanisms controlling certain physiological systems—
temperature and pulse are notoriously unstable, as is, for instance, the
regulation of blood sugar. Lately it has been found that the PHI state
associated with dreaming likewise involves great variability and ir-
regularity of pulse, blood pressure, and respiration (Snyder, 1963).
Again this suggests that at least some conditions associated with a
PSI state of diminished free will are characterized by poor homeostasis in PHI.

We might take this as a very general aspect of the PHI state we
are investigating, but it should be possible to be more specific. Unfortunately we know next to nothing about the important neuro-

physiological details of the PHI states involved in neurosis, hypnosis, or drive domination. Any knowledge here could be very useful; it might be feasible to a limited extent to study PHI changes accompanying sudden insight, a sudden relief of depression, etc., but this remains to be done. However, some help may be afforded us by a great body of recent work defining the PHI state concomitant with dreaming (the D state). Certain of its peripheral characteristics have been mentioned above. Decreased muscle tone in most species and the well-known rapid eye movements should also be included. However, the more central neurophysiological findings, derived of course from animal work, are of greater interest here. These include an activated (low-voltage fast) cortex (Dement and Kleitman, 1957), an activated (theta rhythm) hippocampus (Cadilhac et al., 1961), active single neurons in the mesencephalon and in the visual pathways (Evarts, 1962; Huttenlocher, 1961), and a large number of other neural characteristics, many involving the "visceral brain," all initiated by an area in the central pons (Jouvet, 1962) and probably controlled by the accumulation of a neurohumoral substance, possibly serotonin (E. Hartmann, 1965).

These characteristics now constitute a well-defined state, a PHI state concomitant with dreaming. It is quite likely that many of its characteristics—the eye movements, for instance—are specific to dreaming sleep; however, I should like to pose the question: Is it possible that the central aspects of this state actually constitute the PHI state concomitant with the MP state: "prevalence of primary-process thinking," and thus also concomitant with the PSI state: "decreased or absent free will"?

There is no direct evidence at the moment for this vertical speculation, nor is there evidence against it since the work would have to be done on human beings in various of the other conditions involving increased primary process and decreased free will, and there is no satisfactory way so far of examining or altering these subtle central characteristics (pontine function or humoral levels in the brain stem) in the intact human being. However, there are no theoretical obstacles, and such investigations will probably be possible in the near future.

In any case up to now the work on dreaming offers almost the only hint available about possible central PHI states involved in at least one of the conditions I have considered involving prevalence of primary-process thinking and a decreased feeling of free will.

Again, conditions involving a possible increase in the feeling of free will should be examined, but here we find that we know even less about the relevant PHI states. Certainly we can characterize the ordinary alert waking state as one involving an activated cortex, an active ascending reticular system, and a certain general level of discharge in various central nervous system neurons; but none of these conditions are very specific, and we do not know the crucial changes that may occur at a moment of release from depression or other illness, or that might accompany the state of hypomania or euphoria I have discussed. Another class of conditions I have mentioned, but not previously discussed because they have been dealt with in PHI research far more than in MP, are the pharmacological states. There are numerous drugs that appear to produce some sort of euphoria. The opium derivatives and other narcotics are often associated with a happy contented feeling, but generally a feeling close to lethargy or sleepiness and certainly not involving an increased feeling of free will. The psychotomimetics, mentioned previously, cause a state involving, if anything, a decrease in the feeling of free will. A third class of drugs sometimes associated with euphoria is the amphetamine group; the effect of these drugs varies considerably from individual to individual, but there are persons who describe a subjective state after Dexedrine that appears to involve an increased feeling of free will. It is quite possible, of course, that this is once more only a rebound effect, associated with a transient lifting of depression or drowsiness. In this case, at least, we are able to characterize the relevant PHI state to some extent, in that it involves the central activity of the drug, producing specifically an increased excitation of the ascending reticular activating system.

Looking at the various conditions I have studied in a slightly different way, the conditions I have characterized as associated with greater feeling of free will might be considered as states in which there is a capacity for more efficient information handling, for switching impulses along specific pathways with a minimal expenditure of energy—and certainly secondary process can be described in this way in terms of the amount of "psychic energy" expended (Rapaport, 1951). This sort of information handling involving a "fine adjustment" regulation is again most easily associated with the waking activity of the ARAS-cortical pathways.

Thus, my tentative conclusion is that a feeling of free will in system PSI may be concomitant with a "strong" ego and the prevalence of secondary-process thinking in system MP; and concomitant with the homeostatic maintenance of various physiological variables and a "waking" activation of the ARAS-cortical pathways (as opposed to no activation or the very different activation involving humoral mechanisms acting on the pons and visceral brain) in system PHI.

Present knowledge does not allow us to go further, and in fact I must plead guilty to having already passed well beyond the bounds of what is strictly supported by present data. However, I hope this essay may have been of some slight use in several ways:

I have tried to indicate the usefulness of having a clearly defined scheme for considering mind-body relationships. I do not insist that the one I have presented is the best possible, but I have attempted to demonstrate its possibilities, specifically by an example of vertical research.

Secondly, I have tried to indicate, only schematically of course, how psychoanalytic theory, if it is to be a universal human psychology, might fit into a general scheme for research on the human mind.

Lastly, I have tried to show that one of the ancient and eternally debated problems of man has not yet been debated to the point of futility; and that this problem may be eternal not as a sterile exercise or paradox, but as a central factor in the working of our minds.

Nietzsche suggests that a full knowledge of our own determinism will eventually make us supermen. I can offer no opinion on this eventuality, but I have tried to show that it is possible to study even free will in our essentially deterministic framework, and that free will despite its nonexistence may yet teach us much about ourselves.

BIBLIOGRAPHY

Bradley, R. D. (1962), Determinism or Indeterminism in Microphysics. *Brit. J. Phil. Sci.*, 13:193-214.

Cadilhac, J., Passouant-Fontaine, T., & Passouant, P. (1961), Modifications de l'activité de l'hippocampe suivant les divers stades du sommeil spontané chez le chat. *Rev. Neurol.*, 105:171-176.

Dement, W. & Kleitman, N. (1957), Cyclic Variations in EEG during Sleep and Their Relation to Eye Movements, Body Motility, and Dreaming. *EEG Clin. Neurophysiol.*, 9:673-690.

Evarts, E. V. (1962), Activity of Neurons in Visual Cortex of the Cat during Sleep ·with Low Voltage Fast EEG Activity. *J. Neurophysiol.*, 25:812.

Freud, S. (1921), Group Psychology and the Analysis of the Ego. *S.E.*, 18:67-143.

Goldstein, K. (1944), Methodological Approach to the Study of Schizophrenic Thought Disorder. *Language and Thought in Schizophrenia*, ed. J. S. Kasanin. Berkeley & Los Angeles: Univ. Calif. Pr.

Hartmann, E. (1965), The D-State. *New Eng. J. Med.*, 273:30-35, 87-92.

Hartmann, H. (1939), *Ego Psychology and the Problem of Adaptation.* NY: IUP, 1958.

Huttenlocher, P. R. (1961), Evoked and Spontaneous Activity in Single Units of Medial Brain Stem during Natural Sleep and Waking. *J. Neurophysiol.*, 24:451.

Jouvet, M. (1962), Recherches sur les structures nerveuses et les méchanismes responsables des différentes phases du sommeil physiologique. *Arch. Ital. Biol.*, 100:125-206.

Knight, R. P. (1946), Determinism, Freedom, and Psychotherapy. *Psychiatry*, 9:251-262.

Lévy-Bruhl, L. (1923), *Primitive Mentality.* London: Allen & Unwin.

Rapaport, D. (1951), Toward a Theory of Thinking. *Organization and Pathology of Thought.* NY: Columbia Univ. Pr., 689-730.

―――― (1960), Psychoanalysis as a Developmental Psychology. *Perspectives in Psychological Theory*, ed. B. Kaplan & S. Wapner. NY: IUP, 209-255.

Schilder, P. (1954), *Clinical Psychiatry*, ed. W. Mayer-Gross, E. Slater, & M. Roth. London: Cassell, 246.

Snyder, F. (1963), The New Biology of Dreaming. *Arch. Gen. Psychiat.*, 8:381-391.

Dreaming and Sexuality

CHARLES FISHER, M.D.

Hartmann (1959) has remarked, "Freud held on to the expectation, shared by many analysts, that one day the development of brain physiology would make it possible to base psychoanalysis on its findings and theories. He did not think this would happen during his lifetime, in which he proved to be right" (p. 322). He states further, "We have also to consider the fact that, given the actual state of brain physiology, many and even comparatively simple aspects of behavior of the kind we are dealing with in analysis cannot be explained. To rely on brain physiology alone would mean to renounce explanation of the greatest part of the field that psychoanalysis has set out to explain" (p. 321). Psychoanalysis has always claimed to be biologically based, and one of the important aspects of this claim is Freud's concept of the somatic sources of the instinctual drives. In this connection, Hartmann (1948) points out that the "sources [of the instinctual drives] remain relevant because of their developmental aspects and because insight into the sources may be helpful in classifying the drives. This part of Freud's concept also presents a hope—not the only one—for the future meeting of psychoanalysis and physiology" (p. 72f.).

This paper will be concerned with some new experimental findings that have implications for the problem of the somatic sources of instinctual drives and the physiological, neurophysiological, and biochemical correlates of drive activation and their relation to dreaming. The discovery of the dream-sleep cycle, that is, the occurrence of alternating

From the Institute of Psychiatry, Department of Psychiatry, The Mount Sinai Hospital, New York, M. R. Kaufman, M.D., Director.

This research is supported by U.S.P.H.S. Grant #MHO3267.

This paper is a modified version of the Abraham A. Brill Memorial Lecture, delivered before the New York Psychoanalytic Society on November 23, 1965.

periods of so-called REM and NREM[1] activity which characterizes sleep, is by now well known. Sleep is not a unitary state of being but a progression of rhythmic cycles representing different phases of neural functioning. Dreaming sleep is a special organismic third state associated with marked somatic activation, which extends to all organ systems that have so far been investigated. It is a state of almost frenzied internal activity resembling in many ways that of alert wakefulness, but in spite of all this internal turmoil, the subject is behaviorally and subjectively asleep. The internal activity is correlated with the events of the hallucinatory dream and not with events in the external world. The sleeping organism is sealed off from the outer world by the widespread motor paralysis and the occlusion of incoming sensory impulses that accompanies REM sleep.

Recently, I and my co-workers, Gross and Zuch (1965) at The Mount Sinai Hospital, have demonstrated that one of the important aspects of the physiological activation accompanying REM dreaming sleep is a massive excitation of the sexual drive in the male as manifested by a cycle of penile erections synchronous with the REMPs. We were able to show that about 95 per cent of REMPs are accompanied by some degree of erection: more or less full erection in 60 per cent of instances and partial erection in 35 per cent. Erections are found to occur in close temporal relationship to onsets and terminations of REMPs, so that there may be approximately as much erection during a night as there is dreaming, that is, from one fifth to a quarter of sleep in the young adult male may be spent in a state of full erection. Initially I was reluctant to believe that such extensive erections could be related to dream content and suggested a number of alternative explanations; e.g., that they may represent another aspect of the general REMP physiological activation without necessarily being related to dream content, or that they are manifestations of an overflow phenomenon due to limbic system excitation.

In order to elucidate this problem, I undertook, in collaboration with Gross and Byrne, to study the relationship between REMP erections, their fluctuations, and dream content.[2] I wish to present the preliminary results of this investigation.

[1] REM equals Rapid Eye Movement or dreaming sleep. REMP equals Rapid Eye Movement Period. NREMP equals Nondreaming sleep.

[2] These experiments are extremely arduous, involving prolonged night vigils and scoring of literally miles of records. I wish to acknowledge my debt to my collaborators, Joseph Gross, Edwin Kahn, and Joseph Byrne, and especially to my secretary assistant and laboratory coordinator, Adele Edwards.

Recently, in her excellent study on the nature of inspiration and the phallic phase, Greenacre (1964), in discussing the problem of variations in individual susceptibility to genital excitation, remarked, "It is certainly an area for investigation not yet open to genitograms comparable to cardiograms or electroencephalograms, and we are still dependent on the less precise methods of clinical observation" (p. 14). Fortunately or unfortunately, the day of the genitogram has arrived. The most sensitive method for obtaining such a genitogram, or, in the experiments to be reported, a continuous all-night recording of the degree of penile tumescence, is the mercury strain gauge. The only apparatus attached to the penis consists of an elastic silicon plastic tube about the size of a small rubber band (Figure 1). Minor

FIGURE 1

Photograph of the mercury strain gauge. The scale is in cms. The mercury strain gauge is looped around the base of the penis.

variations in electrical resistance as the tube is stretched during erection can be electronically amplified, quantified in terms of mms. of increase of penile circumference and graphically recorded. Figure 2 is such a graphic representation of the dream-sleep cycle of a subject who showed five REMPs during nine hours of sleep. The x-d line shows the changes in penile circumference during the course of the night. Approximately at the beginning of each REMP, there was an increase of penile circumference of 2½ or more cm., amounting to full erection; detumescence began in close temporal relationship to the termination of each REMP.

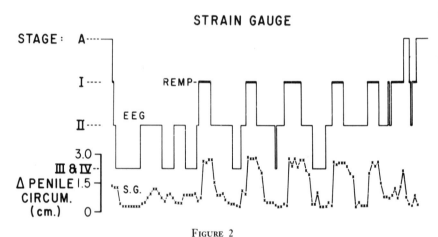

FIGURE 2

The graph shows the stages of the EEG plotted against time. The REMPs are indicated by the darker horizontal lines. Directly below is a graphic representation of the increase in penile circumference in cms. as measured by the strain gauge. The increases are of an order of 2.5 cm. or more, indicating full erection.

Method

Continuous all-night recordings of EEG, REM, and changes in penile circumference were done on 6 paid college student volunteers in their early 20s for a total of 15 nights. On these nights the subjects were awakened from REMPs during some particular state of penile tumescence and detailed accounts of dreams were elicited, especially the content just prior to and at the moment of awakening. The next day I attempted, from a study of 58 dream accounts, including reports of affects and associations to the dreams, to make a blind prediction of the fluctuations of erection in any given instance.

Figure 3 shows a typical erection curve and the points at which awakenings were most often made. The most frequent pattern of erection, present in about 50 per cent of the instances, unfolds in the following way: a slight tumescence begins a few minutes before onset of the REMP and continues for some minutes. Rapid tumescence then occurs during which full or nearly full erection may be attained within a few minutes. The erection may then be sustained throughout the remainder of the REMP or there may be greater or lesser degrees of fluctuation. The initial marked tumescence, however, may begin some minutes before onset of the REMP or as late as 18 minutes after it. In the latter instance, we obtain a prolonged flat record indicating inhibition of erection. We were particularly interested in dream content associated with flat portions of the records (awakenings made at point A on the graph) compared with content from awakenings made at B or C after a considerable degree of erection had been attained. We also paid special attention to dream content from awakenings made at point D following episodes of sudden detumescence.

We have calculated normal baseline data for the degree of erection in 10 subjects for 14 nights during 57 REMPs. We have divided degree of erection into three categories: slight erection, representing 0-7 mm. increase in penile circumference; moderate erection, 8-16 mm.; and full or nearly full erection, 17-20+ mm. During the 57 REMPs there were 68.5 per cent full, 14 per cent moderate, and 17.5 per cent slight erections.

Results

The most successful predictions were in those instances when a sudden sharp detumescence occurred. In seven out of eight such instances my predictions were correct (significant at the .001 level).[3] The prediction was made on the basis of the presence of marked anxiety associated with the events of the manifest dream just prior to and at the time of awakening. All of these dreams contained marked aggressive elements, in five instances the aggression being directed toward the dreamer and in two turned outward toward a second party. In four of the dreams the dreamer was either bitten by an animal or such biting was being threatened, by a dog, fish, snake,

[3] I wish to thank Jacob Cohen for the statistical analyses of the data.

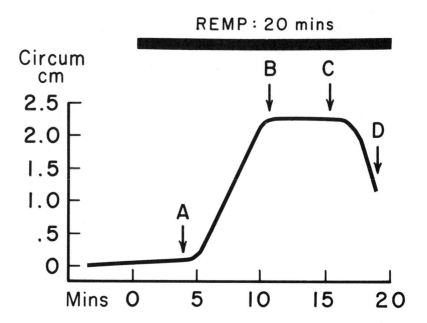

SCHEMATIC REPRESENTATION OF REMP ERECTION SHOWING TYPICAL POINTS OF AWAKENING TO ELICIT DREAM CONTENT:

A. DURING INITIAL FLAT PHASE.

B. AFTER ABRUPT RAPID TUMESCENCE.

C. DURING SUSTAINED MAXIMAL ERECTION.

D. AFTER ABRUPT RAPID DETUMESCENCE.

FIGURE 3

or lion. In the fifth dream, the dreamer was in the process of stabbing an attacker in the abdomen just as the awakening buzzer sounded. In the sixth dream, this same subject was stopped by the police and was very fearful that the knife with which he had done the stabbing would be found in his car. In the seventh dream, the dreamer was aggressively tickling another man to the point where he began to choke and the subject was afraid that he was going to kill him.

A second aspect of the prediction study was also quite successful. In five out of six instances a sharp, sudden increase in tumescence was correctly predicted (significant at the .001 level). In four dreams the prediction was made on the basis of an overtly erotic episode in the manifest dream occurring just prior to and at the moment of awakening. In the fifth instance, the prediction was made on the basis of the symbolic nature of the dream, e.g., the dreamer was going up an elevator with several girls. In two manifestly erotic dreams the dreamer was kissing or petting; in a third the dreamer was thinking of having intercourse with a girl on a stairway and felt excited; and in the fourth, the dreamer was looking at a nude girl and felt sexually aroused.

The following individual examples illustrate the kind of results obtained. The first is the dream of Subject B, who at the time of the experiment had been continent for over a year and had had no sexual outlet whatever, including nocturnal emission or masturbation. He was involved in a difficult and painful love affair with a sadistic Indian girl who treated him badly and rejected any sort of physical intimacy.

Figure 4 shows that the REMP associated with this dream lasted 14 minutes. The initial phase of rapid tumescence began a minute before onset of the REMP and full erection of 2.5 cm. was attained within a few minutes. The initial flat phase of the typical erection curve was not present. The erection was sustained for 10 minutes when a sudden detumescence amounting to 9 mm. occurred in the space of 1 minute, at which time the subject was awakened.

From the dream record, I correctly predicted that there would be a good erection with rapid detumescence at the end. The subject reported a very long dream consisting of three separate episodes, which can be correlated with the different parts of the erection curve. Since rapid tumescence began a minute before the onset of the REMP and full erection was attained within 2 minutes after its onset, it

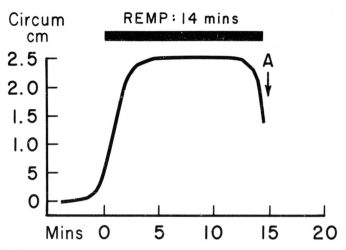

SUBJECT B.

ONSET OF TUMESCENCE 1 MINUTE BEFORE ONSET OF REMP, FULL
ERECTION (2.5 cm) ATTAINED 2 MINUTES AFTER, SUSTAINED FOR 11
MINUTES AND FOLLOWED BY A SUDDEN DETUMESCENCE OF 8 mm.
A = AWAKENING

FIGURE 4

might be expected that erotic content would appear early in the first
dream episode. This turned out to be the case. The subject dreamed,
"We were riding on these glass sheets and I lied down upon it, face
down, and she [his girl friend] does it right next to me. Somehow it
wasn't just her, it was her; she was my brother, too. We looked at
each other and I kissed her almost by accident. . . . We got shoved
against each other or we put our arms around each other."

In the second dream episode the subject is driving with his girl
friend and stops off at a lake where he meets his brother who seems
changed. He likes him better and they begin wrestling playfully and
good-naturedly, rustling one another's hair, etc. It will be noted that
in the first episode on the glass sheet his girl friend turns into his
brother. From this and other material we were aware that the subject had some serious unconscious homosexual conflict, confused his
girl friend with his brother, and in general, because of his anxieties
about girls, tended to turn toward men. The period of sustained erection, up till the final rapid detumescence, appears to be connected
with the thinly disguised homosexual contact with his brother.

The third episode lasted, according to the subject, a matter of minutes. His brother returned to the car and the subject looked at the lake and saw some really strange fish in the water. They were red and had spines and looked like sharks. They came right on the land to get him and he was forced to climb a tree. He was scared that they would bite him, that they would come out of the water, that they would rub against him with their sharp scales and do him in. He was hitting at them with a branch when he was awakened by the buzzer. It was clearly this part of the dream that was associated with the rapid detumescence.

It was evident from the subject's associations that he suffers from severe anxieties about sexual relations with women and that he unconsciously thinks of the female genital as a dangerous, biting organ. For example, in talking about the good-natured fight with his brother, he remarked that he is always fighting with his girl but it's never playful. He said, "There's two levels that men and women get along on, and that, after you have intercourse with a woman, it's much different. It's like a cat, and then you have to really fight, because then it's like after the cat's made the female, the female cat bites the male cat if she can." One can guess that the biting sharks and biting cat are equivalent and stand for the dangerous female genital. I might note, at this point, that direct representations of the strain gauge were very rare in the dream reports elicited. We have five dreams that revolve around being bitten by animals, and it is possible that the loop of the mercury strain gauge around the penis may be transformed in the manifest dream content into a biting mouth.

The next example is of a correct prediction of rapid tumescence at the end of a long dream by the same subject. Figure 5 shows a REMP lasting 18 minutes during which there was marked inhibition of erection. Just before the subject was awakened there occurred a sudden tumescence of 10 mm. over a period of about a minute. The terminal part of the dream had to do with his being in a rowboat and necking with a girl. He was fondling her breasts and just as the buzzer went off he moved his hands down between her legs. It appears certain that this openly erotic episode was associated with the sudden tumescence. Again, as in the previous dream, the subject kept getting the girl with whom he was petting confused with a boy.

The long dream preceding the petting episode was filled with anxious and aggressive content associated with the inhibition of erec-

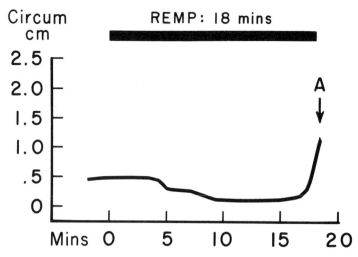

SUBJECT B.

MARKED INHIBITION OF ERECTION FOR 17 MINUTES FOLLOWED BY
ABRUPT TUMESCENCE OF 12 mm IN 1 MINUTE.   A = AWAKENING

FIGURE 5

tion and a feeling of shock. There was a party at a beautiful house where a dam breaks and a deluge occurs; water started pouring onto the lawn and into the driveway and it was dangerous. There was a rainstorm and a stream ran right inside the house, swelled up immensely, and started rolling down the driveway. The water pushed a lot of people in rowboats out to sea and the subject was rowing out with his girl to rescue them when the petting episode occurred. The subject's associations and the symbolism of the "water breaking" suggest that the dangerous flood has to do with anxieties about childbirth.

The next example is that of a dream associated with a nocturnal emission, the only one we have ever observed. Figure 6 shows a REMP lasting 9.5 minutes. During all but the last minute or two of this period there was no erection. Suddenly over a period of about 90 seconds, rapid tumescence occurred with a 2 cm. increase in penile circumference, terminating in a nocturnal emission.

It is possible, in this instance, to delineate the part of the dream content associated with absence of erection and that connected with sexual arousal and nocturnal emission. He was alone in his house

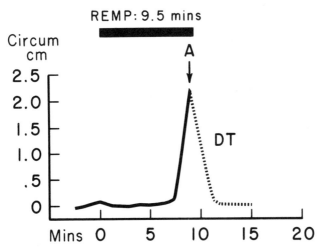

SUBJECT A.

REPRESENTATION OF NOCTURNAL EMISSION BEGINNING 7.5 MINUTES
AFTER ONSET OF REMP. FULL ERECTION (2.1 cm CIRCUMFERENCE)WAS
ATTAINED IN 1.5 MINUTES. NOTE RAPID DETUMESCENCE (DT).
A = AWAKENING

FIGURE 6

looking out the window. There was a crowd before the house. Two
girls from his native country appeared and told him that a friend of
his had committed suicide and he was surprised and unhappy. They
came in and sat down and he began to tease them. One of the girls
wanted some water and the other went to get it for her. When she
returned she dropped something, a pin that girls use to shape their
hair. He picked it up and gave it to her and held her hand. At this
moment he had a wet dream.

The minimal physical contact of holding the girl's hand does not
seem a sufficient excitation to have produced a nocturnal emission.
From other available material I have the impression that the sexual
excitation related to the latent content of the dream, e.g., the symbolic meaning of the falling pin and giving it back. The subject had
an earlier dream in which he was in an airplane returning to his native
country to be reunited with his wife from whom he had been separated in reality for over a year. In the dream, he was holding a knife
in his hand and was walking through the plane to cut a loaf of bread.
In relating this dream, the subject twice unconsciously made a slip

and referred to the "knife" as his "wife." The oral-phallic content of
this dream and indications that the two dreams reported revolve
around some fantasy of a phallic woman suggest that the nocturnal
emission was produced by an exciting unconscious fantasy of phallic
restitution. The part of the dream in which there was no erection was
associated with anxious, unhappy content and with aggressive fantasies, e.g., the suicide of a girl who, his associations revealed, had once
been in love with him. Figure 7 shows the actual EEG-REM, strain-
gauge tracings. Note the 12 ejaculatory spasms.

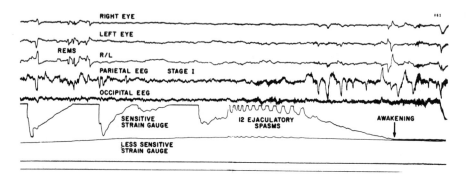

FIGURE 7

Subject A. Showing 60 seconds of the REM, EEG, and strain-gauge recording during
a nocturnal emission. Note the rapid rise of the strain-gauge tracing and the 12 ejaculatory spasms.

The next example is that of a dream associated with failure of
erection to develop, the total increase in penile circumference during
17.5 minutes of a REMP amounting to only 2 to 3 mm. as shown in
Figure 8. This is another dream of Subject B. The dream takes place
in a "wild" concert hall where Nat King Cole is singing from upstairs. "People with oars were going upstairs to the balcony and I was
using one oar to keep the crowd back because they were beginning
to charge up the stairs. So I stuck my oar across the stairway and
caught it in the corners and held the crowd back. Then I got mad
because this stupid redhead was still going up and I wanted to hit
her because she was going to knock against the oar and it wasn't in
very secure. . . . I felt outraged and scared because my oar is only
a little crevice corner type thing, and in the woodwork of the stairway is only like a nook, like a filigree nook, and I'm scared this whole

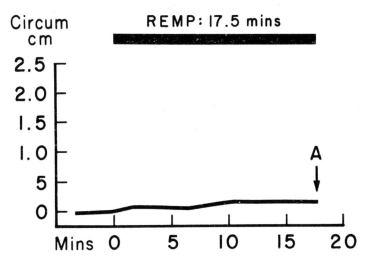

SUBJECT B.

MARKED INHIBITION OF ERECTION. TOTAL INCREASE IN PENILE
CIRCUMFERENCE ONLY 3mm DURING REMP OF 17.5 MINUTES.
A = AWAKENING.

FIGURE 8

crowd is so pent up getting to the balcony they're gonna knock past
the oar, knock it over and mix up his song. . . ."

This is the same subject who had the dream about necking in a
rowboat. It seems probable that oars have some special symbolic
phallic significance for him. The anxiety in the dream revolves around
the aggression of the women, especially the redhead, who are charg-
ing up the stairs and bumping into his oar which "wasn't in very
secure," and with his counteraggression and anger because he felt
threatened. The stairway symbolism and castration content of this
dream are to be noted.

It is of interest that several months later this subject participated
in a second experiment. In the interval, a change had occurred in him
which we would like to believe was an inadvertent therapeutic side
effect of his participation in the experiment. He brought along with
him a small, thin, boyish, masochistic girl who had recently recovered
from a surgical abortion, the result of a pregnancy by a former
lover. With this girl, obviously opposite in temperament to the sadistic
Indian, he had been able to establish a successful sexual relationship.

These partially successful attempts at prediction encourage me to believe that with greater experience and more careful methods even more significant results can be obtained. In addition to the prediction study, a different and promising approach to the data was made, that is, a comparison of the content of the dreams associated with no or slight erection with the content of those dreams in which moderate to full erection was attained, e.g., from awakenings made at Point A as compared to awakenings made at Points B and C on the graph of the typical erection curve (Figure 3). Comparisons were made as to the persons involved in the dream, their interaction with the dreamer, the activities in the dream, with special reference to manifest or latent sexual content, the degree of aggression present, and the quality of affect.

Of the 17 flat records available, indicating no, slight, or inhibited erection, there was not a single instance of the presence of erotic content in the manifest dream, and in no instance was there any direct physical contact of the dreamer with any person in the dream. On the other hand, among the 30 dreams with moderate to full erection there were 8 in which erotic feeling was experienced in the manifest dream. These involved such activities as kissing, petting, holding hands, looking at a girl undressing, etc.

One of the important findings of this investigation is that erection may be associated with disguised, latent, and symbolic erotic content even though there is no erotic feeling in the manifest dream. Fifteen of the 30 dreams with moderate to full erection showed such latent erotic content, and also 7 of the 17 dreams associated with flat records. Combining the figures for manifest and latent erotic content, we see that 23 of 30 dreams with moderate to full erection showed sexual content as opposed to 7 of 17 of the dreams with minimal erection. (This difference is significant at the .02 level.) By latent or symbolic content, I refer to such findings as the presence of at least four dreams involving climbing stairs, a common symbolic representation of sexual intercourse.

An even more significant difference was that the dreams associated with minimal erection contained much more aggressive content, anxiety, and other negative affects such as jealousy, feelings of shock, rejection, and resentment. Thus, 10 out of 17 of the flat records were associated with such content as opposed to only 5 out of 30 of the records of dreams showing moderate to full erection. (This difference is significant at the .01 level.)

I believe that the following preliminary formulations can be made about the relationship of dream content to the accompanying REMP erections and their fluctuations:

1. In instances where there is erotic content in the manifest dream, relatively free from anxiety, erection will occur.

2. In instances where the sexual content is latent or expressed in symbolic form even though there is no erotic feeling in the manifest dream, erection will occur if anxiety-aggressive aspects are in abeyance.

3. If, in the presence of ongoing erection, the dream content shifts to an episode arousing marked anxiety or other negative affect, associated with aggression either directed toward the subject or against someone else on the dreamer's part, rapid detumescence will occur. The anxiety, as would be expected, involves the well-known danger situations related to castration, loss of love, or loss of the love object.

4. If aggressive content associated with anxiety or other negative affect is present in the dream from the very onset of the REMP, erection will not occur or will be markedly inhibited. Such periods of inhibition may last for 15 or more minutes. Whether or not erection occurs appears to depend upon the particular balance in any given dream between aggressive and sexual content and the accompanying anxiety or other negative affect.

5. The initial flat phase of the erection curve, which is present in about 50 per cent of the instances, may not make its appearance if erotic content is present at the very onset of the REMP. In these instances, the initial rapid tumescence may begin shortly before or at the very onset of the REMP.

DISSOCIATION OF ERECTION FROM REMP AND REBOUND EFFECT

During the course of the awakening experiments, we made an interesting observation. We noted that quite often when a REMP was interrupted by awakening, especially if erection had not yet occurred, and while the subject was falling asleep subsequent to the interview, most often in the transition between awakening and Stage 1 sleep onset, varying degrees of erection up to full would occur extending for a variable time into Stage 2, followed by detumescence.

It seemed as if the erection, which had not had an opportunity to develop during the REMP, occurred as a sort of rebound effect during NREM sleep, following awakening. This suggested that the sexual excitation which began with the REMP, if not permitted to develop during it, continued on into NREM sleep, thus becoming dissociated from it and indicating that erection was even more difficult to suppress than other manifestations of REMP activation.

In order to study this phenomenon more systematically, I carried out, in collaboration with Gross and Byrne, a series of REM-dream-deprivation experiments on two subjects by the method of forced awakenings and in two by the administration of Nembutal and Dexedrine plus forced awakenings (Dement, 1965a, b). As a control, we awakened one subject frequently during NREM sleep to investigate the effect of such awakenings on the erection. We observed a variety of rebound and dissociative effects following REM suppression, which did not, however, occur during the control experiment.

Figure 9 shows three rebound erections which occurred during the latter part of the night following three REM interruptions. The variously striped bars across the top indicate the different stages of

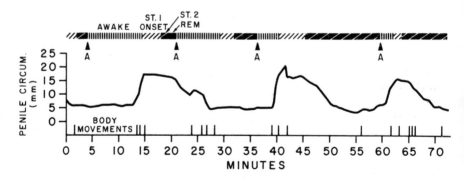

SUBJECT S.W.

SECOND DREAM DEPRIVATION NIGHT SHOWING
REBOUND EFFECT

FIGURE 9

Showing three rebound erections which occurred toward the end of the awakening period following the first, third, and fourth REMP interruptions (A), extending into sleep onset Stage 1. There was no rebound effect following the second REM awakening.

sleep. The solid bar indicates the REMPs. The "A" indicates the awakenings made after a few minutes of dreaming. The rebound in these three instances attained nearly full erection and, as can be seen, occurred at the transition between awakening and sleep-onset Stage 1. The rebound effect was especially evident in the latter part of the night when REMPs are longer in duration and when it becomes necessary to awaken the subject more and more frequently in order to suppress dreaming. At this time, a rebound erection can occur and sustain itself through a series of four or five or more awakenings. Figure 10 illustrates such a rebound effect extending and maintaining itself through Stage 2 and across two additional REM awakenings.

SUBJECT D.A.

SECOND NIGHT DREAM DEPRIVATION
(FORCED AWAKENINGS)

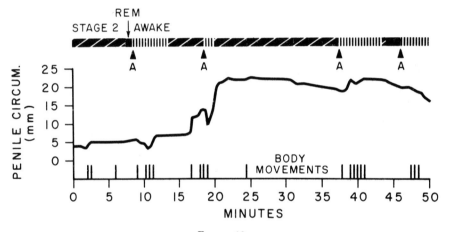

FIGURE 10

Showing rebound erection following REM awakening. The erection continued for more than 15 minutes into Stage 2 and then maintained itself across two additional REM awakenings.

During the first night of dream deprivation with Dexedrine and Nembutal on Subject ST, the REMPs and erections were totally inhibited for the first 5 hours of sleep. The first REMP then occurred from which the subject was awakened after 5 minutes. About 6½ hours after sleep onset a second brief REMP, lasting 4 minutes, occurred (Figure 11) accompanied by a mild degree of tumescence. With the spontaneous termination of the REMP, there was a sudden marked tumescence during Stage 1 sleep onset, a full erection of about 2.5 cm. developing and persisting into Stage 2 for a period of about 7 minutes, followed by rapid detumescence. This example indicates that the rebound effect can take place spontaneously following a REMP even if the subject has not awakened.

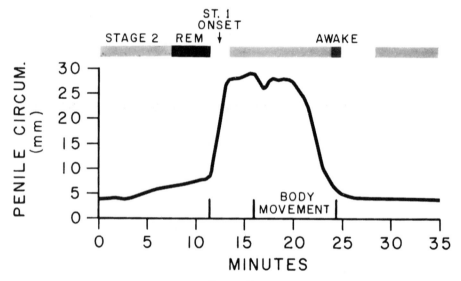

FIGURE 11

Showing a sudden marked rebound erection following spontaneous termination of a brief REMP. Marked tumescence occurred during Stage 1 sleep onset, persisting for a period of 7 minutes into Stage 2 followed by rapid detumescence.

An even more striking variety of dissociation is illustrated in Figure 12. On the second night of dream deprivation with Dexedrine and Nembutal, Subject ST showed complete REMP and erection suppression during the first 3 hours of sleep. About the time that the second REMP would ordinarily have occurred, there was a very brief period of arousal. The subject, however, did not go into a REMP but

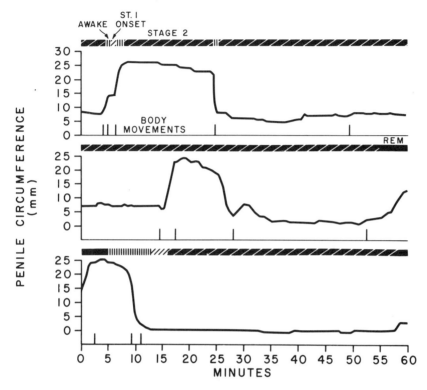

DISSOCIATION OF ERECTION FROM REMP

SUBJECT S.T. SECOND NIGHT DREAM DEPRIVATION
(DEXEDRINE - NEMBUTAL)

FIGURE 12

The top graph shows a 17-minute erection dissociated from the REMP occurring about the time that the second REMP would ordinarily have made its appearance. The erection was initiated by a brief period of arousal and was then sustained through Stage 2. The middle graph shows a second dissociated erection occurring during Stage 2 at the time the third REMP would have normally taken place. The bottom graph illustrates the erection associated with a normal REMP.

continued in Stage 2; simultaneously rapid tumescence occurred with the development of full erection lasting for about 17 minutes. About an hour later when the third REMP would have been due, another 8-minute full erection developed in Stage 2. In these two instances we believe that the erection became dissociated from the rest of the manifestations of the REMPs which were suppressed by the drug.

That is, the erections occurred when a REMP would normally have appeared.

Following three or four nights of REMP deprivation, the subjects were allowed to sleep without interruption and showed the usual compensatory increase in REM time, a compensation which always occurs following a period of REMP suppression. On the first re-covery night, REM time was as high as 40 per cent. Very extensive erections occurred during recovery nights, but relative to the per-centage of REM time there was no more erection than these same subjects showed during control nights. In spite of the large amount of REM erection during the recovery periods, there was also more NREM erection than normally occurs. Figure 13 shows two NREM erections which occurred on the second recovery night in Subject ST preceding a final prolonged REMP. This suggests that in spite of the very extensive REMP erections during recovery nights there was a need for even greater amounts of erection which broke out in Stage 2 NREM sleep.

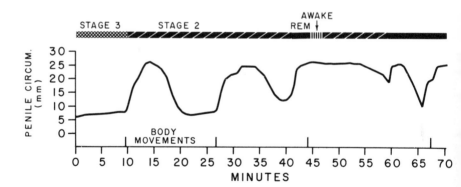

SUBJECT S.T.

SECOND RECOVERY NIGHT SHOWING
NON REM ERECTION

FIGURE 13

Showing two episodes of NREM erection preceding the final REMP of the night. The REMP itself was interrupted by a fairly long period of Stage 2, but the erection was sustained throughout this period of NREM sleep.

ERECTION CYCLE IN MEN OVER 70

I wish to summarize briefly the results of an investigation, carried out in collaboration with Kahn, on the erection cycle in a group of relatively healthy men over 70 whom we had recruited as subjects from various old age clubs around the city. Of seven subjects, three, aged 75, 78, and 74, showed erection cycles which in their extent and duration rivaled those of young men in their 20s. The figures were 61 per cent full, 14 per cent moderate, and 25 per cent slight. Three other subjects showed very markedly reduced erections, but these may have been due either to anxiety or to technical difficulties. All the subjects, with the exception of one, had continued sexual desire and some form of sexual activity, either masturbation, nocturnal emissions, or sexual intercourse. There was no particular relationship between extent of nocturnal erection and the degree of activity in their sexual lives; those who showed markedly reduced nocturnal erection were also sexually active. There were a number of especially interesting subjects. We had one 78-year-old virgin, a rather paranoid man with extreme racist and right-wing tendencies who had an excellent erection cycle. His only sexual activity was a form of nonfrictional masturbation in which he claimed that he was able to produce erection and ejaculation by fantasying sexually exciting situations. Another subject, a minister, aged 72, had both testicles removed because of cancer at the age of 67. He had been sexually active prior to the castration but had lost sexual desire and erectile capacity thereafter. He showed a total absence of erection during REMPs. It is of interest, however, that he was the only subject who reported a dream of nocturnal emission although he knew that he did not have erection and did not actually ejaculate. It is clear that both the erection cycle and sexual desire and activity can endure into extreme old age. Many of these old men would have been sexually more active if they had available partners, especially younger ones, and if they were not afraid that sexual activity was potentially dangerous, liable to cause strain, and especially, as expressed by three or four of them, to bring on heart attacks. Although both the REMPs and erections may persist into extreme old age, there may be gradual waning indicated by some decrease in the total amount of dreaming and the accompanying erections, but the evidence for this is still somewhat ambiguous. Several subjects showed REM time percentages equivalent to those of younger individuals.

ERECTION CYCLE IN THE MONKEY

Because the physiological manifestations of REM sleep in mammals and primates have been reported to be very similar to those described in man, it might be thought that the erection cycle would be present in lower forms also. No systematic observations have yet been made on mammalian forms, although an occasional erection has been described in the opossum and the tree shrew. In collaboration with Gross and Byrne and Elliot Weitzman of the Albert Einstein College of Medicine, who made some monkeys and his laboratory available to us, we have observed several rhesus monkeys, one of which was implanted with electrodes for continuous EEG and eye-movement recordings. In this latter animal especially, slight to moderate and occasional full erections were observed in many REMPs. However, we do not believe that we obtained an accurate picture of the erection cycle in the monkey because in order to make observations the animals have to be physically restrained, which undoubtedly produces much anxiety and inhibition of erection.

Discussion

The observations I have presented demonstrate something that has not heretofore been known—that dreaming in the male is accompanied, on a physiological level, by massive sustained genital excitation.[4] From a psychoanalytic viewpoint this excitation may be considered a periodically insistent physiological concomitant of instinctual drive arousal. The excitation is importantly involved in the sexual nature of dreams, and I have demnostrated that the fluctuations and inhibitions of erection, which represent waxing and waning of this sexual excitation, can to a considerable degree be correlated with dream content. I would suggest the formulation that the erection cycle as a physiological phenomenon is primary and that more or less full erection will occur during every REMP in the absence of inhibitory factors. The chief inhibitory factor appears to be anxiety aroused by dreams with aggressive content especially related to cas-

---

[4] No work has yet been reported on a possible comparable REM-sexual cycle in the female. It is reasonable to assume that clitoral erection may be involved, but it is possible that the sexual excitation in the female may be more diffuse in nature.

tration wishes and fears, although the other well-known danger situations, loss of love or loss of the love object, associated with such negative affects as jealousy and feelings of rejection, are also involved.

Manifestations of the aggressive instinctual drive appear only in connection with the sexual drive, that is, there are always fusions of libido with aggression. As Schur (1966) has indicated, "It is difficult to conceptualize the mental representation of the early gratification of the aggressive drive because the latter's discharge is originally triggered by libidinous demands." It can be assumed that from the neonatal period onward REMP sexual excitation begins to organize memory traces of penile sensations of frustration and gratification, pleasure and unpleasure, pain and anxiety.

Schur (1966) has recently proposed that the id makes use of innate apparatuses in its development in a manner analogous to Hartmann's innate ego apparatuses. Starting from Freud's statement that "The id has its own world of perception," Schur assumes that the id is subject to development, that it utilizes some percepts and memory traces, and that there is an interaction between the development of the id and the development of perception and memory. The early organization of memory traces of penile sensations which I have mentioned are thus of relevance here. Schur advances the opinion that the complex function of dreaming and the erections observable in newborn boys make use of preformed, innate apparatuses.

Recently, Karacan (1965) and his co-workers (1965) have independently confirmed our results on the erection cycle in all its principal features. They have also demonstrated that anxiety inhibits erection. They have observed the same rebound and dissociative effects on erection following dream deprivation; have also concluded that it is more difficult to suppress the erections than it is the other manifestations of the REMPs, and that erection deprivation may need to be compensated for more strongly than the REMP itself. These results, plus the observation that the erection cycle is present in the neonate and may persist in its full intensity into extreme old age, attest to the significance and power of the sexual drive in dreaming. The fact that the erection cycle is present in the monkey indicates that we are dealing with a primitive mechanism which is triggered and regulated by phylogenetically old parts of the brain contained within the limbic system.

Our results more than confirm Freud's (1915) formulations about one of the main characteristics of instinctual drives, namely, their pressure or *Drang*. He stated, "By the pressure of an instinct we understand its motor factor, the amount of force or the measure of the demand for work which it represents. The characteristic of exercising pressure is common to all instincts; it is in fact their very essence" (p. 122). Freud always insisted that instincts maintain an "incessant and unavoidable afflux of stimulation," that their excitation is continuous as opposed to the intermittent nature of external stimulation. Of course, Freud was aware that instinctual drive level changed in response to gratification and also that discharge was regulated by thresholds. The persistent nature of nocturnal sexual excitation is demonstrable only during the REMPs; the excitation is intermittent and geared to the REMP cycle and either absent or very much diminished during NREMPs. As I have indicated elsewhere (1965), the alternating periods of REM and NREM sleep represent a built-in biological cycle, perhaps alternating periods of physiological energy discharge and generation.

Some recently reported experiments of Dement (1965a) and of Jouvet (1965) on prolonged REMP deprivation in the cat are relevant to the issue of the pressure of instinctual drives and their relation to dreaming, and point up the special role of the sexual drive in dreaming sleep. The spontaneous, peremptory, and obligatory nature of dreaming has been demonstrated in the most vivid fashion in the dream-deprivation experiment in which it is shown that when REMPs are suppressed by repeated awakenings or drugs, increasing attempts are made to dream. Subsequently, when subjects are permitted to sleep uninterruptedly, high percentages of compensatory dream time take place. I have suggested that suppression of the Stage 1 REM phase, from the physiological side, and simultaneously of dreaming from the psychological side, would lead one to predict the occurrence of an inhibition of instinctual drive discharge associated with probable intensification of pressure toward discharge. It has been shown that human subjects, deprived of REMPs for 15 or 16 days, develop a psychoticlike state. Following such prolonged REM deprivation no disturbances of genital behavior have so far been reported, but in both humans and animals disturbances of orality have been noted in the form of increased hunger and hyperphagia. Both Dement and Jouvet have deprived cats of REMP for periods ranging from 30 to 70 days. These experiments involved the ingenious method of placing a cat on a rock surrounded by water. Because of the marked loss of muscle tone accompanying REM sleep, the animal will fall into the water if it goes into this state of sleep. The animals must remain in NREM sleep in order to prevent their falling into the water, and in this fashion they can be deprived of REM sleep for many days. Dement reports that six of twelve animals so deprived developed some serious abnormalities of sexual behavior. They became markedly and compulsively hypersexual, would mount and attempt to copulate indiscriminately with other males or females, one cat even mounting an anesthetized animal that was lying in the laboratory. The cats would cling to their partners for prolonged periods. Some of the females came into heat more than once, and Dement (1965c) had the impression that their oestrus behavior was excessive. Other animals became markedly hyperphagic as compared to control animals, especially if they were starved for a period. There appeared to be a reciprocal relationship between hunger and hypersexuality, that is, those animals that became hypersexual did not show hyperphagia and vice versa. The animals were restless and hyperactive but lost aggression. There were evidences of increased excitability of the central nervous system, the animals showing a markedly lowered threshold to convulsions produced by electric shock. Additionally, some of the animals had serious difficulty in learning to run a simple maze for food.

These results attest to the irrepressible force of the sexual drive. It is relatively easy to make a formulation, in terms of psychoanalytic theory, that since the sexual excitation in these animals was not discharged during the REMPs, substitute discharge occurred during waking behavior, the animals in effect acting out in overt sexual behavior what might normally take place in fantasy during the hallucinatory dream of the REMPs. Thus, there may well be some relationship between the polymorphous-perverse hypersexual and hyperoral behavior of the REMP-deprived cats and the normal polymorphous-perverse hypersexuality of the REM state, as manifested by the extensive erections and the profusion of dreams whose essential content is sexual in nature, although admittedly it is dangerous to extrapolate from findings in the cat to man.

There is every reason to believe that during REMP dreaming sleep there is a release from inhibition of the drive centers and circuits located within the so-called limbic system which includes the hypothalamus. These same areas and circuits are also implicated in the triggering of REM sleep. The functions which are regulated by the limbic system have, in the broadest sense, to do with self and racial preservation. In their lighter moments, neurophysiologists refer to these functions as the 4F's, namely, fight, flight, feeding, and . . . mating. There are areas within the hypothalamus that are necessary for the integration of copulatory behavior in the male and mating and maternal behavior in the female. There are other areas and circuits, stimulation of which produce erection and ejaculation, or oral and feeding behavior. It is of great interest that the areas within the hypothalamus that regulate drive activity have been shown to respond not only to neural stimulation but to chemical stimulation as well. Thus, minute amounts of male or female sex hormone when injected into specific areas of the hypothalamus result in sexual behavior. These findings confirm a brilliant speculation that Freud (1905) made in the *Three Essays on Sexuality* at a time when he was interested in the somatic and chemical sources of the drives. He stated, "It seems probable, then, that special chemical substances are produced in the interstitial portion of the sex-glands; these are then taken up in the blood stream and cause particular parts of the central nervous system to be charged with sexual tension" (p. 215). It is highly probable that the somatic aspects of drive, involving complex neural and biochemical relationships within the limbic system, will be fairly completely elucidated within the not-too-distant future, and the investigation of the drive activation of the REM dreaming periods will undoubtedly play an important role in the unraveling of these relationships.

I have been struck by the fact that the group of behavioral disturbances following prolonged REM deprivation in the cat closely resembles the deviations from normal behavior comprising the so-called Klüver-Bucy (1939) syndrome which follows bilateral ablation of the temporal lobes in the monkey. In such ablations, extensive parts of the limbic system are removed. These animals show the most extreme form of disturbance of drive-oriented behavior that has ever been experimentally produced. They show a form of hypersexuality which very closely resembles that following prolonged REM deprivation in the cat. The monkeys manifest frequent erection, long-continued licking and sucking of the penis, oral and manual exploration of the genitalia, various forms of heterosexual and homosexual behavior, and may copulate almost continuously for half an hour, an observation which both Dement and Jouvet made in the REM-de-prived cats. The males compulsively and repetitively mount the fe-males and two males when left together indulge in all kinds of poly-morphous-perverse behavior; they repeatedly mount one another, mutually explore one another's genitalia, etc. They also show markedly disturbed oral behavior, indiscriminately putting objects in the mouth, biting, chewing, licking, touching with the lips and smelling.

It seems possible that extreme REM deprivation in the cat results in a state tantamount to a functional ablation of those parts of the limbic system which ordinarily hold in check and modulate the sexual and other drive centers within the hypothalamus. It is too early to state with certainty that we are dealing exclusively with a disruption of drive activity in economic terms, namely, that the disorganization of drive behavior is brought about when genital and oral drive dis-charge that normally occurs during the REM dreaming periods is prevented from taking place and substitute discharge occurs during the day in the form of hypersexuality and hyperorality.[5] Whatever the complexities of neurophysiological and biochemical disturbance following prolonged REM deprivation turn out to be, Freud's formu-lation of the relationship of instinctual drives to dreaming, especially his emphasis on the role of sexuality in dreaming, remains one of the great products of his genius.[6]

Freud (1900) stated, "The more one is concerned with the solu-tion of dreams, the more one is driven to recognize that the majority of dreams of adults deal with sexual material and give expression to erotic wishes. . . . Let me say at once that this fact is not in the least surprising, but is in complete harmony with the principles of my

[5] Pribram (1961) has minimized the role of drive in these behavioral disturbances and has offered an alternative explanation in terms of the inability of temporal-lobe-damaged animals properly to run off sequences of behavior or to stop a sequence once started. Dement's report of the inability of some of his REM-deprived cats to run a simple maze for food is relevant here.

[6] Snyder (1965) recently stated, "In the broadest sense everything that has been learned during the past decade about the REMS [REM State] seems to complement remarkably Freud's insights concerning the integral relationship of dreaming to basic biological forces" (p. 309). And Dement (1965a) concluded, "Thus, when REM sleep is interfered with in the adult organism, some instigating compound piles up in the nervous system. This accumulation appears to induce a generalized, hyperex-citable state whose main behavioral effect is a potentiation of drive-oriented behavior, to some extent, probably the same behavior patterns that are part and parcel of the rapid eye movement sleep state itself" (p. 407).

explanation of dreams. No other instinct has been subjected since childhood to so much suppression as the sexual instinct with its numerous components; from no other instinct are so many and such powerful unconscious wishes left over, ready to produce dreams in a state of sleep. . . . The assertion that all dreams require a sexual interpretation, against which critics rage so incessantly, occurs nowhere in my *Interpretation of Dreams*" (p. 396f.). Freud gives as exceptions the simple wish-fulfillment dreams of children; dreams stimulated by hunger, thirst, and other somatic needs; and dreams of mere convenience. Considering that dreams of convenience are rather rare and that dreams of hunger, thirst, or excretory need are very readily libidinized, one may legitimately contend that practically all dreams have an erotic component and that Freud's (1905) comment, "It may well be that nothing of considerable importance can occur in the organism without contributing some component to the excitation of the sexual instinct" (p. 205), is especially true of dreaming.

It may also be necessary to modify our views of the role that repression plays in bringing about the multiplicity of sexual dreams. The physiological sexual excitation of the REMPs is primary, present in the neonate and the monkey, and antedates the establishment of repression as a defense mechanism. It is more likely that repressed, erotic, unconscious sexual wishes in the id are activated each night during the periodic waves of REMP sexual excitation, independently of repression, or better still, that the REMP excitation, occurring as it does in a state of sleep, is instrumental in lifting such wishes and their derivatives from repression.

As I have noted, physiological activation of the sexual drive is present at birth and the erection cycle may persist in full force into extreme old age, at least up until 80. Both Karacan and I have made the observation that it does not appear to be particularly influenced by the recency of sexual gratification. The first erection period of the night may take place within an hour or two after intercourse. Karacan made the interesting observation that one of his subjects who had a nocturnal emission during the fourth REMP of the night went on to have a full erection during the final fifth REMP about an hour later. This observation demonstrates the imperative nature of the genital excitation.

It seems likely that there are, from the beginning of life, relationships between genital excitation and pregenital experience so that the genital participates in the pregenital phases of development, that is, that oral-genital and anal-genital interactions are of great developmental significance, as Greenacre (1950) has stressed. Halverson (1940) has shown that the male infant when frustrated in its nursing activities develops penile erection, and Wolff (1966) that in the neonate erection can substitute for sucking and vice versa.

In our experiments we observed that erections take place with pregenital dreams, especially oral ones. It may well be that no oral dream, however primitive, is devoid of some connection with genital excitation. The famous blank dream of Lewin's (1950) hypomanic patient was accompanied by orgasm, the blankness itself representing the flattened-out image of the breast. The concept of oral-genital relationships receives neurophysiological support from MacLean's (1962) observations. He has shown that excitation in certain areas of the limbic system involved in oral mechanisms readily spills over into closely adjacent areas concerned with genital function. He states, "This close neural relationship helps in understanding the intimate interplay of behavior in the oral and sexual spheres, examples of which we are accustomed to see in the activities of our domestic animals" (p. 295). MacLean points out that the so-called limbic lobe is bent upon itself and that nature apparently arranged it this way in order to afford the olfactory sense close participation in both oral and anogenital functions.

Attempts by investigators to correlate the content and affects of dreams with the physiological processes that accompany them have so far not been very successful. Snyder (1965) and his co-workers (Hobson et al., 1965) have demonstrated that more active and affectively intense dreams are associated in a global way with increased respiratory rate and variability and have observed a specific relationship between periods of respiratory apnea and such respiratory content in the dream as laughing, choking, speaking, etc. The most significant correlation of content with physiological variation is the relationship that we have shown between fluctuations in erection and dream content. Correlation of affective content in dreams with physiological fluctuations is fraught with difficulties. Freud (1900) has pointed out that the dream in general is poorer in affects than the psychic material from the manipulation of which it has proceeded. The dream work brings about suppression, displacement, or turning of affects into their opposite. It is, therefore, necessary to elucidate the latent dream content, a difficult task with experimental subjects, in order to make appropriate correlations between content and physiological fluctuations. In addition, Freud advanced the suggestion that the state of sleep itself may bring about a weakening of affects independently of the dream work or other factors. I have proposed that there may be a certain discontinuity or lack of parallelism between dream content and the underlying physiological affect and drive processes. For example, it has been shown by Money (1960) that quadriplegics who have total spinal cord transections do not experience sexual and genital pelvic sensations but nevertheless continue to have dreams of seminal emission with orgasm imagery, almost as though it were the real thing. I have mentioned one of our elderly subjects, aged 74, castrated for cancer some years before, who showed no erection during his REMPs. He nevertheless had a dream of nocturnal emission in the absence of erection or ejaculation. This suggests that once the experience of nocturnal emission obtains psychic representation, dreams of nocturnal emission can occur in the absence of the usual physiological accompaniments of such dreams. This raises the important problem of the extent to which psychic content and affects may be dissociated from the underlying physiology (Snyder, 1965).

One of my chief theoretical concerns has been that of linking the instinctual drive concept of psychoanalysis to the recently discovered physiological and neurophysiological processes that have been shown to accompany the dream as a psychic event. In discussing the possibilities for future developments in psychoanalysis, Eissler (1965) remarked, "It is possible that a new technique will be required, to give psychology a boost equal to the one it obtained when hypnosis and free association were placed at its service. It is my personal belief that this boost may come one day from electrophysiology, refinements in which may be carried to unimaginable subtleties and depths" (p. 8). He may well be correct in his belief that electrophysiological investigations may be of great value for psychology and the recent break-through in the understanding of sleep and dreams provides an example of the significance of electrophysiological research. I agree with Eissler that the port of entry of biology into psychoanalysis is the study of the id. He states, "Inextricably connected with the Id and its elements, the instinctual drives, is the concept of a task or demand imposed on the psychic apparatus. This task can be objectively described in physiological terms. The dynamic relationship between the psychic apparatus and an instinctual drive; the pleasure-pain and constancy principles which characterize the ways in which this relationship is consummated—these are cornerstones of psychoanalytic psychology, belonging to the biological sphere" (p. 128).

It is my hope that the work I have presented represents a contribution essentially to the psychobiological investigation of the id and has brought somewhat nearer that hope, mentioned by Hartmann, for the future meeting of psychoanalysis and physiology, and that was Freud's ultimate goal. I do not believe that we will ever have a complete understanding of mental functioning without breaching the mind-body problem. Psychoanalytic theories can lead us to hypotheses about the workings of the central nervous system, and neurophysiological findings can have an impact on our views of psychic functioning. I do not wish to imply that psychology will ever be *reduced* to neurophysiology but only that one can be *translated* into the other (see Rubinstein, 1965). As Kety (1960) has said, there may someday be a biochemistry of memory but never of memories. The same can be said of dreaming and dreams, which will always require psychological interpretation. Eissler (1965) has remarked, "For a new generation of neuropsychiatrists, however, for whom the inventory of psychoanalytic mechanisms has become a matter of mere routine, while the new discoveries in the field of neurophysiology, neuropathology and biochemistry seem to be quite promising and even awe-inspiring, the temptation to dissolve the world of human conflicts into enzymes must be irresistibly attractive" (p. 355).

In this connection, Milton Miller (1965) has said, "Admittedly, intuition, poetic hypotheses, and speculations based upon non-quantified observation are in a state of current disrepute. The existence of the brand new science of sleep causes us to wonder whether we will ever again believe that cadre of authorities which includes the lovers of all times, the poets, and the 'unscientific dreamers' of the world. . . . Yet in the face of the facts and figures which will emerge from the new laboratories of sleep, we must be careful not to lose sight of the significance to the individual of his dreams and of his dreaming" (p. 4f.). And he concludes with the following little poem:

> One mystery alone remains
> Of my beloved's sleep:

We've solved the movement of her eyes
And why they do repeat;
We know what brings her breath in sighs;
We've tracked her EEG;
The haunting doubt that still remains
Is does she dream of me?

BIBLIOGRAPHY

Dement, W. (1965a), Recent Studies on the Biological Role of Rapid Eye Movement Sleep. *Am. J. Psychiat.*, 122:404-408.

—— (1965b), An Essay on Dreams. *New Directions in Psychology*, 2. NY: Holt, Rinehart & Winston.

—— (1965c), Personal communication.

Eissler, K. R. (1965), *Medical Orthodoxy and the Future of Psychoanalysis.* NY: IUP.

Fisher, C. (1965), Psychoanalytic Implications of Recent Research on Sleep and Dreaming. *J. Am. Psa. Assn.*, 13:197-303.

—— Gross, J. & Zuch, J. (1965), A Cycle of Penile Erection Synchronous with Dreaming (REM) Sleep. *Arch. Gen. Psychiat.*, 12:29-45.

Freud, S. (1900), The Interpretation of Dreams. *S.E.*, 4 & 5.

—— (1905), Three Essays on the Theory of Sexuality. *S.E.*, 7:125-245.

—— (1915), Instincts and Their Vicissitudes. *S.E.*, 14:111-140.

Greenacre, P. (1950), Special Problems of Early Female Sexual Development. *Psa. Study Ch.*, 5:122-138.

—— (1964), A Study on the Nature of Inspiration. *J. Am. Psa. Assn.*, 12:6-31.

Greenfield, N. S. & Lewis, W. C., eds. (1965), *Psychoanalysis and Current Biological Thought.* Madison & Milwaukee: Univ. Wisc. Pr.

Halverson, H. M. (1940), Genital and Sphincter Behavior of the Male Infant. *Pedag. Sem. & J. Gen. Psychiat.*, 56:95-136.

Hartmann, H. (1948), Comments on the Psychoanalytic Theory of Instinctual Drives. *Essays*, 69-89.

—— (1959), Psychoanalysis as a Scientific Theory. *Essays*, 318-350.

Hobson, J. A., Goldfrank, F., & Snyder, F. (1965), Respiration and Mental Activity in Sleep. *J. Psychiat. Res.*, 3:79-90.

Jouvet, M. (1965), Behavioral and EEG Effects of Paradoxical Sleep in the Cat. *Proc. XXIII Int. Cong. Physiol. Sci.*, 344-353.

Karacan, I. (1965), The Effect of Exciting Presleep Events on Dream Reporting and Penile Erections during Sleep. Doctor of Medical Science thesis.

—— Goodenough, D. R., Shapiro, A., & Witkin, H. A. (1965), Some Psychological and Physiological Correlates of Penile Erection during Sleep. Assn. Psychophysiol. Study of Sleep.

Kety, S. S. (1960), A Biologist Examines the Mind and Behavior. *Science*, 132:1861.

Klüver, H. & Bucy, P. C. (1939), Preliminary Analysis of Functions of the Temporal Lobes in Monkeys. *Arch. Neurol. Psychiat.*, 42:979.

Lewin, B. D. (1950), *The Psychoanalysis of Elation.* NY: Norton.

MacLean, P. D. (1962), New Findings Relevant to the Evolution of Psychosexual Functions of the Brain. *J. Nerv. Ment. Dis.*, 135:289-301.

Miller, M. H. (1965), On Building Bridges. In: Greenfield & Lewis (1965), 3-10.

Money, J. (1960), Phantom Orgasm in the Dreams of Paraplegic Men and Women. *Arch. Gen. Psychiat.*, 3:373-383.

Pribram, K. H. (1961), Implications for Systemic Studies of Behavior. In: *Electrical Stimulation of the Brain*, ed. D. E. Sheer. Austin: Univ. Texas Pr.

Rubenstein, B. B. (1965), Psychoanalytic Theory and the Mind-Body Problem. In: Greenfield & Lewis (1965), 35-36.

Schur, M. (1966), *The Id and the Regulatory Principles of Mental Functioning.* NY: IUP.

Snyder, F. (1965), The Organismic State Associated with Dreaming. In: Greenfield & Lewis (1965), 275-316.

Wolff, P. H. (1966), *The Causes, Controls, and Organization of Behavior in the Newborn. Psychol. Issues,* 17.

Toward an Integrated Psychoanalytic-Physiological Theory of Psychosomatic Disorders

MORTON F. REISER, M.D.

I

Freud (1915) considered the mental apparatus obligated to negotiate the biological needs of the body vis-à-vis the adaptive opportunities and difficulties of the environment. And, as is well known, he always considered the brain to be the "organ" of the mind, i.e., he believed that mental phenomena would ultimately yield to explanation by the physical-chemical nature of brain function when these were finally understood (1940). It is probably one (of many) measures of his genius that he delimited his theory of mind to the psychological parameters of mental life despite his "belief" in its physical roots (1950, p. 264; 1937). A major factor in this decision seems to have been the lack of relevant physiological facts. Rich clinical data and theoretical speculations about the mind itself continually called for corresponding extrapolations into the physical sphere. However, these gave rise to unwieldy (and unfounded) theoretical constructs of unending complexity. All the same, as Amacher (1965) and others have pointed out, Freud's theory of the mind was strongly influenced by the neurological models of his time. Conversely, with the exception of early considerations of the innervation phenomena possibly involved in major hysterical conversions (1894, 1910), and later extrapolations into neurovegetative function implicit in his last theory of anxiety (1926), Freud was resoundingly silent in respect to the possible role of the mind in relation to the abnormal physiology of medical illness —the field we now subsume under the term psychosomatic medicine.

Chief, Division of Psychiatry, Montefiore Hospital and Medical Center; Professor of Psychiatry, Albert Einstein College of Medicine, Yeshiva University.

Moreover, despite the rich accumulation of new facts in psycho-physiology and in vast areas of brain–behavior research, and the substantial and rapid enrichment and maturation of psychoanalytic ego psychology since the publication of Hartmann's conceptualizations (1939), a satisfactorily integrated formulation of mind-body inter-relationships has not yet been achieved. It can be argued that we are not yet ready to attempt it. I shall not here belabor the semantic, methodological, and conceptual difficulties involved; these have been extensively discussed elsewhere (Reiser, 1961; Weiner, 1962). I would rather suggest an approach which I believe may be more realistic and ultimately more productive—i.e., to develop parallel psychological and physiological theories, in each case as the facts permit. This approach might lead us toward integration through gradual convergence of the two lines of development. Or, as suggested by von Bertalanffy (1964), we may achieve integration via ultimate emergence of intermediate theoretical templates which are isomorphic in respect to both the physiological and the psychological models.

II

From the recent psychoanalytic literature a rather extensive overview of the general metapsychology of psychosomatic disorders can be extracted. To me, the most useful central conceptualization is that advanced by Schur (1953, 1955), who maintains that, from a psychological point of view, patients with active pathological somatization reactions demonstrate ego regression in several important respects. He emphasizes primarily alterations in the ego's capacity to perceive and evaluate certain dangers, and regression to extensive use of thought processes organized according to the primary process as well as to the use of unneutralized energy in resomatized reactions to perceived danger signals. Consideration of the topographic dimension of altered level of consciousness, as discussed below, may aid in understanding these reactions. In any case, the alterations in ego state (and levels of consciousness) are not total and homogeneous; rather, they are uneven, partial, and limited to (split-off) spheres of regressed function. In most respects, such patients display highly mature and adaptive ego functions, e.g., intelligence, memory, general reality testing, synthetic function, etc. Defensive ego functions are also unevenly disrupted, but, in general, regression to more primitive defenses is seen with the altered ego state. This is particularly apparent in the ego's eventually unsuccessful attempts to master the external and internal pressures of the stressful situations that precede the onset of the clinical disorder (Binger et al., 1945). In this connection, Giovacchini's very interesting studies (1959, 1965) of the ego state in relation to psychosomatic disorders contain some important observations and worth-while leads. It would be important in future investigations to compare the ego pathology in psychosomatic patients with that of patients with schizophrenia. Such an undertaking would be the subject of a separate study. We are indebted to Hartmann (1953) for elucidating and specifying the metapsychology of schizophrenia. A similar task remains to be done in the psychosomatic field.

The internal instinctual pressures involved in the reactivated conflicts appear to be extensive and to involve derivatives of all varieties of instincts and psychosexual levels, but with main emphasis on pregenital libidinal issues and difficulties with unneutralized aggression. Accordingly, the psychogenetic traumatic experiences are postulated to have occurred very early, perhaps in the immediate perinatal and earliest neonatal epochs. Some authors (Greene, 1959; Sontag, 1944) have even suggested that such effects are evoked *in utero*. Engel (1962) has emphasized the possible role of object loss and the reactive affects of helplessness and hopelessness as central issues in the ego reactions associated with serious medical illness. Schmale (1958), in particular, has studied and emphasized the role of separation—real, symbolic, or threatened. The exact relation of these affects to depression is not yet fully elucidated, but these formulations serve to emphasize the importance of object relations and the variety of major affects which may be involved. In contrast, much of the previous literature has emphasized anxiety and activation ("fight-flight") states.

The preceding overview summarizes psychological dimensions which are general, rather than specific, with respect to distinguishing why individual patients develop one disease rather than another. Nor, for that matter, do we understand why individual patients develop a psychosomatic illness rather than a predominantly psychological disorder, such as a major functional psychosis. To deal with the problems of specificity, physical factors must be considered. Alexander (1950) and his colleagues have extensively written on the issue of specificity. His views have been critically discussed elsewhere and I shall therefore not undertake a detailed examination of his theory and the idea of specific unresolved core conflicts (and associated affects with concomitant physiological patterns of arousal). However, I wish to emphasize that Alexander added a constitutional (perhaps genetic) predisposition to his conceptual scheme. At its present stage of development, then, the theory is a multiple-factor one which proposes specific necessary, but not sufficient, causes in both psychological and physiological spheres. Others, such as Grinker (1963), Deutsch (1953), and Schur (1953, 1955), also recognize and acknowledge the incompleteness of the psychological description alone, but tend more to see choice of organ system as dependent mainly upon genic factors and/or early conditioning-like psychophysiological fixations, rather than specific physiological concomitants of well-developed affects, such as those encountered in the adult. In other words, they believe that specificity is determined by genetic factors or by early psychophysiological life experiences, which may have occurred at crucial developmental stages. As mentioned above with reference to Schur's work, more primitive and global affect states are postulated.

Mirsky (1958) has further refined the Alexander concept. He has identified what he believes to be the physiological (genetically determined) condition necessary, but not sufficient, for the development of duodenal ulcer, i.e., the hypersecretion of pepsinogen into the blood. Mirsky postulates that this inborn trait also plays a central role in personality development and in determining the types of social conflict situation that will be pathogenic for the individual in adult life. This somato-psychosomatic theory holds up well in respect to empirical data. Both psychological and physiological aspects of it have been subjected to experimental tests which yield consistent results (Weiner et al.,1957). Its psychological characteristics resemble those of Alexander's theory, but it differs in an important respect, i.e., it identifies specific combined genetic-experiential factors, rather than purely experiential factors, as determinants of the adult personality structure.

III

Incorporation of nonpsychological specificity factors into the general theory of psychosomatic illness has the potential drawback of precasting (or committing) the psychological parameters, and of thereby contaminating, misleading, or prematurely closing off further development of the psychological parameters of the theory—which are by no means settled or complete. Instead, the more general, nonspecific psychological ideas summarized above can be regarded as incomplete and open-ended. This minimizes the danger of their being confounded by what might be termed spurious physical feedback—spurious in the sense that it may result in an attempt to accommodate incomplete psychological understanding to incomplete physiological information.

The clinical conditions most commonly regarded as falling into the psychosomatic area are diseases of unknown multi-factor etiology—peptic ulcer, bronchial asthma, essential hypertension, neurodermatitis, thyrotoxicosis, rheumatoid arthritis, and ulcerative colitis, being the classic "big seven." Their pathogenesis is unknown, and understanding of the pathological physiology is incomplete (although this varies somewhat with the different conditions). In any event, from time to time, our conceptualizations of these disease entities require alteration in the light of new data, as illustrated by Engel's classic studies of ulcerative colitis (1954).

Accordingly, at this point I would like to list some generalizations pertaining to "nonpsychologized" physiological parameters, which might be considered in parallel with the psychological parameters summarized above.

First, a major feature of the pathological physiology of most, if not all, psychosomatic conditions is profound disturbance in vegetative (autonomic nervous system) functions. These dysfunctions include excessive lability and range as their primary characteristic, but abnormal sustained levels of activity (both overactivity and underactivity), and exaggerations or disturbances of integrative patterns (synchronization) of autonomic mobilization responses and homeostatic mechanisms are also importantly involved. The degree to which these changes are general and widespread (i.e., involving organs and structures other than the primarily diseased ones) varies with the different conditions, but some degree is probably present in all. For example, patients with rheumatoid arthritis often display marked generalized peripheral and cutaneous vasomotor lability; patients with essential hypertension frequently display functional disturbances of gastroenteric tract activity, etc.

These features of autonomic nervous system physiology are strikingly similar to, but not necessarily identical with, autonomic functions in the neonate and infant (Richmond et al., 1962; Bridger and Reiser, 1959). Although very little is yet known of the developmental physiology of the vegetative nervous system, certainly a cardinal characteristic of its maturation is the development of modulating, restraining, patterning, and homeostatic regulating mechanisms. Snyder's studies (1963, 1965) of the physiology of REMP sleep show that the most prominent characteristic of autonomically innervated functions during this phase of sleep is increase in range and lability.

Second, endocrine malfunction is involved in these conditions. The disturbances range from activation of the adrenal medulla and acute releases of epinephrine and norepinephrine to widespread alterations in secretory levels of virtually all of the endocrine glands. Although the endocrine changes characteristic of activation of the hypothalamic anterior pituitary adrenal axis have been studied most extensively, and hence are best known, more recent data from Mason's laboratory (1963) implicate most of the endocrine glands, and Mason believes that significant changes are reflected in alterations in multiendocrine profiles (constructed from an array of the levels of the products of many glands). Again, the degree of endocrine dysfunction, and the extent to which it is general rather than specific, varies in different conditions, but some endocrine dysfunction is probably present in all.

Third, stimulation and ablation studies of the brain have demonstrated that the deeper visceral functions involved in the various psychosomatic disorders may be profoundly altered by manipulation of subcortical and paleocortical structures, particularly the amygdala and limbic system, as well as various hypothalamic and brain-stem centers (MacLean, 1949; French et al., 1956). And neurophysiological studies in animals have shown that some of these same areas, e.g., the amygdala, are involved in major general behavioral functions, such as eating, sexual activity, and aggression (Klüver and Bucy, 1937, 1938, 1939; Schreiner and Kling, 1953). In man, studies of medial temporal lobe structures and amygdala in patients with temporal lobe epilepsy have shown these areas of the brain to be related to social behavior and memory as well (Mahl et al., 1964). Mason et al. (1960) have clearly delineated separate circuits from the hippocampus to hypothalamic nuclei which are differentially involved in stimulating releases of various adrenal hormones, presumably via the pituitary-adrenal axis.

Finally, immune mechanisms and the proteogenic immunological functions of reticulo-endothelial structures have been implicated, e.g., in rheumatoid arthritis (Moos and Solomon, 1965; Solomon and Moos, 1965), in addition to their relatively well-established role in bronchial asthma and neurodermatitis. (It is interesting to note that immune mechanisms, both local and general, demonstrate strikingly persistent and specific biological "memory," as witness the Schwartzman and Arthus phenomena.)

IV

In attempting to follow each of these parallel—or possibly converging —arrays of data and speculation toward a concept of pathogenesis, it may be helpful to consider the process of pathogenesis under at least three separate categories: (1) considerations of the premorbid state; (2) conditions and mechanisms of precipitation; and (3) mechanisms of maintenance, exacerbation, and remission.

CONSIDERATIONS OF THE PREMORBID STATE

1. *Physiological premorbid conditions:* I find it most helpful to think of the individual who will eventually develop a psychosomatic disorder as being "preprogramed" for it—much as in Freud's analogy of the dream to the firework (1900), the dream having been constructed over a relatively long period, but playing off to display relatively quickly under proper conditions. This hypothesized preprograming would involve: (a) local tissue factors in the organs to be involved (e.g., gastric hypersecretory capacity); and (b) central nervous system factors, i.e., circuitry for activating appropriate autonomic and endocrine mechanisms. These local tissue and central nervous system factors could well be intimately related, and would most likely be of genic origin and/or result from early developmental and experiential sensitizing events—disease, trauma, conditioning (?).

The new concept I wish to state and emphasize here relates to the central nervous system circuitry. I would hypothesize: (a) that the central connections for all such diseases are part of the normal structure of the brain; (b) that preference or predisposition to sustained activity in a particular circuit (or circuits) in specific individuals is determined genically and/or experientially; and (c) that such predisposing (preprogramed) circuits do not ordinarily discharge into the body, but are capable of doing so under appropriate conditions. (By this I mean that their potential output does not ordinarily have access to neural pathways to the endocrine and visceral structures, but that under certain conditions the necessary outflow connections to the body become available to them and are activated.)

2. *Psychological premorbid conditions:* With respect to these issues, I would refer to Mirsky's (1958) concepts of the nature of per-

sonality structure, its developmental relation to specific constitutional (given) vulnerabilities, and to the types of social stress situations under which ego defenses may fail, as the most appropriate ones available.

CONDITIONS AND MECHANISMS OF PRECIPITATION

In this section the two lines of psychological and physiological evidence do converge for a brief segment. Although it has been known for some time that "stress" can activate the autonomic nervous system and the pituitary-adrenal axis, and that "stress" can be either physical or psychological, recent data have endowed these ideas with far greater precision. It is now quite clear from the work of Friedman et al. (1963) and Wolff et al. (1964) that there is a reciprocal relation between the effectiveness of ego defenses and the level of adrenal activity under chronic sustained stress. The studies of Sachar et al. (1963), and, more recently, of Bunney and his co-workers (1965) and Knapp et al. (1964, 1966) all show that in situations of acute psychological decompensation there is a reciprocal relationship between the effectiveness of ego defensive operations and the level of adrenal cortical and medullary hormone output.

1. *Physiological conditions of precipitation:* In response to adaptive psychological breakdown, the acute neuroendocrine changes already referred to, and possibly anabolic ones hypothesized (but not yet demonstrated) by Engel (1965), may in the first place act physiologically in a nonspecific way to facilitate or permit development of disease. Secondly, as mentioned above, under appropriate conditions, in predisposed individuals medically pathogenic brain circuits and neural pathways may be triggered and allowed to initiate more specific changes in body tissues. One physiological state that may be capable of something like this—i.e., that may provide the appropriate condition—is REMP sleep, or dreaming sleep. Furthermore, there have been occasional reports of greater than usual changes in level of physiological function (both hyper and hypo) under hypnosis (Sachar et al., 1965). Such phenomena may also be seen under conditions of unusual brain pathology or experimental stimulation of the brain (French et al., 1956).

2. *Psychological conditions of precipitation:* In this regard, I would refer to Schur's description of alterations in ego state that follow in the wake of adaptive ego defensive breakdown and "the return

of the repressed" (summarized above) as most appropriate. I believe it brings us still closer to convergence with the physiological aspects if we regard these altered ego states as also involving altered states of consciousness, perhaps similar to the original hypnoidal state referred to by Breuer and Freud (1893/95), and recently rediscussed by Holzman (1959).

3. *Psychophysiological speculations about precipitation:* Ego state or level of consciousness fluctuates regularly with the 24-hour circadian rhythm. In addition, probably throughout the daytime period itself, there are definite, if slight, alterations in level—daydreaming, periods of hyperalertness with activation, etc. It is even probably that the acute neuroendocrine discharge of distress affects the cortical state. There is some evidence that this may be so and that certain psychologically expressed cortical functions may be affected (Callaway and Thompson, 1953; Pollin and Goldin, 1961).

At this point I wish to hypothesize a way in which the psychological and physiological parameters may be reconciled or integrated.

(a) *Failure of ego defenses and reactivation of conflictual instinctual pressures may so stress the individual that acute nonspecific neuroendocrine mobilization of the autonomic adrenal system occurs.*

(b) *Simultaneously, affective arousal and regressive changes are seen in the ego (state and level of consciousness). These may enhance and be enhanced by the physiological hormonal reaction just referred to above in "a": $a \rightleftarrows b$.*

(c) *A reaction thus reinforced and sustained may result in an altered state of the brain which provides the necessary condition for central nervous system recircuiting in such a manner that the medically pathogenic circuits become activated and gain access to outflow paths to the periphery of the body.*

MECHANISMS OF MAINTENANCE, EXACERBATION, AND REMISSION

Once a disease is triggered or activated, the individual is changed—physiologically and psychologically. It is probably important to distinguish between the psychological condition which allow for original activation of disease and the psychological states which may subsequently affect its course. For example, rage and anxiety may elevate the arterial blood pressure of the hypertensive patient, but may not necessarily have been the conditions involved or responsible for triggering the disease in the first place. Further, it is well known that once it is clinically established, disease acquires psychological meaning and is incorporated into the ongoing psychology (self image, etc.) of the individual. This may even occur when its onset is imminent, but the disease is not yet clinically manifest. The point is that it is not possible to separate original causes from psychological epi-phenomena without prospective longitudinal study.

Probably, many of these diseases are capable of self maintenance once they have been active long enough. (For instance, essential hypertension may become established via possible renal hormonal changes.) It is also possible that various intense affects can influence the clinical course in a nonspecific way, although I doubt that such influences ordinarily exert profound effects. On the other hand, the reoccurrence of states capable of precipitating the onset of disease, such as those described above, namely, states which permit connection of central pathogenic impulse discharge patterns to the periphery, perhaps provides the prerequisite condition for acceleration or precipitation of major, even fatal, exacerbations, such as malignant hypertension, intractable status asthmaticus, etc.

V

In summary, I have attempted to review separately the psychological and physiological data and related lines of speculation concerning psychosomatic disease. At one point in the review an area of convergence appeared—the relation of the effectiveness of ego defenses to the degree of adrenal reaction, as measured by levels of hormones associated with stress. In the main, the physiological substrate of psychosomatic disorders in susceptible people was hypothesized as ultimately residing in dormant central nervous system circuits which are ordinarily inactive, but are capable of affecting peripheral organs under certain conditions. The psychological substrate for the precipitation of disease was seen as consisting of altered state of consciousness and an altered (regressed) ego state, as previously described by Schur. In suggesting an approach toward an integrated theory, it was hypothesized that those physiological states of the brain which permit pathways for peripheral discharge to dormant medically pathogenic central nervous system circuits may be the same ones which are detected psychologically as altered ego (consciousness) states. It is hoped that these formulations may have heuristic value in that they may contain material for the generation of hypotheses capable of experimental test.

BIBLIOGRAPHY

Ader, R. & Friedman, S. B. (1965), Social Factors Affecting Emotionality and Resistance to Disease in Animals. *Psychosom. Med.*, 27:119-122.

Alexander, F. (1943), Fundamental Concepts of Psychosomatic Research, Psychogenesis, Conversion, Specificity. *Psychosom. Med.*, 5:205-210.

—— (1950), *Psychosomatic Medicine*. NY: Norton.

Amacher, P. (1965), *Freud's Neurological Education and Its Influence on Psychoanalytic Theory*. *Psychol. Issues*, 16.

Binger, C. A. L. et al. (1945), *Personality in Arterial Hypertension*. NY: Am. Soc. Res. Psychosom. Problems.

Breuer, J. & Freud, S. (1893/95), Studies on Hysteria. *S.E.*, 2.

Bridger, W. & Reiser, M. F. (1959), Psychophysiologic Studies of the Neonate. *Psychosom. Med.*, 21:265-276.

Bunney, W. E., Jr., Mason, J. W., & Hamburg, D. A. (1965), Correlations between Behavioral Variables and Urinary 17-Hydroxycorticosteroids in Depressed Patients. *Psychosom. Med.*, 27:299-308.

Callaway, E., III & Thompson, S. V. (1953), Sympathetic Activity and Perception. *Psychosom. Med.*, 15:433-455.

Deutsch, F., ed. (1953), *The Psychosomatic Concept in Psychoanalysis*. NY: IUP, 175-177.

Engel, G. L. (1954), Studies of Ulcerative Colitis. *Am. J. Med.*, 16:416-433.

—— (1956), Monica, a Study of an Infant with a Gastric Fistula: Section I. *Psychosom. Med.*, 18:374-398.

—— (1962), *Psychological Development in Health and Disease*. Phila.: Saunders.

—— (1965), Some Considerations of the Psychoanalytic Theory of Psychosomatic Disorder. Presented at the Fall Meetings of the Am. Psa. Assn.

French, J. D. et al. (1954), Experimental Observations on "Psychosomatic" Mechanisms: I. *AMA Arch. Neurol. Psychiat.*, 72:267-281.

—— —— (1956), Experimental Gastroduodenal Lesions Induced by Stimulation of the Brain. Abstr. in: *Psychosom. Med.*, 18:516.

Freud, S. (1894), The Neuro-Psychoses of Defence. *S.E.*, 3:43-68.

—— (1900), The Interpretation of Dreams. *S.E.*, 4 & 5.

—— (1910), The Psycho-Analytic View of Psychogenic Disturbance of Vision. *S.E.*, 11:209-218.

—— (1915), Instincts and Their Vicissitudes. *S.E.*, 14:109-140.

—— (1926), Inhibitions, Symptoms and Anxiety. *S.E.*, 20:77-174.

—— (1937) Analysis Terminable and Interminable. *S.E.*, 23:209-253.

—— (1940), An Outline of Psychoanalysis. *S.E.*, 23:141-207.

—— (1950), *The Origins of Psychoanalysis*. NY: Basic Books, 1954.

Friedman, S. B., Mason, J. W., & Hamburg, D. A. (1963), Urinary 17-Hydroxycorticosteroid Levels in Parents of Children with Neoplastic Disease. *Psychosom. Med.*, 25:364-376.

Giovacchini, P. L. (1959), The Ego and the Psychosomatic State. *Psychosom. Med.*, 21:218-227.

—— & Muslin, H. (1965), Ego Equilibrium and Cancer of the Breast. *Psychosom. Med.*, 27:524-532.

Greene, W. A., Jr. (1959), Role of a Vicarious Object in the Adaptation to Object Loss: II. *Psychosom. Med.*, 21:438-447.

—— & Miller, G. (1958), Psychological Factors and Reticuloendothelial Disease: IV. *Psychosom. Med.*, 20:124-144.

Grinker, R. R. (1963), Some Current Trends and Hypotheses of Psychosomatic Research. *The Psychosomatic Concept in Psychoanalysis*, ed. F. Deutsch. NY: IUP, 37-62.

Handlon, J. H. et al. (1962), Psychological Factors Lowering Plasma 17-Hydroxy-corticosteroid Concentration. *Psychosom. Med.*, 24:535-542.

Hartmann, H. (1939), *Ego Psychology and the Problem of Adaptation.* NY: IUP, 1958.

——— (1953), Contribution to the Metapsychology of Schizophrenia. *Essays*, 182-206.

Holzman, P. S. (1959), A Note on Breuer's Hypnoidal Theory of Neurosis. *Bull. Menninger Clin.*, 23:144-147.

Klüver, H. & Bucy, P. C. (1937), "Psychic Blindness" and Other Symptoms Following Bilateral Temporal Lobectomy in Rhesus Monkeys. *Am. J. Physiol.*, 119:352.

——— ——— (1938), An Analysis of Certain Effects of Bilateral Temporal Lobectomy in the Rhesus Monkey, with Special Reference to "Psychic Blindness." *J. Psychol.*, 5:33-54.

——— ——— (1939), Preliminary Analysis of Functions of the Temporal Lobe in Monkeys. *AMA Arch. Neurol. Psychiat.*, 42:979-1000.

Knapp, P. H. et al. (1964), Steroid Excretion, Emotion, and Asthmatic Crises. Abstr. in: *Psychosom. Med.*, 26:631.

——— ——— (1966), Asthma, Melancholia and Death: I & II. *Psychosom. Med.* (in press).

MacLean, P. D. (1949), Psychosomatic Diseases and the "Visceral Brain." *Psychosom. Med.*, 11:338-353.

——— (1963), Phylogenesis. *Expression of Emotions in Man*, ed. P. H. Knapp. NY: IUP, 16-35.

Mahl, G. F. et al. (1964), Psychological Responses in the Human to Intracerebral Electrical Stimulation. *Psychosom. Med.*, 26:337-368.

Mason, J. W. (1959), Psychological Influences on the Pituitary-Adrenal Cortical System. *Recent Prog. in Hormone Res.*, 15:345-389.

——— (1963), Comments on the Psychoendocrine Approach to Psychosomatic Research. Discussion in: *Proc. 44th Ross Conference on Pediatric Research.* Columbus, Ohio.

——— et al. (1960), Limbic System Influences on the Pituitary-Adrenal Cortical System. Abstr. in: *Psychosom. Med.*, 22:322.

——— ——— (1961), Concurrent Plasma Epinephrine, Norepinephrine and 17-Hydroxycorticosteroid Levels during Conditioned Emotional Disturbance in Monkeys. *Psychosom. Med.*, 23:344-353.

——— ——— (1963), Psychoendocrine Differentiation of Emotional Responses in the Monkey. *Proc. Res. Nerv. Ment. Dis.* (in press).

Mirsky, I. A. (1958), Physiologic, Psychologic, and Social Determinants in the Etiology of Duodenal Ulcer. *Am. J. Digest. Dis.*, 3:285.

Moos, R. H. & Solomon, G. F. (1965), Psychologic Comparisons between Women with Rheumatoid Arthritis and Their Nonarthritic Sisters: I & II. *Psychosom. Med.*, 27:135-149.

Pollin, W. & Goldin, S. (1961), The Physiological and Psychological Effects of Intravenously Administered Epinephrine and Its Metabolism in Normal and Schizophrenic Men: II. *J. Psychiat. Res.*, 1:50-67.

Porter, R. W. et al. (1958), Some Experimental Observations on Gastrointestinal Lesions in Behaviorally Conditioned Monkeys. *Psychosom. Med.*, 20:379-394.

Reiser, M. F. (1961), Reflections on Interpretations of Psychophysiologic Experiments. *Psychosom. Med.*, 23:430-439.

Richmond, J. B., Lipton, E. I., & Steinschneider, A. (1962), Autonomic Functions in the Neonate: V. *Psychosom. Med.*, 24:66-74.

Sachar, E. J. et al. (1963), Psychoendocrine Aspects of Acute Schizophrenic Reactions. *Psychosom. Med.*, 25:510-537.

————— (1965), Influence of the Hypnotic Trance on Plasma 17-Hydroxy-corticosteroid Concentration. *Psychosom. Med.*, 27:330-341.

Schmale, A. H., Jr. (1958), Relationship of Separation and Depression to Disease: I. *Psychosom. Med.*, 20:259-277.

Schreiner, L. & Kling, A. (1953), Behavioral Changes Following Rhinencephalic Injury in Cats. *J. Neurophysiol.*, 16:643-659.

Schur, M. (1953), The Ego in Anxiety. *Drives, Affects, Behavior*, ed. R. M. Loewenstein. NY: IUP, 1:67-103.

————— (1955), Comments on the Metapsychology of Somatization. *Psa. Study Ch.*, 10:119-164.

Snyder, F. (1963), The New Biology of Dreaming. *Arch. Gen. Psychiat.*, 7:381-391.

————— (1965), Progress in the New Biology of Dreaming. *Am. J. Psychiat.*, 122:377-391.

————— et al. (1964), Changes in Respiration, Heart Rate, and Systolic Blood Pressure in Human Sleep. *J. Appl. Physiol.*, 19:417-422.

Solomon, G. F. & Moos, R. H. (1965), The Relationship of Personality to the Presence of Rheumatoid Factors in Asymptomatic Relatives of Patients with Rheumatoid Arthritis. *Psychosom. Med.*, 27:350-360.

Sontag, L. W. (1944), Differences in Modifiability of Fetal Behavior and Physiology. *Psychosom. Med.*, 6:151-154.

von Bertalanffy, L. (1964), The Mind-Body Problem. *Psychosom. Med.*, 26:29-45.

Weiner, H. (1962), Some Psychological Factors Related to Cardiovascular Responses. *Physiological Correlates of Psychological Disorder*, ed. R. Roessler & N. S. Greenfield. Madison: Univ. Wisc. Pr., 115-141.

————— Thaler, M., Reiser, M. F., & Mirsky, I. S. (1957), Etiology of Duodenal Ulcer: I. *Psychosom. Med.*, 19:1-10.

Wolff, C. T. et al. (1964), Relationship between Psychological Defenses and Mean Urinary 17-Hydroxycorticosteroid Excretion Rates: I & II. *Psychosom. Med.*, 26:575-591; 592-609.

Some Thoughts on the Concept of Primary Autonomous Ego Functions

HERBERT WEINER, M.D.

The concept of primary autonomous ego functions—one of the many clarifications and extensions of theory brought about by Hartmann —has been justly acclaimed as one of the major advances in psycho-analytic theory. First proposed more than twenty-five years ago, its impact has since been felt in many areas of psychoanalysis and psychology—in research, in theory making, and in the clinic. As a result of its heuristic power, this concept has stimulated investigation in developmental psychology; it has fostered the integration of findings of clinical and experimental psychology into the body of psycho-analytic theory; and it has supplied a conceptual hinge for the articulation of intrapsychic phenomena and social and other environmental processes and events (Hartmann, 1939, 1944; Erikson, 1950). In brief, the concept of primary autonomous ego functions has broadened the range of interest of psychoanalysis by contributing to the formulation of a more comprehensive psychoanalytic theory of personality, and has provided a base for the development of a general psychology (Hartmann, 1964) which goes beyond motivational and conflict psychology. (Within the framework of conflict psychology, however, primary autonomous ego functions determine how the environment is to be experienced, and in consequence are necessary, if not sufficient, in predisposing to conflict.)

Further, this concept has illuminated some of the difficulties which the experimental psychologist often chooses to ignore. Those ego functions which Hartmann (1939, 1950) has called "primary au-

Professor of Psychiatry, Albert Einstein College of Medicine and Associate Chief, Division of Psychiatry, Montefiore Hospital and Medical Center, New York, N. Y.

tonomous," such as perception, do not exist in isolation; therefore, they cannot be studied as though they were single cells in tissue culture. Perception may interact, for instance, with motives, values, defensive and regulatory mechanisms, memory and other cognitive processes. In addition, the psychoanalytic concept of perception derives from inferences about internal perceptions which manifest themselves at many different topographic levels.

It is the purpose of this paper to attempt to integrate into the concept of primary autonomous ego functions and their origins some of the data which have been accumulated in other fields. Although the need to test psychoanalytic observations and hypotheses has been emphasized repeatedly, past experience has shown us how difficult it is to design such research and how "piecemeal" such attempts have been (Hilgard, 1952; Kubie, 1952; Hartmann, 1959). Yet when observations are confirmed by experiment, then validation is achieved and/or the observations are further specified. Furthermore, experiments are welcome, if only because they permit the pooling of efforts and the integration of the findings of all those interested in mental functioning.

Apparatuses Underlying Autonomous Ego Functions

Freud (1937) postulated that there might be congenital or genetically determined variations in ego functioning. As is well known, the developmental concept of primary autonomous ego functions states that the rudimentary apparatuses underlying these functions are present at birth. Clearly, the testing of this hypothesis, which may link psychoanalytic propositions with the new field of behavior genetics, is called for (Hartmann, 1950).

Obviously, an attempt to determine whether a specified apparatus is present at birth can be expected to present serious problems. Yet, suggestive evidence confirming the presence of one such apparatus has been gathered by psychophysiological techniques (Bridger and Reiser, 1959). Perhaps monozygotic twins who have been separated at birth might prove suitable subjects for the study of such variables. Concordance studies in such twins for certain traits, functions, capacities, or clinical syndromes are unlikely to identify with any degree of accuracy the relative contributions of environment and heredity (Hartmann, 1934/35). However, monozygotic twins separated at birth might show concordance for certain functions, which, if stable over time, could then be attributed to heredity alone. This does not mean, of course, that we could expect such a method to be infallible, for there may be congenital physiological differences between the members of a monozygotic pair, caused by differential factors of placentation, natal and prenatal experience. Such factors would favor discordance for whatever apparatus and its emerging functions were being studied. On the other hand, in another pair, in which congenital factors played no role, concordance for the same functions might be found.

Unfortunately, the studies on monozygotic twins reared apart which have been reported to date are rather gross in terms of their behavioral and psychological parameters. They are mentioned only because of the methodology they employed—methods which psychoanalytically trained observers might refine and use in the future in order to learn more about genic factors in the development of primary autonomous ego functions.

The studies referred to measured intelligence by I.Q. tests: on the average, nineteen pairs of monozygotic twins separated at birth differed only slightly more than monozygotic twins who had been reared together. However, the monozygotic twins separated at birth did not differ as much as dizygotic twins who had been reared by the same parents, and not nearly as much as members of the general population. The differences in I.Q. of a few of the monozygotic twins reared apart, when compared to the twins reared together, accounted for the trend in group scores; in these cases, differences in intelligence were due to marked discrepancies in the educational opportunities available to members of the pair (Newman et al., 1937).

Shields (1958, 1962) studied forty-four pairs of monozygotic twins (not all separated at birth, however), and found striking similarities between the members of each pair with regard to mannerisms, gestures, vocal intonation, sociability, interests, and activities. Of some further relevance to the topic of ego development, and possibly that of defense, was Shields's conclusion that an adverse family environment favored the development of neurotic symptoms or character pathology only when a predisposition was present.

If it can be established that uniovular twins are alike in certain ways without the operation of subtle intrafamiliar and intertwin relationships, it might be possible to study not only autonomous ego development but also other commonalities of personality development.

We may then be able to obtain information about their earliest manifestations which might be under genic control. Such data may also help in specifying which ego functions are more or less impervious to formative environmental influences.

Infant observation (Wolff, 1959) has also provided some meaningful, though indirect, data to substantiate the hypothesis that at birth, or very soon thereafter, there are "processes characteristic of ego apparatuses . . . [which] have a definitely inhibitory aspect" (Hartmann, 1950), and might be characterized as thresholds.[1]

The "Average Expectable Environment" and Autonomous Ego Functions

Primary autonomous ego functions mature and develop in an "average expectable environment." At each point along the developmental curve, these functions are said to be coordinated and to proceed from coordinations with the "average expectable environment" (Hartmann, 1939). From birth, a state of adaptedness exists, guaranteed not only by existing sensorimotor coordinations but by the rudimentary apparatuses previously mentioned. Therefore, it is of some interest that "attention" to visual stimuli has been demonstrated to be present at birth (Hershenson, 1964; Hershenson, Munsinger, and Kessen, 1964). In addition to the protective mechanisms with which the infant appears to be equipped, he can also make simple discriminations, at least of auditory stimuli (Bridger, 1962).

The "average expectable environment" encompasses more than just the human object, although this particular coordination has been studied most thoroughly by psychoanalysts. Moreover, these investigations have dealt primarily with the consequences of the disruption or failure of such coordinations (e.g., Spitz, 1945; Mahler, 1952). Coordinations of the infant and child with the object for need and drive satisfaction, sublimated or not, and fulfillment of these needs by the environment have also been well studied. In fact, the environment also provides the social and educational opportunities which permit additional coordinations. The processes of adaptation which thereby come about and the adaptive achievements which ensue may still require further study.

---

[1] In this context, the term "threshold" does not carry with it any particular physiological implication. However, it might be possible to investigate the mechanism underlying such thresholds in young animals at some future date (see below).

Of particular interest, however, is the observation which has been brought into focus only recently, as the result of the work of many men, that a part of the "average expectable environment" is a persisting "screen," or arrays of stimuli, against which changes in stimulus conditions occur. Generally speaking, this background activity, e.g., the gravitational pull, does not intrude into awareness, but it may (Gibson, 1959; Helson, 1959; Klein, 1965).

Psychoanalytic research has focused on the stimulus conditions in the analytic situation under which introspection proceeds best (Freud, 1900), and the factors which adversely influence such functioning, such as the "active" therapeutic intervention which Ferenczi (1920) proposed. However, much recent research has been carried out in other disciplines on the manipulation not only of the contextual background, but also of varying stimulus conditions within a change in context. For example, two such investigations have focused on how normal and organized changes are processed and experienced when the "average expectable environment" is changed by zero gravity (Brown, 1961) and sensory deprivation (Solomon et al., 1961), and the effects of this change on dependent ego operations, such as performance, and their subserving ego functions.

It is of interest that in the highly controversial area of sensory deprivation the phenomena that have been reported, such as regressive ones, appear not to be simply a function of withdrawal of the "average expectable environment," that is, of withdrawal of "the arrays of constant stimulus levels" in the "average expectable environment" (Klein, 1965). These phenomena are, in addition, a function of changes in stimulus conditions when such arrays are absent. Furthermore, under such conditions one can study which ego operations and their subserving ego functions are resistant to dedifferentiation or regression and which are not. Thus Vernon et al. (1961) have shown that depth perception, strength of grip, and response to delayed auditory feedback are impervious to change, whereas color perception, motor coordination, mirror tracing, and rotary pursuit ability are not.[2]

Further insight into the nature of the "average expectable environment" has been provided by experiments in which the subject listened to his own voice. The effects on the subject's cognitive proc-

[2] Of course, many others have also studied the perceptual and cognitive changes and the appearance of regressive phenomena under conditions of sensory deprivation.

esses of a delay in the usual feedback of his voice against a background of undifferentiated noise have been thoughtfully studied by Klein (1965). It seems that such feedback is a necessary condition for "monitoring spoken thought, for inhibiting peripheral lines of thought," and for reality testing. In its absence, regressive thought processes occur, and drive derivative contents emerge with inferably exaggerated defensive and controlling effects. It would be of considerable interest to study the interaction of such variables with personality variables (for instance, different ego organizations), as well as the effects of the independent experimental manipulations described above on a wide range of ego functions (both of primary and secondary autonomy), defenses, and object relationships.

Although this kind of experiment does tell us a great deal about specific situational variables in the "average expectable environment" and their effects on ego functioning, one tends to overlook the fact that in most people ego functions are remarkably stable. Here, again, psychoanalytic theory in general, and ego psychology in particular, have led the way. We know that inhibitions or deviations in functioning occur only when specific ego functions are drawn into conflict. Under other circumstances, these functions are characterized by remarkable stability and slow rates of change, although perhaps this is more common in adults. Moreover, these functions remain equally stable when certain perceptual-cognitive styles are used as criteria, despite quite dire need states (Klein, 1954).

The results of Kohler's experiments (1964) are also relevant to a discussion of the disruptive consequences of interference with information obtained from the environment—such as self-produced movements. But one is even more impressed with the rapidity with which the processes of adaptation occur to the reversed retinal image —or, in other words, with the stability of perception, a fact that is easily predicted from the concept of the conflict-free sphere of the ego. Perception is an activity of continuous exploration of the environment, in the course of which coordinations between the organism and the environment occur (Gibson, 1964). With specific reference to Kohler's experiments, these coordinations involve a process of adaptation to the spectacles, not to the retinal image.

Autonomous Ego Functions and Psychosis

Among the many benefits that have accrued from the concept of primary autonomous ego functions is a shift in emphasis in the theory of psychosis, specifically with respect to schizophrenia. Hartmann (1953) states that "deficiencies in primary autonomous factors in the ego contribute to the vulnerability of defense and of neutralization (and of other ego functions), and thus represent an etiological factor in schizophrenia" (p. 204). In this paper, Hartmann postulates an increased tendency toward conflict in schizophrenic persons as well as a diminished capacity of their defensive ego to deal with such conflict. However, it would certainly seem that conflicts per se are not specific to schizophrenic persons; rather, the defect in the schizophrenic ego is considered a primary etiological factor (e.g., Hendrick, 1951; Bak, 1965).

Hartmann further points out that the precursors of defense, which he classifies among the primary autonomous ego functions, may be deficient in schizophrenia. In view of the complex disturbances of object relationships in psychosis, and the ontogenetic interrelationship of object relationships to defense, the impairment of one such mechanism may interact with and contribute to the impairment of the other. The matter is more complex, however. As Hartmann (1953) points out, the "building up and structuring of the object and partly also of the inner world" (p. 188) are in part the products of intentionality, attention, and anticipation. Presumably, these functions enter as variables into the building up of object representations during ontogenesis, and if their functioning is impaired, this may lead to disturbances both in object representations (e.g., Jacobson, 1954) and in object relationships. Since intention, attention, and anticipation are also classified among the primary autonomous ego functions, if the apparatuses which underlie them are deficient at birth, this deficiency may antedate the well-known disturbances in object relationships which characterize the childhood psychoses and adult schizophrenias.

It is of some interest then, though perhaps not directly relevant to the foregoing, that much recent research has focused on attentional processes in schizophrenia. In the nineteenth century, disturbances in attention, e.g., the "apperceptive dementia" of Weygandt, were considered to be of central importance among a large number of symptoms, formal disturbances of psychological function, and behavior patterns (Jung, 1907). Kraepelin and Bleuler, however, believed attentional processes to be derivative phenomena. The former ascribed changes in active attention as secondary to disturbances in volition; the latter ascribed them to changes in "affectivity."

More recently, Shakow (1962) performed reaction-time experiments on schizophrenic subjects and conceived of his results in terms of an "inability to maintain set." The performance of schizophrenic subjects in such experiments is adversely affected by the context of the task, and by irrelevancies in that context which prevent the subject from "focussing on the to be responded to stimulus." During the preliminary scanning process, the subjects were unable to select the information relevant to the performance of the task at hand. Perhaps, instead, such persons attend to all the characteristics of the stimulus field, or only to some, though these are not relevant. Indeed, a considerable body of research data has been accumulated which relates scanning to attentional processes. These investigations have shown that the degree to which stimuli are sampled when a perceptual field is registered is a function of a characteristic "style," which operates outside of conscious awareness and is correlated with a number of personality variables (Gardner et al., 1959; Klein, 1958; Silverman, 1964). However, shifts in attention toward or away from stimuli are closely related to changes in degree and direction of scanning of objects in the environment (Luborsky et al., 1963; Santos et al., 1963).

Other workers have also commented on the primary role of deviations in attentional processes in schizophrenia (Buss and Lang, 1965). Yet, all in all, neither experimental work nor clinical observation has confirmed the presence of any single form of attentional difficulty in schizophrenia. In some schizophrenic patients there is a tendency at first to be overly attentive to many, or all, often irrelevant, stimuli; later, they reduce their attention to these stimuli, or even exclude them. Some patients are excessively vigilant and attentive to stimuli, or increase the intensity of stimuli; others do not. Still other schizophrenic patients may idiosyncratically select or respond to stimuli which are inappropriate, or are more likely to respond to certain types of stimuli, while avoiding those which represent a threat or are otherwise affectively tinged.

These findings are based on work done with adult schizophrenic patients. Unfortunately, there is no information available regarding the presence of such disturbances *prior* to the onset of illness, or their presence in children who later become psychotic. Therefore, it is impossible at present to determine whether such attentional deficits are primary, present since birth, or concomitants of the psychosis. In fact, there is some suggestion in the literature that such attentional deficits are secondary to "arousal," such as anxiety might produce. It has also been stated that the "sensitivity" of schizophrenic subjects to input, whether or not it leads to accurate perceptions of the environment (Harway and Salzman, 1964), may, in itself, by flooding the subjects with unassimilable percepts, produce anxiety (McReynolds, 1960). In this connection, some authors maintain that apathy and withdrawal stem from attempts to reduce percepts (McReynolds, 1960) or "arousal" (Venables, 1963). Admittedly, such hypotheses sound rather "thin" to the psychoanalyst's ear; yet, they do link autonomous functions with conflict, anxiety, and even defense.

Hartmann (1953) has also pointed out that certain primary autonomous functions, and for that matter secondary ones, are involved in some forms of schizophrenia but not in others. Moreover, in the same patient, different ego functions may be involved at different phases of his illness. In this regard, it might be noted that many complex problems of clinical psychoanalysis, some of which have not yet been resolved, might be clarified by the reformulation of psychopathology within the framework of ego psychology, as exemplified by Hartmann's paper.[3] For example, why do certain classes of conflicts produce formal disturbances of autonomous functions, while others do not? Why does a constellation of conflicts produce certain classes of symptoms (such as phobias) in childhood, but lead to a different class of symptoms (such as hysterical "tunnel vision," or paralysis), involving the primary autonomous functions, in the adult? Perhaps the answer does indeed lie in the regressive reactivation in conflict situations of earlier, successful modes of mastery by the ego (Kris, 1950). Clearly, then, one important variable in the etiology of neurosis or psychosis is variation in the endowment of ego functions capable of mastering conflict, which, in turn, may lead back to genic factors, apparatuses underlying such functions, drive endowment, and innate tendencies toward organization, defense, and structure formation (A. Freud, 1963). Thus the shift in emphasis to primary autonomous ego functions and their implication in various clinical syndromes, as well as in conflict, has broadened our perspectives with respect to etiology, while preserving the pathogenic explanations of symptom formation so clearly elucidated by Freud and his coworkers.

[3] See, for instance, Wangh's paper on the structural determinants of phobia (1959).

Some Factors in the Organization of Ego Functions

Discussion of the ego as a coherent organization is somewhat hampered by the fact that its components have not yet been fully enumerated (Hartmann, 1950). It is, of course, well known that besides the primary autonomous functions, secondary autonomous functions, affects, object relations, "ego interests," defenses, and object and self representations are included in this generic category. Furthermore, although these have not all been worked out, extensive interactions between these functions exist. More precisely, some of these functions, but not all, are involved in certain "tasks," such as the control and regulation of motives, conflict solution and mastery, and self preservation. Again, all of the functions may be involved in certain processes of adaptation, but not in others. In the course of conflict solution it is not clear why certain regressions or dedifferentiations of one or another function occur in some personalities and not in others.

In addition to conflict solution, in every psychic act integrations and coordinations of "tendencies" from reality, id, and superego (Waelder, 1930), and that tendency which is conceived of as the repetition compulsion, must occur either passively or actively (Hartmann, 1939). Intrasystemic conflicts must be integrated as well. The manner of such integration will depend on whether the conflict involves a reality problem or an intrapsychic one. The relationship of reality to drive derivatives is not reciprocal, as some authors have implied (e.g., Holt, 1965).

In the process of integration of the tendencies mentioned above, contradictory ones must be eliminated. Yet, if I have understood Hartmann correctly, during the course of such synthesis, and because to a certain degree adult personality variables are not wholly static and result in further differentiation of ego functions, new syntheses are continually required. Perhaps such synthetic processes are more easily observed in the child, in the course of personality development, than in the adult. The consequences of the suspension of synthesis in the creative act might also be studied (Kris, 1952). But one wonders, in view of the personality changes wrought in the course of analysis, whether the analytic setting would be an appropriate "laboratory" for such observations. This statement does not gainsay the enormous yield of data and theory from the analytic situation. Yet the situation is a very special one in which the impact of reality is temporarily suspended.

Studies of sensory deprivation and their conceptualization (Rapaport, 1951, 1958; Miller, 1962; Holt, 1965) yield another dimension. Further study of interactions between tendencies may yield data which will in no way refute the concept of the ego as an organized unit, but may further test, specify, and extend it to incorporate situations other than the analytic. For example, it might be possible by systematically manipulating situations, by altering the "average expectable environment" during various motivated states and other states of the ego, to study ego operations which involve specific functions. It might also be necessary to consider personality variables in order to account for all the observed variations in results.

In the following experiments, the kind of incentives used, though motives of behavior, are not the kind of dynamic motives which psychoanalysts study. The latter, as one form of personality variable, might also have to be taken into consideration in such experiments. These experiments concentrated on specified tasks involving ego operations and functions, and tested these against graded and experimentally controlled levels of arousal, interference by noise, and incentives. Wilkinson (1961) has shown that, as might be expected, the effect of sleeplessness is to reduce efficiency in a particular task, if the sleeplessness reduces "arousal." On the other hand, applying incentives to this task results in a much greater improvement in performance among sleepless men than among normal men, so that, to some extent, the incentive is able to cancel out the effects of sleeplessness. Similarly, Corcoran (1962) and Wilkinson (1963) have shown that noise will increase the efficiency of sleepless men, but will not affect the efficiency of people who have slept normally.

The existence of such interactions makes it clear that efficiency does not rise uniformly as the level of arousal rises, but this finding does not, in itself, imply that working efficiency will actually decrease at very high levels of arousal. This was suggested, however, by the introduction of noise with the intensity of 100 decibels as one of the stimulating conditions in the experiments mentioned above. Such noise produces very high levels of stimulation which, among subjects who have slept normally, is known to cause inefficient performance on specified tasks (Broadbent, 1953). It is plausible to attribute this inefficiency to overstimualtion, which in turn affects integration adversely. On this basis, one would expect, from what has been said, that the effects of noise would be most serious when the level of incentive applied was high; this expectation has been confirmed by Wilkinson (1963). There are good reasons, therefore, for thinking, first, that there is a general level of efficiency which increases with stimulation, arousal, and incentive, and also that there is an optimum point beyond which further increases in arousal produce a deterioration in performance. Such experiments suggest that the interrelationships between certain classes of motives, arousal, stimulation, organismic states, and ego functions are complex; and they tell us something about adaptive functioning which could not otherwise be gleaned in the clinical setting. In any case, the relationship of efficiency to arousal for certain types of ego operations, and for the functions which subserve them, may be of the inverted U-type, so that paradoxical interactions of incentive and arousal may occur. Such data might be incorporated into a model which would specify the interaction of motives and external events, and their interaction.

The Question of Neural Correlates of Autonomous Ego Functions

There is another benefit accruing from modern ego psychology. Because of its emphasis on function and organization, ego psychology provides a conceptual framework which may lead to the translation of some of the data into physiological terms, as Freud (1895) and Hartmann (1950) anticipated. But here some general principles of such translation might be kept in mind. First, psychoanalytic theory teaches us that statements made about one function must be related to the over-all functioning of the entire system, and that the interactions between these functions account for ego organization. In the same manner, statements which apply to particular physical changes in the brain must be related to the actual functioning of the entire system before one can be certain of the validity of such explanations. Second, psychoanalytic observations provide data about the plasticity of functioning, or the interaction of functions—qualities which, for example, need to be explained in terms of physiological mechanisms (Weiner, 1965).

Other properties of the system which will have to be included in a physiological mechanism, or explanation, are the interaction of part functions of the ego, their coordination, and the capacity of the unit to integrate external stimuli and events with internal processes, such as motivations. These interactions may either be "cooperative" or they may be disruptive in relation to other functions. Eventually, it may also be necessary to test experimentally the hypothetical physiological mechanism against behavior or ego functioning. One cannot understand the workings of any system unless one is properly informed about the properties of that system and the functions which that system serves. Once function is understood, one can approach the details of the mechanism.

It seems likely that one might begin with the translation of ego functions, rather than the neurobiological basis of drives. A considerable amount of information has been gathered about the neuroendocrinology of sexual behavior in animals and some of the neural mechanisms of their aggressive behavior. But we are left with the insuperable problem of how neural events in man, and the endocrine factors which instigate them, are translated into psychological events —specifically, into drive derivatives. For example, it is possible to make certain generalizations about the way hormones influence reproductive or sexual behavior. Hormones seem to play less of a role in the sexual behavior of those animals which are higher on the phylogenetic ladder. However, even in male mammals which are lower on the scale, the effects of castration on sexual activity varies according to the age of the animal at the time of operation, the species to which it belongs, and its previous sexual experience (Grunt and Young, 1952). In lower mammals, both male and female, fragments of copulatory patterns seem to be under the control of centers in the spinal cord, but the differential and more complete hormonal activation of these patterns requires the integrity of a more rostrally located neural site, most probably above the level of the lower midbrain (Bard, 1940). In female mammals, the maintenance of mating behavior requires only subcortical centers—and estrogen; but the initiation of such behavior requires an intact neocortex, in the presence of sex hormones (Goldstein, 1957).

From much recent work it is possible to conclude that in female cats there is an important integrative site for sexual behavior in the hypothalamus, anterior to its ventromedial nucleus and medial to, or within, the area of the median forebrain bundle. Lesions of this area produce anestrus; yet, despite the lesions, stimulation of the ventromedial nucleus results in ovulation. Thus the area anterior to the ventromedial nucleus does not appear to be crucial in the maintenance of ovarian integrity. More posterior regions are, however, since lesions in these areas are followed by pituitary atrophy. Even when anestrus follows more caudal lesions, animals will mate when exogenous estrogen is supplied (Sawyer and Robison, 1956).

In the rabbit, separate "mating" and gonadotrophic integrating sites are present. The mechanism of action of sex hormones on such integrative centers in the nervous system and on peripheral receptors is largely unknown. But it is almost axiomatic that sex hormones, when released, act to suppress their specific pituitary substances, possibly by their action on hypothalamic centers. Evidence that bursts of high amplitude electrical activity in the anterolateral hypothalamus can be recorded in estrus cats, during and after vaginal stimulation, further implicates the hypothalamus in mating behavior (Porter et al., 1957). Sex hormones may also have less specific effects on neural centers, or more general behavioral effects: For example, in the first five hours following subcutaneous injections of progesterone, the threshold for cortical desynchronization on stimulation of the mesencephalic reticular formation was progressively lowered by unknown mechanisms (Sawyer, 1958).

Such findings must not be rashly extrapolated to man, first, because they deal only with the correlation of external behavior, mating, estrus and neuroendocrine events. Psychoanalysis has taught us that much, if not most of mental life may proceed without any external manifestations. (Much neural activity does too, but there still is no way of correlating it with any psychological parameter.) Second, our inability to use such experimental data is based, in part, on our failure to solve the mind-brain problem, and to deal with the translation of neural events into fantasy, motives, or other kinds of drive representations. Yet, such data specify how the same hormone differentially affects neural structures, and thus leads to different facets of a behavioral act.

This does not mean that other psychological parameters could not be translated into physiological terms. As mentioned previously, refined and detailed description of psychological functions and their components, tested perhaps by experimental findings, might be our starting point. Once we have defined the properties and organization of ego functions, we might then be able to account for the known properties of their functioning. For instance, a molar analysis of the part functions of the ego might lead us to postulate the functional requirements of an isomorphic physiological mechanism, to account for its properties.

Once again one might choose attention as a paradigm. Recent evidence suggests that there is not just one kind of attention, but at least three. A suggestive neural mechanism has been worked out for one of these. If a subject is asked to listen to a stream of speech directed into one ear, and to repeat its content as rapidly as it is presented, while at the same time speech is directed into his other ear, the subject soon learns to "ignore" what has been going on at his neglected ear, and is unable to identify any of the words presented to it (Cherry, 1953). Desmedt (1960) has found that there is a central control of incoming auditory impulses, which does not occur at the round window of the cochlea, and is not an artifact or a microphonic, but is a diminution in the response of the first interneurone. The gating does not occur peripherally, but perhaps at the cochlear nucleus. However, the kind of attention which involves the selection of one sensory channel, followed by the selection of stored information which has arrived by another sensory channel, has not yet been explained by any neural mechanism. There is no reason for assuming, therefore, that any particular ego function is unitary—or that it has only one neural analogue.

Conclusion

The fruitfulness of the concept of primary autonomous ego functions and its heuristic power of the integration of recent experimental findings into psychoanalysis are well known. This paper has perhaps overemphasized data which have been acquired by techniques other than psychoanalytic observation, but which might be incorporated into this concept in order further to specify it. The only rationale for this approach is the history of Hartmann's own research which began with investigative work in the clinic and which pointed the way to the integration of data and concepts from many other fields. For instance, his work on the Zeigarnik effect (1933) reveals a wide-ranging knowledge of Kurt Lewin's experimental work, and emphasizes the need to complement the results of these experiments by psychoanalytic concepts, particularly with respect to the dynamics of affect and drives.

One learns from Hartmann that whatever information may advance a general theory of behavior and our understanding of the mind's functions has some value, provided this new information is not used to dispense with the tried and true. His hard dispassionate thought and taste serve as a model for all who value the accomplishments and achievements of psychoanalysis.

BIBLIOGRAPHY

Bak, R. C. (1965), Comments on Object Relations in Schizophrenia and Perversions. Abstr. in: *Psa. Q.*, 34:473-475.

Bard, P. (1940), The Hypothalamus and Sexual Behavior. *Assn. Res. Nerv. & Ment. Dis. Proc.*, 20:551-579.

Bridger, W. H. (1962), Sensory Discrimination and Automatic Function in the Newborn. *J. Am. Acad. Ch. Psychiat.*, 1:67-82.

———— & Reiser, M. F. (1959), Psychophysiologic Studies of the Neonate. *Psychosom. Med.*, 21:265-276.

Broadbent, D. E. (1953), Noise, Paced Performance and Vigilance Tasks. *Brit. J. Psychol.*, 44:295-303.

Brown, E. L. (1961), Human Performance and Behavior during Zero Gravity. *Weightlessness*, ed. E. T. Benedikt. NY: Plenum Pr., 156-170.

Buss, A. H. & Lang, P. J. (1965), Psychological Deficit in Schizophrenia. *J. Abnorm. Soc. Psychol.*, 70:77-106.

Cherry, E. C. (1953), Some Experiments on the Recognition of Speech, with One and with Two Ears. *J. Accoust. Soc. Am.*, 25:975-979.

Corcoran, D. W. J. (1962), Noise and Loss of Sleep. *Q. J. Exp. Psychol.*, 14:178-182.

Desmedt, J. E. (1960), Neurophysiological Mechanisms Controlling Acoustic Input. *Neural Mechanisms of the Auditory and Vestibular Systems*, ed. G. L. Rasmussen & W. Windle. Springfield, Ill.: Thomas, 152-164.

Erikson, E. H. (1950), *Childhood and Society*. NY: Norton.

Ferenczi, S. (1920), The Further Development of an Active Therapy in Psycho-Analysis. *Further Contributions to the Theory and Technique of Psycho-Analysis.* NY: Basic Books, 1952, 198-217.

Freud, A. (1963), The Concept of Developmental Lines. *Psa. Study Ch.*, 18:245-265.

Freud, S. (1895), Project for a Scientific Psychology. *The Origins of Psychoanalysis.* NY: Basic Books, 1954.

———— (1900), The Interpretation of Dreams. *S.E.*, 4:101.

———— (1937), Analysis Terminable and Interminable. *S.E.*, 23:209-253.

Gardner, R. W. et al. (1959), *Cognitive Control. Psychol. Issues*, 4.

Gibson, J. J. (1959), Perception as a Function of Stimulation. *Psychology: A Study of a Science*, Vol. I, ed. S. Koch. NY: McGraw-Hill, 456-501.

———— (1964), Introduction to I. Kohler, *The Formation and Transformation of the Perceptual World. Psychol. Issues*, 12:5-13.

Goldstein, A. C. (1957), The Experimental Control of Sex Behavior in Animals. *Brain Function and Behavior*, ed. H. Hoagland. NY: Academic Pr., 99-123.

Grunt, J. A. & Young, W. C. (1952), Differential Reactivity of Individuals and the Response of the Male Guinea Pig to Testosterone Propionate. *Endocrinology*, 51:237-248.

Hartmann, H. (1933), An Experimental Contribution to the Psychology of Obsessive-Compulsive Neurosis. *Essays*, 404-418.

———— (1934/35), Psychiatric Studies of Twins. *Essays*, 419-445.

———— (1939), *Ego Psychology and the Problem of Adaptation.* NY: IUP, 1958.

———— (1944), Psychoanalysis and Sociology. *Essays*, 19-36.

———— (1950), Comments on the Psychoanalytic Theory of the Ego. *Essays*, 113-141.

———— (1953), Contribution to the Metapsychology of Schizophrenia. *Essays*, 182-206.

—— (1959), Psychoanalysis as a Scientific Theory. *Essays,* 318-350.

—— (1964), *Essays on Ego Psychology.* NY: IUP.

Harway, N. I. & Salzman, L. F. (1964), Size Constancy in Psychopathology. *J. Abnorm. Soc. Psychol.,* 69:606-613.

Helson, H. (1959), Adaptation Level Theory. *Psychology: A Study of a Science,* Vol. I, ed. S. Koch. NY: McGraw-Hill, 565-621.

Hendrick, I. (1951), Early Development of the Ego. *Psa. Q.,* 20:44-61.

Hershenson, M. (1964), Visual Discrimination in the Human Newborn. *J. Comp. Physiol. Psychol.,* 58:270.

—— Munsinger, H., & Kessen, W. (1964), Preference for Shapes of Intermediate Variability in the Newborn Human. *Science,* 147:630-631.

Hilgard, E. R. (1952), Experimental Approaches to Psychoanalysis. *Psychoanalysis as Science,* ed. E. Pumpian-Mindlin. Palo Alto: Stanford Univ. Pr., 3-45.

Holt, R. R. (1965), Ego Autonomy Re-evaluated. *Int. J. Psa.,* 46:151-167.

Jacobson, E. (1954), Federn's Contribution to Ego Psychology and Psychoses. *J. Am. Psa. Assn.,* 2:519-525.

Jung, C. G. (1907), *The Psychology of Dementia Praecox.* NY: Nerv. & Ment. Dis. Monogr., 1944.

Klein, G. S. (1954), Need and Regulation. *Nebraska Symposium on Motivation,* ed. M. R. Jones. Lincoln: Univ. Nebraska Pr., 224-274.

—— (1958), Cognitive Control and Motivation. *Assessment of Human Motives,* ed. G. Lindzey. NY: Rinehart, 87-118.

—— (1965), On Hearing One's Own Voice. *Drives, Affects, Behavior,* ed. M. Schur. NY: IUP, 2:67-117.

Kohler, I. (1964), *The Formation and Transformation of the Perceptual World. Psychol. Issues,* 12.

Kris, E. (1950), Notes on the Development and on Some Current Problems of Psychoanalytic Child Psychology. *Psa. Study Ch.,* 5:24-46.

—— (1952), *Psychoanalytic Explorations in Art.* NY: IUP.

Kubie, L. S. (1952), Problems and Techniques of Psychoanalytic Validation and Progress. *Psychoanalysis as Science,* ed. E. Pumpian-Mindlin. Palo Alto: Stanford Univ. Pr., 46-124.

Luborsky, L., Blinder, B., & Mackworth, N. (1963), Eye Fixation and Recall of Pictures as a Function of GSR Responsivity. *Percept. Mot. Skills,* 16:469-483.

Mahler, M. S. (1952), On Child Psychosis and Schizophrenia. *Psa. Study Ch.,* 7:286-305.

McReynolds, P. (1960), Anxiety, Perception and Schizophrenia. *The Etiology of Schizophrenia,* ed. D. Jackson. NY: Basic Books, 248-292.

Miller, S. C. (1962), Ego-autonomy in Sensory Deprivation, Isolation and Stress. *Int. J. Psa.,* 43:1-20.

Newman, H. H., Freeman, F. N., & Holzinger, K. J. (1937), *Twins.* Chicago: Univ. Chicago Pr.

Porter, R. W., et al. (1957), Localized Changes in Electrical Activity of the Hypothalamus in Estrus Cats Following Vaginal Stimulation. *Am. J. Physiol.,* 189:145-151.

Rapaport, D. (1951), The Autonomy of the Ego. *Bull. Menninger Clin.,* 15:113-123.

—— (1958), The Theory of Ego Autonomy. *Bull. Menninger Clin.,* 22:13-35.

Santos, J. F., Farrow, B. J., & Haines, J. R. (1963), How Attention Influences What Is Perceived. *Bull. Menninger Clin.,* 27:3-14.

Sawyer, C. H. (1958), Activation and Blockade of the Release of Pituitary Gonadotropin as Influenced by the Reticular Formation. *Reticular Formation of the Brain,* ed. H. H. Jasper et al. Boston: Little, Brown, 223-230.

—— & Robison, B. (1956), Separate Hypothalamic Areas Controlling Pituitary Gonadotrophic Function and Mating Behavior in Female Cats and Rabbits. Abstr. in: *J. Clin. Endocrinol.,* 16:914-915.

Shakow, D. (1962), Segmental Set. *Arch. Gen. Psychiat.*, 6:1-17.
Shields, J. (1958), Twins Brought up Apart. *Eugen. Rev.*, 50:115-123.
—— (1962), *Monozygotic Twins Brought Up Apart and Brought Up Together.* NY: Oxford Univ. Pr.
Silverman, J. (1964), The Problem of Attention in Research and Theory in Schizophrenia. *Psychol. Rev.*, 71:352-379.
Solomon, P., et al., eds. (1961), *Sensory Deprivation.* Cambridge: Harvard Univ. Pr.
Spitz, R. A. (1945), Hospitalism. *Psa. Study Ch.*, 1:53-74.
Venables, P. H. (1963), Selectivity of Attention, Withdrawal and Cortical Activation. *Arch. Gen. Psychiat.*, 9:74-78.
Vernon, J. A., et al. (1961), The Effect of Human Isolation upon Some Perceptual and Motor Skills. *Sensory Deprivation*, ed. P. Solomon et al. Cambridge: Harvard Univ. Pr., 51-57.
Waelder, R. (1930), The Principle of Multiple Function. *Psa. Q.*, 5:19-36.
Wangh, M. (1959), Structural Determinants of Phobia. *J. Am. Psa. Assn.*, 7:675-695.
Weiner, H. (1965), Psychoanalysis as a Biological Science. *Psychoanalysis and Current Biological Thought*, ed. N. S. Greenfield & W. C. Lewis. Madison: Univ. Wisconsin Pr., 11-34.
Wilkinson, R. T. (1961), Interaction of Lack of Sleep with Knowledge of Results, Repeated Testing and Individual Differences. *J. Exp. Psychol.*, 62:263-271.
—— (1963), The Interaction of Noise with Sleep Deprivation and Knowledge of Results. *J. Exp. Psychol.*, 66:332-337.
Wolff, P. H. (1959), Observations on Newborn Infants. *Psychosom. Med.*, 21:110-118.

Ontogeny of Ritualization

ERIK H. ERIKSON

To treat an issue epigenetically means to describe the steps, each built upon preceding ones, which are essential to its development through the individual's life cycle. To do so with "ritualization" (here put in quotation marks until we can release it from them) we must first set aside three now dominant connotations of the term. One, the oldest, is the *anthropological* one which ties it to rites and rituals conducted by communities of adults (and sometimes witnessed by children or participated in by youths) for the purpose of marking such recurring events as the phases of the year or the stages of life. I shall attempt to trace some of the ontogenetic roots of all ritual-making, but I shall not deal with adult ritual as such.

A more recent connotation of "ritualization" is the *clinical* one. Here the term "private ritual" is used to conceptualize obsessional behavior consisting of repetitive solitary acts with highly idiosyncratic meanings. Such behavior is vaguely analogous to the aimless repetitive behavior of caged animals, and thus seems to provide a "natural" link with a possible phylogenetic origin of "ritualization" in its more stereotyped and driven forms.

It seems important to set aside this clinical connotation in order to take account of newer insights both in ethology and in psychoanalysis. There is now a trend in the ethological literature (recently summarized by Lorenz, 1964) which follows the original suggestion of Sir Julian Huxley to use the word ritualization, and this explicitly

This paper is based on a communication, "The Ontogeny of Ritualization in Man," presented to the Royal Society in June, 1965 as a contribution to a symposium on "Ritualization in Animals and in Man." The whole symposium in its original form will appear in due course in the *Proceedings of the Royal Society.*

without quotation marks, for certain phylogenetically preformed ceremonial acts in the so-called social animals. We may remember here the greeting ceremonial by which the newborn gosling Màrtina (a name perhaps as significant in ethology as Anna O. is in psychopathology) insisted on teaching Konrad Lorenz a lesson. To paraphrase him: when the gray-lag gosling has managed to slip out of the egg and lies there in a little wet heap, its neck limply extended, there is one reaction which can be elicited promptly. If one bends over it and emits some sounds reasonably reminiscent of those of a mother goose, it raises its head, stretches its neck—and greets the world around it with a thin but clearly recognizable sound. Before it can walk, stand up, or eat, then, it can produce an early form of that greeting ritual which comparative behaviorology has shown to have phylogenetically evolved out of threatening gestures. The newborn gosling's life and growth depend on the fittedness of this earliest response, for it is normally responded to (as it is elicited by) the mother goose.

Thus, what has come to be called "ritualization" in *phylogeny* clearly points away from pathology, in that it reveals the bond created by the reciprocal message contained in such behavior. This also means that repetitive forms of display or of posturing or of signalizing would not, by themselves, qualify as "ritualizations" in the full sense except in phylogenetically given reciprocal contexts. Human behavior, in turn, in order to be called "ritualization," would have to go beyond mere methods of formalizing, routinizing, or conventionalizing, not to speak of pathological stereotypy. For, as Heinz Hartmann said as early as 1939, "we must not take every repetition for an expression of the repetition compulsion" (p. 96)[1] and again "reality-regulated ego tendencies . . . must use the repetition compulsion's tendencies selectively" (p. 98). To free the word from the indignity of quotation marks we should, therefore, begin by postulating that behavior to be called ritualization in man must consist of an agreed-upon interplay between at least two persons who repeat it at meaningful intervals and in recurring contexts; and that this interplay should have adaptive value for the respective egos of both partici-

---

[1] In the following, except where indicated otherwise, all quotations are from H. Hartmann's pioneer work *Ego Psychology and the Problem of Adaptation*. I restrict myself to this work because of its early and singular emphasis on phylogenetic and ontogenetic adaptation.

pants. I would submit that these conditions are, for example, fully met by the way in which a human mother and her baby greet each other in the morning.

In attempting to anchor human ritualization in the earliest stage of the life cycle and to carry the matter through to maturity, I feel encouraged (as I have felt in approaching comparable tasks [1966a]) by Heinz Hartmann's advocacy, going back to my student days, of the study of man's "primary equipment"; of the role of the ego in that "most crucial adaptation . . . to the social structure"; and to the "ego's share in building tradition" (p. 30).

Infancy and the Numinous

I shall treat ritualization, then, as a *special form of everyday behavior*. The awakening infant conveys a message to his mother and immediately awakens in her a whole repertoire of emotive, verbal, and manipulative behavior. She approaches him with smiling or worried concern, brightly or anxiously voicing a name, and goes into action: looking, feeling, sniffing, she ascertains possible sources of discomfort and initiates services to be rendered by rearranging the infant's condition, by preparing food, picking him up, etc. If observed for several days (and especially in a milieu not one's own) it becomes clear that this daily event is highly formalized, in that the mother seems to feel obliged (and to be not a little pleased) to repeat a performance arousing in the infant predictable responses, which encourage her, in turn, to proceed. Such formalization, however, is hard to describe. It is at the same time *highly individual* ("typical for the mother") and also tuned to the particular infant; and yet it is also *stereotyped* along traditional lines—as we can see best in cultures, classes, or families other than our own. The whole procedure is, of course, superimposed on the periodicity of vital physical needs; it is an *enhanced routine* which keeps close to the requirements of survival. We have every reason to believe, however, that it is much more than this, and that, as an *emotional* as well as a *practical* necessity for both mother and infant, it can be properly evaluated only as a small but tough link in the whole formidable sequence of generations. Psychoanalysis reveals the way in which "man lives, so to speak, in past generations as well as in his own" (p. 30), and a mother's procedures envelop an infant in this process without delay.

She may call the infant by a nickname or a name. The name may have been carefully selected and certified in some name-giving ritual, held to be indispensable by the parents and the community. Whatever has thus given meaning to the name, that meaning now exerts a decisive effect on its pronunciation during the greeting procedure, joining other emphases of caring attention which have a very special significance for the mother and eventually for the child.

There is much to suggest that man is born with the need for such regular and mutual affirmation and certification: we know that its absence can harm an infant irreversibly, by diminishing or extinguishing his search for impressions which will verify his senses. But once aroused, this need will reassert itself in every stage of life as a hunger for new and more widely shared experiences which repeat such "recognition" of the hoped-for face and voice.

I would, therefore, suggest that this mutuality of recognition, attached as it is to the first necessities of mere survival, becomes the ontogenetic root of a pervasive element in human ritualization and, in fact, in mature ritual. Such ritualizations range from daily greetings affirming a strong emotional bond, to singular encounters of a sudden and mutual fusion in love or inspiration, to the aura of Madonna-and-Child images, and to the mass surrender to a leader's "charisma." The first dim affirmation thus becomes one basic element in all ritual: I would call it the *numinous* element, the sense of a hallowed presence. This conclusion betrays my intention to follow the earliest ritualizations to the last rituals: and, indeed, in *religious observances,* the believer confesses by gestures of humility his dependence and his childlike faith and seeks, by appropriate offerings, to secure a sense of being lifted up to the godhead, which in the visible form of an image may seem to respond graciously, perhaps with the faint smile of an inclined face. The emotional effect is a sense of *separateness transcended,* and yet also of *distinctiveness confirmed.*

I have now already gone "the whole way," by offering as intrinsically related two sets of phenomena, namely, ritualization in the nursery (as an enhancement by playful formalization of the routine procedures which assure mere survival) and religious rituals (which provide periodical reaffirmation for a multitude of men). This is my first example of an affinity of themes, which seem to "belong" to entirely different "fields" but are necessarily brought together by psychoanalytic insight. By suggesting such far-reaching connections, however, I do not mean to reduce formalized ritual to infantile elements, but rather, to recognize an ontogenetic beginning to be re-integrated on each higher level of development. The relationship of the earliest ritualization and of mature ritual is twofold: as adult ritual evokes in its participants residues of their earliest experiences, it also supports them (as we shall see later) in the task of ritualizing selected aspects of their children's lives. Thus, both infantile ritualiza-tion and adult ritual are parts of a functional whole, of a cogwheeling (as David Rapaport was fond of calling it) of the generations, and of a cultural version of human existence. As Hartmann puts it, "Re-ligions are the most obvious attempt to cope both with these [the inner] mental institutions and with social adaptation . . . by means of synthesis" (p. 79).

I shall now try to summarize a few of the basic elements of ritualization which we can already recognize in the first, the numi-nous, context. Its mutuality is based on the *reciprocal* needs of two quite *unequal* organisms and minds; yet, it unites them in *practical reality* as well as in *symbolic actuality*. It is a highly *personal* matter, and is yet *group-bound;* by the same token it heightens a sense both of *belongingness* and of personal *distinctiveness*. It is *playful*, and yet *formalized*, and this in *details* as well as in the *whole* procedure. Be-coming *familiar* through repetition, it yet renews the *surprise* of recognition which provides a catharsis of affects. And while the ethologists will tell us that ritualization in the animal world must, above all, provide an *unambiguous* set of signals so as to avoid fatal misunderstanding, we suspect that in man, the *overcoming of am-bivalence* is an important aim of such ritualization. For what we love or admire is also threatening, awe becomes awfulness, and benevo-lence is in danger of being consumed by wrath. Therefore, ritualized affirmation, at first playfully improvised, becomes indispensable as a periodical experience and must find new forms in the context of new developmental actualities. Its perversion or absence, in turn, leaves a sense of dread or impoverishment. Thus, the earliest affirmation soon becomes reaffirmation in the face of the fact that the very experi-ences by which man derives a measure of familiarity also expose him to a *series of estrangements*. The first of these is a sense of *separation by abandonment* to which corresponds, on the part of the mother, a chilling sense of not being needed: both must be prevented by the persistent, periodical reassurance of familiarity and mutuality. Such reassurance later remains the function of the numinous, whether it is dominant, as in the religious ritual, or subsidiary, as in all ritual. If one chooses to see in such reaffirmation an element of regression to a "primary narcissistic state" of "fitting together," and of "being one with the object," Hartmann reminds us that "Even this regressive tendency may, under certain conditions, serve adaptation" (p. 53). These "certain conditions," as I shall now attempt to show, include an institutional or creative setting in which ego integration and cultural solidarity are maintained and enhanced.

In another context (1964), I have suggested that the most basic strength of human life, *hope*, emerges unbroken from early familiarity and mutuality and provides for man that sense of fitting (into his personal and cultural environment) which the animal seems to derive (in his environment) by the fittedness of its instincts. Hope is subsequently replenished by all those ritualizations and rituals which combat a sense of abandonment and hopelessness and promise instead a mutuality of recognition, face to face, all through life—until "we shall know even as also we are known."

The Pseudo Species

Before reviewing other stages of life which contribute epigenetic elements to and receive meaning from human ritualization, I must introduce a few theoretical considerations of an incomplete and still controversial nature.

Since ritualization in animals is for the most part an intraspecies phenomenon, it must be kept in mind throughout that man has evolved (by whatever kind of evolution and for whatever adaptive reasons) in pseudo species, i.e., tribes, clans, classes, etc., which behave as if they were separate species created at the beginning of time by supernatural intent. Thus each develops not only a *distinct sense of identity*, but also a conviction of harboring *the* human identity, fortified against other pseudo species by prejudices which mark them as extraspecific and inimical to "genuine" human endeavor. Paradoxically, however, newly born man is (to use Ernst Mayr's term [1964]) a *generalist* creature who could be made to fit into any number of pseudo species and must, therefore, become "specialized" during a prolonged childhood—certainly a basic fact in ontogeny which is served by familiarization through ritualization.

But what is the role of instincts in such adaptation? Whenever we use the noun instinct, it is helpful to ask ourselves whether the corresponding adjective would be "instinctive" or "instinctual," i.e., whether we intend to emphasize an *instinctive pattern* of behavior, or an *instinctual drive or energy* more or less divorced from inborn patterns of adaptiveness. It will appear, then, that we usually mean instinctual drives, and this with the connotation of a quantitative measure more or less out of proportion with the instinctive quality, the pattern of fittedness, in the behavior described. For, in man, "It is a long step from the pleasure principle to the self-preservative instinct; the intentions of the two of them are very far from coinciding from the start" (Freud, 1933, p. 94). Hartmann has provided an adaptive rationale for what we may call an estrangement of instinctuality: "No instinctual drive in man guarantees adaptation in and of itself, yet on the average the whole ensemble of instinctual drives, ego functions, ego apparatuses, and the principles of regulation, as they meet the average expectable environmental conditions, do have survival value" (p. 46). "Average expectable," however, can only be what has evolved as universal in all human conditions, so that any healthy organism, any intact ego, and any adequate society can live by it—all three in mutual adaptation to each other. But no pseudo species can, by definition, be universal; in fact, it must take chances with man's adaptability for the very reason that each tends to over-emphasize selectively a unique combination of evolved human elements, giving play to selected instinctual and defensive extremes and, at the same time, trying to contain them in a specific style of adaptation. That such specialization tends to violate the limits of the "average expectable," thus exposing man to sickness, neurosis, and anomie —this, after all, is the crux of Freud's discovery. At any rate, the evolutionary rationale for a freely available quantity of instinctuality lies in the very fact that man, the "generalist animal," is born to invest relatively nonspecific drives in a specialized cultural universe, in which learning experiences and social encounters are to establish, during a long childhood, a special combination of mutuality, competence (White, 1963), and identity—all supported most affirmatively by appropriate ritualizations.

I say "most affirmatively" because, as we know only too well, the mere containment of instinctuality by the negative emphasis of moral prohibition and inner inhibition is apt to be as excessive and mal-adaptive as the drives which are meant to be counteracted. Could it be, then, that true ritualization represents a creative *formalization* which avoids both impulsive excess *and* compulsive self restriction, both social *anomie* and moralistic *coercion?* If so, we could see at least four vital functions served by the simplest ritualization worthy of that designation:

1. It binds instinctual energy into a pattern of mutuality, which bestows convincing simplicity on dangerously complex matters. As mother and infant meet in the first ritualization described so far, the infant contributes his searching needs, his drives as subsumed under "orality," and an inner capacity to have disparate experiences made coherent by proper mothering—a capacity which we may well consider the precondition for the ego. The mother in her postpartum state, however, is also needful in a complex manner: for whatever instinctive mothering she may be endowed with, and whatever instinctual gratification she may seek in being a mother, she needs to be a mother of a special kind and in a special way. This she becomes by no means without some anxious avoidance (sometimes outright phobic, often deeply superstitious) of "other" kinds and ways typical of persons or groups whom she more or less unconsciously dislikes, despises, or fears as godless or evil, unhealthy or immoral—and this can, of course, have come to include (wherever the generations themselves become pseudo species) some of the ways of those who, at one time, mothered her.

2. In permitting the mother to "be herself" and to be at the same time an obedient representative of a group ethos, ritualization protects her against the danger of instinctual arbitrariness and against the burden of a thousand small decisions. If, in Hartmann's classical formulation, "the normal ego must be *able* to control, but it must also be *able to must*" (p. 94), then one can well see that ritualization helps her to maintain this combination even with a sense of playful choice.

3. In establishing mutuality in the immediacy of early needs, ritualization also does the groundwork for lasting mutual identifications between adult and child from generation to generation. For the mother is reaffirmed in her identification with those who mothered her well; while her own version of motherhood is reaffirmed as benevolent by the increasing responsiveness of the infant. The infant, in turn, develops a benevolent self image (a certified narcissism, we may say) grounded in the recognition of an all-powerful and mostly benevolent (if at times experienced as malevolent) "Other."

4. Thus, ritualization also provides a first step for the gradual

development of an independent identity which in adolescence will be sealed by various rituals of "confirmation" representing a "second birth."

Early Childhood and the Judicious

Any ontological discourse suffers from the fact that it must begin to enumerate its guiding principles at the obscure beginning. The plausibility of first generalizations, therefore, remains dependent on the demonstration of their explanatory usefulness in later stages. The dimensions of ritualization suggested so far must now reappear on higher levels of mutuality between the growing person and that increasing number of adults with whom he becomes ready to interact. In each stage of development, we should be able to locate the affirmation of a new mutuality by a new form of ritualization, and this in the face of a new kind of estrangement. This ritualization, in turn, should contribute an essential element to adult ritual.

The best term for the second kind of human ritualization to be discussed would seem to be *judicial,* because it combines *jus* and *dicere,* "the law" and "the word." At any rate, the term should encompass methods by which the *discrimination between right and wrong* is ontologically established. The ontological origin of this second element is the second stage of life, early childhood, which is characterized by a growing psychosocial autonomy and by rapid advances in general development. But as *locomotion* serves increased autonomy, it also leads to the boundaries of the permissible; as *discrimination* sharpens, it also serves the perception of conduct which does or does not "look right" in the eyes of others; while *language development* (obviously one of the strongest bonds of a pseudo species) distinguishes with finite emphasis what has meaning in the verbalized world, and what remains outside, nameless, strange, *wrong.* All of this is given strong connotations by anal instinctuality and its eliminative and retentive emphasis. But there is also a new sense of estrangement: standing upright, the child realizes that he can suffer shame and lose face. Involuntarily giving himself away by blushing, he feels furiously isolated, realizing that he may be outcast if he does not cast out part of himself. His elders, in turn, feel compelled to utilize and thus to aggravate this trend. And yet, is it not again in the ritualization of approval and disapproval, in recurring situations of high symbolic meaning that the adult speaks as a mouthpiece of a supra-individual righteousness, damning the deed but not necessarily the doer?

I share, I am sure, with all anthropologists (professional and amateur) the astonishment with which one encounters "in the field" old people who will describe what is appropriate in their culture with a sense of moral and aesthetic rightness unquestionably sanctioned by the universe. Here is an example of what I was told among the Yurok Indians in Northern California, who depended on the salmon and its elusive ways (long hidden from naturalist observation) of migrating and propagating.

> . . . once upon a time, a Yurok meal was a veritable ceremony of self-restraint . . . a strict order of placement was maintained and the child was taught to eat in prescribed ways; for example, to put only a little food on the spoon, to take the spoon up to his mouth slowly, to put the spoon down while chewing the food—and above all, to think of becoming rich during the whole process. There was supposed to be silence during meals so that everybody could keep his thoughts concentrated on money and salmon. This ceremonial behavior may well have served to lift to the level of a kind of hallucination that nostalgic need for intake which may have been evoked by the early weaning from the breast [quite extraordinary among American Indians]. . . . Later, . . . [in] the "sweat house" the older boy will learn the dual feat of thinking of money and *not* thinking of women. [And the adult] Yurok could make himself see money hanging from trees and salmon swimming in the river during the off season, and he believed that this self-induced hallucinatory thought would bring action from the Providers [Erikson, 1963, p. 177].

This ceremonial style invested similar ritualizations along the whole course of Yurok life, for cultures (so we may remind ourselves in passing) attempt to give high coherence and continuity to the whole schedule of ritualization. While the example is an extreme one, coming from a culture with a special elaboration of compulsive potentials, it will be easily seen that all cultures have unofficial ritualizations—often hardly recognizable as such—which give special emphasis to rightness and wrongness and to ways of undoing wrongness already committed.

The judicial element of ritualization is differentiated from the first (the numinous) primarily by an emphasis on the *child's free will*. In the ritualizations of early infancy avoidances were the mother's task and responsibility; now the child himself is trained to "watch himself." To this end parents (and here the father and other men appear significantly as judges) compare him with what he might become if he (and they) did not watch out. Here, then, is the ontogenetic source of the "negative identity" which is so essential for the maintenance of a pseudo species for it embodies everything one is supposed *not* to be or to show—and what one yet potentially is. The negative identity furnishes explicit images of real or imaginary pseudo species (neighbors, enemies, witches, ghosts) which one must *not* resemble in order to have a chance of acceptance in one's own. Behind the dreaded traits are often images of what the parents themselves are trying not to be and therefore doubly fear the child might become, and thus *potential* traits which the child must learn to imagine in order to be able to avoid them. The self doubt and the hidden shame attached to the necessity of "eliminating" part of himself as well as the suppression of urges create in man a certain righteous rage which can turn parent against parent, parent against child, and the child against himself.

This is a sinister matter because it is the ontogenetic origin of the divided species. Moral self discrimination is sharpened by an indoctrination of hate against evil others, on whom the small child can project what he must negate in himself, and against whom he can turn that moralistic and sadistic prejudice which has become the greatest danger of the species man. Not only is "prejudice against himself" at the bottom of his proclivity for compulsive, obsessive, and depressive disorders. Irrational prejudice against others, if joined with mass panic, clumsy leadership, and modern weaponry, may yet mark the premature end of a species just on the verge of really becoming one.

At any rate, true ritualization on the level of the pseudo species appears again to be a supra-individual formalization of rules of conduct which help the adult to minimize the expression of ambivalence disguised as arbitrary righteousness, and help the child to "learn to must" in complying with demands which he can comprehend and in situations which he can manage. In its adult elaboration into a *judiciary procedure*, however, this judicious element is reaffirmed on a grand scale, making all-visible on the public stage what has developed in each individual as an inner process. The law is untiringly watchful as is, alas, our conscience. It locates a suitable culprit who, once in the dock, serves as "an example," on which a multitude can project their inner shame. The conflicting evidence which parades past the parental judge, the fraternal jury, and the chorus of public opinion matches the unceasing inner rumination with which we watch ourselves. Judgment, finally, is ceremoniously pronounced as based on sanctified agreement rather than on passing outrage or personal revenge; and where repentance is not strong enough to ask for punishment, the verdict will impose penalties for the culprit's "own good" (K. Erikson, 1966).

I trust it will not be necessary to demonstrate in detail the fact that both the ritualized establishment of boundaries of good and bad in childhood and the judiciary ritual in the adult world fulfill the criteria for ritualized procedures as suggested earlier: meaningful regularity; ceremonial attention to detail and to the total procedure; a sense of symbolic actuality surpassing the reality of each participant and of the deed itself; a mutual activation of all concerned (including, or so it is hoped, the confessing culprit); and a sense of indispensability so absolute that the need for the ritualization in question seems to be "instinctive" with men. And, indeed, the judicial element has become an indispensable part of man's phylogenetic adaptation as well as his ontogenetic development. It is hard to think of a ritual which does not include a judicial discrimination between the sanctioned and the out-of-bounds, the holy and the profane, the elect and the damned —to the Last Judgment.

In seeing the judicial element at work, however, in public and in private, we can also perceive where this form of ritualization fails in its adaptive function, and this means in the convincing transmission of boundaries from generation to generation. Failure is indicated where *fearful conformity* replaces free assent to what is felt to be right; where thus the *obsessively formalistic* becomes dominant over the convincingly ceremonial or where considered judgment is swamped by instinctual excess and becomes *moralistic sadism* or *sensational voyeurism*. All of this increases the hopeless isolation of the culprit and aggravates an impotent rage which can only make him more "shameless." Thus, the decay or perversion of ritual never creates an indifferent emptiness only, but always a void with explosive possibilities—a fact to which the theorists of social change have every reason to pay careful attention. For it explains why "nice" people who have lost the art of imparting values by meaningful ritualization can have children who become juvenile delinquents; and why church-going but ideologically inconsistent nations can so act as to arouse the suspicion of murderous and exploitive intent.

Here, again, the psychopathology of individual misfunction and of social anomie are closely related. The breakdown of judiciousness leads to an alternation of impulsivity and compulsivity, of excess and self-restriction, of anarchy and autocracy.

Childhood: The Dramatic and the Formal

I have now attempted to isolate two elements in human rituals which seem clearly grounded in ontogenetic stages of development. It seems important to reiterate that I am not suggesting a simple causal rela-tionship between the infantile stage and the adult institution, in the sense that adult rituals "only" satisfy persisting infantile needs in disguise; rather, they support (among other things) what Hartmann has called "adaptation by a detour through regression." The image of the Ancestor or of the God sought on a more mature level is by no means "only" a replica of the mother's inclined face or the father's powerful countenance; nor is the idea of Justice "only" an externali-zation of a childish bad conscience. Rather, man's epigenetic develop-ment assures that each of his distinct and protracted childhood stages specializes in one of the major elements (i.e., the numinous, the judi-cial) which hold together human institutions, each binding together a new set of instinctive patterns and of instinctual energies, of mental and of social capacities so as to assure the continuity of that element, throughout the individual's life and through the sequence of genera-tions. In all epigenetic development, however, a ritual element, once evolved, must be progressively reintegrated on each higher level, so that it will become an essential part of all subsequent stages. The numinous element, for example, reappears in judicial ritualizations and in judiciary rituals as the aura which attaches to a personified or abstract image of Justice, or to the concrete persons who as justices are invested with the symbolism and the power of that image. But this also means that neither the numinous nor the judicial elements, although they can dominate a particular stage or a particular institu-tion, can "make up" a ritual all by themselves: always, the whole inventory must be present. Of this inventory, we must still discuss the elements (and the ontogenetic sources) of *dramatic elaboration,* of *competence of performance,* and of *ideological commitment.*[2]

The *dramatic* element, I believe, is grounded in the maturational advances of the play age which permits the child first to manipulate available images and objects in solitary play, and then to join his peers in games which tend to have a *coherent plot, dramatic turns,* and a *climactic conclusion.*

While the second, the "judicial" stage was characterized by the internalization of the parental voice, the play-and-games age offers the child a microreality in which he can escape adult ritualization and prepare his role as future ritualizer. In play, he can now relive, correct, and recreate past experiences, and anticipate future roles and events with the spontaneity and repetitiveness which are part of all ritualization. His themes, however, are often dominated by the usurpation and impersonation of adult roles; wherefore the principal inner estrangement which finds both aggravation and resolution in play is the sense of *guilt.* One might think that this sense should be subsumed under the judicial sphere. Yet, guilt is an inescapable sense of self condemnation not restricted to the degree of public culpability. It does not even wait for the fantasied deed to be actually committed, or, if committed, to be known to others, or, if known, to be judged by them. In fact, as we have learned in "play therapy," there is a potential isolation in all solitary play which therefore—for all its inner wealth—does not qualify as a full-fledged ritualization except as it leads to playful communication, to the jointness of games, and —eventually, to the child's work, learning.

The *theater* is, of course, adult man's "play" and the theme of secret guilt and of potential total self-destruction or isolation dominates the great tragedies. In fact, the play on the toy stage and the plays enacted in official drama and magic ceremonial have certain themes in common which probably helped to induce Freud to give to the dominant "complex" of the play age the name of a tragic hero: Oedipus. That common theme is the conflict between hubris and guilt, between father murder and self sacrifice, between freedom and sin. The theater, then, has become the home of the *dramatic ritual;*

---

[2] At this point, it may be well for the interested reader to consult the epignetic chart (see p. 615). It reads from the top down, assigns to each element of ritualization a stage of psychosocial development, and lists in the bottom line the inventory of ritual elements discussed in this paper.

Suggested Elements in the

EPIGENESIS OF RITUALIZATION

	NUMINOUS	JUDICIAL	DRAMATIC	FORMAL	IDEOLOGICAL	GENERATIONAL SANCTION
Infancy	Mutuality of Recognition					
Early Childhood		Discrimination of Good and Bad				
Play Age			Dramatic Elaboration			
School Age				Rules of Performance		
Adolescence					Solidarity of Conviction	
Elements in Adult Rituals	NUMINOUS	JUDICIAL	DRAMATIC	FORMAL	IDEOLOGICAL	GENERATIONAL SANCTION

but it cannot do without the numinous and the judicial, even as they, in any given ritual, rite or ceremony, cannot dispense with the dramatic.

The psychopathology of the play age is the weight of excessive guilt in the isolated individual, his repression in thought, and his inhibition in action. This pathology is dramatically expressed in *Hamlet*, the tragedy of the *actor* (in every sense of the word) who tries to solve his inhibitive scruples by the invention of a *play within the play*, but only succeeds in preparing his perdition in and by it.

The *school age* adds another element to ritualization, that of *perfection of performance*. A binding discipline must hold all the other elements of the ritual mood and the ritual act to the minute sequence and arrangement which are indispensable to ceremonial magic. The mental and emotional capacity for such accuracy arises only in the school age; or rather, because it *can* arise then, children are sent to "schools." There, with varying abruptness, play is transformed into work, game into cooperation, and the freedom of imagination into the duty to give full attention to the details which add up to a satisfactory performance. Ritualization here encompasses the whole arrangement called "school," that is, the social interplay and the prescribed tasks which are structured according to the prevailing technology. This, I submit, is the ontogenetic source of that *formal aspect* of rituals which is so convincing to the senses and so supportive of the ego's active tension because it is *order perceived* and yet also *participated in*. But we also recognize in the perfection of the formal the danger of overformalization and of empty ceremonialism, the collective counterpart to the compulsive "ritual" of the neurotic, for both are aberrations in which true ritualization in our sense is lost.

Adolescence and Beyond: The Ideological and the Generational

The foregoing review has focused on some of the elements of "unofficial" ritualization in childhood. From here, one could continue in two directions, in that of further improvised ritualization or in that of planned ritual. One could follow the further ontogenetic trend of *unofficial* improvisations by which adolescents spontaneously ritualize their relations to each other and demarcate their generation as (slightly or decidedly) different both from the adult haves and the infantile have-nots. However, having emphasized throughout the elements contributed by earlier ritualizations to the formal rites and rituals of adulthood, I should now point out that it is in the formal rites of confirmation, induction, etc., that adolescing man is enjoined for the first time to become a full member of his pseudo species, and often of a special elite within it. All the elements developed in the ontogenetic sequence already discussed now become part of formal rites which add to the existing inventory the *ideological element*, that is, the element providing a coherence of ideas and ideals. Only now can man be said to be adult in the sense that he can devote himself to ritual purposes and can eventually be trusted to become the everyday ritualizer in his children's life.

What the ethologists describe as the reciprocal mechanisms by which adult and young animals *complete* the "instinctive" interplay of their respective inborn patterns can be said to be paralleled in man by no less than the *whole period of childhood and youth* sketched so far. To be fully grown in the human sense means the readiness to join not only the technology but also certain irreversible commitments to one's pseudo species; which also means to *exclude* (by moral repudiation, fanatic rebellion, or warfare) inimical identities and foreign ideologies. In a number of publications (1965a, 1966b) I have undertaken to delineate the emergence in youth of a sense of psychosocial identity and the readiness for the ideological style pervading the ritualizations of his culture. Only an integration of these two processes prepares youth for the alignment of its new strength with the preservation or the renewal of society. I have called the corresponding estrangement *identity confusion*. Clinically (i.e., in those so predisposed), this expresses itself in withdrawal or in lone-wolf delinquency; while it is often a matter of psychiatric, political, and legal definition whether and where borderline psychosis, criminality, or dangerous fanaticism may be said to exist. At any rate, the role of *spontaneous ritualization* in conformist as well as in extremist youth must be obvious. Much of youthful "demonstration" in private or in public represents a dramatization of a spontaneous search for new forms of artful or ideological ritualization invented by or for youth itself. Challenging and mocking, rarely riotous, and often deeply sincere, such new ritualizations attempt to counteract (sometimes with a romantic revival of past tunes and costumes) the meaninglessness of existing conventions—in our time, the impersonality of mass production, the vagueness of confessed values, and the intangibility of prospects for either individualized or truly communal existence. Above all, they show up the necessity to find entirely new forms of ritual meaning in a technology changing so rapidly that change becomes the period's ethos.

We have also witnessed in our time totalitarian attempts at involving new generations in organized mass rituals combining the numinous and the judicial, the dramatic and the precise in regimented gatherings on the largest scale. These seem to provide for masses of young individuals an ideological commitment encompassing perpetual revolutionary change and, in fact, marking all traditional (in the sense of prerevolutionary) values either as dialectic precursors of the future or as aspects of a decidedly negative identity.

I point to all this in the present context primarily because of a pervasive problem in all epigenesis: steps must not only be fitted to each other, they must also add up to a definite direction and perspective. In adolescence, previous development, present direction, and future perspective must jointly provide an ideological blueprint, and this for the sake of the adolescent ego (even in its struggle with sexuality) as well as for that of society. What is in question is, at the same time, the necessary coherence and continuity between childhood ritualization and pervasive technological and political trends, and the integration of a humanist past with the technological age now emerging worldwide.

We add the ideological element, then, to the numinous and the judicial, the dramatic and the formal elements of ontogenetic development. I cannot be sure, of course, that this is a complete list; it corresponds to the developmental stages which I have been able to discern. The game of demonstrating the joint presence (or to account for the absence) in any complete ritual of all these elements must be left to another occasion. But there remains one epigenetic issue which must find at least a tentative answer in this paper. The parents are the earliest ritualizers in their children's lives; at the same time, they are the consumers of the available rituals in which the ritualizations of their childhoods find an echo and a reaffirmation. What, then, is the prime contribution of adult ritual to the ontogenesis of ritualization? I think it gives *sanction* to adults to *become* ritualizers.

Marriage rituals, for example, provide for adult "strangers" the license to enter these new familial associations which will transmit tradition to the coming generation. I will recount here, as my final illustration, a wedding ceremony which took place not long ago in a small town in the French Alps; for "foreign" experience often reveals the nature of the familiar. Two young Americans were to be married. They faced the mayor; the tricolor was wound round his middle (which was soon to be regaled with ceremonial champagne). Above and behind him, le Général looked most distantly out of a framed color print into new greatness; and above him a white bust of l'Empereur stared vacantly into the future, the brow wrapped in laurel; while even higher up, the afternoon sun streamed through a window. In its light the mayor read phrases from a Code, to which a young bride from America could have agreed only with some reservations, had she fully understood them. Yet we few, in a foreign land, felt well taken care of, for the Western world shares many ceremonial values and procedures; and the couple accepted from the mayor a standard booklet which provided for the entry of the names and birth dates of a dozen children.

Whether the ceremonies of the adult years call on personal ancestors in the beyond or on culture heroes, on spirits or gods, on kings or leaders, or, indeed, on the sovereign creators of new ideas (who are ceremoniously quoted to justify newer ones), they sanction the adult in his double role as the agent of daily ritualization in the life of the younger generation and as the consumer, as it were, of those formalized rituals which integrate his own childhood ritualizations. We have, I think, overestimated the regressive component in such participation, that is, the insistence on being a child once more; and we have overlooked the importance to the adult ego of (to use Hartmann's term) a "detour through the archaic" in order to gather up the strands of re-progression to a higher level of integration, in the face of what remains forever unknown. The adult's mature needs include the need to be reinforced in his role of ritualizer, which means not more and not less than to be ready to become a numinous model (always endangered by ambivalence) in his children's and in the next generation's minds, and to act as a judge and the transmitter of traditional ideals or of innovating ideas. This last element in the ontogenetic series I would call the *generational*, which includes parental and instructive, productive, creative—and curative endeavors. The clinician encounters it every day in the form of transference.

Conclusion

In establishing a psychoanalytic rationale for the adaptive value of ritualization in man—corresponding to its survival value in animals—one becomes only too aware of the decrease of ritual reassurance from the ceremonial resources of a passing age. Fading rituals, however, may at this time be giving way to ritualizations of a new kind, dictated above all by new methods of communication and not always recognizable to the overtrained eye fixated on the cultural history of the past. Each era develops new forms of ritualization—technological and mercantile, political, professional, and intellectual—which establish an aura of sanctity, propriety, and necessity resting more on rationalization than on reason. The emerging world image is held together by the scientific ethos, the methods of mass communication, and the replacement of "ordained" authorities by an indefinite sequence of experts correcting and complementing each other. In viewing the over-all scene, and in searching for emerging ritualizations, we should not overlook the beginnings of a new professional ritualization which psychoanalysis has created at the gates of the unconscious both for the sake of her students and for that of her patients. Here, too, self analysis may lead to new insight.

In the future, new forms of numinous and judicial affirmation as well as of dramatic and aesthetic representation will probably come from a new spirit embodying an identification of the whole human species with itself and a universal sense of responsibility for each child planned and born. In the meantime, the transition compounds our estrangements, for could it not be that much of the ritualization discussed in this paper owes its inescapability to a period in mankind's evolution when the pseudo species was dominant? Will a more inclusive human identity do away with the necessity of reinforcing the identities and the prejudices of many pseudo species—even as a new and more universal ethic may make old moralisms obsolete?[3]

Here I must pay tribute once more to Heinz Hartmann who saw decades ago that the emergence of psychoanalysis in this period of history "does make possible a synthesis and a further development of adaptation-forms" (p. 70) and thus itself represents a step in hu-

[3] For one major example of creative ritualization in the modern era, namely, Gandhi's nonviolent technique (which has striking analogies to the pacific ritualization in the social animals), see Erikson (1965b).

man evolution. But he also warned that "At a certain level of development intelligence becomes aware of its own role as one function among others, sees its own activity in correct perspective among the other mental tendencies" (p. 69). The rationality of knowing, therefore, and of supporting reason as an organizing function, must not "lead to a disregard of the significance of the irrational" (p. 73). This significance, I would submit in conclusion, can also be seen in the arational and prerational way in which persons interdependent on each other create significant ritualizations.

At any rate, there can be no *prescription* for ritualization, for far from being merely repetitive or familiar in the sense of habituation, any true ritualization is ontogenetically grounded and yet pervaded with the spontaneity of surprise: it is an unexpected renewal of a recognizable order in potential chaos. It thus depends on that blending of surprise and recognition which is the soul of creativity, reborn out of the abyss of instinctual disorder, confusion of identity, and social anomie.

BIBLIOGRAPHY

Erikson, E. H. (1963), *Childhood and Society*, 2nd ed. NY: Norton.
—— (1964), *Insight and Responsibility*. NY: Norton.
—— (1965a), The Concept of Identity in Race Relations. *Daedalus.*
—— (1965b), Psychoanalysis and Ongoing History. *Am. J. Psychiat.*, 122:241-250.
—— (1966a), The Human Life Cycle. *International Encyclopedia of the Social Sciences*. NY: Crowell-Collier (in press).
—— (1966b), Identity, Psychosocial. *International Encyclopedia of the Social Sciences*. NY: Crowell-Collier (in press).
Erikson, K. T. (1966), *Wayward Puritans*. NY: Wiley.
Freud, S. (1933), New Introductory Lectures on Psycho-Analysis. *S.E.*, 22:3-182.
Hartmann, H. (1939), *Ego Psychology and the Problem of Adaptation*. NY: IUP, 1958.
Lorenz, K. (1964), *Das sogenannte Böse*. Vienna: Borotha-Schoeler.
Mayr, E. (1964), The Determinants of Evolution. *Proc. Nat. Acad. Sci.*, 51:834-841.
White, R. W. (1963), *Ego and Reality in Psychoanalytic Theory*. *Psychol. Issues*, 11.

Notes on Work

MARIE JAHODA

Christian mythology presents work as punishment for man's original sin. But throughout recorded history work has meant many things for many people: achievement, fulfillment, salvation as well as drudgery, degradation, damnation. The Protestant ethics of capitalism has made work an ultimate virtue; and without the benefit of religion communism rivals capitalism in its attitude to work. But notwithstanding official ideologies, people continue to love and hate their daily work, to be bored or excited by it, to dream of escaping from it or into it.

This limitation of the power of ideology over human feelings is, perhaps, not surprising. For, above all, work is a necessity, a condition of being alive. In its most global definition, work is the expenditure of energy; and even in the narrower sense in which work is used here as the actions in which people engage in order to make a living, it is ubiquitous in all known societies as the major activity, consuming most of the waking time of the vast majority of all individuals. The great utopias from Thomas Moore onward have not conceived of a world without work, but have used their imagination to change the conditions under which it was to be done.[1] Even the early Church Fathers could not imagine Paradise without work. They "were intrigued as to what Adam did before the fall; in the variety of speculations, none assumed he was idle. He devoted himself to gardening, 'the agreeable occupation of agriculture' said St. Augustine" (Bell, 1956).

[1] There is, perhaps, one exception: Grimm's Schlaraffia. However, the conditions of reaching this country where nobody has to work are truly forbidding even to imagination: one has to eat through a mountain of rice pudding! The moral of Grimm's story is to me that a life without work is not worth the effort.

With so universal a phenomenon found at all times in all cultures and even in man's dreams of a better society, attitudes to work must reflect the infinite variety of life in its meaning to individuals. Accordingly, when the human sciences came of age and in innumerable studies made work the subject of their researches, they produced a vast variety of approaches to it. Questions were asked about the conditions which make work satisfactory or unsatisfactory, how morale relates to productivity, how people choose their occupations and acquire the skills necessary for them, how wage incentives affect output, what workers want from their jobs, and so on.

If one surveys these studies, one is struck by their inconclusiveness, an inconclusiveness which defies efforts to summarize their results. To be sure, some naïve assumptions, still powerful in the "real" world, have been convincingly disproved. While people continue to believe that the industrial worker's main motive is the pay check, study after study has demonstrated that this is not the case. While early studies seemed to demonstrate that satisfaction with work leads to high productivity, later investigations have shown that there is no systematic relation between the two factors. While repetitive work as required in industrial production was assumed to be unsatisfactory by definition, there are many studies to show that it is highly satisfactory to some people. But with all the knowledge that has built up, the literature remains fragmented; so much so that Mason Haire (1954), a recognized expert, called the literature on the subject almost incomprehensible. "We know the strength of group-induced forces in restraining productivity, in policing a group culture, and the like, but we do not have the theoretical formulation to handle these phenomena adequately. The most glaring weakness is probably in the field of morale, where we are most abundantly supplied with empirical data. Here we are beginning to amass a body of information that is all but incomprehensible for the lack of good motivational theory."

In my own studies bearing on the meaning of work for the individual (Jahoda et al., 1933; Jahoda, 1942a, b, 1963), which have all the limitations that Haire criticizes in the literature, I was helped by an almost casual remark which Freud made in a footnote in *Civilization and Its Discontents* (1930, p. 80). He said that work is man's strongest tie to reality. This essay is an attempt to see whether the intellectual comfort that Freud's metapsychological statement had offered me in the past could be transformed into an explicit psychological approach to the study of the meaning of work for the individual.

Freud made his statement about the meaning of work at a stage when his thinking about reality had undergone several changes. According to Rapaport (1960), there are three distinguishable ways in which Freud thought about reality. At first his concern was with the role of reality in understanding his patients' symptoms and feelings. Reality, in that context, was the enemy interfering with the drives, against which a person defended himself as best he could. This idea is obviously far removed from his later statement about work. Freud's second conception of reality was based on the realization that drives needed real objects for discharge, and that human drives are more flexible in their relations to external objects than those of most animals. Put another way, human beings can make choices between external objects which satisfy their basic needs, and this fact implies that their ability to distinguish between such objects, i.e., their ability for reality testing, has a biological survival function; such reality testing depends on secondary thought processes which convey a "true" knowledge of the external world. This second idea differs from the first in an important aspect that bears on the meaning of work: in the first conception the pleasure principle and the reality principle are tendencies that pull in opposite directions. However, once it was clear that reality could perform a positive function in the discharge of drives, it was recognized that these two regulatory behavior principles need not be at odds with each other and at times could even pull in the same direction. This is an essential assumption if reality adaptation is to deal with both the pleasure and the pain of work.

But the full force of reality as a determinant of psychological functioning emerged only in the third stage, in which both drives and reality were accepted as motivating factors. The ego is now regarded as relatively independent of drives; hence, it is capable of objectivity with regard to reality; moreover, the ego is itself largely shaped by a person's contact with reality. It was in this last stage of conceptualization that Freud made his remark about work, with its clear implication that this strong tie to reality is a biological necessity, not just an economic necessity.

Freud's ideas on reality were emphasized, elaborated, and further developed by Hartmann (1939). A central idea in Hartmann's work is that the human organism has, through evolutionary processes, acquired adaptedness to reality, an adaptedness which in the course of ontogenetic development is further strengthened by processes of adaptation, largely based on secondary processes. Hartmann's major contribution to the subject is contained in his "Notes on the Reality Principle" (1956). Two ideas in this paper seem important for an understanding of the meaning of work. First, he states, "the pleasure principle itself has a history too . . . it is, of course, not the essential characteristics of the pleasure-unpleasure principle by which we define it (that is the striving for pleasure and avoiding of unpleasure) that change in the course of development; what does change are the conditions of pleasure and unpleasure" (p. 249). It follows that the pleasure principle is, as it were, dependent on the proper functioning of the reality principle. An individual who has not developed his "tendency to take into account in an adaptive way . . . whatever we consider the 'real' features of an object or a situation" (p. 244) (Hartmann's definition of the reality principle in its broad sense) will not be able to derive pleasure from his work situation or to avoid pain. He will be liable to accidents, he will make mistakes, he will not get a bonus or receive recognition for achievement and mastery.

The second important thought in Hartmann's essay is his distinction between different types of knowledge of reality. First, one can know about reality in a manner comparable to the methods of science, that is, by applying certain specified methods to discover whether external objects really behave as one thinks they do. Anybody who has ever observed a small child fitting blocks into each other will realize that this "scientific" knowledge of reality is not limited to the adult, let alone the adult scientist. A second type of knowledge of reality is what Hartmann calls "conventional" or "socialized" knowledge of reality. It stems not from the application of certain methods to the world around us, but from accepting views about the world. The child's first knowledge that the earth is round is, notwithstanding the good scientific evidence on that point, for him "conventional" knowledge: the teacher said so.

Hartmann distinguishes a third type of knowledge about reality; this is neither objectively validated knowledge nor acceptance of opinions about what is verified knowledge: it is the knowledge of the world of immediate experience. This is, perhaps, akin to what Kurt Lewin called the "life space" of a person.

The question now arises whether these concepts and ideas have the power of binding together some of the empirical research literature on work.

I shall begin by turning Freud's statement around: that is, if work is man's strongest tie to reality, then the absence of work should leave him less solidly in touch with reality. This is indeed the case, as several studies of unemployment have demonstrated. For example, in Marienthal, an Austrian village in which virtually the total population was unemployed as the result of the closing of its only factory during the depression in the early '30s, withdrawal from reality could be observed in a variety of manifestations. The unemployed men lost their sense of time. When asked at the end of a day what they had done during it, they were unable to describe their activities. "Real" time entered their descriptions at the biologically incisive points, getting up, eating, going to bed, but the rest was vague and nebulous. Activities such as fetching wood from the shed, which could not have consumed more than ten minutes, were recorded as if they had filled a morning. Yet the women complained that their menfolk were unpunctual for their meals. The men's waking day was shortened to twelve or thirteen hours. Rational budget planning, now if ever extremely important, was abandoned in favor of expenditure on trinkets, while essentials could not be paid for. Even though the unemployed had so much more time and newspapers were made available free of charge, they did not bother to read them, and the use of the local library dropped severely.

It would, of course, be foolish to say that these unemployed men had no knowledge of reality; on the contrary, they knew all too well the bitter reality of their economic situation, which was the reality of direct experience. They certainly had the conventional knowledge of reality acquired through a lifetime. What they were missing was the time and goal structures provided by their previous jobs, and the necessity to exercise continuous reality testing, the objective kind, in Hartmann's terms. What these men knew of reality put them in a situation comparable to patients who have to defend against reality (Freud's first notion). The world in which they lived did not permit the mutual reinforcement of pleasure and reality principles to which Hartmann drew attention. Their only choice was withdrawal. Their behavior recalls the experience of many old people who have retired from work.

It is at this point that a further development in psychoanalytic ego psychology helps to understand the situation of the unemployed. In *Ego Psychology and the Problems of Adaptation* Hartmann (1939, p. 46) emphasized that "The functions of all the mental and physical ego apparatuses mentioned can become secondarily sources of pleasure." This idea was elaborated in White's concept of competence when he says (1963, p. 188): "The objective stable world is . . . a construction based upon action. Knowledge about the environment is knowledge of the probable consequences of action." And he goes on to say that this active reality testing is gratifying in itself. This emphasis on the enjoyment that stems from continuous reality testing is perhaps most relevant to Hartmann's objective type of knowledge of reality. In the same way that the scientist needs to engage in action (including thought, of course) to acquire and enlarge knowledge, the ordinary man needs to put his objective knowledge continuously to the test of reality. He needs to experience consequences of his actions. Both conventional knowledge of reality and the reality of one's world of immediate experience are unavoidable; they are not acquired in deliberate action; they happen to man. Yet the unemployed suffered in these areas too. The world of their immediate experience was impoverished and lacked stimuli. Their previously acquired conventional knowledge of reality was, however, in one particular aspect in sharp contrast to their direct experience: their existence as unemployed could not be reconciled with a probably universal aspect of conventional knowledge which is supported both by objective knowledge and by immediate experience, i.e., man's existence is based on his interdependence with others; the purposes of any single individual are conceivable only through the existence of others; the combined purposes of men are greater and longer lasting in their consequences than any individual's life goal. As Freud said in that same footnote (1930, p. 80): "No other technique for the conduct of life attaches the individual so firmly to reality as laying emphasis on work; for his work at least gives him a secure place in a portion of reality, in the human community."

From this consideration of the psychological situation of the unemployed can be derived some major aspects of the manner in which work can tie a person to reality. They are: work strengthens the experience of the passing of time, an experience that is based on "organized action and thought" (Hartmann, 1956) and therefore closer to operations occurring on the level of the secondary process; work encourages the continuous action necessary to maintain objective knowledge of reality; work permits the pleasurable experience of competence; work adds to the store of conventional knowledge, in particular to the knowledge that men's purposes transcend man's; work provides enrichment of the world of immediate experience; work permits the mutual reinforcement of pleasure and reality principles as regulators of behavior, under conditions where infantile sources of pleasure are replaced by adult ones.

That men do indeed seek these elements in work becomes evident if one looks at the research literature, even though the more specific and limited purpose of each individual study does not permit the meaning of all these elements to be jointly demonstrated, as could be done for the unemployed whose total life situation was investigated. A few illustrative examples must suffice here.

1. Satisfaction in work is a function of the imposed time structure, so that satisfaction will be greater if the task prevents time experiences that are closer to primary processes.

Many investigators of industrial work on the shop floor (see, e.g., Wyatt and Langdon, 1937; Jahoda, 1942b; Klein, 1964) have pointed out that the manner in which time is experienced enters into a worker's satisfaction with his job. Workers prefer jobs which "pass time quickly" to jobs which do not. Conversely, a major resentment in industrial workers is created by having to wait for a job or tools, not only when they are on piecework but also on day work. As Wyatt et al. pointed out, boredom results when the task is so automatic that it cannot hold the attention of the worker. In other words, boredom in this case sets in because the job at hand does not provide sufficient stimuli and incentives to engage a person's secondary-process functioning and to sustain his attention cathexis. The actual time span for which an individual requires external structure will, of course, vary from individual to individual, depending on his equipment, abilities, and experience. Individual differences with regard to the amount of time a person can retain the attention cathexis necessary for reality orientation—in this case, job orientation—and avoid being flooded by fantasies are, according to Jaques (1956), the best indicators of levels of work.

The absence of adequate externally imposed time structures has probably much to do with the work difficulties many housewives experience when their children are grown up and when few things have to be done at a given time. Their wish for work outside the home even when economic need does not drive them to work is probably in part a recognition of the psychological support that derives from "regular hours."

2. Work will be experienced as more satisfying if it permits the experience of competence, i.e., the acquisition and testing of objective knowledge.

Many repetitive jobs in industry are unsatisfying, precisely because they do not provide an opportunity for the individual to test his skills. The entire discussion of different degrees of satisfaction among skilled and unskilled workers is relevant here. But the need for this particular type of relation to reality is so strong that workers use great ingenuity and wit in performing even unskilled work in a manner that permits them to see the consequences of their actions. Klein (1964) describes in detail the manner in which operators vary their task and speed, apparently in an effort to experience the consequences of their own actions.

Herzberg et al. (1959) conclude from a study of critical incidents which led to satisfaction or dissatisfaction in work that "the individual should have some measure of control over the way in which the job is done in order to realize a sense of achievement and of personal growth," a recommendation which is beginning to carry more weight in the organization of work than a mechanical efficiency concept which prescribes every motion. It is in keeping with people's need to realize their competence through action that these authors found that satisfaction was derived mostly from the task itself, while dissatisfaction stemmed from the conditions surrounding the task. Early time and motion studies seemed to indicate complete ignorance of the need for activity in reality testing. Yet Taylor, the originator of this approach to the organization of work, knew very well that his efficiency measures made any satisfaction in work impossible, as can be seen in a notation in his diary (quoted in Brown, 1954): "It's a horrid life for any man to live not being able to look any workman in the face without seeing hostility there, and a feeling that every man around you is your virtual enemy." And he wrote this after he had increased the workers' earnings by 60 per cent!

3. Satisfaction in work is a function of the degree to which it supports and enlarges the conventional knowledge which a person brings to the work situation.

While it is not easy to single out a specific research finding demonstrating how satisfaction in work is increased by obtaining knowledge that remains untested by the individual but is shared with others, virtually every single study implies this point. Descriptions of the discomfort experienced by a newcomer to a work situation who discovers that the others share norms and beliefs which are strange to him are relevant here. So is the practice in many companies of passing on information about their policies and plans even when these do not directly affect employees.

The bulk of conventional knowledge is, however, undoubtedly built up in direct informal contact between a person and his colleagues. Hence the actual content of that knowledge varies from working group to working group, and up and down the industrial hierarchy.

That it is difficult to quote more precise research findings on this point probably has to do with the casual informal way in which such knowledge is acquired. Direct questioning about satisfaction and dissatisfaction in work will therefore hardly ever elicit responses referring to it. Yet those concerned with the introduction of change neglect concern with these intangibles at their peril. Where the conventional knowledge acquired in a working group and shared by its members is not in keeping with a suggested change, resistance to this change will appear.

The knowledge of participating in an enterprise with a real purpose—Freud's link to the human community—is again demonstrable only by anecdotes. One factory manager reports that when he set a group of workers on a task of no consequence to production but disguised as such to deal with a temporary redundancy, the workers discovered his maneuver and responded with a colossal drop in morale. Engineering training sometimes proceeds via such fictitious jobs; they are resented by the trainees who want to learn while doing useful work; when trainees are, with the best intention of giving them an overview of the company, assigned to watch various departments for a week at a time, the response is frustration of a similar kind (Jahoda, 1963).

4. Motivation to work grows to the extent that work enriches a

person's direct experience of the world. This point is almost self-evident. Once again, the nature of many industrial tasks enriches the direct experience of a worker only in the initial stages when he learns the job. When he has mastered it, it is as a rule only the social side of industrial life which provides this particular tie to reality.

5. Satisfaction in work is in proportion to the extent that these various forms of reality testing lead to pleasurable experiences on an adult level. Freud, in that same footnote (1930, p. 80), makes this point when he says: "The possibility it [work] offers of displacing a large amount of libidinal components, whether narcissistic, aggressive or even erotic, on to professional work and on to the human relations connected with it lends it a value by no means second to what it enjoys as something indispensable to the preservation and justification of existence in society." This point foreshadows Hartmann's explicit statement about the compatibility of the pleasure and reality principles; here it raises the question: what sort of reality in a work situation will give rise to instinctual pleasure, not just the pleasure that derives from the experience of competence?

Needless to say, not every kind of work or working condition provides such pleasure, and one must assume considerable individual differences in this respect. Whatever it is that makes little boys want to be engine drivers, only some persons manage to combine this urge with the sane reality of adult working conditions. That the actual nature of work which civilized society requires is not always of a kind which permits pleasant gratifications, Fourier recognized in his socialist utopia, which was built on the idea that everyone would work according to his interest and inclination. This principle had him deeply worried about who in his dream society would do the sewage cleaning, until he hit upon the idea that this job would provide considerable pleasure to young boys.

There is some information on the nature of work which provides instinctual pleasure and pain under adult conditions. A recent study of some psychological factors which lead to success among managers in the durable household goods industry suggested that a man's unconscious attitude toward women may have something to do with the energy (and hence success) that he put into providing them with goods designed to ease their lives (Rogers, 1963).

On the negative side, a penetrating study of nursing (Menzies, 1960) has demonstrated that the nature of the nursing task is such that it often evokes powerful emotions which most people have not faced since early childhood when they learned to repress them. To deal as a daily routine with suffering, pain, anxiety, and death requires great emotional maturity, or the development of defense mechanisms which can easily warp the individual nurse or interfere with her task, or both, though the performance of her task is undoubtedly also sustained by the gratification of the specific motives which originally influenced her choice of profession.

Freud (1930, p. 80) thought that "Professional activity is a source of special satisfaction if it is a freely chosen one—if, that is to say, by means of sublimation it makes possible the use of existing inclinations, of persisting or constitutionally reinforced instinctual impulses." But he implied that this was a rare exception when he added: "The great majority of people only work under the stress of necessity." That sublimation in work may be a more widespread phenomenon than this remark suggests is in keeping with Hartmann's elaboration of this concept (1955); his suggested change in terminology from sublimated to neutralized energy leaves room for thinking about sublimation not only in terms of mankind's great achievements in science and art, but of a process which occurs in every human being at work.

To summarize: Freud's statement on work in conjunction with Hartmann's contribution thus fulfills one function of a useful theory: it binds together some empirical knowledge in the area of work. But a theory should also show the way toward the acquisition of further knowledge. Not that the first function is negligible; *post-factum* explanations are suspect only when they refer to a single set of data. Where they have the power to subsume a diversity of empirical findings, their usefulness can hardly be doubted. But what about the power of these ideas to predict behavior so that they can be verified or falsified by "real" events? This is crucial. For notwithstanding the power of the theory for summarizing research, it is possible that this agreeable function stems from the theory being too global. It might explain everything, which in the end means that it remains in the realm of metapsychology; a convenient way of thinking, but not inevitably or directly linked to evidence, of heuristic rather than predictive value. Psychoanalytic psychology has so often been accused of being just this and no more, that the question cannot be ignored. But neither can it be answered by speculative argument. Nobody has yet tried to put these ideas to a systematic empirical test. At this moment all I wish to claim for them is that they help to think in an area where "facts" are infinitely more numerous than thoughts.

BIBLIOGRAPHY

Bell, D. (1956), *Work and Its Discontents*. Boston: Beacon Pr.
Brown, J. A. C. (1954), *The Social Psychology of Industry*. London: Penguin.
Freud, S. (1930 [1929]), *Civilization and Its Discontents*. S.E., 21:59-145.
Haire, M. (1954), Industrial Social Psychology. *Handbook of Social Psychology*, ed. G. Lindzey. Cambridge: Addison-Wesley, 2:1104-1123.
Hartmann, H. (1939), *Ego Psychology and the Problem of Adaptation*. NY: IUP, 1958.
—————— (1955), Notes on the Theory of Sublimation. *Essays*, 215-240.
—————— (1956), Notes on the Reality Principle. *Essays*, 241-267.
Herzberg, F., Mausner, B., & Snyderman, B. B. (1959), *The Motivation to Work*. NY & London: Chapman & Hall.
Jahoda, M. (1942a), Incentives to Work. *Occup. Psychol.*, 16:20-30.
—————— (1942b), Some Socio-Psychological Problems of Factory Life. *Brit. J. Psychol.*, 31:191-206.
—————— (1963), *The Education of Technologists*. London: Tavistock.
—————— Lazarsfeld, P. F., & Zeisel, H. (1933), *Die Arbeitslosen von Marienthal*. Allensbach & Bonn: Verlag für Demoskopie, 2nd ed., 1960.
Jaques, E. (1956), *Measurement of Responsibility*. London: Tavistock.
Klein, L. (1964), *Multiproducts Ltd*. London: H.M.S.O.
Menzies, E. P. (1960), A Case-Study in the Functioning of Social Systems as a Defence against Anxiety. *Hum. Relat.*, 13:95-121.
Rapaport, D. (1960), *The Structure of Psychoanalytic Theory. Psychol. Issues*, 6.
Rogers, K. (1963), *Managers: Personality and Performance*. London: Tavistock.
White, R. W. (1963), *Ego and Reality in Psychoanalytic Theory. Psychol. Issues*, 11.
Wyatt, S. & Langdon, J. N. (1937), *Fatigue and Boredom in Repetitive Work* [Report No. 77, Industrial Health Research Board]. London: H.M.S.O.

Disturbances of Representation and Reference in Ego Deviations

VICTOR H. ROSEN, M.D.

> "Do you mean that you can find the answer to it [the riddle]?" said the March Hare. "Exactly so", said Alice. "Then you should say what you mean", the March Hare went on. "I do", Alice hastily replied, "at least I mean what I say, that's the same thing, you know." "Not the same thing a bit", said the Hatter. "Why, you might just as well say that I see what I eat is the same as I eat what I see."—CARROLL, 1865

This is a preliminary attempt to study the effect of ego deviations on language and to examine the possibility that some language distortions may be used to identify ego deviations. An effort will also be made to correlate current concepts of linguistic reference with Freud's theory (1915) of "word-thing" presentations. The problem is vast, encompassing the whole range of language and communication theory within its sphere. I shall deal with only a fragment of this material through the analysis of a few clinical examples of the relationship between ego deviations and disturbances of linguistic reference.

Hartmann (1951) refers to these problems in discussing the "Technical Implications of Ego Psychology." He says, "Finally, the influence of the superego on speech and language is familiar to us,

I am indebted to the members of a graduate study group in linguistics and psychoanalysis, which has been meeting for several years in the New York Psychoanalytic Institute, for the exchange of many of the ideas that have led to this discussion. A special debt of gratitude is owed to Dr. Henry Edelheit who has served as the secretary to this group and often as its mentor. Without his diligent spade work and constant stimulation we would not have been able to proceed. I am also indebted to Dr. Elise Wechsler Snyder for editorial revision and valuable suggestions concerning the content of the paper.

DISTURBANCES OF REPRESENTATION

especially from psychopathology. This is to say that the different aspects of speech and language, as described by psychologists and philosophers, become coherent and meaningful if viewed from the angle of our structural model, and that in this case actually all the structural implications have today become relevant for our handling of the analytic situation. In trying to clarify the technical aspects of the problem involved, we are actually following the lead of structural psychology" (p. 150).

Encouraged to associate freely, the patient frequently "misunderstands" these directions as license for ambiguous and obscure reference. Not only is this a misinterpretation of the "basic rule" by the patient, but it exposes the therapist to the possibility of a technical error if he does not make clear that an understanding of the manifest meaning of an utterance is usually necessary before an interpretation of the latent meaning is possible. One may suspect an "ego deviation"[1] or at least an unconscious defensive maneuver when the patient is consistently unable to make the "reference" of his utterance explicit. Furthermore, the multiple choices and ambiguities inherent in the internal structure of language afford unconscious intentions, fantasies, and conflicts various opportunities for linguistic expression. The individual's representation of self, object, and external world (Jacobson, 1964) determines in many cases the phonetic variant, the lexical alternatives, and the syntactic structures of words and sentences used in communicating ideas.[2]

Two extreme language phenomena encountered in the psychoanalytic situation cannot be understood simply as "defenses," but require a further examination of the language function itself. In one

---

[1] The term "ego deviation" (Beres, 1956) is used here instead of "defect" since it implies any departure from average expectations in ego functions, whether in the direction of decreased or increased effectiveness. Hyperfunctions of various kinds in one area may produce concomitant distortions in other sectors (Rosen, 1955, 1958).

[2] Roman Jakobson (1941, 1964), who studied linguistic aspects of aphasia, states that many different styles of discourse fall into two major categories. He says, "the development of a discourse may take place along two different semantic lines: one topic may lead to another either through their similarity or through their contiguity. The 'metaphoric' way would be the most appropriate term for the first case and the 'metonymic' way for the second, since they find their most condensed expression in metaphor and metonymy respectively. In aphasia one or the other of these two processes is restricted or totally blocked—an effect which makes the study of aphasia particularly illuminating for the linguist. In normal verbal behavior both processes are continually operative but careful observation will reveal that under the influence of cultural pattern, personality and verbal style, preference is given to one of the two processes over the other" (Jakobson and Halle, 1956, p. 76).

of these extreme forms of disturbed reference, the patient alludes to thoughts for which he cannot find adequate verbal expression and often assumes that they are too complex or too removed from shared experience to be verbalized. In the other extreme, words follow each other glibly and rapidly with few pauses and in bewildering profusion. One has the impression that the patient only knows what he is thinking by listening to what he says. This relationship between speech and thought was well summarized by an apocryphal elderly lady who, when asked her opinion about a certain matter, said that she did not know what it was until she heard what she had to say about it. Lewis Carroll's not-so-mad Hatter referred to the same problem.[3] Between the libidinized speech that is apparently empty of conceptual thought and the mental content that cannot be rendered in words lie a large variety of clinical phenomena which can be studied from a semantic viewpoint.

The process of communication in words, the one absolutely indispensable feature of psychoanalytic therapy, is itself often involved in the psychopathology that brings the patient to treatment. Part of the time consumed in any analysis is employed in developing a common vocabulary. When ordinary words cannot convey subtle idiosyncratic aspects of experience, despite a sufficient community of experience to share the idea if the right word or combination of words were available, difficulties in understanding arise. More often, however, the highly differentiated languages of man suffice for the communication of even the most uncommon event in the life of the individual (Sapir, 1921). Most commonly, the cause of disturbances in understanding the manifest meaning of an utterance lies in some distortion of the phonetic, syntactic, or semantic conventions of either the speaker's or the listener's linguistic code.

Ideally, when two individuals engaged in an ordinary dialogue[4]

---

[3] The word "mean" in this context may have several connotations. "I mean what I say" is usually construed as a statement of intention; i.e., you can count on my being reliable, rather than the more absurd implication that I speak before I think and then assume that what I have said is what I "really" think. Even in the more usual context, however, an individual who places a higher value on the spoken word for its own sake than on the semantic will sometimes carry out or defend an unintended statement simply because it "passed his lips."

[4] See Jakobson and Halle (1956) with regard to the six primary functions of language. "Ordinary dialogue" in this context would correspond to a dialogue that is devoted to a "referential" interchange in his terminology. These remarks would have to be radically qualified in the case of "poetic," "phatic," "conative," and "expressive" modes of communication. The sixth or "metalinguistic" category is also "referential" in that its reference is language itself.

are "on the same wave length," they know that the arbitrary meanings of the words they are using are the same, not only because they understand each other's idea, but also as a result of the opposite event. They know that they do not understand each other when the idea being expressed is unfamiliar as an experience, unfamiliar because of a logical ambiguity, or unfamiliar because a strange word is used or an unaccustomed meaning attached to a familiar word. Such a misunderstanding is often signaled by the listener's feeling that his attention has lapsed. At such times, the listener usually requests repetition of the statement. It is only when the repetition of the utterance fails to bring enlightenment, even with the aid of paraphrasing, word substitution, or examples, that the listener is sure that he has misunderstood or that the speaker has failed to make his meaning clear. When a speaker and listener are "on the same wave length," the meaning is clear to the listener, even when the experience described is recognized as an unfamiliar one.

In the "transference neuroses," the patient's referential utterances are usually unambiguous in their manifest content. Such precision in reference does not eliminate the possibility that some expressible thoughts are withheld and that some unconscious ideas are unavailable to language. The opposite case, typified by the florid psychoses, is one in which the language process is so severely disorganized that we know, without question and without the need for closer scrutiny, that failures of communication result from the use of unfamiliar language. In the frank "narcissistic neuroses," an understanding of the dynamics of the patient's illness through the communication of experience in terms of manifest meaning is largely an academic problem. We speak quite reasonably in these cases of "schizophrenic language," even though the phonetic and syntactic structure of the patient's speech may simulate the gross features of the communal language code. Initially, when confronted with the schizophrenic disorganization of language, the problem of understanding is similar to that of being faced with a foreigner speaking an unfamiliar language. In the case of the former, paralinguistic and kinesic behavior may suggest that, even after the code has been deciphered, communication of meaningful experience will not be easy because other problems in communication exist; while in the case of the normal foreigner, behavioral signals may reassure us that could we but speak the same language, we would find our thoughts easy to share. In neither case can we be certain of ideational congruence, until the varying code conventions are reconciled by mutual agreement or through the services of an interpreter. Both varieties of confusion—ideas disconnected from words and words disconnected from ideas—appear concurrently and serially in severe obsessional neuroses, borderline conditions, and those other syndromes which arise from deviations in ego functioning.[5] This same problem may arise as a result of the therapist's failure to realize the ambiguity of the task imposed on both the patient and the therapist when "thought," "language," and "speech" are not defined at the time free associations are requested. What we intend by the "basic rule" has yet to be formulated in linguistic terms. What does the patient understand when we ask him to tell us "all the thoughts that come to his mind" and fail to distinguish between "all the thoughts in his mind" from "all the words" that come to his tongue? Fortunately this distinction is usually unnecessary, but in some cases its absence becomes a severe obstacle to progress. It is also necessary to recognize some of the regressive effects upon communication that our technique per se imposes. When we ask a patient to relate, for example, his fantasies, in response to an accidental event in the analysis (such as a session canceled at the analyst's behest), he must resort to signal reactions, i.e., stereotypic possibilities arising from a single stimulus without the opportunity for cognitive discrimination. A disturbance of the secondary process should not be inferred from the character of such responses.

Freud was greatly interested in the problems of language. His early monograph on aphasia (1891) reveals his interest in the psychopathology of language. There are several specific references in his writings to the psychopathology of reference (1891, 1910, 1913, 1915). These are most succinctly summarized in the last of his metapsychological trilogy, the paper entitled "The Unconscious" (1915).

In this discussion of schizophrenic communication difficulties, Freud did not distinguish between "speech" and "language." When he stated, "In schizophrenics we observe—especially in the initial stages, which are so instructive—a number of changes in *speech*, some of which deserve to be regarded from a particular point of view"

---

[5] Both of these forms of semantic disturbance have been exploited as literary devices. In the "Theater of the Absurd," for example, Samuel Beckett's (1961) Winnie in *Happy Days* makes her "point" by a stream of verbigeration which appears to precede reflection, while Jonathan Rosepettle in Kopit's (1960) *Dad, Poor Dad . . .* conveys the oppressive influence on a boy's development of an overpowering and devouring mother through his inarticulate stammering and uncompleted sentences.

(p. 197), he seemed to have "language" in mind. He then described a peculiar disorganization of communication and some examples of literal interpretations of metaphor in psychotics. This phenomenon he called "organ speech" or "hypochondriacal speech." Freud then suggested that in schizophrenics, words are subjected to the same process which makes dream images out of latent dream thoughts. "They undergo condensation, and . . . transfer their cathexes to one another in their entirety" (p. 199). In pointing to the fact that the word in schizophrenia is used as if it had a primitive sexual symbolic reference, Freud concluded, "If we ask ourselves what it is that gives the character of strangeness to the substitutive formation and the symptom in schizophrenia, we eventually come to realize that it is the predominance of what has to do with words over what has to do with things" (p. 200). He believed that this substitution was the result of similarities between the words themselves, rather than between the things and a sexual part or object. "Where the two—word and thing—do not coincide, the formation of substitutes in schizophrenia deviates from that in the transference neuroses" (p. 201). The next paragraph is quoted *in extenso* since it represents the key to Freud's idea on meaning and its disturbance in schizophrenia.

If we now put this finding alongside the hypothesis that in schizophrenia object-cathexes are given up, we shall be obliged to modify the hypothesis by adding that the cathexis of the *word*-presentations of objects is retained. What we have permissibly called the conscious presentation of the object can now be split up into the presentation of the *word* and the presentation of the *thing;* the latter consists in the cathexis, if not of the direct memory-images of the thing, at least of remoter memory-traces derived from these. We now seem to know all at once what the difference is between a conscious and an unconscious presentation. The two are not, as we supposed, different registrations of the same content in different psychical localities, nor yet different functional states of cathexis in the same locality; but the conscious presentation comprises the presentation of the thing plus the presentation of the word belonging to it, while the unconscious presentation is the presentation of the thing alone. The system *Ucs.* contains the thing-cathexes of the objects, the first and true object-cathexes; the system *Pcs.* comes about by this thing-presentation being hypercathected through being linked with the word-presentations corresponding to it. It is these hypercathexes, we may suppose, that bring about a higher psychical organization and make it possible for the primary process to

be succeeded by the secondary process which is dominant in the *Pcs.*
Now, too, we are in a position to state precisely what it is that repression denies to the rejected presentation in the transference neuroses:
what it denies to the presentation is translation into words which shall
remain attached to the object. A presentation which is not put into
words, or a psychical act which is not hypercathected, remains thereafter in the *Ucs.* in a state of repression. [Freud further states:] Probably, however, thought proceeds in systems so far remote from the
original perceptual residues that they have no longer retained anything
of the qualities of those residues, and, in order to become conscious,
need to be reinforced by new qualities. Moreover, by being linked
with words, cathexes can be provided with quality even when they
represent only *relations* between presentations of objects and are thus
unable to derive any quality from perceptions. Such relations, which
become comprehensible only through words, form a major part of our
thought processes [p. 201f.].

Freud also suggests that it is the restitutive attempt in schizophrenia which brings about this state in which the word presentation
alone is cathected. In an attempt to regain the lost object, the ego
begins by cathecting the verbal part of it (the object) but then finds
itself obliged to be content with the word instead of the thing.

These formulations of the essential features of the disorganization
of the process of communication in schizophrenia have shed new light
on the meaning of psychotic utterances. In several respects, however,
Freud's hypotheses are ambiguous and too highly condensed to be
applicable to other aspects of normal, neurotic, and psychotic communication. There are four major ambiguities in Freud's formulations.
(1) He failed to distinguish between speech and language. (2) "Unconscious thing presentation" was never clearly defined. (3) He did
not relate the process of linkage of "word" and "thing presentation"
to the ontogenesis of language. (4) He did not note the preintellectual
speech processes or the preverbal thought processes and the part
they play in the development of language.

The first ambiguity has been studied extensively by the structural
linguists. They emphasize that both the intrinsic structure of language
as well as the mental processes that deal with it must be considered
in any attempt to explain disturbances of communication. Modern
linguists distinguish carefully between "speech" and "language."
"Speech" refers mainly to the acoustical forms of words and the

vocal-articulatory processes. "Language" is the mental representation of a complex learned code for communication. There are methods of communication that do not employ "speech" such as writing, Morse code, etc. These depend, however, upon the same "language" structure for their comprehension. Speech and language can, within certain limits, be independently disturbed, either by organic or functional processes.[6]

It is probable that Freud was using the term "speech" to mean "language" in his topographic formulation of "organ speech" in schizophrenia. There are, however, other problems unclarified by this distinction. In schizophrenia, for example, the relatively autonomous processes of speech and language might remain intact, and the communication difficulty might be the result of disturbance in their integration rather than in their intrinsic structure.

With regard to the "unconscious thing presentation," modern studies find little evidence that the conventional shared meaning of words in ordinary communications requires an image or "thing presentation." They depend rather upon concepts or referential categories. These meanings are based upon the identifying attributive features of classificatory schemata rather than upon images. In topographic terms, these schemata seem to have almost exclusively preconscious rather than conscious representations. It is probable that only some proper names of individuals or specific places have a "representation" as distinct from a "reference" which is attached to the acoustical image of the word. In schizophrenics who use many words divorced from their lexical meanings, it would *seem* to be the referential category rather than the "thing presentation" that loses its connection with the word; or the structure of the categories themselves is disturbed, perhaps as a result of a deviation in ego structure.

The third and fourth points raised with regard to Freud's formulation are intimately related. To postulate the presence of an "unconscious thing presentation" suggests that thought develops before language. Psychoanalytic constructions concerning early preoedipal phases refer regularly to preverbal thinking but rarely to preintellectual speaking. The work of some developmental psychologists presents fairly compelling reasons for considering both phenomena (Werner and Kaplan, 1963). Vygotsky (1934), for example, believes that

[6] For example, "language" may be quite intact in stuttering, while "speech" can remain relatively intact in aphasia.

thought and speech may have different roots. He adduces phylogenetic and ontogenetic reasons. The anthropoid apes display an intellect like man's in certain respects; for example, they employ tools in an embryonic fashion and have the beginning of a social organization. They are capable of emitting a wide variety of phonetic sound variations which they employ in a way similar to the expressive function of man. The close correspondence between thought and speech which has been defined as language is, however, absent. Vygotsky (1934) says, "In the phylogeny of thought and speech, a prelinguistic phase in the development of thought and a preintellectual phase in the development of speech are clearly discernible" (p. 41). Some observations of infant speech also suggest the existence of a prelinguistic phase of thinking and a prethought phase in the material of vocal and articulatory sound making. The child's activities at certain stages of development indicate an ability to conceptualize (as seen in the way in which he manipulates objects), but without the ability to describe the concept in words. At the same time the child may imitate words and even use sentences without communally valid referential implications.

During the phase of questioning, the child feels a need for meaning and tries actively to learn the signs attached to objects (Jakobson, 1941, 1960; Piaget, 1923; Ranken, 1963; Székely, 1962). As Vygotsky (1934) put it: "He seems to have discovered the symbolic function of words" (p. 43). Speech at this stage enters its intellectual phase and thought begins to acquire its linguistic aspects. "At this point the knot is tied for the problem of thought and language" (p. 43), and from this point on "thought becomes verbal and speech rational" (p. 44). Vygotsky (1934), Piaget (1923), and others (Werner and Kaplan, 1963) have suggested that this convergence in concept formation has successive nodal points, each one of which initiates a new and higher level of abstraction. The intrinsic structure of language may be expected to reflect concomitant ego functions.

Semantics is usually considered a subdivision of the field of semiotics or the theory of signs. It has two complementary models, much like the structural and topographic models of our own metapsychology. Both models are necessary for the investigation of meaning in language. The *referential* point of view is based upon the well-known "Ogden-Richards Triangle" (1923). The second, called the *operational* or *contextual* model, is less easily diagramed.

In the referential model of meaning, (1) the word symbol, (2) the concept or "reference," and (3) the "referent" ("thing," object, etc.) are schematized as the three apices of a triangle. The side of the triangle which indicates the relationship between the word symbol and the "reference" (or concept category) is often in classic semantics called the "name-sense complex." It is a learned, culturally determined relationship. The causal connections are the result of arbitrary convention and are shared by the members of the whole language community. Most linguists consider it the central issue in the question of manifest meaning. The line connecting the "referent" ("thing") and its "reference" is also considered a causal one. Unlike the first, it is largely determined by individual psychological events and the development, especially, of perception and cognition. The link between the word symbol and the "referent" is usually portrayed as a dotted line to indicate that the relationship is an imputed rather than a causal one (see Ullman, 1962).

Freud's model of the relationship of the conscious word with the thing presentation and the relationship depicted by the "semantic triangle" differ in the origin assigned to "meaning." Freud believed meaning was determined by the link between the word symbol and its "referent," while in the semantic model, a reciprocal relationship existing between the word symbol and its "reference" is called "meaning." This complex has its own relationship with the "thing" or "referent." In the reciprocal relationship between word and sense the experience of "meaning" is evoked by their mutual availability. Thus, a word symbol evokes a "reference" and a "reference" ("sense") evokes a word symbol. From this union, the basic semantic unit is born. Other reasons exist for assuming that the phonetic shape of the word is attached to a concept category rather than a "thing presentation." Such categories are partially determined by word networks established in most languages through synonym-homonym-antonym complexes (Ullman, 1962).

How are the "reference categories" formed which bring "name" and "sense" together in "meaning"? This is the meeting ground of structural linguistics and developmental psychology. Brown (1958) describes a hierarchical order of "reference categories" built upon the "criterial attributes" of the referent classes that are named. The semantic unit can be identified as (1) the linkage between the invariant distinctive features which constitute the acoustic form of a word with (2) certain "references" in certain contexts. Brown describes four general classes of such semantic categories. (1) *Simple categories:* These are words that are defined by a single criterial attribute, usually of sensory immediacy as in the experience of a primary color. (2) *Conjunctive categories:* Most nouns fall into this category. Here two or more criterial attributes, when conjoined, define a thing. (3) *Disjunctive categories:* These are words that refer to events that have different attributes but are linked in some way by their context, such as the rules of a game; then these categories are defined by the same word and have the same meaning despite their referential differences.[7] (4) *Relational categories:* This group consists of the terms which define the special relationship of one object to another in a "family" constellation. Unlike the "disjunctive category" in which arbitrary features are grouped under a common name, in relational categories the names of the objects are arbitrary but the context is determined by a natural order rather than arbitrary rules. This natural order, for example, would define the referents in the words "mother," "father," and "son" as members of a biologically determined family group.

In the second model of meaning, the operational or contextual, the true meaning of words is sought in what language does with them in ordinary operations. Wittgenstein (1922), for example, states that the "meaning" of a word is its "use in language." He likens the word to a tool or a piece in a game of chess. Equivalences are determined by word substitutions. Thus it can be shown that the verb "to be" is not a single semantic unit but has several meanings.[8] The "operationalist" asserts that the contextual meanings, discovered by this method, would remain obscure to those using the referential method. In the contextual model words are categorized like "lexical substitution counters" by the slot into which they fit. In practice, dictionaries employ both referential and contextual methods for defining words.

---

[7] An example given by Brown is a "strike" in baseball. Sometimes the batter does nothing and it is called a "strike." Sometimes he swings and misses the ball and it is called a "strike." Sometimes he swings and his bat connects with the ball, and it is still called a "strike." The categorization of these disjunctive events in this case is determined by, and can be known only through, the rules of the game of baseball.

Certain terms in analysis, such as "acting out," should be similarly considered as "disjunctive categories."

[8] For example, in the two sentences: "the violet *is* blue" and "twice three *is* six," the word "equals" can be substituted for "is" in the second sentence, but not in the first.

These investigations of the intrinsic structure of language and of the development of thought, speech, and meaning require some revision of our psychoanalytic model (of meaning). Such a revision might facilitate the construction of more precise schemata for the identification of the borderline or intermediate stages of disorders of reference. It is thought that secondary-process thinking emerges as delays in instinctual gratification lead to hallucinatory wish fulfillment in the form of images. The ability to distinguish between hallucinatory wish fulfillment and real gratification arises interdependently with the separation of the self from the object, and thus is related to the formation of self and object representations within the ego. In this formulation, words are seen as later forms of images (here, acoustical ones). They become, through association with the primary love object, linked in Freud's terms to the visual "thing presentation" (see also Werner and Kaplan, 1963). An alternative model conceptualizes a parallel development of primitive thought in the form of images and of speech sounds which have no referential connections. Piaget and Vygotsky suggest that language as a symbolic system does not arise until the two are joined by a crucial conceptual act at a certain stage in ego development. This is the model which postulates the progressive episodic convergence of more and more abstract categorical references (thought) with speech development. This concept seems to me to be better suited to explain some of our clinical observations.

The two forms of semantic disturbance—ideas without suitable words and words without formulated ideas—may be the result of a regression to both preverbal thought in the former and to preintellectual speech in the latter. A most extreme form occurs as an alternating phenomenon in some cases of catatonia (mutism and echolalia).

If language is a synthesis of thought and speech, a theory of language disturbance must also involve the synthetic function. In any dialogue, the speaker must simultaneously cathect and synthesize the following functions or objects: (1) the coding process of translating thought into language; (2) the self representation; (3) the representation of the object; (4) time, place, and purpose, or the environmental and social context. For the listener it is the decoding process or the translation of language into thought that is cathected, while 2, 3 and 4 are analogous to the same functions in the speaker. It is the synthetic function which organizes and integrates these various systems. In other words, in order to engage in a meaningful dialogue, the speaker and listener each need a common linguistic code, a sense of time, place and person, for the self and the other, along with an awareness of the phenomena about them.

The following is an attempt to extend the features of the apices of the "Ogden-Richards semantic triangle" to include these aspects of the communication process.[9]

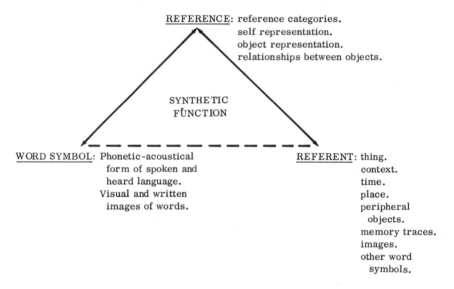

REFERENCE: reference categories.
self representation.
object representation.
relationships between objects.

SYNTHETIC
FUNCTION

WORD SYMBOL: Phonetic-acoustical
form of spoken and
heard language.
Visual and written
images of words.

REFERENT: thing.
context.
time.
place.
peripheral
objects.
memory traces.
images.
other word
symbols.

In this expanded semantic triangle, meaning is determined by the reciprocal evocation of word symbol and reference. Included in the "reference" are the lexical and syntactic features of conceptual categories, the personal identities of the speaker and listener, contextual awareness, and reciprocal interaction with the "referent" ("thing presentation").

The failure to integrate any of the items in the word, reference, referent, or representation, with the rest of the process will result in a semantic dislocation. The structure of several such confusions can be illustrated in terms of the "psycholinguistic" diagram. In each instance the ambiguity derives from a different aspect of the "meaning" complex and is related to the major unconscious conflict or to a distortion of ego function.

[9] The diagram is intended heuristically rather than definitively.

1. *Faulty word-reference integration in a disjunctive category in the service of ambivalence.* A wealthy middle-aged borderline woman was involved in an affair with an indigent, uneducated young man in a kind of Lady Chatterley relationship. Having to support him and to buy his clothes made her uncertain of the sincerity of his feelings for her. She was, however, ashamed to be seen with him in public in his unkempt clothing and wanted him to have an "ivy league" appearance which, she felt, would obscure the incongruity of their appearance together. Thus, against her will, she was forced not only to pay for his clothing but to select it herself since she could not rely upon his taste. One day she reported that she had been shopping for neckties for him, but had been unable to find what she wanted because they were all "too expensive." As she rarely questioned the cost of her purchases I asked what she meant by "too expensive." She was surprised by my question since she thought her meaning was self-evident. She was not short of money when she was shopping, the ties were of standard quality and price. I explained that the word "expensive" was usually employed relative to some standard such as one's budget, the average retail price, etc. To this, the patient remarked that she had suddenly become angry at what she was doing and did not *want* to buy ties for him any longer. Thus the word "expensive" acquired an idiosyncratic meaning. The price was too high in relation to her desire for the young man. In order to disguise her ambivalence toward her lover she employed a semantic shift. Referring to the ties as "too expensive" implied that although her desire for the ties remained unchanged, her feelings for her lover had undergone a reversal.[10]

2. *The affective connotations of a proper name in the service of confusion in identity.* The adolescent son of wealthy, first-generation Mediterranean parents had been sent to an aristocratic Eastern preparatory school. His parents' contradictory attitudes toward their cultural background and their own inability to decide whether to adhere to Old World or American customs had produced great confusion in the boy. There were two friends in his class whose favor and esteem he valued. One, L., a Jewish boy, was the ranking scholar

---

[10] In such patients, when there is a repetitive tendency to such ambiguous unreflective utterances, it is sometimes helpful to make a suggestion that may sound like the antithesis of the basic rule. The patient may be urged not to speak immediately but to organize the words in which he expresses his thoughts so that he is reasonably sure that they make his "meaning" clear.

of the class and admired by the patient for his intellect. The second, R., fair haired, of old American family, and Captain of the football team, was admired for his athletic ability and his social standing. On the patient's return from a winter vacation in Florida, a deep tan was superimposed upon his usual swarthy complexion. As he was standing at a school dance with his friend L. and their girl friends, he was approached by R. who said in the hearing of the rest, "Hello, Rastus, how is you all?" The patient replied, "I'se fine, massah." At this point his friend L. said in a low tone to the patient, "You disgust me," and walked away with his girl. The patient could not understand what had happened. L. was even more disgusted by the patient's failure to sense the nuances of the interchange than by the event itself. The patient became depressed and developed the following obsessional fantasy, "I wish I were a New England Yankee, a Jew or a Negro." The meaning of the fantasy became evident in treatment. Because of the patient's underlying sadomasochistic identity confusion and his uncertainty as to his place in the social strata of the school, he had not known whether the reference to "Rastus" was meant as the good-natured ribbing of an equal or as an insult flung at a denigrated inferior. The fantasy suggested that, if his identity could have been clarified, he would have understood the various implications of the incident. It was not until years later that he understood L.'s reaction as the response that is often elicited by one "victim" when another "victim" identifies himself with the "aggressor."

3. *Allusion in the service of faulty reality testing.* During consultation, a borderline patient referred to relatives and friends by various locutions such as "a close relative of mine" when she meant her husband. "A business acquaintance of long standing" was a reference to her employer. Later, as the result of a casual question of the patient, it became clear that she had misidentified a covered typewriter as a tape recorder. These allusive references were the result of misdirected discretion that fostered and served to rationalize her underlying paranoid tendencies, and perpetuated her poor discrimination of reality together with her inadequate object relations.

4. *Word-finding difficulties (pseudoanomia).* The inability to find an appropriate word occurs often during free association. The following incident demonstrates the role of empathic problems in a patient with a severe compulsive character disorder and a disturbance of object relations. The patient was an intelligent young graduate stu-

dent who did very well scholastically in those disciplines which did not place a premium on verbal skills. In spite of an excellent education, his verbal style had the "tough" quality of a teen-age gangster. His "toughness" was a defense against early castration anxieties and it precluded any sentimental, tender, or sympathetic references. On one occasion, he had great difficulty in finding the appropriate adjective to describe the quality of an article on addiction in a popular magazine. He derided his girl friend for reading the magazine piece and then turned his scorn on the narcotic addicts portrayed in it. Finally admitting that his attack was neither against his girl friend nor against the subjects of the article, he attempted to find an adjective that would convey his criticism of the writing itself. After much searching on his part, I offered the word "sensational" which the patient had been trying to evoke. The analysis of this small linguistic event indicated that some sympathy for the subjects of the article as "sick people" was a necessary prerequisite for finding the critical adjective for the magazine article. It was necessary to view them sympathetically as inappropriate objects for a side-show display to evoke the "criterial attributes" of the word "sensational." This admission of a "soft" attitude was prohibited by the patient's defense and thus inhibited his word-finding abilities.

In other patients in whom affect blocks, disturbances in orientation and confusion in self and object representations are found, similar disturbances of reference can be illustrated. The transference neurosis is particularly likely to evoke these latent tendencies. Disturbances of identity, ambivalence toward the object, and marginal defects in the testing of reality implicit in the psychoanalytic situation disturb the synthetic balance upon which the integrity of the semantic function depends. A regressive redistribution of cathectic energy between self representation, the representation of the object, and the "presentations" of the external world may become manifest in a semantic disturbance before other ego functions are recognizably involved. This disturbance of semantic function may in turn engender further regression with increasing language disorganization and subsequent involvement of other ego functions as the process extends in scope.

Most attempts to describe ego defects, to classify them, or to provide diagnostic criteria for their identification have dealt with functional disturbances of one or more of the elementary "ego functions." Beres (1956), for example, designates the functions of the ego under seven headings: (1) the testing of reality, (2) the regulation and control of the drives, (3) the mediation of the relationship of the self to objects, (4) thinking, (5) the defensive activities, (6) the autonomous processes, (7) the synthetic function. Most authors concur in general with this classification. Beres gives examples of disturbances in each of these functions which he considers to be symptomatic of ego deviation. As a diagnostic tool, this traditional procedure is often unsatisfactory. Except for gross disturbances of function which are obviously outside the range of "normal" behavior, it is difficult to establish sufficiently precise quantitative norms for such activities as reality testing, drive regulation, or object relationships to serve as reliable indicators of "ego disturbances" as distinct from neurotic symptoms. Thus such standards are impressionistic, vulnerable to subjective distortion and the influence of social value judgments which may substitute for the careful delineation of psychological norms. Nor can the clinician feel confident with these tests that his observations are primary rather than *post hoc* assumptions based upon a diagnosis already established from other signs. In many cases discussed in the literature, one wonders whether a given "borderline" phenomenon would be considered pathognomonic in the absence of obvious signs of severe psychopathology.

A delineation of specific types of language disturbances should provide less ambiguous signs of ego-deviational states. Reasons for the usefulness of such a tool may be summarized briefly. (1) The appearance of the ego as a psychic structure and the beginning of language development seem to be more or less simultaneous in the infant. There are undoubtedly important reciprocal relations between the two, making it likely that a disturbance in one during early developmental phases will be reflected in the other. (2) All the *functions* of the ego (as distinct from its apparatuses) (Hartmann, 1950a, b, c, 1951, 1952, 1953) must be investigated via the language function. Thus even the accuracy of our picture of the other functions of the ego is called into question when language itself is involved in the ego deviation. Furthermore, when one considers such ego functions as thinking, memory, reality testing, etc., it is difficult to separate them from their linguistic substrate. (3) Since the major function of language is communication, it has become the most carefully conventionalized and coded of all human activities. This results in a high degree of systematization of its form and a relative intolerance for idiosyncratic alteration in its internal structure. Thus, language retains invariant characteristics for the average members of a language community. Since, with language, the rules upon which the system is based and which govern its use may be formulated, a more objective assessment of impairment and a more microscopic measure of degrees of deviation from a known *external* standard is possible than in the study of impairment of other ego functions. (4) Object relations, whose disturbance is one of the key indicators of ego deviation, depend so much upon communication and therefore language, that it is difficult to imagine how the one can be impaired without concomitant disturbance in the other. While there is a considerable body of experience correlating ego deviations and grossly observable disturbances of language, the more microanalytic relationships between psychopathological states and various distortions of language in communication remain to be studied.

Greenson suggested the following characteristics of borderline psychopathology: (1) impulsivity, (2) confusions in identity and role, (3) severe affective disturbances, (4) disturbances of reality testing, (5) confusion between past and present, (6) reactions to part objects, (7) disturbed synthetic function, (8) exaggerated sexual and aggressive fantasies, (9) disturbed autonomous functions (see Rangell, 1955). In any patient, these characteristic borderline features may exist alone or in combination. Some linguistic correlates of these disturbances are the following. Impulsive patients frequently react to words as signs or signals rather than to the referential meanings of words (Michaels, 1959). Individuals with identity confusions may reveal their disturbance by pronoun transpositions, affectations of speech due to their propensity for imitation and role playing, and phonetic and stylistic peculiarities due to failure of the imitative process. Often these patients produce incomplete sentences or sentences with such syntactic errors as to make them all but incomprehensible. In such patients the confusion in identity results in a failure to maintain a clear separation between addressor and addressee. The speaker verbalizes his inner thought process without consideration for the addressee's confusion when he is called upon to decode the message. In instances where the choice of words or of word order to ensure clarity of reference depends upon an accurate appraisal of the context of the auditor, patients who distort reality or use massive denial may reveal their psychopathology (Stein, 1958). Patients with disturbed object relationships, especially those who react to a part object as if it were the whole, may have difficulty in using metaphor (Sharpe, 1940). Where empathy is required, these patients (see case 4) have difficulty in finding the correct modifiers for nouns and verbs. Disturbances of the synthetic function (Rosen, 1955, 1961) may reveal themselves in a variety of ways. Usually the larger units, such as the sentence or the paragraph, are involved. Written language may be involved more than speech. Often it is difficult to know whether the confusions between past and present, revealed in consistent distortions of tense, are the result of a disturbance primarily in thinking or in language. Finally, disturbed autonomies (such as memory or perceptual defects) may reveal themselves in functional aphasias, word-finding difficulties, and parapraxes of pronunciation, spelling, and grammar.

The formulations previously discussed and the clinical examples suggest that a revision of Freud's topographical model of language disturbance (particularly in the narcissistic disorders) would be of value. In such a revision along "structural" lines the term "manifest meaning" or "linguistic reference" could replace what Freud called the "word-thing presentation" in consciousness. "Reference" in normal language function is a synthetic product. It includes mnemic acoustical patterns of speech, syntactic structure, and conceptual categories of meaning, none of which are completely independent of the complex of self, object, and environmental representations in the ego. In this integrated structure, a disturbance of any one of the linguistic buttresses is felt in all other parts of the representation-reference system, and not only in the referential use of words whether in speaking or in understanding. Less crippling ego deviations than frank schizophrenic disorders give rise to language disturbances as a result of the simultaneous and reciprocal development of ego structures and of language (Glauber, 1944; Greenson, 1950; Kubie, 1934; Laffal, 1965; Lidz, 1963; Székely, 1962). Often such language disturbances are the presenting signs and the most sensitive indicators of the ego deviations themselves. "Semantic shifts" have diagnostic implications and can be an important technical aid to therapy when they are analyzed.

BIBLIOGRAPHY

Balkányi, C. (1964), On Verbalization. *Int. J. Psa.*, 45:64-74.

Beckett, S. (1961), *Happy Days*. NY: Grove Pr.

Beres, D. (1956), Ego Deviations and the Concept of Schizophrenia. *Psa. Study Ch.*, 11:164-235.

Brown, R. W. (1958), *Words and Things*. Glencoe: Free Pr.

Bühler, K. (1934), *Sprachtheorie*. Jena: Fischer.

Carroll, L. (1865), *Alice's Adventures in Wonderland*. Boston: Boston Books, 1932.

Cassirer, E. (1923), *Language and Myth*. NY: Harper, 1946.

De Saussure, F. (1916), *Cours de Linguistique*. Paris: Payot.

Freud, S. (1891), *On Aphasia*. NY: IUP, 1953.

—— (1910), The Antithetical Meaning of Primal Words. *S.E.*, 11:153-161.

—— (1913), *The Philological Interest of Psycho-Analysis*. S.E., 13:176-178.

—— (1915), The Unconscious. *S.E.*, 14:159-209.

Glauber, I. P. (1944), Speech Characteristics of Psychoneurotic Patients. *J. Speech Dis.*, 9:18-30.

Greenson, R. R. (1950), The Mother Tongue and the Mother. *Int. J. Psa.*, 31:18-23.

Hartmann, H. (1950a), The Application of Psychoanalytic Concepts to Social Science. *Essays*, 90-98.

—— (1950b), Psychoanalysis and Developmental Psychology. *Essays*, 99-112.

—— (1950c), Comments on the Psychoanalytic Theory of the Ego. *Essays*, 113-141.

—— (1951), Technical Implications of Ego Psychology. *Essays*, 142-154.

—— (1952), The Mutual Influences in the Development of Ego and Id. *Essays*, 155-181.

—— (1953), Contribution to the Metapsychology of Schizophrenia. *Essays*, 182-206.

Hochett, C. F. (1960), The Origins of Speech. *Sci. Amer.*, 203:88-96.

Jacobson, E. (1954), Contribution to the Metapsychology of Psychotic Identifications. *J. Am. Psa. Assn.*, 2:239-262.

—— (1959), Depersonalization. *J. Am. Psa. Assn.*, 7:581-610.

—— (1964), *The Self and the Object World*. NY: IUP.

Jakobson, R. (1941), Kindersprache, Aphasia und allgemeine Lautgesetze. *Uppsala Universitets årsskrift*, 1-83, 1942.

—— (1960), Why 'Mama' and 'Papa'? *Perspectives in Psychological Theory*, ed. B. Kaplan & S. Wapner. NY: IUP, 124-134.

—— (1964), Towards a Linguistic Typology of Aphasic Impairment. *Ciba Foundation Symposium on Disorders of Language*, ed. A. V. S. de Renck & M. O'Connor. London: Churchill.

—— & Halle, M. (1956), *Fundamentals of Language*. Hague: Monton.

Kopit, A. L. (1960), *Oh Dad Poor Dad, Momma's Hung You in the Closet and I'm Feeling so Sad*. NY: Hill & Wang.

Kubie, L. S. (1934), Body Symbolization and the Development of Language. *Psa. Q.*, 3:430-444.

Laffal, J. (1964), Freud's Theory of Language. *Psa. Q.*, 33:157-175.

—— (1965), *Pathological and Normal Language*. NY: Atherton Pr.

Lidz, T. (1963), *The Family and Human Adaptation*. NY: IUP.

Loewenstein, R. M. (1956), Some Remarks on the Role of Speech in Psycho-Analytic Technique. *Int. J. Psa.*, 37:460-468.

Michaels, J. J. (1959), Character Disorder and Acting upon Impulse. *Readings in Psychoanalytic Psychology*, ed. M. Levitt. NY: Appleton, 181-196.

Ogden, C. K. & Richards, I. (1923), *The Meaning of Meaning*. NY: Harcourt Brace, 1959.

Peller, L. E. (1964), Language and Its Prestages. *Bull. Phila. Assn. Psa.*, 14:55-76.

Piaget, J. (1923), *The Language and Thought of the Child*. London: Routledge & Kegan Paul, 1948.

Rangell, L. (1955), Report on Panel: The Borderline Case. *J. Am. Psa. Assn.*, 3:285-298.

Ranken, H. B. (1963), Language and Thinking. *Science*, 141:48-50.

Rosen, V. H. (1955), Strephosymbolia. *Psa. Study Ch.*, 10:83-99.

——— (1958), Abstract Thinking and Object Relations. *J. Am. Psa. Assn.*, 6:653-671.

——— (1961), The Relevance of 'Style' to Certain Aspects of Defence and the Synthetic Function of the Ego. *Int. J. Psa.*, 42:447-457.

Rycroft, C. (1958). An Enquiry into the Function of Words in the Psycho-Analytical Situation. *Int. J. Psa.*, 39:408-415.

Sapir, E. (1921), *Language*. NY: Harcourt Brace.

Seboek, T. A., ed. (1960), *Style in Language*. Cambridge: M.I.T. Pr.

Sharpe, E. F. (1940), Psycho-Physical Problems Revealed in Language. *Int. J. Psa.*, 21:201-213.

Stein, M. H. (1958), The Cliché. *J. Am. Psa. Assn.*, 6:263-277.

Székely, L. (1962), Meaning, Meaning Schemata, and Body Schemata in Thought. *Int. J. Psa.*, 43:297-305.

Ullman, S. (1962), *Semantics*. Oxford: Blackwell.

Vygotsky, L. S. (1934), *Thought and Language*. Cambridge: M.I.T. Pr., 1962.

Werner, H. & Kaplan, B. (1963), *Symbol Formation*. NY: Wiley.

Wittgenstein, L. (1922), *Philosophical Investigations*. Oxford: Univ. Pr., 1953.

On Nonsense

PHYLLIS GREENACRE, M.D.

I

This paper will deal with nonsense and its relation to aggression and anxiety. It draws largely on the study of the nonsense of Lewis Carroll's Wonderland and Looking Glass countries, and somewhat less on that of the nonsense rhymes of Edward Lear. But before discussing the nonsense of these two authors we must first approach the question of what we mean by nonsense anyway. Very many definitions of nonsense have been given by the various critics of this field of literature. Of these only a few will be mentioned.

Emile Caemmerts (1925) points out that the general opinion of nonsense is that it consists of anything which displeases you or any statement with which you emphatically disagree, and that there are as many different nonsenses as there are individual opinions, so that it would be a hopeless task to distinguish between them, or to attempt to draw up a list of them. He argues further that what is nonsense for one person is very often sense for another—similar to the situation of one man's meat being another man's poison. Someone else has remarked in regard to science fiction and scientific theory that yesterday's scientific nonsense becomes today's scientific sense. Be that as it may, Caemmerts introduces this view of multiple nonsense with a quotation from H. G. Wells's *Christina Alberta's Father*, which describes Mrs. Preemby's nonsense thus: "She said it was nonsense. And when your dear mother said it was nonsense, it only made things disagreeable if you agreed it was anything else."

Caemmerts then proceeds to give his own version of poetical nonsense, seeing it as arising from the same matrix as nursery rhymes, viz., the "innocent exuberance of childhood." He believes that writers of nonsense, referring especially to Lear, Carroll, and Kipling (and here it seems he stretches a point to include the *Just So Stories*), wrote their nonsense out of memory of this joyously restless state of childhood and to please child friends of later life. This point of view would certainly oppose the theory that many of the Mother Goose rhymes originated as slyly disguised political satires which only later were incorporated into the lore of childhood. But there is at least some disagreement from another angle, and I would point out that Lear did not have a happy childhood and felt burdened by the obligation to teach children later—gradually becoming somewhat irritable toward them. In his adult life their noise almost literally set his teeth on edge. And Carroll's friendly relationship to children, almost exclusively to little girls—for he had an open aversion to little boys—was an exceedingly complex one. "Stuff and Nonsense," or "Fiddlesticks," has a considerable excluding aggression in it, like Mrs. Preemby's declaration of nonsense. It is an attitude which may become playfully elaborated when it has gone through another stage of development, achieving some degree of emotional detachment. But Mrs. Preemby could never achieve this and so was always stuck with an argument.

Another writer, Elizabeth Sewall, an English philosopher dealing with the *Field of Nonsense* (1952), goes to considerable length to show that nonsense is an intellectual game with its own rules, and is really a manifestation of the mind's force toward order, and the establishment of order over a counterpull to disorder. Having a stance just the opposite of Mrs. Preemby's, she seems to take nonsense entirely away from any emotional connections. She sees in the extraordinary meticulousness of both Lear and Carroll only an indication of their spontaneous pleasure in "being that way," since they were not compelled by *external* events to behave in this fashion. She seems to see mental health and balance in terms of derangement or no derangement, and scouts the idea that there was emotional disturbance of any importance in either man, ignoring the painfully disturbing symptoms associated with Lear's severe epilepsy during his adult life, and his constant anxiety about money. The fact that neither man married or was known to have a sexual interest in any adult woman appears to her insignificant.[1] The nonsense of these men, she says, represents their sanity and reason. I shall return to look at this from a little different angle later.

Max Eastman (1936), looking at nonsense more from the angle of the effect of the finished product than from that of the process, says that nonsense is only effective if it pretends to make sense, i.e., if in some way it gives the illusion of being sensible. It appears, then, that part of its effectiveness has an element of the practical joke in it; one laughs at oneself for reaching for something that isn't there. Koestler (1964), who quotes Eastman and himself writes only briefly of nonsense, turns his attention at once then to tickling; and it seems possible that there is a connecting link between the two: both are threats that were only play after all.

This discussion will deal chiefly with the nonsense of Carroll in the *Alice* books, but will rely also on the *Hunting of the Snark* and the Songs of the Mad Gardener in *Sylvie and Bruno*. No one can talk about nonsense in any serious, sensible way, however, without considering the nonsense rhymes in the *Book of Nonsense* and *More Nonsense* by that master, Edward Lear. These two, Lear and Carroll, are certainly the outstanding professors and practitioners of nonsense. But here may we add the name of another literary man whose work would not generally be considered nonsensical at all, but only gruesome, eerie, and nightmarish. Yet his writings, especially *Metamorphosis, Amerika,* and *The Trial,* contain many of the ingredients of nonsense, without the detachment which permits comical effectiveness. I refer to Franz Kafka.

What do *we* mean by nonsense? Obviously, the word means no sense, i.e., without sense. This would seem to be clear enough. But

---

[1] Lear's ideas about marriage seemed to be part of his whimsey. According to Holbrook Jackson (who edited the 1950 edition of the complete works of Lear), Lear "puzzled over the problem of marriage in much the way he puzzled over so many things that are not quite obvious." At 41, thinking of marriage in the abstract at a time when he felt a renewal of energy and spirit after cutting two new teeth, he reflected that if he married he was sure he would paint less well, and besides the idea of an infant a year would make him frantic. He felt that he saw few happy marriages around him, and that marriage could not even be relied upon to be a corrective to the loneliness of old age. In Corfu at 50 he was wishing that he were married to a clever, good, nice, fat little Greek girl, and had twenty-five olive trees, some goats, and a house. And again he said that if he went to heaven, he would ask the polite angels to leave him alone, but after he had become established in the course of a million or two years, he might have an angel for a wife. In fact, he had the same man servant for thirty years, and the same cat for seventeen.

sense is not so clear-cut in meaning as one might at first think. *Sense* at once suggests the intellect and reason, and nonsense would then consist in words or actions which convey an absurd meaning or no meaning at all. But sense also refers to the ability to receive and to respond to stimuli. The senses considered as a total bodily function are distinguished from intellect and movement. Thus the word *sense-less* may mean unconscious, or it may refer to something unreasonable, foolish, and apparently meaningless in content. My scrutiny of the nonsense of Lear and Carroll will encompass both meanings of the word *sense*, for it seems to me that the intellect and reason emerge developmentally from the hinterland of the bodily senses, and that the separation of the two areas of functioning is never complete. This becomes more obvious with the examination of the content of the nonsense productions which critics like the philosophically minded Sewall would rule out of the field altogether.

It is an interesting fact that the term nonsense, except when said in a very emphatic tone of voice, is rarely applied to a production without some qualifying adjective. There is "just nonsense," "mere nonsense," "utter nonsense," "sheer nonsense," or, in the extreme, "absolute nonsense." These qualifying adjectives convey the subjective judgment of the spectator or listener, and go all the way from a relatively mild feeling: "I don't understand what you are talking about (or doing). It does not seem reasonable to me," to the extreme judgment of "absolute nonsense," implying: "What you are saying is so unheard of, so generally incomprehensible, that it disturbs me unbearably unless I think that no one can be expected to understand it." Now, absolute nonsense, with the meaning of a complete elimination of any kind of coherence or even cohesiveness of content, and associated with an inability to receive or respond to stimuli from others—the elimination of any degree of relationship whatsoever would mean such a state of disorganization and psychophysical disintegration as to be scarcely compatible with life itself. Like its extreme opposite, absolute perfection, it then becomes static, isolated, and approaches lifelessness. When Lear speaks of his rhymes as "absolute and pure nonsense"—as he does in the introduction to the book *More Nonsense* (1872)—he is using the phrase not to indicate the degree of nonsensical quality, but rather to indicate that his nonsense does not contain any hidden attack on any specific individuals or any sly political satire.

II

In studying nonsense from the productions of Lear and Carroll, we have to realize further that neither of these men could possibly have come very close to absolute nonsense, not only because of the practical inaccessibility of that chaotic, disorganized, anarchic state except for a babbling idiot incapable of writing or of definite language formation; but because both Lear and Carroll were gifted men, perhaps men of genius. This in itself gives an obligatory inner organization with some extra capacity for rhythm and patterning both in awareness and in execution. Absolute nonsense is incapable of representing itself.

The garden variety of judgment of nonsense may represent the frame of mind of the spectator or listener rather than having much to do with the product itself. Thus, as in Mrs. Preemby's case, it may show rather the antipathy of prejudice with an *accompanying* aggressive wish to rid oneself of the disquieting intrusion. The aggression then may be largely on the part of the spectator, although it is felt by him as a justified reaction to the aggressively nonsensical intruder who must be banished. But with Lear and Carroll, the object of the nonsense and the subjective audience are essentially the same person—the author of it. The public is only taken in by accident, as it were.

Lear was a painter of considerable ability, and Carroll was a mathematician and an Oxford don, although trained to be a clergyman. Neither made the writing of nonsense his primary profession, and both were puzzled or even annoyed at winning fame more through their nonsense than through their serious professions. Charles L. Dodgson, the Oxford don, was so annoyed, in fact, that at one time he disclaimed knowledge of Lewis Carroll and refused to receive mail directed to Carroll at his, Mr. Dodgson's, address. Carroll's nonsense works have been translated into some thirty to forty different languages, and it is reported that in English-speaking countries the *Alice* books rank next to the Bible in the frequency with which they are quoted. Almost the whole world knows some, at least, of Lear's rhymes, though relatively few know anything of his painting.

III

The form of the work of the two men is rather different, although the ingredients of nonsense contained in it are strikingly similar. Lear was probably best known for his rhymes in the *Book of Nonsense* and *More Nonsense*. In these books the rhymes were entirely in the limerick form, in which there is usually a single verse consisting of five lines, rhyming *aabba*, with the third and fourth lines half the length of the others. This verse form, usually facetious in content, and at least in some way related to doggeral, anagrams, punning riddles, and even charades, had originated in England about 1820, i.e., when Lear was 8 years old, and had a certain vogue in his young manhood. The continued popularity of the limerick seems to have been sustained, however, by Lear's indefatigable productions. The term *Limerick* was not applied until 1898, ten years after Lear's death.

Lear wrote some songs not in limerick form, of which *The Owl and the Pussycat* is probably the best known. He also wrote a few very short stories for children and several nonsense alphabets. All of these were greatly enhanced by his own illustrations, which are more captivating than his words. At 34 (1846) he published his *Book of Nonsense* containing 112 nonsense verses. These show a certain uniformity of structure and content. In all of them the third and fourth lines are combined into a single line contracting the verse to a four-line outline. The last line is generally an actual or approximate repetition of the first. This has a soothing, letting-down effect rather than the stimulating effect of the punch line so common in limericks. Many of the verses begin: "There was an old man of Crete . . ." (or some other place). Proper names of individuals are never intruded; it appears as though the person were hardly an individual, but only to be seen as part of the place. Most of the rhymes are mildly comforting in content, in that they offer nonsensical answers to ridiculous dilemmas or infirmities (which are understated or overstated, but not presented in reasonable proportions). The last line goes back to a repetition of the first, as though to say: "Well, that's the way it was anyway." For example:

> There was an old Person of Annerley
> Whose conduct was strange and unmannerly;
> He rushed down the Strand, with a Pig in each hand,
> But returned in the evening to Annerley.

or:

> There was an old Person of Spain,
> Who hated all trouble and pain;
> So he sat in a chair with his feet in the air,
> That umbrageous Old Person of Spain.

One has meandered a bit, but after all nothing has changed.

In 84 of the 112 rhymes in the *Book of Nonsense*, the rhymes have to do with old men who are generally (57 of the 84 times) referred to as "There was an old man of . . . ," but in 27 the central character is referred to only as an "Old Person," and the rest of the limerick shows him to be an old man. Never once does he make a young man or a boy the main character of a rhyme. In 28 of the 84 limericks, the central figure is female, who (in 21 of these 28 verses) is referred to gallantly as a "Young Lady," and in two as a "Young Person." Once he introduces a "Young Girl," and there is one Old Person who turns out to be female rather than male. There are three Old Ladies in the galaxy. His gallantry toward the female sex is in his words rather than in his drawings, which show many of them as misshapen old creatures. All of his characters, male and female, tend to be restless persons, as he himself was, and seem to be dashing about with their elongated arms and legs so flung out that they seem in danger of becoming detached from the body. On the other hand, there is not the same emphasis on the cutting off or spontaneous loss of a body part as occurs in the *Alice* books of Carroll, and is seen in purest culture in the German *Struwwelpeter*. One young lady loses her head and one male loses his thumbs. Lear's ladies often have big noses and sharp chins, like the one of the rhyme:

> There was a young lady whose chin,
> Resembled the point of a pin;
> So she made it sharp, and purchased a harp
> And played several tunes with her chin.

And they do not often redeem themselves by their behavior. Daughters especially seem to be trials or at least irritations rather than comforts to their parents.

Lear became known for his *Book of Nonsense*, which is supposed to have been written for the children of the Earl of Derby into whose household Lear came as an illustrator for the Earl's considerable ornithological collection. But the Earl and then the whole family of the House of Derby served as Lear's patrons, so that during his long life Lear was to know the benefit of patronage of four generations of Earls. A dedication dated 1862 is to the great-grandchildren, grand-nephews, and grandnieces of Edward, 13th Earl of Derby, but he puts in parentheses: "The greater part of which were originally composed for their parents." This is a slightly ambiguous statement, and Lear's relationship to children was complicated by his pathological sensitivity to the noise from which he was frequently trying to escape. While in Corfu, he wrote that he was much distressed by people next door who had twin babies and played the violin, but one of the twins died and the other had eaten the fiddle—so peace was again established. His sensitive nerves were always aroused by young women practicing singing or violin playing, and in those nonsense rhymes which do deal with young ladies, there is the repetition of the young lady playing on a harp with sufficient frequency to make one wonder whether one of his many sisters intruded on him in this way in his childhood.

In 1871, twenty-five years after the *Book of Nonsense* first appeared, Lear published, at the age of 59, *Nonsense Songs, Stories, Botany and Alphabets;* and in the next years, *More Nonsense, Pictures, Rhymes, Botany etc.* In 1877, at 65, he brought out *Laughable Lyrics, a Fourth Book of Nonsense Poems, Songs, Botany and Music, etc.;* while in 1895, seven years after his death, *Nonsense Songs and Stories* appeared. It would seem that as he grew older he became more reconciled to or philosophical about being famous as a writer of non-sense rather than as a painter.

When one examines the "one hundred nonsense pictures and rhymes" of the *More Nonsense* volume, it turns out that there are only 96 of the nonsense rhymes. The rhymes are limericks having much the same, almost stereotyped form as the first batch had had twenty-five years earlier. No young men and no girls appear in this *More Nonsense* group. Men are not designated as "Old Man" as often (only 33 out of 96 possibilities) but are referred to as "Old Person" (42 out of the 96), who is shown to be male by the rest of the rhyme and the drawing. "Old Person" is also applied more frequently to his female characters and fewer of the latter are dubbed "Young Lady" (only 5 in the 96 verses; as in contrast to 21 out of the 112 in the first series). On the other hand, "Young Person" is the designation for 10 young women and is not used at all for young men. If we can draw any conclusions at all from this kind of analysis, it would be to say that as he got older Lear tended to think of those around him even more as persons than as male and female.

In his limericks in general, even though they were dedicated to children, he did not deal with children but with adults. His appeal to children was not through presenting pictures of their adventures or antics, but rather through lampooning adults—often thinly disguised versions of himself—for the children, and making the lampooning foolish or nonsensical enough to take the sting out of any irritability he may have felt toward them. He thought of himself as "an old cove," and once referred to himself as a frisky and energetic old cove. He once confessed that with few exceptions he found all human beings awful idiots. But one gets the impression from his journals and his letters that at least some adults could be quiet and this he appreciated. Here one remembers that Lear was the next to the youngest of twenty-one children and must really have been subjected to a great amount of varied stimulation. It has seemed to me that Lear may never have felt quite at home in the world—as a child feeling like an older person and as a man feeling like a child. I cannot quite agree with Holbrook Jackson (1950) that his rhymes and his drawings are sexless. The drawings especially show rather the perpetual preoccupation with sex in one who feels shut out from its enjoyment.

Lear's underlying sensitivity was very great indeed and may have been part of his creativity as well as associated with his epilepsy and possibly secondarily with his severe and chronic asthma. He was conscious of being influenced to an extreme by everything in natural and physical life, i.e., atmosphere, light, shadow, and all the varieties of day and night. He wondered whether it was a blessing or the contrary but decided that "things must be as they may and the best is to make the best of what happens." One feels that this is what he is unconsciously aiming at in his nonsense limericks—temporarily and repetitively to insensitize himself by laughing at his infirmities so that he may get back to his real work of painting. The lack of real joyousness in Lear's limericks is conspicuous. It is only when he deals with animals or with inanimate objects which he animates that he can let go in joyous fun rather than in the fun of the comic in his nonsense. The latter tends to have a reduction and an attack in it—surely often primarily against himself—*even* though he over and over again attains a kind of recovery through bringing the last line back to the first. If one compares the mood of the nonsense limericks with the joyousness of the love affair of the owl and the pussycat or the flirtatious walk of the table and the chair who danced on their heads till they toddled to their beds, one realizes that something was probably felt as dangerous in the relations between human beings.

Lear's stories are relatively few, are short, and do contain children as characters. The chief one is the story of four little children who went around the world. They are personalized to the extent of having names and definite sexes: Violet, Slingsby, Guy, and Lionel. There is a certain amount of play with reversals as in the case of an island of water surrounded by earth and a great gulf stream that runs over evanescent isthmuses. There is some play with alliterative and rhyming words and a few coined words, but the whole story is more at the level of the absurd than the nonsensical.

The vehicle of Carroll's nonsense is quite different from Lear's, for Carroll was known primarily for his stories, especially the *Alice* stories. These are interlarded with rhymes and nonsense poetry, but he seldom uses the single verse, except for the Songs of the Mad Gardener in *Sylvie and Bruno*, and he does not use the *aabba* form (the limerick) as Lear did. Many of his poems are parodies and all abound in original word forms—for Carroll was a master at these bumptious creations and has contributed more to the English language than even Lear did. His verses are more elaborate, more sprightly, and do not show any of Lear's tendency to stick to one form in an almost stereotyped way.

In each of the *Alice* stories there is a central theme, though it is almost lost sight of in the nonsensical meanderings of its pursuits. According to Carroll, Alice is a little girl of 7½, though she talks and acts more like a prepuberty child of 9. The aim of Alice's adventures in the first book is to find a secret subterranean garden, toward which she has been led by her curiosity in following a white rabbit, dressed as a gentleman, whom she sees as he disappears into a hole in the ground. In the pursuit of this goal she wanders through a wonderland confused and bewildered. She is never quite sure who she is and time itself is quite mixed up and runs one way and another. In fact, nothing, not even ideas and knowledge, remains reliable. She thinks of bats in connection with rats and mice and then finds herself in a confused doubting "Do rats eat bats? Do bats eat cats?" and a little later she is wondering whether she is herself or Ada who has ringlets or Mabel who is rather stupid. She is constantly growing up or shrinking down and is fearful that she may go out like the flame of a candle, but what is the flame like after it is out? She encounters animals who behave like human beings and human beings who behave like savages. Her hands and feet grow so large and distant that they seem to have identities separate from her own, and she considers sending a letter in order to communicate with her right foot, but realizes that she is talking nonsense. Her voice is so strangely hoarse that it too hardly belongs to her. There are many tears in Wonderland, and once the diminutive Alice nearly drowns in a pool of tears wept by Alice the Great. In general, however, she maintains a somewhat addled philosophical poise through all the faultfinding, bickering, and threats of open savagery. Decapitation is the favorite threat of those in power.

No one laughs much. But the Cheshire cat grins in his superior fashion since he can withstand decapitation by allowing his own body to disappear leaving his grinning head, which in turn fades with the grin, the last part to go. The story begins by Alice being bored at the book her sister is reading to her until she drops to sleep, and dropping to sleep with boredom, even in the thick of an argument, remains one of the retreats of minor character in the tale. At one point, when with a spurt of growth Alice finds herself so large that the room will no longer contain her and she is pressed against all its sides, she considers that when she is (really) grown up she will write a book about herself describing all this. This evidently is the task undertaken then by Lewis Carroll, even though Alice herself could not decide whether it was better to risk growing up to old womanhood or remaining young and doing other people's bidding, even that of cats and rabbits. Then again in a diminished phase when she is very small indeed, she gets into an argument with a caterpillar who, seated on a toadstool smoking a hookah, defends the idea that metamorphous changes need not be upsetting. He admonishes her to curb her temper and directs her to recite that erotically suggestive rhyme about Father William. Soon she is growing so big again that a wandering pigeon mistakes her elongated neck for a serpent.

In her protest that she is only a little girl (and she has jiggled herself small again) she continues to look for the secret garden, and then comes to a diminutive house in the wood. Here she encounters a grotesque version of maternity, in a ferocious duchess who is impatiently nursing her baby while she sings "Speak roughly to your little boy . . ." as she is anxious to be off to a croquet game with the Queen. Complete pandemonium soon reigns. The baby's nose is cut off by a flying saucepan hurled by an enraged cook. The baby himself is thrown into Alice's arms, but quickly turns into a pig and runs off into the woods. The Cheshire cat appears or disappears, as the case may be, and directs Alice to the Mad Hatter, who quickly lands her in the Mad Tea Party, all of whose members are male. She is no better off here, for all her remarks are turned around and used against her until she doesn't know the meaning of anything she has said. The Hatter's remarks seemed to have no sort of meaning at all and yet certainly were in English. (Here Alice certainly seems to agree with Max Eastman's views about effective nonsense.) Confusion is piled on confusion. Time and size are mixed up individually and together. Alice is accused of having beaten Time in her music lessons, and the Hatter is threatened with decapitation for having murdered Time. But in the end Alice does find the door to the secret garden and enters.

This, the royal garden, is as chaotically angry a place as the Duchess's kitchen had been. A rampageous croquet game is in progress. All humans, regardless of sex, age, or rank, look exactly alike from the rear, as they are really animated playing cards. The balls and the mallets, however, are animals who contribute to the general anarchy by doing whatever they please while the Queen threatens decapitation to anyone who displeases her. The Cheshire cat materializes out of his grin and escapes execution, though the King argues that anything that has a head can be beheaded, and the Queen threatens to execute everyone unless a way can be found to execute the cat. The game ends with everyone, even the wickets, being taken into custody, leaving Alice alone with the King and Queen while the King whispers a pardon to all whom the Queen has executed or imprisoned. Alice is taken in charge by the Gryphon, a hideous composite of lion, eagle, and dragon, who explains to her that the executions are only the Queen's fancy. "They never execute anybody you know." After an interlude of a satirical and whimsically nonsensical discussion of education with the Gryphon and the Mock Turtle (who suffers from sorrow which is only fancy since he is only a *mock* turtle and the source of Mock turtle soup), the messily confused day ends in a trial. The King with the Queen by his side is an uneasy judge fearful lest his own crown may fall off. The Knave of Hearts is being tried for stealing tarts. But execution is threatened to nervous witnesses and then for good measure to nonnervous ones as well. A general atmosphere of execution prevails.

Alice feels herself suddenly growing up, getting too big for all this nonsense. When she at last is called as a witness she has so far outgrown any trepidation that she tips over the jury box with the edge of her skirt and has to pick up the spilled jurors and return them to the box for the trial to go on. Alice's testimony that she knew nothing whatsoever about the business is considered important or unimportant, as the case may be, until an argument arises about it, and Alice herself is ordered out of the court as being too high and mighty. But before she leaves, an incriminating bit of evidence against the knave is discovered in an unsigned set of verses not in the knave's handwriting which prove beyond the shadow of a doubt that the knave is a dishonest man. For why else would he have not signed his name and further gone to the trouble of imitating someone else's handwriting! Alice declares that the verses have not one atom of meaning in them, but the Queen demands the sentence first and the evidence later, while the King thinks that he detects some meaning somewhere. Alice, now full size, declares the whole thing stuff and nonsense, while the Queen shrieks, "Off with her head," and Alice retorts, "Who cares for you, you are nothing but a pack of cards!" Whereupon they all rise up in the air and come flying down at her. She wakes to find her sister brushing away dead leaves that have fluttered into her face. And in the epilogue, when Alice tells her sister the dream, she herself begins to dream Alice's dream and then, half awake, muses that this little sister of hers will soon be a grown woman with children of her own.

I shall not go to as much length in describing *Alice Through the Looking Glass*. It is a less spontaneous production and seems more consciously contrived than *Wonderland*, almost as though Alice herself had become a little more settled. It too is played against the background of a game involving a royal family, the game of chess in which the characters are now three- rather than two-dimensional, and the sexes can be distinguished even from the rear. Alice's aim in this game is to become a queen. There is not quite as much riotous confusion as in *Wonderland*, but the bipolarity of constant doubt is paramount. Many experiences appear in opposites, and many characters are in pairs: Alice and her mirror image, the black kitten and the white one, the Red King and Queen, and the White King and Queen, Tweedledum and Tweedledee, Haigha and Hatta, etc. Alice's size does not change so much as was true in *Wonderland*, but the creatures around her are often outsized, especially the insects; and space and time have a way of extending and contracting themselves that is bewildering.

In the end Alice does find a crown on her head, but her maturity is at once challenged by the Red and White Queens, who then succumb to the fatigue of their own arguments and fall asleep on her shoulder. In the last scene, a coronation banquet is given for Alice who arrives late and is scolded like a bad child. Nothing can be eaten, however, as the food is all animated, and the various dishes behave like guests as soon as they are introduced to Alice. The whole party ends in a riot with the White Queen disappearing into the soup tureen, while the mutton sits in a chair. Alice and all the plates and the candles fly up in the air while the guests lie down in the remaining dishes. Alice completes the destruction by pulling the tablecloth off and dumping everything left onto the floor. She again awoke to find it all a dream.

The Red Queen whom she thought she was scolding for having instigated the mischief turned out to be the Black Kitten whom she had been admonishing for tangling up the yarn at the time she had gone to sleep. In talking to the Black Kitten (alias the Red Queen) Alice gives a valuable clue to the meaning of all this nonsense, when she says, "Let us consider, who it was dreamed it all. You see Kitty, it must have been either me or the Red King. He was part of my dream—but then I was part of his dream too. *Was* it the Red King, Kitty? You were his wife, my dear, so you ought to know—*do* help to settle it!" It may be worth noting, too, that in *Wonderland*, Dinah (Alice's cat) does not actually appear unless we are to consider her reincarnated as the Cheshire cat—and there is no mention of kittens. In the *Looking Glass* world, it is Alice's play with the kittens that initiates her adventurous exploration. Perhaps we may guess that the kittens or the thoughts of kittens have arrived in Alice's life between *Wonderland* and *Looking Glass*. But I shall have more to say of content later.

Carroll's nonsense rhymes are quite different from Lear's in form. They are generally interspersed through his stories, and many among them are parodies. He did not use the *aabba* rhyme form;[2] and his single-verse rhymes, appearing mostly as the Songs of the Mad Gardener in *Sylvie and Bruno,* achieve a comical effect largely through the utter incongruity of the fused pictures and ideas presented.

Thus the rhymes:

> He thought he saw an Elephant
> That practiced on a fife.
> He looked again and found it was
> A letter from his wife.
> 'At length, I realize,' he said
> 'The bitterness of Life!'

or:

> He thought he saw an Argument
> That proved he was the Pope:
> He looked again and found it was
> A bar of Mottled Soap.
> 'A fact so dread,' he faintly said
> 'Extinguishes all hope!'

> (from *Sylvie and Bruno*)

These rhymes spoof the dilemma, critical though it may be, by making it ridiculous, and the rhythm and utter absurdity of the solution have a stimulating, almost staccato effect. This is different from the returning monotony of Lear's last lines in his limericks and is also in contrast to the word distortions and creations of new words which reach their height in the *Jabberwocky*. This is not only written backward in mirror writing, but it contains twenty-six newly coined words in its five stanzas.

[2] There is one exception to this—a verse addressed to one of his little girl favorites, Miss Vera Beringer. It runs as follows:

> There was a young lady of station,
> "I love man" was her sole exclamation;
> But when men cried, "You flatter,"
> She replied, "Oh! no matter
> Isle of Man is the true explanation."

Here the punch is obviously in the last line in contrast to Lear's form.

It is interesting to see that in the *Complete Works of Lewis Carroll*, introduction by Alexander Woollcott (1936), this is headed "A Limerick." According to other authorities, the term *limerick* did not come into use until 1898, and Carroll died on January 14, 1898. The limerick form *aabba* had been popular, however, since the early nineteenth century.

IV

What are the ingredients in the picture of nonsense? The feeling of nonsense materialized by Lear and Carroll has a general background of confusion against which a central bewildered explorer struggles with the problems of life. One aspect of the main problem is that of maintaining a sense of his own identity. With this in jeopardy, there can be no definite decision about which course to take, what road to pursue, or even whether to move forward, go backward, or attempt to stay where he is. This uncertainty of the identity is felt variously not only concerning the self and the own body, but also about all the elements (animate and inanimate) of the environment, which are generally anthropomorphized as well. Activity is the order of every situation, as is shown endlessly in Lear's drawings and in Carroll's prose. This multiplies the confusion since no one—whether Alice or the animals she meets or the path she travels—seems able to keep straight who or what he is; is supposed to be doing; or how it can be done. Even the words get out of hand and cannot be relied upon. A variety of verbal switches are utilized with punning based on klang associations, alliterations, spoonerisms, malapropisms, portmanteau condensations, neologisms, etc. Humpty-Dumpty tries to master words by making them mean whatever he wants them to, but very often, in the struggle, the words themselves win out and seem to go their own way.[3] In other words, even words lose their identity in losing their uniqueness of form and meaning, and seem to run off in various directions. Sometimes the word self-consciously maintains two opposite meanings (as indeed may be the case even with well-behaved words), but in the *Looking Glass* especially, opposites seem like nearly identical twins who are bound in an eternal wrangle as in the case of Tweedledum and Tweedledee.

The portmanteau word is a descriptive phrase originating with Carroll, who applies it to a combination of a number of words in one single one which contains at least the remnants of them all. Thus just as the *snark* is a monstrous combination of animals, so the word itself, like a composite photograph, contains snake, shark, snail, and probably

---

[3] Humpty-Dumpty would also take liberties with body configurations; it is he who suggests to Alice that she cannot be distinguished from others, as her features are arranged like everyone else's; "Now, if you had the two eyes on the same side of the nose for instance—or the mouth at the top—that would be some help in identifying you."

many others. *Jabberwocky*, too, is such a portmanteau word, designating a terrifying animal composed of several others. There is one word play used by both Carroll and Lear which has never been given a special name. It consists in the snapping off the end of one word and adding it to the word next to it. Thus in *Jabberwocky*, the "slithy toves did gyre and gimble in the wabe." As it is explained later, *wabe* comes from "*way-be*fore" and "*way-be*hind" the sundial in the garden. Lear spoke of a "sill kankerchief," "a nempty stomach," etc. But he was in any case an inveterate tamperer with words, combining phonetic spelling with colloquialism in a way which may make sense to the ear but is grotesquely unfamiliar, when printed, to greet the eye.

A certain compulsiveness appears in Lear's punning, for his journals and letters are heavy with it. To me, at least, it becomes tiresome in its monotonous cuteness, as though it were a repetitive plea not to be taken seriously, and not to be held responsible. In *Looking Glass* in which accusation and trial seem always in the air (and the trial has actually taken place in *Wonderland*) the compulsive nature of the punning is clearly indicated. While Alice finds herself riding in a railroad carriage over the chessboard of life with a variety of animals dressed as humans, as fellow travelers, she hears a hoarse voice down the car a way and thinks to herself that it sounds like a horse. At the same time a very small voice close to her ear says, "You might make a joke of that—something about 'horse' and 'hoarse' you know." When presently she wishes that she could go back to the wood she has just left, the same little voice echoed, "You might make a joke on *that*, something about 'you would if you could, you know.' " It was a gnat that had lodged in her ear and was directing her travels punwise. And just as a bee she had seen only a while ago had become an elephant diving into enormous flowers with his great proboscis, so the gnat flew into a tree and became the size of a chicken.

Tampered-with words resulting in distortions of their form and meaning are obviously closely bound up with problems of their identity, whether these have to do with flora,[4] fauna, or the human species,

---

[4] Lear's *Nonsense Botany*, illustrated, includes "small tooth-combia Domestica," "Phatfacia Stupendia," "Many peeplia Upidownia" as well as other rare flowers; while the Garden Live Flowers in the *Looking Glass* world is guarded by a tree which has a protective bark and whose branches are called *bough-woughs*. Both Lear and Carroll have a playful time with snapdragons and tiger lilies. Insects seem to loom large to both, and both have the experience of seeing dishes and tableware rise up in the air in sportive love or anger. And so it goes.

and involve in turn changes in size and apparent distortions of part or all of the body. Gross changes in size overtake Alice and many of the animals whom she encounters. But since these change individually rather than in an epidemic wave, there are many discrepancies and incongruities. In Lear's rhymes and stories there are more distortions of body shape with accentuation or a practical loss of some body part than changes which involve the entire body. There is not the same fluidity of form as occurs in Carroll's productions. In Lear indeed the body distortions are much more apparent in the drawings than in the rhymes.

The basic sexual identity of the characters is maintained at least in outline by both nonsense writers. Alice does not change into a boy, nor does she behave like a boy; and there is no frank change from one sex to the other as there is in Thorne Smith's stories or in *Orlando*. But there is a thinly disguised set of sexual problems in Alice's quest for the secret garden and for queenship. Her dilemma is rather: "What does it mean to grow up, be a woman and have children? How do the two sexes really get together? Is it after all an enviable state to be grown up?" At times it is as though she were saying, "What is happening to my body anyway? It is getting out of hand in its demands on me, and I can't stop it, or can I?" Older people whether men or women are, on the whole, unappetizing and as unpredictable as children in Alice's worlds. But one must remember that Carroll was next to the oldest of eleven children, and a crowded parsonage may well have been tempestuous. In Lear's drawings, many of the men have enormous heads and large bellies, but spindly arms and legs that wave like banners in the breeze. His women are nearly always thin, boardlike creatures with sharp noses, chins, and long pointed toes.

Lear much more openly than Carroll indicated his feeling of inadequacy as a man. Carroll seemed to side-step masculine goals in many ways and identify with the prepuberty girl who was doubtful but inquisitive about growing up.[5] In some of Lear's rhymes, one about a man is followed by one about a woman, with very obvious comparisons, but clear-cut contrasts are evaded. For example:

> There was an Old Man with a beard
> Who said, 'It is just as I feared!—

[5] In my book on *Swift and Carroll* (1955) I have examined the life story and concluded that Carroll probably had an unusually close relationship and identification with his sister, Louisa.

> Two Owls and a Hen, four Larks and a Wren
> Have all built their nests in my beard!'

and:

> There was a Young Lady whose bonnet
> Came untied when the birds sate upon it;
> But she said 'I don't care! All the birds in the air
> Are welcome to sit on my bonnet.'

A last major ingredient of the nonsense picture, and one which is also part of the identity complex, has to do with the loss of body parts, either in actual fact or threatened as accident or punishment. In Lear's rhymes this is a less frequent occurrence than it is in Carroll's writings. Lear describes the Old Man of the Nile who loses his thumbs as the result of sharpening his nails with a file, and another old man who just escapes catastrophe when he is offered a hatchet with which to kill a flea that is biting him sorely. Then there is the famous Pobble that has no toes, as well as one young person who loses her head by its being fanned off by a too-attentive uncle. Lear also works this theme of loss in reverse in his accentuation or enlargement of body parts and members. It is perhaps most dramatic in his nonsense song of the Dong who fell in love with a Jumbly girl and so grieved when she sailed away and left him that what little sense he had in his head also left him. Consequently, as he wandered disconsolately over the world hunting her, to light his way at night he made an artificial nose with a luminous light on its end, which served as a beacon. He became celebrated then as the Dong with the Luminous Nose.

Lear's "nonsense" pictures of body mutilations and compensatory exaggerations are readily recognizable by anyone familiar with the psychology of the unconscious as expressions of severe castration fear which is being expressed directly or in an extreme form of denial.

In the *Alice* books, this is presented differently. Decapitation and extinction by fading out are more frequent threats than those of damage to or loss of a body part. To be sure the baby does lose its nose, sliced off by a flying pan; and the extinction of the Cheshire cat proceeds bit by bit rather than through a massive fading. Decapitation in a less corporeal form is suggested too by Alice's recurrent fear of loss of memory even of her own name and whereabouts, so that she is frequently testing her own mental functioning.

V

It is not my intention to go into a very extensive or detailed interpretation of the thematic content of the nonsense productions of Carroll and Lear. I have attempted this somewhat, for Carroll's stories and nonsense poems in an earlier work (1955). The thread of the stories in the *Alice* books shows quite clearly the major crises of growing up, with attempts to solve the problems of sexual identity and identification. But the fears of castration and annihilation are so vivid and repetitive as to suggest chronic anxiety of panic proportions. All this is in the general setting of oedipal guilt; but is complicated by the persistence of infantile rage in the case of Carroll,[6] and by real epileptic attacks in Lear. What is striking, however, is that the situations which might produce panic are presented in so exaggerated and confused a way as to appear ridiculous. The panic is quickly muted. The beheading is anticipated on the scale of the French Revolution or worse, only actually "They never behead anyone," and it is all in the Queen's mind anyway. Certainly the sadistic aggression, which is a component of all anxiety and especially of that arising in anticipation of cruelty, is then compounded and directed against the self in guilt— the conscience is on a veritable rampage, until the voice of reason steps in and says, "This is all mental, a dream, a game." In this sense Sewall is right—that with the ability to get some distance, the force of reason prevails over the destructive forces. This control by the rarified counteraggression of reason—the superiority of the mind over primitive instincts—is personified by the Cheshire cat sitting aloft, grinning a superior (rather than a merry) grin, which is the last to go.

But there may be another determinant in the fear of beheadment, to be found in the nature of extreme rage. The enraged person then

---

[6] About the time of puberty or early adolescence, the boy Charles Dodgson began writing a small family newspaper in which he was already developing some skill at humorous verse writing. Among these early verses are some dealing with the *First Ear Ring*. This was a pun for "ringing in the ears" following a severe box on the ears. The story was that this had been administered by a father who had lost patience with his son and in his counteranger had boxed the child's ears so severely as to impair his hearing slightly but permanently. The young Charles seemed to get some of his talent for nonsense from this same father. In Derek Hudson's life of Lewis Carroll, he reproduces a letter from the father written apparently in the hope of counteracting the angry disappointed outburst he anticipated from his young son when he was unable to bring the child certain ardently desired things which the father had promised on a shopping trip in a nearby town. This letter contains elements of the same sort of nonsense which Charles was later to use so effectively in the *Alice* books.

"loses his head"—he loses his sense of direction and becomes disorganized. He acts, we say, like a chicken with its head cut off. Some think indeed that the epileptic convulsion is intrinsically related to and represents repressed rage. This is a state very close to absolute nonsense. But the ability to write, or to paint, or to reproduce this in a communicable form saves the person—here Lear or Carroll—from being devastated by it. It is my suspicion that communicating nonsense always requires considerable talent. This is a way of saying that talent provides ways of leaving the purely individual personal experiences, pains, and pressures of life; and through channels of empathic association not open to the less gifted, talent permits the maintenance of a distance from which to hear the collective or even the cosmic beat or see the outlines of organization and feel relationships in that which would otherwise be personally devastating. Communicated nonsense is a defense against destructive forces. But it may be more than a defense in that its very ability to maintain an equilibrium against such odds contains a constructive force offering, at the very least, continuity of existence rather than complete annihilation or disintegration. One might liken it to the expectation of rebirth which sometimes accompanies the intention of suicide.

Earlier in this discussion I have mentioned that some of the stories of Franz Kafka contain many of the ingredients present in the nonsense rhymes and stories, and especially in the full-length productions of Carroll. There is the same feeling of bewilderment and questioning, both about the self and the surroundings, the distortions of and changes in the body form and functioning, the becoming too small to cope with the people in the environment, the almost constant awareness of senseless frustration and of being unreasonably held responsible for all manner of happenings, of being threatened with punishment, and ultimately having to stand trial. But in the *Alice* books these are presented in what may be called a focus of absurdity with all manner of diverting incongruous detail; whereas in Kafka's stories the nightmare scenes are recounted with the most meticulously realistic details, especially in regard to the subjective feelings and perceptions of the central character.

If we compare, for example, Kafka's description of the opening of the door of his room by the cockroach who used to be Gregor Samsa with Alice's various attempts to open the door into the little garden, the contrast is striking. In Alice there is nothing to compare with the exquisite horror of the cockroach's attempts to turn the key in the lock of his door: first using his tiny legs with their sticky exudate to give some purchase on the wall, then turning the key in the lock with his mouth with such effort that a brown saliva covers the key and drops to the floor—in the meantime circling round and round the lock, holding on with his mouth, pushing on the key as required or pulling it down again with all the weight of his body until the lock yields.

With Kafka, there are symptoms of chronic panic from guilt, probably largely in relation to his father. He seems as though caught in the eddy of hostile aggressive feelings with the hostility absorbed into a sadistic conscience turning it mercilessly and eternally toward himself. Several times in Kafka's stories, the central character tells himself that these monstrous events must be nonsense, but is unconvinced and unrelieved. I shall not attempt any detailed analysis or interpretation of Kafka or his works, but I would point out that Kafka comes as close perhaps as is possible to presenting the destructiveness that actual nonsense is, whereas Carroll and Lear use the sense of nonsense in a defensive way to allay panic. The sadism is then diluted but is to be detected again in the triumph of the comic, the persistent grin of the Cheshire cat which disappears last of all. Rage and panic can in the extreme reach a state approaching annihilation of reason.

Kafka would seem to be a man doomed to slow self destruction and indeed he died at 41 (1924). Yet he seems to me somehow more of a piece even in his endless struggles and his profound chronic depression than Carroll or perhaps Lear. Carroll seemed to take leave of his masculinity and to present rather the clinical picture of a negative fetishism through his identification with a little prepuberty girl. There was in fact some indication of perversion in his great absorption in photographing little girls of 9 or 10 either in the nude or as close to it as a Victorian setting permitted.

While the typical fetishist has always to have an object which will be a phallic representative for him if he is to function sexually at all, there is no evidence that Carroll had any sexual interest in any woman, except his lost mother. But just as the fetishist must have his fetish not only for sexual adequacy but for the narcissistic completion of his body image, so Carroll, I suspect, in his voyeurism and intensive interest in prepuberty girls was repetitively confirming his identification with them, thus denying his need for masculine genital adequacy.

But this very denial could not help but contribute to a sense of unreality and alienation from his actual body and from the pursuits of family life which constitute so much of the emotional foundation for most of us. It permitted, however, the development of a defensive critical distance in which a sense of nonsense could develop and flourish. It is interesting, too, that whereas Kafka remained painfully faithful to his interest in writing and is known for the scrupulosity of his writing, which won him posthumous fame, both Lear and Carroll have become renowned for their nonsense writing, and were less productive and attained less recognition in the fields in which their major interest presumably was involved.

BIBLIOGRAPHY

Caemmerts, M., 1925, *The Poetry of Nonsense*. London: Routledge.
Carroll, L. (1865), *Alice in Wonderland* [published as *Alice's Adventures Underground*]. London: Macmillan, 1876.
—— (1871), *Through the Looking Glass*. London: Macmillan, 1876.
—— (1876), *Hunting of the Snark*. London: Macmillan.
—— (1889), *Sylvie and Bruno*. London: Macmillan, 1893.
Eastman, M. (1936), *Enjoyment of Laughter*. New York: Simon & Schuster.
Greenacre, P. (1955), *Swift and Carroll*. NY: IUP.
Hudson, D. (1954), *Lewis Carroll*. London: Constable.
Jackson, H. (1950), Introduction. *The Complete Nonsense of Edward Lear*. London: Faber & Faber.
Kafka, F. (1916), *Metamorphosis*. London: Vanguard, 1947.
Koestler, A. (1964), *The Act of Creation*. London: Hutchinson.
Lear, E. (1846), *Book of Nonsense*. London & NY: Frederick Warne, 1905.
—— (1872), *More Nonsense*. London & NY: Frederick Warne.
Sewall, E. (1952), *Field of Nonsense*. London: Chatto & Windus.
Woollcott, A. (1936), Introduction. *The Complete Works of Carroll*. NY: Modern Library.

Publications by Heinz Hartmann

1917

(& L. Zila) Über die sogenannte Chiningewöhnung. *Münch. med. Wochschr.*, 64:1597-1598

1918

(& L. Zila) Das Schicksal des Chinins im Organismus. *Arch. exper. Pathol. & Pharmakol.*, 83:221-234

1922

Ein Fall von Depersonalisation. *Z. Neurol. & Psychiat.*, 74:593-601

Zur Frage der Selbstblendung. *Jb. Psychiat. & Neurol.*, 41:171-188

1923

(& P. Schilder) Zur Klinik und Psychologie der Amentia. *Z. Neurol. & Psychiat.*, 92:531-596

1924

Ein Beitrag zur Frage der katatonischen Pupillenstarre. *Wien. klin. Wochschr.*, 37:1013-1015

(& S. Betlheim) Über Fehlreaktionen bei der Korsakoffschen Psychose. *Arch, Psychiat. & Nervenkr.*, 72:278-286

    English: (condensed) On Parapraxes in the Korsakow Psychosis. In: *Organization and Pathology of Thought,* ed. & tr. D. Rapaport. NY: Columbia Univ. Pr., 1951, 288-307; *Essays* (1964), 353-368

Halluzinierte Flächenfarben und Bewegungen. *Mschr. Psychiat. & Neurol.*, 56:1-14

(& P. Schilder) Zur Klinik und Psychologie der Amentia. *Mschr. Psychiat. & Neurol.*, 55:321-327

1925

Ein Beitrag zur Lehre von den reaktiven Psychosen. *Mschr. Psychiat. & Neurol.*, 57:89-108

Kokainismus und Homosexualität. *Z. Neurol. & Psychiat.*, 95:79-94

(& P. Schilder) Zur Psychologie Schädelverletzter. *Arch. Psychiat. & Nervenkr.*, 75:287-300

Ein weiterer Beitrag zur Selbstblendungsfrage. *Jb. Psychiat. & Neurol.*, 44:31-36

(& P. Schilder) Hypnoseversuche an Paralytikern. *Jb. Psychiat. & Neurol.*, 44:194-202

1927

Zur Frage organische Amnesie und Hypnose: Versuche an Korsakoffkranken. *Wien. klin. Wochschr.*, 40:1507-1508

(& P. Schilder) Körperinneres und Körperschema. *Z. Neurol. & Psychiat.*, 109:666-675

Die Grundlagen der Psychoanalyse. Leipzig: Thieme
  English: Chapters 1 & 2: Concept Formation in Psychoanalysis. *Psa. Study Ch.*, 19:11-47, 1964; Chapter 3: Understanding and Explanation. *Essays* (1964) 369-403

1928

(& F. Stumpfl) Ein zwillingspathologischer Beitrag zur Frage: Idiotypus, Paratypus und Neurose. *Wien. med. Wochschr.*, 78:911-915

Psychoanalyse und Wertproblem. *Imago*, 14:421-440

Kokainismus und Homosexualität. *Dtsch. med. Wochschr.*, 54:268-275

1929

Über genetische Charakterologie, insbesondere über psychoanalytische. *Jb. Charakterol.*, 6:73-96

1930

Abreagieren. Assoziationen. Fausse reconnaissance, déjà vu, déjà éprouvé. Komplexreaktionen. Psychische Energie. Psychoanalyse. Tagträume. Traum. Trieb. Unbewusstes. Verdrängung. [Atricles in] *Handwörterbuch für medizinische Psychologie*, ed. K. Birnbaum. Leipzig: Thieme.

(& F. Stumpfl) Psychosen bei eineiigen Zwillingen. *Z. Neurol. & Psychiat.*, 123:251-298

Gedächtnis und Lustprinzip: Untersuchungen an Korsakoffkranken. *Z. Neurol. & Psychiat.*, 126:496-519

1931

(& E. Stengel) Studien zur Psychologie des induzierten Irreseins. *Arch. Psychiat. & Nervenkr.*, 95:584-600

(& A. Adler) Malariabehandlung einer schwangeren Paralytikerin. *Dtsch. med. Wochschr.*, 57:2018-2019

(& M. Weissmann) Zur Decholinbehandlung der Melancholie. *Med. Klin.*, 27:1819-1820

1932

(& E. Stengel) Studien zur Psychologie des induzierten Irreseins. *Jb. Psychiat. & Neurol.*, 48:164-183

Zwillingsforschung in der Psychiatrie. *Wien. klin. Wochschr.*, 45:1592

(& M. Weissmann) Photodynbehandlung bei Melancholie. *Wien. med. Wochschr.*, 82:1526

1933

Psychoanalyse und Weltanschauung. *Psa. Bewegung*, 5:416-429

Der entwicklungspsychologische Gedanke in der Neurosenlehre. *Wien med. Wochschr.*, 83:971-973

Über Zwillingsforschung in der Psychiatrie. *Wien. med. Wochschr.*, 83:781-785; 809-811

Psychiatrische Zwillingsstudien. *Jb. Psychiat. & Neurol.*, 50:195-242; see also *sub* 1934-1935

   English: (condensed) see *sub* 1964

Ein experimenteller Beitrag zur Psychologie der Zwangsneurose: Über das Behalten erledigter und unerledigter Handlung. *Jb. Psychiat. & Neurol.*, 50:243-278

   English: An Experimental Contribution to the Psychology of Obsessive-Compulsive Neurosis: On Remembering Completed and Uncompleted Tasks. *Essays* (1964), 404-418

(& F. Stumpfl) Ein Beitrag zum Thema: Zwillingsprobleme und Schizophrenie und zur Frage der Vererbung musikalischer Begabung. *Z. Neurol. & Psychiat.*, 143:349-380

1934-1935

Psychiatrische Zwillingsstudien [contains the paper with the same title listed under 1933 and the paper on twins listed under 1935]. Berlin: Springer; Leipzig: Barth.

   English: (condensed) Psychiatric Studies of Twins. *Essays* (1964), 419-445

1935

Das Korsakowsche Syndrom. *Wien. klin. Wochschr.*, 48:457-459

Zur Charakterologie erbgleicher Zwillinge. *Jb. Psychiat. & Neurol.*, 52:57-118; see also *sub* 1934-1935

   English: (condensed) see *sub* 1964

1936

Sigmund Freud: Zum achtzigsten Geburtstag. *Neue Freie Presse*, May 5, p. ii.

1939

Ich-Psychologie und Anpassungsproblem. *Int. Z. Psa.*, 24:62-135

   English: (condensed) Ego Psychology and the Problem of Adaptation. In: *Organization and Pathology of Thought*, ed. & tr. D. Rapaport. NY: Columbia Univ. Pr., 1951, 362-396; see also *sub* 1958

Psychoanalysis and the Concept of Health. *Int. J. Psa.*, 20:308-321; *Essays* (1964), 1-18

1943

Psychiatry: Its Relationship to Psychological Schools of Thought. In: *Psychiatry and the War*, ed. F. J. Sladen. Springfield, Ill.: Thomas, 17-28

1944

The Psychiatric Work of Paul Schilder. *Psa. Rev.*, 31:287-298

Psychoanalysis and Sociology. In: *Psychoanalysis Today*, ed. S. Lorand. NY: IUP, 326-341; *Essays* (1964), 19-36

1945

(& E. Kris) The Genetic Approach in Psychoanalysis. *Psa. Study Ch.*, 1:11-30; *The Yearbook of Psychoanalysis*, 2:1-22. NY: IUP, 1946; *Psychol. Issues*, 14:7-26, 1964

  German: Die genetische Betrachtungsweise in der Psychoanalyse. *Psyche*, 3:1-17, 1949

1946

(& E. Kris, R. M. Loewenstein) Comments on the Formation of Psychic Structure. *Psa. Study Ch.*, 2:11-38; *Psychol. Issues*, 14:27-55, 1964

  Spanish: Comentarios sobre la formación de la estructura psíquica. *Rev. Psicoanál.*, 8:222-248, 1951

1947

On Rational and Irrational Action. *Psychoanalysis and the Social Sciences*, 1:359-392; *Essays* (1964), 37-68

1948

Comments on the Psychoanalytic Theory of Instinctual Drives. *Psa. Q.*, 17:368-388; *Essays* (1964), 69-89

1949

The New York Psychoanalytic Treatment Center. *Bull. Am. Psa. Assn.*, 5:11-13

(& E. Kris, R. M. Loewenstein) Notes on the Theory of Aggression. *Psa. Study Ch.*, 3/4:9-36; *Psychol. Issues*, 14:56-85, 1964

  Spanish: Notas sobre la teoría de la agressión. *Rev. Psicoanál.*, 8:402-429, 1951

1950

The Application of Psychoanalytic Concepts to Social Science. *Psa. Q.*, 19:385-392; *The Yearbook of Psychoanalysis*, 7:81-87, 1951; *Essays* (1964), 90-98

  German: Die Anwendung psychoanalytischer Begriffe auf die Sozialwissenschaft. *Psyche*, 18:367-374, 1964

Psychoanalysis and Developmental Psychology. *Psa. Study Ch.*, 5:7-17; *Essays* (1964), 99-112

  German: Psychoanalyse und Entwicklungspsychologie. *Psyche*, 18:354-366, 1964

Comments on the Psychoanalytic Theory of the Ego. *Psa. Study Ch.*, 5:74-96; *Essays* (1964), 113-141

   German: Bemerkungen zur psychoanalytischen Theorie des Ichs. *Psyche*, 18:330-353, 1964

1951

Technical Implications of Ego Psychology. *Psa. Q.*, 20:31-43; *Essays* (1964), 142-154

(& E. Kris, R. M. Loewenstein) Some Psychoanalytic Comments on "Culture and Personality." In: *Psychoanalysis and Culture*, ed. G. B. Wilbur & W. Muensterberger. NY: IUP, 3-31; *Psychol. Issues*, 14:86-116, 1964

1952

The Mutual Influences in the Development of Ego and Id. *Psa. Study Ch.*, 7:9-30; *Essays* (1964), 155-181

   German: Die gegenseitigen Beeinflussungen von Ich und Es in der psychoanalytischen Theoriebildung. *Psyche*, 9:1-22, 1955

1953

(& E. Kris, R. M. Loewenstein) The Function of Theory in Psychoanalysis. In: *Drives, Affects, Behavior*, ed. R. M. Loewenstein. NY: IUP, 1:13-37; *Psychol. Issues*, 14:117-143, 1964

Contribution to the Metapsychology of Schizophrenia. *Psa. Study Ch.*, 8:177-198; *Essays* (1964), 182-206

   German: Ein Beitrag zur Metapsychologie der Schizophrenie. *Psyche*, 18:375-396, 1964

1954

In: Problems of Infantile Neurosis: A Discussion. *Psa. Study Ch.*, 9:16-71; *Essays* (1964), 207-214

1955

Notes on the Theory of Sublimation. *Psa. Study Ch.*, 10:9-29; *Essays* (1964), 215-240

   German: Bemerkungen zur Theorie der Sublimierung. *Psyche*, 10:41-62, 1956; *Entfaltung der Psychoanalyse*, ed. A. Mitscherlich. Stuttgart: Klett, 1956, 41-62

1956

Notes on the Reality Principle. *Psa. Study Ch.*, 11:31-53; *Essays* (1964), 241-267

   German: Bemerkungen zum Realitätsproblem. *Psyche*, 18:397-419, 1964

The Development of the Ego Concept in Freud's Work. *Int. J. Psa.*, 37:425-438; *Essays* (1964), 268-298

   German: Die Entwicklung des Ich-Begriffes bei Freud. *Psyche*, 18:420-444, 1964

1957

Ernst Kris, 1900-1957. *Psa. Study Ch.*, 12:9-15

1958

Ego Psychology and the Problem of Adaptation [Journal of the Ameri-
    can Psychoanalytic Association Monograph No. 1], tr. D. Rapa-
    port. NY: IUP.
    Spanish: La psicologia del yo y el problema de la adaptacion. Mexico,
        D.F.: Cesarman, 1960
    Japanese: Tokyo: Seishin Shobo (in press)
    Italian: Torino: Boringhieri S.P.A. (in press)
    French: Paris: Presses Universitaires de France (in press)
    German: see *sub* 1960
Comments on the Scientific Aspects of Psychoanalysis. *Psa. Study Ch.*,
        13:127-146; *Essays* (1964), 297-317
Discussion of A. Freud: Child Observation and Prediction of Develop-
    ment. *Psa. Study Ch.*, 13:120-122

1959

Psychoanalysis as a Scientific Theory. In: *Psychoanalysis, Scientific
    Method, and Philosophy*, ed. S. Hook. NY: N.Y. Univ. Pr., 3-37;
    NY: Grove Pr., 1960, 3-37; *Essays* (1964), 318-350
    German: Die Psychoanalyse als wissenschaftliche Theorie. *Psyche*,
        18:445-474, 1964

1960

Psychoanalysis and Moral Values [The Freud Anniversary Lecture Series
    of The New York Psychoanalytic Institute]. NY: IUP
Ich-Psychologie und Anpassungsproblem. *Psyche*, 14:81-164; *Ich-Psy-
    chologie und Anpassungsproblem.* Stuttgart: Klett
Toward a Concept of Mental Health. *Brit. J. Med. Psychol.*, 33:293-298

1962

(& R. M. Loewenstein) Notes on the Superego. *Psa. Study Ch.*, 17:42-81;
    Psychol. Issues, 14:144-181, 1964
    French: Notes sur le surmoi. Rev. Franç. Psa., 28:639-678, 1964.

1964

Essays on Ego Psychology: Selected Problems in Psychoanalytic Theory.
    NY: IUP
(& E. Kris, R. M. Loewenstein) *Papers on Psychoanalytic Psychology.
    Psychological Issues*, Monogr. 14. NY: IUP
Concept Formation in Psychoanalysis. *Psa. Study Ch.*, 19:11-47
Understanding and Explanation. *Essays*, 369-403
Psychiatric Studies of Twins. *Essays*, 419-445

Key to Abbreviations Used in Bibliographies

C.P.	*Collected Papers*
Essays	*Essays on Ego Psychology: Selected Problems in Psychoanalytic Theory.* New York: International Universities Press, 1964.
Int. J. Psa.	*International Journal of Psycho-Analysis*
IUP	International Universities Press
J. Am. Psa. Assn.	*Journal of the American Psychoanalytic Association*
Psa. Q.	*Psychoanalytic Quarterly*
Psa. Rev.	*Psychoanalytic Review*
Psa. Study Ch.	*The Psychoanalytic Study of the Child,* currently 20 Vols., ed. R. S. Eissler, A. Freud, H. Hartmann, M. Kris. New York: International Universities Press, 1945-1965.
Psychol. Issues	*Psychological Issues,* currently 17 Monographs, ed. G. S. Klein. New York: International Universities Press, 1959-1966.
S.E.	*The Standard Edition of the Complete Psychological Works of Sigmund Freud,* 24 Vols., translated and edited by James Strachey. London: Hogarth Press and the Institute of Psycho-Analysis, 1953-